Teaching the Arab-Israeli Conflict

Teaching the Arab-Israeli Conflict

Edited by Rachel S. Harris

Wayne State University Press
DETROIT

Copyright © 2019 by Wayne State University Press, Detroit, Michigan 48201.
All rights reserved. No part of this book may be reproduced without formal permission.

ISBN 978-0-8143-4677-8 (paperback); ISBN 978-0-8143-4676-1 (printed case);
ISBN 978-0-8143-4678-5(ebook)

Library of Congress Cataloging Number: 2019930526

Wayne State University Press
Leonard N. Simons Building
4809 Woodward Avenue
Detroit, Michigan 48201-1309

Visit us online at wsupress.wayne.edu

In memory of
Michael Kotzin, 1941–2015
Michael Feige, 1957–2016

Contents

Preface	xi
Acknowledgments	xxvii
Maps	xxix

Introduction to the History of the Region and the Conflict

The Path to Genuine Peace? Historical Perspectives on the Arab-Israeli Conflict   3
JACOB LASSNER

Teaching Skills, Facing Challenges: What Happens in the Classroom?

"Why Can't We Just Create New Sacred Holy Sites?" Teaching the Arab-Israeli Conflict in a New England Public Liberal Arts University   21
CAITLIN CARENEN

Comics and Conflict: Using Graphic Narrative to Wrestle with the Complexities of Israel/Palestine   28
JANICE W. FERNHEIMER

Joe Sacco, Comics Journalism, and Representations of Israel   43
MARTIN B. SHICHTMAN

Teaching the Conflict as a Critical Thinking (Dis)course   51
ASHLEY PASSMORE

Teaching Students How to Think, Not What to Think, about the Middle East Conflict   58
DONNA ROBINSON DIVINE

Empathy, Access, Language, and Education: Learning to See the Other

Teaching Literature to Arab and Jewish Students in Israel: Between National Identities, Languages, and Genders   65
ADIA MENDELSON-MAOZ

Victim or Terrorist? On the Perils of Misreading and the
Creative Writing Classroom as Border Crossing   72
MARCELA SULAK

Representing the Homeland: Israel and Palestine Onstage   81
ELLEN W. KAPLAN

Darwish in the Transnational Classroom   90
BEVERLY BAILIS

Surprised by Complexity: Empathy, Narrative, and Conflict
in the Classroom   99
RANEN OMER-SHERMAN

Fictional Literature in Interdisciplinary Studies of the
Arab-Israeli Conflict   108
MARILYN R. TAYLER

Communication, Conflict, and the Arab-Israeli Conflict   114
RANDALL G. ROGAN

Competing Interpretations and Multiple Narratives: Teaching Diversity

The Arab-Israeli Conflict: Competing Narratives as a Focus   123
ALAN DOWTY

Teaching the 1948 War at the United States Naval Academy   127
SHAYNA WEISS

Borders, Boundaries, and Barriers: Depictions of Land in
Israel/Palestine through Film   133
AMY WEISS

Teaching Competing Narratives through Film   141
OLGA GERSHENSON

Teaching Jewish-Israeli, Arab-Israeli, and Palestinian Poetry Together   147
CARY NELSON

Dual Narrative Learning: Experiential Education in Palestine/Israel   180
OREN KROLL-ZELDIN

A Course on Zionism and the Novel   187
RUSSELL A. BERMAN

History, Politics, and Religion: Putting the Class(room) in Context

Challenges of Teaching Middle Eastern Politics in a Non-Jewish, Non-Arab Muslim Country with an Imperial Past in the Region 203
UMUT UZER

India: Teaching Israel to the "Other" 210
P. R. KUMARASWAMY

Exploring Middle East Politics in Various Classroom Settings 216
HUSAM MOHAMAD

How Resources Shape Pedagogy: Israel Studies at Cairo University 227
MENNA ABUKHADRA

Where to Begin? Teaching the Conflict at San Diego State University, Jewish History, and John le Carré's *The Little Drummer Girl* 235
PETER C. HERMAN

Jerusalem: Holy City of Conflict and Desire 243
RACHEL FELDHAY BRENNER

Teaching the Value of Conflict: Intellectual Hospitality, Humanistic Pedagogy, and the Poetry of Yehuda Amichai 250
HOLLI LEVITSKY

Teaching Pluralism via the Arab-Israeli Conflict at a Catholic University 258
JEFFREY BLOODWORTH

Teaching about the Establishment of Israel in Florida's Public Schools Using Primary Sources 265
TERRI SUSAN FINE

The Personal and the Political: When the Outside World Intrudes on the Sacred Class Space

Feeding Minds: Using Food to Teach the Arab-Israeli Conflict 275
ARI ARIEL

Letting Politics into the Israeli-Palestinian Relations Classroom 282
MIRA SUCHAROV

Seeing the Israeli: Teaching Palestinian Students 288
MYA GUARNIERI JARADAT

Teaching the Palestinian-Israeli Conflict in the
Community College Classroom — 294
SUSAN JACOBOWITZ

Grappling with the Arab-Israeli Conflict at a Historically Black
College and University: Reflections on an Accidental Journey — 301
ROLIN MAINUDDIN

Thinking Differently and Creating New Paradigms: Teaching Israel/Palestine without Repeating History

Teaching Israel/Palestine Studies — 311
LIORA R. HALPERIN

Teaching Israel/Palestine: A Contrapuntal Reading of Savyon Liebrecht's
"A Room on the Roof" and Ghareeb Asqalani's "Hunger" — 318
PHILIP METRES

Israeli Narratives: Charting New Territories — 333
SHIRI GOREN

Women On-Screen: Teaching Gender but Not History — 339
RACHEL S. HARRIS

Conclusion: How What We Teach Changes (and Changes Us)

Teaching beyond the Conflict — 347
JOEL S. MIGDAL

Time Line: The Arab-Israeli Conflict in Historical Context — 355

Selected Bibliography — 377
Annotated Filmography — 395
List of Contributors — 405
Index — 417

Preface

In 1929, violent rioting broke out in Palestine. This Arab revolt against Jewish immigration and British rule resulted in a week of terror throughout the Mandate. Maurice Samuel, a British Jewish journalist and translator newly arrived in the country, wrote his assessment of the situation in a book that appeared six months after the events and before the official government reports.[1] He described the growing tensions in the days before the violence and his participation in a delegation from the Zionist Executive that visited the inspector-general of police, Alan Saunders, on August 23, requesting he deputize Jewish men. When Saunders declined, they approached the acting high commissioner, Sir Harry Charles Luke. According to Samuel, Luke expressed his concerns that deputizing the Jews would be seen as a provocation but conceded that the police force was too small to withstand an Arab attack.[2] In order to mitigate the situation, Luke authorized Saunders to recruit every able-bodied British man who was willing to supplement the meager forces.

That summer, forty theology students from Wycliffe Hall were brought by Rev. George Francis Graham Brown (1892–1942), principal of the Anglican college at Oxford University, who "began that excellent scheme of taking parties of young students in his charge to Palestine to get the knowledge that only sight of that land gives."[3] As divinity students, they were supposed to be attending the college's "usual programme of lectures and tutorials,"[4] poring over religious texts, visiting churches, and generally taking in the sites and history of the Holy Land as groups had done in previous years as part of a travel-abroad study program. Instead, caught up in the outbreak of hostilities, they volunteered as special constables for the understaffed police force in the face of mounting tensions between Arabs and Jews. The students executed their duties with aplomb, and the British High Commissioner, Sir John Chancellor, praised their service, subsequently writing to them, "If Palestine has given you less than you had hoped of her, you have bestowed upon Palestine most timely services, which will not be forgotten."[5] Though one student was shot in the shoulder and was delayed by hospitalization, the others returned to England at the end of the summer to resume their studies.

I first read about this incident as I was preparing my master's thesis as part of my degree in Middle Eastern Area Studies at the School of Oriental and African Studies in the summer of 2001. My research examined the relationship between the historical facts around the events that took place on the morning of Saturday, August 24, 1929, in Hebron and the interpretations that they were given by the British, Jews, and Arabs. The participants narrated these events to score political points and entrench their position, a path that not only prolonged the situation in the short term but also formed the basis of ideological myths that informed all sides for decades. But the events were also given interpretations by journalists in the British press, who were concerned about the danger to British forces; the Jewish press in Britain, who were worried not only about their brethren in Palestine but also that the British government would betray its commitment to Jewish self-determination promised in the Balfour Declaration; the Hebrew and Arabic press in Palestine, whose diverse range of positions reflected political and ideological divisions in approaching the situation; and the European press, who were critiquing the British right to the Mandate.[6] As I sat in the idyllic surroundings of the English countryside writing more than seventy years later, a wave of suicide bombings were taking place in Israel, whose interpretation in the British, Israeli, Arabic, and Jewish press were framing the contemporary events in light of the region's history. The resonances between the past and the present seemed at the heart of why my work mattered.

Later that year, I began my doctorate in Israeli literature at the University of Oxford and ultimately wrote my dissertation on the ways in which fiction and poetry have commented on national narratives. Between my training (first in Islamic studies as an undergraduate, then Middle Eastern studies, and finally Israel studies) and my research interests, I had arrived at a deep underlying and very personal understanding of the Arab-Israeli conflict that informed my scholarship from thence onward. I believed that studying the historical facts could only tell us part of why the situation was so difficult to navigate socially, politically, and intellectually and that the focus on politics tended to emphasize the perception, ideology, and achievements of the leadership without considering the social and cultural impacts. In turn, this also marginalized the voices that had informed and shaped the mythologization of history. Art, I felt, offered a way to analyze myths and see how they shape our understanding of the past, and ultimately art made space for the voices on the fringes, including women and minorities.

With this in mind, I created my first course, "War and Peace in Israeli Poetry," for a continuing-education program for young adults at the Reform Synagogues of Great Britain. Despite the title, the course included poems by Palestinian authors. For, as Liora R. Halperin explains in her essay in this book, "Though one may make pretensions to study Israel without Palestine or Palestine without Israel, on the basis of one's topic of interest, the practice of scholarship requires facing both Israel and Palestine." The course was divided into six topics: "The Role of the Sabra," "Memory and Memorials," "Contested Land," "Human Relations," "Daily Life," and "War Cries and Peace Songs," and in later iterations of the course I added "A Perfect Peace." The readings included poems by women, Mizrahi authors, disabled authors, and veterans. I have taught it in a variety of guises including public lectures, academic-credit courses, and to undergraduates at two different universities in the United States where I have been on the faculty (SUNY Albany and the University of Illinois at Urbana-Champaign). Later I created a second complementary course, "The Arab in Hebrew Literature" (which I taught first in England and then in the United States), which explores mainly fiction and includes writing by Palestinian authors who write in Hebrew (Sayed Kashua and Emile Habibi) and a Palestinian author who was born in Lebanon, lives in Britain, and writes in English (Samir El-youssef). The course includes works by Mizrahi authors on the experience of being both Arab and Jewish (Tikva Levi, Sami Shalom Chetrit, and Yechezkel Rachamim). More recently at Illinois, I created an Israeli film course that includes modules on Palestinian films and filmmakers (Hiam Abbas, Elia Suleiman, Suha Arraf, Hany Abu-Assad, and Ibtisam Mara'ana) and that I have also taught in a variety of adult-education and community settings.

Yet having been deeply embedded in this field for my entire professional academic career, I felt my teaching becoming stale. I was helped by becoming a fellow and participating in the Brandeis Summer Institute for Israel Studies (SIIS), a three-week intensive program for faculty, as have many of the contributors to this volume, but there were few other pedagogical resources available within the field for faculty working in the arts. In recent years, several new textbooks suited for use in history and political science courses have been published, and there is a longer history of resource collections, such as Walter Laqueur's *The Israel-Arab Reader: A Documentary History of the Middle East Conflict* (1969), now in its eighth, revised and updated edition, coedited with Dan Schueftan (Penguin Books, 2016). Nevertheless, like many such "comprehensive" resource books meant for classroom use, there is an absence of female voices or documents from other minority groups. There are few comparative works, textbooks, readers, or anthologies designed for university instruction in the many other disciplinary fields in which the Arab-Israeli conflict is taught. There is a dearth of suitable English-language resources for undergraduate (and graduate) courses. For the most part, faculty cobble together courses with homemade readers, trading materials like samizdat. Whereas once conferences were the only opportunity to corner colleagues to discuss teaching, today Facebook has become a space for crowdsourcing suggestions for texts, assignments, and class activities. But as with all social media, the record may be permanent, but finding the informative thread, even a few days later, may prove challenging.

Wide-reaching historical changes in the eighteenth and nineteenth centuries and two world wars in the twentieth century transformed the modern political landscape, creating nation-states where once there had been ruling empires. The global reach of these epoch-changing historical events played out in the localized region of Palestine, an administrative district of the Ottoman Empire from 1517 until it became a British Mandate in 1918 and an area often known as the Holy Land. This territory on the eastern shores of the Mediterranean has been a contested landscape for as long as history has been written. The site of successive waves of settlement and military attack for millennia, it also serves as the home of important religious sites for three major monotheistic religions: Judaism, Christianity, and Islam. While the contemporary Arab-Israeli conflict has modern political roots, this religious historical context has meant that the events in the region are of interest in large parts of the world, particularly where Christians and Muslims live, far outweighing the economic or geographic size of the land.

The Arab-Israeli conflict emerged in the shadows of European colonialism that began in the seventeenth and eighteenth centuries. European powers raced to control natural resources in the New World and the Far East and later engaged in land-grabs during the nineteenth century that included taking control of parts of Africa and the Middle East. With the Ottoman Empire's central location between the European West, and the Great Powers' resources and political ties in the East and in Africa, Britain, France, and Germany began to see the sultan as an obstacle to their enrichment. At the same time, the presence of the Ottoman Empire limited Russian expansion beyond the Black Sea. Thus, during the nineteenth century, the Ottoman Empire faced external attacks by Russia (Russo-Turkish Wars), a desire for its dismantlement by the Great Powers (through treaties), and internal factionalism as a result of the growth of nineteenth-century nationalist political movements that began with the Greek Wars of Independence (1821–27).

The region's connection to the Bible had made Mesopotamia, Egypt, and particularly Palestine important sites of religious pilgrimage. But these expeditions had often proved treacherous. With the introduction of steam-powered ships and the railway in the middle of the century, travel became affordable and relatively safe. In turn, this increased accessibility intensified interest in the region for scientists, botanists, historians, archaeologists, and tourists. There are more than three thousand travelogues including books and paintings of Palestine during the nineteenth century, created by primarily European and North American travelers, which further sparked public interest. In 1869, with the opening of the Suez Canal, the travel agency Thomas Cook began leading tours of the region, opening it up as one of the most desirable destinations for international travel.

In Europe, changes since the Middle Ages had affected the nature of citizenship and the attitude toward Jews. Following the French Revolution, Jews first gained political emancipation, which spread through parts of Europe with Napoleon Bonaparte's conquests. Yet it took until the end of the nineteenth century for all of western Europe and parts of central Europe to grant Jews full legal equality. In the Russian Empire, such political emancipation did not arrive until the Russian Revolution in 1917. Yet even with nineteenth-century political emancipation, blood libels and waves of antisemitism continued. "The Jewish Question"—the concern that Jews somehow were not quite the same as the other Europeans among whom they lived—destabilized the very meaning of inclusion that emancipation promised.

New political ideologies began to develop both in Europe and in the Ottoman Empire, and though they started as consciousness-raising efforts by groups of intellectuals, they eventually developed widespread appeal, flowering into mass movements for political self-determination. For Jews in the nineteenth century, Zionism began as an effort at national consciousness-raising among a small elite, and waves of immigration to Palestine served to situate a modern territorial claim to a historic and spiritual homeland. Palestinian national consciousness developed locally in the Levant among the elite, in response to the collapse of Ottoman identity, as well as to Jewish immigration, and driven by the same nationalist ideologies as other movements of the time. While it found mass expression among the local population in the "Peasant's Revolt" of 1936–39, the Second World War and the Arab losses in 1948 led to the movement's suppression until its reemergence with the Palestinian Liberation Organization (PLO) in the 1960s.

The Western powers remained attentive to the Middle East in the late nineteenth and early twentieth centuries, motivated by a rush to control former Ottoman territories and the protection of financial interests in the region. Later, the discovery of oil and the opening of the Suez Canal and the Hijaz railway served to provide new strategic interests that kept Britain, France, and Russia in competition for Palestine leading into the First World War, resulting in British and French control of regional mandates after it. The Cold War and the alignment of powers following the Second World War also encouraged the United States and the European Union to continue regional investment out of concern over Russian influence in the newly created Arab states.

It is these geopolitical and historical forces that have meant that the Arab-Israeli conflict is a global issue. Nevertheless, it is not a single war. Rather, it is a number of smaller conflicts between different countries and political groups over a range of regional issues. These disputes include territorial debates over land, water rights, and gas fields in the Mediterranean. Changing political alliances in the region, between Arabs, Iranians, and Turks, particularly with regard to religious issues; the Syrian conflict and Russian involvement; and the rise of extremist religious groups engaged in terrorism against other Muslims and Christians also affect Israeli-Arab relations and lead to changing allegiances in response to facts on the ground. Hence, the Arab-Israeli conflict should not be regarded as an inevitable, long-standing, and unresolvable historical conflict but a dynamic, complex, and constantly changing engagement whose parameters are dictated by issues of the day.

The most well-known of these smaller Arab-Israeli conflicts, and the one that has been at the center of most of the regional issues since the beginning of the twentieth century, is the Israeli-Palestinian conflict. While this conflict is no less global, its interests are localized. At its heart is the fact that two groups both claim the right to sovereignty over the same territory, and both groups claim Jerusalem as their capital. Neither Jews nor Palestinians can be considered monolithic in their political positions, religious identities, or geographic histories. Nor do all Palestinians or all Jews, even Israeli Jews, live in the territories under dispute. But we have come to think of these two groups as opposing camps engaged in a political struggle based on the competing desires for governance of the region, with diasporic communities whose reach extends the conflict beyond the land's boundaries.

The creation of the State of Israel in 1948 led to the end of British control of Palestine, though it covered a smaller territory than the mandate. The remaining territory was occupied by Israel's Arab neighbors: Egypt, Jordan, and Syria. In 1967, in a war with several Arab countries, Israel conquered these and additional territories containing large populations of Arabs, many of whom had originally lived within areas of mandate Palestine that came under Israeli rule in 1948.[7] These areas have come to be known as the occupied territories. While some of these territories have been absorbed into the suburbs of Jerusalem and thus fall under Israeli law, the majority of them remain under a separate legal system of Israeli military rule.[8] Since 1948, Israel has frequently been at war with its neighbors, though it has also made peace treaties with Egypt and Jordan. From 1964 onward, the Palestinian Liberation Organization (PLO) and then other Palestinian groups worked to raise international consciousness about the Palestinian cause, through both political and violent means, but in 1987, the First Intifada, a grassroots Palestinian uprising, moved the fight from a struggle masterminded by a leadership to a popular rebellion. This served as the precursor to the beginning of a peace process between Palestinians and Israelis. While aspects of the process remain in place, the negotiations broke down, and waves of terror and suicide bombings in Israel, known as the Second Intifada, began. In recent years, it has seemed that Israelis and Palestinians have reached a stalemate. The intractability of this conflict lies not in the inability to propose technical solutions to political issues but in the deep emotional trauma that has resulted from more than a century of violence. As with other long-standing conflicts, however, there is no reason to imagine that a resolution is impossible.

Teaching the Arab-Israeli conflict is approached from numerous historical and disciplinary perspectives that include the geopolitical role the conflict has played and the global actors that continue to influence the political reality, including the European Union, the United Nations, the United States, Turkey, Iran, and the Arab states that surround Israel and the Palestinian territories. But it is also explored and situated in the more localized context of Israel/Palestine. The essay contributors here have chosen different roots to approach this topic, and the variety—including that of terminology—often reflects the particular contexts the instructors are framing.

Though there continue to be many ongoing conflicts throughout the globe, few have held the international interest of the Arab-Israeli conflict, and there are few conflicts that have been as literary or that have engendered as much scholarly attention. All sides have created fiction, poetry, and films reflecting their perspectives, while historians and political scientists have fought over the facts, the narrative, and the impacts to the political reality. Anthropologists and sociologists have sought to understand these societies from within. They consider the impact of the conflict on microcosms such as the religious community, settlers, development towns, the kibbutz system, Russian and Ethiopian immigrants, Bedouin, women, and the Arab Israeli population. Scholars have studied the ways in which reality is processed by individuals (through travel or military service) and as a society at large (through memorial culture). Literature, communication, and film departments have worked to understand the ways in which communities are represented or represent themselves. Urban planners consider the situation and impact of development projects; musicians and dancers explore cultural innovations and their roots in traditions; and lawyers examine the implications of everything from the absence of a formal constitution to the impact of ruling a population that is not part of a country's citizenry. That is to say that there are a wide number of ways to approach the study of the conflict and the region. There are courses in many fields including religion, conflict resolution, demography, economics, comparative literature, Jewish studies, film studies, gender studies, security studies, geography, tourism, education, peace studies, food studies, Mediterranean studies, international relations, urban planning, dance, music, and law. Military institutions teach the conflict in order both to use it as a case study for other regions and to prepare students should they find themselves deployed. Religious studies programs teach about the sacred sites; communications departments use it to consider children's educational programming as a way of peace building. Planning programs teach about the conflict as a way for thinking about urban segregation and the challenge of two communities sharing water, power, air space, and telecommunication networks. In fact, there are few fields within the humanities and social sciences where the Arab-Israeli conflict would not prove a relevant case study. *Teaching the Arab-Israeli Conflict* is designed to help faculty planning a course to consider approaches to the topic, find relevant resources, think through possible assignments, navigate institutional settings, and consider the ways the political climate may intrude on the classroom space.

This book explores different pedagogical aspects that arise in teaching the conflict. It begins with a historical overview by Jacob Lassner. The first section, "Teaching Skills, Facing Challenges: What Happens in the Classroom?," brings together essays that engage directly with classroom skills, such as close readings, critical thinking, debate, and tolerance for diverse opinions in the class space. The second section, "Empathy, Access, Language and Education: Learning to See the Other," considers the meanings of othering and otherness. These essays recognize diversity not only within the conflict but also within the classroom. The focus on empathetic readings is meant to create an understanding about not only the complexity of the conflict but the ideological and lived experience that students bring when they study courses in the humanities and social sciences that engage with conflict and real-world questions. The selections of texts used in classes discussed here provide models for comparative reading that ultimately facilitate student engagement with difference. The third section, "Competing Interpretations and Multiple Narratives: Teaching Diversity," questions the nature of narrative. The scholars here discuss teaching materials and in-class exercises that force students to retain a sense of competing political positions simultaneously. These chapters develop models for complete courses, particularly in literature and film, but also think about the impact of discipline on the ways we use materials. The fourth section, "History, Politics, and Religion: Putting the Class(room) in Context," brings us to reflect on the institutional, political, and religious contexts in which we teach. These essays draw our attention to the particularity of teaching location in framing course content and finding the right angle for sharing the conflict's complexities. These essays particularly consider institutional and social cultures and their potential opportunities and constraints. They also suggest ways of navigating these complexities by drawing on other local reference points for providing a starting point for access to the topic and materials. The fifth section, "The Personal and the Political: When the Outside World Intrudes on the Sacred Class Space," considers the political implications of the conflict as they impact the personal lives of students and faculty. Here many teachers share their own conflicted personal journey navigating the tension between their discipline and belief system. The sixth section, "Thinking Differently and Creating New Paradigms: Teaching Israel/Palestine without Repeating History," provides a series of essays that offer practical advice on creating a syllabus and framing a course. Though they refer to logistics, they also provide different theoretical models that can help faculty set out course objectives before selecting the course content and materials. The conclusion is the testimony of one faculty member's constantly changing classroom journey. It is a reminder that as teachers we are also students.

The essays contain their own citations, but the book includes a selected bibliography of works (primary and secondary) to help instructors prepare materials for class. The annotated filmography provides information about feature, short, and documentary films, including ways to stream or purchase them. The time line situates the Arab-Israeli conflict within the larger global historical context of the past two centuries. It is meant for quick reference and contextualization, and it may prove useful in creating class exercises.

In the introduction to this book, Jacob Lassner provides an overview of the history of the region and its political ramifications. He carefully frames the competing interpretations of history, challenging any notion that the conflict is a binary between Palestinian and Israeli. Instead, he situates history into a contextualization of competing ideological positions—expanding beyond Israelis and Palestinians as homogeneous categories. His essay situates the conflict within the larger landscape of the Arab world and the Middle East and addresses the diversity within all camps, reminding us that this conflict has never been about two coherent groups with competing agendas but many groups brought under larger umbrellas who may have as much intragroup conflict as intergroup divisiveness. Some understanding of the facts of history may be necessary in teaching courses on the Arab-Israeli conflict—one that reaches well beyond a discussion of Palestine/Israel and takes into consideration competing political forces within the region. But as Marcela Sulak notes in her essay about creative writing courses that she teaches in English at Bar Ilan University, it is not only what we read but how we read that shapes our understanding. Caitlin Carenen's history courses, Janice W. Fernheimer's courses in rhetoric and composition built around comics, and Donna Robinson Divine's politics courses are the subjects of just a few of the essays that directly explore this relationship between content and analysis, thinking through the ways in which we teach our students to engage with representations of these facts.

Courses on the Arab-Israeli conflict are often, by their very nature, interdisciplinary, and Donna Robinson Divine, Amy Weiss, and Marilyn R. Tayler direct our attention to a variety of texts that can facilitate such engagement. Several essays consider the balancing act between teaching within a discipline and teaching context. Often faculty will use examples from other disciplines to elucidate an idea—a historical document is provided in a poetry class, or a film is screened in an anthropology course. Tayler discusses her experience of teaching literature in a jurisprudence course, in which she wants students to understand the "conflicting interests of Jewish and Arab Israelis, represented by Israel's security concerns, on the one hand, and the opposition of Arab Israelis to Israeli-imposed civil rights limitation on Arab Israelis, on the other." She explains that in her class, "fiction frees students from many of their conscious and subconscious biases and preconceived notions and engages them intellectually and emotionally at a human level." Amy Weiss, for similar reasons, discusses teaching film in a history course, in which the discussion about borders and boundaries acquires a visual reality, emotionally charging the students' encounter with the facts, so that they gain greater insight into the real costs to daily life.

For literary courses, it is frequently desirable to provide historical and political context or to explain the sociological situation that may give birth to art. Russell A. Berman through the novel, Cary Nelson through poetry, Olga Gershenson through film, Beverly Bailis through a reading of Mahmoud Darwish, Peter C. Herman using the British novel *The Little Drummer Girl*, Martin B. Shichtman referencing Joe Sacco's comic *Palestine*, Philip Metres in his comparison of two short stories by women, and others engage with the contextualization of literature, providing close readings of several texts in poetry, fiction, comics, and film.

Metres, Halperin, Alan Dowty, Shiri Goren, Joel S. Migdal, and I, in my own essay, also provide examples of thinking structurally about the creation of courses and the ways in which we constitute the students' engagement with material. These essays share a clear pedagogical focus directed at helping teachers create courses and select suitable texts that offer complex readings of the situation, while stimulating students' engagement.

The literate nature of the region has particularly facilitated the emergence of a range of voices in the modern period. Teaching this diversity is integral to disrupting the prejudices created through propaganda, social media, and the press that students bring to the classroom. For Rachel Feldhay Brenner, tracing the shared history of Jerusalem as a sacred space offers an avenue to ensure that students see the shared cultural history of the region; thus, reading Christian, Muslim, Jewish, Druze, and Baha'i writing together elucidates the central place that the Holy Land occupies in several religious traditions. Writing by women is replete in both Arabic and Hebrew, the two major languages of the conflict (though texts in Persian, French, and English may also provide additional perspectives), and offers an opportunity to consider female experience within cultures that revere masculinity and militarism, asking whether women's shared experience may transcend that of national difference. Moreover, the diversity within Palestinian and Israeli culture also reveals issues of race, privilege, and the staking out of multiple diasporic sites. In Hebrew, one can use writing by Mizrahi Jews (Jews who lived in Muslim countries before the twentieth century), Arab citizens of Israel, Vietnamese immigrants, Ethiopians, and Russians, as many of the contributors here do, including Gershenson, Ranen Omer-Sherman, Berman, Nelson, and Bailis. These relationships complicate our conceptions of identification with the nation-state and the place of the individual within the conflict. At the same time, the Palestinian diaspora not only writes from within Gaza or the West Bank or in the Arabic language but also has emerged as a literary force writing in Hebrew in Israel; across the Arab world; and in an English-speaking diaspora in the United Kingdom and the United States. As Berman explains, the multiplicity of these voices allows us to consider the impact of the conflict on daily life in the region and also the shaping of diasporic identity for those who consider it a geographical point of identification but are no longer situated within it.

Oren Kroll-Zeldin, Bailis, Rolin Mainuddin, and Mira Sucharov also offer discussions of the ways in which courses on the Arab-Israeli conflict serve to address contemporary social justice issues within the United States and Canada. While not collapsing the distinctions between different regions and historical situations, these parallels draw students into an immediacy that reflects other conversations with which they are already familiar. It can also work to give a face to Palestinian suffering and situate contemporary movements within a larger global debate about privilege, oppression, and government responsibility.

Several essays consider the ways in which teaching frames the material that students encounter and the role the instructor plays in crafting the narrative of the historical context and what terms are used to describe wars, events, borders, nations, and peoples, including essays by Goren and Ashley Passmore. Fernheimer addresses the issues that arise in defining terms of reference that potentially evoke the region's tensions, characterized for example in the ways in which Arab Christians and Muslims who live within Israel are defined: as Arab citizens of Israel, Arab Israelis, Palestinians, Palestinian Israelis, the Arab minority—terms that may or may not be hyphenated. Moreover, these terms pretend to specificity, but the reality is that the groups to which these given terms refer are also debated. Are Druze and Bedouin separate groups, are they identified with the Arab minority within Israel, and can they be called Palestinian or choose to identify themselves as such?

The sites of classrooms also shape the kinds of labor demanded by instructors. The United States is only one among a large number of countries in which there are course offerings on the Arab-Israeli conflict. These include Australia, Britain, Canada, China, Cyprus, Denmark, Egypt, France, Germany, India, Ireland, Israel, Japan, Jordan, Malaysia, Poland, Qatar, Romania, Saudi Arabia, South Africa, Turkey, UAE, the West Bank and Gaza, and Zimbabwe, to name but a few. The historical, political, and social context of the institutions and geographic locations play a role in the work of faculty. Umut Uzer reflects on the legacy of Ottoman colonialism in discussing the Middle East and the complex relationship that Turks have with Arabs and Jews. P. R. Kumaraswamy outlines the issues of teaching Israel studies in India, where the conventional frames of reference that function within Western culture are absent. Like Uzer, Husam Mohamad shows in his essay that even a single faculty member may need to modify his or her teaching depending on location, for teaching within the Islamic world or another country embroiled in its own regional conflict; Mohamad found that teaching in Cyprus is not the same as teaching at an institution with a large evangelical Christian population in Oklahoma. Menna Abukhadra outlines the changing history of teaching the conflict in Egypt and the impact that the World Wide Web has had on creating immediate access to resources, news, and people.

Mya Guarnieri Jaradat found that the conflict intruded into the classroom, when as a Jewish woman she was told her presence was unwelcome teaching Palestinian students in the West Bank. She questions whether there are limits to what can be taught, by whom, and where, but as Adia Mendelson-Maoz shows in her discussion of running the Open University literature department in Israel, we can continue to work to make education accessible, even when that requires us to rethink our materials. Moreover, in different areas within the United States and different kinds of academic institutions, the student encounter is shaped by factors that exist beyond the classroom walls. Not only do politics on campus, including Birthright, the debate over Hillel's relationship to Israel, Apartheid Week events, and Boycott, Divestment and Sanctions (BDS) campaigns, affect student engagement, but the economic and social demands that students encounter must also be part of our broader discussion about enfranchising student learning. Sucharov, Berman, Guarnieri Jaradat, and Ari Ariel consider the ways BDS can and does play a role in considering how and what we teach. Even as course objectives continue to focus on enabling students to develop the apparatus for critical, reasoned thinking and civil discourse, in an age of trigger warnings, faculty more than ever are asked to respect students' feelings and backgrounds. Ariel's discussion of hummus maps out the issues that arise in tying identity to the conflict and considers learning in relation to BDS efforts to single out Israel. Berman discusses his own political activism against BDS outside the classroom and his refusal to treat the classroom space as a captive audience for his political positions.

The essays in the volume include examples from two-year colleges, regional public universities, small liberal arts colleges (SLAC), a U.S. military service college, state universities, private universities, institutions with a religious mission, a historically black college and university, and elite schools both in the United States and abroad.

Several essays here consider physical and experiential learning experiences in order to create empathic responses. Ellen W. Kaplan uses theater, asking students to take on the roles of Palestinians one week and Israelis another so that they learn to embody their awareness of the other. Divine teaches respect for the other by asking students to defend different political positions each week, and Passmore enables students to speak in the voice of characters as they work through their understanding of the conflict. Kroll-Zeldin and Jeffrey Bloodworth use travel to Israel and the West Bank, including walking through checkpoints, as a way to have students experience the conflict; while Randall G. Rogan has students act out conflict resolution, and Divine also invites students to participate in a model UN debate—all examples that help students engage in experiential learning. Goren using maps at Yale and Shayna Weiss using a battle plan at the United States Naval Institute invite students to reconstruct the very process of history and highlight the shaping of narratives and the ways they inform ideology.

Many of the essays address institutional requirements and their application in courses on teaching the conflict, such as Carenen's comparison of lower- and upper-division courses, Passmore's essay on her institution's critical thinking curriculum, or Berman's observation that adding learning requirements moved his student enrollment from fifteen students to fifty. Terri Susan Fine's essay focuses on the ways in which middle school and high school curriculums with requirements to teach Israel and the Holocaust engage in discussion of the conflict within the tightly regulated structures of mandated instructional criteria. Though her essay focuses on a specific institutional setting, it maps out the ways of engaging with institutional language that may also form part of having courses listed for general education requirements.

Many essays move beyond this broader discussion to consider the instructor's own personal experiences of encountering the materials and changing in the face of the classroom experience, including those by Susan Jacobowitz, Guarnieri Jaradat, and Sucharov. As Sucharov explains, "we carefully and deliberately analyzed the many dynamics of activism we observe . . . on campus and social media," but keeping politics out of the class proved an uncomfortable struggle that worked against the principles of her discipline. Learning to embrace the discussion instead, she harnessed the tension within her instruction in order to make the engagement a relevant practical lesson. Jacobowitz's horror at encountering apathy from students toward Palestinians, while wrestling with her own ambivalence toward the occupation, due in part to being a daughter of Holocaust survivors; Sherman's discussion of the tensions he experiences as a Zionist opposed to the occupation; Guarnieri Jaradat's conflict between her beliefs in educational counterargument and her students' perceptions of her as a Jewish woman; and Mainuddin's identity as a Bangladeshi Muslim, which marks him out as an object of suspicion when teaching political science about the conflict, are studies in navigating the personal encounter that faculty have with the material. Many of the essays in this volume consider whether there is a moral and political responsibility in the ways in which we teach the conflict. Can the lessons in the classroom facilitate an awareness of the region's complexity that eschews simplistic explanations, thereby combating propaganda in the face of rigorous intellectual analysis? Can we use education to help us build bridges and work toward compassion in an effort to tear down prejudice and aim for the higher ideals of empathy and tolerance?

The book's contributors were given two principles: first, that the essay should provide insight for someone who might face the same pedagogical problems, offering assignments, activities, and lists of resources that could be used effectively by a person in a similar disciplinary context; second, that the essay should prove useful for scholars and educators in other fields, institutions, or locations, by providing reflection on guiding principles or exploring challenges that extended beyond a specific area of study. The essays range from short, practical guides to extended analyses of the field and institutional context. I have learned from all of the essays as I have edited this collection, and often by translating ideas through my own disciplinary lens, I have enriched my syllabus as well as my teaching practice.

With these goals in mind, the book is organized by thematic topics, across disciplinary lines. Adjacent essays (even across sections) expand on related ideas. The book can be dipped into for quick inspiration or read from beginning to end—though the essays can be read in any order—as part of course planning. As such, there is some repetition among the essays—of philosophy, texts, and assignment ideas. I have left these in place so that readers will find what they most need wherever they look. Rather than impose standardized terminology, contributors have chosen the terms they prefer to use for referring to historical events, wars, and peoples, though as most of the essays show, the discussion of terminology serves a pedagogical role within the class itself.

In discussions of travel-abroad programs, Holli Levitsky, Kroll-Zeldin, and Bloodworth all consider students' encounters with the reality of life in the region. They encourage connecting with Israelis and Palestinians, and Bloodworth's students also stay in Jordan, where they meet Christian and Muslim Arabs—both Jordanian and Palestinian—who view Israelis and the conflicts in very different ways. Yet all of them address in some ways the need to keep their students safe on the trips. It is jarring to think that in 1929, the Wycliffe Hall students were willing to sacrifice their own security to stabilize the region. It may not be the objective of today's travel-abroad programs to directly participate in this same task, but all of these courses serve in some ways a similar end. For all of the contributors to this volume, helping students understand the regional complexity is part of a process that leads toward a responsible citizenry. We hope that critical thinking, empathy, and respect will inform their approach to the conflict, and perhaps our students may go on to be journalists, politicians, soldiers, activists, or scholars whose actions could ultimately play a direct role in shaping the future of the region.

Notes

1. Maurice Samuel, *What Happened in Palestine: The Events of August, 1929, Their Background and Their Significance* (Boston: Stratford, 1929).
2. Ibid. In Luke's diaries, there is nothing written for the five days of the riots. For a man who wrote prolifically in his diaries, this lacuna is decidedly curious. Middle East Archive, St. Anthony's College.
3. *Living Church* 106 (January 1943): 5.

4. "Wycliffe Hall Students Who Helped to Defend Palestine Jews in 1929 Outbreak Again Visiting Palestine," JTA (Jewish Telegraph Agency), August 13, 1931, www.jta.org/1931/08/13/archive/wycliffe-hall-students-who-helped-to-defend-palestine-jews-in-1929-outbreak-again-visiting-palestine.
5. Letter in the archives of Humphrey Ernest Bowman (1879–1965), St. Anthony's College Middle East Centre Archives.
6. Rachel S. Harris, "Shooting Yourself in the Foot: Hebron 1929" (master's thesis, Middle Eastern Area Studies, School of Oriental and African Studies, University of London).
7. Though large populations of Arabs came under Israeli rule, many had also fled during the 1948 and 1967 wars and moved to other parts of the Arab world and later the United States and Europe. Among the major issues in resolving the Israeli-Palestinian conflict has been the situation of Palestinian refugees since 1948. While many Palestinians were displaced, the actual numbers are contested by both scholars and the United Nations. Since one of the negotiating points has been a Palestinian claim to a "right of return" for these individuals and their descendants, or in some cases there has been the suggestion of remuneration and reparations, the establishment of precise numbers is relevant for those who are negotiating a final peace agreement. For a detailed analysis of this question of numbers, see Efraim Karsh, "How Many Palestinian Arab Refugees Were There?," *Israel Affairs*, April 1, 2011, www.meforum.org/articles/2011/how-many-palestinian-arab-refugees-were-there; Benny Morris, *The Birth of the Palestinian Refugee Problem, 1947–1949* (Cambridge: Cambridge University Press, 1987); and Alan Dowty, *Israel/Palestine*, 3rd ed. (Cambridge, UK: Polity, 2012).
8. In 2005, Israel withdrew from Gaza, leaving a Palestinian population to internal self-determination, while continuing to control the access of goods to the area, some infrastructure (such as airspace), and maintaining the Erez border crossing into Israel, which is generally restricted to humanitarian passes. The main route into Gaza is through the Rafah crossing with Egypt. By contrast, the West Bank is divided between areas of Palestinian rule and areas of Israeli rule, with some overlap, and Israel continues to control access from the West Bank into Israel.

Acknowledgments

Teaching a living conflict is for many people both an intellectual exercise and a deeply profound experience. I am grateful to the contributors here, who have reflected on the professional and personal challenges they have encountered, and their willingness to share their journeys toward making the classroom a thoughtful, reflective, and inclusive space.

This book grew out of my own need to revisit my teaching (the result is a course on women's filmmaking that I discuss in the volume), my need to connect with other practitioners in the field to overcome the inevitable isolation of the classroom, and my awareness of the increasing globalization of this area of study, with its inherent complications. As the fields of Israel studies, Palestine studies, and Middle East studies continue to expand not only at universities in North America but across the globe, a book that helps faculty engage with the pedagogical challenges of teaching the Arab-Israeli conflict becomes ever more necessary. I want to thank Kathryn Wildfong at Wayne State University Press, who supported the project from the beginning; Kristin Harpster, my ever-patient editor; and Andrew Katz, Kristina Stonehill, and Rachel Ross at Wayne State for their expertise and trust. I am grateful to the Academic Engagement Network for a subvention grant to help with the manuscript preparation; and Martin B. Shichtman, who served as a sounding board and thoughtful reader throughout the project. I also want to thank the anonymous reviewers and the network of fellows from the Brandeis Summer Institute for Israel Studies (SIIS), many of whom contributed essays or helped connect me to potential authors. I would like to express my very great appreciation to the Washington Institute and Aviva Weinstein for arranging access to their shape files for the West Bank, settlements, and the barrier, as well as areas A, B, C. Using these and by sourcing population data from both the Israeli and Palestinian population bureaus, who kindly shared their materials, Gregory Newmark was able to make original maps for this book, and I am thankful for these resources and his work to make them happen. I owe a huge debt of gratitude to Randy Deshazo, my husband, for the significant amount of invisible labor he contributed toward creating the time line, as well as all those who advised and reflected on it, including Helene Sinnreich, Joshua Shanes, Jarrod Tanny,

Jacob Lassner, Katja Vehlow, Liora Halperin, Mira Sucharov, Michal Raucher, and Husam Mohamad.

This project became deeply personal when two close mentors who had dedicated their careers to ensuring the teaching of the Arab-Israeli conflict through interdisciplinary engagement died early in its development. It is dedicated to the memory of Michael Kotzin, at the Jewish Federation of Metropolitan Chicago, a literary scholar and administrator who fought bravely against the disease that claimed his life, working to advance Israel studies until weeks before his death; and to the memory of Michael Feige, a sociologist and anthropologist at Ben Gurion University of the Negev and the Ben Gurion Research Institute for the Study of Israel and Zionism who was a friend and collaborator and whose works have informed many of the essays here. Feige's support of this volume and our early conversations on the shape it would take were a manifestation of his intellectual generosity. We had been discussing his participation in the project when in June 2016, he was one of four Israelis killed in a terrorist attack on the Sarona Market in Tel Aviv. In a eulogy, his research institute paid tribute to him by describing him as "the incarnation of a man of reason, tolerance, and peace." He lived the qualities that I hope this book embodies.

Maps

The Middle East

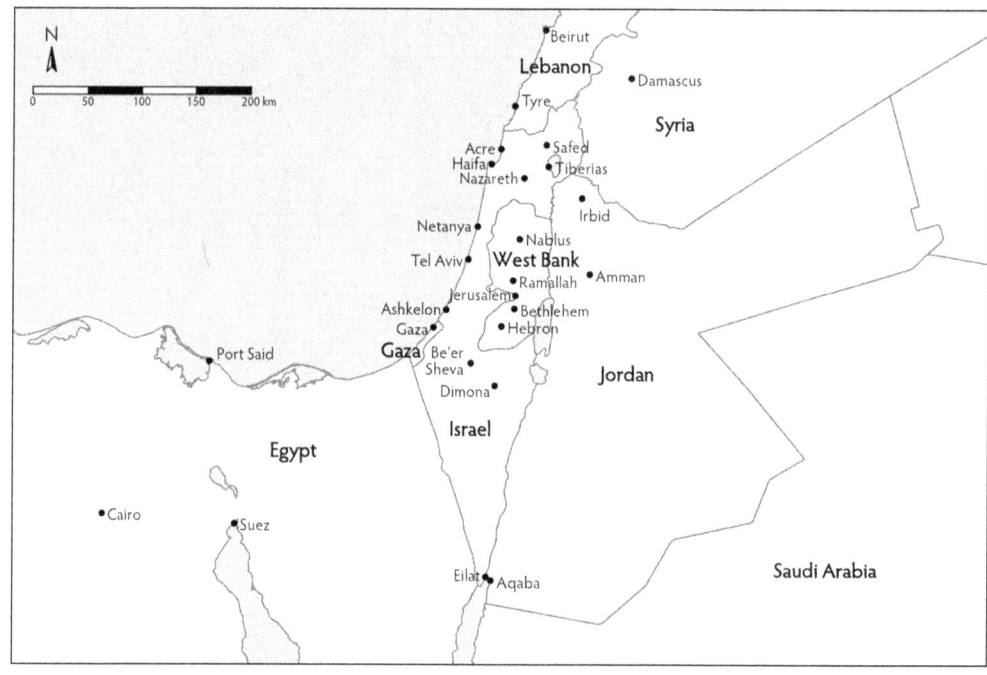

Southeastern Mediterranean

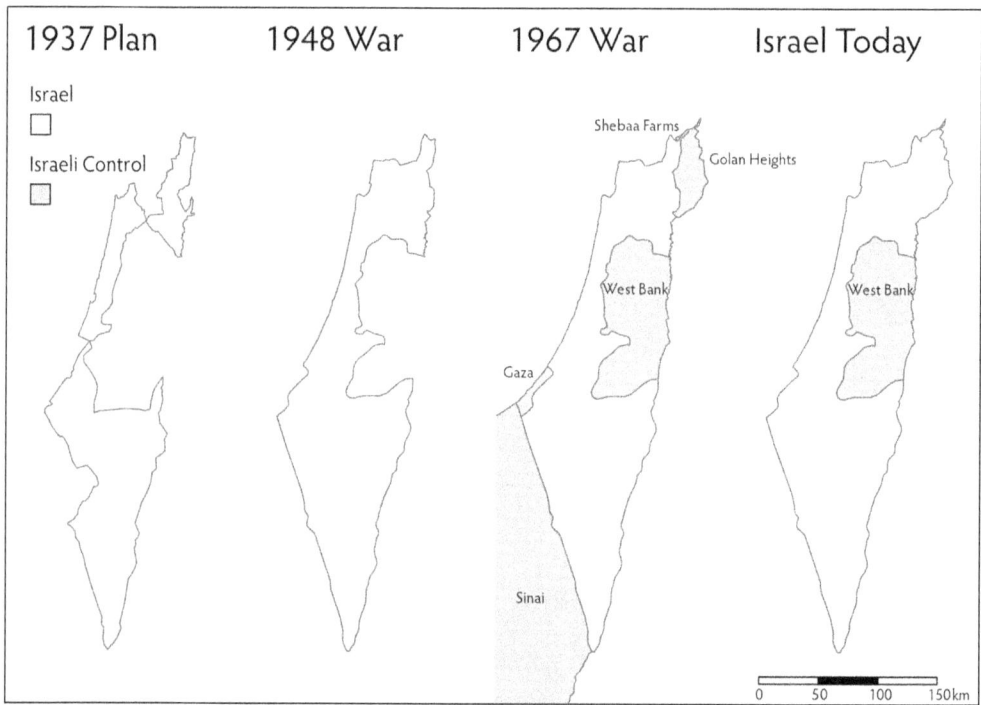

Territory of Israel/Palestine

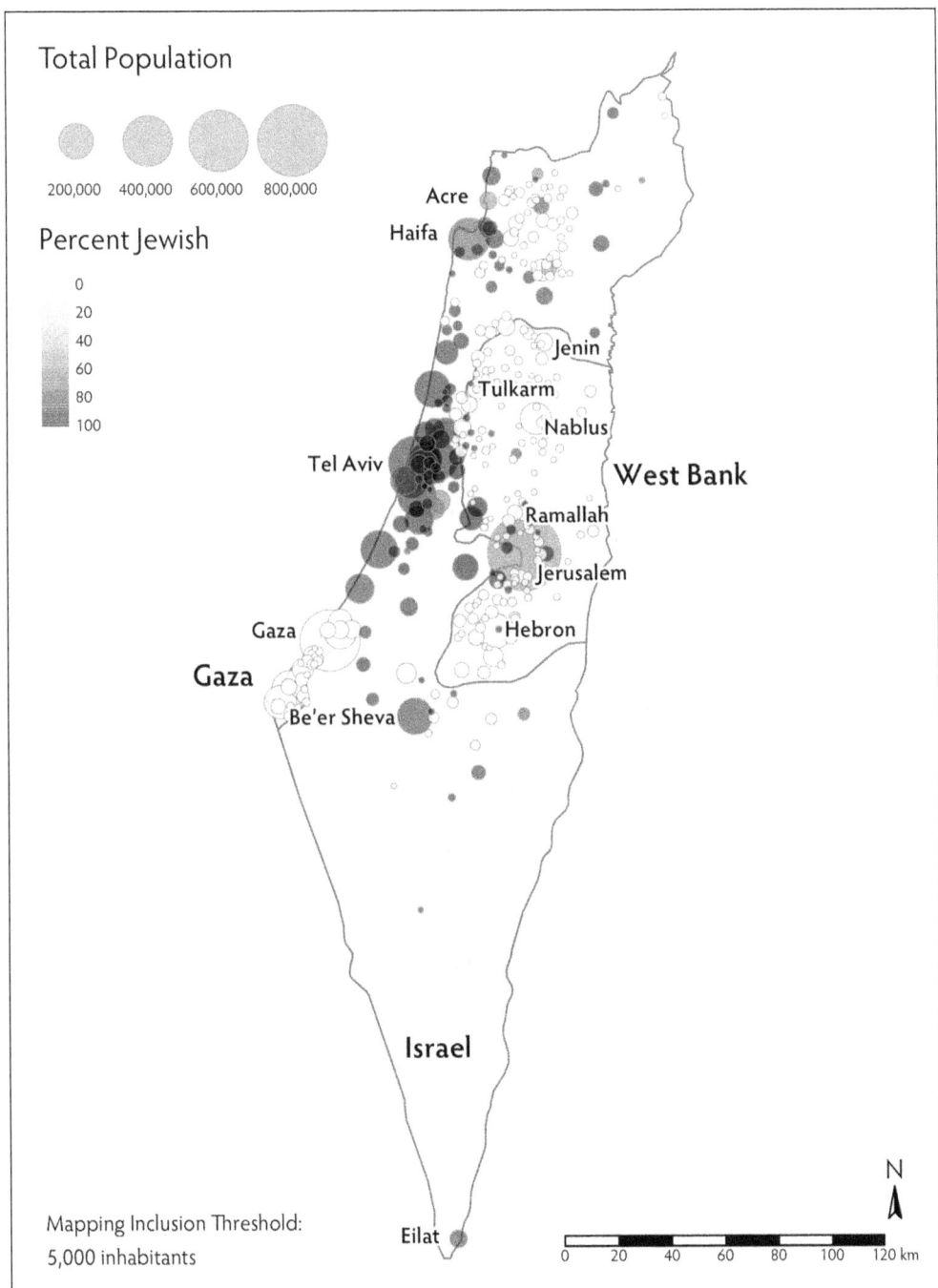

Population distribution

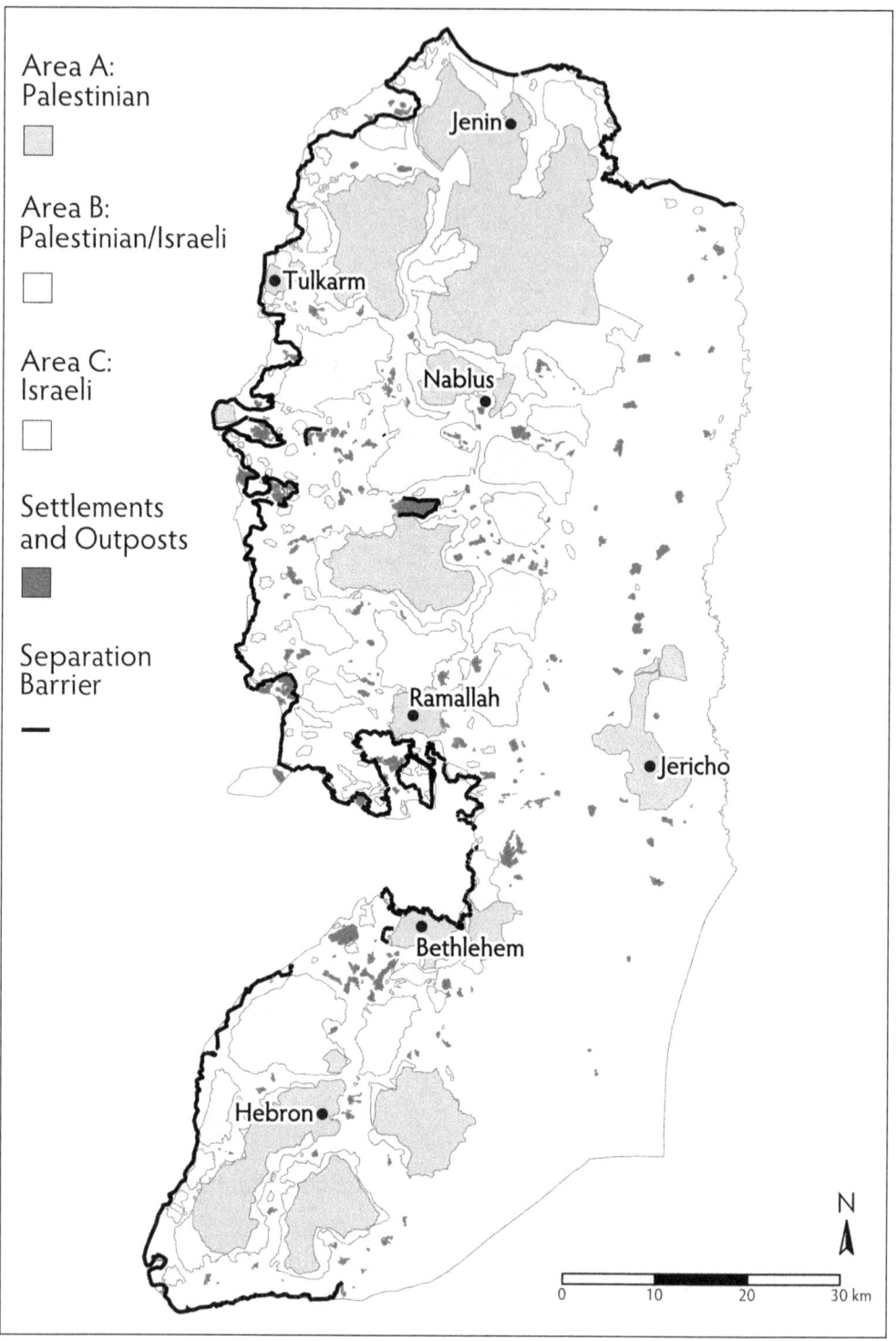

West Bank administrative divisions

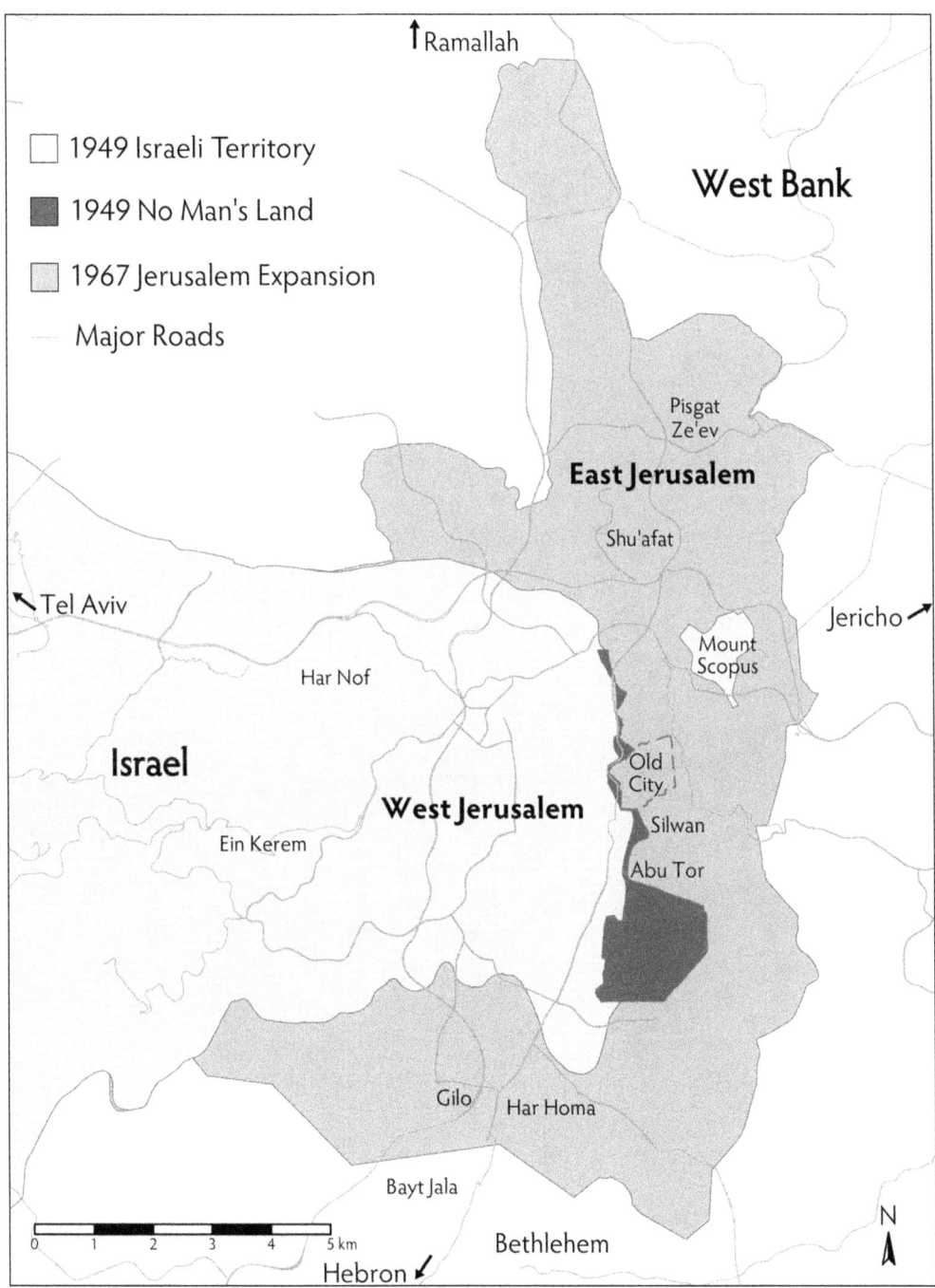

Jerusalem occupied and expanded

Introduction to the History of the Region and the Conflict

The Path to Genuine Peace?

HISTORICAL PERSPECTIVES ON THE ARAB-ISRAELI CONFLICT

JACOB LASSNER

It is now almost seven decades since the creation of the Jewish state, and yet the Arab-Israeli conflict endures, a dispute that engulfs all the nations of the region as well as much of the wider world beyond. Complex and morally vexing, "the conflict" has all the outward appearances of a theatrical tragedy, a performance that exhausts actors and audience alike even before the final act has begun. What is it that makes the Arab-Israeli conflict, and in particular the dispute between Israelis and Palestinians, so resistant to some sort of resolution, a question easily posed but given to varied answers, depending in large part on how past and present events in the region are interpreted.

There is a tendency among many, if not most, Western observers to view the Arab-Israeli conflict—the outgrowth of what before the establishment of Israel was called the Palestine Problem—from two distinct and, at times, seemingly incompatible points of view. The first characterizes the dispute between Israel and its Arab neighbors and between the Jewish state and the as-yet-stateless Palestinians as a dispute between modern political movements, one Jewish, the other Arab, both inspired by the rise of European nationalism in the nineteenth century. Analysts who maintain that the Arab-Israeli conflict, and specifically the dispute between Israelis and Palestinians, is driven essentially by modern politics contend that the issues dividing the parties should and could be resolved by political means: namely, extensive negotiations that build trust between the contending parties, a trust that can then lead to the kind of give-and-take that will point the way to a permanent settlement. In this scenario, cooler heads and gifted leaders will prevail. Peace has a compelling logic on its own.

The second perspective recognizes that the Arab-Israeli dispute is in many respects the outgrowth of interlocking political events that have unfolded in modern times.

But it also places great stress on residual attitudes from a distant past. Those who hold this view maintain that the current situation between Israel and the Arab states is in essence an existential conflict between two faith communities, both deeply rooted in the Holy Land. That is, most Arabs are seen as tied to long-standing and deeply felt religious traditions that preclude the very existence of an independent Jewish state in the Islamic heartland. And so any political settlement that legitimizes any Jewish state compromises Islamic principle and degrades the Muslim body politic. In these circumstances, Muslims, who represent well over 90 percent of those who identify themselves as Arabs, will find it difficult to reach any sort of agreement that fully sanctions an independent Jewish polity in Palestine. Any agreement reached between Israel and an Arab state, and specifically between Israel and the Palestinians, might address broadly defined Arab concerns of the moment and satisfy Israel's quest for normalcy. But there is no guarantee the agreement will endure when Israel is perceived as weak and susceptible to Arab pressures. Palestinians may eventually sign peace agreements with Israel, as have the Egyptians and the Jordanians, but in the end, they will not hold to the contract indefinitely—or so those who embrace the existential argument believe.

Understanding the Conflict's Roots

Any serious analysis of the first perspective begins with a thumbnail sketch of the aims of two rival nationalist movements, political Zionism and Arab nationalism, with particular emphasis on the formation of Palestinian national identity. Political Zionism, which emerged in the nineteenth century in an age of national movements, promoted an agenda that embraced a two-thousand-year-old Jewish yearning to return to the land of their ancestors and celebrate life as did Jews in days of yore. But, rather than passively await the coming of the Messiah to occasion that return, Zionists, mostly secular in outlook, opted for a politically proactive program that included intensive Jewish settlement in what Jews long called the Land of (*Eretz*) Israel. At the same time, representatives of the Zionist movement lobbied internationally for the creation of a Jewish polity therein. The ultimate objective was to reconstitute the Jewish people in the ancient Land of Israel, or as the original wording of "Hatikvah," the anthem of the Zionist movement, put it, "We have not yet lost our two-thousand-year hope to return to the land of our forefathers and to the city [Jerusalem] to which [King] David came and settled." In May 1948, the State of Israel was declared in part of modern Palestine, and the Jews of the Diaspora altered the words of "Hatikvah" to coincide with the national anthem sung by Jews who settled Palestine and created the Jewish state: "to be a free people in our land, the land of Zion and Jerusalem [according to our ancient dream]." The newly minted State of Israel was defended in an armed struggle with the native Palestinians and their Arab allies. Having beaten back the Arab challenge and established itself on a firm footing, the fledgling Jewish state gained admittance to the United Nations and thus became a recognized member of the world community. For Jews, the emergence and then survival of the state in a hostile environment was the fulfillment of the Zionist dream. After two thousand years of exile in foreign lands, the Jews had a national home like other peoples of the world, a place that could give refuge to their brethren when necessary and serve as the place in which to forge a modern Jewish culture reflective of Jewish values.

Still, for decades thereafter, no Arab nation formally recognized the existence of the Jewish state, let alone its legitimacy. It was not until a peace treaty was signed between Israel and Egypt in 1978 and between Israel and the Hashemite Kingdom of Jordan in 1994 that the state of war between these countries was brought to an end and full diplomatic relations were established between former adversaries. The rest of Israel's Arab neighbors who warred with the Jewish state at its inception remain officially at war with Israel, a state of belligerency that has now extended for nearly seventy years. As a result, there are no recognized borders between Israel and the neighboring Arab states with which it has no peace treaty. There are only the boundary lines that were drawn when armistice agreements were signed in 1949, the diplomatic initiative that signaled the end to Israel's war of independence.

Usually, an armistice leads to signing a peace treaty following intensive face-to-face negotiations. However, once the armistice agreements were signed, the Arab world boycotted all official contact with representatives of the Jewish state. Travel by Israelis or people bearing passports stamped in Israel were denied entry to Arab countries. Even Muslim citizens of Israel were unable to make the obligatory pilgrimage to Mecca, as their official travel documents would have signified the very existence of the state that claimed their allegiance. Any encounters between Israeli and Arab representatives outside the region were carefully monitored to avoid face-to-face contact. Even maps of the region were altered so that the contours of the Jewish state disappeared along with the name "Israel."

Like political Zionism, Arab nationalism is the outgrowth of nineteenth-century European trends in nation building, which in this case percolated into the Arabic-speaking provinces of the Ottoman Empire. Hitherto, Arab (Arabic: *'Arab*) had been a term that signified a Bedouin or someone linked directly or by ties of clientage to an Arab tribal configuration. More often than not, the designation *'Arab* carried with it a pejorative connotation ranging from "uncouth" to "uncivilized" and individuals and groups "given to anarchic behavior." With the rise of modern Arab nationalism, the term came to signify a proud person and people identified with a great cultural heritage and historic achievements on the field of battle. Arab nationalism began as a movement to liberate the Arabic-speaking provinces of the Near East from the yoke of the Turkish Ottoman Empire. The original aim of the Arab nationalists was not to create nation-states independent of the empire, as did the Christian communities of the Ottoman-ruled Balkans. Rather, the Arab nationalists sought greater license to administer regional and local affairs and to promote a culture based on the Arabic language rather than Turkish. Indeed, at the time, the very concept of a nation-state was foreign to Muslim thinking. The only truly legitimate polity was the Islamic Ummah, the universal community of Muslims that theoretically transcends all boundaries of ethnic, linguistic, or regional and local affiliation. The concept of the all-encompassing Ummah dates back to the very origins of Islam, and although it was always more theoretical than real, it remains for Islamists the idealized polity for all the faithful. The Islamic State in the Levant (ISIL) has gone so far as to declare itself the linchpin of a newly founded Ummah; its leader, Abu Bakr al-Baghdadi, claims to be a caliph, or successor to the Prophet Muhammad, the leader of the first universal Islamic community.

To be sure, Christian Arabs had a different view. Among them, Arab nationalism was tied from the outset to the concept of a nation-state and citizenship within a polity bounded by universally recognized borders. They found these European ideas of nationalism particularly appealing because, based on the model of the liberal countries of the Western world, the nation-state would have offered them citizenship and legal equality with the Muslims instead of the subordinate status of a protected minority (*ahl al-dhimmah*), a condition dictated by Islamic law and enforced by the Ottoman authorities, if loosely at times. It would appear that modern nation-states of the Middle East have yet to fully allay the concerns of their rapidly diminishing Christian minorities.

Despite recent appeals by the more strident Islamists to reconstitute the Ummah, given the world order of the moment, the current polities of the Arab world retain the structure of nation-states. However fractured some of these states may seem, they still are regarded by the world community as discrete political entities with recognized borders, although given present trends in the region, we may witness a redrawing of current boundaries and the establishment of autonomous regions, if not indeed new national entities seeking universal recognition within the world community.

How does the evolution of the Arab nation-state affect understanding of the Arab-Israeli conflict? With the dismemberment of the Ottoman Empire at the end of World War I, the Arabic-speaking provinces east of Egypt were carved up by the international community and awarded as mandates to be administered by the British and French until such time when they were fit for independence. With that, Arab nationalism was redirected to a new goal: ridding the region of foreign influence and establishing Arab nation-states within the artificial borders of the mandated territories. These areas included the British-administered Palestine Mandate, a newly established geographical entity carved out of what had been the Muslim province of al-Sham, the "Greater Syria" of ancient and premodern times. But who was to rule Palestine when it was seen as fit for independence, Arabs or Jews?

The Palestine Problem

When in 1917 the British government issued the Balfour Declaration, a loosely worded document that called for the establishment of a "Jewish national home" in Palestine, it handed the Zionist movement the basis with which to argue its legal case before the court of world opinion. The declaration, combined with the long association of Jews with their ancient land, whose history was firmly entrenched in the imagination of Bible-reading Christians, served as the legal foundation of the Zionist claim. The Arabs of Palestine did not foresee at first the potential threat posed by the Zionist movement. But they, along with other Arabs, understood the skill with which Zionist spokespersons maneuvered within the corridors of international power. Their initial antipathy toward the Jews in Palestine was governed largely by religious considerations. Indeed, a distinctive Palestinian national identity did not cohere until the early 1930s, when all hopes of reestablishing a Greater Syria that included Palestine were abandoned as the Levant had been divided by the European powers. The French controlled the mandates of a truncated Syria and Lebanon, and the British administered the Palestine Mandate, creating thereby several potential nation-states with boundaries that bore little, if any, resemblance to those of previous times.

As a discrete Palestinian nationalism took root and sprouted, Arabs became ever more vigilant of mounting Zionist settlement and the threat that it represented to their evolving national aspirations. The Jewish population of Palestine, about 40,000 when the Balfour Declaration was issued, had grown to some 400,000 by the mid-thirties, and following World War II, the roughly 650,000 Jews in Palestine exceeded one-third of the total population. The growth of the Jewish community and the resistance of the Arabs to any form of Jewish polity made for a combustible situation. Not surprisingly, the years following World War II were marked by rekindled nationalist fervor and, with that, internal strife in Palestine despite the presence of 100,000 British troops and police. With security declining, the United Nations Organization, as the UN was then called, sent a commission to investigate a possible solution that might satisfy both Arabs and Jews. Its decision, which was shaped into a United Nations resolution, resurrected an idea that had been proposed in the 1930s and that had previously been rejected by both parties, namely, to partition modern Palestine into two sovereign states: one Jewish, one Arab. In turn, Jerusalem was to be given special status as a place holy to three faiths and was to be administered as an international city. The leaders of the Jewish community in Palestine accepted the resolution; the Arabs of Palestine and all the established Arab nation-states rejected it. The partition resolution made its way in November 1947 to the UN's General Assembly, where it passed thirty-three for, thirteen against, with ten abstentions. Immediately thereafter, resistance to the plan, initiated by the Arabs of Palestine, precipitated armed conflict with the Jewish community.

Following the withdrawal of the last vestiges of British authority in Palestine in May 1948, the leaders of the Jewish community proclaimed the birth of the modern State of Israel. With the last British troops gone, Arab armies from the surrounding states came to the assistance of the Palestinians and the volunteers that had previously entered the country to lend their support for the Palestinian cause. In the end, the combined Arab forces, save for Jordan's Arab Legion, suffered a humiliating defeat. The nascent State of Israel expanded its boundaries beyond those stipulated in the partition plan. An estimated five to six hundred thousand Palestinians (Arabs contend that the figure is upward of eight hundred thousand)[1] fled their homes, never to return again, partly in an attempt to flee the battle zone and partly the result of forced expulsion when Israeli forces attempted to establish direct and secure links between the embattled and isolated areas of Jewish settlement. At the conclusion of the 1947–49 war, the only areas of Mandate Palestine that were not in Israeli hands were the Gaza Strip, a narrow ribbon of land along the Mediterranean bordering Egypt, and parts of the West Bank of the Jordan River. Jerusalem was divided in half; the Jordanians occupied the sacred territory of the Old City and its environs as well as all the eastern neighborhoods; the Israelis, all of West Jerusalem.

Having occupied the West Bank of the Jordan and part of Jerusalem, the Jordanian authorities did not relinquish their spoils of war to the Palestinian Arabs. Instead, they annexed the occupied land to their own domain and declared the Palestinians dwelling therein citizens of an expanded Jordanian state. Nor did the Egyptians cede the territory they held to the Palestinians. Instead, they made the Gaza Strip into a rump state with a rump parliament that was subjected to a heavy-handed Egyptian administration. Aside from 1956–57, when Israel took control of Gaza as a result of the Sinai campaign, only to be forced out by U.S. intervention, the Palestinians were under foreign Arab rule for nineteen years. No attempt had been made by either the Egyptians or the Jordanians to grant the Palestinians a state of their own. Nor did the disgruntled Palestinians rise up in rebellion. Moreover, exiled Palestinian nationalists who were anxious to confront Israel by force of arms found their activities carefully monitored by the neighboring Arab governments, which were fearful of unwanted consequences. The cross-border incursions by Palestinians and the reprisal raids by elite Israeli forces did not lead to any substantive changes to the status quo.

The Six-Day War and Its Aftermath

Following Israel's withdrawal from Gaza and the Sinai Peninsula in 1957, the situation remained more or less static until the Six-Day War of 1967, when, responding to a prolonged provocation by Egypt and Syria, Israel unleashed a preemptive strike against the combined forces of the neighboring Arab states. Once again, Israel conquered the Sinai Peninsula and Gaza as it did in 1956, but this time it added the remaining areas of the West Bank, including East Jerusalem, having seized the opportunity to capture this territory when Jordan reluctantly entered into the conflict. In addition, the Israel Defense Forces (IDF) overran the Golan Heights, an area of the Holy Land that had been ceded to the Syria Mandate by the European powers following the defeat of the Ottomans in World War I.

The Six-Day War might truly be considered a turning point in the modern history of the Middle East and the Arab-Israeli conflict in particular. For one, it demonstrated the great strength of Israel's armed forces and its modern society. Although a number of leading Arab statesmen were well aware of the power Israel could project, they made no serious effort to counter the Arab public narrative that explained away the defeats of 1947–49 and the debacle of the Sinai War of 1956. The former, labeled the Nakba or "catastrophe," was attributed to corrupt politicians who sent Arab contingents into the field without proper equipment to confront the Jewish army. The 1956 disaster, in which the Egyptian army was driven from Sinai and Gaza in one hundred hours, was described as an orderly retreat in order to confront the British and French forces that had invaded Egyptian territory along the Suez Canal. As the United States successfully pressured all three invaders to withdraw, the Arab narrative of these events proclaimed a great victory. This version of history became conventional wisdom in the Arab street along with the betrayal of 1948–49.

No such rewriting of history was possible in 1967. Arab expectations of a monumental victory, so high in the days before the outbreak of hostilities, juxtaposed with an Israeli victory that was so thorough and swift, left no room for a counternarrative that could mitigate the shameful disaster. There was at first some serious soul searching among Arab intellectuals regarding Arab culture and the very fabric of their societies. There were even critiques of Islam. Be that as it may, such critical reflection did not penetrate deeply and in any case was short-lived. Shamed by the enormity of the defeat, the Arab states rejected a public Israeli offer to return the conquered territory in exchange for a genuine peace treaty, that is, a treaty that would have formally ended the state of war between Israel and the Arab states, recognized Israel's standing within the world community, and established full diplomatic and economic relations with the Jewish state. It is unlikely that Israel would have ceded all the conquered territories—certainly not the venerable Jewish Quarter of Jerusalem's Old City, which had been conquered by Jordan's Arab Legion in 1948. But the official Arab response to this teasing offer was so negative that it created no room for serious negotiations.

In the meantime, Jews returned to settle a rebuilt Jewish Quarter, reoccupied settlements near Jerusalem from which they were forced out by Jordan's Arab Legion during the War of Independence, and expanded Jewish settlement in hitherto-unoccupied areas of the holy city. The Israeli government also established a Jewish presence in the holy city of Hebron, the burial site of the Jewish patriarchs Abraham, Isaac, and Jacob and three of the matriarchs. A caretaker was appointed to look after the tomb of Rachel (the fourth matriarch), which was situated outside Bethlehem. As the years drifted by with no end to the conflict, various Israeli governments gave in to pressure to establish any number of Jewish settlements throughout the West Bank, the ancestral homeland of the ancient Israelite tribes. Together with a newly created ring of Jewish settlements in the Jerusalem area and along the old Green Line that separated Israel from the Hashemite Kingdom west of the Jordan River, the settlements of the ancient Israelite highlands, an area labeled by Jews according to the biblical toponyms Judea and Samaria, have become home to an estimated six hundred thousand Israelis, some of them uncompromising religious nationalists.[2] This region is also referred to by those who oppose Israeli presence in the area as "the occupied territories," within which the settlements have become a bone of contention, as well as a serious obstacle to any projected peace agreement between Israelis and Palestinian Arabs.

The Six-Day War also produced far-reaching changes in Arab politics. On the heels of the disgraceful defeat in 1967, Arab nationalism or, to be more precise, the notion of Arab unity was shattered. The unifying force of pan-Arabism was superseded by the resurgence of Islam. It was widely felt in certain quarters that the Arab states could only meet the challenge of Israel and Western political and cultural influence by returning to the pristine Islam of the early and universal Ummah. The return to Islam has led ultimately to movements such as Hamas, Islamic Jihad, al-Qaeda, and so far the most extreme manifestation of pan-Islam, the Islamic State of the Levant (ISIL). Another sign of the shattering of pan-Arabism was that the individual Arab nation-states looked to their own narrowly defined interests rather than partake of a grand Arab military alliance against Israel, an alliance that might call for premature action and lead to disaster, as occurred in 1967. This loss of nerve and the disgrace that the Arab states bordering Israel bore for their shameful effort on the field of battle proved beneficial to the Palestinians. Unable or unwilling to create a Palestinian state or even give meaningful lip service to the rights demanded by the Palestinians, the Arab nation-states hosting the Palestine Liberation Organization (PLO), which had been formed in 1964, gave the Palestinians license to act on their own. But despite some high-profile terrorist activities that drew wide attention, the PLO failed to make any significant headway.

The surprise Egyptian-Syrian attack on the Jewish Day of Atonement in 1973 created the embers that resulted in the Israel-Egypt peace agreement of 1978. Although the Israelis recovered from the initial assault and within three weeks had extended their hold on the Golan Heights and penetrated the Egyptian heartland, the initial Arab success produced positive results, at least for the Egyptian leadership. The Israeli advance into Egypt was halted by U.S. intervention, giving the impression that the United States was prepared to broker future agreements between old adversaries. Having taken the fight to Israel, Egypt had salvaged its honor and could therefore anticipate a future agreement with the Jewish state that would return all of the Sinai Peninsula to Egyptian control.

Serious Arab thinkers drew a clear lesson from the 1973 war: the Israelis could not be defeated in any conventional conflict, but they could be pressured with the assistance of the United States to enter into negotiations that might be of mutual benefit to the two states that were still technically at war. The result was a diplomatic effort that led to the peace agreement of 1978, in which Egypt recovered the lost Sinai Peninsula in stages in return for certain security guarantees and the normalization of relations between the two countries. The stunning turn of events did not resonate favorably within the Arab world. Israel's traditional enemies treated the historic agreement that the United States brokered with animosity. This was especially true of the Palestinians, as Egypt had ended the hostilities with Israel and normalized relations with the Jewish state without addressing Palestinian desires for self-determination.

The role of the Palestinians, enhanced by their headline-grabbing actions against Jewish targets, may have won them considerable sympathy in the Arab world and even in certain Western circles. However, a subsequent sequence of events undermined this temporary fame and eventually forced the leadership of the PLO to do what seemed unfathomable, that is, to recognize the Jewish state in return for Israel's recognition of the Palestinians' right of self-determination. Having been ignominiously forced by the Israelis from their bases in Lebanon in 1982 and made a pariah in the rest of the Arab world by their endorsement of Iraq's invasion of Kuwait in 1991, the Palestinians eventually turned their political agenda on its head and entered into secret negotiations with the Israelis. The talks, held initially in Oslo, Norway, led to the signing of a 1993 agreement known as the Oslo Accords in which both parties broadly accepted the validity of the other's national claims.

With the 1993 agreement, the Palestinians, save the Islamists among them, started a process that many observers hoped would be a second major step in resolving the long-standing Arab-Israeli problem. Shortly thereafter, the Jordanians gave up their claim to the West Bank, paving the way for a possible Palestinian state, and then joined the Egyptians in making peace with Israel and normalizing relations. Many people now expected that this was the long-awaited breakthrough that would create a climate of stability for the troubled region. There had been public talks between Israelis and Arabs representing various governments of the region in Madrid in 1988. However, the participants to the Madrid conference had no license to enter into a serious give-and-take. Still, the very fact that Israelis and representatives of different Arab countries were sitting together was an encouraging sign.

The Oslo Accords served as a series of agreements between PLO representatives and Israeli officials. These included Palestinian recognition of the State of Israel and Israeli commitment to Palestinian self-determination, beginning with a plan laid out for the division of 97 percent of territory in the West Bank, while further talks would determine the final boundaries of a Palestinian state, which would include territories in Gaza, at the time under Israeli control. The accords led to the creation of the Palestinian Authority (PA) and a three-part division of the West Bank into Areas A, B, and C. The PA has responsibility for Area A, which comprises the major urban population centers, with exclusive control over both security and civilian issues. In Area B's more rural locale, the PA only has civilian control. While the Jewish population in Area C is administered by a regional Jewish council, the Palestinian population is administered indirectly by the PA, including responsibility for education and health care. However, Israel is responsible for all infrastructure construction in Area C.

The interest stirred by the proceedings in Madrid and the initial euphoria that accompanied the understanding between the leaders of the PLO and the Israeli government has given rise neither to a Palestinian state nor to a final peace agreement with any of the Arab states that are still technically at war with Israel—this in spite of numerous attempts at actual negotiations and efforts to restart stalled talks. The two major issues that proved a sticking point in the negotiations with Palestinians and ultimately led to the peace process stalling were an inability to resolve the status of (East) Jerusalem as the capital of a Palestinian state and the right of Palestinian refugees to return, though many reasons have been proffered for the lack of progress. Considerable blame has been apportioned to all the partners in the dispute and to those outsiders seeking to intervene on behalf of peace. Ultimately, the manner in which one views the current situation is dependent on whether one sees the search for peace as forged on the anvil of modern Near Eastern history or conditioned by cultural factors deeply rooted in the region's past.

With this brief historical survey behind us, we can return to the two historical perspectives with which we began our discussion: conceptualizing the Arab-Israeli conflict (1) as a political dispute that has to be solved by political mean or (2) as an existential conflict that by its very nature resists normal attempts at conflict resolution.

Perspective One: The Arab-Israeli Conflict as a Political Problem

As noted, the 1967 war and especially the failed 1973 surprise attack demonstrated to thoughtful and realistic Arabs that Israel could not be defeated in a conventional war at any time in the foreseeable future. Unconventional war (Arab terrorism) and asymmetrical conflict (rocket launches on Israeli civilian centers), however much they satisfied Arab needs for action, have also proved no substantial threat to the very survival of the Jewish state. Recognition of the power that Israel is capable of wielding and the resiliency of its people in the face of all challenges has led many analysts of Middle East politics to conclude that despite the current climate, in which both Israelis and Palestinians appear frozen in their positions, there remains now, as before, only the possibility of a political solution. In this case, they point to a solution based on the creation of two states within the area of the original Palestine Mandate. Should the Israelis and Palestinians agree to such an arrangement and actually carry through on implementing it, the same analysts expect other Arab nations to follow suit and make peace with the Jewish state. Indeed, the mechanisms for such an arrangement have been in place ever since the conclusion of the Six-Day War.

After the events of 1967 and again in 1973, Israelis seeking peace had for the first time real bargaining chips: namely, the Sinai Peninsula, the West Bank, and the Golan Heights, which were being held concurrently. Moreover there were two United Nations resolutions, 242 and 336, that could serve as the legal basis for a comprehensive settlement between Israel and the Arabs. Each of these resolutions embraced the principle of exchanging conquered land in return for a durable peace and the normalization of relations between the Arab states and Israel, a formula that led to the aforementioned peace agreements with Egypt and Jordan, agreements that have also led to strong, if at times subdued, relations between former adversaries. That being the case, why not actively pursue the partitioning of the former Palestine Mandate into respective Jewish and Arab states, the seeming objective of the agreement signed between Palestinian and Israeli leaders in 1993?

Astute observers realized that despite the euphoria following the historic agreement of principles through the Oslo Accords in 1993, there were many outstanding issues that could delay and even thwart the onset of real peace. Successive Israeli governments have called for a two-state solution, the most recent right-wing government with seemingly great reluctance. The Palestinian leadership of the West Bank has also accepted the concept of partition, but there seems to be no movement toward a political solution. Some twenty-five years have come and gone since both parties agreed to recognize each other's national aspirations, and yet the final act to end the long-standing dispute is nowhere in sight. To be sure, seasoned observers of Middle East politics understood from the start that the task of resolving the problem of Palestine would be difficult. Although a two-state solution seemed eminently sensible, there were critical issues that could doom attempts at reaching a final agreement.

What were to be the borders of the two respective states? In particular, how could one arrange for direct access from the Gaza Strip to the West Bank, areas of the future Palestinian polity presently separated by the Israeli heartland? Since any map would produce kissing points between areas of Israeli settlement and the future Palestinian state, there are obvious security concerns in Israel about protecting the heartland against terrorist assaults. This manifested itself in the erection of a much-debated security fence (also called a separation barrier or wall) dividing the West Bank from major areas of Israel proper. There are also compelling emotional issues. What is to be the fate of Jerusalem, the holy city of three faiths? For Israelis, Jerusalem, the city founded by the biblical King David three thousand years ago, is their eternal capital, a city never to be divided again or withdrawn from Israeli control. For Muslims, Jerusalem is the third-holiest city in the Islamic world, in many ways comparable to Mecca and Medina. It is their intention to establish the city as the capital of the future Palestinian state. Above all, there is the contentious issue of how to resolve the problem of the Palestinian refugees, whose ranks include not only those dispossessed by the fighting in 1947–49 but also the subsequent generations of Palestinians who insist on the right to return to their homes or the homes of their parents and grand- or great-grandparents. Israelis have made it clear that no such mass return is possible, as it would alter the Jewish character of their state. From the Israeli perspective, the best the Arab refugees and their descendants can hope for is financial compensation, balanced against compensating the eight hundred thousand Jews who fled their homes in Arab lands in the years following the creation of the Jewish state.

Over the years, foreign nations, be they Arab, European, or the United States, have attempted to lessen tensions and/or broker a final agreement to end the dispute between Israelis and Palestinians, thus paving the way to an all-embracing permanent solution to the Arab-Israeli conflict. None of these efforts has succeeded. There are indeed observers from all camps who think that the two-state solution is all but dead, but none among them has a realistic idea of what is likely to follow if that indeed is the case. The thought of abandoning the two-state solution is too depressing to contemplate for those realists who see it as an essential path to creating a stable environment in the region. As a result, those who seek a political solution to what in essence they declare to be a political problem still hope for successful diplomacy.

Perspective Two: The Arab-Israeli Conflict as an Existential Problem

On the other hand, there are those so-called experts who tend to weigh their understanding of current events largely in favor of a history that is long past. They do not deny the influence of the upheaval created by European colonialism and the emergence of a powerful Jewish state. But, according to them, these occurrences, as shocking as they have been to Muslim sensitivities, are best understood in light of an ongoing history of complex Jewish-Muslim relations. This second school of thought stresses the traditional enmity shown by Muslims to Jews, negative attitudes and at times hostile behavior that begins with the very birth of Islam and continues until this very day. They refer to the daily vitriol found in the Arab media and in the textbooks that Muslim Arab children are given to read. While many recognize that until modern times Jews were generally better off in Arab lands than they were in contemporaneous Christian Europe, they dismiss altogether the notion of a Jewish Golden Age under Islamic rule. Given the negative views of Jews and Judaism found in the Qur'an and the vast and ongoing literature and public preaching to which Muslim scripture has given rise, those who see the past through darkened lenses see little reason for Muslims to recognize the validity of a Jewish state in their midst. Jews were unthreatening when they were a docile minority in Islamic empires, but as proud possessors of a powerful polity on Muslim land, there can be no permanent accommodation with the Zionist enterprise.

If there is ever a peace agreement between Israel and the Palestinians or, for that matter, between the Jewish state and the Arab states with which it is still at war, the agreement is bound to be limited in time. A strong Israel might be able to secure a formal peace with the Palestinians and all the Arab polities of the Middle East, but it will never be able to overcome the anti-Jewish sentiments that have shaped Muslim attitudes and behavior into the present. There may be a peace agreement occasioned by pragmatic concerns related to Israeli strength and Arab weakness. However, this will not lead to psychological acceptance of a Jewish state in the Abode of Islam. The peace is likely to be de facto even though on paper it is declared de jure. As the skeptics see it, the agreement will collapse at the first sign of genuine Israeli weakness. Some holding to this view even forecast a new Holocaust, this time at the hands of Muslim extremists. The recent activities of ISIL have given the pessimists much food for thought.

There is, moreover, the long-standing Muslim belief that any lost territory that was at one time subject to Islamic law must be reclaimed by the Muslim faithful. Such a view takes precedence over any treaty that relinquishes control over lands that were once governed by the authorities of the Ummah. Hamas, the Palestinian Islamist movement that controls the Gaza Strip, has formally rejected any treaty recognizing the Jewish state. Moreover, it has concocted an Islamic tradition that declares Palestine a *waqf*, or sacred trust of the Ummah. As such, it cannot be sold or otherwise transferred to any foreign or individual Muslim client. Hence, there would be no legal basis for recognizing the legitimacy of Israel, not now or ever. There is the expectation among Hamas supporters that somehow the Israelis will lose heart under constant pressure and will go the way of the Crusader states before them.

The example of the Crusaders is frequently cited by Palestinian nationalists and other Arabs who oppose Israel and the encroachment of the West. From the very outset, Muslims have exhibited a triumphal attitude toward external adversaries. Until modern times, they had much reason to believe that history was on their side. The early Muslim conquests were swift and decisive. It took eight hundred years, but the Muslims put an end to their principal rival, the Christian Byzantine Empire. Until the fifteenth century, and following that the rise of the West, the only significant Muslim losses to nonbelievers were to the Crusaders and the Mongols. The Muslims outlasted the Crusaders, whose kingdoms withered and disappeared, and the Mongols soon converted to Islam. It was only some three hundred years ago that the Ottoman armies stood at the gates of Vienna, poised to bring western Europe under Islamic rule, as they had done earlier to the Christian lands in the Balkans.

The rise of the West and, linked to that, the emergence of the Jewish state, which is seen as an extension of the West, has shaken Muslim self-confidence. But recent years have seen the resurgence of Islamist tendencies in the Arab world, as reflected in the activities of the long-established Muslim Brotherhood, Hezbollah, Hamas, Islamic Jihad, a number of splinter groups fighting in Syria, and especially al-Qaeda and its offshoot ISIL. The latter two movements have taken the fight against the West beyond the region in which they were spawned. One cannot predict with any accuracy, if at all, what the future holds; but as long as the Islamists are a force to be reckoned with, there is danger to the existing Arab regimes, and with that, any agreements concluded with their established rulers will be, in the worst scenarios, subject to revocation. Given this outlook, the pessimists who embrace the notion of an existential conflict have little, if any, faith in the durability of any negotiated settlement.

Is all this pessimism warranted? The Muslims were forced from the Iberian Peninsula after having created a flourishing culture there that lasted nearly nine hundred years. The same could be said for Sicily and more recently the Balkans. And yet there does not seem to be any formal attempt to establish a clandestine movement or Muslim expeditionary force to reclaim these former Islamic lands. That being the case, what prevents the current Arab states and even the Islamists from being reconciled to the existence of Israel and establishing formal relations with the Jewish state? One should be clear that all the Muslim lands lost were on the periphery of the Abode of Islam; Palestine is at the epicenter of the Muslim Arab world and has enormous religious importance. The Islamists are convinced that at some undisclosed time in the future, all the world will turn to Islam. But that vision of Islam's ultimate triumph is expected at some future apocalyptic moment. Israel is a problem of the present.

Afterthought

Is there, then, no way out of the morass that has been created in the Middle East? A review of Islamic tradition and history offers several clues on how to deal with the Arab-Israeli problem and the more narrowly circumscribed dispute between Palestinians and Israelis. Some people may suggest that we ought to fully understand the complexity of the issues and strive not for a permanent resolution of the conflict but for effective crisis management. Arab Muslims will never accept the legitimacy of a Jewish state in the Abode of Islam, but there are various mechanisms allowed by Islamic law and tradition that can produce a temporary accommodation that might be extended for long periods of time. And there is precedent for this idea, given that the Muslim states and Byzantine Empire lived cheek to jowl for eight hundred years, a period marked by intermittent fighting and truces, usually along the frontier, and of diplomatic missions and frayed relations that, taken as whole, took on the appearance of a ritual dance. Muslim law allows for temporary truces with unbelievers, albeit a halt in fighting that is designated for a limited period of time of up to some fifteen years. Needless to say, no responsible government in Israel will formally agree to such an arrangement, especially because such a truce (*hudnah*) can be legally broken at any time that Muslims feel they have the upper hand. However, there is in this kind of arrangement the possibility of a peace that can last well beyond fifteen years. As long as the Jewish state is seen as fully able to protect itself and has an increasing role to play in the Arab politics of the region, a situation that is currently unfolding, any number of parties in the region including the Palestinians can see the benefit of a formal peace, as opposed to periodic disturbances that can morph into a major conflict that will further destabilize an unsettled region. Israel's more recalcitrant Arab neighbors might not explicitly recognize Israel as the state of the Jewish people, but why should the leaders of Israel insist on this public declaration? That Israel is the state of the Jewish people is an established fact. All that the current enemies of Israel should have to acknowledge is that the international community fully recognizes the legitimacy of the Jewish state and that Muslim Arabs are reluctantly obliged as partners in the international community to follow its dictates as regards Israel. The Palestinians and their Muslim brothers may think otherwise and hold another view in their hearts. They may also fervently believe that at some undisclosed time in the future, God will redeem the national rights of the Palestinians and restore the glory of the Islamic world as in days of yore.

Israel and the world should be able to live with that messianic vision. Dreams, however vivid, are surely preferred to foolish and in the end self-destructive actions.

Notes

1. Efraim Karsh, *Palestine Betrayed* (New Haven, CT: Yale University Press, 2010), 272 (583,121–609,071).
2. According to population statistics from the Israel Central Bureau of Statistics, approximately 401,500 Jews live in the West Bank, and a further 273,000 live in East Jerusalem. Israel Central Bureau of Statistics, "Population in Localities by Sex, Age and Statistical Area [Hebrew]," data file, 2016.

Teaching Skills, Facing Challenges

What Happens in the Classroom?

"Why Can't We Just Create New Sacred Holy Sites?"

TEACHING THE ARAB-ISRAELI CONFLICT IN A NEW ENGLAND PUBLIC LIBERAL ARTS UNIVERSITY

CAITLIN CARENEN

My university, a public liberal arts university in a small town in rural, eastern Connecticut, boasts approximately five thousand students who are predominantly in-state residents, with a smaller percentage primarily gleaned from the states of Massachusetts, New York, and Rhode Island. I have taught "History of the Arab-Israeli Conflict" as an upper-division history course and as a smaller interdisciplinary colloquium as part of my university's honors program. My university's location in small-town New England means that I rarely encounter the committed Christian-evangelical Zionist (unlike my previous teaching experiences in the Deep South, where I attended graduate school) or Zionists in general. Most of my students are not particularly religious, and only once (of which I am aware) have I taught a Jewish student (who self-identified as Jewish, secular, and openly nonpartisan). Despite this liberal and secular New England context, however, most students approach the class convinced that while they do not know much about the Arab-Israeli conflict, it must surely be a religious war between Judaism and Islam. For example, after reading an introductory chapter on the significance of Jerusalem to the world's three-largest monotheistic faiths and the inherent difficulties stemming from that real estate reality, one very bright honors student offered a classically pragmatic American solution: just create new holy sites in different locations. We start, in other words, with a tabula rasa.

Course Goals and Inherent Challenges

Whether I am teaching an upper-level course to history majors or an interdisciplinary honors colloquium, one consistent and clear challenge remains: teaching a deeply complex topic to students who generally have no background or prior knowledge of the conflict. They have "heard" about it, of course, but that is usually the extent of their exposure. Perhaps they have also, at some point, "liked" a Facebook post about the conflict (usually one that benignly calls for peace in the Holy Land). When the class begins, many are even unsure of Jerusalem's location. But they are there because they genuinely want to learn more, to become educated about a complex, entrenched struggle, and are keenly aware that learning about the conflict makes them better global citizens. From my perspective as an instructor, that is an excellent starting point. Ignorance can be educated, but apathy is difficult to overcome.

The overriding goal, then, is to move beyond the facile Facebook "like" to profound, unsettling (and even upsetting), thoughtful, and informed contemplation of one of the world's most notorious conflicts. Teaching the conflict immediately brings to the forefront one problem students often have with needing absolutes. They crave universal truth, absolutes, and clear "good guys" and "bad guys." Throughout the semester, I witness students struggling to determine "whose side they are on." Repeatedly they vocalize that they are not sure, and it is frustrating to them that their "side" keeps changing, the more they are exposed to a variety of primary sources. This pressure is certainly not forced by me (that would surely constitute poor pedagogy) but by their own internal pressure to keep the gray at bay. Introducing them to multiple perspectives not only is necessitated by the subject material (and class title) but is good historical practice and serves a useful pedagogical function by constantly challenging comfortable assumptions and positions.

For historians, the benefit of hindsight offers a simultaneous blessing and curse: this is particularly acute in studying conflict. What might appear obvious now can sometimes prevent a critical appreciation for the decisions humans made in their historical moment. Forcing students to consider sources in their particular moment in history is a hard task and one that I, as their professor, frequently have to remind students to undertake. I have found that students gravitate to historical "what ifs," and while that can be an interesting speculative exercise, it remains in many ways outside our discipline's boundaries. Teaching students to consider actions and motivations *in their historical context* is the metagoal of all history professors, regardless of subject material.

Finally, the tendency of students to apply their own twenty-first-century personal context as well as their strong inclination to substitute emotional conviction for critical analysis makes teaching this course particularly challenging. When a student supplants reasoned argument with feelings and contemporary values, I pause and reframe the comment in a way that shows them the necessity of evaluating their statement against their primary sources (the old-fashioned Socratic method is particularly useful here). To minimize this tendency from the beginning, I overexaggerate the point in a way that gets their attention. I tell them at the start of the course that in history, "we don't care about your feelings." I say this somewhat tongue in cheek and quickly modify the statement by explaining that I deeply care about them as human beings but that history, as a discipline, does not. I encourage them to avoid the verb *feel* in written and oral work. At first, they find this somewhat paralyzing, but by the end of the semester, we have a humorous call-and-response. I begin by asking, "What do I not care about?" They respond in unison (with giggles), "Our feelings!" All of this is perhaps a little simplistic, but I have found that it works. Students are careful to frame their discussion comments and essays in ways that rely on sources, and critical interpretation of those sources, rather than emotional and shallow responses. In fact, the transformation in the degree and sophistication of their analysis is often quite dramatic from the beginning of the semester to their final-exam essays.

Reading Materials and Assignments

The upper-division history course is capped at twenty-five students, while the honors colloquium is capped at fifteen. The difference of ten students has been a profound one and has led to the creation of two fairly different syllabi and, to a certain extent, learning objectives. Nonetheless, "beginning at the beginning" is required for both. During the course of the semester, both classes take multiple map quizzes to learn geography, both are given basic theology instruction on Judaism and Islam, both are provided a general introduction to pre-1897 history of the region, and both classes complete a final mock-UN debate session on a proposed two-state solution. From that point, however, the structure divides.

In the upper-division history course, I have used Charles D. Smith's *Palestine and the Arab-Israeli Conflict: A History with Documents* (8th ed., Macmillan, 2013). I chose this book for several reasons: it offers a broad historical survey of the topic and concludes each chapter with primary sources from a variety of players. It begins with Ottoman-controlled Palestine and concludes with post-Oslo realities through 2012. It includes maps in appropriate places as well as a small selection of black-and-white photos. The usually abbreviated primary sources, ranging from three to six, try to offer multiple perspectives. Interestingly, however, some students have commented that they detect a pro-Palestinian bias in Smith's narrative. I find this surprising since, as I have already noted, most students have no background in the history of the conflict. When prompted to explain, students have responded along the lines of "I don't know, it just seems/feels that way." These comments have proven useful in generating class discussion by prompting me to ask in what ways, specifically, they perceive bias and how they might rewrite sections to present a more neutral tone, given the available material (they also get a gentle reminder about the use of the word *feel*). This also provides an opportunity to address the challenges of writing "neutral" history about a continuing conflict.

In addition to Smith's text, I assign two other books to conclude the semester. The first semester I taught the history course, I assigned Shlomo Ben-Ami's *Scars of War, Wounds of Peace: The Israeli-Arab Tragedy* (Oxford University Press, 2007). Ben-Ami's narrative of the conflict, from his well-placed position as a negotiator for the Israeli government (he was the former Israeli minister of foreign affairs), offers students an Israeli perspective of the conflict. The students' reaction to it has been lukewarm. They tend to find it overly detailed and too tightly focused on diplomacy (an asset, from my perspective), but they concede that it teaches them how excruciatingly difficult it is to conduct diplomacy and provides them with an appreciation for the complexities that are too often ignored by the general public. The final reading is from the Palestinian perspective: Sari Nusseibeh's *Once upon a Country: A Palestinian Life* (Farrar, Straus and Giroux, 2007). This is generally a favorite. Despite complaints of "wordiness," students find the framework of Nusseibeh's memoir engaging, relatable, and thought-provoking (again at this point, I find students struggling with which "side" they are on). Ending the course reading assignments with two memoirs helps students see the human impact of the conflict and makes what they have learned all semester much more accessible. Students appreciate ending, rather than starting, with these, as they now have a clearer sense of the course of events and can appreciate the finer details and first-person accounts.

With every reading, students are expected to complete a list of five discussion questions that reflect the totality of the assigned readings. These must be formal and typed (mainly to avoid students trying to complete the homework in class). These cannot be questions answered with a quick yes or no, nor can they be what I call "list" questions. List questions are questions that require only a simple recitation of a list of facts, events, or the like. At first, students in the general history course gravitate to these two types of questions, but rapid and thorough feedback tends to correct the problem. I explain to the students on the first day that while this assignment is intended to check their reading, it is also intended to help them concentrate and focus on what might be most significant from the readings. During each class discussion, one student "leads" the discussion by offering his or her five discussion questions to the class first. The quality of the discussion can somewhat vary, but even poor questions can be restated to provoke excellent discussion.

The honors colloquium students also have to construct discussion questions, though they are asked to write ten questions instead of five. However, they are exposed to a more significant reading load. In addition to a variety of scholarly articles that I provide, they read a large number of primary sources from *The Zionist Idea: A Historical Analysis and Reader* (Jewish Publication Society, 1997) and *Israel in the Middle East: Documents and Readings on Society, Politics, and Foreign Relations, Pre-1948 to the Present* (2nd ed., Brandeis University Press, 2008). The latter includes a mix of Israeli, Palestinian, Egyptian, and Jordanian sources translated into English. In addition, for the end of the semester, I have assigned Sandy Tolan's *The Lemon Tree* (Bloomsbury, 2006), Nusseibeh's memoir, and most recently Sarah Glidden's graphic novel *How to Understand Israel in 60 Days or Less* (Vertigo, 2010). I rotate between Tolan and Glidden; both are very popular with students, but Glidden's American perspective finds a sympathetic audience among my students.

The remainder of the graded assignments for both the history course and honors colloquium are composed of map quizzes. These start from a broad understanding of the region to the more narrowly focused areas of the conflict; three in-class open-notes, open-book essays in which they are asked broad questions that they must answer by direct and constant reference to their sources; and finally a mock United Nations debate. In this fictional debate, I break the class into two teams: Team Palestine and Team Israel. They have to debate the nature of a two-state solution (even as we have learned that not all agree with this solution) and center on five issues of contention: travel/roadways, security, economic cooperation, refugees, and the status of Jerusalem. If, during the course of the semester, I detect a student leaning toward one side, I will purposely assign him or her to the opposite team. Otherwise, it is a random team assignment. This is, by far, the most popular assignment all semester.

Students are given time in class and expected to work outside of class to prepare their team to debate each issue and turn in all their research in individual folders (so I can make sure all students do the work). Both teams give an opening address, break to meet with their counterparts, and then reassemble to present their final proposals. The students take this very seriously, work very hard, and in some cases, show an astonishing dedication to their task. This assignment, despite its admittedly simplistic approach, does create a deeper sense of how negotiation works and what is at stake. Observing the students working feverishly in their teams is gratifying. In the formal debates, I have witnessed previously quiet students red-faced and passionate about their perspectives, students quoting statistics and geographic details like experts, and some coming up with unusual solutions (in one course, a student designed a "Shotguns for Shekels" weapons buy-back program to improve security). In one of the honors courses, the students could not agree on the final status of Jerusalem and kept working long after the three-hour class ended. Eventually, I had to tell them that time was up and that their distress at not solving the problem was poignant.

Conclusions, Successes, and Failures

The always-popular debate is one of the most successful assignments of the class. It reveals to students the knowledge they have acquired throughout the semester. I always end that class by reminding them of how little they knew at the beginning, by asking them, "How could you have done this on day one? Think of how much you know now." Inevitably, every student smiles widely, revealing a much-deserved sense of pride. Some students have even gone on to pursue careers in international relations as a result of the course. Many more have accompanied me on intense study-abroad trips to Israel, Jordan, and the West Bank. But above all, success can be measured by the students' improved sense of perspective and appreciation of the conflict's complexity. At the conclusion of the debate for the most recent course I taught, one thoughtful and quiet student commented as he was leaving the room, "We got really into that. But we don't have anything personally at stake. Imagine if we did."

I have never had an assignment fall totally flat (yet). I have struggled, however, with overloading students with too much information. Particularly in the more intensive honors course, I assign a huge amount of reading. Part of this comes from intentionally designing the class to be as challenging as it can be for our most gifted students, but part of it comes from my impulse to expose them to as much primary source material, as many perspectives, and as many conflicting accounts as I can. Intellectually this is justified. Practically, however, it creates a bit of a "forest for the trees" problem. Working on streamlining readings to be the most effective, in part by editing the number and length of readings, would probably be more effective. And while not a failure, one of the issues that is difficult to observe is the emotional effect that studying this conflict can have on students, particularly sensitive ones. Many students over the years have commented on how "depressed" the subject makes them. Many leave class quiet and conflicted. The Arab-Israeli conflict *is* depressing, and my students' American pragmatism is at odds with this entrenched conflict rooted in historical memory. Quickly they learn that we cannot create new sacred holy sites, and they despair with the realization of the conflict's complexity. It is difficult to watch, but I restrain myself from any attempts to offer comfort. I instead constantly encourage them to consider deeper study over paralysis.

During my first research visit to Jerusalem, the director of the institute where I was a scholar in residence told me a now-familiar adage: the longer you stay, the more you study, the fewer solutions you have. I tell my students this story at the beginning of the semester, and I find it fulfilling that by the semester's end, they, too, have learned to avoid the easy, uninformed positions that are so ubiquitous in today's social media and dinner conversations, even among the educated. The final essay question I pose to my students is a seemingly simple one: What have you learned about the conflict this semester? This open-ended question forces them, as their last act in class, to reflect on the totality of the course. I get a variety of answers, of course, but my favorites are those that recognize the ambiguity inherent in the conflict—something that previously made them deeply uncomfortable. One student who was not a history major wrote, "There is blood on both sides, and who is 'right' and who is 'wrong' is . . . impossible to determine. Truth, as Nusseibeh would say, is never what it seems, especially when it is mixed in propaganda." Another concluded, "In all, each of these [readings] did their part in illustrating just how connected each side is to the region, and all of the hardships they have had to endure. My takeaway as a result, is that out of respect for both sides, I need to do my best to remain unbiased and open with regards to the conflict." If these were Facebook postings, I would be tempted to click "Like."

Comics and Conflict

USING GRAPHIC NARRATIVE TO WRESTLE WITH THE COMPLEXITIES OF ISRAEL/PALESTINE

JANICE W. FERNHEIMER

My scholarly path has been deeply entwined with my experiences in Israel/Palestine, and my teaching reflects this influence. In 2000–2001, I was fortunate enough to receive a Dorot Fellowship, enabling me to study abroad in Jerusalem and expand my knowledge of Hebrew language, Jewish culture, and Israeli society. Little did I know that I would be living in Jerusalem during the onset of the Second Intifada. Needless to say, I came back with firsthand experiences that complicated what I had learned in Hebrew/Sunday school about Israel.

I returned to the United States that fall to teach my first-ever, first-year writing class at the University of Texas at Austin, which took place the semester of the 9/11 attacks. It is no surprise that my experiences living amid the violence of the Second Intifada and returning to a United States responding to violence made me think carefully about the alternatives to violence that rhetorical theory and teaching might provide. I began to realize both how important and how difficult it is to teach others how to become informed about complicated issues and decide for themselves how they engage these issues in the classroom and beyond. Providing a method to wrestle with complexity and a means to translate that nuanced knowledge into action are two of the main things I try to do in all the courses I teach, but especially in the courses about Israel/Palestine that I have been offering since the early 2000s. In what follows, I show how the strategic juxtaposition of graphic narratives helps students to focus on multiple perspectives simultaneously and how this strategy helps students "wrestle with complexity" in their thinking, research, and academic writing. Before I turn to these strategies, I first provide some background about the course(s) I teach on Israel/Palestine and their conflict(s).

Background

As of spring 2017, I have taught five sections of three different courses at three different institutions (University of Texas at Austin, Rensselaer Polytechnic Institute, and University of Kentucky) over the span of fifteen years. Across the years and institutions, my students were quite different in their preparedness for college, not to mention advanced work in the humanities. Yet they all shared at least one thing in common: a familiarity with Israel/Palestine from the headlines they read in the news but little in-depth historical knowledge of the specific region, the greater Middle East, or the cultural heritages of either Jews or Palestinians.

The courses I design and teach serve a crucial introductory function in several respects: they introduce students to Israel as a nation and Palestine as a national entity, to Israeli and Palestinian cultures, to rhetorical concepts for critical analysis, and to strategies for academic research and writing. The first course I designed and offered in 2002–3 focused on the "rhetoric of the conflict" and aimed to help students satisfy the upper-division writing requirements at the University of Texas; it was a required course with no prerequisites. The second version I taught in fall 2009, "Representing Israel and Its Conflicts," was an introductory seminar aimed at first-year students and the first-ever course in Israel or Jewish studies offered at Rensselaer Polytechnic Institute. It aimed to introduce mostly STEM students to humanities-based research and inquiry while advancing their academic-writing strategies.

The course I now offer most consistently, though its name has changed with each iteration, is currently titled "Comics and Conflict in Israel/Palestine." I offered the course in fall 2012, fall 2014, and spring 2016 at the University of Kentucky, where I also direct the Jewish Studies program. It is an upper-division rhetoric class designed for majors in writing, rhetoric, and digital studies (WRD). Since the WRD major was only recently approved in 2014, the class has mostly attracted English and English education students looking to satisfy an upper-division writing requirement for their major. The course has no prerequisites. Though it "counts" toward the Jewish Studies minor, I have had few students enroll in it to further their minor studies.

Students at the University of Kentucky come mostly from in-state and across the Kentucky Commonwealth, many with little to no experience outside Kentucky, much less outside the United States. Sometimes I am the first Jewish person they have met, and often their limited knowledge of Judaism or Jewish culture comes to them filtered through an evangelical lens. Thus, in addition to furthering students' exposure to rhetorical theory and graphic narrative, the course often provides a first exposure to Jewish and Palestinian cultures as well as their "conflict(s)." I offer this background to emphasize the important introductory role this course plays, despite its upper-level designation and curricular design to help rhetoric majors develop disciplinary knowledge. Since this course serves as a first exposure to Israel/Palestine and an entrée to the larger global issues their conflicts call to the fore, I have worked to carefully set up its trajectory to expose students to multiple perspectives while also building critical, interpretive, and writing skills that enable them to make sense of these many, often-conflicting voices. One way I have done that is to shift the primary course readings from daily news stories, selected films, and historical texts to focusing on comics, or more specifically long-form graphic narratives.[1]

Why Comics?

I did not begin to teach "the conflict" through comics because I started out as a comics expert. I confess, I did not stay up late reading them in childhood or spend hours in comics stores as a teen. Rather, I was looking for a way to make difficult and nuanced content more accessible. As a pedagogue, I was drawn to comics because I found them immersive and engaging, and I wondered if they might provide an "easier," more powerful way for students with little background or familiarity to identify with multiple perspectives that are foreign to their own. The visuals help make a place far away in both geography and culture seem incredibly immediate and present; they hold out the promise of ease in identification, or what Scott McCloud terms "amplification through simplification,"[2] and perhaps most importantly for the way I teach the conflict(s), they offer a way for incommensurable narratives to be present simultaneously. As an educator offering an introduction to a complicated topic, I feel deeply responsible for how that introduction is shaped and how it in turn shapes how students think about the region and its peoples. This ethics-of-introduction aspect is even more important because many of my students will become the next generation of Kentucky's public school teachers in the not-too-distant future, soon providing introductions of their own.

Consequently, the specific ordering of texts and selection of graphic narratives has evolved as more graphic narratives in English are published and as I have gained more firsthand experience working specifically with University of Kentucky students. Joe Sacco's *Palestine* burst on the scene in 2001,[3] and since then at least fifteen graphic narratives that focus on some aspect of the conflict have been published. I list them here starting with the most recent: Amy Kurzweil's *Flying Couch* (2016),[4] Miriam Libicki's anthology of comics essays *Toward a Hot Jew* (several focus on Israel/Palestine; 2016),[5] Leila Abdelrazaq's *Baddawi* (2015),[6] Boaz Yakin and Nick Bertozzi's *Jerusalem: A Family Portrait* (2013),[7] Harvey Pekar and J. T. Waldman's *Not the Israel My Parents Promised Me* (2012),[8] Guy Delisle's *Jerusalem: Chronicles from the Holy City* (2012),[9] Galit and Gilad Seliktar's *Farm 54* (2011),[10] Sarah Glidden's *How to Understand Israel in 60 Days or Less* (2010),[11] Joe Sacco's *Footnotes in Gaza* (2009),[12] Oreet Ashery and Larissa Sansoor's *The Novel of Nonel and Vovel* (2009),[13] Naji al-Naji's *A Child in Palestine: The Cartoons of Naji al-Naji* (2009),[14] Miriam Libicki's *jobnik!* (2008),[15] Rutu Modan's *Exit Wounds* (2008).[16] Some are more accessible than others, and clearly there are now too many texts to teach all in one fifteen-week semester. Despite the steady release of narratives about Israel/Palestine, surprisingly little scholarly attention focuses on them,[17] much less the way they serve to represent and introduce readers (often for the first time) to Israel/Palestine, which makes the area ripe for students and teachers alike to make significant contributions to scholarly conversations.

Though which texts stay and go varies each semester, my aim is always to provide a multitude of perspectives: of foreign-born journalists who come to the region with a particular "representative" aim to focus narrative attention on the Palestinians' plight, such as Sacco; of those who end up there by chance with no particular religious or other tie to the region, such as Delisle; of those whose Jewish American educations shape the way they encounter Israel, whether on a "Birthright trip," such as Glidden or Kurzweil, or because they elect to make aliyah and join the Israel Defense Forces, such as Libicki; or of those who grew up in Israel, such as Rutu Modan, and of Palestinians living in the West Bank, Gaza, and Israel.

The first time I offered the course in 2012, it bothered me that the only way students learned about Palestinian perspectives was through the eyes of others, whether they were non-Jewish foreigners or Jewish Americans and Israelis. Until very recently, the only Palestinian-authored text in English that I was able to include was a one-page comic about West Bank water issues, written and illustrated by Amer Shomali, a multidisciplinary Palestinian artist and cartoonist whom I came to know through his monthly Arabic-language cartoons published in the *Filistin ashabab* (Palestine youth) magazine of Palestine and his animation work at ZAN studios; he was gracious enough to share his work with me after we met in person in 2012. When the Palestinian American Leila Abdelrazaq published *Baddawi* in 2015, I was grateful to be able to include a book-length narrative in English authored by someone of Palestinian descent who was not much older than the students enrolling in the course, adding another example to the growing list of powerful young authors writing comics.

Course Overview

Since competing narratives are so central to the rhetoric of "the conflict(s)," I aim for the course to provide critical tools to help students talk specifically about narrative and its important function in persuasive discourse. There are four main ways that I hope to enable students to critically engage competing narratives. While that probably seems overly ambitious, my general philosophy is to "overexpose" in the hope that students will find something that helps them further develop their critical apparatus for textual analysis. The frameworks I establish early on include the following: (1) a baseline understanding of stereotype, trope, and rhetorical topoi to better understand how pre/misconceptions shape people's understandings; (2) a rhetorical/historical/symbolic interpretive context using "myth" to frame and understand narrative incommensurability and emphasizing the traumatic impact of the Holocaust and Nakba on collective identity; (3) McCloud's theory of comics to better understand the medium through which we are learning; and (4) a brief "history" of Israel/Palestine to introduce students to the most basic elements of the complicated, controversial, and ever-expanding historical time line.

From the first class, we begin to investigate our preconceived notions about the place and its peoples when we watch Ari Sandel's Oscar-winning short musical comedy *West Bank Story* (2005). Based on the more popular and well-known *West Side Story*, this short piece follows the star-crossed love of the Jewish Israel Defense Forces (IDF) soldier David and the Palestinian falafel heiress/cashier Fatima, who meet while David is serving in an unspecified part of the West Bank, where there are dueling falafel restaurants: the Jewish-owned Kosher King and the Palestinian-owned Hummus Hut. At just over twenty-two minutes, this short and somewhat silly story helps call attention to stereotypes and narrative tropes that we continue to unpack over the course of the semester. Its rhetorical efficacy lies in its humorous play on conventional stereotypes, drawing attention to these tropes: for example, one of the menu items at Hummus Hut is "death by suicide bombing chocolate cake." Although suicide bombings are no laughing matter, the inclusion of this riff on the "death by chocolate" cake title pokes fun at the woefully inaccurate stereotype that "*all* Palestinians are suicide bombers" while calling attention to the fact that something as simple as naming chocolate cake can be politicized in this context. The importance and power of naming is something we continue to investigate throughout the semester as we learn the ever-changing historiographic time line, where something deceivingly simple—naming a war, even one of the most important wars, that of 1948—sheds light on whose point of view is privileged; "The War of Independence" privileges Jewish Israeli perspectives, whereas "Nakba" privileges Palestinian perspectives and experiences.

The second "frame" I offer is, not surprisingly, a rhetorical one, and though John Rowland and David Frank's *Shared Land/Conflicting Territory: Trajectories of Israeli and Palestinian Symbol Use* (2002) is a required text for the course,[18] we begin with their more recent *Communication Studies* article, "Mythic Rhetoric and Rectification in the Israeli-Palestinian Conflict" (2011),[19] which provides a theoretical framework for understanding the rhetorical importance of "myth" while also giving a brief historical background that attempts to answer why the conflict is as of yet unsolved. There is always a tension about where to begin and end the "coverage" aspect of this complicated history, and part of the reason we read Rowland and Frank's article "Mythic Rhetoric" early on is because the authors call attention to the way historiographic framing both opens up and limits the type of political resolutions possible. As we learn rhetorical concepts such as *ethos*, *pathos*, and *logos*, we also discuss the importance of the way baseline assumptions and definitions shape and frame how people think about historical events and chronologies. Connecting what we learn about the importance of myth to collective identity narratives, we move immediately from general ideas about collective identity myths to specific examples, reading graphic narratives and scholarly essays about the traumas that are most central and significant for Jewish and Palestinian identity myths in the Israeli/Palestinian context: the Holocaust and the Nakba.

While it is not always possible to find graphic narratives that provide equally complex representations from different points of view, I prefer to offer students narratives told from different perspectives to highlight the deep impact and sometimes polarizing differences of incommensurable narratives and their interpretive frameworks. Frames 2 (rhetorical concepts) and 3 (comics vocabulary) work together well to highlight the importance of putting multiple perspectives in conversation. Juxtaposition is a concept that is important both in the analysis and definition of graphic narratives. In *Understanding Comics*, Scott McCloud defines comics as "juxtaposed pictorial and other images in deliberate sequence, intended to convey information and/or to produce an aesthetic response in the viewer."[20] His definition emphasizes the important rhetorical and aesthetic effects of position in the comic medium, and strategic juxtaposition of multiple perspectives told in separate graphic narratives enables us to put disparate narratives in conversation. Through such strategic juxtaposition, we can sometimes see another, more encompassing narrative emerge—one that would be impossible to see without hearing multiple perspectives, often told from the privileged position of first-person autobiography, in quick succession.

Such strategic use of juxtaposition also offers an opportunity to consider why some rhetorical strategies are more effective than others and how/why the logistics of Israel/Palestine make it literally impossible for certain individuals to see or experience what others do. For example, the type of free mobility and access that Guy Delisle, a Western foreigner with no religious ties to the region, reports of his experiences in West Jerusalem are simply unavailable to the Palestinians living in Gaza with whom his wife's Doctors Without Borders work brings his family into contact. They are equally unavailable to Palestinians living in East Jerusalem and the West Bank. Key issues such as freedom of access/mobility/security as well as the lasting impact of collective trauma are broached and brought into conversation this way.

Frames 2 and 3 thus work together to provide a comparative look at how collective trauma is illustrated in the conversation between Jewish Art Spiegelman's *Maus* and

Palestinian American Leila Abedelrazaq's *Baddawi*. Both are told from the perspective of a son/daughter working to represent the father's traumatic experiences. Though the texts cannot be equated—*Maus* helped to establish the medium as worthy of literary and scholarly attention, whereas *Baddawi* was just recently published—reading both texts in quick succession creates narrative bridges across the experiential and historical divides. Students begin to get a sense of the significance of collective trauma for both peoples, even for those who did not directly experience it.

Once strategic juxtaposition helps to underscore the importance of the Holocaust and the Nakba for Jewish and Palestinian narratives, we delve more deeply into Scott McCloud's *Understanding Comics* to learn additional comics vocabulary to better understand how they work as a narrative medium. As McCloud observes, "The Cartoon is a vacuum into which our identity and awareness are pulled, . . . an empty shell that we inhabit which enables us to travel in another realm. We don't just OBSERVE the cartoon, we BECOME it."[21] He suggests that the reader's ease of putting him- or herself in the narrator's place is inversely related to the level of detail used in the representations, so the more cartoony and less detailed, the more likely you are to see yourself in the characters and the more likely you are to see the characters' experiences as universal. Given that for many people, Israel/Palestine is often cloistered off as a place whose issues have to do only with "Jews" and "Arabs," the use of comics offers a way to universalize very particular experiences, especially those of young-adult Jewish women, foreign travelers who come to the region to report or write, Palestinians living under occupation, Israeli soldiers, and Palestinian Americans, to list just some of the perspectives that students encounter. Finally, we take a step back to the larger historical picture, and I use Alan Dowty's introductory history *Israel/Palestine* in combination with Rowland/Frank's rhetorical analysis in *Shared Land/Conflicting Territory* to teach history and historiography as part of narrative's important persuasive work. After establishing these theoretical and conceptual "lenses," we encounter a plethora of graphic narratives about the region itself.

Space will not permit a full discussion of the daily schedule or assignments;[22] so I will first focus some attention on the writing assignments I give, and then I will discuss the way Sarah Glidden's *How to Understand Israel in 60 Days or Less* (2010) models the type of critical wrestling that I hope to teach students to adopt.[23] The writing assignments I include are intended to help students develop a better grasp on the theoretical concepts and historical background while also gaining practice in the important areas of close reading (including visual analysis), scholarly research and critical summary, and textual analysis and scholarly argumentation. For the final research project, I also allow students to write graphic essays that follow Libicki's models in *Toward a Hot Jew* (the title essay of what is now an anthology of short comic essays; it began as the senior project for Libicki's BFA).[24] Although I do not require a specific format or topic for students' research-based graphic essays, the most successful graphic essays have tended to provide a literacy autobiography of the way the course has helped students become better informed about Israel/Palestine.

The comics author Sarah Glidden became better informed about Israel/Palestine through a combination of her personal research and experiences as a self-reflective participant on a Birthright trip, as her graphic novel *How to Understand Israel in 60 Days or Less* details. Her title clearly plays with our yearning for quick and simple understandings, and she employs the graphic autobiography/memoir to narrate the experiences of a young American woman who goes to Israel to learn about the culture, the conflict, and herself.[25] She skillfully juxtaposes visuals and text to offer space for multiple, incommensurate narratives to coexist in both the narrator's and audience's minds, thus pointing toward possibilities across the narrative divides in Israel/Palestine. In so doing, she provides a model for the kind of engaged wrestling that I think good college writing courses, and especially those about Israel/Palestine, should foster. As she explained in an interview with David Wolkin, published in *Comics Alliance* on November 2, 2010,

> All I did was read. I did not make my boyfriend and my friends happy. I would get home from work and I would just read all these big books. And then I thought that being there for two weeks would seal the deal and I would know everything. Clearly you're not going to ever understand such a complicated place in such a short amount of time, but I really wanted to try. So this book is about that attempt at trying to figure it out because when I got there, I realized it was a lot more complicated than I thought.[26]

In fact, the phrase "it's more complicated than that" serves as a kind of refrain, appearing multiple times throughout the text.[27] From the moment Glidden arrives at the airport, going and also watching others go through the difficult security checks, she struggles to hold multiple narratives in her head at the same time: those of her ideologically based understanding as what she defines as a "progressive liberal" and the "propaganda" that she expects that Birthright will offer her.[28] In a conversation with one of the Israeli Birthright leaders, Nadan, she clarifies this tension: "I'm Jewish so that means I'm supposed to support Israel no matter what. But according to a lot of people any support for the Palestinians means that you don't support Israel. At the same time, when it comes to politics, I'm left wing and progressive and if you're progressive you're supposed to be anti-Israel, any sympathy with Israel means that you don't support the Palestinians. So See? I'm stuck."[29] Struggle as she may, she skillfully uses the comic medium to keep the parallel but competing narratives in focus and tension.[30]

As the intense rhythm of the trip moves forward and across the nation, Glidden also offers a visual way to build a narrative bridge across them. The panels at the center of the text on pages 100–101 offer the narrative climax of Glidden's evolving relationship to her preconceived ideas, the place where her feelings overpower her intellect and where she literally and emotionally breaks down, overwhelmed by her own shifting identifications and the incommensurability of both the narratives and the competing elements of her own multifaceted identity. Yet what she leaves the reader with is a set of complex visuals that layer and compress multiple narratives into a series of three panels.[31] Though she has not (yet) found a way to put the narratives in dialogue, through the visuals she is able to let them coexist simultaneously in the same physical space. The panels include images of Nazis beating up Jews and an iconic drawing of Anne Frank, followed by images of Israeli soldiers confronting Palestinian women and children in front of the wall and then one image that offers a montage of experiences from both sides in contemporary Israel/Palestine: the charred remains of a bus, presumably left over from a terrorist bombing; the bloody remains of Israeli citizens; a civilian taking the pin out of a grenade; an Israeli soldier pointing (a firearm?) at Palestinian women and children while a rocket points at him; an armed Palestinian whose weapon points to crying, bloody people, while he faces the reader directly, punctuated by Glidden herself looking to the right and bursting into tears.[32] These panels appear in the middle of the two-hundred-page graphic text, where Glidden is forced to confront the conflict of competing narratives.

Later in the interview with Wolkin, Glidden calls attention to the importance of the event and the panels that represent it:

> I was upset because I was finally starting to see the Israeli point of view on things that I had rejected for so long and that was really terrifying because I felt like I was being . . . I didn't know whether I was really feeling that, whether I really wanted to feel that, or whether I had been successfully manipulated and it's scary to think that maybe you're being controlled by someone else, or maybe you're not. Maybe you're just changing your mind, but changing your mind is a terrifying thing too. We're so used to having our convictions and our beliefs and I think people are really afraid of . . . it's like losing a part of your identity, almost. This thing that you thought was part of you, this idea, this political belief system. If that goes away then it's like part of you is being cut off.[33]

From this point forward in the graphic novel, Glidden attempts to accommodate the multiple narratives, rather than simply pitting one against the other. These panels, like the text as a whole, begin with a lot of iconic images yet end up in a more complicated space of competing but coexisting narratives. Similarly, her text begins with a lot of stereotypes but ends up troubling those easy assumptions about the author herself, about Birthright, and about Israel and its citizens. It ends perhaps where any trip to such a complicated place should end, with a lot of unresolved questions. As Glidden sips tea with other tourists in a Turkish hostel, they ask her, "What's the deal with that place anyway?" She responds by ambivalently not answering, "Well . . ."[34] Glidden's text offers key insights into the way young adults wrestle with new ideas, especially new ideas they discover through research and experiences that trouble or complicate identities and commonplace beliefs that they have held dear, perhaps unquestioningly so, throughout their young lives. It also demonstrates how writing takes place both within and across multiple media.

Perhaps most importantly for a course interested in using juxtaposition as a method to "wrestle" with complexity, the Glidden quotes just presented—which highlight the way the author changed her understandings in response to the things she read and the people and places she encountered and the ways changing her mind was a visceral and complex process that unfolded over time—suggest that wrestling with new ideas requires intellectual commitment and rigor, an understanding that you write, read, rewrite, and reinterpret to better know and comprehend the world and that intellectual growth requires a willingness to be open to changing one's opinion. Glidden's ideas were constantly evolving in response to new situations and stimuli, and writing is also an iterative, recursive process that changes in response to instructor and peer response and further research. If students come away from a writing course focused on graphic narratives of Israel/Palestine with a deeper appreciation of complexity and the importance of acknowledging what may at times seem like incommensurable narratives and with more questions than answers, then perhaps that is the best kind of introduction one can hope for, given such nuanced topics and limited time.

How to Get Students to Wrestle with Complexity: Some Strategies for Teaching

Given that my aim is to get students to wrestle with complexity through strategic juxtaposition, my hope is that the course structure can accomplish what the very "dual tract" of the graphic medium makes possible[35]—keeping competing, sometimes incommensurable narratives simultaneously present and, through that simultaneous albeit cacophonous presence, perhaps creating some narrative, imaginative space across them. On the basis of my experiences teaching writing courses whose content focuses on Israel/Palestine, I offer the following advice to teachers who hope to incorporate either comics/graphic narrative or Israel/Palestine content in their future courses. Some of the more successful assignments and pairings that have helped to accomplish meaningful classroom discussions include the following:

(1) To get at the very painful circumstances surrounding suicide bombings—both the extreme desperation that leads individuals to consider such horrific actions and the tragic loss that results from them—I have put the following texts in conversation: the 2005 film *Paradise Now*, whose very structure puts the audience in the ethically ambivalent position of identifying with an otherwise-"ordinary" young man in Palestine,[36] who through a combination of choices and happenstance becomes a potential suicide bomber, with the 2003 documentary *No. 17* (*Ha-harug sheva esreh*), about the 2002 Meggiddo suicide bombing that killed seventeen people, only sixteen of whom were initially identified; the documentary shows how the unidentified victim was eventually identified while telling the stories of many others impacted by the horrific event.[37] A similar suicide bombing in Hadera provides some of the narrative premise around which the love story unfolds in Rutu Modan's graphic novel *Exit Wounds*.[38]

Moving from a graphic novel in which a suicide bombing and the "situation" it metonymically represents provide more of a background soundtrack around which the graphic novel's plot unfolds, to a documentary that asks the audience to identify with the victims and family members of a 2002 suicide bombing, to *Paradise Now*, a film that asks the audience to identify with/as a potential suicide bomber, students begin to understand the multifaceted human perspectives involved in such horrific events. I have yet to teach a class in which this sequence has not resulted in some very poignant and perspective-expanding discussions. It usually comes toward the end of the class, when students are comfortable enough to talk about very uncomfortable and disconcerting topics, and the questions raised often linger beyond the course itself.

(2) In addition to giving a midterm that requires students to apply and demonstrate their knowledge of conceptual and analytic terms, I have found it useful to have every student in the class give an encyclopedia-style "Contextualizing Presentation," in which they choose a topic from a curated list to introduce the class to topics or groups of people whom students may not otherwise know anything about but whose presence is important to Israeli and Palestinian societies. For example, until someone gives a presentation on Christian Palestinians, many students are not aware that there are substantial Palestinian and Arab populations who are not Muslim. Until someone gives a presentation on Ethiopian Jews and the Israeli Black Panthers, some students may not know that all Jewish Israelis are neither phenotypically "white" nor culturally Ashkenazi. Presentations on the following topics have helped to ensure that students are exposed to the diversity of Palestinian and Israeli societies: Bedouins, Druze (and Circassians), West Bank/Gazan Palestinians, Israeli-Palestinians (also sometimes called Israeli-Arabs or Arab-Israelis), Christian Palestinians, Samaritans, Ethiopian

Jews, Russian Jews, Mizrahi Jews (Moroccan, Iraqi, Iranian, Kurdish, and Yemenite Jews), Israel Defense Forces, Ultra-Orthodox Jews (Haredim), Jewish settlers, Israeli Black Panthers, Palestinian Jerusalemites, Irgun, Deir Yassin, rhetorical/historical importance of the 1967 war, First Lebanon War, Second Lebanon War, IDF and Israeli ethos, Birthright/Taglit.

(3) Each time I teach the course, I require students to open a Twitter account and follow the news of the region from a multitude of sources. They follow each other, journalists, various outlets for news (official and unofficial), and me. Though we often do not have a lot of time to discuss current events in class, just having them read the news regularly has helped them gain a better understanding of how complex the region and representations of it are. It also enables them to put the critical and conceptual vocabulary we are learning in class into action.

As an instructor who uses "strategic juxtaposition" as a guiding principle to set up the overall trajectory of the course to facilitate greater wrestling with complexity, I have grappled with how best to organize the course. Does one organize chronologically, and if so, where does one begin with the history? Does one begin thematically, with careful attention to concepts with important cultural and symbolic significance? And how does one handle the fact that the historical time line is ever expanding?

Given how much I value the model that Glidden's text offers, it should come as no surprise that the first time I taught the comics course, I began with it. It was good to begin with a model of the type of researched, reasoned changing of one's mind that her narrative represents, but starting with her text also privileges the perspective and position of Jewish Americans. The second time I taught the course, in 2014, I had just returned from a research trip in Israel/Palestine amid the Israel-Gaza conflict of 2014—referred to by (most) Israelis as *Miv'tzah Tzuk Eitan*, or Operation Protective Edge, and referred to by others as the 2014 Gaza War. To help students better understand the multiple perspectives of these recent events, I adjusted the syllabus to include a selection of short stories authored mostly by Palestinian students during the 2008–9 Gaza conflict, culled from *Gaza Writes Back* (2013) and *The Book of Gaza: A City in Short Fiction* (2014), as well as the short story "Pastrami," by Etgar Keret,[39] and a short comic by Koren Shadmi about his experiences visiting Israel during the 2014 Israel-Gaza conflict, "Snapshots from Israel."[40] I began the course with *Maus* and some of the short stories about the Nakba to introduce the collective traumas that are so foundational to Jewish Israeli and Palestinian identity narratives and to open the course with Jewish and Palestinian voices rather than the perspectives of others who visit.[41] To me, including these voices (even though they are not always in comics form) is beneficial because they point to the ever-evolving historiographic time line and the important ways that writers, sometimes even students such as the ones enrolled in our courses, help to shape the way these events are perceived and understood.

Part of the complexity that the course highlights is the need to sit with difficulty and not immediately move to try to push it aside, to write or speak over it, in order to get to some other kind of possibility, but to be present with the complexities and the way art provides a beautified lens through which to get a glimpse of someone's experiences instead. Although teaching about Israel/Palestine is not without difficulty, if anything, these narratives have also demonstrated that it is also not without tremendous value. Through the distanced and self-reflexive remove of artistic representation, there is the possibility of teaching about difficulty and finding beauty, joy, and delight in students' discoveries of the everyday normalcies in Israel/Palestine that exist beyond the narrative divides and polarizing headlines.

Notes

1. Hillary Chute coined this term in her "Comics as Literature? Reading Graphic Narrative," *PMLA* 123, no. 2 (2008): 452–65.
2. Scott McCloud, *Understanding Comics: The Invisible Art* (New York: Paradox, 1993), 30.
3. Joe Sacco, *Palestine* (Seattle: Fantagraphics Books, 2001).
4. Amy Kurzweil, *Flying Couch: A Graphic Memoir* (New York: Black Balloon, 2016).
5. Miriam Libicki, ed., *Toward a Hot Jew* (Seattle: Fantagraphics Books, 2016).
6. Leila Abdelrazaq, *Baddawi* (Charlottesville, VA: Just World Books, 2015).
7. Boaz Yakin and Nick Bertozzi, *Jerusalem: A Family Portrait* (New York: First Second, 2013).
8. Harvey Pekar and J. T. Waldman, *Not the Israel My Parents Promised Me* (New York: Hill and Wang, 2012).
9. Guy Delilse, *Jerusalem: Chronicles from the Holy City* (Montreal: Drawn and Quarterly, 2012).
10. Galit and Gilad Seliktar, *Farm 54* (Castalla-Alicante, Spain: Fanfare/Ponent Mon, 2011).
11. Sarah Glidden, *How to Understand Israel in 60 Days or Less* (New York: Vertigo, 2009).
12. Joe Sacco, *Footnotes in Gaza* (New York: Metropolitan Books, 2009).
13. Oreet Ashery and Larissa Sansoor, *The Novel of Nonel and Vovel* (Milan: Edizioni Charta, 2009).
14. Naji al-Naji, *A Child in Palestine: The Cartoons of Naji al-Naji* (London: Verso, 2009).
15. Miriam Libicki, *jobnik!* (Coquitlam, BC: Real Gone Girl Studios, 2008).
16. Rutu Modan, *Exit Wounds* (Montreal: Drawn and Quarterly, 2008).
17. For commentary on Glidden and Libicki, see Tahneer Oksman, *"How Come Boys Get to Keep Their Noses?": Women and Jewish American Identity in Contemporary Graphic Memoirs* (New York: Columbia University Press, 2016), chap. 4. On Birthright, see Shaul Kelner, *Tours That Bind: Diaspora, Pilgrimage, and Israeli Birthright Tourism* (New York: NYU Press, 2010). For interviews and commentary on contemporary

Israeli graphic novels and an interview with Libicki, see Samantha Baskind and Ranen Omer-Sherman, eds., *The Jewish Graphic Novel* (New Brunswick, NJ: Rutgers University Press, 2008). See also Stephen Tabatchnik, *The Quest for Jewish Identity and Belief in the Graphic Novel* (Tuscaloosa: University of Alabama Press, 2014), chapters 3 and 7; and Derek Parker Royal, ed., *Visualizing Jewish Narrative: Jewish Comics and Graphic Novels* (London: Bloomsbury, 2016). There is a significant critical body of work focusing on Sacco's and Delisle's graphic narratives.
18. John Rowland and David A. Frank, *Shared Land/Conflicting Territory: Trajectories of Israeli and Palestinian Symbol Use* (East Lansing: Michigan State University Press, 2002).
19. John Rowland and David A. Frank, "Mythic Rhetoric and Rectification in the Israeli-Palestinian Conflict," *Communication Studies* 62, no. 1 (2011): 41–57.
20. McCloud, *Understanding Comics*, 93.
21. Ibid., 36.
22. The full syllabus is available in its most recent iteration here, replete with assignment prompts: http://wrd401.fernheimer.org.
23. Sarah Glidden, *How to Understand Israel in 60 Days or Less* (New York: Vertigo, 2010).
24. Miriam Libicki, *Toward a Hot Jew* (Seattle: Fantagraphics Books, 2016). See Libicki's essay about the origins of *Toward a Hot Jew*, the drawn essay and collection of drawn essays: "The Big Idea: Miriam Libicki," *Whatever* (blog), September 23, 2016, http://whatever.scalzi.com/2016/09/23/the-big-idea-miriam-libicki/.
25. Elsewhere, I have argued that Glidden's text uses the very subjective, personal mode of confessional graphic memoir to offer us new insights into some of the more "universal" commonplaces surrounding Israel/Palestine while also pointing to more complex truth(s) about the Israel that they and their audiences have imagined. See Fernheimer, "'It's More Complicated than That': Confessing the 'Conflict' and Coming of Age in Women's Graphic Representations of Israel," Association of Israel Studies, University of Haifa, Israel, June 25, 2012.
26. David Wolkin, "Sarah Glidden Explains 'How to Understand Israel in 60 Days or Less' (Interview)," *Comics Alliance*, November 2, 2010, http://comicsalliance.com/sarah-glidden-how-to-understand-israel-in-60-days-or-less-interview/.
27. Glidden, *How to Understand Israel*, 25, 76, 139.
28. Ibid., 8, 7, 6.
29. Ibid., 77.
30. Wolkin, "Sarah Glidden Explains."
31. Glidden, *How to Understand Israel*, 95–100, esp. 100.
32. Ibid., 100.
33. Wolkin, "Sarah Glidden Explains."
34. Glidden, *How to Understand Israel*, 206.
35. Chute, in "Comics as Literature?," refers to the visuals and texts of graphic narrative as dual, parallel tracts (452) and this doubling as a formal structure particularly apt

for ethical engagement with trauma (457). She also highlights how these structural qualities allow graphic narratives to represent trauma not "through the lens of unspeakability or invisibility" but through "inventive and (various) textual practice" (459).

36. *Paradise Now*, directed by Hany Abu-Assad, DVD, 2005.
37. *No. 17*, directed by David Ofek, DVD, 2003.
38. Rutu Modan, *Exit Wounds* (Montreal: Drawn and Quarterly, 2008).
39. Atef Abu Saif, ed., *The Book of Gaza: A City in Short Fiction* (Manchester, UK: Comma, 2014); Refaat Alareer, ed., *Gaza Writes Back: Short Stories from Young Writers in Gaza, Palestine* (Charlottesville, VA: Just World Books, 2014); Etgar Keret, "Pastrami," *New Yorker*, November 20, 2012, www.newyorker.com/books/page-turner/pastrami.
40. Koren Shadmi, "Snapshots from Israel," *New York Times*, August 5, 2014, www.nytimes.com/interactive/2014/08/06/opinion/opart-snapshots-from-Israel.html; also available at www.korenshadmi.com/works/comics/?id=296.
41. Art Spiegelman, *Maus: A Survivor's Tale* (New York: Pantheon Books, 1986).

Joe Sacco, Comics Journalism, and Representations of Israel

MARTIN B. SHICHTMAN

I teach "Imagining the Holy Land" at Eastern Michigan University (EMU) in Ypsilanti, Michigan. This is a general education, English department class, offered primarily to lower-level undergraduates—generally to students enrolled in the university's Honors program. Taking a close look at literatures supporting various claims to possession of "the Holy Land," particularly claims to the city of Jerusalem, "Imagining the Holy Land" asks students to consider why the three "peoples of the book," Jews, Christians, and Muslims, have engaged in centuries of nearly continuous conflict. Students are encouraged to think about how, in the case of Israel, religious, racial, and political identities are fashioned, how these identities are represented in texts, and how these identities become, often enough, inextricably associated with territory.

EMU calls itself a "school of opportunity," a largely working-class institution just eight miles away from the far more prestigious, far wealthier University of Michigan. EMU justifiably celebrates diversity, drawing student populations from, among other places, the Middle Eastern communities of Dearborn and the Jewish communities of West Bloomfield. Conversations about Israel can, therefore, get heated, and often the texts read, from Karen Armstrong's *Jerusalem: One City, Three Faiths* (Knopf, 1996) to the short stories in Robert Alter's *Modern Hebrew Literature* (Behrman House, 1975) to the poetry that Salma Jayyusi includes in *The Anthology of Modern Palestinian Literature* (Columbia University Press, 1992), ignite the passions. Toward the end of the class, we take on Joe Sacco's journalistic comic *Palestine* (Fantagraphics Books, 2001). I ask my students both to appreciate Sacco's political intent—his advocacy for Palestinians, who he believes are subjects of intense Israeli discrimination and abuse—and to analyze how that intent is, on occasion, undermined as Sacco's narrative plays out. Sacco's primary move is always to call his own journalistic credibility into question; this becomes both a virtue and a problem as he seeks to advocate for Palestinian rights. In students' initial reading, they immediately take to Sacco's primary arguments—lulled, I think, into a slightly less critical attitude by the comic medium. As we discuss *Palestine* in class, they realize that Sacco's arguments are far more complicated and that the comic medium is able to contain such complexity.

In *Palestine*, Joe Sacco looks to the medium of the comic book to bridge the gap between journalism and memoir and to address a number of social, cultural, economic, and political issues underlying the Israeli/Palestinian conflict. Sacco—an American born in Malta—deploys this "children's" medium in an effort to find something like objectivity, to uncover Truth about the ongoing struggles for power and identity that stand at the heart of Israeli/Palestinian dispute(s). What he produces instead, however, is a compellingly subjective narrative that deconstructs the notion that there is a discoverable truth to be found in Israel/Palestine. He very intentionally draws himself into disparate, often competing story lines that complicate his own preconceived positions on the Israeli/Palestinian struggle, his own desire to be fair and balanced—can any medium be fair and balanced?—and his obligation both to his subject(s) and to his audience. For students expecting the simplicity and straightforwardness of either the DC or Marvel universes, Sacco's comic book, in both style and substance, problematizes the spaces between history and literature, truth and fiction, high art and low, even as it endeavors to shed light on the volatility of the arguments and the actions that divide Israelis and Palestinians. In so many ways, reading Sacco becomes as much an exercise in the expansiveness of the comic medium as it is about a particular journalist's understanding of the Israel/Palestine conflict.

Sacco says that he writes comic books. But there is nothing juvenile about either his craft or his ambition. He calls himself a "cartoonist . . . doing journalism in comics form" and is uncomfortable with the description of his texts as graphic novels. Like Art Spiegelman, who once went to war against the *New York Times* because his Holocaust memoir, *Maus*, was listed in the category of best-selling fiction, Sacco argues that through meticulous research and numerous eyewitness testimonies, he is writing history, that his compositions convey "people's pain." In an interview with *Mother Jones* concerning his 2010 book *Footnotes in Gaza*, Sacco stakes out his position, "I want people to be able to look at this situation in a historical context and understand the layers of hard history that the Palestinians have endured, and get a sense of why perhaps there's resentment in the region—it doesn't come out of the blue. You might not want to excuse it, but it doesn't come out of the blue. It bothered me personally that so much history gets lost. In some ways, I want this book to prompt an Israeli historian to really do a thorough research job from that end."[1]

But how does Sacco imagine succeeding where Israeli historians—and American journalists, for that matter—have fallen short? What is the lost history he hopes to recover? Sacco makes no claim to providing an objective reading of the situation in the Middle East, and he mocks such aspirations in the *Mother Jones* interview: "I don't really believe the idea of objective journalism. . . . I find a lot of the journalism that's written as if you're a fly on the wall is really sort of phony. And it has this pretense of being very fair-minded and removed, and that's not true at all. . . . I'd rather just get rid of that completely and say: It's me, these are my prejudices, these are my doubts, and I'm writing about this, and you're seeing it through my eyes."[2] In fact, Sacco's aggressive subjectivity provides for the illusion of evenhandedness, his willingness to inject himself into the narrative, his determination, as Aryn Bartley suggests, to record the "stories of those who are positioned as victims."[3] Edward Said—a hero of Sacco's whose book *Orientalism* he pictures himself reading—writes that Sacco "is tugged at by the forgotten places and people of the world, those who don't make it on to our television screens, or, if they do, who are regularly portrayed as marginal, unimportant, perhaps even negligible were it not for their nuisance value which, like the Palestinians, seems impossible to get rid of."[4] Students studying the Israel/Palestine conflict need to come to terms with their roles as observers, as tourists of pain. Sacco too understands that he is always just visiting, and because he acknowledges his own status as an outsider, he is able to build a relationship with the reader. We join him in trying to make sense out of a generations-old hostility. It is important, however, to appreciate that Sacco is never impartial, even in his claims to critical distance. He insists, "I've come to meet Palestinians"; "I've heard nothing but the Israeli side most of my life"; "it occurs to me that I have seen the Israelis, but through Palestinian eyes—that Israelis were mainly soldiers and settlers to me now, too."[5]

In *Palestine*, Sacco buys into two conflicting—yet mutually accommodating—stereotypes of Israelis. On the one hand, he sees Israelis as objects of desire—the new, hard-bodied Jew, strong, tough, beautiful. Even though he has come to interview and learn more about Palestinians, he cannot help but fall in love with an image of the Israeli that has always already been available since the birth of the state, an image that he accepts with considerable irony and, yet, somehow also devoid of irony. He writes "as an international jetsetter with an opportunity (if not a mandate) to compare such things": "I would place Israeli women way high in the global hot looks sweepstakes, . . . and in uniform—particularly those olive green pullovers—they're peerless. . . . And what about the boys? Ooo la la!! I mean, look at this dude! He's taking five on the Old City ramparts . . . gazing over annexed Arab land . . . doing a Welcome-To-Marlboro Country. Even *I'm* pressing my legs together!!" (16). As if this were not enough, he continues to describe the soldiers as "beefcake" (17). Sacco generally peoples his cartoons with ugly characters—his cartooning style owing much to R. Crumb and the underground comix movement of the 1960s, which insisted on the grotesquery of humanity. Before my students read *Palestine*, I ask them to consider the Jewish stereotypes offered up in the cartoons of *Der Stürmer*: hideous, obese, obscene, predatory. I want them to appreciate that there is a difference. Sacco's response to Israel's new, hard-bodied Jew runs, for my students, against the *Stürmer* stereotype—as it should—and opens discussions about the post-1948 Holy Land as a place of radical Jewish self-redefinition.

But Sacco suggests that the very attractive coin portraying the Israeli Jew holds a much nastier flip side. He also presents Israeli men as hypermasculine morons, capable of turning ugly—both physically and emotionally—belligerent, and violent. Israeli men are golems, brainless, soulless, unfeeling creatures who have lost sight of their original purpose—protecting their people from antisemitic violence—and, instead, have, themselves, become a source of uncontrolled, and uncontrollable, force. For Sacco, there is no Rabbi Leow to master the Israeli monster. In fact, it is almost as though Sacco is incapable of imagining an intellectual Jew in Israel—where are all the small, bespectacled technocrats, businesspeople, newspaper editors, college professors? As Sacco sees it, the power associated with the casual "gazing over annexed Arab land" has so corrupted Israeli men that they have become monstrous, evil, irredeemable. Sacco stops just short of projecting Nazism onto the figure of the IDF soldier, but that analogy hovers above the text, requiring my students to address this particular charge. We use *Palestine* as a foundation to talk about the rationales for state violence and, in the case of Israel, to consider if that violence has a particularly racist agenda. The question that Sacco poses for my students is, What is the price of Jews reimagining themselves as powerful and beautiful? (And the corollary: Who pays that price?) They need to consider whether this question itself creates new, equally objectionable stereotypes of Jews.

In my students' discussion of Sacco's portrayal of Israeli women, they address not only the corrosiveness of stereotype but, perhaps even more important, whether Jews should be held to higher standards than other people. Israeli women are oversexed princesses, according to Sacco, vain and indifferent to the crushing misery that their conspicuous overconsumption of other people's resources has caused. In Jerusalem, he befriends two women: Paula, whose "roots are Eastern European," and Naomi, whose "grandparents came from Germany? Germany!!" (262). Sacco's unease with the women's Ashkenazy heritage is exacerbated by their nervousness around Palestinians—Naomi's refusal, for instance, to explore the Old City because she fears being knifed by an Arab. Should Paula and Naomi really have any rights to the land they call home? How can their rights to this land possibly compare to the claims of the many Palestinians whom Sacco has interviewed? While he recognizes that the two women are highly educated—architects—and have given some thought to issues such as the (in)correctness of new settlements, Sacco is largely dismissive of them: "probably one or both of them have the hots for me, and on a day like today, who can blame them?" (260). They are spoiled, superficial, banal. Naomi insists, "We just want to live our lives, okay? We have *our lives*! We have jobs and families and we go out and live just like *you* do. . . . We don't think about this stuff all the time, and we get a bit tired of hearing about it!" Paula counters, "It's not that we're tired. . . . But when you hear it over and over you get . . . tired" (264). There appears to be a peculiar double-standard at work here—and students are called on to ponder its significances. Sacco says that he hopes his writing will have some larger effect: "People read it and maybe they change their ideas or they get interested like I got interested. That can happen too."[6] But Paula and Naomi are interested. They have thought about the matter to distraction—and they seek distraction from the matter. What does Sacco want Paula and Naomi to do? In what other ways, what greater ways, can they show their interest? Sacco's journey toward political enlightenment is a kind of "dark tourism," and given the opportunity, he readily leaves the Palestinian plight behind him to flirt with Paula and Naomi, first in Jerusalem and later in Tel Aviv, where he relaxes with them by the beach. He will ultimately abandon the muddy streets, the ruined homes, the scarred bodies and minds of his subjects to get on with his life, return to the safety and security of the United States. How and why should he expect more from Paula and Naomi?

In fact, Sacco seems to have some problems with Western women in general. He seems to prefer the domesticity of women he finds on the Palestinian side. He never raises questions about his ability to sit for hours speaking with groups of men—"the boys" (141), as he calls them—while women supply endless cups of tea; he never wonders how, or from where, the meals he consumes miraculously originate. Nor does he ever consider the cost of such gifts—and if there might be some expectation of a return gift. After a long meditation on the politics of the hijab, during which he notes that "Hamas followers began threatening women and sometimes beating them for going outside without a head covering," Sacco records testimony of a woman who tells him, "I saw a lady physician driving her car right by the hospital. She wasn't wearing the hijab. Three or four youths began stoning her car, injuring her, she was bleeding" (140). Nevertheless, Sacco allows himself to be convinced of the appropriateness of the hijab, that Palestinian women want to wear it, when "two attractive young women, decked out with cosmetics," tell him about their commitment to the veil: "Not just in the streets. I want to *really* believe in wearing it" (140). Rather than pressing his subject on the nature and depth of her beliefs—as he surely would have Paula and Naomi—Sacco responds, "I tell you what throws me for a loop, and I see the gulf between us. . . . I realize I've forgotten what it's like to have faith. . . . I mean I've forgotten what it's like to want to have faith" (140).

The matter of the hijab is of note on the Eastern Michigan University campus, with many Middle Eastern women choosing some form of veiling. On the one hand, students' perceptions are formed by liberal democracy's anxieties about religion and the public space and by exposure to Western feminism. On the other hand, students participate in activities in which they wear a "hijab for a day," during which they experience the othering that Muslim women endure in the United States. They readily appreciate Sacco's difficulty in coming to terms with a social/political structure dominated by faith, a culture at once oppressive, as in the case of the physician, and liberating, as it is for the "attractive young women." Ultimately, they inquire, Can it be that the hard-nosed journalist Joe Sacco is so charmed when "two attractive young women, decked out with cosmetics," offer professions of faith that he conveniently forgets the horrific fate of the lady physician?

The egregiousness of Sacco's cultural relativism becomes evident in a section called "Law," wherein the journalist/cartoonist visits an attorney working on a case of "family honor." Christopher Hitchens, writing about "shame" in the Middle East, argues that for cultures where self-fashionings of manhood vacillate between hypermasculinity and anxieties concerning emasculation, embarrassment becomes "some vicarious parody of emotion where it is always others—usually women—who are supposedly bringing the shame on you."[7] Certainly my students see these kinds of sexisms working out everyday in their hometowns, their families, their campus—and they find them abhorrent. Discussion about the cultural shaming of women is easy, so long as the conversation focuses on the West. There seems to be greater difficulty in imposing the values of Western feminism on Muslim society. Sacco sees no irony as he talks with a lawyer defending the killers of a fifteen year-old girl: "She was married. She committed adultery with a collaborator" (160). The lawyer insists that this is "a religious case" and that the girl's family had the right to murder her (160). Sacco allows himself to be distracted by the attorney's discussion of cases concerning Israeli abuse and torture, allows himself to be distracted by a barrage of anti-American sentiment offered up by clients sitting in the waiting room. Finally, he justifies the honor killing with this outrageous comparison: "In Gaza you can take your pick: there's one family's version of Islamic law for an adulterous daughter, . . . there's Israeli military justice for kids who may or may not have thrown stones" (163). I find it difficult to take anything Sacco writes seriously beyond this point. My students are more generous—especially because they have been exposed to barrages of Facebook memes posting similar sorts of strained comparisons. My students want to equate U.S. and Israeli injustice with injustices such as "honor killings." I do my best to make the argument that one sort of wrong does not allow for the other.

Nevertheless, Sacco's *Palestine* does make a powerful case for those who are living in the occupied territories, in the camps, the emaciated and frail, who spend nearly all of their lives suffering—and, it seems, talking about their suffering. Sacco investigates Israeli interrogation methods and comments on the proliferation of prisons. He may be too willing to turn a blind eye to the efficacy of a thrown stone, or a Molotov cocktail for that matter, and unwilling to think seriously about what an appropriate response to assault with stones or Molotov cocktails should be, but he succeeds in placing the reader in the shoes of the dispossessed, the marginalized. Sacco creates cartoon documentaries that mock the notion of objectivity, that seek Truth in subjective responses to particular events. It is by meandering through multiple subjectivities that he believes Truth may be recovered. Sacco makes no apologies for his "journalistic" style, and his style is most decidedly anti-Zionist:

> I want to show things from my point of view because I think it's more honest in a way to be subjective. Admit your prejudices; admit those points when you feel uncomfortable in a certain situation. Just admit it. And then beyond all that, I find it very difficult to be objective when to me there is a clear case of a people being oppressed. I'm not sure what objective means in a situation like that. I would rather be honest about what's going on. Which means perhaps the oppressed aren't all angels—but the fact would remain that they are oppressed.[8]

In the end, Sacco's *Palestine* offers itself up as something of a bildungsroman—as much as its author would object to my recognizing a fictive impulse in his journalistic narrative—in which the hero moves from apathy, mostly taking political positions to impress various women, to becoming a genuine, kaffiyeh-wearing Palestinian sympathizer, one who has no problem with the men, of course, at a Palestinian wedding expressing their happiness by singing, "To all the people who hate us, how sweet to die for Palestine. . . . Fatah does not fear death, and Fatah shall liberate Palestine" (228).

Ultimately Sacco leaves his readers, my students, without much hope—he went to Palestine to uncover trauma, and he is satisfied with his success. If Israelis have treated Palestinians horrifically, the victims of such abuse are in no forgiving mood. Sacco's anger at Israelis and their political institutions is magnified exponentially in the hostility of Palestinians that he covers. Sacco leaves his readers at an impasse, made even more treacherous as both sides amp up their rhetorics and their firepower. For my students, who adore this book for its accessibility—especially after trudging through the likes of Armstrong's *Jerusalem: One City, Three Faiths*—*Palestine* ultimately offers more questions than answers. They are left to wonder about the very project of journalism—any kind of journalism—in covering a dispute in which both sides are so remarkably adept in spinning their stories, so adept in "handling" journalists. Sacco holds his vulnerabilities on full display—he likes women, food and drink, flattery—and almost seems to understand when these vulnerabilities are being used against him. But he never entirely appreciates how he is being manipulated, ultimately succumbing to a powerful narrative of suffering without ever really investigating its underpinnings—or choosing, at times, simply to pass over those underpinnings in silence. Sacco understands that the Israeli/Palestinian conflict is complex, but he seems to desire an easy narrative of victim and perpetrator—and by choosing to use a journalistic comic form, he hints to his readers that the story really is easy to understand. The task for my students is to unwind form and content, to see that Joe Sacco's *Palestine* is never easy and that all its assumptions, even as they masquerade as journalism, are always open to question.

Notes

1. Sonja Sharp, "Joe Sacco: Graphic History," *Mother Jones*, January 8, 2010, www.motherjones.com/media/2010/01/joe-sacco-graphic-history/.
2. Ibid.
3. Aryn Bartley, "The Hateful Self: Substitution and the Ethics of Representing War," *Modern Fiction Studies* 54 (2008): 50–71.
4. Edward Said, "Homage to Joe Sacco," in *Palestine*, by Joe Sacco (Seattle: Fantagraphics Books, 2001), iv.
5. Sacco, *Palestine*, 256. Subsequent citations appear parenthetically in the text.
6. Rebecca Tuhus-Dubrow, "January Interview: Joe Sacco," *January Magazine*, June 2003, https://januarymagazine.com/profiles/jsacco.html.
7. Christopher Hitchens, "From Abbottabad to Worse," *Vanity Fair* 53 (2011): 70.
8. Laila El-Haddad, "Interview: Joe Sacco," Al Jazeera, January 18, 2010, www.aljazeera.com/focus/2010/01/201011783113578937.html.

Teaching the Conflict as a Critical Thinking (Dis)course

ASHLEY PASSMORE

Critical thinking is a necessary academic skill for students. It facilitates a capacity to exceed common patterns of thinking and promotes reflection on problems from different perspectives using both analysis and synthesis. The course I teach, intended to develop these skills in students, "The Arab-Israeli Conflict through Film," features films that take different and occasionally opposing stances on the conflict. Teaching about Israel with a focus on critical thinking skills challenges students to recognize unspoken assumptions, to determine whether conclusions they make follow from given information, and to assess generalizations about the conflict from particular images, scenes, characters, or films. Because the films we watch in the course are produced by filmmakers from different nations and political orientations, our classroom discussion of them draws a connection between what the films represent and the perspective of the filmmaker(s). Students in the course make short presentations on the films we view and present each film's outlook on, and visual representation of, the Arab-Israeli conflict. In so doing, students are asked to summarize and reconstruct a perspective on the conflict that is not necessarily their own and thereby reflect on the validity of their own views about the issues discussed. The format of the course as a guided discussion creates an environment in which all students' perspectives are heard and topics debated. Since it is an introductory course at my university, one of the learning outcomes is to model for students how opinions are expressed and debated in the liberal arts classroom environment.

Many of the films we view in "The Arab Israeli Conflict through Film," which I teach one day a week at Texas A&M University as part of the core liberal arts curriculum, problematize conventional views about the conflict by virtue of their production. Some of the films are Arab and Israeli coproductions, some are produced by Jewish Israelis who are nevertheless critical of Israel, while other films highlight the complexity of the situation, such as the lives of Arabs who are also Israeli. To synthesize this new information, which may complicate previously held opinions, students in the course are asked to write a reflective essay at the start of the course about their views about the conflict and what media they have used to learn about it. At the end of the course, students review that original essay to see whether their views have changed over the course of the semester after viewing these films and whether they have been moved to find different media sources for current information about the subject. As a critical thinking seminar, an ongoing aspect of our classroom discussion is about avoiding bias confirmation as we seek out media and information sources.

The Student Composition

While Texas A&M University has the second-largest student enrollment of all universities in the United States, it also has the smallest percentage of Jewish students among Association of American University member institutions: less than 1 percent, or roughly five hundred Jewish students in total.[1] In comparison, the University of Iowa is second to last, with slightly over 1 percent Jewish students, while the average among the top sixty-five research institutions in the United States is between 8 and 12 percent. Therefore, research into the teaching of Israel at Texas A&M yields relatively unique results in the U.S. university landscape. All students in the university's College of Liberal Arts must take one of the Critical Thinking Seminars during their studies, of which my course is but one example. Tenured, tenure-track, and instructional faculty with multiyear contracts may teach the courses. Small class sizes (with a limit of twenty students) and discussion-based classroom activities offer the opportunity for faculty to model classroom debate at the university level while interacting with students on a personal level. It is not unusual for faculty to teach topics in the Critical Thinking Seminars that are not part of any standard degree-program curriculum, or that are controversial in general. The Arab-Israeli conflict is a natural topic for this course format, since it has been the subject of campus protest and controversy in recent years, especially in the era of the Boycott, Divestment and Sanctions Movement on U.S. campuses.

In the most recent semester that the class was taught, the vast majority of students in the class were evangelical Christians, over 60 percent of the class was female, and 5 percent of the class were ROTC students. There was one Mexican American with a recently discovered, crypto-Jewish family history, a Hindu, and two Muslim students, one of whom was American and the other British. Very few students knew anything about Israel or the conflict at the start of class, except for the British Muslim student, who cited social media as the primary source for learning about what was going on with the conflict between Palestinians and Israelis.[2] Roughly 40 percent of the evangelical Christian students knew little about Israel or Palestine other than the stories they learned through Bible study, according to their initial essays. Over the course of the semester, some students began to articulate some of their original sources for understanding Israel and Palestine and thus identified themselves to other students in terms of whether the opinions they held on the conflict qualified as "pro-Israel" or "pro-Palestine." As the course instructor, this was not something I encouraged students to do, but I also did not prohibit them from doing so in class discussion. So long as students adhered to the indicators in the critical thinking rubric for writing and presenting on a film, which I discuss shortly, I let students know that I did not expect them to change their views, nor would I anticipate that the class would come to any consensus. Because the writing prompts, the writing assessment, and the class presentations were highly scripted with regard to the points students had to address, it was possible for many students to maintain some distance from the material and not be required to position themselves politically in the classroom. They could effectively take on someone else's viewpoint—for example, that of a filmmaker or a character in a film—and represent that viewpoint to the class as they formed their own, personal opinions in relative anonymity.

The Format of the Course

The course begins with a critical thinking pre-test in which students are asked to analyze their knowledge of the conflict and the sources of their information in a short essay. To show how challenging it is to find reliable media outlets, students are given a map of metadata compiled by the data scientist Gilad Lotan, showing "pro-Israel" and "pro-Palestine" Twitter accounts during the 2014 war in Gaza and the diversity of media sources cited in their retweets to share information about the conflict.[3] From this image, discussion ensues in class about the media sources one uses when assessing the conflict and acquiring new information more generally. Using a modified version of the VALUE (Valid Assessment of Learning in Undergraduate Education) rubric for measuring critical thinking (published by LEAP, Liberal Education and America's Promise, an initiative of the Association of American Colleges and Universities), I assessed (but did not grade) students' level of critical thinking in their initial reflections on the conflict and the media sources they used.[4] This is an effective way to get students to focus on my expectations in their writing for the class and to align their work to the assessment tool being used.

The same rubric is then used for subsequent, in-class written assignments (four in total) as students are exposed to further content, materials, and interpretations. In their final essays, students are asked to write about how they would share the demonstrable evidence or argumentation that explains and justifies their own views with other people who do not share their views about the conflict. The use of a transparent rubric from the beginning encourages students to write toward that rubric as a thought exercise, with the knowledge that I am not interested in changing their beliefs or views on the conflict. Most importantly, the rubric serves as both a formative and a summative assessment of the ability to think critically when talking about the conflict while in the course. As students gain more knowledge about perspectives on the conflict over the course of the semester, they begin to look at the information they have encountered as part of a dynamic process.

The Films Viewed

In the most recent iteration of the course, one film was shown per week through an intrauniversity streaming service through the library (Media Matrix). The films we viewed about the Arab-Israeli conflict, which formed the basis for class discussion, were the following:

Out in the Dark (2014)
The Attack (2013)
Barriers (2010; produced by Ma'aleh Film)
For My Children (2009)
The Bubble (2006)
On the Frontline (2002)
Five Broken Cameras (2013)
Waltz with Bashir (2009)
Arab Labor, episodes "Independence Day" (season 1) and "The Shelter" (season 3)
Lemon Tree (2009)
Dancing in Jaffa (2013)
Ajami (2009)

Presenting on Films

In addition to in-class writing activities, each student was asked to co-present on a chosen film using a relatively scripted formula that amounts to a rhetorical précis.[5] In the prompt, students were asked to give the following information about the film on which they were presenting:

1. The name of the filmmaker (optional: a phrase describing the filmmaker)
2. The genre and title of the work with the date in parentheses
3. A descriptive verb (or verbs) describing how the filmmaker develops the main ideas of the film, using words such as "asserts," "demonstrates," "implies," "suggests," etc., and a "that" clause containing the film's main assertions, viewpoints, or thesis statement
4. An explanation of how the filmmaker develops and/or supports the main idea of the film, usually in chronological order
5. A statement of the filmmaker's apparent purpose, if known, followed by an "in order to" phrase
6. A description of the intended audience and/or the relationship the filmmaker establishes with the audience: How does the director try to show the validity of the viewpoints he or she is portraying in the film?

The film presentations created a classroom situation in which presenters had to act as the authority on the film and were required to present from the perspective of the film, as if in a role play. With regard to critical thinking capacity, it allowed students to speak on behalf of a particular perspective to develop deep knowledge of that viewpoint or narrative, even when it was not their own. After this, class discussion ensued, which often followed from the topics of the presentations.

Conclusions

There were quite a few critical thinking skills I targeted in the course, though they were addressed in different ways by the class material and through their use in prompt questions for essay writing and classroom discussion. Some of those include the following:

- *To question how and from where you get the information on which you base your decisions.* This was addressed in the initial, critical thinking pre-test essay.
- *To identify and determine causality.* A rhetorical analysis of the message of each film watched and what causal relationships are established in the film was an in-class activity that began with the first film we watched. Teaching students to be skeptical about causal claims can help them to become better-informed consumers of research, ideas, and even products.
- *To display the pros and cons.* One class discussion prompt was the following: "Using a given film, what are arguments in favor of the viewpoint of the film and those that may be against it? What can we infer or are we meant to infer from a given character, scene, or story line?"

- *To synthesize certain viewpoints to arrive at a few "true" statements.* Because the films we viewed showed competing perspectives on issues related to the Arab-Israeli conflict, there was one day toward the end of the semester that I asked students in class to try to synthesize some of the perspectives into a series of statements of commonality, or a few "true" statements from all the films.

There were four writing activities in total; only the final essay was graded, while the others were assessed according to how I viewed them on the critical thinking rubric. The first essay, as I discussed earlier, involved talking about one's own source of information about the conflict. The second asked students to do a rhetorical analysis of a film they viewed that changed their views of the conflict, either in large or small measure. The third writing assignment asked students to compare two films they saw as having different views on the conflict and how they, as viewers, resolved that conflict in their own thinking. The final writing assignment was more significant. Students were asked to build on the third writing assignment by also explaining to someone who does not share their views on the conflict why these films and their perspectives might be important. The students knew the final prompt for a few weeks before the end of the semester and were asked to write on it inside class. Their final essay used the same rubric as before but with point values.

The Arab-Israeli conflict as a topic for this methodology of classroom instruction was not a random choice of mine; rather, I believe it is important and necessary to approach this topic in this manner on the university campus, even if not always so programmatically as outlined here. Not only has the climate of debate about the conflict on university campuses today lacked this element of critical thinking when approaching the subject, but also certainly some scholarship has as well. Several students reported to me in course evaluations that it was a "welcome relief" to be able to use this venue of a small discussion class and the structured parameters of the writing and presentation of information to be able to have the courage to navigate the complexities and ambiguities of the conflict, about which they had only an emerging knowledge. Critical thinking tools gave many students the courage and the interest to dive into the course material before they mastered the facts of the conflict and its intricate history.

Notes

1. Kenneth Kimutai, "Largest Universities in the United States by Enrollment," *WorldAtlas*, September 19, 2016, www.worldatlas.com/articles/largest-universities-in-the-united-states.html.

2. In the initial reflective essay, this student cited social media that he had seen during the 2014 war in Gaza and later and stated that he felt his sympathies were a "product" of his "social media echo chamber," which suggested that he came to the course with an interest in hearing different perspectives.
3. Gideon Lichfield, "There Is Only One Major News Site That Both Pro-Israelis and Pro-Palestinians Read," *Quartz*, August 4, 2014, https://qz.com/244620/there-is-only-one-major-news-site-that-both-pro-israelis-and-pro-palestinians-read/.
4. Association of American Colleges and Universities, "Critical Thinking VALUE Rubric," accessed April 7, 2017, www.aacu.org/value/rubrics/critical-thinking.
5. M. K. Woodworth, "The Rhetorical Précis," *Rhetorical Review* 7, no. 1 (1988): 156–64.

Teaching Students How to Think, Not What to Think, about the Middle East Conflict

DONNA ROBINSON DIVINE

When Israel proclaimed its independence in 1948, it lodged itself in our imagination as a progressive cause celebrated across the globe. But despite the development of a vibrant democracy and robust economy, its titanic struggle for survival has damaged its special status as an enduring symbol of liberation. The story of a people returning to its ancient land to build a new kind of social order and community has been replaced by a tale of Israel as the singular source of much of the world's evils. Once a trope for national redemption, Israel is now viewed as the cause of Palestinian dispossession and dispersion and even of spreading a political agony across the Middle East.

My own teaching, once largely shaped by my own experience as an undergraduate and graduate student, could not remain unaffected by these profound changes. Nor could I ignore that a new set of assumptions about the Middle East conflict now carries significant authority on the U.S. campus. Seeing how I teach about the conflict through the lens of my students conditioned in me the idea of focusing less on why it occurred than on how it unfolded. These two different ways of understanding the conflict lead in different directions. The question of "how" encourages an examination of interactions and decisions that produce outcomes at certain junctures, probing the many ways the available options were defined and accounting for why some were chosen and others rejected. By contrast, the search for the "why" of this conflict may have the appeal of identifying a single cause but also inevitably produces the distorting effect of succumbing to what are defined as long-term trends—not visible at all times—and to rendering judgment and apportioning blame.

But let me take my perspective out of the realm of the abstract and put it into the classroom. The course I offer on the Arab-Israeli conflict is one of many intermediate-level classes in Smith College's Government Department.[1] It fulfills a disciplinary requirement for majors, but it also attracts students pursuing a wide array of studies across the college. There are generally more Arab and Muslim than Jewish students enrolled in this class, which normally includes from twenty-five to forty students. Most say they register for the course to learn something about what appears to be an endless conflict between sworn enemies that continually dominates the headlines.

The syllabus is multidisciplinary insofar as it draws on works of history, sociology, literature, film, and even music. I have translated clips from Israeli and Palestinian films and parts of Hebrew and Arabic songs that give a sense of the experience of living with the conflict. (I sometimes hand out translated and transliterated versions of the recordings I play so that students can join in the chorus.) My pedagogic strategy is indeed reflected in the syllabus and in the emphasis I place on a designated readable history of the conflict. I have changed the texts many times and like to offer a variety of positions, typically choosing texts that do not accord with my own interpretation of certain major events and developments.[2] I want students to wrestle with different viewpoints in order to learn how to assess them.

Another of my more recently adopted strategies involves assigning short papers every few weeks so that writing becomes a frequent and regular task, not something rarely done. Sometimes I ask students to imagine that they are Jews living in tsarist Russia or Arabs in the Ottoman Empire and are exchanging letters about why the land of Israel and/or Palestine has become critical to their survival as a people and civilization. I stress that students need to bear in mind whether the first generation of Zionists and Arab nationalists aimed their arguments at one another or at people within their own communities.[3] Some assignments require students to examine the narratives created on social media and to explain whether they reflect the way in which Jews and Palestinians actually conduct their lives and interactions. Of course, I also pose the kinds of questions that typically punctuate a course on the Middle East conflict: the origin of a particular war; the war's objectives; and its impact on both combatants and on civilians. And the topic of war almost always stimulates questions about prospects for peace, typically triggering spirited but respectful debates among students.

On the first day, I begin by asking students to ponder the appropriateness of the course title: "The Arab-Israeli Conflict." I do so to invite criticism, to suggest that my perspective is not sovereign, and to say, plainly, that the arguments I may put before them need not be taken for granted. My task as instructor is aimed at helping students develop their analytical and critical abilities as well as to make available to them the body of knowledge necessary for making their own informed judgments long after the final examination has been graded. The initial readings, including excerpts from books or articles by Edward Said, Fawaz Turki, Hillel Halkin, Amos Oz, and Aaron Soloveichik,[4] encourage students to confront the fact that this conflict is not only about a piece of real estate: it is also about different and competing conceptions of national identity. And on that topic, Zionists and Palestinians disagree as much within their own communities as across the national divide.

The Edward Said piece introduces students to the notion of Zionism as an appendage of Western imperialism. Zionism is, he claims, no more than an instrument for dispossessing a people and for downgrading a nation into a problem. He heaps scorn on the support for Israel proffered by liberal humanists across the globe. In his book, Said devotes more time to denouncing Zionism than to depicting the nature and characteristics of Palestinian national identity. As Hillel Halkin remarks in his reply, while Edward Said is enraged by what he perceives as the neglect and lack of serious attention directed at the humiliations that continue to be visited on Palestinians, he offers no comparable respect for or recognition of the national right to self-determination asserted by the Jewish people.

Moreover, and perhaps more significantly, Said's polemic makes clear how much the paradigm on political and moral rights has changed. More than thirty-five years ago, when Said's text first appeared, the international consensus evinced sympathy for Israel's struggle for peace and stability. Now the infrastructure of international politics has experienced a shift in the direction of the Palestinian cause as part of the language and institutional commerce of human rights.

Israelis and Palestinians pay a very high price for their nationalist commitments and ambitions, and the reasons for accepting those burdens when their implications are so fully clear must be put front and center of any course on the Middle East conflict. But no less important is an examination of the effectiveness of strategies and tactics and of the reasons why Zionists were far more successful than Palestinians in reaching their political goals. Consider the damages resulting from the Palestinians' decision to stake their political future for so many decades on absolute opposition to the establishment of a Jewish state in any part of Palestine. The class and I talk about the consequences flowing from this principled stance and the very high price paid by Palestinians in lives lost, villages erased, and lands forever gone.

Or analyze, as I gently prod my students to do, the periodic effects of unleashing outbursts of murderous force that pull such large numbers of Palestinians into its cataclysmic center of gravity. Palestinian (and, for that matter, Arab) political leaders have embarked on military campaigns that left their costly expressions in the wreckage of both societies and polities as well as of individual lives. Why, I ask my students, were such leaders as unwilling or unable to prepare adequately for war in 1947 as in 1967, entrapping their people in the kind of chaos that they could not long endure? Examining the decisions of the past builds stronger analytic authority for evaluating the choices made in the present. It comes as no surprise to my class that even after years of unremitting strife presumably altered the official Palestinian standpoint and committed its leadership to engaging in diplomatic negotiations with Israel, violence still seems a compelling means of propelling its cause forward. Thus, the political benefits conferred by the Oslo process produced the outrages of another intifada, as Palestinian leaders seemed incapable of subordinating the promises of a redemptive politics, with its magical goals of wiping away all injustice, to the practical compromises necessary to get a state.

Applying this calculus to Israel, the question for my class becomes whether this country, too, has been rightly led to pursue strategies offering the best chance of escaping the untold expense of continued bloodshed or whether failures of imagination have forfeited opportunities for peace and degraded the capacity to recognize the dangers of remapping the state's borders even after waging wars that were not entirely of its own making. So I ask my students to calculate the costs and benefits of founding settlements in the areas conquered from Jordan in June 1967, part of the historic land of Israel and its landscape of sacred sites. It may have bestowed both a renewed spirit and religious energy on Zionism—arguably an asset—but did it not also impose on Israel major responsibility for the Palestinian problem, an accounting that may have complicated the nation's foreign relations, raised the costs of its common defense, and produced a prolonged policy paralysis with its own downward political dynamic?

The class has had a number of memorable moments, many coming during the debates I structure on some topic that is a current focus of controversy—one year, the security fence or wall; in another, the return to negotiations; a third, on Jerusalem. I ask students to take on positions normally at odds with their own personal preferences or loyalties. I have had students from Saudi Arabia and other parts of the Arab world—some who wear the hijab—represent Israeli Likud politicians, and there are Jewish students who assume the mantle of Hamas or of the al-Aqsa Brigades. Interestingly, my Arab students typically remark that they are happy that their fathers are not around to see them perform. Even before the Middle East conflict sought the shelter of academic freedom across the U.S. campus, I assumed that free speech in the classroom was intended to provide the opportunity to examine this complex emotional political issue in all its dimensions but primarily as a lively intellectual inquiry.

Many of the students have very personal and emotional connections to the issues, none more deeply felt and expressed than to those concerning Jerusalem. To spark discussion and awareness, I encourage students to think about how they might respond if they were born in another country, raised in another religion, and found themselves to be bearers of another history. Moreover, I urge them to think about Jerusalem as a city whose most notable resident is God and, precisely for that reason, a site of endless conflict and perpetual war. Jerusalem may be the house of the one God, but it is the temple of three religions and claimed as the capital of two peoples. It is also said that it is the only city to exist twice—in heaven and on earth—and that means it exists in fact and in the imagination. The Abrahamic religions were born there, and it does not take much imagination to believe in the prophecy that the world will supposedly end there as well.

The feelings stirred up by the conflict between Palestinians and Israelis are so deeply held that examining it without taking sides is difficult. But the terrible toll exacted by this hundred years' war should command intellectual analysis, not political advocacy, or the academy, itself, will become one of its casualties.

Notes

1. Smith is the largest women's college in the United States. Located in Northampton, Massachusetts, it is part of a network of colleges in the Pioneer Valley that includes Amherst, Mt. Holyoke, Hampshire, and the University of Massachusetts. Students are allowed to register for classes at any of the institutions, and my classes typically contain several students from one or more of them.
2. Texts have included Charles D. Smith, *Palestine and the Arab-Israeli Conflict: A History with Documents*, 9th ed. (New York: Macmillan, 2016); David W. Lesch, *The Arab-Israeli Conflict: A History* (New York: Oxford University Press, 2008); James L. Gelvin, *The Israel-Palestine Conflict: One Hundred Years of War*, 3rd ed. (New York: Cambridge University Press, 2014); Alan Dowty, *Israel/Palestine*, 3rd ed. (Malden, MA: Polity, 2012).
3. One sample question to illustrate: "Nationalisms often require an 'other' to define their collective identities, but do they also need an 'enemy'? Who or what served initially as the 'other' for Zionism and for Palestinian nationalism? Has the 'other' changed as these nationalist ideologies developed and confronted one another? To what extent did the definitions of their national identities dispose Arabs and Jews in Palestine to view one another as enemies?"
4. Excerpts from Edward W. Said, *The Question of Palestine* (New York: Times Books, 1979); Fawaz Turki, "The Future of a Past: Fragments from The Palestinian Dream," *Journal of Palestine Studies* 6, no. 3 (1977): 66–76; Hillel Halkin, "Whose Palestine? An Open Letter to Edward Said," *Commentary* 69, no. 5 (1980): 21–30; Amos Oz, "The Meaning of Homeland," *New Outlook* 31, no. 1 (1988): 19–24; Aaron Soloveichik, "The State of Israel: A Torah Perspective," *Tradition: A Journal of Orthodox Jewish Thought* 25, no. 2 (1990): 1–11.

Empathy, Access, Language, and Education

Learning to See the Other

Teaching Literature to Arab and Jewish Students in Israel

BETWEEN NATIONAL IDENTITIES, LANGUAGES, AND GENDERS

ADIA MENDELSON-MAOZ

In an episode from Eran Riklis's film *A Borrowed Identity* (2014) that brings together two of Sayed Kashua's books, *Dancing Arabs* (2002) and *Second Person Singular* (2010), Eyad, the protagonist, sits in the classroom of a prestigious high school in Jerusalem, where he is almost the only Arab student. During literature class, the teacher discusses Amos Oz's novel *My Michael* and specifically focuses on the characters of the Arab twins in the novel and their symbolic role. Determined to prepare her class for the matriculation exam in literature, she drills the students to say what is considered to be the accepted interpretation of the novel. When she asks Eyad a question, he is able to answer exactly what she expects to hear, yet the fact that he is the one who delivers this answer creates a subversive meaning since he, the Arab student, refers to the Arab twins in Oz's text as a source of anxiety. His words reveal the alienation experienced by Arab-Israelis when called on to deal with the Israeli curriculum in literature. Thus, if Eyad wants to get good grades in high school, he has to recite the right words from the Bible, know the official phrasing regarding the history of the State of Israel, and read canonic Israeli literature from a Zionist perspective.

This scene from *Dancing Arabs* echoed in my thoughts during a meeting on the "third hour" project, which provides extra hours to Arab students at the Open University of Israel, where I serve as the chair of the Department of Literature, Language, and the Arts. The Open University of Israel was founded four decades ago and today has forty-seven thousand students (more than any other university in Israel), representing all sectors of Israeli society and all religious and ethnic groups. The Open University aims to make higher education accessible to all individuals. It has an open admissions policy for bachelor's degree candidates, and it offers flexibility and accessibility to anyone who seeks to study. Using a distance-education system, over fifty learning centers throughout Israel, a wide range of courses, materials, textbooks, online lectures, internet forums, and face-to-face interactions with teachers all over Israel, it reaches a broad swath of the population.

This openness and accessibility create a highly heterogeneous body of students. Many of the students at the Open University work and cannot be full-time students. Other students include adults engaged in further education; advanced high school students; soldiers during their military service; people who live abroad and want to learn in an Israeli institution; and people who cannot attend other universities because they live too far away, have disabilities, or have religious and cultural restrictions, such as ultra-Orthodox Jews and students who come from certain Muslim and Bedouin communities.

In the field of literature, the Open University offers a bachelor's degree in Hebrew and comparative literature, as well as a teaching certificate in literature for those who plan to specialize in education. We offer a wide range of courses in Hebrew literature from different periods, from the Bible to the present. There are also courses on the Western canon, including in a comparative context, classics, medieval literature, Shakespeare, nineteenth-century novels, poetry, and literature of the twentieth and twenty-first centuries.

This lengthy introduction to the Open University helps to better situate a unique, perhaps surprising, fact about the students who choose to study literature as their major. First, as is congruent with Western statistics for literature students, most of those who choose literature degrees are women. Second, the majority of students are Israeli Arabs, whose first language is Arabic. Males (both Jewish and Arabs) usually make up roughly 10–15 percent of all literature students. Students (male and female) whose first language is Hebrew constitute about 25–30 percent, and the remaining 70–75 percent are native speakers of Arabic. In other words, Arab women make up more than 60 percent of the students who choose literature as a major, and most of them continue to study toward their teaching certificate in literature. Other students who take courses in literature as part of other programs in the humanities generally have the same profile: most are women, and most of them are Arab.

The reasons for this demographic are varied, including the crisis in the humanities in general, the low status of teachers in Israel (specifically among Jews), and teachers' relatively low salaries, all of which do not attract culturally and economically strong candidates to these disciplines. Though many Israeli Arabs study literature both at Ben Gurion University and at Haifa University, the special nature of the Open University encourages Israeli-Arab women from certain areas to enroll.

Because the Open University has many centers in Israel, it makes education available to any group that seeks to study while making huge efforts to support it. Literature courses can be taken in centers not only in the Tel Aviv, Jerusalem, and Be'er Sheva areas but also in Wadi Ara, Shfar'am, Nazareth, the Golan Heights, Bedouin areas of the Negev, and other locations in Israel. Some of these centers have a diverse student body, that is, both Jews and Arabs (as in Wadi Ara), whereas other centers cater only to Arab students. Thus, students who cannot leave their villages to become full-time students in other universities (mostly due to the restrictions imposed by religious or traditional families) can study and earn their degrees within their community.

I will not elaborate on the huge difficulties involved in teaching literature (mostly Hebrew literature) to these students. The first barrier is the language. At the Open University, Hebrew is the language of instruction, and students are required to read, write, and submit papers in Hebrew (in Hebrew literature classes but also in classes in comparative literature). Several courses are oriented toward Arabic, in which although the books are in Hebrew, students can study with tutors in Arabic and write assignments in Arabic. However, they can only take a maximum of three courses in Arabic. While most of the Israeli Arabs who go to Haifa or Tel Aviv University have experience speaking Hebrew and living among Jewish Israelis, some Muslim women who are not allowed to travel by themselves but can attend the Open University center are unfamiliar with Hebrew language and culture. Furthermore, because the university has an open admission policy, the disparities in education backgrounds and scholarly abilities (with regard to skills, prior knowledge of materials, and aptitude) among students can be considerable.

The Open University in general and our department in particular focus on developing students and encouraging them to succeed by overcoming these particular obstacles. Each teacher is assigned students, who receive special assistance in Hebrew and are taught study skills. For every two hours of teaching delivered to Hebrew-speaking students, Arab-speaking students receive an additional hour. This is known as the "third hour" project.

But while we can help students learn Hebrew, and Jewish or Israeli culture, the content and the context of the literature we teach are removed from the experiences of most of our students. Not only do they study in a foreign language, about a literature that is informed by Zionist ideology, but it is this very ideology that led to their own minority status within the country. As in Kashua's poignant scene, these students learn about the background of nineteenth-century Jewish eastern European villages (*A'yara*) that produced authors such as Bialik, Agnon, Shofman, Berdichevsky, and Steinberg, but they learn nothing about Arab or Palestinian literature and identity (Mahmoud Darwish, Anton Shammas, Tawfiq Zayyad, Ghassan Kanafani, Nathalie Handal).

Nevertheless, these students choose to study and later teach Hebrew literature, because it is considered a respectable profession in their villages. I was shocked a few years ago when the class on Palestinian cinema (the only course we have in our department that truly explores the Palestinians' history and identity) had no enrollment at the Open University center in Wadi Ara, while a class on the works of the Hebrew writer S. Y. Agnon was full. That cinema crosses into the territory of forbidden and therefore censored content (particularly for religious students) may explain part of the lack of interest for the Palestinian cinema course, but in general the lack of enthusiasm for it stems from the strong pragmatic belief in Israel's Arab communities that it is more respectable to study Hebrew literature.

What can we do to help these students not only to succeed in their literature degrees but to see literature as a source of personal contemplation? How can we encourage them to feel that literature can affect their lives, and promote understanding and dialogue about literature and nationality, literature and personal identity? As teachers and faculty, we can tackle this issue in two ways. First, we can use what we already offer but give it a new perspective, and second, we can develop new courses that will foster a more balanced dialogue.

Working with What We Have

Courses at the Open University use textbooks made for the program that cannot be changed from semester to semester. Teachers at different centers have to teach the same material since the assignments and exams administered every year are identical for all students in all centers taking the course. Rather than viewing heterogeneous groups as a source of difficulties for teachers and the course coordinator, who monitors and supervises all the groups, faculty are encouraged to consider the fixed material from multiple perspectives.

Here are two possible examples that make literature relevant to all students:

(1) The introductory drama class, which is obligatory for the teaching certificate, introduces fundamental concepts in drama and theater and outlines milestones in the history of the theater and its conventions. This course has Arabic support and thus is very popular among Arab students in literature as well as other students in the humanities. There are around twenty groups and around three to four hundred students who take this course throughout Israel every year. The course coordinator, Dorit Ashur, who has extensive experience in teaching mixed groups of Arab- and Hebrew-speaking students, strives to make the course relevant to Arab students. Thus, although the course focuses on the (Western) history of the theater and its conventions, she invites

Arab actors and producers to class, and she draws attention to the theatrical treatment of ideological and gender issues.

The highlight of the course is the mandatory requirement to attend a preselected theater performance. The Open University buys the tickets and arranges buses. Ashur decides which production students see and has been sensitive not only to the pedagogical issues she wishes to raise in regard to theater but also to the social and cultural nuances that might prevent a female student from a traditional or religious background from being able to view the play. Some years ago, the Be'er Sheva Theater performed Ibsen's play *A Doll's House*. Ashur felt that this would be the right play for her students, since most of them are women (Jews and Arabs). However, when watching the production herself, as she always does in advance, she discovered that in the last scene, the actress playing Nora removes her shirt, exposing her chest as an expression of her independence. This was something that could not be shown to her Arab students. She talked to the theater, explained the importance of the play despite its problematic ending, and eventually arranged for the Open University to buy all the seats for one performance, on condition that the actress would not take off her shirt. On the day of the performance, she sat nervously afraid that the actress would forget to change the last scene; but the play went well, and all the students were excited by the play and its content. Many of Ashur's students had not seen a live theater production before, and they were strongly impacted by the experience, with some drawing connections with their own lives, such as women's struggle for independence and the role of patriarchy within the family. The play had provided them with language to discuss personal issues that they had not previously considered in light of global female experience. In turn, this gave them a new appreciation for the role of literature as a medium of personal exploration, rather than an externalized and removed area designated purely for scholarship.

(2) The Hebrew poetry course "Israeli Poetry of the 1950s" familiarizes students with poetic changes from modernism and the Palmach generation (Natan Alterman, Haim Gouri) to the poetry of the State generation (Dalia Ravikovitch, David Avidan, Natan Zach). Teaching the course in Wadi Ara to a mixed group of Arab and Jewish students, I found it difficult to talk about the poetry of the 1948 war that is a major feature of the Palmach generation's work. To my mind, the focus on Hebrew literature excluded the narrative of the Palestinians. When Mei-Tal Nadler taught the course, she included Palestinian poetry by Mahmoud Darwish, Taha Muhammad Ali, and other Palestinian writers. Drawing out concepts of "national poet" versus "personal poet," she was able to mark parallels between Palestinian and Israeli thematics. Although she does not know Arabic, she encouraged her students to find the original poems online and to read other works as well. The students, Arab and Jews, were more engaged in the material, were more independent in their reading, and actively

searched out additional texts. By redefining the boundaries of the course, Nadler created a dynamic and engaged learning experience.

New Prospects

In conclusion, I want to consider the ways in which we can look to future endeavors to facilitate a richer experience for native Arabic speakers, one that I believe will also inform a more complex classroom dialogue that also serves to augment Jewish and native Hebrew speakers' learning experience.

A national writing competition under the auspices of the Arditi Foundation has a short-story category open to submissions in Hebrew or Arabic. Like other Israeli universities, the Open University participates in the competition, but unlike other places where the majority of student submissions are in Hebrew, 50 percent of our submissions are in Arabic. The introduction of a creative writing workshop led by the Israeli author Matan Hermoni helps fuel some of the Hebrew interest, and more recently, I have promoted a workshop for creative writing in Arabic, to give Arab-speaking students the opportunity to express themselves in their native language within a literature framework. Not only does this serve to facilitate greater respect for Arab-language students, but it also recognizes the lack of scholarly focus on writing literary Arabic that is a lacuna of the Israeli education system. As Kashua has said of his own uneasy relationship with Hebrew, while he may forever remain a foreigner in Hebrew, he cannot write in Arabic. Thus, such a course would also help preserve Arabic cultural and literary heritage.

The second initiative that I hope to promote is a new course in our department that will be bilingual in Hebrew and Arabic and will discuss the Israeli-Palestinian conflict through literature. Moving beyond the canon of recognized male authors (both Palestinian and Israeli), the course would focus on women's literature, thereby refocusing discussions of the conflict on the broader social impact. Given that most of the literature students are female, it also recognizes women's personal and unique experiences and voices.

Palestinian and Israeli women's writing on the conflict reveals different perspectives that can help better explore the conflict and encourage empathy, such as texts by the Palestinian authors Suad Amiry, Shajid Husseini, Sahar Khalifeh, and Liana Badr, in major genres such as the personal memoir and the family and historical novel. These can be read alongside Jewish authors such as Netiva Ben Yehuda, Shani Boianjiu, Orly Castel-Bloom, Savyon Liebrecht, Michal Govrin, Ronit Matalon, and Dorit Rabinyan.

These texts are diverse with regard to genres, style, language, context, and content. However, they share mutual issues. Motherhood, nationalism, resistance, and the relationship between mothers and daughters crisscross most of the literature. The connection between the Holocaust and the Nakba appears in different ways in both the Palestinian and the Israeli texts. Themes such as women's coming of age, militarism, and chauvinism can facilitate a comparative discussion. Finally, a discussion of genres of women's writing can shed light on the different literary norms of women writing in Hebrew, in Arabic, or in English.

The department is currently planning a new syllabus that thematically pairs Palestinian and Israeli texts, including a significant number of works by women. The texts are available in both Arabic and Hebrew in order to proactively facilitate greater engagement for Arab students, offering them an equal opportunity to participate and feel that there is space for them to freely express their thoughts about literature.

These many differing models (a drama course, a poetry course, a writing workshop, and a course on bilingual literature) showcase ways in which diverse bodies of students can be engaged with simultaneously. In this way, literature courses become a site of and a model for dialogue that not only teaches sympathy and even empathy for the other but also serves to shape personal discussion—all the while placing the Arab-Israeli conflict within a broader context of literary trends, feminist and ethnic experience, and a universalizing expression of humanity.

Victim or Terrorist?

ON THE PERILS OF MISREADING AND THE CREATIVE WRITING CLASSROOM AS BORDER CROSSING

MARCELA SULAK

"Are you a victim or a terrorist?" writes R., the feminist Muslim graduate student in the 2014 documentary poetics workshop. Her thesis is a collection of poems entitled *Schizophrenia*, in which she explores the gender inequality felt by a woman in the Arab world, "a woman who has to respect the values and traditions of God." As a woman and an Arab living in Israel, she notes, "I am doubly silenced." Another way of putting the issue, she says, is how to be "'real' in Is-rael."

Two years later, "terrorist," rather than "victim" (or the more charged "martyr"), is how the police officer from Nazareth decided to translate the Arabic *Shahid* into Hebrew in Dareen Tatour's poem "Resist my people, resist them." Dareen Tatour had posted the poem on Facebook in the fall of 2015, during a period of Palestinian car rammings and stabbings in Israel, to bring attention to recent and numerous violent acts committed against innocent Palestinians by Israelis. She had recorded the poem and used it as the soundtrack to images of Palestinians in violent confrontations with Israeli security forces, including rock throwing. Although the Jewish police officer had no qualifications as a scholar of Arabic literature or as a scholar of poetry (he spoke Arabic at home, and he possessed a "love of the Arabic language"), his non-contextualized reading was taken as evidence, over the more nuanced reading of the Jewish scholar of Arabic literature who had been called in for the defense in court in the spring of 2016. Tatour was held under house arrest until her conviction in May

2018 and was sentenced in July 2018 to five months' imprisonment. If, as Tatour has stated, the poem was misunderstood and she herself had not called for violence, she was being convicted for the police officer's misreading of a poem, for his failure to close-read properly, and because he brought his own associations to the poem, rather than entering into the world of the poem and humbly listening to it.

I do not believe that poetry necessarily saves anyone's life. But I do believe that participating in the dialogic possibilities it creates when two or more people gather together might help us not to imprison one another in homes, jails, or ideologies. This essay describes three kinds of creative writing workshop that I have been teaching for the past seven years as the director of the Shaindy Rudoff Graduate Program in Creative Writing at Bar-Ilan University.

The Shaindy Rudoff Graduate Program offers a master of arts degree through the Department of English Literature and Linguistics at Bar-Ilan University. For the past ten years, students from at least sixteen countries and thirteen different native languages have written poetry, fiction, and creative nonfiction together. To enter the program, students must submit a portfolio in their intended genre; once enrolled in graduate studies, they participate in three to four writing workshops, two to three literature seminars, and the William Solomon Jewish Arts Seminar, which is optional for non-Jewish students.

Bar-Ilan University, founded in 1955 with the goal of "fostering Jewish values and continuity," also requires of all graduate students in all departments and programs two formal Jewish studies courses, to be taken in the Department of Jewish Studies. Non-Jewish students may choose to substitute two general studies courses in any department. Each year my program enrolls between fifteen and twenty-six new students, of which at least 80 percent are Jewish. The program is designed to take two years, but students have finished course work in a single year, if they must return abroad; some have taken three years, if they are working full-time and have families.

Although the graduate program is in English, upward of 30 percent of the students enrolled do not speak English as a native language. And contrary to what one might imagine, this is precisely the reason some of the students enroll. The Europeans who study with us do so in languages that are not their own because they want to be in Israel, outside of their own culture; because they want to write in a Jewish context; or because there is no writing program in their country in their language. For the Palestinian-Israeli students, English is a neutral language. Hebrew would signal to them their inferior social status. And they cannot write what they need to write in Arabic, a language they feel confines their thoughts, imaginations, and literary creativity by holding them to the social, familial, and cultural roles expected of them. The genderless English language emboldens native Hebrew and Arabic speakers and frees them somewhat in their literary bodies.

Documentary Poetics

Given the student population of our program and the background of the graduate students—a surprising number of whom have been journalists—as well as my beliefs about what poetry is and what it is for, I developed a workshop called "Documentary Poetics," which is available to poetry and nonfiction students in the program. The course's "statement of merit" or underlying principle can be summed up in a couple of lines from William Carlos William's poem "Asphodel, That Greeny Flower":

> It is difficult
> to get the news from poems
>   yet men die miserably every day
>   for lack
> of what is found there.

In this workshop, which I teach in odd-numbered fall semesters, I ask each student to identify an obsession or a subject that their poetry will engage in the course of the semester. This external focus helps prevent the poetry from becoming propaganda, and it also allows us to address emotional material by way of external frameworks. The participants have chosen such subjects as the Mahane Yehuda Shuk in Jerusalem, compasses, Herod the builder, the history of tear gas, Ramadan recipes, the "Lone Woman" of San Nicolas Island, gender-based violence, Israeli checkpoints, mothering toddlers, and Arab-Israeli feminism. Often the final projects from this course have turned into master's theses.

In addition to weekly writing and workshop, we typically read about five outside poetry collections and emulate their research methods and composition techniques. These texts will typically include an example of the scientific and/or researched poem, such as Kimiko Hahn's *Toxic Flora*, for which the *New York Times* Science section provided inspiration. We include texts that demonstrate how nations are narrated constructs and how words can eviscerate maps by erasing continents: Craig Santos Perez's trilogy, *Unincorporated Territory*, about Guam, or Jena Osman's mapping of New York, *The Network*. We read texts that show the political nature of language, such as Martha Collin's *White Papers*, and texts that weave various source materials and testimonies into poetry, such as Muriel Rukeyser's *Book of the Dead* or C. D. Wright's *One with Others* or *One Big Self*. I change the reading list each semester.

Each four-hour workshop is divided into an hour to discuss the assigned reading and then three hours to discuss the poems that students bring into class. This discussion is called the "workshop," and we follow an etiquette in this workshop and in the other two I describe later:

The most helpful workshop feedback demonstrates an understanding of what the poem is trying to accomplish and HOW it means. Workshop feedback should avoid subjective statements such as "I like" and "I don't like." Instead, preface your feedback with reference to the world of the poem and the poem's overall structure and goals.

The poet whose work is under discussion will be silent during the discussion, though he or she may ask a question at the end.

I give very open-ended writing assignments each week. The assignments are based on form and method, not on content. At the beginning of the semester, in addition to identifying the subject each student will explore, the student must create a bibliography or research plan.

A typical writing assignment would be "Read Martha Collins's *White Papers* and write a poem about your topic in which you note all the words that are taboo or off-limits for you to use. How do you censor yourself?" For Martha Collins, as well as many of my students, we censor ourselves by designating "us" and "them" and feeling fearful in the presence of "them."

For this writing assignment, R. wrote a long poem critical of the patriarchy of the Arab states and also their thirst for oil and power. Another student, a Peace Now activist studying fiction who also volunteers to observe the checkpoints between West Bank and Israel, to make sure that soldiers do not abuse their power, informed R., "You cannot say that about Arabs!"—as if, in the intimacy of the workshop, R. was not "an Arab" but "one of us." This was a shock to me, if not to R.; maybe it was a shock to the checkpoint observer, as well—that even in guarding one another's humanity, we still think in terms of "us" and "them."

But "us" and "them" also come up in gender—the native Hebrew speaker who was writing about her own experience of gang rape, as well as her experience of teaching women in refugee camps in Darfur how to become midwives, made the men uncomfortable. "Whenever I look at her, I can't get her suffering out of my mind, and I don't know what to say. I am a man." There was no easy answer to this, and we never fully solved this problem. But we *began* to solve it by approaching the content through the structure—by focusing on use of language, on pronouns. Some of the characters in the midwife's poems had ambiguously marked genders, for example. She did not do this to make the men in the room comfortable, but it did allow for an interesting discussion about how outer appearance (how people appear and how they represent themselves through language or clothing, including how we gender people) affects our encounters with them.

At the end of the semester, the students put together a dramatic reading of the Israeli poet's work about gender-based violence. We called it *Hysteria* and performed it in Jaffa, the ancient port city, the Arab-majority city that preceded and lies next to Tel Aviv. This student, now an alumna, is currently working with the Knesset to establish adequate facilities for women recovering from gender-based violence and trauma.

Perhaps it is not a coincidence that many students end up writing about borders and boundaries; their work is obsessed with crossing. There is Jane, whose work traverses the "permeable membrane" between the secular and the sacred. Her poems are archeological digs into the landscape around her and into language; they are prayers, they are complaints, and they are exegeses on the Jewish texts she had studied for twenty years. Jillian's thesis, *Breaking Hannah Szenesh*, traverses national boundaries as it follows Szenesh from Hungary to Palestine, then, as a paratrooper, back across the border for the last time. Her Hannah Szenesh invaded her dreams, and her narrator conversed with her subject, interrogated her, held her close. Joanna, a former *Newsweek* journalist working in the Palestinian Territories and in Israel, wrote a thesis called *Check.Point*.

However, there was one student whose poetry resisted the here and now. This poet lived beyond the Green Line in the Palestinian Territories and wrote lyrical poems praising the mythical, biblical past, with its David's harp and Zion. Speaking to her privately, I discovered that she was not unaware of her place in the world; nor was she without material to write about. In fact, she confessed to me, once she had fallen asleep at the wheel, and her car had stopped at the edge of a cliff. She could have easily fallen into a ravine. A Palestinian man risked his life to save her and pulled her from the car. Then she realized she had not been wearing her *sheitel*, her wig, which religious women wear to cover their own hair as a sign of modesty. It was in the trunk. She insisted that the man get it, and he did. "A Jewish man would never have risked his life for my modesty, but this Palestinian did," she explained, "because he understood." Poetry, for her, had nothing to do with the life of the physical body in the here and now. It was, for her, a spiritual exercise. "Why don't you write about this experience?" I suggested. She did not say.

Poetic Prosody, Genre, and Form

There is a fine balance in teaching, between enabling students to write about what they wish to write about and in encouraging them to dig deeper into concerns that one feels ought to be acknowledged, if not directly addressed. However, when dealing with poetry, I find it is most liberating to approach content only indirectly and, instead, to focus directly on form, prosodic technique, exploring the history of poetic genres in symphony with current developments, and researching interests that are not explicitly biographical. In this way, content can be approached slantwise—what are the limits of language, of form, for exposing thoughts for which there is no vocabulary, situations that are exquisitely new and current? The workshop in poetic prosody, genre, and form has been a successful approach. Here is the description:

> Poetic forms and genres emerge in response to the way people and cultures have expressed over time their most intense feelings and their most vital stories. They shape readers' expectations, they shape poets' arguments and perceptions, and, most importantly, they allow poets to glean from the past the ideals, values and stories that shape our present moment. In this seminar, we will practice using various formal tools to shape feelings and perceptions into music by writing poetry in specific forms, and by participating in workshop sessions. We will also become familiar and confident with the interpretative tools that enhance our understanding and enjoyment of poetry, and that allow us to communicate about this multifaceted art form in a clear and thoughtful manner.

As in the documentary poetics workshop, we read about five contemporary collections written in poetic forms and genres and mix a discussion of these collections with our participation in workshop. The writing assignments dictate form, not content. So a typical assignment in this workshop would be to write a sonnet, a sestina, an ode, a prose poem, and so forth.

I struggle to take the long view when I teach poetic prosody, genre, and form; I want students to challenge themselves, not only as writers but also as thinkers, not only as historians of genre but as innovators. I wish for them to embrace whatever religious feelings and ideologies they have but also to question the relevance of them. It is fine if the questioning confirms their original stance. But ideological poetry is not particularly interesting to anyone except those who are already of like minds. And for me, poetry is a transformative encounter with the Other.

Early in the semester of prosody, genre, and form, I worried for A., the new immigrant mother of three children under the age of five whose religious conversion to Judaism had not yet been accepted by the State of Israel. We all wondered if race had anything to do with it—she was African American—or if it was simply that her conversion was performed under the auspices of the Conservative movement. No sooner had she arrived in Ashkelon than the Gaza war (2014) had begun, and she often could not come to class because she was sitting with her children in a bomb shelter all day for the duration of the war. And yet her poems for the genre class were funny abecedarians about feeding her children breakfast, giving in to their requests, and finally forcing them to choose between ice cream and pie. Or they were accentual verse about potty training. Yes, motherhood was a valid topic—who was I or anyone else to say what was not a valid topic for poetry? The second year, after the summer of so many unarmed black boys killed by police in the United States, she ended the documentary poetics class with powerful critiques of the U.S. militarization of the police force. She is also a performance artist and, after graduation, has been giving extremely effective performances and workshops in performance. Only after her conversion was officially accepted, it seemed, did she have a position of security and authority from which to criticize. This is the limit of a poetry workshop—no matter how much group trust and acceptance is built, no matter how many friendships and support networks are in place, the workshop and its aftermath are only a microcosm. They are not the world.

Hybridity

There was still one more part of the writing experience in our classroom that I was eager to address. In Israel, among many of the Muslim and Jewish communities, there is not a large shared history, not a common consensus on historical facts that appear basic to one side or the other. Perhaps this is what R. had meant when her essay had asked "how to be real in Is-rael."

With that in mind, and driven by universal budget cuts that required staff to be creative in designing courses that fulfilled multiple needs, I developed an upper-division, undergraduate course in hybrid writing. It began as a multigenre course, but it soon rebelled against the idea of genre as a fixed entity. Instead, we considered genre as a collection of affinities and alliances. Out of this course, and in collaboration with a like-minded coeditor, Jacqueline Kolosov, I created the Rose Metal Press anthology *Family Resemblance: An Anthology and Exploration of 8 Hybrid Literary Genres*. My understanding of genre was that different generic affiliations expressed different kinds of truth claims, different registers of experience, and different perspectives. The idea was that in combining generic methods and goals, one could express multiple points of view and truths. For distinctions between "history" and "myth" or between "memoir" and "folk story" have long been used to bolster particular versions of "truth" that most efficiently disenfranchise, incarcerate, or otherwise innervate people of color and their personal and cultural narratives. Perhaps this is why the Haifa-born Emile Habibi's books are all described as "part memoir, part political commentary, part fairy tale."[1] Hybrid works imagine ways of being that have not yet been articulated and, therefore, do not exist in the cultural map of the master social narrative, though they exist in the physical world. Hybridity is also used as a joyful force of destruction that can clear received notions of thought. What Miriam, a choreographer who had lived and worked in tens of countries and who had been seeking a way to translate dance into literature, discovered about the lyric essay could be true to the workshop in general: "In this form of the essay, the narrative is presented in blocks or linked fragments of prose and prose poems, layering experience, offering neither conclusion nor judgment, thereby representing the limits of narrative control." It was just this limit of narrative control that we all found to be the catalyst of some of our most important and moving work.

The hybrid course attracted a diversity of students—twenty-five the first year, which made workshop challenging. I divided the class into five graduate and undergraduate workshop groups and circulated among them. Later iterations of this workshop were smaller and more intimate. In addition to the stunning work the students created in multiple forms, we also spoke together and shared stories. Students found the workshop personally empowering, and we all encountered one another with openness. I believe it was one of the most beautiful and expansive experiences I have had in teaching. Thus it happened that a Druze student came out to us as lesbian. Another student revealed her disappointment with the marriage candidate whom her parents had selected; they did not marry. A newly immigrated Russian security guard wrote about and discussed his bipolar condition. In a word, we accomplished more than writing. We encountered one another in a way that I could not have imagined happening anywhere else.

Most of the students enrolled in the program feel themselves to be hybrids of sorts, because of their immigration into a new culture and language, their religiously mixed backgrounds, their temporary or permanent "otherness" status granted by student visas, their nonmajority cultural status. There was I.J., a young student, a teacher, sincerely and joyfully religious, possessing what seemed to be a complete trust in Allah and the prohibitions and rituals to which her life was structured. She wrote ecstatic, lyrical poems about food. She brought food to class. The students partook to the extent that their kashrut prohibitions allowed. She wrote as if she had never suffered at all as a woman or as an Arab-Israeli (not to mention as a high school teacher in Lod). Toward the end of her studies, however, she submitted a powerful lyrical essay on buying food in a *sook* (market) in the West Bank for Ramadan; how her mother mixed her Arabic with Hebrew in the *sook*, much to her discomfort; how her mother explained, "But we are also Israeli, so it is natural that we use Hebrew too. We are not purely Palestinian." This is a woman who would ask directions in Tel Aviv in English, not Hebrew, of the Israelis in the street. She would rather speak English, a neutral language. And perhaps that is why she was enrolled in our English-language creative writing program. In her essay, called "The Meal," she describes returning from the *sook* and being stopped at a checkpoint to discover that her mother does not have her identity card and will not be permitted back into Israel. After much consternation—would they have time to prepare the festive meal for breaking the Ramadan fast that night?—she leaves her mother at the checkpoint and returns home, to discover that her mother has left her identity card on the kitchen table. The mother is retrieved, and the festive meal is hastily composed. You can hear this essay in its entirety at https://

tlv1.fm/israel-in-translation/2017/06/07/your-id-haji-preparations-for-ramadan/. I.J. was able to say in the essay what she did not feel poetry had the space to explain. Which is fitting; her lyrical essay was a hybrid, just as she is, as the essay asserts—or, at least, just as her mother feels that they are. The author appears more skeptical.

Other students have come from Haredi communities to pursue secular art forms. Some have been rejected by family or religious communities for their sexual orientation. Sometimes the experiences they wish to document cannot be aptly narrated within the confines of any one genre. Although some students choose to write standard lyric poetry of witness or researched poetry, others blend genres to push the boundaries of journalism and poetry. These theses were often among the most interesting, and they include, in addition to those mentioned earlier, Geula's essay "The Beginnings of Fire," which witnessed "a personal story of sexual abuse which had its roots in sexual repression in religious cultures." It wove together first-person testimony with biblical stories and midrashim about covering the body and was conveyed through a magical realist style. Shoshana's thesis *Traverse Babel* overlays personal geographies of the Ukraine, Crimea, Israel, Maryland, and Alabama like transparencies, and Batnadiv's essay describes the recovery of her Rosh Yeshiva grandfather's Hebrew-language journal, which he carried with him in hiding in Siberia during the Shoah. He had died in America without her ever having known he spoke anything but Yiddish.

These experiences have been consistent in the seven years I have taught in Israel. It is a tiny country that contains unimaginable complexity, and no matter how much we disagree, we have to come home to one another. The creative writing classroom, in my experience, has given boundaries and borders an elasticity as we cross them, move them, renegotiating them again and again. I do not believe that poetry will necessarily save anyone's life. It will not change policies. But, as the case of Dareen Tatour demonstrates, when you misread poetry, it can have dire consequences.

Notes

1. "A Fairy Tale: Emile Habibi's 'Saraya, the Ogre's Daughter,'" podcast for TLV1, June 21, 2017, https://tlv1.fm/israel-in-translation/2017/06/21/a-fairy-tale-emile-habibis-saraya-the-ogres-daughter/.

Representing the Homeland

ISRAEL AND PALESTINE ONSTAGE

ELLEN W. KAPLAN

The great Norwegian dramatist Henrik Ibsen once asked how "the Jewish people—the aristocracy of the human race—have kept their place apart, their poetical halo, amid surroundings of coarse cruelty? By having no State to burden them. Had they remained in Palestine, they would long ago have lost their individuality in the process of their State's construction, like all other nations" (letter to George Brandes, February 17, 1871).

Ibsen's admiration of Jewish exile was linked to an idea that political normalcy was irreconcilable with "spiritual adventure, religious virtuosity, and intellectual creativity." But the historical consequences of statelessness have been shattering. Without a territorial anchor, a *homeland*, history has shown that Jews are vulnerable.

In creating a national homeland for the Jews, the problem of Palestinian statelessness has also been created, one that deserves no less attention. For Israelis and Palestinians, the consequences of diaspora, the geography of exile, and the effects of assimilation and deracination on the construction of a spiritually and historically meaningful identity center on a single question: What is the importance of the land?

At Smith, a liberal arts women's college in Massachusetts, I teach acting, directing, and dramatic literature. In this essay, I focus on "Israel: Homelands, Borderlands, and Debate," a course that examines the multiple and fractious identities within and beyond Israeli borders; this essay examines how we address the Israeli-Palestinian conflict. Students are typically juniors and seniors with little to no prior knowledge of Zionism or of Israeli and Palestinian history. A majority are Jewish identified, secular, curious—but committed to a flattened, ahistorical narrative characterized by a single-minded identification with the perceived "underdog." Engaging with students means challenging narratives that portray an atavistic Israel, devoid of history or context, and upending a simplistic oppressed/oppressor paradigm.

Theater offers *theoretical frameworks* and *operational toolboxes* for use in the classroom. Nonpartisan, nonideological teaching strategies, grounded in an artistic discipline, encourage compassionate listening and dialogue across difference and are useful in any classroom that addresses social conflict. By using theatrical texts as the principal course readings and deploying strategies of applied theater to examine contentious issues and conflicting narratives, students consider multiple voices across a range of viewpoints.

In theater, *we tell stories*. A story told onstage, through the "optics of the theater" (as Harold Clurman terms it), makes visible something larger than itself. Stories tell us who we are; they create, and reflect, the "social imaginary."[1] Through the enacted story, we better understand others and ourselves.

Theatrical practice mobilizes empathy. Acting requires a compassionate and engaged presence in relationship to another; as the ethicist Elaine Scarry asserts, relationship is the heart of all ethical action. And Amos Oz refers to the goal of literature as "enhanc[ing] our ability to imagine each other."[2] Engaging the other through imagination makes us more human, more *humane*.

Good dramatic writing presents complex characters in contention: it moves beyond expectation and stereotype, to offer multiple voices and perspectives. Dramatic characters strive against each other, against society, and against themselves. For the actor, the *specificity* of characterization works against stereotype and allows access to the heart and mind of a *particular person*. By speaking the words of others and enacting their desires, we begin to see the world through their eyes. One reading for the course, *How to Cure a Fanatic* by Amos Oz, defines the zealot as a person who is not willing to listen to alternative definitions of justice and who insists on converting others to his or her own (rigid) belief system. Our aim in the course is to challenge zealotry and to encourage pluralism, while insisting on rigorous analysis and critical thought.

We read a series of plays that offer perspectives on the 1948 war and the experience of exile; identity formation and the role of gender; representing the "other"; the progressions of history and evolving ideologies; the move from rational discourse to zealotry; and departure from conciliatory viewpoints and hope for compromise to the pessimism of recent years.

We begin with Jonathan Sobol's *Ghetto*, written in 1989 and set in 1941–43. This trenchant look at the Vilna Ghetto uses a theatrical performance as its point of departure. The play looks at the vicious humiliation of the Jews and conditions that led directly to the murder of fifty thousand Jews. It is also a study of the pressures on the chief of Jewish Police and leader of the ghetto, Jacob Gens, who collaborates with the Nazis as a means of saving some Jewish lives.

We compare Sobol's play with two Palestinian plays set in Israel/Palestine in the pivotal year 1948. *I Am Yusuf and This Is My Brother* (2009) by Amir Nuar Zuabi is a searing look at exile, seen through the eyes of child-like Yusuf, whose mental "slowness" prevents his brother Ali from marrying his beloved. As the British make ready to depart, Arab armies attack, and war begins, we see the tragic effects of exile on a family, a village, and a people. The Palestinian displacement stands in contrast to a British soldier who has been stationed in Palestine and longs to return home. The bitterness of exile, the separation from the land, and the loss of the beloved are painted in vivid images and with a delicate poetry. Life and death become surreal, as the ghosts of dead refugees surround a dying Ali. Yearning is all that is left.[3]

Plan D by the Irish-Palestinian playwright Hannan Khalil (2010) is inspired by oral histories from Palestinians who lived through the Nakba (catastrophe); Khalil examines the human cost of losing your home and how to decide whether to flee or fight. By portraying three generations of a fictional family—children who struggle to keep an injured mouse alive, a grandmother who is killed trying to recover the family gold she has buried, and a father who narrates the tragedies they see as they flee—Khalil conveys the perpetuation of Palestinian trauma and the experience of exile.[4]

After reading and discussion, we speak aloud sections of these three plays. Each student selects a character to explore, then moves through a series of exercises, beginning with solo work in which the actor develops a psychological and physical portrait of the character. By stepping into this imagined body and finding the physical manifestations of its wounds and losses, students begin to find visceral connections. Students enact a day in the life of the character; they write a letter to someone they love and speak it aloud to the imagined recipient. Finally, the characters write a "letter to the editor," a public statement about a crucial issue in their lives.

Another set of improvisations brings the characters from each world together, in small groups, to explore familial relations. They use their bodies to silently "sculpt" tableaux that spatialize their connections, dreams, desire, and situation at a specific moment in time. After the frozen images are shared, the tableaux come to life as characters speak a line or phrase that expresses their innermost thoughts, and the sculpture begins to moves forward in time.

To explore the lived experience of exile, we gradually move from the given circumstances of the plays to imagined scenarios. These include responding to an image, such as the discovery of a bloodied piece of clothing, a lost child, or an unnamed threat. Each group improvises a story that responds to the challenge of what they hear, see, or find. At the end of the exercise, we debrief, first by individual free-writing, followed by discussion in pairs and then among the whole group.

Physical experimentation, body sculpting, writing in role, character development, free-writing, and improvisation are entry points to deep reflection and discussion. As an acting teacher, I am well aware of the need to establish guidelines and respect boundaries; as in all theater work, each student retains personal autonomy and remains in charge of what he or she chooses to explore. Students are encouraged to withdraw and process their experiences in a "safe space," writing in private journals or simply observing, as needed. With full respect for students' emotional vulnerabilities, I continue to encourage bringing personal discoveries into the broader discussion; reflecting on written texts and embodied exploration lays the groundwork for a reasoned analysis of social and historical factors that create the political situation and what it means to live in what the Israeli novelist David Grossman calls "a disastrous region like ours."[5]

How to represent the "other" onstage is a vexed question. In Israeli theater, it has taken decades to begin to write intentionally and explicitly about the Arab "other." Even the acclaimed Israeli author Hanoch Levin, whose early plays *You and Me and the Next War* (1968) and the satirical cabaret *Queen of the Bathtub* (1970) excoriate Israeli nationalism and the madness of war, rarely portrayed Arab characters, and then only as stereotypical victims.[6] In *Bathtub*, Levin created the Arab character Samatocha, a dishwasher in an Israeli café who is subservient and nonthreatening and who is distinct from the "bomb-throwing" Arabs. "Don't hurt the Arab. . . . There are loads of dirty dishes in the kitchen."[7] There are various iterations of "Samatocha" on the Israeli stage; Levin, in *The Patriot* (1982), has an Arab say of the Israelis, "They divided the world between us / They shit and I clean."[8]

In analyzing Levin's oeuvre, the Israeli theater historian Dan Urian says, "The implicit perception that those who suffer most from the conflict are the Arabs is common to all such Israeli plays. . . . Although the Jews pay a heavy price, they are shown to be the stronger side." In Levin's early work, "exploitation of the Arab is juxtaposed with fear of [his] violent response."[9] The corollary here is that "the Arab" is drawn as a monolithic character with no individuality. The victim "suffers" at the hands of the all-powerful state and its (indifferent, vicious, or oblivious) representatives.

Jonathan Sobol, in his play *Shooting Magda (The Palestinian Girl)* (1985) creates Palestinians with more depth. The play has Arabs and Jews collaborate to shoot a film about a Jewish nationalist and a Palestinian woman who fall in love. The play-within-a-play structure highlights the chasm between social roles and personal desire. A Jewish actress plays the Arab woman who wrote the "script" for the film, telling the story of how she was mistakenly taken for a Jew and beaten by the Israeli thug who then becomes her lover. As characters step in and out of role, the play attempts to elide and undermine set political "positions," as they inevitably stand in the way of human connection and understanding.

This complex piece also questions whether a Jew can truly present a nuanced characterization of an Arab.

An Arab actor says to a self-avowed 'anti-racist' Jew, "You don't want to present an Arab who behaves dishonourably."[10] David, the former Jewish nationalist who falls in love with Samira/Magda, says, "I feel guilty toward you" (243), and Adnan, an Arab character, says, "The Jews are doing another production about the Arabs to calm their crummy conscience" (250). The compression of time and place—twenty-four hours in a TV studio—heightens the urgency and metaphorically highlights the necessity of recognizing the "other," but liberal guilt and Arab anger complicate the task. Conversely, in most Palestinian plays, the Jew is absent from the narrative; presence is assumed but not embodied. Or Jews may be deliberately villainous or well-intentioned but ineffectual.

Women's roles are tenuous and unstable in both societies. In *Shooting Magda*, the Israeli actress playing the Arab woman feels vulnerable ("naked") and threatened by the "real" Arab woman, Samira, with whom she is in competition both sexually and artistically. Yet Samira has conflicted feelings about her allegiances and the violence tainting her life.

Handala (2011), adapted by Abdelfattah Abusrour, is based on a cartoon series by the Palestinian Naji Al-Ali. Handala is a ten-year-old boy who stands frozen in time, his back turned to the viewer; he will remain frozen until Palestinians return to the land and "reclaim our true histories."[11] Meanwhile, a Palestinian refugee, Fatima, whose husband is in prison, writes political tracts under a male pseudonym, the only way she can be published and heard.

Considering gender in Fatima's world, and as it impacts Palestinian and Israeli women in different ways, brings us to discuss broader social systems. We look at social power in the broader political contest: although power ostensibly remains with the Israelis, the larger picture reveals two people locked in an existential struggle. Cycles of violence, in which each side passes on its pain through injury to the other, leading to ever-more-extreme positions and to retaliatory violence, are addressed in several of the plays; in class, students are asked to consider their own relation to spheres of power, vulnerability, and victimhood and how social "identities" often overlap. From here, we discuss the factors that contribute to radicalization and to violence.

The Black Eyed (2007) by the Palestinian American Betty Shamieh looks at violent reprisal through the eyes of four Arab women from different millennia as they debate the ethics and efficacy of terrorism. They each see themselves as victims of history. They wait outside a door leading to a closed section of Heaven reserved for martyrs and discuss oppression of Arabs and of women and the repercussions of political violence.

The opening line of the play has Aiesha, a suicide bomber, say, "I do someone good dead. I do someone dead good."[12] The other characters are Delilah, who betrayed Samson to save her people; Tamam, whose brother killed Crusaders to avenge her rape; and The Architect, a Westernized woman who rejects terrorism and resents the traditional attitudes that would restrict her if she lived in Palestine (60).

Aiesha explains why she becomes a martyr: "no one would give a shit about my people's plight unless I blew myself up and took others with me" (35). Tamam, referring to the Crusades, explains why her people rejoice when a boy is born: "Because times like these call for soldiers, to fight / the Europeans and their Holy War, crusading against we people who lived here before, / and will live here afterwards" (38). Still, Tamam rejects the "intoxication of hate." She believes peace can be achieved by peaceful means. It is braver "to live in a place / where no one wants us to live / than to die" (45). Aiesha disagrees.

As Amos Oz has written, fanatics value justice over human life. But in Shamieh's play, Aiesha, the suicide bomber, asks a key question: "How do you survive in a violent world and not be violent?" (82).

In the most striking image of the play, Aiesha and Tamam say, "Oppression / is like a coin maker. / You put in human beings / press the right buttons and watch them get squeezed, shrunk, flattened / til they take the slim shape of a two-faced coin / One side is a martyr, / the other is a traitor" (42).

Shamieh has taken the character of Tamam and created a free-standing monologue, in which Tamam is now a present-day Palestinian woman. She goes to visit her imprisoned brother and is raped by Israeli guards. Tamam still stands against the killing of innocents, but she also understands why her brother, released from prison, blows up a bus. She is caught in contradictions, but to her, Palestine is Utopia and must be saved.

As pessimism sets in, earlier efforts to represent and engage the "other" disappear. Coexistence is not an option. There is no absolution and no way forward. Compromise is no longer possible.

Several plays implicate political leadership in the failure to reach genuine solutions. In *Handala*, the character Hamdoul, who represents a composite of Arab and Palestinian leadership, conspires *against* the Palestinian people. He says, "Concerning the massacre of Palestinians, we have all agreed not to lift a finger" (211). Leadership cannot be trusted to protect Palestinians and take back (all) the land.

In *Tennis in Nablus* by Ismael Khalidi (2010), compromise was, and remains, an impossibility. The play takes place in 1939 as Yusef, "a notorious Palestinian rebel," argues that his brother Tariq, a successful businessman in partnership with Samuel Hirsch, a Jew, is following an impossible dream. When Yusef and Tariq are jailed, Hirsch tries to get Tariq released, but Hirsch has no power. Compromise is impossible; the problems are structural, and no amount of "goodwill" can change the equation.[13]

Motti Lerner, a popular Israeli playwright often produced in the United States, is insistent on the deleterious effects of violence on society and how the brutality of war spills over into daily life. In *At Night's End* (2011), Lerner focuses on an Israeli family whose sons have taken divergent paths. They have become cynical, materialistic, or nihilistic, and they perpetrate verbal and physical violence on the women in the family. Lerner is saying that we brutalize ourselves with our violence, whether state sanctioned or not.

Perhaps the most pessimistic Israeli play is *Murder* by Hanoch Levin, first produced in 1997—two years after the assassination of Rabin. In this, Levin's last play, the characters are anonymous, created as types with names such as "Pale Soldier" or "Flushed Soldier" or "Bride." The conflict is insoluble; cycles of retaliation will continue without end.[14]

"*Murder* is a series of violent acts. . . . Its beginning is the *Intifada*, when Israeli soldiers abuse and kill a Palestinian youth."[15] The chain of violence is carried forward by the anonymous injured who go on to injure; no one is innocent, no one is safe. An Arab Father who finds his son dead, his eye gouged, confronts the soldiers who killed the Boy. The Boy's ghost "doesn't relent. It demands its own."[16] The Father must revenge his lost son. He comes upon a couple about to marry. He murders the Groom, rapes the Bride, and shoots her in the face. A crowd assembles. A Whore stabs the Father in the chest. The Pale Soldier has gone blind. A Messenger comes with the news: there will be no end.

These plays call into question the premise and project of this course and of "people to people" efforts. During the Second Intifada, many coexistence efforts simply collapsed due to this new understanding. A report by Neve Shalom/School for Peace in November 2001, looking at Arab and Jewish relations since the intifada, said, "There is a very real conflict between the two peoples, and . . . inter-personal encounters can contribute little to our understanding of that conflict. They certainly do nothing that might lead us to finding solutions to the conflict."[17] According to this view, two national groups with mutually opposed goals cannot resolve their issues through dialogue alone. Our efforts in the classroom also must go beyond attempts at "mutual understanding" if we are to approach the issues through critical analysis and structural critique. But given the polemics on campus that fuel monovocal narratives of a complex situation, it is imperative that our students learn to question and consider the cultural realities that have created the present impasse. Sloganeering and inflamed rhetoric lead nowhere; ignorance of the "other" is a prescription for increased violence.

Our final readings are written by Jewish Americans who have lived in Jerusalem and know it well. My own play, *Pulling Apart* (2004), has been accused of being both too pro-Palestinian and too pro-Israeli. A family is torn between religious and secular, between left and right, and by the challenge of going into a burning Hebron. I ask students to write three-line monologues, selecting one of the characters; first they express their point of view, and then they speak from an opposite perspective. To criticize, to persuade, to convince—what do they say to this person they care for but with whom they violently disagree? These monologues help us to unpack the difficult choices facing the characters, whether they are American or Israeli Jews, or Palestinians, living in Hebron.

We end with *Crossing Jerusalem* (2002), by the American author Julia Pascal. A family tries to befriend a Palestinian man, but history taints everything, even the kindest gesture. It is already too late. As Varda, the Israeli mother says, "You know the problem. Too much history, not enough geography."[18]

Ultimately, this course is aimed at encouraging analytical thought and respect for diverse groups that have legitimate but competing interests. Liberal democracy requires us to accept compromises that are less than perfect solutions; the alternative is unceasing violence, aiming to force the "enemy" to capitulate. Until we fully recognize the legitimate claims of all, we will not accept any restraints. Our ability to find (inherently partial) solutions erodes and disappears. Any path to peace includes compromises that are difficult, but not impossible, to reach.

Notes

1. Harold Clurman, *On Directing* (1972; repr., New York: Fireside, 1997), 162. The phrase "social imaginary" was coined by Cornelius Castoriadis, in *L'institution imaginaire de la société* [*The Imaginary Institution of Society*] (Paris: Seuil, 1975).
2. Elaine Scarry, "The Difficulty of Imagining Other Persons," in *The Handbook of Interethnic Coexistence*, ed. Eugene Weiner (New York: Continuum, 1998), 40–62; Amos Oz, *How to Cure a Fanatic* (Princeton, NJ: Princeton University Press, 2010), 66.
3. Amir Nuar Zuabi, *I Am Yusuf and This Is My Brother* (London: Methuen, 2010).
4. Hannan Khalilin, *Plan D*, in *Inside/Outside: Six Plays from Palestine and the Diaspora*, ed. Naomi Wallace and Ismail Khalidi (New York: Theatre Communications Group, 2015).
5. David Grossman, "Uri, My Dear Son," in "Hamas and Kadima: Are They Up to the Challenge?," special issue, *Palestine Israel Journal* 13, no. 3 (2006), www.pij.org/details.php?id=880 (these are published excerpts from the eulogy Grossman read at his son's funeral).
6. Nurit Yaari, "Life as a Lost Battle: The Theatre of Hanoch Levin," in *Theatre in Israel*, ed. Linda Ben-Zvi (Ann Arbor: University of Michigan Press, 1996).
7. Quoted in Dan Urian, *The Arab in Israeli Drama and Theatre*, trans. Naomi Paz (Amsterdam: Harwood, 1997), 48.
8. Quoted in Dan Urian, "The Arab in Hanoch Levin's Works—From 'The Queen of the Bathtub' to 'Murder,'" *Hebrew Studies* 43 (2002): 226.
9. Ibid., 219, 225.
10. Joshua Sobol, "Shooting Magda (The Palestinian Girl)," in *Modern Jewish Plays*, ed. Jason Sherman (Toronto: Playwrights Canada, 2006), 247. Subsequent citations appear parenthetically in the text.
11. Abdelfattah Abusrour, *Handala*, in Wallace and Khalidi, *Inside/Outside*, 199.

12. Betty Shamieh, *The Black Eyed*, in *"The Black Eyed" and "Architecture"* (New York: Broadway Play, 2009), 13. Subsequent citations appear parenthetically in the text.
13. Ismael Khalidi, *Tennis in Nablus*, in Wallace and Khalidi, *Inside/Outside*.
14. Hanoch Levin, *Murder*, in *The Labor of Life: Selected Plays*, trans. Barbara Harshav (Stanford, CA: Stanford University Press, 2003).
15. Urian, *Arab in Israeli Drama and Theatre*, 228.
16. Ibid., 221.
17. Rabah Halabi, "Arab and Jewish Relations since the Intifada," trans. Bob Mark, in *School for Peace Annual Report, 2000–2001* (Wahat al-Salam, Israel: School for Peace / Neve Shalom, 2001).
18. Julia Pascal, *Crossing Jerusalem*, in *Crossing Jerusalem and Other Plays* (London: Oberon Books, 2003), 77.

Darwish in the Transnational Classroom

BEVERLY BAILIS

I teach at a major public urban university in Brooklyn with over seventeen thousand students from 150 countries. One of the courses I teach, "Introduction to Israeli Literature in Translation," is an introductory course for undergraduates that is cross-listed with the Judaic Studies and the Comparative Literature departments. Many of the students who find their way into my course are Jewish, and their backgrounds reflect the diverse Brooklyn Jewish landscape. I have ultra-orthodox students from Hasidic families and "Black Hat Yeshivish" students raised in traditional and deeply religious environments, along with religious and secular first- and second-generation Russians, Bukharians, Syrians, and Israelis and students whose families have lived in New York City for generations. The course also draws students from the West Indies and the Dominican Republic, as well as other Brooklynite students from different ethnic, religious, and cultural backgrounds. Some of the students identify with Israel, tend to know a great deal about Israeli history from a specifically Zionist perspective, and even have friends and family in the Israeli army. For other students, the topic of Israel is brand new, and they are interested and excited to learn about the literature of a new place. For nearly all of the students, the actual authors and literary texts we read together represent new territory.

My course covers texts from the prestate period until today, and I include a number of Palestinian and Palestinian-Israeli authors on the syllabus to offer students a wide variety of literary perspectives on Israel. These readings serve as a window into the different ways Israel's statehood has impacted the lives of both Jews and Palestinians. One of the most consistently productive and, in my mind, successful teaching experiences I have had in this course, when nearly all of the roughly twenty-five students actively and quite passionately participate, is when we discuss the poetry of Mahmoud Darwish (1942–2008). Darwish, who is considered the Palestinian national poet, has been especially noted for giving "unprecedented voice to the lived experience of Palestinians living in Israel."[1] His poetry has also frequently been viewed as offering a counternarrative to the more "official" national narrative of the State of Israel.

When I teach Darwish's poetry, two main challenges or opportunities arise. On the one hand, many students are confronted with a perspective that is diametrically opposed to their own. My task is to guide their reading to enter the subjective perspective of the poetic "I" and to read the poem on its own terms. This causes some students to confront, and at times to reevaluate, many of their prior assumptions and core beliefs. On the other hand, another interpretive issue that arises is when students read Darwish's poetry about his experiences as a Palestinian living in Israel in the mid-1960s, and they hear it as if it is about the "here and now," where aspects of the conflict "over there" resonate with students' everyday experiences here in Brooklyn. This essay discusses my experiences of teaching two of Darwish's well-known poems, "Passport" and "Identity Card." Alongside close readings of these poems, I demonstrate how I have taught this material to a diverse group of millennials in Brooklyn with these issues in mind.

Before reading Darwish's poems as a class, I explain to the students that they do not need to agree or disagree with the ideas expressed in the poems but rather that we are reading these texts as *poems*. We are looking at figurative language, the construction of the poetic "I," and contemplating the world of the poem that is presented to us. I also ask them to think about why one reads fiction or poetry in general and that while sometimes we read to reaffirm what we think or what we know, other times the subjective world of others presents us with something new or different or something that might even be antithetical to our own worldview. I underscore how these different reading experiences help shape critical thinking, which is ultimately what courses in the humanities are attempting to foster.

It is also important that students have some background information regarding the life of Darwish, such as how in Israel he was considered a "present-absentee," a term designating Palestinians who fled or were driven from what became Israel in 1948 but who returned subsequently to live in Israel under its military administration. Since the poems I read with the class mostly date to his early poetry from the 1960s, I mention the difficulty he experienced traveling between cities within Israel and how during this period he was subjected to frequent imprisonment for writing political poetry and traveling to public readings. We also speak about how he decided to leave Israel in 1970 and then lived in other places, including Cairo, Beirut, and Paris, before returning to the region to live in Ramallah in 1996.[2]

Darwish and the Poetics of Empathy: Reading the Poem "Passport"

The first poem we discuss, "Passport," was written in the early 1970s, shortly after Darwish left Israel. It tells of the speaker's connection and disconnection to the space of Israel/Palestine through its central titular symbol. Beginning with the title, I ask students about their associations with "passports," while reflecting on the fact that the document is not actually a "passport" but a *Jawaz as-Safar*, or "travel document" (the word *safar* literally means "departure" or "journey," from *safara*: to travel, leave, or depart).[3] Whereas both passports and "travel documents" seemingly allow passage, freedom, and mobility, this state-issued document becomes a symbol of rupture and dispossession from place. The opening lines, "They will never recognize me in the shadows / that suck away my color in the passport,"[4] also present the reader with a paradoxical inversion: while the speaker shares this identificatory document with the reader, his image is unrecognizable.

We then focus on the speaker's image. The black-and-white photo reveals an image that is alien, as it turns the speaker's own sense of organic wholeness into a fragment, into something reified and detached from his surroundings. The shadowy chiaroscuro imagery points to the color and vitality that should be there but that is missing. The image of shadows is likewise evocative of a concretization of the seemingly oxymoronic state of "present absentee," since shadows designate both absence and presence, or the presence of absence, underscoring the contradictions of this legal status.[5] The speaker's sense of alienation continues in the lines "To them my wound is an exhibit / For a tourist who passionately loves to collect photographs." The pronominal opposition between "I" and "they" (presumably the creators of the passport, the Israeli authorities) returns from the opening lines, along with the speaker's sense of estrangement, as the object of their gaze.[6] The "wound" that is on display, a central symbol that appears throughout Darwish's work, becomes another way for students to enter the speaker's subjective world. It may be read as a reference to the very color that is drained from him or, following other scholars, a Christian symbol of Jesus's pain and suffering or a reference to the Nakba, the original defeat of 1948, along with the accompanying sense of loss. It may also refer to the present pain of his departure from the land.[7] In the stanza's closing simile, "Don't leave me pale like the moon," the pale moon is both an object of sublime beauty and a symbol of the existential void of night, or the very state of nonbeing that the speaker is fearful of slipping into. The removal of his personhood that began with the draining of his color is now concretized in the image of the pale moon; both images frame the stanza, forming a chiastic structure that further entraps the speaker in this state.

The second stanza then shifts from the static image of the withering black-and-white photograph to images of dispersion signified by birds and an airport. The image of the airport leads to a series of different spaces, locations and other nouns held together by the anaphoric *kul* or "all": "All the wheat fields, / All the prisons, / All the white graves, / All the boundaries, / All the waving handkerchiefs, / All the dark eyes, / All the eyes, / Are with me, but they dropped them from this passport!" The stanza's rhetorical structure invites readers to find connections between these nouns and to contemplate the relation between them. Through directed class discussion, students are readily able to identify fragments of the poet's autobiography and references to experiences, such as his departures from one country to another and his time spent in prisons. The graves also speak to traces of history in this place; they become markers of the speaker's ancestors, who have been buried in this location over generations. Students are then encouraged to look closer at the list of physical spaces and to piece together the connections between them. For example, they notice how the expansiveness of the wheat fields is set against the smaller spaces of prisons and then the white graves, suggesting movement from freedom to increasing confinement. The white graves are then understood as a form of ultimate containment, where former associations between paleness and lack of color and nonbeing are made further explicit. The juxtaposition of the wheat fields with the more "negative" spaces of prisons and graves brings into sharp relief a memory of "freedom" associated with the geographic and spatial experience of Palestine and "home," with more recent infringements on this freedom. The lingering presence of the fields likewise emphasizes that while the fields are still there, the speaker does not have free or unmediated access to them.

These concrete spaces are then set against "all the boundaries" (*hudud*), or literally "sharp demarcations," which move the poem to a deeper level of abstraction. For students who speak Hebrew, connecting the term *hudud* with the Hebrew cognate, *Had* (sharp), helps to convey a more visceral sense of this term. This less concrete noun opens the discussion for students to speculate on the many possible meanings of these "boundaries": the term may suggest the boundaries between different nations or countries or the boundaries of the laws or rules that disconnect the speaker from this space, designating where he can and cannot go, the demarcations between the self and the land. These borders may be interpreted even more abstractly as boundaries between freedom and containment, between being connected or disconnected from a place, and especially following the image of the graves, the boundary between life and death, being and nonbeing.[8] Finally, the shift at the end of the stanza from spaces to people evokes either individuals from the speaker's past or metonymic representations of the Palestinian collective. The use of metonymy (waving handkerchiefs) and synecdoche (dark eyes) likewise presents these human figures as fragments, amplifying the speaker's own sense of fragmentation.

At this point, the students are able to make connections between the first and second stanzas: all of these things, the totality of these experiences, places, and memories, are "dropped" or effaced by the passport picture. The incantatory repetition of "all, all . . ." lists what cannot be seen in the speaker's picture; it reverses the process of dehumanization and erasure, by filling in these omissions in an act of rehumanization. The last stanza continues the process of rehumanization; as opposed to the mechanical world of technology in earlier stanzas, where the camera and airplane become indicators of fragmentation and dispersion, here the lines "Don't ask the trees for their names, / Don't ask the wadis their origin" turn to the realm of nature. The use of merism, or "high" and "low" features of the landscape (the "trees" and the "wadi"—a valley or dried riverbed), a common literary device found in biblical Hebrew poetry and the earliest Arabic poetry, suggests a sense of totality and wholeness that works against the process of fragmentation of the earlier stanzas. Students are then asked to put these lines into their own words, such as, "to ask me for this travel document is as absurd as asking the trees or the wadis for theirs, since, like theirs, my identity is self-evident; I am rooted and of the place, I am a part of the very landscape."

The closing lines of the poem, "From my forehead gushes the sword of light / and from my hand flow rivers. / All the hearts of every man is my nationality / so rid me of this passport," continue the symbolic merging of the speaker with the land, indicating "that he has become a primary vein of both land and people."[9] As opposed to the first stanza, where the speaker's identity and vitality are drawn from him, through the course of the poem the speaker restores his sense of self and connection to place in language as he becomes reembodied in the larger national body. The personal experience of the poet is then connected to the larger national experience, as his voice becomes the voice of the Palestinian people.

The students, notwithstanding the fact that many of them come to the poem with views and experiences that are quite different from those expressed in the poem, are able to connect with the feelings of the poem's speaker. The poem presents the speaker's subjective experience of living under Israel's military administration, while conveying what it *feels* like to be displaced from a natural, organic connection to home, through the use of concrete images, which students can readily grasp, understand, and identify with. While the poem's speaker searches for wholeness and connection, the students likewise become actively involved in this poetic process. They must piece together what they know from the poet's experiences to connect the different fragmented images and parts of the poem in a search for meaning and wholeness. The text invites empathy and underscores poetry's unique ability to "share the language of real people across the barrier of ideology."[10]

Darwish's "Identity Card": The Arab-Israeli Conflict, American Racism, and the Politics of Reading

The poem "Identity Card," one of Darwish's most famous and commented-on poems, in contrast, invites a different kind of readerly engagement. Written in 1964, the text is a poetic reenactment of a concrete situation: the speaker addresses an interlocutor, presumably an Israeli officer who is inspecting his identity card, and the poem that follows is a forceful statement on the speaker's identity and connection to place. In each stanza, the speaker proclaims an aspect of his identity, including details about his family, ancestors, profession, ties to the land, and physical characteristics, held together with the anaphoric lines: "Write it Down / I am an Arab" and "Does this anger you?"[11] The poem thus expresses feelings of defiance and enacts a direct confrontation with the "you" of power and authority.

When the poem is read aloud in class, students' immediate responses become registered kinesthetically: some students respond with looks of anxiety, while others nod their heads in solidarity. It becomes clear that the students' immediate reactions depend on their complex identifications with the text and whether they identify with the poem's speaker or with his interlocutor. In my experience, these identifications are manifested in two main entangled claims and interpretive directions: some students assert, "this poem is antisemitic," while for others, it activates associations with racialized acts of policing in the United States. The teaching of this poem, then, leads to a disentangling of issues that are bound up with the poem's language and meaning, specifically the way it is "translated," both from Arabic to English and from the "original" social, cultural, and political context of the poem to the immediate classroom context.

An illustrative example of a student's claim that the poem is antisemitic appears in the lines "Write it down! I am an Arab / Employed with fellow workers at a quarry. / I have eight children. / I earn their bread, / clothes and books / out of these rocks. / I do not beg for charity at your doors. / Nor do I kneel / on your marble floor. / So does this anger you?" These lines, especially the images of "marble floors" and "charity," evoked in the student's mind the antisemitic stereotype linking Jews and money. The student then argued that the poem mobilizes this stereotype to negate the Jewish figure's claim to the land, since this figure is then set against the figure of the Palestinian, who is presented as connected to the land through the hewing of rough stones in the quarry. While there is a contrast between the smooth stones associated with the poem's Israeli interlocutor and the rough rocks of the workers that ostensibly points to a difference in class, a closer look at the text uncovers a different, perhaps larger claim that stands at the heart of the poem. An alternate reading of the parallelism "I do not beg for charity at your doors. / Nor do I kneel on your marble floor" suggests that these lines have less to do with differences between "rich and poor" individuals or ethnic-religious groups and literal "charity" than with the subject's relationship to power. The word translated as "doors" or "gates" (*bab*) carries with it larger historical and cultural meanings. During the Ottoman Empire, this word was associated with the "Sublime Porte," or the "Imperial Gate," the door of the palace of the sultan, which stood metonymically for the whole empire or "political house." It represented a symbolic entryway and implied the act of going to an official to get what one needs. In this sense, the speaker's liminal status outside the gates suggests his lack of access to the smooth floors of the establishment (i.e., its municipal buildings and court rooms) and the ease with which (some) citizens gain access to the protections of the state. Read this way, the poem points to the unequal citizenship afforded to "present-absentees" such as the speaker and their limited access to state resources.

This analysis, especially coupled with the concrete situation of the speaker who is stopped by an officer, in turn triggers other students' associations and experiences of racism in the United States.[12] Instances of African Americans, Muslims, and other people of color being stopped, searched, "policed," harassed, or even fatally harmed by people in authority have become a focal point in the discussion of race relations in the United States and a central component of the experiences and identities of many students. The pedagogical challenge that arises when teaching this poem is, on the one hand, how to manage the "conflation" of political and social situations and contexts, where a poem about the Arab-Israeli conflict in the 1960s is heard in the Brooklyn classroom as a poem about the here and now.[13] On the other hand, how the students hear the poem also points to a need to take into account the "relational" aspects of the poem and how the poem speaks to students' familiarity with patterns of power structures.[14]

One way to address these issues is to historicize the specific context of the poem within the history of the Arab-Israeli conflict. This involves delineating the history of the conflict and the struggle over territory (which is referenced in the poem's many claims to the land and the desire not to have it taken).[15] It likewise entails explaining how this conflict is between two groups, each with historical claims to the land, who have not recognized each other's right to self-determination, which has led to a protracted conflict. At the same time, how students hear the poem also points to an alternate history that resonates in a transnational context. As Feldman has recently argued, especially after 1967, connections have been made by political activists in the United States between the experience of inequality felt by African Americans in the United States and that felt by Palestinians living in Israel and the Palestinian territories. For example, he explains how "conjunctures" between these two groups became manifested in the culture work of Black Power movements in the 1960s and '70s, which saw "links between Black freedom struggles and struggles for Palestinian national liberation." He also looks to the writing of African American feminists, such as June Jordan, who in the 1980s wrote about the war in Lebanon and the Sabra and Shatila massacre, while offering a transnational critique of state-sanctioned violence.[16] These examples point to the ways that such activists have looked across the borders of countries to find similarities between experiences of inequality and how these similarities have resonated in "local" political discourse. In other words, such perceived and felt similarities have their own history, and the legacy of this history is always already present in the classroom, whether it is explicitly articulated or not. For these reasons, articulating this history can help students name, understand, compare, and differentiate between these experiences of state power.

One pedagogical strategy that is useful in this situation is the practice of journaling. Having students write personal responses to the text, and expressing what it evokes for them, helps foster awareness both for the student and for the professor of the different parallels, connections, and personal associations that are activated by the text. Following this, more formal writing assignments could entail bringing Darwish's poems into conversation with other Israeli literary texts, such as the stories and poetry of Almog Behar or Sami Chetrit. These Mizrahi writers have overtly drawn on Darwish's work, to express both identification with a shared Arab identity and experiences of marginalization in Israeli society, while they also underscore important distinctions between their experiences as Jews and as Israelis. Similar assignments could also include comparing other literary works with Darwish's, by Israelis or writers from other countries, to elucidate points of relation and difference between the experiences of transnational literary subjects. Such writing exercises can be both a way of building bridges between texts and experiences and underscoring structural issues regarding the effects of state power, while encouraging students to appreciate the differences and uniqueness of different subject positions and political and social contexts. In this sense, Darwish's poems, even when they are initially threatening, hitting buttons and sensitivities, resonate beyond their original context and give students immediate reference points that are emotionally familiar in the here and now. The dialogical poetic engagement that these texts initiate helps students relate to the complexities of the Arab-Israeli conflict, while serving as a basis for critical analysis.

Notes

1. Jerome M. Segal, "The Palestinian Nationalist Who Tried to Heal the Israeli-Palestinian Conflict—with Poetry," *Washington Post*, August 10, 2016.
2. Other aspects of his political life are also addressed, such as his serving on the executive committee of the PLO and his drafting of the Palestinian Declaration of Independence in 1988. For more on Darwish, see Khaled Mattawa, *Mahmoud Darwish: The Poet's Art and His Nation* (Syracuse, NY: Syracuse University Press, 2014).
3. This term is a translation of the Hebrew *t'eudat ma'avar*, or a laissez passer "travel document." This document is commonly issued to noncitizens in lieu of a passport.
4. This translation is based on the translation found on PoemHunter.com, with a few alterations for a more literal rendering of the original text: www.poemhunter.com/poem/passport.
5. For more on the symbol of shadows in Palestinian writing and political discourse, see

Keith P. Feldman, *A Shadow over Palestine: The Imperial Life of Race in America* (Minneapolis: University of Minnesota Press, 2015), 221–30.

6. The simile of the tourist is also a subtle and subversive role reversal: whereas the creators of the travel document imply that he does not "belong" to this place, by likening them to tourists, the speaker calls into question the very notion of belonging. The "they" are here perceived as the transient ones, passing through and trying to capture something of "the native."

7. For more on the symbol of the wound in Darwish's oeuvre, see Kamal Boullata's "Dimensions of a Wound," in his introduction to *Mahmoud Darwish: Stranger in a Distant City* (Washington, DC: Arab American Cultural Foundation, 1981).

8. As Najat Rahman points out, in Arabic the word "'place' (*makān*)," like the word for "being" (*kawn*) "is derived from *kāna* (to be, to exist, to take place)." Following this, the inverse of "place" or "displacement" may be equated with nonbeing or a symbolic death. Rahman, *Literary Disinheritance: Home in Writing in the Work of Mahmoud Darwish and Assia Djebar* (Madison: University of Wisconsin Press, 1999), 54. For an analysis of the related Hebrew word for "place" (*makom*) and its resonance in Jewish thought, see Barbara Mann, *Space and Place in Jewish Studies* (New Brunswick, NJ: Rutgers University Press, 2012).

9. Hanoud Yahya Ahmed and Ruzy Suliza Hashim, "Resisting Colonialism through Nature: An Ecopostcolonial Reading of Mahmoud Darwish's Selected Poems," *Holy Land Studies* 13, no. 1 (2014): 97.

10. John Conyers, quoted in Feldman, *Shadow over Palestine*, 213.

11. Translated by Khaled Mattawa, in *Mahmoud Darwish*, 8–9.

12. These connections were made even prior to Black Lives Matter introducing the question of Palestine into their formal platform, which occurred during the writing of this chapter.

13. Willa Johnson's essay on "proximal knowledge" helps elucidate how students frequently process new learning material by associating it with past experiences or knowledge. As she illustrates, this phenomenon either can prevent students from properly absorbing the new material or can be used, in a reflective manner, to help students make meaningful connections to the new information that is learned. Johnson, "From My Place: Teaching the Holocaust and Judaism at the University of Mississippi Fifty-Three Years after James Meredith," *Teaching Theology & Religion* 19, no. 1 (2016): 57–75.

14. The term "relational" refers to a way of perceiving connections between different events and situations that are incommensurable yet at the same time share certain features and can be viewed as interconnected, analogical, or forming a parallel. See Feldman, *Shadow over Palestine*, 9–12.

15. See, for instance, the lines "You have stolen my ancestor's orchards, / the land I farmed / with my children. You left us nothing / except for these rocks. / Will your State take them too / as it's been said?!"

16. Feldman, *Shadow over Palestine*, 6; he discusses these examples in chapters 2 and 5.

Surprised by Complexity

EMPATHY, NARRATIVE, AND CONFLICT IN THE CLASSROOM

RANEN OMER-SHERMAN

Some years ago, I was struck by an observation made by the renowned French graphic novelist Johann Sfar in an interview reflecting on his experiences visiting secondary school classrooms:

> I met some young Arab gang boys, you know, tough kids in the back of the classroom. They asked me about being a Jew, because the only Jew they saw was Ariel Sharon on TV. I said "yes, but my grandmother used to speak Arabic." "How do you dare speak Arabic? You are Jew!" But I said there have been Jews in Algeria for a long time. They say "we come from Algeria, we are the Arabs!" But I said "no my friends, you are not the Arabs, you are Kabyle (Berber) and you have been Arabized by force, as my ancestors were. And you know, my ancestors and yours, they used to fight together against the Arabs." We spoke for over an hour, and afterwards they did not love me, they just said—and this was precious to me—they just said "you, you are complicated!" This made me so happy! When you can complicate life a little bit to a young mind, you are useful. I hate clear and simple answers. I like them to be confused. I like to end my book without knowing if I'm a believer or not, if I'm religious or not, what I think about these characters. I like to put my finger on the political problems but not to solve them. I'm just the storyteller.[1]

This anecdote has lingered with me for a number of reasons but primarily because Sfar's young audience's candid exclamation ("you, you are complicated!") gets to the very essence of the kind of epiphany I hope my own students will reach at some point on their own terms. In an age when many of us find ourselves working at increasingly corporatized institutions, which demand that our humanities syllabi spell out "Student Learning Outcomes," "specific and measurable" mastery of various skills, and "Assessment Measures" (thus subordinating what we do to the reductive rhetoric of the social sciences), I stubbornly cling to the hope that this kind of challenging disruption to complacency and stereotypes still drives much of what we most desire our students to gain from their encounter with narratives of all kinds. For students who are all too acculturated to the reductive rhetoric concerning the Israel-Palestine conflict that has long overtaken college campuses (as though it were a kind of violent football match in which they must take sides, rooting for one "homeland" over another), it is often revelatory for them to encounter the strikingly congruent ways that Jews and Arabs write about exile and diaspora, in nuanced language that frequently transcends the notion of extraterritorial life as an exclusively abject condition.

The introduction to my syllabus is designed to put students who may have no background in the conflict whatsoever at their ease, while alerting others that I intend for us all to be a little unsettled and challenged in our habituated thinking. So alongside Sfar's remarks, they will find the work of another comics artist, Alex Gregory's sublimely funny cartoon of two dogs, caught deep in conversation. One of them remarks to the other, "There they were, sitting around the dinner table, knocking off a bottle of Côtes-du-Rhône and blathering about the Middle East—you've never heard such shallow, simplistic reasoning in your life—and one of them turns to me and says, 'And what do you think, Barney? What do you think we should do?' and all I could come up with was 'Woof.' I felt like such an ass"[2] Given the intensely polarizing nature of this class, the caption strikes me as a winningly disarming way of putting us all on the same page, so to speak, before the course even begins. It signals to them that we all need to challenge ourselves to escape from our comfort zones from time to time.

Over the years, I have taught variations of this course (usually at an introductory level but sometimes for graduate students) in several institutions in both Europe and the United States. In recent years, the semesters that have been most challenging but also most enjoyable and enriching for the students themselves were those in which some of them happened to be Jews whose parents are from Israel or even grew up in Israel themselves (on more than one occasion, I taught students whose "winter break" involved returning to Israel to serve in the reserves), as well as Arab citizens of Israel. And, inevitably, the course usually attracts a fair number of Taglit (Birthright) alumni. Generally that combination produces all the heated exchanges that one might anticipate, but over time, that volatility softens as the students learn to listen to, respect, and even develop friendships with one another. For those students with no prior exposure whatsoever to the conflict, those tense conversations can make for very active learning indeed.

Whether Palestinians or Jewish Israelis, whether the conflict has become part of the fabric of the student's being or a student is entirely new to it, my hope is that Gregory's arch caption will remind each of us that when it comes to the labyrinthine complexity of the Israel-Palestine conflict, we are all "asses." None of us can fairly presume total mastery of its painful historical past or present nor absolute certainty about any possible way forward. That paradigm further prepares students for the pedagogical assumption that underlies the entire course, namely, that we will be grappling with dual, and dueling, narratives that may ultimately prove unbridgeable.

What can be achieved in the wake of such a bleak foregone conclusion? My fervent hope is that students of all backgrounds emerge not just with a more nuanced historical understanding than they brought with them but that they achieve the kind of empathy that artists and writers often seem most capable of provoking. While I have been teaching a comparative course on the Israeli-Palestinian conflict organized around the theme of "empathy" for the past fifteen years, I was heartened by a promising study published in recent years indicating that literary fiction just might have a scientifically measurable impact on empathy and emotional intelligence. At the end of the semester, I share that (and the findings of a few related studies) with my students and ask them to share their impressions based on their own literary journeys.

My first experience teaching a comparative literature approach to the Israel-Palestine conflict and historical memory was in a team-teaching context where my colleague, an accomplished Arabist, taught seminal Palestinian narratives, and my role was to introduce students to Israeli narratives. We began with 1948, so it seemed a great opportunity to launch the discussion with S. Yizhar's (Yizhar Smilansky) 1949 novel *Khirbet Khizeh* (Ibis, 2008), a morally searing work written and inspired by events in the final months of the war and published shortly after its end. Yizhar served as an intelligence officer during the war, and his lyrical prose juxtaposes the stunning natural landscape with the troubled actions and thoughts of its soldier protagonists. The story's agitated narrator (though he remains mostly passive) bears witness to the violent expulsion of Palestinian villagers from their homes by ordinary men. At more than one point in *Khirbet Khizeh*, Jewish memory and the devastating actions are placed in uneasy juxtaposition, culminating in this late recognition: "Something struck me like lightning. All at once everything seemed to mean something different, more precisely: exile. This was exile. . . . This was what exile looked like. . . . I had never been in the Diaspora, . . . but people had spoken to me, . . . taught me, and repeatedly recited to me, from every direction, in books and newspapers, everywhere: exile. They had played on all my nerves. Our nation's protest to the world: exile! It had entered me apparently, with my mother's milk. What, in fact, had we perpetrated here today?" (104–5). In David Shulman's critical remarks in the volume's afterword, Yizhar succeeds in skewering "the prevalent nationalist myth that, like all nationalist myths, blames everything unpalatable on the ever-available 'enemy'" (115). Read nearly seventy years later, the disquiet of *Khirbet Khizeh*'s narrator still reads as an important milestone in the tradition of Hebrew authors who discover traces of the self in the dispossessed Other.

So what about the other side, whose works I have also been teaching for some years? Just what has surprised my students or otherwise complicated their perceptions of Palestinian writers over the years? Perhaps first and foremost, Karen Riley's fine translation from the Arabic of Ghassan Kanafani's (1936–72) novella "Returning to Haifa" (*A'id Ila Hayfa*). The longest narrative included in *Palestine's Children* (Lynne Rienner, 2005), a collection otherwise dominated by Kanafani's portrayal of the grim realities of adults and children living in refugee camps, it has often been extolled by critics as the consummate example of the intertwined role of art and armed resistance in twentieth-century Palestinian culture. And for my classroom purposes, it provides an opportunity to explore themes that are likely to be just as present in Modern Hebrew narratives, reclaiming what has been lost or suppressed, the confluence of place and selfhood, the aftermath of trauma, and a great deal more.

Kanafani's story is set in the wake of the 1967 war, when a middle-aged married couple, Said and Saffiyya, refugees who fled Haifa in 1948 and now live in the West Bank, return to their former home in Haifa, hoping to determine just what happened to Khaldun, the infant they had left behind two decades earlier. The novella delineates their bitter temporary reunion with their abandoned home, now occupied by others. A still-greater shock occurs when they eventually meet the former Khaldun, now Dov, proudly wearing an IDF uniform; they are appalled. The soldier lashes out, accusing them of abandonment.

Until now, Said and Saffiyya had treated their lost son as dead, and the reality of their boy standing, transformed into the enemy, leaves them at a loss: "How could the past come rushing in now by the back door in such an extraordinary way?" (159). But by far the most resonant development in this story is the barbed exchange between the Palestinian couple and those who raised their child, who turn out to be Holocaust refugees who arrived from Poland in 1948. In this story that contrasts martial heroism with an intimate and terrible loss through not-altogether-likely incidents, what passes between the two couples is an episode that wields genuine moral and dramatic force, an artful juxtaposition of Jewish and Palestinian exile, bereavement, and suffering. Kanafani's portrayal of that encounter, in its essence, expresses uncompromised empathy and compassion but also sets forth a stern judgment.

Throughout, Kanafani juxtaposes the plight of the individual with the grand sweep of historical forces. Moreover, the author reveals a surprisingly deep familiarity with the Zionist narrative, literally so, as when Iphrat Koshen, the Jewish husband, recalls his reading of Arthur Koestler's highly influential 1946 novel *Thieves in the*

Night, a romanticized epic about the *chalutzim*. Kanafani sensitively captures the not-unreasonable ignorance and naiveté of the Jewish immigrant regarding what transpired in the months before his arrival in Haifa with a convoy organized by the Jewish Agency: "He had never met a single Arab in his entire life. In fact it was in Haifa that he came upon his first Arab, a year and a half after the occupation," and subsequently encountered nothing to disrupt the "mythical picture" and "perfect harmony" of the Palestine of his imagination (167).

In this often-startling story, what I find most remarkable, aside from its deeply consequential inclusion of the enormity of Holocaust suffering (rare, if not unheard of, in Palestinian narrative of its time) is the further leap it takes in refusing to portray the Jewish enemy as a one-dimensional straw man of malicious intent. Miriam Koshen, who lost her father and little brother to the Nazis, is rendered, in contrast to her sometimes-blinkered husband, as someone all too aware that her refuge has come at a terrible cost for others. Whereas Iphrat is stirred by the quiet of a "true Jewish Sabbath" in their early Haifa days, Miriam sheds tears because there will no longer be "a true Sabbath on Friday, nor a true one on Sunday" (168). Kanafani devotes substantial space capturing Miriam's enlightened, penetrating gaze, her deep distress and courage in confronting uncomfortable truths.

Later, in a tearful exchange with Iphrat, Miriam is shocked to her core by the sight of the bloodied corpse of an Arab child (which immediately conjures the horrific memory of the moment her brother was murdered by the Germans):

> "How did you know it was an Arab child?"
> "Didn't you see how they threw it onto the truck, like a piece of wood? If it had been a Jewish child they would never have done that." (169)

Kanafani's implicit take on Holocaust suffering and Zionist hegemony apparently comes down to this rebuke delivered late in the story by Said to those who are occupying his old home: "I know that one day you'll realize these things, . . . that the greatest crime any human being can commit, whoever he may be, is to believe even for one moment that the weakness and mistakes of others give him the right to exist at their expense and justify his own mistakes and crimes" (186). In other words, while the story is unavoidably a call to Palestinian arms, it is also something else: an examination of the failure of empathy and its lasting consequences.

There is of course another side to Kanafani's life that must be addressed. If he was eager for both Jews and Palestinians to recognize that they shared a great deal of common ground, as a leader and spokesman for the Popular Front for the Liberation of Palestine (PFLP), he also concluded that in the immediate future, only violent struggle would improve the Palestinians' plight. On May 30, 1972, members of the Japanese

Red Army (JRA) enlisted by the PFLP massacred twenty-six Israelis and Christian tourists at Lod Airport. In response, on July 8, 1972, Kanafani was blown up in a car bomb in Beirut by the Mossad.

Ultimately, I leave it for the students to sort out the question of innocence and culpability, perhaps gently reminding them that in Israel most citizens are also soldiers and that for some the term "terrorist" can be a slippery one. No matter how much they may support one or another side of the conflict, there is culpability to go around. That is as far as I will go.

Yet following this discussion, I do incorporate a sort of addendum. Students are often surprised (as I once was) to learn that though Kanafani's provocative narrative was originally published in 1969, few Jewish Israelis had ever encountered it prior to the Cameri Theater's bold decision to stage an adaptation of it by Boaz Gaon decades later, in 2008. Performed by a Jewish and Arab cast, the production was also staged in Jaffa, where the director Sinai Peter hailed the play for providing "an arena for people of both sides to listen to each other's narratives."[3] Nobody missed the rich symbolism that the debut of Kanafani's narrative in Hebrew, at one of Israel's oldest and most prestigious theaters, came at a richly symbolic moment, the sixtieth anniversary of the establishment of the state.

Naturally, the play caused a storm of controversy even before opening, with small crowds of protesters charging that a play written by a "terrorist" had no place on an Israeli stage. I always strive to alert students to issues of audience reception, and given the course's governing ethos, I could not be happier in sharing with them two representative responses from audience members attending the play's opening night: Nivan Kour, who identified herself as a Palestinian Israeli, called the play a "mirror to reality" that might enable the two peoples to better understand each other, a sentiment shared by a Jewish Israeli man named Uri Yarkoni: "People need to see there are two sides to this story or we will be bombing and killing each other for another 100 years."[4] While American students are generally surprised to learn about the unexpected influences and affinities of Israeli and Palestinian writers, I suspect that even Israelis would find it revelatory to learn that Sami Michael's acclaimed novel *Doves in Trafalgar* (*Yonim be'Trafalgar*) owes its inspiration to Kanafani's story.

Another novel that I have found very rewarding to work with in the classroom (both for its relative brevity and for its shimmering prose) is *A Lake beyond the Wind* (Interlink, 1998), Yahya Yakhlif's elegiac story about the impact of the Nakba on a single Palestinian village, Samakh, at the southern edge of Lake Tiberias. Whereas Hebrew narratives of the same period understandably emphasize the fraught beginnings of statehood and Jewish survival, Yakhlif (a native of Samakh) delineates the destruction of Arab nativeness, through language exuding the atrophy of the fabric of indigenous life and a palpable sense of an entire world or topocosm meeting its end:

> The whistle of the Haifa-Deraa train didn't sound now. There was nothing to fill the space of the small town except anxiety; nothing, any more, to evoke a sense of security. . . . Coffee wasn't ground in a mortar anymore. . . . The men no longer told tales of hyenas and foxes and jackals. All the talk revolved around the coming days, whose terrors would turn the blackest hair white. Even the sparrows sensed the fear. . . . A disaster was coming and there was a sense of the earth starting to tremble. Around this time, the time of siesta, the trees and the wind fell silent. Even the waves of the lake were still. It was like the silence and stillness before an explosion at the stone quarries. (1, 2)

Aside from the deeply moving ways the novel chronicles the plight of both memorable individual characters and the collective itself as they respond to the trauma of war and dispossession, *A Lake beyond the Wind* can be productively compared to S. Yizhar's "The Prisoner" (1949), Benjamin Tammuz's "The Swimming Race" (1951), or other Hebrew narratives from the same era that do not withhold criticism of political, military, and other institutions whose callous actions often compound disaster for a society. Yakhlif's lean novel is structured around the journey of a bulletproof vest as it passes through various hands, innocent and naïve foot soldiers to corrupt bureaucrats and cowardly officers, ultimately revealing the multifaceted nature of Palestinian society, its virtues and blemishes, even as it approaches collapse.

In the end, readers are left with a sense of both catastrophic loss and, in spite of imminent exile, the displaced villagers' fierce devotion to the Palestinian landscape, the subtle inclusion of untranslated Arabic names for plants, birds, animals, and fish underscoring the people's *sumūd*, or steady perseverance, through the eyes of the young narrator, who observes a fisherman who sought glory in the war but has just returned from its devastations and knows that the past is gone forever:

> Najib stopped under an ancient carob tree and looked out at the sunset and its reflection in the lake, breathing in the smell of Samakh. . . . He was talking to people he could see but I couldn't, to men and women, and to trees and horses too, in words that were tender, simple and almost broke my heart. . . . He addressed the fennel and the vetch, the marar and the wild mint. He talked to the surface of the lake, that was like the underbelly of a doe, and the musht fish, the karseen, the athathi, the balbout and the marmour fish. (214)

Without insisting on false equivalencies, I sometimes juxtapose Yakhlif's voice with Jewish Israeli writers such as Sami Michael or Samir Naqqash (a Jewish writer in Hebrew who insisted on writing in Arabic and thus suffered a double marginalization). In spite of their ostensible belonging to the "Jewish State," they embrace the identity of "Arab Jew" and their works delineate their own lost Iraqi worlds.

Whenever possible, I gravitate toward narratives that show the fissures, border crossings, and contradictions that open students' eyes to what lies beyond supposedly homogeneous identities. By way of one recent example, in the Palestinian writer Khulud Khamis's novel *Haifa Fragments* (New Internationalist, 2015), the young female protagonist, a Palestinian citizen of Israel, anxiously contemplates the implications of her first illicit excursion to a West Bank village:

> During the 40 minutes it takes them to reach Tal E-Zeitun, the reality begins sinking in. I'm not welcome in this part of the world. I'm not one of them. I'm a citizen of the state that occupies their land. I have a blue ID in my wallet. I'm a traitor. I have running water and I don't need to worry that my home could be demolished at any moment, or that soldiers could raid my house in ungodly hours of the night. . . . It is the first time she is going to the home of a Palestinian family living on the other side—so close yet worlds apart. Will they accuse me of betraying our people? Our land? (11)

The permeable nature of the "us" and "them" of this and related passages in Khamis's multilayered novel (a wonderful work exploring the nexus of feminism, sexuality, and nationalism) lures readers into new appreciation for the messy contradictions and slippages of the Israeli-Palestinian divide.

Though it may not fully satisfy the expectations for those pesky and reductive "learning outcomes" that our corporatized universities increasingly demand of us (and that many would perhaps prefer to disregard altogether), my syllabus does explicitly stress the hope that students, through their encounter with a truly diverse array of genres and texts, will gain a Sfar-like inclination: "We will see how Israeli and Palestinian literature and cinema both often challenge the rigid lines formed in ideological narratives to distinguish the 'West' from the 'East,' ultimately exposing the contradictions in homogeneous narratives."[5] By the end of the semester, my greatest hope for the students is that they emerge with a stronger capacity to appreciate, no matter how difficult it clearly is to bridge Israeli and Palestinian readings of history and collective trauma, that the two peoples are remarkably similar to each other in their anxieties and aspirations.

In that regard, I strive to be mindful of something that Shoshana Gottesman, the musicologist and Israel-Palestine coexistence educator, says about the conflict: "Educators . . . often experience an emotional toll as well, since we are not separated from our vulnerability in relation to discussing and teaching about these topics. After all, like our students, we also all have our own collective memory and trauma, which have constructed the strands of our identities within the Israeli-Palestinian conflict itself. How should we as educators face vulnerability in front of our students? Is it fair to share this vulnerable space with our students?"[6] Though every instructor must answer this question for him- or herself, the years have affirmed for me that such candor can be transformative for everyone involved.

Somehow, teaching the stories of Israel and Palestine deprives many of us of the luxury of the kind of neutrality that our colleagues might have in, say, a nineteenth-century American literature or British Romanticism class. I have yet to meet anyone who teaches this conflict who is not in some way personally implicated and involved. Like some of our students, we have lost loved ones and friends to its violence. Hence, I recognize that my students deserve honesty and transparency, deserve to know just what perspective guides my own encounters with the narratives we read together; I need to expose my own biases. So I begin by briefly sketching out the critical milestones of my own story, from my earliest encounter with the seductive fantasia of Uris's *Exodus* to teenage *oleh*, IDF combat soldier, and kibbutznik and on to academia and a somewhat-chastened and more skeptical critical citizenship—undoubtedly just like my students, when it comes to facing the Middle East, still a work in process.

Notes

1. Johann Sfar, interview by Nan Rubin, November 15, 2005.
2. Alex Gregory, *New Yorker*, August 11, 2003.
3. Rebecca Harrison, "Provocative New Play Evokes Sympathy for Jews, Palestinians," Reuters, April 15, 2008, www.reuters.com/article/arts-stage-palestinians-israel-dc/palestinian-child-raised-as-a-jew-in-israeli-play-idUSL1576760820080415?sp=true.
4. Ibid.
5. Sfar interview.
6. Shoshana Gottesman, "On Nationalism, Pluralism, and Educators Actively Questioning Our Identities," *Journal of Critical Thought and Praxis* 6, no. 2 (2017): 108.

Fictional Literature in Interdisciplinary Studies of the Arab-Israeli Conflict

MARILYN R. TAYLER

Using fiction outside of literature courses offers students the opportunity to take an empathic and emotional approach to the Arab-Israeli conflict. It forces students to move beyond a factual, right/wrong consideration of the situation, by taking human suffering into consideration. I teach an interdisciplinary undergraduate course in Israel Studies for political science and jurisprudence students. Students are sophomores, juniors, or seniors, representing a diverse cross-section of the student population at Montclair State University, a large suburban public institution in New Jersey. Most students in the class are from the United States, while a small number are students of Arab or Israeli background. These students have had no prior academic exposure to the Arab-Israeli conflict.

In the course, we explore the central issue of Israel's conflicted identity as a Jewish and democratic state through the interdisciplinary research process, as articulated for entry-level interdisciplinary courses in Allen Repko's *Introduction to Interdisciplinary Studies*. The six steps described by Repko in the broad model entry-level interdisciplinary research process are identifying the research issue, justifying the need for an interdisciplinary approach, identifying the most relevant disciplines, conducting literature searches in those disciplines, critically analyzing disciplinary insights gained from reading the literature and recognizing conflicts among the insights, and reflecting on how the interdisciplinary research process has enlarged one's understanding of the research issue.[1]

This interdisciplinary approach engages students in an intellectual exploration of areas such as democracy in Israel, government and politics, religion and state, and Israel's unusual personal status laws of marriage and divorce.[2] We explore these areas primarily through readings in the disciplines of political science, law, religion, sociology, and history. Also, as part of Repko's interdisciplinary research process, we explore the origins of the Arab-Israeli conflict through the discipline of fictional literature.

Fiction provides a completely different way for students to relate to historical and political perspectives of the Arab-Israeli conflict. Fiction frees students from many of their conscious and subconscious biases and preconceived notions and engages them intellectually and emotionally on a human level.

Before studying the fictional literature, we read and discuss a series of nonfiction political and historical texts about Israeli Arabs—defined as Arab inhabitants of prestate Palestine who remained in Israel and became Israeli citizens after the establishment of the state in 1948, as well as their descendants who were born after the establishment of the state. Students develop an understanding of the conflicting interests of Jewish and Arab Israelis, represented by Israel's security concerns, on the one hand, and the opposition of Arab Israelis to Israeli-imposed civil rights limitations on Arab Israelis, on the other.[3] For example, my students learn that for Israeli Arabs, the country's Independence Day is not viewed as a day of celebration. Instead, they call it the "Nakba" (catastrophe), because it marks the loss of previously Arab land to Israel. Through these readings, students begin to perceive and explore two narratives, the Jewish narrative and the Arab narrative. We consider the implications of their competing and at times dissonant frames, considering the subjective aspects of each historical narrative.[4] We consider the ways in which these are built on the perspectives, personal opinions, and biases of Jewish and Arab authors, as distinct from factual history.[5]

As preparatory reading for fictional literature, I assign students a book chapter by the historian Benny Morris. According to Morris, "the process by which some 700,000 Arabs departed Jewish/Israeli territory over 1947–1949 was multi-staged, varied and complex."[6] Morris describes four stages of the departure, some of which were voluntary and others involuntary. In the first stage, many of the upper- and middle-class Arabs, fearing heightening hostilities, left because they did not want to live in a Jewish state and could afford to live elsewhere. In the second stage, many of the lower classes left because they saw their Palestinian Arab society in Israel crumbling. In the third stage, Arab militias and irregulars were enticed to leave Israel for surrounding countries by local Arab commanders and the Arab High Command, in preparation for the fight to recapture Israel from the Jews. In the fourth stage of the departure, Israel forced the evacuation of certain Arab villages that were deemed to pose a security risk to the Jewish population.[7] Morris's nuanced description challenges the oversimplification of both the traditional Jewish narrative that the Arab exodus was voluntary and the traditional Arab narrative of a systematic expulsion of Arabs by the Jews. By reading Morris's article, my students are able to see that each side's narrative represents only that side's interpretation of the full picture and that the full picture is more complex than either side's narrative.

In an interdisciplinary course, literature represents a different discipline's approach to the material. It is more open-ended and personal than are the disciplines with which the students have previously engaged in the course. It allows for multiple interpretations and possibilities. In order to prepare students to read and analyze a work of literature, I prepare explanations on the key aspects of a literary work and literary analysis—plot, theme, characters, point of view, setting, atmosphere, style, and the like—as preparatory assigned readings for my students. Having previously considered different fact-based disciplinary perspectives on Israel, students are better equipped to apply those disciplines to gain insights into the fictional work about the Arab-Israeli conflict. Students learn to appreciate the quality and impact of the fictional work both as literature and also for the work's significance in portraying the historical and political circumstances from the point of view of a fictional character with whom the students can identify intellectually and emotionally.

The Fictional Literature and Its Contribution

After reading the fact-based Morris chapter and my prepared material on literary analysis, we read the novella *Khirbet Khizeh*.[8] I will go into some detail about the novella, so that other teachers may assess the potential benefits of using this novella, or similar fictional literature, in their courses.

Khirbet Khizeh takes place near the end of the 1948 war, which immediately followed the establishment of the State of Israel. The author, S. Yizhar, fought as an Israeli soldier in the 1948 war. His novella deals with the forced evacuation of the remaining Arab residents of the fictional village of Khirbet Khizeh in an operation by a small Israeli Army unit. Students are able to apply their prior interdisciplinary studies about Israel to the complex historical, political, and legal perspectives of the involuntary forced expulsion of the Arab villagers by a group of Israeli soldiers, balanced against Israel's security needs to consolidate its hold over its territory. The nameless Israeli soldier who is the main character and first-person narrator in the novella declares, "I conjured up before my eyes all the terrible outrages that the Arabs had committed against us. I recited the names of Hebron, Safed, Be'er Tuvia and Hulda" (87), as he attempts to rationalize the Army operation in the Arab village.

We discuss the interplay of the three main threads woven throughout the novella: the vividly depicted images of the striking scenery, the mission of the soldiers to evacuate the village, and the inner conflict of the nameless soldier narrator. These threads underscore the novella's literary aspects and are also a vehicle for teaching about the Jewish and Arab narratives of the Arab-Israeli conflict.

In the vivid descriptions of scenery in the novella, there is ample use of poetic devices. The beauty of the surroundings described in the novella contrasts with the often-cruel treatment of the villagers by the soldiers. Some of the village animals are admired by the Israeli soldiers for their beauty and are treated better than the villagers are. The description of "fields that would never be harvested, . . . [a]nd already from those fields, accusing eyes peered out at you, that silent accusatory look as of a reproachful animal, staring and following you so there was no refuge" (89), personifies the sense of desolation and destruction of the Israeli Army operation. Students see how literary artistic prose is used to expose the horror and the ugliness wrought by the soldiers carrying out their mission.

While the mission of the soldiers—the evacuation of the village—is announced on the second page of the novella, there is a slow buildup to the actual forced departure of the Arabs. As the soldiers approach the village, they shoot at runaways, although the original plan had been to let them go. The soldiers enter the village and assemble the women, the old, the blind, the lame, and the children at a concentration point for evacuation. It is understood that all of the able-bodied men have already gone ahead to fight against the Israelis from the other side of the border. The humanity of the frightened Arabs is personified in a woman who realizes that "her home and her world had come to a full stop and everything had turned dark and was collapsing" (76). By transporting the inhabitants to the other side of the cease-fire border, the soldiers are effectively sending them into exile, with many ending up homeless and in refugee camps.

The thoughts and words of the nameless soldier narrator reveal his anguish at the role of the soldiers. The narrator gives voice to the creation of a Palestinian Diaspora when he reflects that "this was what exile looked like" (105), as the Jews have become "peddlers of exile, and our hearts have coarsened in the process" (112).

Yizhar's novella, originally published in 1949, is prescient in its observations about Palestinians who were forced to leave Israel. Among those being evacuated is a woman, described as a "lioness," who is holding the hand of a little boy. The narrator declares, "we could also see how something was happening in the heart of the boy, something that, when he grew up, would only become a viper inside him, that same thing that was now the weeping of a helpless child" (104). The novella ends with the stillness, silence, and emptiness of the evacuated village. The nameless soldier narrator's state of mind is pivotal to an exploration of the moral dimensions of the work. He is a soldier who is conflicted about the mission, though he must ultimately follow orders.

The Beneficial Effects of Including Fictional Literature as Part of an Interdisciplinary Approach

Considering *Khirbet Khizeh* in light of the four phases of Palestinian departure described by Morris in the historical chapter that students had previously read, the novella clearly falls into the fourth category of Palestinians who were involuntarily evacuated from their homes and exiled from Israel. This leads to a discussion of each side's narrative of the issue—the justice or injustice of the removal of Arab inhabitants from their land and their homes as weighed against the question of Israeli national security. If students had not read the Morris article prior to reading the novella, they would not have had an accurate and complete understanding of the subject or be able to situate this evacuation within the larger context of Arab refugees from Palestine. But without the novel, they would not have an emotional understanding of the subject.

The Palestinian exiles who left Israel in 1948–49, such as those represented in *Khirbet Khizeh*, and their descendants have not been integrated into the societies of the countries to which they were exiled. Morris affirms that "the subsequent decades of humiliation and deprivation in the refugee camps would ultimately turn generations of Palestinians into potential or active guerillas and terrorists."[9] In the novella, the image of the viper that was growing in the heart of the little boy helps students to gain insights into hostilities between Israel and Palestinians still living in other countries, continuing to the present day as an aspect of the Arab-Israeli conflict. Through the use of this interdisciplinary approach, my students learn that each side's narrative has indelibly colored its ability to objectively perceive and deal with any possible resolution of the conflict.

In an Israel Studies course whose central theme is Israel's conflicted identity as a Jewish and democratic state, *Khirbet Khizeh* provides an opportunity to expand the scope of the course to include an aspect of the complex wider Arab-Israeli conflict through the vehicle of fictional literature. The prereading of the Morris chapter provides balance, context, and historical perspective. While it would be possible to introduce the Arab-Israeli conflict exclusively though fact-based readings, the use of the novella adds the disciplinary perspective of fictional literature and provides the opportunity for students to study and discuss a politically charged subject in the context of a work of fiction. It provides the opportunity for students to integrate more fully the insights of history, political science, and law that they have gained throughout the Israel Studies course. As a measure the success of our interdisciplinary approach, my students have indicated that reading the novella has given them an opportunity to see the different sides and narratives in this very complex issue and gain a more personal, comprehensive, and nuanced understanding of the Arab-Israeli conflict.

Notes

1. Allen F. Repko, with Rick Szostak and Michelle Phillips Buchberger, *Introduction to Interdisciplinary Studies* (Thousand Oaks, CA: Sage, 2014), 202.

2. For a full application of the interdisciplinary research process to a topic in Israel Studies, see Marilyn R. Tayler, "Jewish Marriage as an Expression of Israel's Conflicted Identity," in *Case Studies in Interdisciplinary Research*, ed. Allen Repko, William Newell, and Rick Szostak (Thousand Oaks, CA: Sage, 2012), 23–51.
3. See Marilyn R. Tayler, "The Transformation from Multidisciplinarity to Interdisciplinarity: A Case Study of a Course Involving the Status of Arab Citizens of Israel," *Issues in Interdisciplinary Studies* 32 (2014): 28–52.
4. For a historical perspective on the narratives, from 1882 to 1949, students read Paul Scham's "Israeli and Palestinian Traditional Narratives of Their History: A Distillation," in *The Routledge Handbook on the Israeli-Palestinian Conflict*, ed. Joel Peters and David Newman, Routledge Handbooks Online (2013), www.routledgehandbooks.com/doi/10.4324/9780203079553.
5. See Motti Golani and Adel Manna, *Two Sides of the Coin: Independence and Nakba 1948—Two Narratives of the 1948 War and Its Outcome* (Dordrecht, the Netherlands: Institute for Historical Justice and Reconciliation, 2011), 1–23.
6. See the chapter by Benny Morris, "The Origins of the Palestinian Refugee Problem," in the first edition of *New Perspectives on Israeli History: The Early Years of the State*, ed. Laurence J. Silberstein (New York: NYU Press, 1991), 43. There is an expanded second edition, but the first edition is more straightforward for an entry-level class.
7. Ibid., 43–52.
8. S. Yizhar, *Khirbet Khizeh* (Jerusalem: Ibis Editions, 2008). Quotations from the novel are cited parenthetically in the text.
9. Morris, "Origins of the Palestinian Refugee Problem," 55.

Communication, Conflict, and the Arab-Israeli Conflict

RANDALL G. ROGAN

I am professor of communication and a former administrator at a private, southeastern liberal arts university where student enrollment in the undergraduate college accounts for 84 percent of the student population; the graduate school enrollment, excluding business, law, and medicine, adds another 16 percent. Undergraduate students are 9 percent international, 53 percent female, and 28 percent nonwhite, with 51 percent coming from the southern United States. Finally, 78 percent of 2016 first-year students placed in the top 10 percent of their high school class. For more than 150 years, the institution had strong ties with the Southern Baptist Convention. However, the past 25 years has witnessed a withering of that relationship. Although a Christian theological orientation still serves as the dominant institutional ideological framework, faith leaders from other religions (e.g., Judaism, Islam) have been added to the Office of the Chaplain. Historically, the university would have been described as generally conservative in its political orientation, but today it is fulsomely liberal and progressive. These changes reflect the increasing religious and broader diversity within the student population and faculty.

Undergraduates are required to take courses across all five academic divisions, Humanities, Literatures, Fine Arts, Social Sciences, and Math and Natural Sciences, during their first two years and typically do not declare their chosen academic major until the spring semester of the second year. The basic and divisional required courses include a foreign language, history, English, religion, philosophy, fine art, music, science, social science, and a writing course. Most upper-level courses, such as my 300-level course on communication and conflict, are composed of mostly juniors and seniors. Graduate students can also enroll in the course as a 600-level course that counts toward their graduate credit requirement. As a consequence, by the time students take my course, they have acquired a reasonable basic knowledge about human and geopolitical affairs, complemented by generally solid writing, thinking, and expressive skills. Yet their actual knowledge of the Arab-Israeli-Palestinian conflict is woefully inadequate and usually informed by their consumption of web-based "news." Unlike a sister institution a mere twenty miles down the road, there is presently no on-campus Students for Justice in Palestine group or an active BDS movement.

As a recovering administrator, having served in that capacity outside my home department for eight years, I am just now returning to full-time service as professor. My disciplinary field is communication, with a specialization in conflict interaction. For the first twenty-plus years of my career, my scholarship focus was the communicative dynamics of crisis and hostage negotiation. Early on, I was fortunate to have developed a working relationship with the Crisis Hostage Negotiation Unit of the Federal Bureau of Investigation, stationed at the Quantico facility in Northern Virginia, as well as with agents in the Behavioral Sciences Unit. As a result of these relationships, I had the opportunity to work on some interesting cases dealing with barricade standoff interactions, threat assessments, and identification of unknown authorship, the most notable being the Unabomber case. These engagements with government and law enforcement agents privately and at international professional venues earned me a visit to Israel several years ago to meet with Israeli police and military officials in order to learn about Israeli responses to violence and terrorism. During that visit to Israel, I was inspired to learn more about the causes and manifestations of the violence and, in particular, the historical and contemporary nature of the Arab-Israeli-Palestinian conflict. Since that first trip, I have returned to Israel many times, mostly to attend and speak at the World Summit on Counter-Terrorism but, more critically, to further increase my knowledge and understanding of the Israeli-Palestinian dynamic. In fact, my most recent trip was to meet with and interview Palestinians, Israelis, and U.S. officials about the Palestinian city project of Rawabi. I share this personal background information in order to highlight the applied perspective of my scholarly work that I bring to the classroom.

The Course: Communication, Conflict, and the Arab-Israeli Conflict

Over the years, I have taught varying iterations of this course, yet all have been marked by the integration of theory and application. Prior to my first trip to Israel, I introduced students to crisis and hostage negotiation to demonstrate the application of communication-grounded theories and concepts. The highlight of the course was the concluding class exercise of a terrorist-motived hostage taking that pitted students against each other as they struggled to negotiate a peaceful conclusion. Sadly, such an ending was never realized in the many semesters in which the course was offered. Yet the lessons that students took away from the interaction about the challenges of negotiating for peace and the manifestation of theories and concepts made the course material real for the students. As violence continued to erupt between Palestinians and Israelis, subsequent offerings of the course introduced the Arab-Israeli-Palestinian conflict into the mix, with the final course dramatization being an Israeli-Palestinian engagement. The current iteration of the course has a more robust dedication to studying the Arab-Israeli-Palestinian conflict.

Given my disciplinary grounding in human communication, I believe that communication is the sine qua non of human interaction and therefore is a critical perspective for understanding the dynamics of human conflict. Toward this end, I have established five goals for the course: first, to provide students with a basic knowledge and understanding of fundamental conflict concepts and principles; second, to provide students with a working knowledge of the various theories of conflict interaction and management processes, with particular attention given to communication-based perspectives; third, to provide students with an overview of current conceptualizations of appropriate and effective skills for managing conflict situations, with special attention to the cultural processes that affect conflict dynamics; fourth, to introduce students to practices of principled nonviolence and negotiation; and finally, to guide students in the investigation of the Arab-Israeli conflict as informed by communication theories and concepts. Students conclude the course by demonstrating a basic knowledge and understanding of fundamental conflict concepts and principles; a working knowledge of the various theories of conflict interaction and management processes; a knowledge of appropriate and effective skills for managing conflict situations, with special attention to the cultural processes that affect conflict dynamics; a demonstrated knowledge of principled nonviolence and negotiation practices; and a demonstrated capacity to apply this cumulative knowledge to the Arab-Israeli conflict.

I have bifurcated the course into a theoretical and conceptual portion for the first half of the semester, followed by an application of theory in the second half. For the first portion of the course, I employ the text *Working through Conflict* by Joseph P. Folger, Marshall Scott Poole, and Randall K. Stutman (7th ed., Pearson, 2013). The text does an excellent job of introducing some critical psycho-social and communication-grounded theories of conflict. Further, the text devotes a significant portion of coverage to the well-established conflict interaction goals of power, relational issues, face concerns, and identity. Cultural impact on conflict interaction is likewise well covered. Additionally, from my particular theoretical point of view, the text does a nice job of introducing the centrality of framing theory and narratives as essential conditions for understanding human conflict interaction. Still I supplement this portion of the text with readings from my own framing-based research (e.g., William A. Donohue,

Randall G. Rogan, and Sandra Kaufmann, eds., *Framing Matters: Perspectives on Negotiation Research and Practice in Communication* [New York: Peter Lang, 2011]). This first half of the course also includes an introduction to Gandhian nonviolence, as well as principled negotiation as first introduced by Roger Fisher and William Ury.

The second half of the course is devoted to studying the Arab-Israeli-Palestinian conflict. For this purpose, I use Abdel Monem Said Aly, Shai Feldman, and Khalil Shikaki's *Arabs and Israelis: Conflict and Peacemaking in the Middle East* (Palgrave Macmillan, 2013). I really like this text for several reasons. First, its authors are an Egyptian, a Palestinian, and an Israeli academic who have collaborated to provide a comprehensive, thoughtful, and multidimensional presentation of the conflict. This collaboration alone is a profound statement of conflict management and personal relationships in facilitating reconciliation. Second, the text does not merely provide a historical accounting of the essential events in this seemingly intractable conflict but more critically seeks to examine these events from the tripartite perspectives of the parties involved. And of particular significance for me and my focus in the course, the authors explore the dynamics of the interaction from a narrative perspective, devoting much attention in each chapter to accounting for the narratives of the three perspectives: Arab, Israeli, and Palestinian. Their strong presentation of significant historical events, wedded with an analysis of those events in terms of the narratives constructed to account for the conflict dynamics, facilitates my guiding of student exploration of the conflict from a communication perspective.

During this portion of the course, I task students to take turns (in cohorts of two or three) in presenting the material within each chapter. Admittedly, there is a great deal of information to cover in only seven weeks; the text has thirteen chapters. Consequently, I am restricted in my ability to wander too far afield from the primary text or to devote too much time to any particular portion of the history of the conflict. Yet my goal in the course is not to dwell too extensively on the history of the conflict, though it is critical for students to possess a modicum of that knowledge. I do encourage students to explore suggested supplemental material (e.g., UN resolutions, the Hamas Charter, etc.) on their own outside of class time. During each class session, we devote our attention to discussing and discerning the nature of the conflict goals manifested in the unfolding events and in the authors' narratives. I also challenge students to apply a particular theoretical lens in analyzing the historical events described in each chapter.

In addition to the two required primary texts, students are instructed to explore various web materials in order to glean other potentially relevant perspectives. As the focus of the historical events becomes increasingly contemporary (late twentieth century), I introduce students to websites such as Palestinian Media Watch (PMW), Middle East Media Research Institute (MEMRI), Committee for Accuracy in Middle East Reporting in America (CAMERA), and UN Watch, to name just a few.

I challenge students to interrogate the narratives of these entities in light of their newfound knowledge about the historical narrative dynamics of the conflict. One particularly powerful media resource that I use is a DVD that I received, from Katie Green at the Ma'aleh School of Television, Film, and the Arts in Jerusalem, during a visit there as an academic fellow in the Brandeis Summer Institute for Israel Studies in July 2016.

The video is a graduate-student production titled *Barriers*. It is a powerful film depicting the heightened tensions at an IDF checkpoint when the soldiers on duty are ordered to close the checkpoint, due to a bomb threat, and are challenged to decide the fate of a young Palestinian girl suffering from an acute diabetic attack being transported in an unregistered Red Crescent ambulance. Without sacrificing the particulars of the interaction and the consequent outcome, the video takes one on a roller-coaster ride of emotions.

I have viewed many videos provided by the IDF and other agencies that provide footage of terrorist events and clashes between soldiers and Palestinians at border crossings, and although this film is a fictional creation, I believe that it effectively portrays the existential challenges of both the Israeli soldiers on duty at border checkpoints striving to thwart potential terror events and the Palestinian workers who are simply seeking access into Israel for employment. The film effectively captures the myriad dimensions of the conflict as manifested between the Israeli soldiers and the Palestinian workers, who all simply desire an uneventful morning; among the three Israeli soldiers, about how to manage the situation while striving to do the right thing; between one of the Israeli soldiers and his mother, who is a member of Machsom Watch; and among the Palestinian workers, as their opportunity for daily employment slips away. Furthermore, the film provides a critical visual context within which students can see the characters as individuals and watch the events unfold along that hot, dry stretch of road. My goal in showing the film is to help students translate the abstract interstate-level dimensions of the conflict to the concrete individual level. Postviewing discussion explores students' emotional reactions to the film, as well as its impact on their understanding of the day-to-day interactions between Palestinians and Israeli soldiers. The film can be purchased directly from the Ma'aleh website (www.maaleh.co.il).

As this is an upper-level course, the requirements and assignments are geared toward providing students with opportunities to demonstrate their gained knowledge and comprehension of course material. Further, the assignments are designed to facilitate and assess student learning outcomes associated with critical reasoning, written communication, and oral communication. As such, students complete an essay-format midterm exam in which they are required to demonstrate their understanding of communication and conflict theories and concepts presented in the first half of the semester. Students complete a final essay-format exam that assesses their ability to apply conflict theories and concepts and to address those particularly to the Arab-Israeli-Palestinian conflict. As students present various portions of the Aly et al. text in class, course participation accounts for a percentage of their final grade. Finally, students are required to submit a term paper in which they investigate a specific conflict event according to course theories and concepts.

Lessons Learned and Thoughts for Future Offerings

On the basis of end-of-the-semester course evaluations and individual student feedback, this course is consistently well-received by students. In fact, enrollment demand for the course has historically exceeded enrollment capacity. While students value the opportunity to increase their knowledge about conflict theories and concepts, they really resonate with the application of that knowledge to an actual conflict event. And given the significance of the Arab-Israeli-Palestinian conflict in geopolitics, they welcome the challenges of interrogating this incredibly multifaceted and complex phenomenon. Perhaps the most meaningful aspect of the course for students has been my integration of firsthand knowledge and expertise in researching and working with individuals on the ground in the region who are somehow involved in managing the conflict. Toward this end, I frequently invite professional associates in the U.S. government and military, as well as associates in other military or law enforcement capacities, to speak to my students. The students always value these guest speakers for their candor and real-world knowledge. As I returned to the classroom after several years away, I was excited to reengage with a new generation of students in order to provide them with the opportunity to learn about the Arab-Israeli-Palestinian conflict and some of the more current developments, such as the Palestinian city of Rawabi. My students were equally excited by the course.

In past years, one comment frequently articulated by students during in-class discussions of material was, "I'm a senior in college. Why am I only learning about this now?" Although it is somewhat disheartening to realize that students of the caliber attending my institution are not fully aware of the myriad events unfolding in the Middle East and the multidimensional aspects associated with them, I regard it as a personal mission to help expand their knowledge and understanding of these issues. As a professor at a liberal arts university, it is my firm belief that a liberal education, grounded in the liberal arts disciplines, is the bedrock on which an educated and informed citizenry is developed, a citizenry that challenges itself to strive for the highest ideals of human dignity and freedom, a citizenry that challenges the status quo in order to solve a problem or meet a human need. It is this same liberally educated citizenry that advances the core principles of liberty, equality, freedom of speech, and freedom of action that are basic to our democratic society. As scholars of the Arab-Israeli conflict, we must play our part in creating a liberally educated citizenry, domestically and globally, as we strive to create a better world for all people.

Competing Interpretations and Multiple Narratives

Teaching Diversity

The Arab-Israeli Conflict

COMPETING NARRATIVES AS A FOCUS

ALAN DOWTY

I taught in the Department of Political Science at the University of Notre Dame for twenty years before offering a course specifically on the Arab-Israeli conflict. In part this was due to pressure to cover basic courses: international relations, U.S. foreign policy, international relations of the Middle East. It also reflected the lack of a natural constituency, since Notre Dame had few undergraduate Jewish or Arab students or students from the Middle East. But when I offered a senior writing seminar on Israeli politics, the high level of interest demonstrated by students with no background in or ties to the region led me to believe that an advanced undergraduate course on the Arab-Israeli conflict might find a ready audience and help to fill out the department's offerings in a region of the world that was underrepresented, despite historical religious linkages. And so it proved; the course was filled to capacity every time it was offered.

Choosing a suitable undergraduate text as a framework for the course proved to be more challenging than expected. At the time, roughly twenty years ago, the introductory texts fell into two distinct categories: shorter analytical works that reflected a distinct point of view, and lengthier histories that maintained neutrality by focusing on factual detail. The history seemed essential to me; the basic vocabulary and most of the debates attached to the conflict are rooted in its evolution over time. But at the same time, the detailed histories devoted much space to past episodes that were not essential to an understanding of the conflict today, leaving less space for other course materials that would fill in the analytical dimension of the conflict and illustrate current controversies.

The shorter analytical texts, on the other hand, often offered less history than I was looking for but more importantly usually had a definite point of view—pro-Palestinian or pro-Israeli—embedded in the book's structure and texture. This is of course not an absolute disqualification; how many of us in the field, and how much of the vast literature on the conflict, can be said to be magisterially neutral? But it would require, at a minimum, some offsetting discussion in class to help students understand the perspectives and predispositions of the authors they are reading. Or this could be done by using two texts, representing opposed points of view, and leaving the students to work out the clashing claims.

But using a comprehensive history *and* two opposed texts in an undergraduate course would clearly make it unwieldy. My short-term solution was to use one of the more detailed histories (either Mark Tessler, *A History of the Israeli-Palestinian Conflict*, 2nd ed. [Bloomington: Indiana University Press, 2009]; or Benny Morris, *Righteous Victims: A History of the Zionist-Arab Conflict, 1881–2001* [New York: Knopf, 1999]) in a selective way and complement it with articles representing clashing views on specific episodes or issues. This did indeed demonstrate to the students the presence of these opposed viewpoints, but it did not equip them to put the clashes into perspective or understand how reasonable spokespersons on two sides of an issue can see things differently without being willfully blind or deceitful. "Somebody has to be lying," a student would blurt out in frustration. What students needed at this point was a sense of the overall narratives of the conflict, on both sides, that would help them make sense of impassioned arguments over specific issues. This sense of the narratives needed to be woven into the basic historical framework so students could understand the perspectives that the parties brought to bear: "where they were coming from," in common terms.

I therefore began to provide, in the course lectures, running narratives of both sides as they developed over time. What did the Jewish settlers in the late nineteenth century think and say about the Arab population they encountered? How did the Arabs (and Turkish authorities) perceive the European Jewish immigrants? How did both sides view the establishment of the British Mandate? Why did most Jews in Palestine favor the 1947 partition plan, while nearly all Arabs rejected it? In what way could both sides argue that the 1967 war was, from their own perspective, a defensive war? How do the opposed narratives complicate realization of a two-state solution to the conflict, despite its acceptance in principle by leaders of both sides? Over time, presentation of the perceptions and claims of the parties became central in the organization and content of the lectures.

It quickly became clear that, to avoid confusion, the presentation of these narratives needed to be clearly labeled and distinguished from other passages in the lectures on the basis of my own interpretations. I adopted the practice of placing a small Palestinian or Israeli flag on the podium when I was expressing the respective narrative, which also made it possible to drop the circumlocutions of "Israelis argue that . . ." or "Palestinians feel that . . ." and simply present the respective case in the direct language that an advocate would use. I also used a third flag to indicate when I was speaking for myself (just for fun, a skull and crossbones). The students seemed to adjust to this somewhat-unorthodox procedure with no difficulty; in fact, they were quick to remind me when I forgot to fly the proper flag at the beginning of a narrative or to take it down at the end.

Critics will certainly point out, quite correctly, that neither side has a single shared narrative but rather a spectrum of narratives. There are of course some common threads to various positions taken by various factions, assumptions with which the vast majority of the respective public would identify, and these form the basis for the narrative to be presented. Other than that, one looks for the best articulated arguments that could be described as mainstream and then notes important variants or even opposed positions from important segments of the community. On subjects such as attitudes toward West Bank Jewish settlements in Israel or support for renewed intifada among Palestinians, it is essential to convey the complex diversity that exists within the respective publics.

One question that arose fairly quickly was how to deal with the extremists on both sides. By definition, they are not part of the dominant narrative of their own public, but neither can they be left out of a serious analysis. It occurred to me that the extremists do play a big role in the narrative of *the other side*—which typically sees them as expressions of the enemy's "real" face. So this is where I put the extremists in presenting the narratives. For most Israelis, for example, Hamas suicide bombers are a key element in their own perceptions of Palestinians, and for many, they reveal the "true" nature of the threat that Israel faces. By the same token, Palestinians see violence perpetrated by some West Bank settlers as verification of Israeli intent to annex the West Bank and force out its Arab population. In other words, the extremists on either side validate the more hawkish elements on the other and are an important element in their narrative. I do have to admit, however, that presenting the extremists as part of the other side's narrative was not always perfectly understood. A pro-Palestinian student, for example, would object to the portrayal of suicide bombers, saying they were marginal among Palestinians—and forgetting that they were being presented as part of the *Israeli* narrative, just as Baruch Goldstein's massacre of Muslims in Hebron formed part of the Palestinian narrative.

A focus on competing narratives does not necessarily mean a retreat to pure relativism. Dealing with the best formulations of the respective narratives should help students appreciate the complexity of the analytic and ethical issues involved, particularly if they came to the class with simplistic notions about these issues. But it is also important to provide some tools, and some models, for criticism of the narratives they encounter. Some of the more controversial passages in the conflict cannot simply be left hanging between two sets of claims, where even the basic facts are in dispute. Sowing some confusion in the minds of students, particularly those who come with fixed ideas, is a positive step forward. But confusion is not an end in itself; the next step requires access to factual frameworks that are generally recognized as sound scholarship. The most prominent example, perhaps, is the creation of the Palestinian refugee problem in 1947–49, where good use can be made of the work of Benny Morris and others who have provided at least some empirical path through the polemical landscape.

Eventually, the lectures incorporating the competing narratives, together with a historical factual framework incorporating my own interpretations, came together as a single integrated classroom book (Alan Dowty, *Israel/Palestine*, 4th ed. [Polity Press, 2017]). By now, however, there are also other texts available that show sensitivity to the narratives of both sides and offer a solid historical framework. Had I embarked on this journey today, I might never have felt the need to strike out on my own path.

More recently, I have pulled together the primary sources I have used to illustrate the competing narratives in the first-person voices of the practitioners; this book structures the materials in line with the textbook *Israel/Palestine* so that it can either stand alone or be paired with the textbook in classroom usage: *The Israel-Palestine Reader* (Polity, 2019).

Whatever the material used, it is in my view essential in an introduction to the Arab-Israeli conflict to expose students to the conflicting viewpoints in their most authentic voices and in full intensity. Only in this way can students gain real understanding of the complexity of this historical clash and of the tragedy of right versus right.

Teaching the 1948 War at the United States Naval Academy

SHAYNA WEISS

As my students file into the classroom, I hear them discussing the multiple names of the events covered by their reading, struggling to keep the eponyms straight as they attempt to classify the monikers of Nakba, 1948 War, and War of Independence. Before class begins, I repeat the adage that multiple labels reflect multiple narratives and that each one has something to teach us, students of the Israeli-Palestinian conflict.

My students are midshipmen, attending the Naval Academy, one of the five service academies in the United States. They are young men and women who, upon graduation, will become junior officers in the Navy and Marine Corps. In lieu of paying tuition, midshipmen pledge to fulfill an active-duty service obligation of at least five years. The Academy also hosts exchange students from service academies across the world. In my time at the Academy, I have encountered students from Cambodia, Gambia, Japan, and Korea, who will return to their home countries to complete their service requirements. Due to a STEM-heavy core curriculum, all students graduate with bachelors of science, whether they are majors in English or electrical engineering. I work with a mix of civilian and military faculty, and together we are enjoined to uphold the moral, mental, and physical missions of the Naval Academy.

As the Distinguished Visiting Scholar in Israel Studies, I have a joint appointment in the History and Political Science Departments, and most of my students are from these majors. Another source of students is midshipmen majoring in Arabic, one of three languages that offer a major at the Academy. (The other two are Chinese and Russian, and there are several other languages that offer minors. You can draw your own national security conclusions.) Due to the scarcity of safe places to study Arabic in an immersive environment, many midshipmen choose to do summer Arabic-language immersion in Haifa out of a very short list of accepted programs. While not originally particularly interested in this slice of the Middle East, several students take my courses due to their increased interest in the region after spending a summer in Israel studying Arabic. Some are advanced enough that they read Arabic news and primary sources in the original language. Finally, I also encounter students who choose my course as one of their humanities/social science electives, a requirement for all STEM majors, often due to some previous exposure to the Middle East. Many are Jewish midshipmen curious about their own connection to the region. Others, children of military families, spent time stationed in the Middle East and wish to know more about their previous homes.

In addition to new courses I have created, I teach the Israeli-Palestinian conflict course, an upper-level elective that was already on the roster. I was nervous at first about the course, to teach about a conflict is not only controversial but deeply personal. I include in my teaching points of personal connection, including assigning scholarship by a mentor who was killed in a terrorist attack—and telling my students the fate of the author. I do so not just for my own therapeutic reasons but also to remind students of the multiple ways that the conflict touches daily life. Despite my original trepidation, I have been surprised by how rewarding the course has been for myself and the midshipmen, not despite but because of its heartbreaking content. While decoding the chronology of a conflict, we confront together the essential questions of how peoples fight and why they do so—lessons that transcend Israel and Palestine and are especially relevant for a military institution.

I am constantly asked by my colleagues at other institutions to characterize my students and asked why midshipmen need to learn about Israel and Palestine. Many academics have very little interaction with the U.S. military, for reasons that speak to the deep divide between the U.S. Armed Forces and the majority of the American public. I explain that inside my classroom, it is not so different from any other undergraduate class at an elite institution, once you become accustomed to being the only one not in uniform. Nevertheless, when I stroll around the yard and see my students in formation or overhear discussions of the particulars of service selection, I am starkly reminded that I am a civilian employee of the Department of Defense and that my students will soon be junior officers. Furthermore, my midshipmen are acutely aware that their chosen career will likely take them abroad. When I ask my students why they chose to take my classes, the most common answer cited is that they figure they may be deployed in the Middle East during their service and should therefore know more about the region where they may find themselves.

For this reason, I design my course on the Israeli-Palestinian conflict with that fact in mind, asking myself what a future officer, likely to be stationed in the Middle East at some point in his or her career, should know about the Israeli-Palestinian conflict. As in all the courses I teach, my approach is firmly grounded in repeated exposure to primary sources. I train students in how to read these materials so that they not only learn factual material about the period in question but also are trained to think analytically and critically across genres. By guiding the midshipmen to expand their powers of observation and teaching them to ask basic questions about provenance and meaning, I help them to appreciate the intricacies of multiple, competing narratives. Following Clifford Geertz's call to make the strange familiar, I choose sources that serve as an entry point between my students and the course material. At the Naval Academy, that means a focus on the role of the military on the battlefield and in the negotiating room, whether the topic is the U.S. Marines' role in the 1982 Lebanon War or cooperation between Israeli and Palestinian security forces during Oslo. I stress that as they encounter conflict in their careers, they will not have the luxury of indecision due to conflicting information. I use my course as a staging ground for tough decision-making in the midst of controversy—a controversy with lives on the line.

Despite my aforementioned affection, the challenge of teaching the 1948 war and its aftermath provoked more anxiety than any lesson on the syllabus. I designed a two-part lesson, roughly divided into history and memory, which took place over two class meetings. For the first meeting, midshipmen read the sections of their textbooks that relate to the 1948 war.[1] For the second meeting, the readings focused on historiography, examining Israeli revisionist history and the Palestinian response to such developments.

Plan D, known in Hebrew as *Tochnit Dalet*, connected the two lessons.[2] The previous plan, Plan C, had prescribed limited defensive strategy since December 1947. However, shortly after the outbreak of hostilities in early 1948, serious losses for the Yishuv (the Jewish community in Mandate Palestine) forced the main Jewish fighting force, the Haganah, to reconsider its strategy. Authored by the Haganah, the Mandate-era Jewish paramilitary force that became the core of the current Israel Defense Forces, the plan dates to March 1948. The document detailed a set of guidelines to regain control over Mandate Palestine in order to declare an independent Jewish state in anticipation of the end of British rule, set to expire May 15, 1948. The Haganah correctly predicted it would fight against a combination of small local forces together with semiregular and regular forces affiliated with the Arab League and other neighboring countries. Plan D is hotly debated, with Israeli historians tending to argue that it was a defensive strategy and Palestinian academics often labeling the document a master plan for the ethnic cleansing of the Palestinian people. By using Plan D as the centerpiece, my objectives were twofold: first, to examine how scholars use varying genres of primary sources and, second, to analyze the role of historical memory in the contemporary discussion surrounding the conflict, being cognizant of how those perspectives, especially regarding Palestinian refugees, changed over time.

I began the first class with a lecture covering the end of the Mandate period and the basic outline of the 1948 war, emphasizing that it is best understood as two wars:

the civil war between local Jewish and Palestinian forces and the first Arab-Israeli war between Israeli forces and five Arab armies. Once students had a basic understanding of chronology, I briefly introduced the debate over who bears responsibility for the approximately 750,000 Palestinian refugees after the war.[3] I then returned to the civil war, the war before May 14, 1948, a particularly rough period for the Yishuv with regard to civilian casualties. I explained that for the Jewish forces, one of the biggest concerns was the danger posed by potentially hostile Arab villages and their ability to harbor enemy forces.

It is at this point that I handed out copies of Plan D, explaining that Plan D signified a shift in the trajectory of the 1948 war. To pique students' interest, I mentioned that they now possessed a copy of the most controversial document of the entire war. I purposefully did not explain why, explaining that it was their task to determine the reason for such controversy. To decode Plan D, I chose to employ the strategy of think-pair-share. Students read the documents on their own, then broke out into groups of two or three to discuss for about roughly fifteen minutes, a technique I frequently employ, so students are already familiar with the process. During the breakout period, I rotated between the groups, eavesdropping, making myself available for questions and concerns, and inserting myself into the conversation when helpful. (It also is a way to ensure that students stay on task.) Small groups give shy students a chance to express themselves in a lower-stakes environment and force active engagement with texts in the highly effective dyadic format, in which meaning derives from conversation. After the breakout period, the class reunited to discuss what they had learned, modeling respectful disagreement and close-reading skills.

I asked students to answer one question: was this document a declaration of an offensive or defensive strategy? As I rotated during the breakout discussion, I noticed that midshipmen compared Plan D to other strategy plans they had seen in their other courses. Some color coded the document into offensive and defensive language to guide their analysis. Others asked if the document reflected the reality of what actually happened on the battlefield and how one should weigh Plan D against what had "actually" happened. A few noted that hostile villages potentially harboring enemy soldiers were a feature of many modern conflicts, and they were interested to learn that this tactical issue was not a recent development in warfare. Many noted the difficulty of classifying the document, which seemed contradictory at times. In the discussion following the breakout sessions, many students restated these comments, and the conversation focused on how we should understand Plan D specifically and military strategy more broadly in the conflict. Many students argued that Plan D felt closer to an offensive strategy, but other students strongly disagreed. Class adjourned on a cliffhanger.

For the next course meeting, students read works by Benny Morris and Nur Masalha discussing the rise of the new Israeli historiography of the 1980s and 1990s.[4]

I chose selections that focused on analysis of Plan D, so that students could see that their comments mirrored what historians had said about the document. I used the readings as the basis for a lecture on the New Historians and their critics, charting the shift in attitude regarding the blame for the Palestinian refugee crisis as my focus and demonstrating how much this analysis depended on how one read the intentions of Plan D. I mentioned briefly attempts to solve the Palestinian refugee crisis in the first few years following Israeli statehood in order to provide context for the global refugee crisis in the decade after World War II.[5]

After my lecture, I shifted the discussion from the historical to the contemporary. I asked students to reflect on why I might have decided to dedicate a large portion of class time to study Plan D. Students spoke of the importance of narratives, of mutual recognition, and of the refugee issue in current discussions of the conflict. Many admitted they had heard terms such as "right of return" discussed without fully understanding its genealogy or why Palestinians, even those not directly displaced, considered themselves refugees. Other midshipmen responded with parallels from their own experiences regarding shifts in historical thinking or attempts at collective justice. Several mentioned reparations for African Americans or the controversy over Columbus Day, which served to remind our classroom that U.S. history is not immune from similar controversies, once again helping to make the strange a bit more familiar.

I ended our unit on the 1948 war with a discussion of the Nakba law. After the class read about the Israeli attempt to ban state funds to mark the 1948 Palestinian exodus, students debated the propriety of such legislation. We discussed the relationship between history and memory and particularly how analyzing the politics of commemoration can reveal clashes about a society's most deeply held truths—particularly helpful for a course focused on understanding contradictory narratives. Later in the semester, when students encountered the fate of Palestinian refugees as a final-status issue in the Oslo negotiations, they drew on their previous discussions of Plan D to reflect on the issue's contentious nature and on the relationship between the refugees and other issues such as security arrangements and final borders.

Even as I teach about the Israeli-Palestinian conflict, the relevance of applied decision-making for my midshipmen is far wider. In their careers as military officers, my students will not have the luxury of abstaining from decisions because of their awareness of multiple narratives. They will have to use their knowledge to make tough calls that rely on a complex understanding of a region that has hopefully been made a little less foreign to them due to a semester in my classroom far away in Annapolis, Maryland.

At the start of each class at the United Sates Naval Academy, the section leader calls his or her fellow students to attention. Nearly in unison, they rise and wait, until I grant permission to be seated. At first, the cries of "all hands on deck" struck me as bizarre. Quickly, my discomfort faded away. After a few shorts weeks, I relished our ritual, a way to signify that we are an intentional community, together and ready to learn. As each meeting class ends, the section leader calls the class to order once again. They stand at attention and wait until I formally dismiss my midshipmen. As they file out of the room, I imagine their future deployments. Perhaps, like many of my military colleagues, they will have time off in Haifa, a popular stop for U.S. naval vessels in the Mediterranean. During their vacation, I hope they remember our classroom discussions of Plan D—not just as observers of the conflict but as officers who will probably be tasked one day with writing their own strategic plans in a part of the globe that is far from their homes. I know it is quixotic to hope that their knowledge of the past can prevent tragedies of the future. I do it anyway.

Notes

1. I used the following textbooks for the course: Ian J. Bickerton and Carla L. Klausner, *A History of the Arab-Israeli Conflict*, 7th ed. (Boston: Routledge, 2014); James L. Gelvin, *The Israel-Palestine Conflict: One Hundred Years of War* (New York: Cambridge University Press, 2014); Abdel Monem Said Aly, Shai Feldman, and Khalil Shikaki, *Arabs and Israelis: Conflict and Peacemaking in the Middle East* (New York: Palgrave Macmillan, 2013).
2. I use the version of Plan D as it appeared in the *Journal of Palestine Studies* 18, no. 1 (1988), translated by Walid Khalidi. It is online here: www.mideastweb.org/pland.htm. Due to the interests of time, I chose not to distribute Plan C, but that can easily be worked into this lesson, especially for those who choose to have students read Plans C and D at home.
3. Alan Dowty, *Israel/Palestine*, 3rd ed. (Cambridge, UK: Polity, 2012), 98 (600,000–750,000; UN estimate at 726,000), citing Benny Morris, *The Birth of the Palestinian Refugee Problem Revisited* (Cambridge: Cambridge University Press, 2004), 589.
4. Students read Benny Morris, "Revisiting the Palestinian Exodus of 1948," in *Rewriting the Palestine War: 1948 and the History of the Arab-Israeli Conflict*, ed. Eugene L. Rogan and Avi Shlaim (Cambridge: Cambridge University Press, 2001), 37–59; Nur Masalah, "A Critique of Benny Morris," *Journal of Palestine Studies* 21, no. 1 (1991): 90–97.
5. For more background on the immediate debates after the 1948 war, students also read Ronald W. Zweig, "Restitution of Property and Refugee Rehabilitation: Two Case Studies," *Journal of Refugee Studies* 6, no. 1 (1993): 56–64.

Borders, Boundaries, and Barriers

DEPICTIONS OF LAND IN ISRAEL/PALESTINE THROUGH FILM

AMY WEISS

Although scholars have disagreed about the origins of the Arab-Israeli conflict, disputes about territory have served as one of its defining features.[1] Visual renderings of the land, through an examination of films as well as accompanying images and documents, reveal how new countries in the Middle East have formed and how borders have changed over time. To this end, I typically introduce students to the Arab-Israeli conflict through an examination of maps. This initial examination of the geography of Israel/Palestine provides students with contextual information about the places we will discuss throughout the semester. Beyond maps, however, I have also come to rely more on films and documentaries for their pedagogical use in emphasizing the significance of land in the Arab-Israeli conflict.

The history department at City College, one of the senior colleges constituting the City University of New York (CUNY) system, offers the Arab-Israeli conflict as a historical examination of the cultural, economic, political, religious, and social issues that have affected the people and the region over time. It is an upper-level elective without any prerequisites. On the first day of the semester, I ask students to introduce themselves, including a statement about why they enrolled in the Arab-Israeli conflict class. Although a few students considered the course's twice-weekly evening meeting time as more of a selling point than its subject, the majority of students have expressed past involvement in political causes or trips to the region that prompted their enrollment decision. Others have family members living in Israel/Palestine, and some students have relatives in the larger Middle East. Students, therefore, typically begin the course with prior knowledge of the Arab-Israeli conflict. My goal throughout the semester is to offer multiple perspectives about the people, places, and events covered throughout the course to encourage students to formulate their own evidence-based opinions, aided by the use of films and documentaries.

The genres of film and documentary lend themselves to critical examinations of Israel/Palestine. Audio and visual components enable students to engage with a particular story line, without needing to master the nuances of cinematography. For students who have not previously traveled to the region, films and documentaries provide a way for them to empathize with the subjects they see on the screen.[2] It is this affinity for, or in some cases dislike of, the individuals that draws them into the story, perhaps more so than many one-dimensional primary source documents. Despite limitations, including artistic license and directors' or producers' biases, films and documentaries have intrinsic value for teaching the Arab-Israeli conflict.

Films made by Israelis and Palestinians abound, but three in particular provide noteworthy commentary on land-related issues associated with the Arab-Israeli conflict. *The Settlers* (2016), a documentary film by the Israeli filmmaker Shimon Dotan, underscores the contested nature of Israel's borders through an investigation of a more radical segment of Israeli Jews choosing to live in West Bank settlements. *Waltz with Bashir* (2008), an animated film by Ari Folman, reveals that the geographic boundaries of the Arab-Israeli conflict extend beyond Israel or the Palestinian Territories. Julia Bacha's *Budrus* (2009), a documentary about a Palestinian town that successfully protested the construction of a physical barrier between Israel and the West Bank, explores larger questions about territorial loss and acquisition. These films, especially when paired with an examination of primary source material, advance students' comprehension of the Arab-Israeli conflict as taught in humanities courses.

Borders

The Settlers examines the impact of the growth of Israeli settlements in the West Bank after the 1967 Arab-Israeli war on Israeli and Palestinian societies. Although interviews with religious settlers dominate the documentary, the film offers multiple perspectives on how settlements have transformed the land of Israel and the people who live there. Occasional references to or appearances by Palestinians reveal the practical complexities of determining land rights. The settlers' own words can make them either empathetic or reviled subjects, such as when an Israeli Jew living in a West Bank settlement self-identifies as a racist or when an interviewee glosses over an alleged attack on a Palestinian village. Dotan intermixes these recent interviews with past video footage of early settlement activity to provide context for the Israeli government's shifting settlement policies. This emphasis on change over time may particularly appeal to historians or political scientists teaching a course on the Arab-Israeli conflict.

The landscape literally and figuratively serves as a backdrop for larger discussions about land in the documentary. It begins with individuals interrogating what it means to be a settler and if they regard themselves as one, as they stand before various landmarks or scenery. Yet Dotan quickly reveals that these individuals are not actually being filmed throughout the country but rather are standing in front of a green screen so that the appearance of their locations can be altered during postproduction. Chroma key compositing, the visual effects technique that enables interviewees in a film studio or home to appear to be elsewhere, underscores the filmmaker's goal to have viewers rethink the reality with which they are presented regarding settlement activity.

The documentary's beginning serves as a useful device for understanding the remainder of the film. The audience is now tasked with unpacking each interview, questioning the extent of the performative nature of settlers' statements and how they reflect the larger settlement movement. When interviews are indeed conducted in outdoor settings throughout the West Bank later on in the documentary, viewers are attuned to the fact that what they see may not represent the only reality. For instance, when Dotan asks settlers about their neighbors, the camera zooms out to show the Palestinian towns or villages that are often in close proximity to the Israeli settlements. The land again serves as a framing device, illustrating the geographic nearness of these Israelis and Palestinians, but the ideological divide between them becomes all the more apparent when some of the more radical settlers suggest that this living arrangement is only temporary. Follow-up inquiries from the filmmaker reveal these settlers' beliefs that they will eventually inhabit more (if not all) of the West Bank, illustrating their desire to use their homes as permanent markers of Jewish living in this contested space.[3]

Although the documentary traces the shifting involvement of subsequent Israeli governments in the growth of the settlement movement, the film lacks any discussion of the current administration's attitude toward settlements. This limitation, perhaps indicating Dotan's personal politics, offers students the opportunity to learn more about contemporary Israeli political leaders' policies on settlement construction.[4] Pairing this documentary with an examination of policy statements that Benjamin Netanyahu has issued during his time as prime minister, from 1996 to 1999 and again from 2009 to the present, enables students to compare Netanyahu's approach toward settlements with the attitudes of former prime ministers. Students can then compare these findings with statements made by Palestinian politicians and Israeli opposition leaders, who either reject settlements outright or call for a ban on settlement expansion, to learn more about the attitudes of those in political office. Lastly, an analysis of overall viewpoints on Israeli settlements among the larger Israeli and Palestinian populations further demonstrates how *The Settlers* successfully captures a more extremist segment of Israeli Jews, while acknowledging the multiplicity of dissenting voices related to settlement activity in the West Bank.

Boundaries

A discussion of the geographical reach of Israel/Palestine extends beyond an analysis of settlement activity, particularly as questions about borders highlight the significance placed on demarcating access to land. These borders, defined in resolutions and represented in maps, nonetheless denote varied perspectives, since individuals within or outside the region do not universally accept them. The fluidity of these boundaries is further tested during times of war. Opposing forces often send people or launch weapons into contested spaces in attempts to gain a foothold in the territory and to psychologically or physically harm civilians. Screening film clips from *Waltz with Bashir* underscores war's disruptive nature within the Arab-Israeli conflict.

Waltz with Bashir depicts Ari Folman's real-life quest to seek out fellow infantry soldiers who served with him during the 1982 Lebanon War. After a friend had confided that he suffered from repeated nightmares of twenty-six dogs chasing him, which he attributed to his involvement in the invasion of Lebanon, Folman realized that he lacked any recollection of that period from more than two decades before. The animated film intersperses interviews in the present day with Folman's flashbacks as he begins to recall his participation in the 1982 war. For instance, he remembers lighting flares outside the Sabra and Shatila refugee camps, which he later learned had illuminated the way for the Phalange militia to carry out atrocities against the Palestinian residents. Israeli Prime Minister Menachem Begin and Defense Minister Ariel Sharon had sought to weaken the Palestine Liberation Organization's presence in Lebanon, which was likely to reduce the political activity of Palestinians, thereby creating a situation in which Israel could prolong its presence in the West Bank and Gaza Strip.[5] The Phalangists, originally instructed by the Israel Defense Forces to rid the camps of PLO adherents, instead committed a massacre in the refugee camps as retaliation for the assassination of Lebanon's president-elect Bashir Gemayel. Toward the conclusion of *Waltz with Bashir*, Folman realizes that he had repressed his memories as a way of dealing with the guilt associated with the tangential role he played in facilitating the massacre.

Waltz with Bashir concludes with real footage of the massacre's aftermath, thereby further underscoring the connection between war and borders. Folman created a psychological border when he successfully blocked memories associated with the massacre at the Sabra and Shatila refugee camps for more than twenty years to lessen his own trauma from that period. The film also creates a visual divide. Despite the voice work of several real-life people playing themselves, animation is used to further distance the reality of war.[6] Juxtaposing the video footage at the film's end with everything that had come before drives this point home for students. Yet I suggest showing this last scene only after having students explain what insight this film, minus the final scene, has provided on the Arab-Israeli conflict. When confronted with the raw emotion of the massacre survivors, the viewer is forced to rethink *Waltz with Bashir*'s analysis on war, particularly Israel's 1982 invasion and later continued presence in Lebanon. This film, in production during the outbreak of the Second Lebanon War in 2006, also serves as a critique of Israel's twenty-first-century entanglements beyond its borders.

While several scholars have addressed the role of memory and animation in *Waltz with Bashir*, the significance of borders has not received as much attention.[7] The Arab-Israeli conflict's vast geographical reach is emphasized when Folman's unit rolls into Lebanon in 1982 from within the safety of their tank. The cheerful song "Good Morning Lebanon," sung by the Israeli soldiers as they witness a seemingly serene landscape, belies the devastation that ultimately follows. Pairing the animated film with the graphic novel *Waltz with Bashir: A Lebanon War Story*, by Ari Folman and David Polonsky, can further tease out these nuances in physical demarcations of space. Students, tasked with illustrating a new scene from the film but using the speech constraints of the novel, can identify moments, real or imagined, when land functions as a competing factor in the wars between Israel and Lebanon.

Waltz with Bashir's use of language further illuminates the geographical and ethnic boundaries that exist in the Arab-Israeli conflict. The characters in the film speak Hebrew, yet students unfamiliar with Hebrew will likely view it using subtitles in their primary language. The addition of subtitles, or even the dubbing of the Hebrew dialogue, removes viewers from the original viewing experience. Language becomes even more critical during the film's conclusion. The documentary footage depicting the aftermath of the Sabra and Shatila massacre reveals the anguish of people as they scream in Arabic about the atrocities committed in the refugee camps. Yet, as the only section that includes live footage, it lacks subtitles.[8] Whose voices does this film capture? For whom does Ari Folman speak? How do subtitles add to or distract from one's understanding of the film? By asking students, in small groups, to answer these questions, I facilitate a dialogue that considers the boundaries that Folman depicts in *Waltz with Bashir*, illustrating that the Arab-Israeli conflict exists both within and outside the borders of Israel/Palestine.

Barriers

The creation of a physical barrier has further complicated the political and geographical borders of Israel and the Palestinian Territories. In 2002, Israel began construction of a material boundary that not only separated Israel proper from much of the West Bank but also cut off Palestinians' access in the West Bank to agricultural lands and jobs. *Budrus* investigates the nonviolent protests of the residents of the eponymous

Palestinian town from 2003 to 2009 who successfully worked to change the location of the proposed barrier that would have isolated its residents. Produced in collaboration with Israelis and Palestinians associated with Just Vision, an organization whose "overarching goal is to contribute to fostering peace and an end to the occupation," this film focuses on the barrier's effects on Palestinian communities.[9]

The inclusion of *Budrus* in a course on the Arab-Israeli conflict provides a grassroots examination of Palestinian life in the West Bank. Its focus on the community organizing work of Ayed Morrar, for instance, reveals how this Budrus resident unified the opposing political groups of Hamas and Fatah in a shared goal of changing the route of the physical barrier. This film, therefore, emphasizes moments of cooperation among Palestinians, particularly when the organizing efforts of Budrus's women play a prominent role in the fight against the proposed barrier. Although most protests, both in Israel and Palestine, have been unsuccessful in affecting the barrier's construction, *Budrus* provides an example for how this physical boundary affects all aspects of a community's existence.[10]

Through the screening of *Budrus*, I have facilitated an analysis of the physical contours of the Arab-Israeli conflict. An assignment related to the film includes researching the actual path that the barrier has followed. Students investigate where the barrier closely aligns with the Green Line, the 1949 armistice agreement made between Jordan and Israel, and where it cuts deep into the West Bank. In mapping the barrier, students learn that an electronic fence, with security access roads and ditches, makes up the majority of the structure, while a twenty- to twenty-five-foot concrete wall makes up approximately 5–10 percent of the remaining section.[11] Understanding the actual location and physical makeup of the barrier provides students with important information for comprehending the support or protests that this structure has received from both Israelis and Palestinians (notwithstanding international reactions). To this end, striving to incorporate a discussion of primary source evidence from individuals living on both sides of the structure enables students to evaluate the ecological, psychological, and visual impact that the barrier has had on Israel/Palestine.

An examination of such primary sources reveals the disparate terms used to describe the physical barrier. This essay employs the word "barrier" as a neutral term, indicating that Israel has erected a physical structure of roughly 430 miles (or about 700 kilometers).[12] Yet those who consider the structure as a legitimate tool in preventing terror attacks may call it a "security" barrier. Terminology such as "separation" barrier or "apartheid wall" are often used by those who are opposed to the structure's existence, underscoring Israel's perceived goal of annexing land in the West Bank and effectively separating Palestinians from their land and the larger society.[13] Screening *Budrus* therefore provides students with an opportunity to examine the significance of the barrier from multiple perspectives.

Conclusion

Films serve as a useful pedagogical tool for teaching courses on the Arab-Israeli conflict. Oftentimes, students enter the classroom with a superficial understanding of the issues at hand, from what they either see on the news or view on social media. Yet films and documentaries can add an empathic element to the discussion, particularly as it pertains to land in Israel and Palestine. Viewing the films, along with classroom debriefings of the themes and questions addressed in them, helps students consider the conflict from several viewpoints. Examining Israel and the Palestinian Territories with a focus on land, particularly concerns about borders, boundaries, and barriers, captures a fundamental aspect of the Arab-Israeli conflict.

Notes

1. See for instance Hillel Cohen, *Year Zero of the Arab-Israeli Conflict: 1929* (Waltham, MA: Brandeis University Press, 2015); Walter Laqueur, *The Road to Jerusalem: Origins of the Arab-Israeli Conflict, 1967* (New York: Macmillan, 1968); Amy Dockser Marcus. *Jerusalem 1913: The Origins of the Arab-Israeli Conflict* (New York: Viking, 2007); Jonathan Schneer, *The Balfour Declaration: The Origins of the Arab-Israeli Conflict* (New York: Bloomsbury, 2010).
2. For more information on film and empathy, see for instance Alan S. Marcus, Scott Alan Metzger, Richard J. Paxton, and Jeremy D. Stoddard, *Teaching History with Film: Strategies for Secondary Social Studies* (New York: Routledge, 2010), 27–68.
3. Michael Feige, "Soft Power: The Meaning of Home for Gush Emunim Settlers," *Journal of Israeli History* 32, no. 1 (2013): 109–126. In this article, Feige investigates the significance of the home, both the physical structure and settlers' presence on the land itself, as part of an ideology in which settlers establish and maintain roots in the West Bank.
4. "An Interview with Shimon Dotan, Filmmaker and Director of *The Settlers* (2016)," *Journal of Religion and Film* 20, no. 2 (2016): article 25.
5. Anita Shapira, *Israel: A History* (Waltham, MA: Brandeis University Press, 2012), 379.
6. Yosef Raz, "War Fantasies: Memory, Trauma, and Ethics in Ari Folman's *Waltz with Bashir*," *Journal of Modern Jewish Studies* 9, no. 3 (2010): 317–22.
7. Examples of such works include Yuval Benziman, "'Mom, I'm Home': Israeli Lebanon-War Films as Inadvertent Preservers of the National Narrative," *Israel Studies* 18, no. 3 (2013): 112–32; Alison Patterson and Dan Chyutin, "Teaching Trauma in (and out of) Translation: *Waltzing with Bashir* in English," in *Media and Translation: An Interdisciplinary Approach*, ed. Dror Abend-David (New York: Bloomsbury Academic, 2014), 221–44; Judith Kriger, *Animated Realism: A Behind-the-Scenes Look at the Animated Documentary Genre* (Waltham, MA: Focal, 2012): 1–16; Raya Morag, *Waltzing*

with Bashir: Perpetrator Trauma and Cinema (New York: I. B. Taurus, 2013); Garrett Stewart, "Screen Memory in *Waltz with Bashir*," in *Killer Images: Documentary Film, Memory, and the Performance of Violence*, ed. Joram ten Brink and Joshua Oppenheimer (New York: Columbia University Press, 2012), 120–26; Joram ten Brink, "Animating Trauma: *Waltz with Bashir*, David Polonsky," in ten Brink and Oppenheimer, *Killer Images*, 127–35.
8. Patterson and Chyutin, "Teaching Trauma," 224–25.
9. Just Vision, home page, accessed March 22, 2017, www.justvision.org.
10. Uri Ben-Eliezer and Yuval Feinstein, "'The Battle over Our Homes': Reconstructing/Deconstructing Sovereign Practices around Israel's Separation Barrier on the West Bank," *Israel Studies* 2, no. 1 (2007): 171–92.
11. Alan Dowty, *Israel/Palestine* (Malden, MA: Polity, 2012), 185.
12. Gabriel Sheffer and Oren Barak, *Israel's Security Networks: A Theoretical and Comparative Perspective* (New York: Cambridge University Press, 2013), 105.
13. Dowty, *Israel/Palestine*, 172.

Teaching Competing Narratives through Film

OLGA GERSHENSON

At the start of my teaching career, my department received a number of complaints about my Israel-related courses. As one of the students put it, "Professor is not sufficiently pro-Israel." Other complaints were nearly identical and came from Jewish students indoctrinated in their Hebrew schools and synagogues into an unconditional, unquestioning support of Israel. "What am I to do?" I asked James E. Young, who was then my department chair. "I never propagate any kind of position, pro- or against Israel. I just teach students the best research there is on Israeli culture. Some of it is pretty critical, but it's not like I can scratch it from my syllabi to appease my students." "Teach them about competing narratives," he said. James was a good mentor. Like other things that he told me back then, these words became my teaching mantra.

I changed my teaching. I still give my students "the best of" contemporary writing on Israel, but I also make sure that I cover more ground, teaching cultural expressions that represent competing points of view.

The University of Massachusetts is a big public university in an overall liberal-progressive state, and my students' composition reflects this fact (many of our students are from in state). The Department of Judaic and Near Eastern Studies, in which I teach, has a small number of majors, and in order to survive in the current climate, where enrollment is emphasized above all else, I structure my courses to satisfy general education requirements. This means that my courses on Israel attract students from majors all over the campus—some of them committed Jews with a strong Zionist background and a few Palestinians (or students of Palestinian descent)—but most of my students have no particular agenda or background and are there to fulfill a general education requirement by taking a course on a subject that is vaguely familiar from their news feeds. Some students take the course to fulfill requirements in the Film Studies program or simply because it is "fun," as my courses usually deal with film and popular culture. Most students are white, but there are also African and Asian Americans, as well as a smattering of international students. For this diverse student audience, teaching competing narratives proved to be a critical strategy in making the courses successful. It is a way for me to introduce the uninitiated to the lay of the land and to let the believers and ideologues soak in the arguments from the other side. Here is how I do this in one of my courses, "Film and Society in Israel," a 300-level (i.e., relatively advanced) seminar capped at thirty students, a course that qualifies for both the Judaic Studies and Middle Eastern Studies majors, as well as the Film Studies Program, and fulfills general education requirements.

First, let me define the terms: What are these competing narratives as I regard them? Whose narratives are they, and why are they in competition? The most immediate answer I offer is Israeli and Palestinian narratives: what for Israel is a triumphant War of Independence is a tragic Nakba (catastrophe) for Palestinians. What for Israel is a heroic Six-Day War is the start of the occupation in Palestine. The list goes on and on. Often there are no unified terms to discuss historical or present events; by just naming something, we commit to a position. If it is difficult to agree on terms, it is nearly impossible to arrive at a mutual understanding of historical facts. It is a familiar story. But these are not the only competing narratives: there are also different voices within each narrative. Zooming in on Israel, we have the Zionist and the post-Zionist narratives. The question here is not, for instance, whether Palestinians in 1948 were expelled by Zionist forces but, rather, how we assess this event today from an Israeli perspective. Was the expulsion justified? The so-called post-Zionist perspective is a part of the Israeli narrative, but it is a more critical, more probing examination of its assumptions and foundations. So both sets of narratives are competing, but in the first case, the competition is over the actual story, whereas in the second, it is over how to tell it—the perspective, the assessment. These two sets of narrative tensions reflect the biggest ideological divides, but the course on film and society in Israel is not limited only to those questions. In units dealing with Jewish immigration, for instance, the competing narratives may occur between insider and outsider representations (films made by Mizrahi or Russian-immigrant filmmakers and talent versus films made by Israeli filmmakers who are not members of the community they are portraying). These films may have similar plots but tell very different stories. Another set of competing narratives can be generational, as in artistic production and representations of Holocaust survivors and their second- and third-generation descendants, also covered in this course. I do not want to reduce "competing narratives" to Israeli-Palestinian ideological divides but rather take an approach based on dialogue—on defining and understanding different stories.

Second, let me define my methodology. Since I am interested in exposing students to competing narratives, I structure every class meeting around competing representations: two films telling somewhat similar stories in profoundly different ways. For instance, in a class about the foundation of Israel, I place side by side a Hollywood blockbuster, *Exodus* (1960, dir. Otto Preminger) and a much-later art film, *Kedma* (2002, dir. Amos Gitai). Both films deal with the events taking place in Israel/Palestine in 1947–48, including illegal Jewish immigration to Palestine and relations between Zionist Jews and Palestinian Arabs; yet the overall messages of the films are dramatically different. *Exodus* represents a Zionist narrative, whereas *Kedma* can be described as representing a post-Zionist narrative. But if I wanted to focus on competing Israeli and Palestinian narratives, I would choose a different pairing of films, such as an early Israeli film of the so-called heroic-nationalist genre, *Hill 24 Doesn't Answer* (1955, dir. Thorold Dickinson), versus a sweeping family drama, *The Time That Remains* (2009), by an exilic Palestinian filmmaker, Elia Suleiman. It is easy to notice that these films differ not only in their conflicting ideological positions but also with regard to their genres, styles, and times of production. In fact, in-depth analysis of the films' representational strategies is an excellent way to arrive at their ideology and politics. The focus is always on a close-up; the movement is always from the specific to the general; the method is always inductive.

The pairings of the films are accompanied by readings—usually a reading per film. But sometimes one reading focuses on the actual history (or subject), and the second reading focuses on film. This choice depends both on the availability of film research and on the need to provide background to students. For instance, in a session dealing with terrorism/freedom fighting, I pair an Israeli Oscar-contending thriller, *Bethlehem* (2013, dir. Yuval Adler), with an equally engaging thriller, *Omar* (2013), by an Israeli-Palestinian filmmaker, Hany Abu-Assad. Both films revolve around a similar idea—an ambivalent relationship between an Israeli handler and a Palestinian informer—but from very different perspectives. Since this is such a loaded subject and the films are new (it usually takes at least a year or two for peer-reviewed research to appear), I assign a research article on Israel's use of Palestinian collaborators along with a critical and comprehensive film review.[1] But in cases where the literature on films is already available and sufficiently covers the background, I may assign only film-specific readings. For instance, in a session that approaches the Israeli-Palestinian relationships through the prism of romantic love, I pair Israeli films on the subject (such as *My Michael* [1974], *Hamsin* [1982], or the more recent *Trumpet in the Wadi* [2001] or *Jaffa* [2009]) with two chapters in Yosefa Loshitzky's book on Israeli cinema.[2] In this case, the conversation with the students is not about Israeli versus Palestinian perspective but rather divergent Israeli attitudes to Israel's "internal others": the Palestinian Arabs. Considering films made in different eras and taking different artistic approaches gives students a chance to trace the nuanced changes that took place in Israel over time and to articulate their significance.

Here is how it takes place on a practical level, made possible entirely, I should say, by technology. The course meets once a week for a three-hour session. The first hour and a half is a discussion, the second hour and a half is an in-class screening of a film to be discussed the following week. Usually, I screen a more challenging or simply less accessible film in class, leaving it to students to watch the second film at home. All the homework films, which the library streams for my class, are linked to the course's web module (currently Moodle, but I have used others). All the readings are available on the Moodle site as well. But the most important part of this course is homework, identical for each week, also due on a discussion forum on Moodle. The homework is to post a three- to four-hundred-word response to my question based on the two films and the two readings, forcing the students to consider the films' divergent ideologies and aesthetics. The questions are open and do not have a "right" or "wrong" answer.[3] However, they are structured to make students articulate positions expressed in the films and in the readings, rather than voice their personal opinions or attitudes. (In fact, I teach them to watch films "differently"—for learning and understanding, not for entertainment or pleasure.)

To encourage students to do their homework, I assign a large chunk of the final grade to it (usually 40 percent of the final grade does the trick). Moreover, along with posting their own responses, students are required to read everyone's posts. To motivate them to do that, I ask them to bring their favorite quotes from others' responses to class. I open the class by asking a couple of students to share and briefly discuss their favorite quote. These quotes become the launching pad for discussion.

To allow for all this to happen, and also to give me a chance to read and grade, the online responses are due two days in advance of the class meeting, and late responses do not receive credit. As a result, before the class, I know what students understood, how they perceived the films and the issues raised in them, and consequently, how I need to structure the in-class discussion. Also, this assignment and grading structure creates a classroom culture in which it is not acceptable to come unprepared. Because it is so challenging for students (as well as for me) to sort out the distinct positions of the two films and the relationships between them, to incorporate the voices of critics or scholars analyzing the films, and then to express it in their own writing, the work endows students with internalized knowledge and understanding of the material. It forces them to develop almost a stereoscopic view of the issue. This is the goal of the method.

The in-class work opens with small-group discussions. These discussions are structured; I usually design the questions for discussion on the basis of the online responses, allowing students to review and expand what they found out on their own at home. I circulate in between the groups, listening and answering questions and taking notes for the larger discussion. When we come together, the groups share their findings (a large chunk of the participation grade counting toward the final helps), and I conclude with a summary and more theoretical take on the material. I will often add discussion of related works from other cultural genres—visual arts, music, poetry—which complicate the narratives.

The midterm assignment in this class also contributes to developing this kind of dialogical perspective on the issues. I call this assignment "An Interactive Presentation," and it consists of a small group of students (two to three people) facilitating a brief discussion on the film clip of their choice. Each presentation lasts just a few minutes, but a staggering amount of preparation goes into it. Students form their own groups and choose a film to work on. I am available for guidance, but overall, they have to pick on their own something that is relevant to the course but has not been included in the syllabus. Then they research the film and its historical and cultural context, select a film clip, and meet with me to discuss their clip and a plan for their in-class discussion. Usually, students are socialized to perform monologically—and to the singular audience of a professor. This assignment flips a classroom, as they are required now to listen more than to talk, and to rely on their peers (as copresenters and as discussants) for the success of the assignment. Their goal is not to show their own understanding or mastery of the material (although it is necessary) but to engage other students in a discussion of the film clip in relation to the classroom material. It is this reversal that results in the most profound revelations for students; as a final stage in this assignment, they are required to write pieces reflecting on what they learned in the process. Although they all talk about learning a lot about their particular film, mostly their writing is about learning to listen, to interpret, and to connect. In other words, this assignment that cultivates dialogical thinking serves the principle of teaching competing narratives.

The final paper is a traditional academic paper, but dialogical aspects are present even there. Students are required to work on it in a system of multiple drafts, developing each draft on the basis of feedback received at different stages of writing, not only from me but also from their peers, during structured review session.

Since my first years of teaching, the campus climate (and possibly Hebrew school) has changed. Not a single Jewish student has accused me of being "insufficiently pro-Israel" for years. I would like to think that this a good sign, a sign of American Jews moving beyond their PEP (progressive except on Palestine) position. But the times are changing again, and with the new set of political players, who knows what kind of ideological positions will dominate? Whatever they may be, the dialogical perspective will help us and our students to identify these positions and see them in the context of other competing narratives instead of as received wisdom.

Notes

1. The research article is Hillel Cohen and Ron Dudai, "Human Rights Dilemma in Using Informers to Combat Terrorism: The Israeli-Palestinian Case," *Terrorism and Political Violence* 17 (2005): 229–43. The review is Dorit Naaman, "Oscar Hopeful 'Bethlehem' Yet Another Film That Celebrates Israeli Victimhood," *Mondoweiss*, November 11, 2013.
2. Yosefa Loshitzky, *Identity Politics on the Israeli Screen* (Austin: University of Texas Press, 2001), chapter 5, "In the Land of Oz: Orientalist Discourse in *My Michael*," and chapter 6, "Forbidden Love in the Holy Land: Transgressing the Israeli-Palestinian Conflict," 90–154.
3. A sample question: "Both *Exodus* and *Kedma* reflect a moment in the foundation of the state of Israel—arrival of post-WWII immigrants and an armed conflict with British and Palestinians. But the stories that emerge from the two films are quite different. How so? Discuss the differences in the ways the two movies portray 'sabras,' new immigrants, and Palestinian Arabs. Rely on your notes from watching both films and on readings by Loshitzky and Ginzburg."

Teaching Jewish-Israeli, Arab-Israeli, and Palestinian Poetry Together

CARY NELSON

Defining Issues

Jews and Arabs have had an intersecting history in Palestine for over a century.[1] It is a history in which poetry, once intermittently, eventually persistently, has played an organizing and sometimes defining role. Since 1948 and the founding of Israel, that role has evolved significantly, acquiring increasing linguistic variety, but it has also received seismic and defining shocks from historical events, including the 1967 and 1973 wars. Teaching this poetry comparatively offers an opportunity to place both peoples' aspirations, self-reflections, and accusations in dialogue with each other: to compare, contrast, and confront the most verbally compressed and metaphorically rich versions of their national narratives; to see rhetorical opportunities for engagement, commemoration, and vision that conventional political discourse rarely offers; to enrich our understanding of the genre in a specific historical context; and to encounter sometimes-unexpected local perspectives on the conflict itself. While there are many history and political science courses that aim to teach both sides of the Israeli-Palestinian conflict fairly and comparable courses emphasizing fiction, there seem to be few such courses focused exclusively on poetry. Poetry presents an especially intense challenge to a comparative course because it includes passionate, volatile imagery that requires considerable thought if you want to treat both sides to the conflict sympathetically.

In what follows, I will need not only to explore some of the principles at stake but also to offer illustrative examples from the poetry itself. And I will have to address enough of the relevant poetry to convince readers that such a course is doable and worth doing. That requires commenting on a few poets in detail and drawing together brief quotations from others to suggest broader bases for comparison. Finally, I will try to document the main resources available to teach such a course. The principles guiding the course explored here can underwrite a wide variety of courses about the Israeli-Palestinian conflict, though literature courses in general have at least one inherent advantage over those in most other fields: the built-in guarantee that individual Arab and Jewish voices will be represented.

I must begin, however, by acknowledging that it is easier to design courses devoted exclusively to either Jewish-Israeli or Palestinian poetry. A course on only one people's poetry can cover more of its particular territory and bracket vexing questions raised when designing a comparative Israeli-Palestinian syllabus or attempting to teach from it. Indeed, most anthologies devote themselves only to one people's poetry.[2] But courses limited in this way carry a specific political and cultural risk: that poetry's distinctive capacity for identification, naming, and idealization will be attached to one people alone, thereby increasing rather than ameliorating the distrust and ignorance that already accompanies the Israeli-Palestinian conflict. This is a pedagogy with potential cultural and political consequences with regard to how it affects students' understanding of the world in which they live.

For anyone seriously invested in the history of the conflict and its current status, comparing Jewish-Israeli and Palestinian poetry can be painful and challenging. Even those who are committed to honoring both peoples' narratives may recoil at unwarranted Holocaust comparisons or overly blunt and literal poetic accounts of violence and find them difficult to process and evaluate. The way violence is represented is a frequent problem in antiwar poetry generally, one that was repeatedly in evidence during the anti-Vietnam movement. Poets can also be especially unsparing in their portraits, not only of their adversaries but also of their own people. Poetry engaged with traumatic histories—and both Jews and Palestinian Arabs have them—often seeks uncompromising and essential truths. When poetry opts instead for irreducible complication, that too can leave readers frustrated. To address the poetry about the conflict means to confront the fundamental character of the conflict itself, even while exploring the culturally distinctive functions poetry can serve.

Teaching the poetry comparatively means that Jewish and Arab voices call out to one another in the classroom. There are numerous topics that both groups address and that can be the subjects of assigned readings for one or more weeks. One might compare the following:

- How both peoples mourn their dead lost to wartime or terrorist violence
- How poets address the very different historical contexts and nature of exile
- The ways love and politics intersect
- Songs of affection and lament about Jerusalem, the critical city for both peoples
- Responses to the military occupation of the West Bank

This is not an exhaustive list, but it is a more-than-adequate basis for a course. I will devote a separate section of what follows to the last of these topics. The individual volumes and anthologies cited here include many poems on these and other fruitful topics common to both bodies of poetry.[3] The first topic in the preceding list might pair poems by Jewish poets about people lost in the 1948 war and since with decades of Palestinian poetry about martyrdom. Teaching the poetry separately, as one can see from even this one example, can serve an impulse to instrumentalize it for partisan political ends. That follows the emerging disciplinary inclination to jettison the commitment to complexity that has shaped literary close reading from the new criticism through deconstruction and to substitute it with the belief that interpretation should serve simplicity instead, that interpretation should reduce literature to simple, repeatable truths and serve a specific political agenda. The Jews of Israel and the Palestinians are each consequently either magnificently heroic or obsessively violent, virtually invisible or the world's preeminent victims.

This emerging trend in literary studies can be imposed on either Jewish-Israeli or Palestinian Arab poetry, but it can also follow textual prompts within the poetry itself. That is partly because both bodies of poetry have contributed substantially not only to the ideologies of nationalism but also to the articulation of individual identity models grounded in collective needs, histories, and aspirations. As Michael Gluzman writes, "literature, by permitting an imaginary perception of unity before it is achieved politically and administratively, is instrumental in creating an 'imagined community' and in effecting national unity."[4] In a struggle for new or redefined nationhood, individual identity can be articulated to that ideal of collective unity. Readers nowhere near the Middle East can then empathically internalize the poetry's identity discourses and imagine themselves to be heroes and victims of area struggles. Both peoples have produced poetry in which subjective experience is subordinated to or understood in terms of collective experience and goals. The challenge to the teacher who identifies primarily with one or the other people's traumatic history is to compensate by the selection of poems within each tradition that complicate that impulse toward unitary political commitment and to give full credit to textual evidence of nuance and contradiction. Rather than opt exclusively for simplicity or complication, the poetry, broadly speaking, embraces both.

I believe the goal should be to combine empathy with objectivity, to teach both Jewish-Israeli and Palestinian Arab poetry sympathetically but reserve the right to distinguish between poems that do and do not succeed, between poems that may serve only near-term political needs and those more likely to engage critical attention over time. Both purposes are valid, but they may implicate different evaluative criteria. Both can include the application of appropriate aesthetic standards, but, as I have argued for years, explicitly political or agitational poems can implicate different aesthetic principles.

In the history of modern political poetry, there are few conflicts for which there is a substantial and equivalent body of complex and ambitious poetry from both sides.[5] Here there is, at least in recent decades, and it requires rethinking what counts as and constitutes political poetry. Indeed the history of Jewish-Israeli and Palestinian Arab poetry includes intense debates about the nature and goals of political poetry, debates waged not just in scholarly work but in media outlets contemporary with the poems themselves.

Deciding what poems to assign to a class will depend in part on how each of us addresses such questions. Since few American, Canadian, or European students and literature faculty are proficient in both Arabic and Hebrew, as I am not, most such classes will assign English-language versions of the poems. Outside Israel itself, indeed, that limit will apply almost everywhere. A substantial amount of critical analysis in Arabic and Hebrew remains untranslated, which constrains faculty preparation as well. The reliance on what has actually been translated can distort poetic careers, even though it opens possibilities for classroom discussions about translation that focus in part on which translation offers the most effective version of a poem. Often enough, comparing different translations means discovering that some passages are translated more powerfully in one version, while other passages are better handled in others. Combining elements to produce a new composite translation is sometimes useful both in the classroom and in scholarly analyses.[6] Comparing multiple translations can also help establish what the poet's intentions were. Even translated poems merit detailed commentary on their language, which we need if we are to deal with translated poems *as poems*.

My own view is that such a class should not only cover broad trends in the bodies of poetry, for which individual poems are useful, but also spend time on individual poets' full careers. Time spent on coverage of several poets' full careers would thus balance topical weeks that cover the responses that a number of poets have had to a given subject, such as the five topics listed previously. I will give examples of each. The number of poets comprehensively translated, however, is small. Several more have good representative selections available in English, but many recognizably influential Israeli and Palestinian poets do not. I begin, then, with the two best candidates for comprehensive coverage.

Before embarking on that comparison, however, I should warn that it is unwise to imagine that comparing Jewish-Israeli and Palestinian Arab poems will produce a reconciliation between these competing voices. Exploring the two bodies of poetry comparatively instead foregrounds at once points of convergence and divergence.[7] No tracking of similar or intersecting needs and discursive resources can obscure the fundamental collision of irreconcilable narratives. That is the context, nonetheless, in which a conversation can take place.

Darwish and Amichai

Almost any imaginable comparative course on Jewish-Israeli and Palestinian Arab poetry is likely to include Mahmoud Darwish (1941–2008) and Yehuda Amichai (1924–2000), two poets, respectively Palestinian and Israeli, who are widely considered the foremost modern poets of their peoples.[8] Their prestige and the universally admired caliber of their work is unsurprisingly matched by the fact that they are the poets with the most extensive body of work translated into English, as well as the largest body of criticism of their work available in English. They are also the only two poets with a large number of poems in multiple English-language versions.[9] Here and throughout what follows, poems by Palestinians are presented in translation from the Arabic, and poems by Israeli Jews are presented as translated from Hebrew. Not all poets, however, follow that pattern of language choice. The Druze poet Naim Araidi (1948–) writes in both Arabic and Hebrew, as does Anton Shammas (1950–), a Palestinian who was born Catholic, while Reda Mansour (1965–), also Druze, writes exclusively in Hebrew. Salman Masalha (1953–), a Muslim Druze, also writes in both Arabic and Hebrew.[10] Rashid Hussein (1936–1977) an Arab Israeli, translated some of his own poetry from Arabic to Hebrew, meanwhile translating Chaim Nahman Bialik's Hebrew poetry into Arabic and a number of Arab songs into Hebrew.

Darwish is perhaps the single most prolific and certainly most revered of Palestinian poets. He sometimes saw himself as competing with Amichai. Darwish is unstinting in his condemnation of Israeli policies and their impact on and consequences for Palestinians, though his recommendations for the future varied during the course of his career. For quite some time, he rejected any accommodation with Israel, but eventually he made his peace with the necessity of a two-state solution. In the wake of particularly lethal events, he used poetry to elevate his anger to the level of principle. A poem published in the *Jerusalem Post* (April 1988) in response to the First Intifada, "Those Who Pass between Fleeting Words," met with a firestorm of Israeli protest, as he sought to cast out Israelis for the betrayal of their ideals, echoing the rage of Moses when he descended from Mount Sinai:

> O those who pass between fleeting words
> Pile your illusions in a deserted pit, and be gone
> Return the hand of time to the law of the golden calf
> Or to the time of the revolver's music!

> For we have that which does not please you here, so be gone
> And we have what you lack: a bleeding homeland of a bleeding people
> . . . .
> It is time for you to be gone
> Live wherever you like, but do not live among us
> It is time for you to be gone
> Die wherever you like, but do not die among us
> For we have work to do in our land
> We have the past here
> We have the first cry of life
> We have the present, the present and the future
> We have this world here, and the hereafter
> So leave our country
> Our land, our sea
> Our wheat, our salt, our wounds
> Everything, and leave[11]

If this poem's accusations verge on schematic dehumanization, it is also true that Darwish's poetry often resists that temptation. His 1967 poem "A Soldier Dreams of White Tulips" faults the Jews for what he considers a superficial, invented connection to the land, but the poem is constructed as a dialogue with an Israeli soldier and was widely criticized in Palestinian circles for humanizing the Israeli.[12] Early on, Darwish fell in love with a Jewish woman, Tamar Berkman (Ben 'Ami), giving her the name "Rita" in several poems written over a period of years, from "Rita and the Rifle" (1967) and "A Beautiful Woman from Sodom" (1970) to "Rita's Winter" (1992). The poems have a fundamental duality in common: they are at once exquisite love poems and testaments to the political impossibility that their feelings present. Here is a stanza from "Rita's Winter":

> Rita sips the morning tea
> and peels the first apple with ten irises
> and says: Don't read the newspaper now, the drums are the drums
> and war isn't my profession. And I am I. Are you you?
> I am he, I say
> who saw a gazelle throw her glitter upon him
> and saw his desires stream after you
> and saw the two of us bewildered in unison on the bed
> before we became distant like a greeting between strangers on the pier
> then departure carried us like a paper in its wind

and threw us at the doorsteps of hotels like letters read in a hurry.
She says: Will you take me with you? I would
become the ring of your barefoot heart
if you take me with you
I would become your garb in a country that birthed you . . . to kill you
I would become a coffin of mint that carries your doom
and you would become mine, dead and alive . . . ?
O Rita, the guide is lost
and love, like death, is a promise that can't be refused . . . and doesn't vanish[13]

The poem is remarkable for the intricate way that it interweaves intimate erotics with public conflict. In a willed plea that private affirmation triumph over an overshadowing history, Rita urges Darwish not to read the newspapers, for war is not her profession. And yet they are at once intertwined and "bewildered" in bed. Every moment of psychological distance replicates the political distance between them.

Darwish began publishing in the 1960s, establishing himself as the premier liberation poet of the Arabs of Palestine. The early poetry was direct and partly polemical. I actually find much of Darwish's early work effective and compelling, though Arab critics often share the standard academic bias against more aggressive political poetry and consider his work after 1985 not just different but better. His signature poem of the 1960s, "Identity Card," which opens *Leaves of the Olive Tree* (1964) but was read aloud earlier, repeats the defiant declaration "Write it down, I am an Arab" at the outset of each of its four stanzas. The repeated declaration is hurled in the face of an Israeli official; it became not just an anthem of resistance but also a rousing affirmation of identity. Its recitation of working-class labor made Darwish a people's poet throughout the Arab world:

> Write it down:
> I am an Arab
> & I work with comrades in a stone quarry
> & my children are eight in number,
> For them I hack out
>   a loaf of bread
>   clothing
>   a school exercise-book
> from the rocks
> rather than begging for alms
>   at your door
> rather than making myself small

at your doorsteps.
Does this bother you?[14]

After 1985—the date Darwish identifies as marking a major change in his style—he often embedded political work in more oblique and reflective poems, but the political import is often still strong. To open one of the books Darwish published since 1985 is at once to find yourself in a terrain of inscape and insight. It is territory both familiar—invoking historical and contemporary experience that we should know well—and uncanny, evoking surprising and unsettling forms of alienation, empathy, and anguish. "The girl / The scream" opens his 2008 collection *The River Dies of Thirst*, a remarkable mixed-form book including poetry and prose poems reminiscent of William Carlos Williams's mixed forms from the first decades of the previous century:

On the seashore is a girl, and the girl has a family
and the family has a house. And the house has two windows and a door
And in the sea is a warship having fun
catching promenaders on the seashore:
Four, five, seven
fall down on the sand. And the girl is saved for a while
because a hazy hand
a divine hand of some sort helps her, so she calls out: 'Father
Father! Let's go home, the sea is not for people like us!'
Her father doesn't answer, laid out on his shadow
windward of the sunset
blood in the palm trees, blood in the clouds

Her voice carries her higher and further than
the seashore. She screams at night over the land
The echo has no echo
so she becomes the endless scream in the breaking news
which was no longer breaking news
when
the aircraft returned to bomb a house with two windows and a door.[15]

Of course, this is fundamentally—but not only—a protest poem. For Darwish, the seashore was primarily Lebanon's; reading it now, for us the seashore is also Gaza's, but the planes remain Israeli. The poem is also partly a parable. That house with two windows and a door is symbolic and real, partly a human face with two eyes to see with and a mouth with which to speak, partly a typically modest house of the poor. The personified warship bounces on the waves observing—"having fun" in a phrase that is both innocent and chilling or outrageous—but when the promenaders "fall down," despite the contrast with the diction, it is more than a nursery rhyme or a child's account because they do so from the impact of real bullets. That hazy unknowable hand may be fate's, and Darwish adds an uncanny element of whimsy to the scene when he calls it "a divine hand of some sort." The call to a father resonates with half a century of Darwish poems to his own and others' fathers; when the girl innocently calls to her own father, it serves for the reader at the same time as a call to the father above. "People like us" invokes Palestinians but also all innocent victims of war. The father "laid out on his shadow" is again an uncanny image of the pity of war, fusing the absolute fact of death, something the child cannot understand, with the fleeting character of shadows that are by nature temporary. "The endless scream in the breaking news" with no echo fuses transcendent, unbounded horror with contingency in such a way as to tell us that this is a repeated and ongoing story in which all play parts that seem preordained. It is breaking news "which was no longer breaking news." I do not see this only as an anti-Israel poem but also as a poem about the overall pity of this ongoing war, one that teaches empathy through both anger and sorrow. But it is not simply a universal poem; it keeps pulling us back to a particular history.

A very different particular history is at issue in Amichai's poem "The U.N. Headquarters in the High Commissioner's House in Jerusalem" from his 1955 first book. Written in the wake of the UN partition plan of 1947, the recognition of the Jewish state amid complex political maneuvering the following year, and the partition plan's failure amid the outbreak of war when the Arab states attacked in 1948, it gives a compelling portrait of the vicissitudes of international politics. I use the English translation by Assia Gutmann but the longer title as translated by Chana Bloch and Stephen Mitchell.[16] For the poet, the UN represents not only itself but also the staging ground for the whole international community's investment in the Arab-Israeli conflict. The poem opens with a grotesque portrait of international diplomats and their staffs and assistants all playing their preordained parts, none of them acting out of individual agency:

> The mediators, the peace makers, the compromisers, the pacifiers
> Live in the white house
> And receive their nourishment from far away,
> Through twisting channels, through dark veins, like a fetus.
>
> And their secretaries are lipsticked and laughing,
> And their immune chauffeurs wait below, like horses in a stable,
> And the trees whose shadow shades them have their roots in disputed territory,

And the delusions are children who go out into the fields to find cyclamen
And do not come back.

And the thoughts circle above, uneasily, like scout planes,
And they take photographs, and return, and develop the film
In dark, sad rooms.

And I know that they have very heavy chandeliers,
And the boy that I was sits on them and swings
In and out, in and out, and out, and does not come back.

Later on, the night will bring
Rusty and crooked conclusions out of our ancient lives,
And above all the houses the music
Will gather all the scattered words,[17]
Like a hand gathering crumbs off the table
After the meal while the talk continues
And the children are already asleep.

And hope comes to me like daring sailors,
Like discoverers of continents
To an island,
And they rest for a day or two,
And then they sail away.

This poem—traversed by bitterness, sorrow, and the lament for lost opportunities—could have been written last week, last month. The building in question is still there, but more importantly, the diplomats have not ceased their failed meddling, their disposal of hope from all sides. Benjamin and Barbara Harshav translate the first line as "the mediators, reconcilers, compromisers, appeasers," giving it a still-darker edge, especially with appeasement still in mind from Europe in 1938. The planes that circle overhead suggest UN oversight of the armistice lines as the '48 war ended, but they echo down to the boundary disputes of our own day. Jerusalem is no less disputed territory now than it was then. The fourteen lines that begin with "And" add to a sense of an endless, ongoing political cycle, reinforced by additional uses of "and" midline.

As so often with both Amichai and Darwish, the poem here is woven partly out of representative autobiographical material, autobiography in other words that stands in for generational and national experience. Amichai was eleven years old when his family emigrated from Germany to Israel in 1935. The boy that he was symbolically climbs the ornate chandeliers at the UN's Jerusalem headquarters, dreaming that his hopes will be fulfilled. But the political possibilities in play internationally arrive "from far away, / Through twisting channels, through dark veins," and their engagement with the human needs on the ground can be oblique, compromised, misguided. The political proposals "bring / Rusty and crooked conclusions out of our ancient lives," diminishing an ancient heritage in the process. The lament at the end has the kind of whimsical charm that also animated Darwish's "The girl / The scream," though it embodies hopes that have no material future. "They rest for a day or two, / And then they sail away."

As with Darwish, subtle complication is at the heart of Amichai's poetry. Immediately after the Six-Day War, in "Jerusalem, 1967," when Israelis were ecstatic at the reunification of the city, Amichai began to warn of unforeseen consequences. "Jerusalem stone," he tells us, "is the only stone that can / feel pain"; the city is "built on the vaulted foundations / of a held-back scream." He asks that we think of what Palestinians are paying for the Jewish victory:

On Yom Kippur in 1967, the Year of Forgetting, I put on
my dark holiday clothes and walked to the Old City of Jerusalem.
For a long time I stood in front of an Arab's hole-in-the-wall shop,
not far from the Damascus Gate, a shop with
buttons and zippers and spools of thread
in every color and snaps and buckles.
A rare light and many colors, like an open Ark.[18]

A possible allusion to Joseph's coat of many colors is followed with a suggestion that verges on blasphemy. The Harshav translation makes the comparison that concludes the stanza explicit. The Arab's shop glows "like an open Ark of the covenant." It is a dual reference. The wooden ark held the Ten Commandments that Moses brought down from Mount Sinai. The reference to the sacred ark turns it into a burden for secular reverence. If we cannot honor the commandments as they apply to the Arab in the Old City, we are doomed. But the ark is also now the ark in the synagogue where the Torah is kept, opened, as the poem implies, for the Yom Kippur service. Then the speaker addresses the shopkeeper internally, making a link that warns us violence cannot but echo violence:

I told him in my heart that my father too
had a shop like this, with thread and buttons.
I explained to him in my heart about all the decades
and the causes and the events, why I am now here
and my father's shop was burned there and he is buried here.

"There" is Germany, but Amichai offers the link more with sadness than in accusation.

Amichai can also be fiercely prophetic when he testifies to the consequences of militarization. In the concluding stanza of "I Guard the Children," written—as Chana Kronfeld points out in a fine analysis of the poem—in the wake of Israel's 1982 invasion of Lebanon, Amichai castigates Israel's leaders with rhetoric that also implicates their equals worldwide:

> But I lift up my face and see above us,
> as in some hideous vision, wielders of power,
> uplifted by honor, vaunted and vaunting,
> clerks of war, merchants of peace,
> treasurers of fate, ministers and presidents
> flaunting their gaudy responsibilities.
> I see them pass over us
> like angels of the plague of the firstborn,
> their groin gaping and dripping
> a honeyed dreck like sweetened motor oil,
> and the soles of their feet clawing like the feet of Ashmedai,
> their heads up in the sky, stupid as flags.[19]

The poem opens with an Israeli father meditating while he serves as an armed guard in a schoolyard. At the end, as Kronfeld writes, he "insists that if the schoolchildren are in danger, it is only the politicians' doing."[20] They are compared to Ashmedai, king of demons, said to be here on Earth after millennia in hell. The poem refuses to distinguish Israel's nationalism and its flag from that of any other country.

Though it would help to have a substantial English-language selected poems 1960–85 for Mahmoud Darwish, a volume that would have to include the widely celebrated but untranslated "In Praise of the High Shadow" (1983), there is a considerable amount of his work in translation, enough to base a full course on his work. The extensive body of Amichai translations puts him in the same category. Nonetheless, although Amichai and Darwish are the most widely translated Jewish-Israeli and Palestinian poets, the English-language reader and teacher faces notable challenges. The available translations are scattered across many volumes. If you admire Darwish's 1986 poem sequence *Lesser Roses*, as I do, you may want to assign the only volume of his selected poems that more or less spans his whole career, *Unfortunately, It Was Paradise*, translated by Munir Akash and Carolyn Forché, where you can find the first half of the fifty poems of *Lesser Roses*. You can find four more in the three-poet collection *Victims of a Map*, along with alternative translations of eight of the poems, but that still leaves you twenty-one poems short of the complete sequence. One important additional poem from *Lesser Roses*, "Oh, Father, I Am Joseph," is translated by Reuven Snir in the valuable critical anthology *Mahmoud Darwish: Exile's Poet*.[21]

If you want to teach Amichai's key Jerusalem poems—Adam Kirsch has called him more a poet of that city than of his country[22]—then you can find the compelling poem sequence cited earlier, "Jerusalem, 1967," in Robert Alter's fine 2015 collection *The Poetry of Yehuda Amichai*. But you might want to pair it with his 1974 "Songs of Zion the Beautiful," another intermittently personal poem about the city and its history. Twenty-five of the thirty-nine poems in the 1974 sequence can be found in Alter. Three more are translated in Benjamin and Barbara Harshav's *Yehuda Amichai: A Life of Poetry, 1948–1994*, and still another three are in *Poems of Jerusalem and Love Poems*. Yet one more each are in *Amen* and in Glenda Abramson's critical book *The Writing of Yehuda Amichai*. That gives you a total of thirty-three out of thirty-nine.[23]

If you combine all of the volumes of Amichai translations, you end up with something reasonably close to a collected Amichai, minus a few key omissions.[24] Darwish is a more complex case. His work since 1986 has been widely translated. The sometimes more polemical and agitational poetry he wrote before then has a much spottier translation history.[25] What is more, most of those who translate poems from the first twenty-five years of his career do not tell us which books the poems are from. Some of the information can be gleaned from critical sources, and his three-volume collected poems in Arabic divides the poetry by book; so a complete Darwish table of contents could be translated into English from that source. *Unfortunately, It Was Paradise* presents poems book by book chronologically but adds three poems labeled only "before 1986" at the end as though they are juvenilia.[26]

Poets Confront the Occupation

No credible course comparing Jewish-Israeli and Palestinian poetry can avoid the most pressing political subject, the occupation of Gaza until 2005 and the occupation of the West Bank from 1967 to the present. A good place to begin is with Dahlia Ravikovitch (1936–2005), a Jewish Israeli whose impact on the Israeli scene has been exceptional. Happily, she has a true collected poems in English. Like Amichai, she also felt intimations of disaster in the wake of the 1967 war. In her case, that anxiety found expression in "The Horns of Hitin," published in her 1969 volume *The Third Book*. The poem invoked the Crusaders, who "plundered everything," an allusion that the Palestinians draw on as well. But it was the first war in Lebanon in 1982 that gave Ravikovitch and thousands of Israelis reason for the first time to oppose the government aggressively in the midst of war. When then faced with Palestinian deaths, Ravikovitch refused, as Ilana Szobel puts it, "to take part in the dominant political narrative, which forms the victimized Israeli and which defends only its own existence."[27]

Registering that "As the tiger gnaws at the wild ox, / that's how doubt eats away at me," Ravikovitch reserves most of her empathy for Palestinian victims.[28] "In the valley, the army was hunting down human beings" (213):

> These are the chronicles of the child
> who was killed in his mother's belly
> in the month of January, in the year 1988,
> "under circumstances relating to state security." (215)
>
> but who was that man
> lying there lonely,
> choking on his blood?
> What did he see
> what did he hear
> in the uproar that seethed
> above him? (196)

She wrote "The Story of the Arab Who Died in the Fire" to bear witness to a man burned alive, and she produced "Hovering at a Low Altitude," her most famous protest poem, to put us in the place of a Palestinian shepherd girl who is raped and murdered. It is a complex imaginative exercise that both dramatizes and condemns readerly distance:

> She still has a few hours left.
> But that's hardly the object of my meditations.
> My thoughts, soft as down, cushion me comfortably.
> . . . .
> I am not here.
> I'm above those savage mountain ranges
> . . . .
> Can make a getaway and persuade myself:
> I haven't seen a thing. (175–76)

Ravikovitch is thus also concerned with what the occupation has done to corrupt Jewish Israel and with the irrelevance of this or that camp of opinion in the light of the fundamental violence done to the Palestinians:

No point in hiding it any longer:
We're an experiment that went awry,
a plan that misfired,
tied up with too much murderousness.
Why should I care about this camp or that,
screaming till their throats are raw. (198)

A course in Israeli and Palestinian poetry might pair Ravikovitch's work with the equally uncompromising and poetically inventive anger that a major Palestinian poet, Taha Muhammad Ali (1931–2011), reveals in the evocative translation of his selected poems, *So What: New and Selected Poems, 1971–2005*.²⁹ Once again, as with Darwish and Amichai, we see what perhaps only poetry can contribute to a political struggle. Born in rural Galilee, Muhammad Ali saw his village destroyed in the 1948 war, but he keeps it alive in his poetry. "Sabha's Rope" tells the story of a cow that swallows a rope and has to be slaughtered as she is dying. Only after the village scene is detailed—the cow meat is cooked, but no one is emotionally able to eat it; and Ali tells us that the bitterness of hard times can be savored—does he offer a political message:

and with all my heart I would have agreed,
to swallow a rope longer than Sabha's,
if only
we could have stayed in our village. (105)

"Sabha's Rope," notable for its humanism and its rejection of unqualified anger, is among the poems Muhammad Ali wrote, remarkably, in 1988 in the midst of the First Intifada, when others might have settled for simple rage. In "Fooling the Killers," written the same year, he enlarges on the story of a ten-year-old boy who dies, giving it near-mythic status:

But even if they did it,
Qasim,
if, shamelessly,
they killed you,
I'm certain
you fooled your killers,
just as you managed
to fool the years.
For they never discovered
your body at the edge of the road,

> and didn't find it
> where the rivers spill,
> or on the shelves
> at the morgue,
> and not on the way to Mecca,
> and not beneath the rubble. (57)

Muhammad Ali can also be forceful and uncompromising in political critique, concisely combining outrage at repeated violence with a blunt critique of its religious rationalization:

> In God's name
> they slit my throat
> from ear to ear
> a thousand times (15)

But his narrative inventiveness, his love poems, and his lyricism give us a fully nuanced version of someone who preserves his humanity while solidifying his activist commitment. Thus he can also write in sorrow that haunts us of

>   countless blinded birds
> that have lost their way
> to the heart of the forest (49)

or give a visceral, naturalized, and affecting portrait of his anger:

> my blood rushing
> like the shadow
> cast by a cloud of starlings (123)

while protesting,

> Our land makes love to the sailors
> and strips naked before the newcomers:
> it rests its head along the usurper's thigh (45)

and entertaining a vision in "Empty Words," another of his 1988 poems, in

>   which the young men

from Hebron explode
and offer as a gift to Jerusalem's children,
ammunition for their palms and slings! (109)

From Ravikovitch and Muhammad Ali, we can segue to protest poetry that is still more bluntly unforgiving, as in the work of the Israeli Jew Aharon Shabtai (1939–). His two translated collections, *J'Accuse* (2003) and *War & Love / Love & War* (2010) give a good indication of his formal and thematic range and the ferocity of Israeli poets' critique of the occupation—both of its consequences and of the policies that sustain it. In "The Reason to Live Here," a poem that opens with an indictment of Israeli capitalism, with its increasing concentration of wealth in the hands of the few, he tells us, "The pure words I suckled from my mother's breasts: Man, Child, Justice, Mercy, and so on, / are dispossessed before our eyes, imprisoned in ghettos, murdered at checkpoints."[30] Here, as elsewhere in his work, he insists that the Zionist vision has been corrupted over time, that its origin was not in moral darkness. Part of his aim, as in the title poem, "J'Accuse," is

> to reconstruct the manner
> in which public discourse itself
> is corrupted and turned into refuse—
> . . . .
> words
> are only the skins of potatoes
> with which the stupid are to be stuffed— (18, 21)

He ends the poem "2006," asking what came of the withdrawal from Gaza, with one declaration:

> I see only a single sentence:
> Mothers and children
> in Gaza are searching
> for food in heaps of trash.[31]

"The wells of morality have all gone dry," he writes in "Summer 1997," "the wine of mercy run out" (11). In "Toy Soldiers," he asks,

> What muck have you filled your heads with,
> that you came by night in the driving rain
> to tear down seventy miserable shanties

and toss seven hundred people—
women and children—into the mud? (41)

It is not that Shabtai has no hope. Indeed his poetry aims to shock an oblivious population into the need for reform, but in "The Moral, It Seems, Doesn't Come with a Smile," he warns that "only when the wealthy are drowning in the tears of the poor will it come" (10). In "Lotem Abdel Shafi" (12), he extends the emotions of intimate relations to the political realm, imaginatively welcoming the thought that his daughter might marry the grandson of a Palestinian politician and thereby reconcile two peoples. Yet he reserves his strongest rhetoric for condemnation. In "To My Friend," a poem that recalls the anticapitalist rage of Depression-era poetry, he castigates the corruption of the country in the language of apocalyptic satire:

A man with the head of a pig becomes king;
people mutter gibberish and turn into wolves.
Beautiful women fornicate with apes.
Rabbis shoot pistols, affix mezuzahs to a whorehouse (8)

But Shabtai also knows that even the most savage political critique does not compensate for the damage done to the Palestinian people. In "To Dr. Majed Nassar," he asks a rhetorical question: "Is it any comfort to know that the tanks murdering/ in my name are digging a grave for my people as well?" (38).

At the same time, these observations point to a fundamental difference between what Palestinian and Jewish-Israeli political poets are culturally and politically empowered to do. Both call out and condemn the brutality of the occupation, highlighting its violence. But Jewish-Israeli poets take a further step and ask what Israelis themselves have become as a consequence, who they *are*. This produces a body of oppositional poetry that is arguably fiercer, more fundamental, more unforgiving, and more pervasive than anything Palestinian poets feel able to muster. It is a judgment rendered simultaneously from within and without. That fierce self-critique is partly made possible by the power differential between the Israeli state and West Bank Palestinians, but it also draws on Jewish traditions that date back to the prophets of the Hebrew Bible. It can be compared with a century's pattern of Palestinian Arab poetry that critiques corrupt Arab regimes and their failure to resist the political realities in Palestine. Perhaps alone among Palestinian poets, however, Darwish late in his life issued a challenge to his people to consider what follows anger if they were to achieve a state of their own; he imagined that he would be among the loyal opposition.

After the First Rain: Israeli Poems on War and Peace (1998) gathers poems written in doubt and anguish.[32] Many are poems of foreboding or of a reversal of values and the natural order, as with "The Rain Is Ready to Fall" by Eytan Eytan (1940–1991): "The rain is ready to fall downside up / On the defeated victors" (55). "Unable to cleanse inundations of hate," Shlomo Tan'ee (1919–) writes in "Rains," we are "sucked down to its dark abysses" (133). But there are also specific indictments, as in "Memory of Three Dead" by Yitzhak Laor (1948–): "Lina from Nablus, who was killed in '76, / fleeing from the soldiers; she was slain by the door / to her home" (85). Similar judgments from Israelis occur throughout *With an Iron Pen: Twenty Years of Hebrew Protest Poetry*; first published in Hebrew in 2005, the book includes a number of younger poets. Dvora Amir (1948–) in "Woodcut of a Landscape" sees only "killing in the name of the law."[33] Dahlia Falah concludes "Thursday at Angel's Bakery" by reminding us that "The children on vacation gather rocks to throw at the Jewish soldiers" (36).[34] Oreet Meital (1957–) in "October 2000" concludes, "here, in the darkness, if we breathe in anything / it is forgetting" (75). Tal Nitzan asks "what it means / to bring forth children in sorrow" (83).[35] In a moment of desperation, Tali Latowicki (1976–) cries, "Call in the snakes, let them come and pluck out my eyes, / for I am weary and have no desire to see" (122).

Some Jewish-Israeli poets invoke memories of the Holocaust to bring the ultimate challenge to the country's West Bank policies, not always with appropriate care. Palestinian poets do so as well, with equally varied results. Claims of equivalence, I believe, are historically irresponsible and unwarranted. But one may fairly ask, as Samih al-Qasim (1939–2014) does, what bearing the Holocaust has on how we live now. Along with Mahmoud Darwish one of the two most prominent poets of the Palestinian resistance, al-Qasim is the author of "Buchenwald." Addressed to the Israeli people, "Buchenwald" issues an appropriate question: what are the ethical demands that the memory of the Holocaust brings to contemporary conduct?

> Have you forgotten your shame at Buchenwald?
> Do you remember your flames at Buchenwald?
> Have you forgotten your love in the lexicon
> of silence? Do you remember your panic—
> at the reign of death, in the nightmare of time—
> that the whole world
> would become a Buchenwald?
> Whether you've forgotten or not,
> the dead's images linger
> among the wreaths of flowers,
> and from the dismembered corpses
> a hand emerges,
> a nail in the palm and tattoo on the wrist—

> a sign for the planet.
> Do you remember? Or not?
> Buchenwald—
> whether or not you've forgotten,
> the images of the murdered
> remain among the wreaths of flowers[36]

Jewish-Israeli poets also frequently call on their fellow citizens to use the legacy of the Holocaust to instill mercy and justice in their hearts. In evoking the fear that the world would become an extension of Buchenwald, al-Qasim's lyric honors the scale and gravity of the Holocaust. By linking "a nail in the palm and tattoo on the wrist," he places the murder of six million Jews alongside what Christians understand to be the crucifixion of the son of God.

Many other Palestinian poets as well, first protesting either their exile from their homes or their status in Israel and then castigating the occupation, are in inescapable dialogue with Jewish poets. In "Tent #50 (Song of a Refugee)," Rashid Hussein registers the impossible contradiction of trying to live as a refugee in one of the early camps: "Tent #50, on the left, that is my present, / But it is too cramped to contain a future!"[37] Tawfiq Zayyad (1929–1994) in "Cuba" embodies the anger growing out of exile:

> Within me lies the vengeance of a wounded people
> Thrown into the streets
> A people yearning for their usurped lands[38]

Fouzi El-Asmar (1937–2013), echoing Matthew 16:26 in "The Wandering Reed," captures the impossibility of fulfillment in exile:

> Of what benefit is it, if man were to gain the whole world
> But lose the green almond in his father's orchard?
> Of what benefit is it, if man
> Were to drink coffee in Paris
> But none in his mother's house?[39]

"I shall open a map of the world / to look for the village I lost," writes Anton Shammas in "Prisoner of Sleeping and Waking."[40] Hussein explores a related conceit in "At Zero Hour": "I traced the outlines of my country upon my heart / Turning myself into an atlas for her contours." But then he vents his resulting despair: "While she became the milk of my verse, / Yet nothing has changed."[41] Reading through such poems, one begins to recognize the special ways poetry can build empathy by registering versions of loss that are not typically found in argumentative prose. "How it hurts to see the flocks of birds returning/without us," Harun Hashim Rasheed (1927–) exclaims in "We Will Return One Day,"[42] investing nature's rhythms with Palestinian awareness of exile. Birds are free to travel, but Palestinians are not. Salim Jubran (1941–) makes a similar point in "A Refugee": "The sun crosses the borders/Without the soldiers firing bullets at her forehead."[43] Mourid Barghouti (1944–) ends "The Balcony" with a definition: "A Balcony looking for its demolished home/That is my heart."[44] In "Remainder," Hussein tells us "the bones burn under his skin," capturing pain that will not let him rest.[45] Salim Makhuli (1938–) captures something of the collective passion of the resistance in one image: "we found ourselves/In the furnace of struggle—and we were its fuel."[46]

Few poems, however, carry a greater freight of anguish than the second section of 'Abd Al-Karim Al-Sab'awi's (1932–) "Three Poems to Palestine":

> Abel on my shoulders, how heavy he is!
>   They killed him, yet I must carry him,
>   Roaming the streets with his corpse,
>   Lamenting, wailing, crying, "Abel is dead."
>   Abel, my grief, my dark fate,
>   I did not kill you; I did not beat your head with a rock
>   . . . .
>   For years I have wandered in the wilderness,
>   You upon my shoulders like a curse
>   . . . .
> Your flesh has fallen away, Abel.
> But woe unto me if I refuse,
> Or rebel against my fate and dig a hole
> To fling you in.[47]

Perhaps even more than those poems by Palestinians that compare their suffering with those of Jesus on the cross, of which there are many examples, including examples by Muslim poets, this poem invokes an originary and unresolved violence. The speaker wanders the earth carrying the original murder victim, unburied, on his back. The death is primal; it does more than make an analogy with the Genesis story; it collapses the intervening millennia into a single moral accusation against an Israeli perpetrator. And it treats all Palestinians as members of an extended human family, unable to make peace with their dead until justice is achieved. As Zayyad writes about "our tragedy" in "On the Trunk of an Olive Tree, "It has absorbed us and we have absorbed it."[48] The anger that flows from this reality is not surprising, even if its tropical realization sometimes is. In "Dearest Love II," Salma Khadra Jayyusi (1928–) commemorates 1967's Six-Day War with heightened accusatory language: "the hyenas of June went on the rampage: June cut through the ramparts of the sky."[49] Zayyad in "The Skull Harvest" urges his people "to destroy a system based on oppression / to destroy a system of crime and blood."[50] Rashid Hussein in "Jerusalem . . . And the Hour" tell us, "Anyone born in Jerusalem / is a potential bomb."[51] At times, the rhetoric of protest is brutal. Here are the opening lines of Zayyad's "Taxation":

> Taxes of every type and stamp
> Leave us indigent and penniless
> Our children craving
> Wandering amidst the dump
> To pick some remnants of food
> Abandoned by affluent breed
> While their brats are boneless
> Like balls of fat[52]

Repeatedly in revolutionary Palestinian poetry, however, and perhaps increasingly so as the occupation continued for decades, there is the fatalistic sense that the future failure of the revolution has always already taken place.

Translations

The translations available for this group of poets present somewhat different classroom opportunities. Ravikovitch comes to us in what is, except for a few poems that are deemed impossible to offer in English, a complete collected poems. One may aim to talk productively about her career as a whole or about any of its major elements—from her poems about the occupation to her classic feminist poems to the important role her work played in the rise of the women's peace movement in Israel. Shabtai's two translated volumes make an evaluation of his whole career ill advised, but they do make it possible to discuss his unusual erotic love poems or his distinctive contribution to the poetry of the occupation.

In the case of Samih al-Qasim, one can combine *Sadder than Water*, cited earlier, with *All Faces but Mine: The Poetry of Samih al-Qasim* to obtain a working selection of his poetry and a reasonable assessment of his contributions to Palestinian poetry, although not a full assessment of his career. One should, however, add to those single-author translations the twenty-one al-Qasim poems in *Enemy of the Sun*, which translates poems before 1970, the twelve poems from *Victims of a Map*, and the nine poems in *The Palestinian Wedding: A Bilingual Anthology of Contemporary Palestinian Resistance Poetry*, which collects poems published before 1982, as well as poems from other anthologies.[53] Those collections help flesh out Mahmoud Darwish's early career as well, as do a number of early collections of Darwish poems in English.

I list these examples, along with those provided for Darwish and Amichai earlier, not to provide a comprehensive bibliography of Palestinian and Jewish-Israeli poetry available in English (or not), which would require a substantial document, but rather to alert readers to the kinds of resources that are available, to the distinctions that need to be made, and to the work that has to be done to find what is in fact available in translation. Once specific subtopics are defined, moreover, even poets with very few translated works can have their poems integrated into a discussion of the kinds of poems Jews or Palestinians wrote about given subjects. Palestinian poets with only limited work in English who can be used that way and need also to be credited as significant literary figures in English-language courses include Fadwa Tuqan (1917–2003), Tawfiq Ziad (1929–1994), Mai Sayigh (1940–), Khalil Touma (1945–), Nidaa Khoury (1959–), and many others.

Conclusion

In thinking through the issues at stake in teaching a course on Jewish-Israeli and Palestinian poetry, I have focused on poetry on major political issues. It would be possible, conversely, to base a comparative course on Jewish-Israeli and Palestinian poetry on relatively apolitical humanistic affirmation.[54] Most of the poets mentioned previously write on nonpolitical (or on less centrally political) topics as well. Some poets have written and continue to write autobiographical poetry that is more personal than political. Both Jewish-Israeli and Palestinian poets write love poetry, some of which, unlike Darwish's Rita poems, places politics and history in the background. But to teach only such poems in a comparative course would be to deliberately exclude the poetry that has been culturally and politically most influential. In the United States and Europe alike, one can find countless poems about parents, children, death, religion, and other subjects in which politics and history either have retreated beyond the horizon or have been displaced by sentiment. This is not so recently anywhere in Palestine, on either side of the Green Line, where a substantial body of love poetry by major poets in both groups explicitly mingles love and politics. If one is unwilling to teach poetry at the heart of the Israeli-Palestinian conflict, one might be advised not to teach such a course.

A few further issues, however, need to be briefly noted here. Space does not permit me to offer even a capsule history of the two bodies of poetry, but there are a few points to keep in mind.[55] Teachers should recognize from the outset that the parallelism implicit in a comparative course title does not begin fully to apply historically until about 1960. That was when Arab poets in Palestine began to create a notable poetry of resistance. Until the '67 war, however, as Muna Abu Eid confirms, Arabs in Israel identified as Arab, not Palestinian.[56] A few Jewish-Israeli poets produced work addressing the Arabs in their midst before then, Avot Yeshurun's (1904–1992) long poem "Passover on Caves" (1952) being the most widely debated example, but most Israeli poets who dealt with public issues (and many did not) concentrated on creating a homeland and the identities that could sustain it through the 1950s.[57] As Emmanuel Levinas might have observed, it took some decades before Jewish-Israeli poetry fully recognized and engaged its other. As the Palestinian poet and Israeli citizen Hanna Abu Hanna (1928–) writes in "The Desire's Squint," "I am the burden of the chosen people."[58] Poets overall are well ahead of other segments of Israeli society in confronting that recognition.

The Jews who relocated to Israel beginning in the late nineteenth century included both established writers and young educated people ready to write poetry in the first four decades of the twentieth century. A majority of the Arab population in Palestine had no access to schooling and literacy, and many of the literate Arabs were among the elite who fled or were pushed out in 1947 and early 1948. Both for the Arabs remaining in Israel and those under Jordanian occupation on the West Bank from 1948 to 1967, conditions were not ripe to create a community of writers for many years. Israel meanwhile produced more than one generation of poets.

Both Jewish-Israelis and Palestinians, however, had to go through parallel processes of breaking with the past, though not in the same decade. Jews were focused on turning Hebrew into a modern, secular language. Until that goal was achieved, a viable contemporary poetry was impossible. Both peoples inherited very long histories of highly formal poetry in either Hebrew or Arabic. In the case of the Jews, much of the poetry was religious; for the Arabs, it was a formal tradition of love poetry that had to be superseded before contemporary history could be addressed. Both had a cultural and political need for vernacular poetry, and both peoples in time embraced free verse as a way to produce it.

Finally there is the complex and debatable question of who constitutes a Jewish-Israeli or Palestinian poet. Both peoples also have prehistories that include poetry relevant to the current state of national aspiration and identity. There is an anachronistic tendency to project the label of "Israeli" or "Palestinian" back in time to embrace larger and longer-running national poetries. I prefer an effort to draw distinctions, but it is complicated by individual careers that span multiple periods. As political conditions change, a Hebrew-language poet can become a Jewish-Israeli one; an Arabic-language poet can become a Palestinian one. And their careers can begin to include poetry that addresses identity or political issues that they did not address in their early work. Jews and Palestinian Arabs are both, in different ways and with different temporalities, diasporic peoples; critics of poetry must decide whether poets who emigrate belong to the poetries of their native land, to an adoptive country, or to both.

A few examples can suggest how distinctions can sometimes be drawn. Chaim Nahman Bialik (1873–1934) was the premier poet of European Zionism and of the effort to revive the Hebrew language. Born in a Ukrainian village, he emigrated to Palestine and settled in Tel Aviv in 1924, but he wrote little poetry after 1911 and, despite being recognized as Israel's national poet, arguably belongs with the forerunners of Israeli poetry.[59] One can argue that he never wrote as an Israeli poet. On the other hand, Rachel (Rachel Bluwstein, 1890–1931) did, despite her brief career, sometimes write as a poet of the Yishuv, the Jewish community established in Palestine before the Jewish state. Born in Russia, she was in Palestine briefly from 1909 to 1913; she returned to live there permanently in 1919. Her nostalgia for her time in the Kinneret and later in the Degania kibbutz, the latter cut short due to her worsening tuberculosis, is one of the themes of the poetry she wrote in Palestine, mostly in the 1920s.[60] Her nostalgia for kibbutz life can be compared with Darwish's nostalgia for the lost village of his childhood.

Ibrahim Tuqan (1905–1941), the foremost poet of his generation in Palestine, predates the Palestinian national movement, but his political poetry, partly written in protest of the British presence in the Mandate period (1922–47), makes him a clear precursor poet. Rashid Hussein was born in a village near Haifa and was politically active in Israel until he chose exile to the United States after the 1967 war. He had been under assault from both sides for his support for coexistence. Eventually dying impoverished in a fire in New York, he is clearly a Palestinian poet, on the basis not only of his birth and activities in Israel but also of the political themes in his poetry. Ahmed Dahbour (1946–) was born in Haifa but has lived in exile since 1948; the combination of birth and subject matter makes him a Palestinian poet.

The benefits of a course taking up politically engaged Jewish-Israeli and Palestinian poetry together are considerable. From a broad perspective, Jewish-Israeli and Palestinian poetry raise challenging questions about the relation between individual and collective identity. Both bodies of poetry open a debate over the question of what constitutes a national poetry. Teaching the poems together puts both students' and faculty's political and disciplinary value systems in dialogue and potential conflict with one another. The resulting conversations can be a good way to think about literature itself and to enrich self-understanding and political understanding alike with poetic nuance.

I believe it is easier to conduct this conversation fairly, however, if you feel empathy for both peoples and believe that a political route must be found to honor both peoples' national aspirations. For a literature course, that aim can be fulfilled simply by teaching both bodies of poetry sympathetically. It is not necessary for a poetry or fiction course to commit to a given political solution, though a general sympathy for a two-state solution comports well with sympathetic readings of poems from both sides of the Israeli-Palestinian conflict. It is more difficult, conversely, to produce sympathetic readings of both peoples' poems if you believe that justice resides on only one side of the conflict. My aim in this essay has been to persuade by example, to show how the poetry can be taught. Although I do not like to exaggerate the effect that one course can have on students, I do hope that teaching the poetry this way can lead to greater political understanding. Perhaps such a course can also suggest what pedagogy can enrich and complicate campus debates that can otherwise be unproductively acrimonious.

Notes

Epigraphs: Rashid Hussein, "An Address," in *Enemy of the Sun: Poetry of Palestinian Resistance*, ed. Naseer Aruri and Edmund Ghareeb (Washington, DC: Drum and Spear, 1970), 14. In an effort to demonstrate that the poems it reprints constitute a collective movement, *Enemy of the Sun* takes the unusual step of listing authors' names in the table of contents but not including them with the poems themselves. Throughout this essay, I transcribe Arab poets' names using the English-language version that is most widely used, which may differ from the version used in some of the anthologies I cite. For a substantial biographical essay about Hussein, along with translations of ten of his poems and testimonials from both Arabs and Jews, see Kamal Boullata and Mirène Ghossein, eds., *The World of Rashid Hussein: A Palestinian Poet in Exile* (Detroit: Association of Arab-American University Graduates, 1979). Natan Zach, "Landscapes," in *The Static Element: Selected Poems of Natan Zach*, trans. Peter Everine and Shulamit Yasny-Starkman (New York: Atheneum, 1982), 71. Zach (1930–) was born in Berlin and came to Palestine in 1936. The poems published in *With an Iron Pen* and *No Rattling of Sabers* show him evolving into a critic of the occupation. See Zach, "On the Desire to Be Precise," in *No Rattling of Sabers: An Anthology of Israeli War Poetry*, trans. Esther Raizen (Austin, TX: Center for Middle Eastern Studies, 1995), 138–40; and "A Small Song for the Fallen," "Language," and "Good Intentions," in *With an Iron Pen: Twenty Years of Hebrew Protest Poetry*, ed. Tal Nitzan and Rachel Tzvia Back (Albany: State University of New York Press, 2009), 27, 31, 124–25. The subtitle in the Hebrew edition translates as "Hebrew Protest Poetry 1984–2004." The epigraphs I use evoke the diasporic histories that have shaped both peoples' identities.

1. Regarding the terms in this chapter's title, some Arab poets of Palestine are Israeli citizens, while others are not, though that is often a result of whether their families

remained in Israel or fled or were forced out during the 1948 war. If a family returned after a census was taken, they were not accepted as citizens. There is no meaningful thematic difference between poetry by Arab citizens of Israel and noncitizen Palestinians. There are thus overall two relevant bodies of poetry, not three. I often use "Palestinian" to describe both Arab-Israeli and noncitizen Arab poets of Palestine.

2. Daniel Weissbort's collection *Palestinian and Israeli Poets* (London: King's College London, University of London, 1999) is a valuable exception. Among its virtues is that it offers examples of Palestinian lyricism that include both political and nonpolitical poems, along with some whose political resonance is ambiguous. Equally valuable for demonstrating that lyricism and politics are not mutually exclusive alternatives is Jamal Assadi, ed. and trans., *The Story of a People: An Anthology of Palestinian Poets within the Green-Lines* (New York: Peter Lang, 2012).

3. Poems about Jerusalem are scattered among many of the collections cited here. It is useful, however, also to read a broader selection of Arab poetry and poetry from the Palestinian diaspora about Jerusalem. See Salma Khadra Jayyusi and Zafar Ishaq Ansari, eds., *My Jerusalem: Essays, Reminiscences, and Poems* (Northampton, MA: Olive Branch, 2005).

4. Michael Gluzman, *The Politics of Canonicity: Lines of Resistance in Modernist Hebrew Poetry* (Stanford, CA: Stanford University Press, 2003), 71.

5. Often in modern war, the quality of the poetry from one side of the conflict considerably outweighs that of the other. There was an awesome amount of German poetry produced in World War I, but it is the British poetry that has survived to become canonical. Compelling poetry about the Spanish Civil War in support of the Spanish Republic was written worldwide, but the fascist poetry of the other side is mostly forgotten. Both during and after World War II, the allies produced memorable poems, but Nazi poems are of interest only to see how they contribute to antisemitism and the adulation of Adolf Hitler.

6. Although distinctly successful and unsuccessful translations are worth comparing, my preference in teaching is often to provide students with all available translations of a given poem, even if that means comparing half a dozen translations. That can become a very focused exercise in close textual analysis.

7. I do not assume that the kind of comparative course I am proposing would have to be exclusively comparative. Some weeks could be devoted to only one of the bodies of poetry. A week on Holocaust poetry by Israeli Jews is one possibility. A week dealing with non-Palestinian Arab poetry is another. The Syrian poet Nizar Qabbani (1923–1998), for example, is often grouped with Palestinian poets because he too writes about Arab resistance and about the occupied territories. A section of the course could look more broadly at poetry engaging Arab nationalism.

8. I make no claim to be able to select the ideal representative poem for either poet; their output is simply too rich and varied for that. My choices are of suggestive texts that I wanted to discuss in this context.

9. A substantial number of alternative Amichai translations are available in the major collections cited below. The translation record for Darwish is more complicated, so it may be useful to note some of its highlights here. There are two full translations of Darwish's long poem sequence "A State of Siege" (2002): in Darwish, *The Butterfly's Burden*, trans. Fady Joudah (Port Townsend, WA: Copper Canyon, 2007); and as Darwish, *State of Siege*, trans. Munir Akash (Syracuse, NY: Syracuse University Press, 2010). Akash writes, "I publish this work to remedy the great harm done to *The State of Siege* in English" (x), but whether he is referring only to online versions or also to Joudah's I cannot say. *Mural* (2000) exists in three translations: in Mahmoud Darwish, *Unfortunately, It Was Paradise: Selected Poems*, trans. and ed. Munir Akash and Carolyn Forché (Berkeley: University of California Press, 2013); in *If I Were Another*, trans. Fady Joudah (New York: Farrar, Straus and Giroux, 2009); and as Darwish, *Mural*, trans. Rema Hammami and John Berger (London: Verso, 2009). Writing in the *Nation* on April 8, 2010, Jordan Davis writes, "'Mural' is remarkably sturdy. While neither of the new English versions—nor the one published in 2003 in *Unfortunately, It Was Paradise* . . . is completely satisfying (in fact, all are often frustratingly vague), the poem is nevertheless a tour de force" ("A Caller of the Dove," available at www.thenation.com/article/caller-dove/). Davis also compares Joudah's Darwish collection *If I Were Another* with Mohammed Shaheen's translation of *Almond Blossoms and Beyond* (Northampton, MA: Interlink, 2009): "Shaheen's versions are so much less cluttered, so much more moving, that it may take a few readings to recognize that Joudah is even referring to the same text. (Joudah: 'Dream / slowly . . . no matter how often you dream you'll realize / the butterfly didn't burn to illuminate you'; Shaheen: 'Dream slowly, / and, whatever you dream, understand / that the moth does not burn to give you light.')." On the other hand, Davis praises Joudah's work in *The Butterfly's Burden*. Darwish's *Why Did You Leave the Horse Alone* (1995) exists in three different versions as well, as an independent book translated by Jeffrey Sacks (New York: Archipelago, 2006) and later by Mohammed Shaheen (London: Hesperus, 2014) and as a partial translation in *Unfortunately, It Was Paradise*. A number of individual Darwish poems also exist in more than one version. His last poem, "The Dice Player," is included with the Hammami/Berger version of *Mural* and is also available in a Fady Joudah translation in *VQR* (Winter 2009), available at www.vqronline.org/vqr-symposium/dice-player.
10. For an analysis of the problematics and ambiguities that Arab-Israeli writers confront when they write in Hebrew, see Lital Levy, *Poetic Trespass: Writing between Hebrew and Arabic in Israel/Palestine* (Princeton, NJ: Princeton University Press, 2014).
11. The full poem by Darwish, "Those Who Pass between Fleeting Words," is available at the Middle East Research and Information Project, www.merip.org/mer/mer154/those-who-pass-between-fleeting-words.
12. In *Mahmoud Darwish: The Poet's Art and His Nation* (Syracuse, NY: Syracuse University Press, 2014), Khaled Mattawa comments on "the poems Darwish wrote in Israel before 1970, in which he actively attempts to understand Israelis. These poems provide

compelling portraits of Israeli characters and demonstrate exceptional empathy on his part. Giving the majority of their lines to the Israeli speakers, these poems engage Israeli characters in intimate dialogue, teasing out their vulnerabilities, aspirations, and contradictions" (54).

13. Mahmoud Darwish, "Rita's Winter," trans. Fady Joudah, in *If I Were Another*, 88–93. For an account of the gradual public acknowledgment of the relationship, see Muna Abu Eid, *Mahmoud Darwish: Literature and the Politics of Palestinian Identity* (New York: I. B. Tauris, 2016), 119–21. For an analysis of "Rita's Winter," see Angelika Neuwirth, "Hebrew Bible and Arabic Poetry: Mahmoud Darwish's Palestine—From Paradise Lost to a Homeland Made of Words," in *Mahmoud Darwish: Exile's Poet*, ed. Hala Khamis Nassar and Najat Rahman (Northampton, MA: Olive Branch, 2008), 167–90.

14. I quote the second stanza of "Identity Card" from *Mahmoud Darwish: Selected Poems*, trans. Ian Wedde and Fawwaz Tuqan (Cheadle, UK: Carcanet, 1973), 24, but there are many different translations available. That accounts for the slightly different version of the refrain that I use earlier in the paragraph. Darwish uses details of his own father's life to create the image of a universal Arab worker. The speaker is notably an Arab, not a Palestinian, because the Palestinian liberation movement had not yet coalesced. Darwish revised the poem, moderating its Marxist character. After leaving Israel in 1971, he refused to perform "Identity Card" at readings, despite endless requests to do so, but the poem was set to music and continued to be heard for years nonetheless.

15. Mahmoud Darwish, "The girl / The scream," in *A River Dies of Thirst*, trans. Catherine Cobham (New York: Archipelago, 2009), 3.

16. See Yehuda Amichai, *The Selected Poetry of Yehuda Amichai*, trans Chana Bloch and Stephen Mitchell (Berkeley: University of California Press, 2013); Amichai, *Poems*, trans. Assia Gutmann (New York: Harper and Row, 1968); and Amichai, *Yehuda Amichai: A Life of Poetry 1948–1994*, trans. Benjamin Harshav and Barbara Harshav (New York: HarperCollins, 1994). The Gutmann translation is reprinted in *The Early Books of Yehuda Amichai*, trans. Yehuda Amichai, Assia Gutmann, and Ted Hughes (Riverdale-on-Hudson, NY: Sheep Meadow, 1988).

17. I take the liberty here of substituting "words," from both the Bloch and Mitchell translation in *The Selected Poetry of Yehuda Amichai* and the Harshav translation in *Yehuda Amichai: A Life of Poetry*, for "things" from the version by Gutmann because I think "words" carries the implication more effectively in English. In the Harshav version (p. 8), the "twisting channels" are "sinuous channels" (line 4), and the "immune chauffeurs" are "burly chauffeurs" (line 6).

18. Yehuda Amichai, "Jerusalem, 1967," in *The Poetry of Yehuda Amichai*, ed. Robert Alter (New York: Farrar, Straus and Giroux, 2015), 83.

19. The poem is included in *The Selected Poetry of Yehuda Amichai*, trans. Bloch and Mitchell, 165–66, but not in Alter's *The Poetry of Yehuda Amichai*. I prefer the new translation by Kronfeld and Bloch from Chana Kronfeld's *The Full Severity of Compassion: The*

Poetry of Yehuda Amichai (Stanford, CA: Stanford University Press, 2015), 55–57, which is what I quote from here (57). *The Full Severity of Compassion* includes Kronfeld's analysis.

20. See Kronfeld, *Full Severity of Compassion*, 55–59 (quote on 56).
21. See Darwish, *Unfortunately, It Was Paradise*; Mahmoud Darwish, Samih al-Qasim, and Adonis, *Victims of a Map: A Bilingual Anthology of Arabic Poetry*, trans Abdullah al-Udhari (London: Saqi Books, 1984); and Reuven Snir, "'Other Barbarians Will Come': Intertextuality, Meta-Poetry, and Meta-Myth in Mahmoud Darwish's Poetry," in Nassar and Rahman, *Mahmoud Darwish: Exile's Poet*, 143.
22. See Adam Kirsch, "Amichai: The Tolerant Irony of Israel's National Poet," *Tablet*, December 21, 2015, www.tabletmag.com/jewish-arts-and-culture/books/195955/amichai-israels-national-poet.
23. See Amichai, *Yehuda Amichai: A Life of Poetry 1948–1994*; Amichai, *Poems of Jerusalem and Love Poems* (Riverdale-on-Hudson, NY: Sheep Meadow, 1992); Amichai, *Amen*, trans. Amichai and Ted Hughes (New York: Harper and Row, 1977); and Glenda Abramson, *The Writing of Yehuda Amichai: A Thematic Approach* (Albany: State University of New York Press, 1989). *Amen* uses the title "Patriotic Songs" for "Songs of Zion the Beautiful."
24. In addition to the several selected poems devoted to Amichai cited here, there are two other translations of note: his *Time*, trans. Yehuda Amichai (New York: Harper and Row, 1979), includes all eighty poems from the original 1978 book, whereas Alter selects thirty-five; his *A Great Tranquility: Questions and Answers*, trans. Glenda Abramson and Tudor Parfitt (Riverdale-on-Hudson, NY: Sheep Meadow, 1997), translates all seventy-five poems from the original 1980 book, whereas the Alter collection selects thirty-three.
25. Abdullah al-Edhari's *Modern Poetry of the Arab World* (Middlesex, UK: Penguin, 1986) happily provides first dates of publication for all the poems included, among them fourteen early poems by Darwish and six by al-Qasim. Ian Wedde and Fawwaz Tuqan's *Mahmoud Darwish: Selected Poems* includes thirty poems from the 1960s and nine from 1970, with dates of first book publication supplied. Denys Johnson-Davies's *The Music of Human Flesh: Mahmoud Darwish* (London: Heinemann, 1980) translates thirty-five poems from the 1960s and 1970s, none of them dated, though most can be dated from other sources. Rana Kabbani's *Sand and Other Poems: Mahmoud Darweesh* (London: KPI, 1986) translates twenty-two undated poems from 1985 or earlier. Munir Akash's *Mahmoud Darwish: The Adam of Two Edens* (Syracuse, NY: Syracuse University Press, 2000) translates one poem from 1989 and twelve from 1990–95, though none of them are dated in the book itself. Aruri and Ghareeb's *Enemy of the Sun* translates fifteen undated Darwish poems from the 1960s, while *The Palestinian Wedding: A Bilingual Anthology of Contemporary Palestinian Resistance Poetry*, ed. and trans. A. M. Elmessiri (Washington, DC: Three Continents, 1982), translates ten undated early Darwish poems. Ben Bennai's *Psalms: Poems by Mahmoud Darwish* (Colorado Springs: Three Continents, 1994) translates a seventeen-poem sequence from 1977. Darwish's *I Don't*

Want This Poem to End: Early and Late Poems (Northampton, MA: Interlink, 2017), translated by Mohammed Shaheen, includes thirty-three early poems but does not identify their sources. Khadra Jayyusi's *Modern Arabic Poetry: An Anthology* (New York: Columbia University Press, 1987) is very useful for placing Palestinian poetry in a broader Arab poetic context, but its Darwish selection of four poems, two only excerpts and only one not available elsewhere, is not very helpful.

There is also disagreement among critics about whether *Birds without Wings* (1960) or *Leaves of the Olive Trees* (1964) should be treated as Darwish's first book, since Darwish himself effectively disavowed *Birds without Wings* and did not include it in his first collected poems, issued in 1973. That is why some list *Leaves of the Olive Trees* as his first book, a practice that seems unnecessarily misleading. Wedde and Tuqan explicitly translate two poems from the 1960 collection to open their selected poems (*Mahmoud Darwish: Selected Poems*). Are we to count them as mistaken?

One very important warning to students and teachers: do not assume that your library owns the books necessary to study Israeli or Palestinian poetry. Many do not. A number of the books I have cited are out of print, and a few are rare. A good source of used and out-of-print books, www.abebooks.com, listed only one copy of *The Music of Human Flesh* in January 2017; the price was $2,000.

26. The poems are "A Soldier Dreams of White Tulips" (1967), "As Fate Would Have It" (1977), and "Four Personal Addresses" (1985). The last of these is a prose poem.
27. Ilana Szobel, *A Poetics of Trauma: The Work of Dahlia Ravikovitch* (Waltham, MA: Brandeis University Press, 2013), 121.
28. Dahlia Ravikovitch, "The Horns of Hitin," in *Hovering at a Low Altitude: The Collected Poetry of Dahlia Ravikovitch*, trans. Chana Bloch and Chana Kronfeld (New York: Norton, 2009), 217. All subsequent quotations from Ravikovitch's poetry are from this collection and are cited parenthetically in the text. For a critical introduction to her poetry and a substantial group of translations, also see Yair Mazo, *Broken Twig: The Poetry of Dalia Ravikovich and Modern Hebrew Poetry* (Milwaukee, WI: Maven Mark Books, 2013). Groups of very good alternative translations are available in Warren Bargad and Stanley F. Chyet, eds. and trans., *Israeli Poetry: A Contemporary Anthology* (Bloomington: Indiana University Press, 1986); and in Tsipi Keller, ed. and trans., *Poets on the Edge: An Anthology of Contemporary Hebrew Poetry* (Albany: State University of New York Press, 2008).
29. See Taha Muhammad Ali, *So What: New and Selected Poems, 1971–2005*, trans. Peter Cole, Yahya Hijazi, and Gabriel Levin (Port Townsend, WA: Copper Canyon, 2006). Ali dated a number of his poems, which enables us to place them in specific historical contexts. All subsequent quotations from Ali's poetry are from this collection and are cited parenthetically in the text.
30. Aharon Shabtai, *J'Accuse*, trans. Peter Cole (New York: New Directions, 2003), 5. Unless otherwise noted, all subsequent quotations from Shabtai's poetry come from this collection and are cited parenthetically in the text.

31. Aharon Shabtai, "2006," in *War & Love / Love & War*, trans. Peter Cole (New York: New Directions, 2010), 37.
32. Moshe Dor and Barbara Goldberg, eds., *After the First Rain: Israeli Poems on War and Peace* (Syracuse, NY: Syracuse University Press, 1998). Subsequent quotations from this collection are cited parenthetically in the text.
33. Dvora Amir, "Woodcut of a Landscape," in Nitzan and Back, *With an Iron Pen*, 34. Subsequent quotations from this collection are cited parenthetically in the text.
34. The biographical notes section of *With an Iron Pen* says, "Dahlia Falah is a pen name, and details of her personal life are a secret closely guarded by her publisher" (151).
35. Neither the book's biographical notes nor various internet sites offer a birth date for Tal Nitzan.
36. Samih al-Qasim, *Sadder than Water: New and Selected Poems*, trans. Nazih Kassis (Jerusalem: Ibis Editions, 2006), 65.
37. Rashid Hussein, "Tent #50 (Song of a Refugee)," in Aruri and Ghareeb, *Enemy of the Sun*, 11.
38. Tawfiq Zayyad, "Cuba," in Aruri and Ghareeb, *Enemy of the Sun*, 123.
39. Fouzi El-Asmar, "The Wandering Reed," in Elmessiri, *Palestinian Wedding*, 107.
40. Anton Shammas, "Prisoner of Sleeping and Waking," in Weissbort, *Palestinian and Israeli Poets*, 37.
41. Rashid Hussein, "At Zero Hour," in Elmessiri, *Palestinian Wedding*, 179.
42. Harun Hashim Rasheed, "We Will Return One Day," in Weissbort, *Palestinian and Israeli Poets*, 160.
43. Salim Jubran, "A Refugee," in Assadi, *Story of a People*, 137.
44. Mourid Barghouti, "The Balcony," in Weissbort, *Palestinian and Israeli Poets*, 61.
45. Rashid Hussein, "Remainder," in Assadi, *Story of a People*, 116.
46. Salim Makhuli, "Once We Found Ourselves," in Assadi, *Story of a People*, 164.
47. 'Abd Al-Karim Al-Sab'awi, "Three Poems to Palestine," in Elmessiri, *Palestinian Wedding*, 165.
48. Tawfiq Zayyad, "On the Trunk of an Olive Tree," in Elmessiri, *Palestinian Wedding*, 57.
49. Salma Khadra Jayyusi, "Dearest Love II," in Elmessiri, *Palestinian Wedding*, 77.
50. Tawfiq Zayyad, "The Skull Harvest," in Aruri and Ghareeb, *Enemy of the Sun*, 8.
51. Rashid Hussein, "Jerusalem . . . And the Hour," in Kamal Boullata and Mirène Ghossein, *World of Rashid Hussein: A Palestinian Poet in Exile* (Detroit: Association of Arab-American University Graduates, 1979), 168.
52. Tawfiq Zayyad, "Taxation," in Aruri and Ghareeb, *Enemy of the Sun*, 93.
53. See Samih al-Qasim, *All Faces but Mine: The Poetry of Samih al-Qasim*, trans. Abdulwahid Lu'lu'a (Syracuse, NY: Syracuse University Press, 2015). Also see Aruri and Ghareeb, *Enemy of the Sun*; Elmessiri, *Palestinian Wedding*; and Darwish, al-Qasim, and Adonis, *Victims of a Map*.
54. As it happens, there is a recent anthology of Palestinian poetry so apolitical that it leaves the remarkable impression that no Palestinian ever wrote a protest poem or

a poem on any other political subject: *A Bird Is Not a Stone: An Anthology of Contemporary Palestinian Poetry*, ed. Henry Bell and Sarah Irving (Glasgow, UK: Freight Books, 2014).

55. For surveys of Israeli and Palestinian poetry, respectively, through 1990 or the early 1980s, see Stanley Burnshaw, T. Carmi, Susan Glassman, Ariel Hirschfeld, and Ezra Spicehandler, eds., *The Modern Hebrew Poem Itself: A New and Updated Edition* (Detroit: Wayne State University Press, 2003); and Khalid A. Sulaiman, *Palestine and Modern Arab Poetry* (London: Zed Books, 1984). *The Modern Hebrew Poem Itself* offers close readings of 105 poems plus a forty-page summary history. *Palestine and Modern Arab Poetry* includes valuable coverage of Arab treatments of key issues by poets outside Palestine. For an analysis of the changing cultural, political, and rhetorical options available to Palestinian poets from the 1950s through the first forty years of the occupation, see Khaled Furani, *Silencing the Sea: Secular Rhythms in Palestinian Poetry* (Stanford, CA: Stanford University Press, 2012).
56. Eid, *Mahmoud Darwish*, 135.
57. Michael Gluzman provides both the Hebrew original and an English translation of "Passover on Caves" in his *Politics of Canonicity*, 173–80. His fifth chapter offers a detailed analysis of the poem and a history of its reception.
58. Hanna Abu Hanna, "The Desire's Squint," in Assadi, *Story of a People*, 22.
59. See Chaim Nahman Bialik, *Songs from Bialik: Selected Poems of Hayim Nahman Bialik*, ed. and trans. Atar Hadari (Syracuse, NY: Syracuse University Press, 2000); and Bialik, *C. N. Bialik: Selected Poems*, ed. and trans. David Aberbach (New York: Overlook Duckworth, 2004).
60. See Rachel, *Flowers of Perhaps*, trans. Robert Friend (New Milford, CT: Toby, 2008).

Dual Narrative Learning

EXPERIENTIAL EDUCATION IN PALESTINE/ISRAEL

OREN KROLL-ZELDIN

Beyond Bridges: Israel-Palestine (BBIP) is a three-week immersion program in Palestine and Israel that takes university students of all backgrounds to the Middle East on a journey of comparative conflict analysis and conflict transformation. Combining rigorous academics and practical hands-on training, this study-abroad course allows students to explore questions at the core of all conflicts. The program creates spaces for both personal and collective growth, helping students gain new understandings of the roles they play in international conflicts and how this relates to their social and political identities.

One summer during the program, I went with a group of students to Independence Hall in Tel Aviv. Independence Hall is an Israeli national museum dedicated to teaching visitors about the historic signing of Israel's Declaration of Independence. Each visit to the museum begins with a short documentary video telling the history of the building on the famed Rothschild Boulevard, which was once the house of the Tel Aviv mayor Meir Dizengoff and later an art museum. The video also gives a short history of the founding of the city of Tel Aviv and a brief explanation of the accomplishments of the Zionist movement between its founding and the United Nations partition plan in 1947. In the final minutes of the video, museum visitors see footage of David Ben Gurion declaring the state's independence, followed by a short description of the Zionist narrative of the 1948 war. Immediately after the conclusion of the video, visitors are ushered into the basement of the building, which has been re-created and preserved to look exactly as it did when Israel declared its independence on May 14, 1948.

At the end of the presentation in the museum on the day I brought the group of students, the docent asked everyone to stand while "Hatikvah," Israel's national anthem, played on the speaker system, reproducing the very events that made the building a destination for tourists in Israel. Most of the students I brought to the museum that day found this to be a strange and uncomfortable request. The cultural and ethnic identities of participants in the program were diverse and included Jewish Americans, Arab Americans, and students of Palestinian descent. When they were asked to stand for "Hatikvah," the students were forced to make a quick decision: to stand or not. Would they stand because they were asked to or because they support Israel? Would they refuse to stand up because they had visited a Palestinian refugee camp the day before and struggled to reconcile what they learned from the refugees with what they were exposed to at the museum? The awkward tension among the students was palpable and provided opportunities for rich reflection later that day and for the remainder of the program. Notably, none of the Palestinian or Arab students stood. As an act of solidarity with their Palestinian classmates, some non-Arab students also refused to stand, while others rose at the docent's request. Every single Jewish student rose to their feet during "Hatikvah."

Later that week, after a day of travel in the northern West Bank, the group walked through Qalandiya checkpoint, an Israeli military checkpoint separating Ramallah from Jerusalem. While standing in line to be checked, the group saw an old man trying to cross the checkpoint into Jerusalem. We learned that he had an Israeli permit to enter the city and was meeting family members that night because the following morning he was scheduled to have eye surgery in a Jerusalem hospital. The guard at the checkpoint yelled aggressively at the old man, pointing his gun into the old man's chest, telling him that he could not pass through the checkpoint. Despite the fact that he had a permit and that the guard had already allowed the man's son to pass through the checkpoint, the guard continued his intense verbal assault on the old man. The students watched intently as the man turned around and walked away from Jerusalem, head down and tears in his eyes, unable to cross the checkpoint.

After the old man was denied entry to Jerusalem, the students, all of whom possess U.S. passports, were easily waived through the checkpoint without any difficulty. It was a critical reminder to the students of their own privilege. Why could they, as citizens of the United States, pass through the checkpoint to go to a city they do not necessarily "need" while this old man was denied entry into Jerusalem, a city he relied on for a variety of basic services? How does confronting the lived experiences of Palestinians help students understand the realities of life under occupation? In what ways might that experience shape the students' political awareness and their commitments to conflict transformation? Much like the visit to Independence Hall, the experience crossing Qalandiya checkpoint served as a foundation for critical reflection for the remainder of the program.

These vignettes demonstrate the varied encounters that students have daily while immersing themselves in the complexities of the Palestinian-Israeli conflict. In particular, they provide a critical lens through which to understand the long-standing conflict on a deeply personal level. The diverse perspectives that students observed during these experiences get at the core objective of the program: engaging with multiple narratives in order to make sense of everyday life in Palestine and Israel. Through these encounters, students learned the value of dual narrative learning in ways that challenged them to understand and empathize with the experiences of others through their own, very different lived experiences.

These encounters illustrate the possibilities for learning when confronting the everyday lives of Jewish Israelis and Palestinians. The disparate nature of these two experiences helps students grasp the complexity of the conflict and illustrates the diversity and complexity of everyday life in Palestine and Israel. Not only did these two experiences teach certain elements of the dominant narratives of each community, but they also served as a platform to connect the students' multilayered social identities with the personal and political lives of Palestinians and Jewish Israelis. Furthermore, the unpredictable nature of learning in the field, as exemplified by the disquieting experiences students had at the museum and the checkpoint, encourages students to push the limits of their comfort. In the process, they learn how to ethically participate in and critically respond to possibilities of conflict transformation.

Overview of Beyond Bridges: Israel-Palestine

Beyond Bridges: Israel-Palestine, an immersion program organized by the Center for Global Education at the University of San Francisco, teaches students about the Palestinian-Israeli conflict through travel, workshops, presentations, and group process. During the program, students travel from the program base in Jerusalem throughout Palestine and Israel, meeting with Palestinian and Israeli scholars, activists, and NGOs while also visiting historical, cultural, political, and religious sites that are important to both national groups. These site visits include tours as well as lectures and presentations that cover a wide range of political perspectives, exposing students to as much of the complexities of the conflict as possible within the span of a short, three-week educational program.

From a pedagogical perspective, BBIP is rooted in two main theoretical frameworks: comparative conflict analysis and social identity theory. By taking a comparative approach, BBIP deexceptionalizes this conflict by emphasizing the ways in which certain key themes—such as competing narratives, violence, nationalism, and power—are reproduced in various societies and other conflicts globally. This serves to illustrate for students the possibilities of conflict transformation and encourages them to think about how similar issues may become manifest in their own communities. The second theoretical framework, social identity theory, focuses on the ways individuals' multilayered social identities give them affinity to a particular group while simultaneously informing their beliefs, values, and actions. BBIP, by rooting its approach in social identity theory, helps students explore the roles they play in the Palestinian-Israeli conflict as well as new understandings of how practices of their identities are linked to other social, cultural, and political issues in the world.

During BBIP, students have a wide range of experiences that are meant to expose them to as much of the complexities of the conflict as possible in such a short time. For example, during the program, students visit a Palestinian refugee camp and a Jewish Israeli settlement in the West Bank to meet with both refugees and settlers; go to the Mahmoud Darwish Museum and Yasser Arafat's mausoleum; tour Yad Vashem, Israel's Holocaust memorial museum, and meet with a Shoah (Holocaust) survivor and visit the adjacent Mount Herzl military cemetery; swim in the Mediterranean and Dead Seas; tour a destroyed Bedouin village; meet with a founder of the Israeli Black Panthers, a politician in the Palestinian Authority, and a staffer for an Israeli member of Knesset; and visit religious and historical sites in Jerusalem's Old City. These patchwork experiences "expose students to multiple narratives, cultures, histories, communal truths, and political ideologies, enabling them to draw on the experiences" of those who live the Palestinian-Israeli conflict every day.[1]

In addition to the site visits and presentations, students attend workshops led by BBIP educators that provide the academic backbone of the program. These workshops focus on key themes in the Palestinian-Israeli conflict and teach students about topics such as local history, theories of conflict transformation, gender in society, and the role of the media in international conflict. Lastly, the group-process sessions provide the critical pedagogical opportunity for students to debrief and deconstruct their thoughts and feelings about what they experience every day during the program. Group process is a facilitated dialogue in which students are encouraged to "reflect on their social backgrounds, socialization processes, and systems of knowledge production" in order to help them make sense of their experiences and challenges them to articulate the struggle of learning about the Palestinian-Israeli conflict experientially.[2] Though students are often exhausted by the program's grueling schedule and are initially resistant to the dialogue sessions, in many ways, group process is the most important and successful element of the program, and data from postprogram student evaluations show that students value group process more than they do most other elements of BBIP.[3]

Dual Narrative Learning

I have been involved with close to a dozen peer or educational trips to Israel or Palestine in the more than quarter century since I first visited Israel with my family.

On the basis of those various and disparate experiences, most of which were quite transformative for me personally, politically, and professionally, I believe that BBIP is the most pedagogically interesting and successful educational program in teaching students about the complexities of everyday life in Palestine/Israel and providing a deep understanding of the Palestinian-Israeli conflict. The program's success is predicated on its commitment to a dual narrative approach and its steadfast refusal to engage in any type of advocacy, focusing instead on giving students the tools to critically analyze their perceptions of the conflict.

For example, a visit to a Palestinian refugee camp has tremendous educational value on its own, but it takes on a different meaning when program participants also visit a Jewish Israeli settlement a few kilometers away. Similarly, learning about the Shoah from a half-day visit to Yad Vashem and meeting with a Shoah survivor is a deeply powerful and moving experience. But understanding the impacts of the Shoah on the contemporary political situation in Palestine/Israel is more transformative when students also hear about it from a former Palestinian militant and political prisoner who is now a prominent nonviolent activist. In this particular case, the Palestinian activist with whom students met saw a movie about the Shoah while in Israeli prison and cried when he learned about what happened to Jews during World War II. Juxtaposing the narratives and experiences of Palestinians and Jewish Israelis does not bridge these narratives but rather opens space for the students to critically reflect on the complexities of competing narratives and identities in the conflict.

The location of the program's base at a hostel in Palestinian East Jerusalem, steps away from the walls of Jerusalem's Old City and a short walk from the central downtown area in Jewish West Jerusalem, illustrates the learning potential of the program's unplanned activities. An East Jerusalem program base is strategic and rooted in BBIP's pedagogical underpinnings in dual narrative experiential education. Additionally, some of the most valuable dual narrative learning opportunities for the students occur after official program hours. Safety permitting, BBIP staff encourage students to explore Jerusalem's nightlife in both the eastern and western sections of the city. When debriefing the day with their friends while sitting in local bars or cafes, students often report that other patrons at the establishment overhear their conversations and ask questions about why the students chose to visit Palestine/Israel, which leads to long conversations with people who live the conflict every day. These extracurricular conversations with locals complement the program itinerary well, and students frequently bring what they learned to group discussions the following day. Each exploration outside formal group programming is possible both because students are encouraged to explore on their own and because the location of the program base makes it possible to engage in after-hours dual narrative learning that challenges students to work through what they think when interacting with locals. In this regard, the immersion element of BBIP is multifaceted, with both planned and unplanned activities that collectively provide students with a unique experience to engage with everyday life in Palestine/Israel.

Students cross the invisible Green Line every day, enabling rich discussions about the differences between Jewish Israeli and Palestinian societies as well as the impacts of the cleavages in Jerusalem on both societies. These late nights do not merely provide the necessary opportunity to decompress but are pedagogically rich as well because they offer yet another occasion to experience the lived realities of Palestinians and Israelis. They also enable students to hear from more diverse Palestinian and Jewish Israeli voices, which sometimes reinforce what others have said and sometimes completely contradict what students have learned earlier in the program. This adds to students' understanding of the complexity of the Palestinian-Israeli conflict, leading to more questions and fewer answers.

Final Thoughts

The stories at the outset of this chapter demonstrate the power and possibilities for dual narrative learning, particularly through immersion in the field. Beyond Bridges: Israel-Palestine is a successful educational program because it is committed to engaging with diverse narratives and exposes students to the deep societal divisions that are integral to the intractable nature of the conflict. It gives students the tools to grapple with the educational material not only intellectually but also experientially, thereby enabling a deeper engagement with the complexities of everyday life for Palestinians and Israelis. Furthermore, it allows students to meet people and travel to places they likely would not visit on their own, while providing the space to analyze and deconstruct their learning. BBIP alumni always return to campus and their home communities transformed by what they experienced.

I recently reached out to a few program alumni and asked what specific moments they remembered most about the summer they participated in BBIP. Remarkably, many of them recalled the visit to Independence Hall and the walk through Qalandiya checkpoint. This indicates how impactful those experiences were not only in the moment but many years later as well. One marker of the success of Beyond Bridges: Israel-Palestine as an educational program is the transformative experiences and memories it provides the students. But memories and transformation are important only insofar as they inspire change in individuals and in their community. Personal change is integral to conflict transformation, and BBIP provides the opportunities for students to radically alter the ways they understand and interact with the world.

Notes

1. Aaron J. Hahn Tapper, and Oren Kroll-Zeldin, "Paulo Freire and the Israeli-Palestinian Conflict: The Pedagogy of a Social Justice and Experiential Educational Program in Israel and Palestine," *Revista Internacional de Educación para la Justicia Social* 4, no. 1 (2015): 79.
2. Ibid., 78.
3. Ibid.

A Course on Zionism and the Novel

RUSSELL A. BERMAN

As we in higher education enter into a new period of politicization and activism, the question of the Middle East or, more narrowly, Israel and Palestine is a particular focus of attention. Students and faculty bring passionate engagement to various positions within this debate, while—in addition to the substantive issues about the region—the academic community faces fundamental questions concerning activism and scholarship, politicization in the university, and the implications for learning: Does a pedagogy of active learning imply an obligation to activism? What does critical theory have to say about critical thinking? Should instructors engage in advocacy in the classroom? And what is the responsibility of scholarship in this terrain?

Scholarship implies expertise but also an obligation to learn more; and it involves the willingness to connect expertise and research with teaching and learning. I chose to combine my expertise in the novel as genre with the intention of responding to students' interest in Israel and Palestine. On the broadest level, my goals for the course involve both enabling students to become better readers of literature and encouraging them to think more complexly about the conflict. It is possible to pursue both pedagogic agenda points, aesthetic and political, but only if one points both of them out to students and reminds them of the tension between them.

My undergraduate seminar "Zionism and the Novel" is designed specifically for sophomores and counts toward the comparative literature major. However, it attracts students at all undergraduate levels, including many with no intention of pursuing comparative literature. I was disappointed when it initially drew only small numbers of students, but when I redesigned it to meet a writing and rhetoric requirement, it attracted nearly fifty applicants, for a course with a normal target of fourteen. To fulfill this particular requirement, the course expects each student to write three essays, of increasing length, and, in each case, to submit drafts, on which I provide extensive comments, prior to preparing a final version. In addition, each student must make two ten-minute oral presentations on the reading assignments. These presentations are very productive for classroom discussion because they allow students to respond to each other, rather than to interact in a binary mode with the instructor. When discussion stalls, I divide the group into small groups of three or four students, pose a topic for them all to address, and after ten minutes, ask for reports from each group. This strategy regularly moves the discussion forward.

The course has multiple learning goals. In addition to the focus on writing and rhetoric, the course emphasizes the opportunity to develop an appreciation of literature and to empower students to become more intelligent readers of novels: I see this as the core ambition of the field. However, the course also enables students to address aspects of the Middle East debate, through encounters with complex material and within the conventions of classroom discussion. That final goal is of paramount importance: equipping students with the ability to talk about the conflict from various perspectives while maintaining respect and civility.

The course includes novels by a diverse set of authors, from the diaspora and from Israel, Jews and Arabs, Europeans, Israelis, and Americans. I had to make pragmatic selections with an eye to the constraints of the quarter system as well as to realistic assumptions concerning the amount of reading students might truly complete. As much as I would have liked to begin with George Eliot's *Daniel Deronda*, I determined that it was too long and too distant from students' interest areas. I had to find more accessible texts that would provide students with positive reading experiences, enabling them to grow as readers. Of course, I was limited to texts originally in English or available in English translation.

At the outset of the course, I provide some historical background to Zionism through programmatic documents, both from the Zionist movement and from the Arab opposition to it, but I do not pretend that the course is the full-fledged historical account that a professional historian might provide. The difference between these types of texts, historical documents and literary narratives, allows for a discussion of the relative value of works of art versus political evidence as representations of the complexity of human experience. Novels are typically richer in their descriptions, but their fictionality could be judged a form of escape from the hard facts of political life. In any case, my own disciplinary access to the topic of Zionism is primarily via the study of the novel, and the only way for scholars of literature to address topical political matters in a responsible way is through their particular scholarly expertise, not by pretending to be historians or political scientists.

To set up the course, I also introduce a small amount of relevant theory and connect it to the problem of the material at hand, Zionism in novels. Especially for the aspiring literature majors, this dimension of the course is important. The novel as genre is the epic form of modernity, and if the ancient epic the *Odyssey* described the aspiration to return home, for the foundational theoretician of the novel Georg Lukács, the novel traces the modern protagonist's path in a context of "transcendental homelessness."[1] An irreducible disjunction between the subject and society leaves its trace in any serious novel, so—excepting in the case of kitsch—the novel displays a scar of alienation or an ironic distance or the irritatingly skewed perspective of a foregrounded narrator. This Lukácsian account of the novel as an expression of homelessness stands, it would seem, at odds with the Zionist aspiration for a homeland and, behind that, the attempt to erase the antisemitic imperative that the Jew must always be wandering, never at home. If the novel, as genre, records an ineluctable alienation as the fate of modernity, then the Zionist promise of return appears untenable, since one can never be at home. By the same token, however, a narrative of a Palestinian homeland appears equally regressive from the vantage point of this theory of modernity that implies the anachronism of any paradigm of a nation-state.

This conflict between at least one, highly influential theory of the novel and the politics of homecoming lays out a provocative field in which to discuss the novel and Zionism—perhaps all the more provocative because the founding figures of political Zionism were themselves novelists. I make reference to Theodor Herzl's *Altneuland* (1902) and Ze'ev Jabotinsky's *The Five* (1935), although they are not on the reading list for the course: the former lacks in literary quality, and the latter is only in a very indirect way connected to Zionism.[2] In the novels that we do examine, one finds much less a utopian fulfillment of the Zionist program than the modern, which is to say problematic, character of life in the Zionist context. Ultimately, the selected works are more novelistic, that is, complex and self-questioning, than they are tendentious expressions of political advocacy. This question of the relation of politics to the novel can be addressed very effectively with classic authors of Israeli literature: the course regularly includes A. B. Yehoshua's *Mr. Mani*, but the students also read the contemporary graphic novelist Rutu Modan's *Exit Wounds*, which has proven very effective in providing an opportunity to explore the relationship between image and word.[3] Other works on the syllabus engage students both as literature and as opportunities to evaluate the politics. I will comment on four that have been especially successful.

A. M. Klein's *The Second Scroll* (1951) explores the confluence of the catastrophe of the Second World War with the messianic and scriptural traditions of Judaism, which define the formal structure of the book: the titles of the five main chapters repeat the order of the Pentateuch, from Genesis to Deuteronomy, and a series of seemingly Talmudic glosses follows the main text. It combines ancient form and contemporary content in a modernism reminiscent of Joyce, on whom Klein was an expert. It raises central questions about the position of Zionism in Jewish history, while giving students the opportunity to work with a relatively short but formally complex text that is rich in cultural-historical allusions.

The novel recounts the travels of the protagonist from a Canadian-Jewish community via postwar Europe and through the oppressiveness of the Jewish ghetto in Casablanca to the young State of Israel, as he searches for his uncle, Melech Davidson, or, to translate that name, the king (*melech*) from the House of David, an indication of messianic status. At stake, then, is the ambiguity of the Zionist experience at the moment of the founding of the state: what had once been a thoroughly secular, indeed often socialist, political movement is reread through religious eyes in the aftermath of the trauma of the Shoah.

For students, the gap between the narrator/protagonist and his elusive uncle offers an exercise in probing the formal structure of narrative. About to leave Canada for Israel, Klein's narrator receives a mailing from the long-lost uncle, now a displaced person himself about to leave Europe for Israel, who provides a description of the Nazi atrocities in the family's hometown of Ratno in Ukraine. Characteristically, Klein places these killings in a specifically religious frame, a grotesque repetition of Judaism in a murderous but also modernist inversion, directed by "a young lieutenant who, it soon appeared, prided himself on being a specialist in Semitic affairs": "How shall I tell you, how shall I bring myself to write down, the abominations which took place that day! The Scroll of the Law was polluted: between its rods upon the parchment an infant was set and then tossed in the air—the specialist shouted: '*Hagba*'—was allowed to fall to the ground, its skull cracked crying: 'Father!' Our women were made to strip and circle the room—*hakafos*, explained the specialist—while the soldiery indulged in their obscene jests; and our men were each in turn called up to the improvised pulpit—*aliyoth*, said the authority—to receive their beard-pluckings and blows."[4] In passages such as this and throughout this novel in particular, one needs to explain Jewish liturgical references. The challenge is worth it: there is a significant cohort of contemporary students, Jewish and non-Jewish, with strong curiosity for topics of religion and spirituality.

Here, the liturgical enactment of atrocity is both a desecration and an effort at an interpretation through the invocation of sacred tradition. This framework enables Melech, in the conclusion of the letter, to imbue the departure of the survivors, the displaced Jews leaving Europe for the Middle East, with a messianic content evident even in the colors of the natural world, as he is about to leave from Bari to Haifa: "Already there come to this harbor the rescuing ships of the Israeli navy. . . . I stand on the shore here watching them, it is my one engrossing vision. Before me there extend the waters of the Mediterranean—blue; and its foam—white; an Israeli flag. Above me there stretches the Mediterranean sky—blue; and its clouds—white: an Israeli banner" (33–34). The visual appearance of creation names the fact of divine rescue, rather than military strength. On the contrary, Melech dismisses the power of secular navies: "Oh, let the nations of the world keep their mighty armadas" (34). Instead, the makeshift

Israeli fleet, "these overhauled corvettes, these leaking tubs, these discarded bottoms," are incomparable, "for they carry a cargo unknown to the annals of the sea—a cargo of re-membered bones—and to the last landfall they make their way—a Navy of redemption" (34).

The formal status of the passage involves a letter within the novel, itself a first-person narration, a textual organization that draws attention to competing perspectives and subjectivities. If Melech, at the point of the letter writing, choses a religious idiom and a theological framework, we also have learned that he had previously undergone an emphatically Marxist phase, which had come to a definitive end at the moment of the Hitler-Stalin pact, explicitly denounced in the text. His discourse shows a competition between secular and sacred interpretations of the Jewish condition, and therefore alternative readings of the dialectic of Shoah and aliyah, in the departure for Israel.

The richness of that hermeneutic project virtually explodes in the third appendix, "Gloss Gimel," a passage from another letter by Melech that he had written in Rome on his way to Bari, titled "On First Seeing the Ceiling of the Sistine Chapel." The passage exercises a particular fascination for students. What Klein provides here is a fictional piece of art criticism, an essay by Melech that reflects an interpretive acumen that hybridizes his Talmudic, Marxist, and messianic backgrounds. In Michaelangelo's depictions of creation, the Holocaust survivor finds a prophetic account of catastrophe: "In vain did Buonarotti seek to confine himself to the hermeneutics of his age: the Spirit intruded and lo! On that ceiling appeared the narrative of things to come, which came indeed, and behold above me the parable of my days" (139). The proliferation of flesh on the Sistine ceiling foretells other bodies: "For as I regarded the flights of athletes above me . . . I saw again the *relictae* of the camps, entire cairns of cadavers, heaped and golgotha'd: a leg growing from its owners neck, an arm extended from another's shoulder, wrist by jawbone, ear on ankle: the human form divine crippled, jackknifed, trussed, corded: reduced and broken down to its named bones, femur and tibia and clavicle and ulna and thorax and pelvis and cranium: the bundled ossuaries: all in their several social heapings heaped to be taken up by the mastodon bulldozer and scavengered into its sistine limepit" (140).

Yet this reading of destruction into the depiction of creation gives way, by the end of the letter, to a prophesy of redemption, in a meditation on the Esther story and, ultimately, in a commentary on the ram's skulls in the chapel, which Melech chooses to understand as "rams' horns, sounding liberation" (150), an escape from a mortal threat in Max Horkheimer and Theodor Adorno's antiessentialistic understanding of homeland as flight: "Home is a state of having escaped."[5] This setting, however, raises for students the question of the relationship between the Holocaust and the founding of Israel, a complicated historical connection that also addresses the longer connection between Jews and Israel, since antiquity, as well as the impact of Zionism on the non-Jewish inhabitants. *The Second Scroll* points to these framing questions about Zionism, while giving students a chance to work with a complex modernist form.

The Zionist homeland was not founded in an empty space, which is why inquiring into Zionism and the novel requires considerations of Palestinian experiences and perspectives. This includes the depiction of the Arab world within Zionist novels, such as *The Second Scroll*, but also accounts by Arab authors. While Klein's modernist novel explores the entwinement of archaic and contemporary, sacred and secular dimensions, Sayed Kashua's *Second Person Singular* (2010) investigates the complexity of identities caught in relations of dependency, recognition, and suspicion. The condition of dependency appears in the novel as a foundational fact: one of the protagonists—a very successful (unnamed) lawyer, an Arab Israeli who has moved to East Jerusalem but practices in the western part of the city—discovers a love note in his wife's handwriting in a copy of Tolstoy's *Kreutzer Sonata* that he happens to pick up in a used bookstore. A narrative of obsessive jealousy and passion ensues, but the very starting point, the intertextual indebtedness, points to the inescapable past, the long shadow of Tolstoy, on whom Kashua's text depends.

As the lawyer tries to determine the significance of the enigmatic note, two characters emerge who, along with the lawyer, stake out a complex landscape of identities and allegiances. Like the lawyer, Amir Lahab came from the Arab countryside to Jerusalem, but in contrast to the successful attorney, Amir is a social worker with few resources. (Years before he had once dated Laila, later the lawyer's wife: hence the note.) At stake, though, is the contrast between the two figures, the obsessive lawyer and the insecure social worker, and their respective representation of class differentiation within the Arab-Israeli community, a distinction that contributes to students' grappling with the multidimensional character of the social issues.

We also encounter Yonatan Forschmidt, a young Jewish-Israeli man who, after a botched suicide attempt, exists in a vegetative state. Amir takes a position as his caretaker, and because they are of the same age and build, Amir gradually assumes Yonatan's identity, which leads him to admission to the Bezalel art school, where he finds success as a photographer.

Second Person Singular demonstrates through the identity formations of the lawyer and Amir the Arab the experience of a tension between rural and urban settings in the context of aspirations for recognition and assimilation into Israeli society; indeed for Amir, *Second Person Singular* turns into a novel of passing, the phenomenon that transgresses rigid ethnic divisions. Yet we also find evidence of the everyday inequities that Arabs can face in Israel, combined with a desire for imitation. Thus, Majdi, one of Amir's roommates, "used to say that the green signal at the traffic light for the Arab cars from Beith Hanina and Suafat was the shortest in the city. The settlers' cars got five minutes of green for every half minute they gave us."[6] An intern in a law office,

Majdi insists that he will eventually appeal the traffic light in the Israeli High Court of Justice. "'It's a sure win,' he'd say. 'They'll cover it everywhere in the Arab press. All I need is a good suit for the cameras and I'll be the number-one lawyer in east Jerusalem. You'll see. *If you will it, it is no dream*'" (65). The irony here is that the final phrase is the well-known motto by the Zionist founder Theodor Herzl, here adopted by the Arab law student in a moment of oppositional imitation. Resentment against exclusion combines with a rhetorical mimicry and a desire for recognition.

Second Person Singular also examines structures of identity discourse and prejudice, Jews about Arabs and Arabs about Jews, particularly with regard to questions of gender. Thus, Amir, passing as Yonatan, reports on the stereotypes that circulate among the Israeli students, about Arab men and their putative obsession with sex and simultaneously with a need to protect their sisters from sexual emancipation. Continuing in the first person, Amir states, "I learned that they can get angry fast and that there is no way to know what might set them off. They're unpredictable and can be aggressive. Honor is desperately important to them: in fact, it's all that matters to them—personal honor, national honor, religious honor, family honor. Show respect and avoid dishonoring them, and you're on safe ground" (285). In addition, because of his own relatively modest behavior, he hears the Israelis wondering if he is gay or asexual; but because he can understand Arabic, he learns that the few Arab students also think the same of him. Amir explicitly reflects on the irony of his liminal position and the insight he gains into the prejudices of the Israeli world, which he nonetheless wants to join, as well as the prejudices of the Arabs who participate in that same Israeli world.

Yet while Kashua excoriates Israeli gendered prejudices, he depicts the lawyer's jealous rage in a way that nearly corroborates those very same prejudices: suddenly suspicious that his wife had betrayed him or even merely that she might have had a lover before him, he sees his progressive veneer giving way to an unvarnished patriarchal traditionalism: "The lawyer had never thought that the matter of his wife's virginity was important to him, but now he learned that it was, more so than anything else" (154). Not that long before, he had laughed at others' sexual conservatism: "Only recently he had sat with a friend, the accountant, and laughed at him for saying that he was worried about the Arab-Jewish education he was giving his daughter because he was afraid that as she approached puberty she would think, like the Jews, that it was only natural to have sex before marriage" (155). While we saw Amir reporting the Israeli stereotype of the hypersexual Arab, here we find the symmetrical Arab anxiety about a threat of Jewish promiscuity. The lawyer, once the voice of enlightenment, suddenly tumbles back into regressive attitudes that he had thought he had long ago abandoned: "He, who spoke out against and even lectured now and again about honor killings, he, who opposed the phenomenon and labeled it barbaric, only now saw the error of his ways. He wished someone from her family would kill her" (155). When he contemplates divorce, he calculates that he would have to rush to file first in a Muslim court; if his wife were to submit a petition earlier in an Israeli court, she would benefit from statutes that are more advantageous to women. For all his progressive liberalism, he has plummeted back into deeply patriarchal calculations.

While *Second Person Singular* is a novel of passing, crossing the border between Arab and Jew within Israel, Samir El-youssef's *Illusion of Return* treats the Palestinian experience outside Israel, reflective of the author's own biographical itinerary, which began as the child of refugees in Lebanon until his departure for London. In addition to these different contents, the two novels enable students to observe formal variations of the genre. Kashua's work intertwines two bildungsroman narratives, the alternative lives of the lawyer and the social worker, while *Illusion of Return* is built around a set of four reminiscences bound together by a frame, nearly a collection of short stories rather than a cohesive work. It does cohere, however, because of the organization of memory. The frame takes place at Heathrow Airport, where the unnamed narrator meets a friend, and they recall their young adulthood as Palestinian refugees during the Lebanon War. Israeli military force appears in their recollections but only marginally, as the novel instead emphasizes the flawed life struggles of a group of four friends, each suffering under his distinct burden: the loveless relationship of the parents, the gay brother shunned in a sexually conservative milieu, the hypocrisy of the Marxist from a well-off family, and the suicide of a sister.

Despite the existential character of these challenges, the novel is relevant to the theme of Zionism because of its title, which stakes out an emphatic rejection of the program for a "right to return" for Palestinian refugees, and precisely that issue is addressed directly in the frame story. The narrator has been studying in London, working on a thesis concerning the pattern of refugees' upward mobility into the middle class. Yet such economic success undercuts the ideological obligation to return to the territory that became Israeli. Radical students attempt to dissuade him from continuing with the topic, first through persuasion and ultimately with violence. In this process, a memorable scene involves the narrator's response to the politicized rhetoric of his challengers. One of them complains that the thesis "would serve nobody but our Zionist enemy," a terminology that the narrator in turn rejects with disdain and laughter: "'Our Zionist enemy!' I repeated and couldn't help laughing again. I actually kept repeating these words 'Our Zionist enemy' and laughing, which was embarrassing enough to bring our first meeting to an abrupt end. My giggles attracted the attention of other students in the bar and my companions felt awkward and left at once."[7]

The passage, combined with El-youssef's comments in interviews, challenges students who are accustomed to radical campus rhetoric to question the validity of the insistence on the "right to return." Of equal importance, El-youssef provides them with the opportunity to consider resisting the political pressures that they themselves encounter. *The Illusion of Return* takes students into the lives of Palestinian refugees in Lebanon in the 1980s, but as a novel, it raises questions about the scope of politicization: Is everything always only political? Can one not identify dimensions of one's life that depend on other qualities and relationships outside of putatively overriding political conflict? Or what kind of balance can one find among competing desiderata, some but not all of which are political? *The Illusion of Return* is the opposite of an engaged novel; it is a plea to turn down the political volume, and it can be placed productively in the proximity of James Baldwin's *Notes of a Native Son*.

One of the strengths of the novel as form is the capacity to explore characters' internal concerns while providing for a multiplicity of voices: *Second Person Singular* explores identity and desire in contemporary Israel, complicating one's understanding of Israeli life in ways that tend to drop out of conventional political discourse, just as *Illusion of Return* does for the Palestinian diaspora. The fourth and last example from my syllabus, Howard Jacobson's *The Finkler Question* (2010), takes a different genre route by utilizing the tools of the comic novel to observe the situation of Jews in contemporary London, their encounter with anti-Zionism and its relationship to antisemitism. The humor derives to a large extent from the slapstick treatment of the hapless protagonist, Julian Treslove, a non-Jew obsessed with his former schoolmate and competitive friend, the Jew Sam Finkler; the running gag in the novel is that Treslove redubs the Jewish question as the "Finkler question." Both are comic figures: Treslove, formerly of the BBC, now ekes out his living as a celebrity impersonator, while Finkler has succeeded as a pop philosopher with unsurprisingly best-selling titles such as *The Socratic Flirt: How to Reason Your Way into a Better Sex Life*.[8] Suddenly, however, this lighthearted world of cultural production is interrupted when, near the start of the novel, Treslove is mugged and, he believes, assaulted because he was mistaken to be Jewish.

The Finkler Question explores Jewish London's anxious response to growing antisemitism. It is part of the irony that it is the non-Jew, Treslove, who sounds the alarm, while Jewish Finkler remains dismissive. Responding to the report of Treslove's mugging, he barks, "It's not exactly Kristallnacht. . . . Ring me when a Jew gets murdered for being a Jew on Oxford Street" (82). That precise crime does not take place in the novel, although we do read about an acquaintance whose "twenty-two-year-old grandson had been stabbed in the face and blinded by an Algerian man who had shouted 'God is great' in Arabic, and 'Death to all the Jews'" (153), which took place in England, albeit not on Oxford Street.

Against this backdrop, the novel turns to the encounter with anti-Zionism, not unlike the activism that students in the course encounter on campus. Finkler eagerly joins a group critical of Israel, opportunistically hoping to attach himself to the prominent names he is delighted to find associated with it, but when he attended the meetings, "he was disappointed to see so few of the illustrious actors and comedians," and "only academics with nowhere else to go attended regularly" (144). Eventually the mediocrity of the group and the hypocrisy of its members turn Finkler into a critic of anti-Zionism, as the novel concludes with incidents of anti-Jewish violence in London. With grotesque humor and a complex constellation of figures, *The Finkler Question* takes on the nervous insecurity of British Jewry and its reaction to an increasingly venomous anti-Zionism.

Jacobson's novel brings us straight to one of the more divisive questions in the debate and one that students are seeking a language to address: is anti-Zionism anti-semitic? The answer is, inescapably, no and yes. Criticisms of Israel or Israeli policies are logically distinguishable from animosity toward Jews. The two phenomena are by definition distinct from each other. That could put an end to the matter, but the matter is by no means so simple or narrow.

Contemporary anti-Zionism has increasingly taken on antisemitic overtones; the two phenomena overlap and not only marginally. At stake is not merely the singular and obsessive focus on Israel. Nor is it only a matter of the shrinking of discussion of the "Middle East" on college campuses to Israel and the Palestinians, to the exclusion of the catastrophe in Syria, the oppression in Turkey, the prisons of Iran, and so many other examples. The point is also that anti-Zionists choose to direct their protests at Jewish, rather than specifically Israeli, sites, notably during the riots in Paris in the summer of 2014, when mobs protesting the Gaza War tried to storm synagogues, proving the case that anti-Zionism has become antisemitic. In addition, however, while anti-Israel protesters have an affinity for targeting sites of Jewish worship, they do not conduct anti-Israel protests outside of evangelical churches, although Christian Zionism is much more widespread and, politically, more supportive of Israeli government policy than is much of liberal Jewish American Zionism. Evidently anti-Zionists only protest Zionism among Jews, not among Christians, just as the anti-Zionist movement is predisposed to confront Jewish, rather than specifically Israeli, institutions.

The diverse group of students in my "Zionism and the Novel" class responded well to the readings the first time I offered the course. It just so happened, however, that it took place when the political debates about Israel and Zionism on campus were particularly heated. At some class meetings, students arrived visibly shell-shocked by the tensions on campus, and the course provided a chance to share different reactions and points of view in a nonthreatening environment. Our teaching should give students an opportunity to explore current and controversial issues in ways that are intellectually appropriate and welcoming of diverse opinions.

My decision to design the class was based precisely on that understanding of the university as dedicated to exploring and exchanging ideas, and this is why I oppose the movement to boycott Israeli universities, an aspect of the BDS program to boycott, divest, and sanction Israel whose anti-Israel advocacy on campus was triggering my students' distress. My course familiarizes students with a more complex and nuanced understanding of Israel. I refrain from in-class advocacy: I believe that instructors should not impose their political opinions on their students. However, the course goals include developing a capacity to work with complex literary texts, an agenda that runs counter to the simplistic misrepresentations of BDS. The point of education is enhancing students' capacity to think, but the impact of BDS, the boycott of academic institutions, will necessarily impede the flow of ideas. Universities should have none of that.

An explicit component of BDS involves the prohibition on so-called normalization, that is, comparing the Israeli and Palestinian positions or placing them in dialogue with each other. Instituting such a prohibition limits my academic freedom by, for example, preventing me from teaching a course in which I stage a conversation among Palestinian authors such as Kashua and El-youssef and Israelis such as Yehoshua and Modan. Omar Barghouti, a founding figure of BDS, states, in defense of the boycott, that it is proper to override academic freedom in the pursuit of more important goals: his ends, so to speak, would justify the means of limiting my academic speech.[9] The issues of boycott and academic freedom echo through the course, implicitly, insofar as I attempt to model the possibility of free and nontendentious teaching in order to provide students the space to learn and develop their own political positions and, explicitly, in the references to the movement in both El-youssef's and Jacobson's texts.

While I do not directly expound on the topic of BDS in the class, I have written on it, and some students find my publications easily enough online. I believe that it is important that instructors not harangue students with their politics in classroom settings, but teachers who are so inclined should surely engage in political debate in the public sphere outside of class. In March 2014, I contributed to a series of essays in the *Los Angeles Review of Books* concerning the campaign to boycott Israel. While I articulated criticisms of specific policies of the Israeli government, I explained my opposition to the BDS goal of the elimination of the State of Israel. I do not want to rehearse those arguments here but focus instead on one question of method that was implicit in a lengthy rebuttal by three Stanford colleagues, which concluded with the following remark: "Russell Berman alludes to his criticisms of certain aspects of Israel's handling of the question of the Palestinians. Other liberals have likewise condemned the boycott while asserting their disagreement with the occupation. The question we would pose to Berman and others would be: What are you doing to address these wrongs? Rather than spend considerable energy and effort in mounting lengthy . . . arguments, . . . would it not be better to use the same energy and resources to improve the situation?"[10] For them, clearly enough, one should spend less time in argument and more time in action. Their opposition of argument versus action, or thought versus deed, is reminiscent of Marx's famous complaint in the eleventh of his *Theses on Feuerbach* that philosophers have only interpreted the world; the point, however, is to change it. We should, so their argument goes, actively change the world, and this in turn requires setting aside argument, philosophy, or scholarship: more action, fewer words.

This is a flawed stance that goes to the heart of our teaching mission. It deserves to be called out for at least three distinct reasons. First, by placing a premium on ostensibly practical solutions, it effectively denounces the claims of a right to engage in reflective thinking that is not tied immediately to action. This dismissal of thinking for its own sake is fundamentally anti-intellectual. The imperative to rush into action without thinking is an expression of despair, not of political acumen. Some real-world situations are complex and resist simplistic formulations. Facing intractable problems, there is no need to adopt flawed strategies, solely in order to appear to be doing anything at all. My critics' retort that it is permissible to criticize a particular course of action only if one can propose a superior one is a vehicle for censorship, and their censorious tones reflect the threat to academic freedom that pervades the boycott movement.

Second, my critics suggest a special obligation to address the situation in Israel. We may, as members of political communities or out of general ethical considerations, assume the duty to respond to human suffering anywhere and everywhere: we should not just live our private lives. However, there is no clear rationale as to why one scene of suffering should have absolute priority over others. My colleagues may choose to devote themselves to the cause of the Palestinians, but if I choose to take up a different banner and pursue other reform activities—addressing human rights in Iran and its wave of capital punishment, or the promotion of literacy in the United States, or combating sexual assault on campus—my critics have no basis to claim that my choices are less valid than theirs. The activist bullying that insists that one cause is more important than all others betrays a repressive arrogance that invalidates other points of view. It destroys an environment conducive to student learning.

Third, the exchange was a debate among scholars. My critics assume that scholars have a special obligation to adopt political positions. With an echo of noblesse oblige, for them scholarship obligates activism; engaged scholars are the better scholars, from which it must follow that scholars who are not activist are, for that reason, poorer scholars. Their logic leads to the introduction of political litmus tests into the university. It is not hard to foresee problematic consequences in decisions concerning hiring and promotion, if a candidate with a mediocre research record were promoted primarily on the basis of appropriate political loyalties. That is not a recipe for excellence in higher education. My own position is antithetical to theirs: scholarship involves teaching and research with no political obligation. Indeed, the more that one's research or teaching subordinates the pursuit of knowledge to an advocacy agenda, the more scholarly quality deteriorates.

Scholarship in the pursuit of truth does not have to apologize for its apolitical character: it is appropriate to explore the cosmos or pursue lab science or research literature without engaging in political activism. There is, however, also no reason for scholars to remain oblivious to the concerns of the world and especially, as teachers, to the interests of our students. We scholar-teachers may address topical matters, although there is no obligation to do so. Yet we should treat the specific subject matter that we teach through the strength and preparation provided by disciplinary identities and the structures of scholarly specialization. Concerning Israel and the Palestinians, a civil engineer might teach on the utilizations of water resources, or a professor of law could address human rights issues, and one would hope that such courses would engage students in a complex thinking-through of the material rather than in the one-dimensional campaigning, unnuanced and flat, that too often characterizes our political discourse, inside and outside the academy. Our goal as teachers should not be to train students to agree with us politically but to enable students to become more effective thinkers on their own, capable of differentiated reflection, careful in the use of evidence, and, as in the course described in this essay, better readers of novels.

Notes

1. Georg Lukács, *The Theory of the Novel: A Historico-Philosophical Essay on the Forms of Great Epic Literature*, trans. Anna Bostock (Cambridge, MA: MIT Press, 1971), 41.
2. Theodore Herzl, *Altneuland* (1902), trans. Lotta Levensoh (Princeton, NJ: Weiner Marcus, 1997); Ze'ev Jabotinsky, *The Five: A Novel of Jewish Life in Turn-of-the-Century Odessa*, trans. Michael R. Katz (Ithaca, NY: Cornell University Press, 2005).
3. Abraham B. Yehoshua, *Mr. Mani* (Boston: Houghton Mifflin Harcourt, 1993); Rutu Modan, *Exit Wounds* (Montreal: Drawn and Quarterly, 2007).
4. A. M. Klein, *The Second Scroll* (Marlboro, VT: Marlboro, 1985), 28. Subsequent quotations from this volume are cited parenthetically in the text.
5. Max Horkheimer and Theodor W. Adorno, *Dialectic of Enlightenment: Philosophical Fragments*, ed. Gunzelin Schmid Noerr, trans. Edmund Jephcott (Stanford, CA: Stanford University Press, 2002), 61.
6. Sayed Kashua, *Second Person Singular*, trans. Mitch Ginsburg (New York: Grove, 2010), 64. Subsequent quotations from this volume are cited parenthetically in the text.
7. Samir El-youssef, *The Illusion of Return* (London: Halban, 2008), 7.
8. Howard Jacobson, *The Finkler Question* (New York: Bloomsbury, 2010), 270. Subsequent quotations from this volume are cited parenthetically in the text.
9. "The AAUP's support for a form of boycott against apartheid-era South Africa can be

interpreted or extrapolated to show that when a prevailing and persistent denial of basic human rights is recognized, the ethical responsibility of every free person and every association of free persons, academic institutions included, to resist injustice supersedes other considerations about whether such acts of resistance may directly or indirectly injure academic freedom. This does not necessarily mean that academic freedom is relegated to a lower status among other rights. It simply implies that in contexts of dire oppression, the obligation to help save human lives and to protect the inalienable rights of the oppressed to live as free, equal humans acquires an overriding urgency and an immediate priority. This is precisely the logic that has informed the call for boycott issued by PACBI in 2004." Omar Barghouti, "Boycott, Academic Freedom, and the Moral Responsibility to Uphold Human Rights," *AAUP Journal of Academic Freedom* 4 (2013): 5, www.aaup.org/sites/default/files/files/JAF/2013%20JAF/Barghouti.pdf.

10. Hilton Obenzinger, Joel Beinin, and David Palumbo-Liu, "Let's Have Reasoned Debate, Not Distortion and Calumny: A Reply to Russell Berman," *Los Angeles Review of Books*, April 27, 2014, https://lareviewofbooks.org/essay/lets-reasoned-debate-distortion-calumny-reply-russell-berman.

History, Politics, and Religion

Putting the Class(room) in Context

Challenges of Teaching Middle Eastern Politics in a Non-Jewish, Non-Arab Muslim Country with an Imperial Past in the Region

UMUT UZER

Turkey is the successor state of the Ottoman Empire, which ruled over the Middle East from 1516 until World War I. One would expect ample knowledge on the Middle East as former imperial masters of the region, but this is far from reality. The truth of the matter is after the breakup of the Ottoman state in the aftermath of World War I and the creation of republican Turkey in 1923, the country has radically disengaged from the Islamic world, which culminated in the abolishment of the caliphate in 1924. The radical secular-nationalist revolution of Mustafa Kemal Atatürk (1881–1938), the founding president of the country, aimed at establishing a new Turk who was to be Western, secular, modern, and nationalistic, with little connection with its immediate past. The perception toward the Arabs was usually negative, bordering on outright hostility, characterizing them as ungrateful backstabbers during World War I and backward and primitive. It would be correct to say that Arabs represented the Islamic past from which Turks or at least the leadership wanted to extricate themselves.

Throughout the republican era, there were efforts of alignment or nonaggression pacts such as the Sadabad Pact of 1937 or the Baghdad Pact of 1958 and establishment of a closer relationship with the Muslim and Arab world as well as the Third World in the 1960s, so as to get support for Turkey's Cyprus policy. Prime minister Turgut Özal's (1983–91; also president, 1991–93) opening to the Islamic world for economic reasons was also noteworthy. However, up until the current Justice and Development Party (JDP) government (2002–), with the exception of the Welfare Party government of 1996–97, when there was an Islamist party ruling the country, relations with

Middle Eastern countries were based on national interest such as strategic or economic concerns. That situation continued in the first years of the JDP government, but gradually the Turkish government took a more pro-Palestine, in fact a pro-Hamas, position in line with its Muslim Brotherhood proclivities. Having said that, however, a pro-Palestinian stance was also taken by the Left, as the Palestinians were seen as the underdog in the Israeli-Palestinian conflict. This is particularly interesting because there was no sympathy toward other Arabs at the governmental or societal level and ample racist attitudes toward Arabs, such as perceiving them as dirty and primitive; however, this Orientalist approach was not directed toward the Palestinians. As part of the revolutionary movement, the PLO was commended by the Turkish Left. Therefore, it would be correct to say that there were strong pro-Palestinian sentiments in significant sectors of Turkish society. Consequently, the PLO was allowed to open up an official representative office in Ankara in 1978.

As regards Israel, there was not much sympathy at the societal level; however, there were strategic relations particularly after Israel's secret Periphery Pact of 1958.[1] This military cooperation also entailed intelligence sharing. During the 1990s, however, which was the golden age of Turkish-Israeli diplomacy,[2] military relations were buttressed by economic, technical, and cultural exchanges. The spearhead of the relationship was very much the military and civilian bureaucracy, especially the Turkish Foreign Ministry. While academic relations increased, there was not much of pro-Israel sentiment on the part of the populace at large. With the coming of the JDP government to power in 2002, relations went smoothly for a couple of years but deteriorated as Israel's relations with the Palestinians turned violent. Turkey took an outright pro-Palestinian position, and relations with Israel were downgraded, especially after the Mavi Marmara incident in 2010 (often referred to as the Gaza flotilla), when Islamist Turkish activists were attempting to break Israel's blockade of Gaza but were intercepted in the Mediterranean by Israeli soldiers. On one ship, soldiers used live fire, resulting in the killing of nine Turkish militants and a tenth who died later of wounds sustained at the time. After that incident, the diplomatic representation was downgraded but never severed, as there were chargé d'affaires who remained at the Turkish embassy in Tel Aviv and Israeli embassy in Ankara. In 2013, Israel's Prime Minister Benjamin Netanyahu formally apologized to Turkey's Prime Minister Recep Tayyip Erdoğan on behalf of his country, thereby opening negotiations to resolve the incident. In June 2016, a reconciliation deal was signed to reestablish mutual relations on a more substantial level.

In light of this historical and political background, teaching Middle Eastern politics in Turkey can be a challenge, for emotional and ideological reasons. I have not taught such a course at my current university, namely, Istanbul Technical University, but have taught such a course at two private universities, one in Ankara and the other in Istanbul. Both of these courses were taught in English. At the private liberal arts college in Ankara, I had a course titled "Middle Eastern Politics," and I started the class by teaching about the end of the Ottoman Empire and more specifically the creation of the new state system in the region. I assigned William Cleveland's *A History of the Modern Middle East* and Charles Smith's *Palestine and the Arab Israeli Conflict: A History with Documents*. We discussed the Balfour Declaration, the Mandates system, the UN partition plan, Arab-Israeli wars, and the peace process. Modern Turkey was not included in these courses because in Turkey it is not considered a part of the Middle East, unlike in the United States.

The class consisted of around forty students who were mostly seniors, and since I had known them for the past three years, the class went smoothly in an interactive manner. The students did not have much prior knowledge on the topic, but they seemed interested. In fact, one of the students later on pursued his graduate studies in Israel. The majority of students were secular, but some of them came from traditional backgrounds. It could be speculated that in a more conservative setting in provincial universities, the sympathy toward the Palestinians might be even more explicit. Yet even at an American-style liberal university such as Boğaziçi University, pro-Palestinian sentiments are to be expected due to the influence of Orientalism and left-wing scholarly literature on the subject. In this regard, influence comes from the United States, as most academics in Turkey are educated there. Of course, this is also speculation, as I did not specifically teach a course on the Middle East at Boğaziçi, but I did teach a class on foreign policy analysis in which I detected the strong influence of Orientalist literature among some of the students.

Not only in the Turkish context but at campuses all around the world, sympathy toward one of the protagonists in the conflict makes an objective analysis of the topic difficult. The solution to extreme forms of emotionalism, ideological proclivities, and the influence of scholarship on Orientalism is keeping a balanced approach to the Arab-Israeli conflict, as well as to the literature on this topic. Students should be convinced that a university setting is different from other platforms and that the goal of the scholar as well as the student should be objective analysis, not being a party to the ongoing conflict.

I taught my other course at a private college in Istanbul, and there was less emphasis on Israel since it was a general diplomatic history course. There were around twenty students including Italian and German exchange students. As part of nineteenth-century nationalisms, I also talked about Zionism within that historical context. Students were particularly surprised at the secular elements in that ideology, which they thought was basically religious, and their questions about Israel sometimes resulted in disbelief about modern Israel, which has both secular and religious dimensions. They were ready to listen and discuss what I had to say, but I am not sure how successful I was in teaching them about the country. The problem is that they and many others outside the class have a difficulty in distinguishing between an expert and an uneducated person on Middle Eastern politics. Sometimes they tend to believe what they read on social media or a commentator who makes sensationalist allegations. Consequently, some of them can be stubborn in learning about the realities of the Arab-Israeli conflict, since they already think they know the topic. On the other hand, they would not have such rigid ideas about, say, China, India, or Latin America since there are no sentimental attachments to those countries or regions or any fixation as there is on Israel, and hence they would not claim to have ample knowledge about them.

In these courses as well as in other courses such as those in international relations or diplomatic history, I do bring in the importance of the Holocaust, depending on context. For instance, in courses on Middle Eastern politics, I discuss the influence of Shoah on Israeli national identity, whereas in classes on international relations or history, we discuss it within the context of racism and xenophobia. The Holocaust does not occupy a central position in my lectures, as it would divert from the main topic we need to cover. Having said that, however, the Holocaust shows the calamitous consequences of antisemitic worldviews, and in this sense, students should be sensitized to the repercussions of their views. The Holocaust should serve as an explanation for both Israel's priority over security affairs, including the real threats to its security, and the impact of the delegitimization of a people. Criticism of Israel should be undertaken within the context of conventional political analysis, while at the same time, students should be cautioned against rising populism and Islamism all around the world, which creates a slanted and biased perception of Israel.

I should also add that I have taught Middle Eastern history in the United States at Smith College and Middle Eastern politics at University of Maryland University College. There were no confrontational arguments coming from the students, although I am aware that debates can be heated in the U.S. academy as well. The major difference between teaching in Turkey and the United States was that students were more informed about World War I and Turkey's role in it in the former, whereas they were more familiar with Israeli politics in the latter. Another major difference is that certain Turkish students as well as people in general in Turkey have a greater tendency to believe in conspiracy theories about Jews and Israel.

As mentioned earlier, in Turkey there is a perception of Arab betrayal of the Ottoman Empire, due to the Arab Revolt of Sharif Hussein in 1916, totally disregarding the countless Arab soldiers in the Ottoman army and pro-Turkish sentiments in Egypt—a state of affairs about which even T. E. Lawrence in his *Seven Pillars of Wisdom* complained. Therefore, such negative perceptions about Arabs can also creep in, making it difficult for students to objectively study the subject matter, even though I did not encounter such ideas directly in my classes.

In Turkish academia, scholarship on the Middle East is quite limited, as opposed to the United States, where Middle Eastern studies is well established. Of course, it should be mentioned that in Turkey people do not perceive their country as part of the Middle East, so when I mention Middle Eastern studies, I am referring to the Arab world plus Iran. Admittedly, there are a number of centers or institutes of Middle Eastern studies at universities such as Marmara, Ankara, Sakarya, and Fırat or ORSAM (Center for Middle Eastern Strategic Studies), a think tank in Ankara, but their expertise so far is rather limited. It should also be noted that there is a Department of Hebrew Language and Literature at Erciyes University in Kayseri in Central Turkey.

Regarding Israel, there is not much knowledge, even though students think they know something about Jews, Judaism, Zionism, and Israel. They can be influenced by the general sentiments in Turkish society, where there are numerous conspiracy theories about Israel, so that makes teaching about Israel particularly hard. At one of the private universities where I taught Middle Eastern politics, there were no conspiratorial mind-sets or questions coming from the students. However, at the other private university where I was teaching about Zionism, there were objections regarding Jews and Israel. Students even quoted their teachers from high school on this topic, which surprised me very much since the curriculum at Turkish high schools is quite tight and Israel is not included in the recommended materials. Be that as it may, I was told that history and literature teachers talked about Israel and how it oppresses Muslims. Students also quoted particular independent scholars and the internet, from which they got their misinformation. Needless to say, most of what they repeated is factually incorrect. I tried to explain that neither the teachers nor some of the professors had any expertise on the Middle East and that most of their worldview has been shaped by conspiracy theories.

In fact, it might be useful to mention some of the common perceptions and theories about Jews and Israel in Turkish society. They are by no means hegemonic, and at prestigious universities such as Bilkent, Boğaziçi, Middle East Technical University, and others, the faculty and students do not share these ideas. But among certain sectors of society, not only among Islamists and conservatives but also among some leftist and nationalist circles, such ideas exist.

Some of these misperceptions are that Jews feel superior to other nations, that Jews do not constitute a nationality, that there can be no conversion to Judaism, that the two lines on the Israeli flag represent the rivers Nile and Euphrates,[3] which Israelis want to control, that Israel supports the PKK, that Jews dominate the United States and hence the world, that they are rich, and that Israeli oppression of Palestinians is tantamount to genocide.

As mentioned earlier, while these ideas are not shared by all or even the majority of the Turkish population, they are common enough to be heard repeatedly. Therefore, if a student comes with such prejudices, it is impossible to change his or her mind, since conspiracy theories cannot be refuted by knowledge, as they are based on emotions and half truths. Belief in conspiracy theories requires taking them as a matter of faith, and uncomfortable facts are generally rejected when they are perceived to disrupt an already-established worldview.

In light of this state of affairs, I needed to remind the students of my credentials in Middle Eastern politics and the lack thereof among some of the individuals they mentioned. They at least listened and seemed convinced, but I am not sure if they believed me. Maybe they deferred because of my position as a professor; but I should point out that in my classes, students never shied away from expressing their opinions, and those who did hold such biased opinions were generally few in number.

The problem with the conspiracy theorists is that their knowledge on Israel and Palestine comes from certain conservative teachers, professors, and independent scholars who have no expertise on the subject. Or they perceive the Arab-Israeli conflict from an ideological perspective based on Muslims being oppressed by Jews. Another important point is the articulation of what is the conservative narrative in Turkey. This has its roots among conservative nationalist and Islamist individuals as well as rightist political parties that try to offer a counterhero to Atatürk, the founder of a modern, secular Turkey. Usually they appeal to an alternative in the person of Ottoman Sultan Abdul Hamid II (1876–1909), who is presented as a pious and benevolent ruler who tried to protect Muslims within the empire and beyond against the forces of nationalism. Praise of Abdul Hamid and his rejection of Theodor Herzl's demand for the establishment of a Jewish state in Palestine in return for providing funds is presented as a heroic attempt to save Ottoman territorial integrity against world Jewry. Too much power is attributed to Herzl, who in this narrative supposedly intended to dismantle the Ottoman Empire in the First Zionist Congress in Basel.[4] Among Islamist circles, especially the National Outlook Movement, the image of Palestine has been an important rallying point for many decades because it offers the opportunity to mobilize around Muslim religious interests. There have been demonstrations to "liberate" Jerusalem from what is perceived as the rule of the infidel, and this narrative draws on crusader language and the Ottoman history of rule in Palestine.

Leftists also have a pro-Palestinian position, as mentioned earlier, and there is no pro-Israel group in Turkey—except perhaps the Jewish community, but their numbers are too small (around twenty thousand) to have an influence on Turkish society. Besides, they are very much under verbal attack from antisemites on social media and through other means. However, they have become more visible and more active in the articulation of their ideas and opposition to antisemitic remarks. Furthermore, Holocaust commemorations on International Holocaust Remembrance Day on 27 January are now well established, and there have been seminars by Holocaust-related organizations such as the United States Holocaust Memorial Museum, the Aladdin Project, Yad Vashem, and Anne Frank House. In 2015, the Edirne Synagogue in the European part of Turkey was renovated, and Hanukkah was celebrated for the first time in a public place in Istanbul. Amid this renewed Jewish activism in Turkey, there are certain expressions of pro-Israel sentiments by a few Jewish columnists[5] in the Jewish weekly paper *Şalom* (Shalom).

In conclusion, Middle Eastern studies, including Israel studies, is underdeveloped in Turkey. There has been an increased interest in Middle Eastern affairs for the past decade or so, but so far, it is confined to a few universities. There is a small number of scholars and graduate students who are interested in Israel, a number that might increase in the coming years. The aim of the scholar in Turkey and elsewhere should be to lay out the facts and keep a balanced approach to the Arab-Israeli conflict without getting caught up in extreme forms of emotionalism and ideologically driven comments.

Notes

1. Yossi Alpher, *Periphery: Israel's Search for Middle East Allies* (Lanham, MD: Rowman and Littlefield, 2015).
2. Umut Uzer, "Turkish-Israeli Relations: Their Rise and Fall," *Middle East Policy* 20, no. 1 (2013): 97.
3. In fact, the Israeli flag was inspired by the Jewish prayer shawl, the tallit.
4. In fact, I heard such reporting from the conservative TGRT TV.
5. Especially Mois Gabay, who says that Turkish Jews have ties of love to Israel (*gönül bağı*), "Türk Yahudileri için yeni bir dönem mi?" (A new era for Turkish Jews), *Şalom*, 23 December 2015, http://salom.com.tr/haber-97547-turk_yahudileri_icin_yeni_bir_donem_mi_.html.

India

TEACHING ISRAEL TO THE "OTHER"

P. R. KUMARASWAMY

Whether located within social sciences, humanities, international relations, or other disciplines, teaching Israel has been uniquely challenging in India. This situation is influenced by political correctness, partisanship, and also immediate news value. It raises questions and controversies that are absent or uncommon in similar country-specific or historical subjects. The problem gets acute if one faces an audience that is far removed from ancient or modern Israel and its historical evolution. How does one teach modern Israel and its sociopolitical challenges to a class of students who are unfamiliar with anything Jewish, with regard to history, religion, culture, or sociology? How does one contextualize and communicate modern Israel and its historical evolution in a country where the Jewish presence was historic but minuscule? Hence, India can serve as a model for thinking about the issues that arise in teaching Israel studies when the topic comes with severe challenges and heavier responsibilities.

The first major challenge is the demographic dynamics and its impact on the general understanding of Jewish history. The countries of Asia have only a nodding acquaintance with Jews, and their long historical association with the region is in contrast to the small size of the Jewish population; this is especially true for India. There were commercial links between the coastal regions of southern India with traders centuries before Christ, and the first arrival of Jews on the Malabar coast is often traced to shortly after the destruction of the Second Temple.

At the same time, Hinduism, the dominant faith of India, is theologically non-proselytizing and culturally assimilationist. Hence, the number of Jews always remained small, and at the height of its strength, during the interwar period, the community was around thirty thousand, composed mostly of refugees from Nazi Europe. The latest census of 2001 puts the number of Jews at around four thousand out of an Indian population of 1.2 billion. Most of the Jews in India live in Mumbai, and making a minyan[1] becomes problematic in some cities, especially New Delhi, due to the microscopic Jewish presence. Thus, most Indians are ignorant of Jews and often assume that they are another branch or sect of Christianity.

Christians make up the third-largest religious community in India, after Hindus and Muslims, but their share is just over 2 percent. Except for the northeastern states, the Christian population is scattered. The vast majority of Indians are unfamiliar with the Bible, and in practice, this means that they are not in a position to comprehend the historical-theological link between the Jews and the Holy Land and the importance attached to Moses or the Ten Commandments. Due to the secularizing nature of the society at times, a significant portion of Christian youths in the country is unaccustomed to the Judeo-Christian heritage that has dominated the European understanding of Jewish history during the past couple of centuries.

The relatively small Christian population in India is dwarfed by a much-larger Muslim population that influences the traditional Indian understanding of the Jews and their claims to the Holy Land. During British rule, India had the largest Muslim population in the world, and presently it is home to the second-largest Muslim population after Indonesia. There are more Muslims in India than in Pakistan and Bangladesh, who were also part of the British Raj. The century-old Judeo-Islamic hostility has prevented a more sympathetic view of the Jews and their historical claims to Palestine before the arrival of the Muslim armies of Caliph Umar in Jerusalem in 636–37 CE.

In short, a microscopic Jewish population, a small number of Christians, and a large Muslim community mean that the average Indian understanding about Jews is a combination of ignorance and prejudice, and hence, it is not easy to communicate the Jewish link to a pre-Islamic Middle East that underpins the historical Jewish claim to the modern State of Israel.

Above all, the Holocaust remains marginal in Indian understanding of Jewish or European history. With minor exceptions, the vast majority of Indians do not fit into the four traditional positions on the Holocaust, namely, victims, perpetrators, bystanders, or rescuers. Most Indian nationalists were incarcerated during the Second World War, and once they were freed, they were busy with the daunting task of communal partition, which was opposed in principle by the Indian nationalists, led by the Congress Party. These and the competition with separatist Pakistani nationals resulted in Indian leaders, including Mahatma Gandhi, remaining silent on the human tragedy in Europe. Thus the Holocaust has little resonance in Indian memory. At the same time, with Partition in 1947, India and Pakistan were engaged in their own political conflict, in which millions were displaced.

The historical evolution of Israel cannot be divorced from the contemporary Middle East, especially the Arab-Israeli and Israel-Palestine conflicts. The political rights of the Palestinians and their fight against prolonged statelessness have considerable support in India. Since the mid-twentieth century, Indian nationalists have championed the Palestinian cause, which was partly manifest in the four decades of the recognition-without-relations policy of New Delhi toward Israel. Furthermore, since the June War (1967), Israel's policies on issues such as settlements and borders have been controversial and have evoked considerable anger and criticisms from the informed and uninformed Indian public. Hence, Palestinian statelessness takes precedence over Jewish existence and territorial claims. The narrow reading at times leads to appalling comparisons between Israeli practices in the occupied territories and apartheid in South Africa and even Nazi Germany.

This approach gathers momentum during periods of violence. Discussing Israel's evolution and its right to exist amid the civilian casualties in the Gaza Strip, for example, is challenging. Issues such as justice and human rights violations and prolonged occupation cannot be brushed aside while dealing with Israel, but excessive focus on these contemporary issues would result in a skewed depiction of the larger picture, namely, that Jewish rights to Palestine emanate from the Balfour Declaration.

Except for an incident in Goa when it was under the Portuguese occupation, historically antisemitism has been alien to India. In recent years, however, the unfamiliarity with Jewish history is often accompanied by an excessive focus on the Jewish influence in the West, especially the United States. A significant section of the Indian elite believes in some of the stereotypical depictions in the antisemitic hoax *The Protocols of the Elders of Zion* and that the Jews wield disproportionate influence over the U.S. establishment and "control" its policy toward the Middle East. A critical approach toward Israel at times borders on antisemitism, and there seems to be a lack of clarity between legitimate criticisms of Israeli government policy and antisemitism.

Since the mid-1960s, especially in the wake of the June War, Israel was caught in the East-West ideological debates. Supporting the Arab states and their position has become "politically correct" among many countries and societies, particularly in Asia. This attitude gathered momentum in the wake of the October War (1973) and the oil crisis, which signaled a new Arab politico-strategic influence vis-à-vis Israel. The breaking of diplomatic relations by the then USSR and its allies amid the war presented opposition to Israel as a sign of being "progressive," and hence, many communists and left-wing parties in many countries ignore that the Soviet Union played the role of a midwife during the partition plan and was the second country after the United States to recognize the Jewish state.

These attitudes are reflected in India's joining the Arab-Islamic chorus in November 1975 that culminated in Zionism being equated with racism. Under the prevailing political climate, supporting the Palestinians meant a vociferous opposition to Israel, and even minimal contacts and relations with Israel meant "dilution" of the commitments to Palestinians.

In trying to impart the evolution of Israel, its rights, claims, and policies, one has to adopt a careful mix of pedagogical approaches. An explicit Zionist narrative would forcefully argue the Israeli case and its justification but would be ineffective in a gentile Indian environment. While the depiction of Jewish history has larger convergence, Zionist responses have been diverse; socialist Zionism and revisionist Zionism, for example, differ considerably over resolving the Arab-Israeli conflict. A narrow approach to the subject through a Zionist-centric prism is self-defeating in a society such as India, with its religious, ethnic, cultural, linguistic, and above all caste divisions and cleavages.

A religious-theological approach toward Israel reflects the prevailing view of the two other monotheistic faiths, Christianity and Islam, toward Israel and can be useful in a Christian- or Muslim-majority country. But this approach is irrelevant within the predominantly but not exclusively Hindu India. This issue is further compounded by the traditional attitude of the Indian elite, who tend to view Israel's links to the Holy Land through an Islamic framework.

Locating Israel within a moral paradigm has its advantages and disadvantages. This argument was largely employed in India until 1992 to explain and rationalize prolonged nonrelations with Israel, but there is a fundamental problem with this approach. Indian elites have been selective in their moral revulsion and have largely been indifferent toward the injustice facing various ethnic, religious, and national minorities in the Middle East and beyond. The statelessness of the Kurds or the persecution of Baha'i has rarely evoked scholarly attention. The same holds true for the Turkish occupation of Northern Cyprus or the prolonged Syrian occupation of Lebanon.

Therefore, a Cold War–centric approach may be useful in explaining some features of Israeli politics and choices, especially the role played by the United States. However, this approach is less relevant since the early 1990s, when the international political order has become more diffuse and less coherent. In the Indian context, this approach is less appealing especially when one tracks the political relations between India and Israel, which began in 1992.

Therefore, it is essential to apply a combination of approaches in conveying the history of Jews and the evolution of the State of Israel: history to describe the Jewish dispersal and Diaspora; Zionism to explain the two millennia of Jewish statelessness and the desire for a national homeland; theology to convey the attitude of the two other Abrahamic faiths toward the Jews; morality to convey different international standards and moving goalposts vis-à-vis issues such as occupation, human rights violations, or statelessness.

In practical terms, this strategy means two prime thematic approaches: locating the Jewish longing for statehood within the context of Moses, and tracing the centrality of Jerusalem in the Arab-Israeli conflict. With the biblical injunction and Moses's demand to "let my people go," it is possible to capture the uniqueness of Jewish history as well as its universalizing nature of justice, equality, and fairness. At the same time, it is possible to draw the same line that different groups of Zionists (as well as writers during the Jewish Enlightenment [Haskalah]) drew from the past to the present in order to demonstrate a historical and spiritual connection to the land. Thus the creation of a Jewish national identity has been predicated on the redeployment of religious, historical, and geographical markers in contemporary contexts. Within this political narrative lies the spiritual narrative of the return to Jerusalem and the rebuilding, if only symbolically, of the Temple in Jerusalem that once marked out the city as the capital of a land with Jewish sovereignty. With its annihilation in 70 CE, any hope of Jewish self-determination was erased, leading to the dispersal of Jews throughout the world and the creation of a diaspora, as well as removing the ability to bring sacrifices and worship through the special requirements of a Temple. Though Jews would worship in synagogues after this, they would retain a belief in the importance of Jerusalem, using it as the physical focus for the direction of prayer and as the spiritual focus for a longing to return.

The modern history of Israel has to be far removed from the Balfour Declaration, and for this, the Jerusalem issue has to be viewed within the context of the contested history and claims of the three Abrahamic faiths, namely, Judaism, Christianity, and Islam. Their different theological and national narratives have to be highlighted to appreciate the historical "right" available to the adherents of these three faiths. This also pushes the question of "occupation." If we reconsider the history of Palestine as a series of historical conquests by different groups, we can see that Jewish occupation and self-governance in Palestine precedes both Christianity and Islam. Jewish rule traces to the eleventh century BCE and, after waves of attacks by successive empires challenging Jewish sovereignty, was eventually brought to an end in the first century CE. The Romans who conquered Palestine did not adopt Christianity widely until the third century, and the Muslim conquests of Jerusalem occur as a result of the Siege of Jerusalem (636–37 CE). Despite constant fighting during the crusades between Christians and Muslims over rule of Jerusalem and the surrounding areas, in 1517 the Ottoman's conquered Palestine and held it until 1918. Appreciation of the layers of contested history is essential to appreciate the Arab-Israeli conflict and in the process to locate Israel studies within more balanced moral standards.

For a long time, Israel studies or teaching about Israel/Palestine has been located primarily in the Western world. Imparting the understanding of the situation has been approached through the traditional Christian and, of late, Islamic prisms. However, teaching Israel to the non-Western and non-Islamic world is more complex than is commonly understood and requires an innovative and inclusive approach when there are so many sociocultural and historical differences and cleavages. This context requires more imagination, contextualization, and sociocultural specificities.

Notes

1. A prayer quorum, traditionally of ten men, required to say certain prayers.

Exploring Middle East Politics in Various Classroom Settings

HUSAM MOHAMAD

Over the course of my teaching experience at universities in the United States and abroad, I have frequently offered courses on Middle Eastern politics—a subject that has never had a shortage of controversies in classroom settings. Identified as the cradle of civilizations and the birthplace of the three Abrahamic monotheistic religions—Judaism, Christianity, and Islam—the unstable reality of the Middle East has generated disagreements inside and outside academia. While teaching at a university in Qatar from 2012 to 2015, discussion topics that I focused on included the Arab Spring's uprisings, sectarian tensions along the Sunni-Shiʻa divide, the Syrian refugees, religious and ethnic minorities, and issues surrounding U.S. policy in the region. The events of the Arab Spring that rocked the foundations of entrenched autocratic regimes remains a central theme in classroom debates. At my current university in Oklahoma, where I have taught since 1999, students in my classes tend to express interest in issues relating to Israel (and subsequently the Palestinians), perhaps due to their deeply rooted religious upbringing that inspires them to romanticize the Holy Land and the Judaic-Christian tradition. They are largely supportive of Christian evangelical groups whose activities are centered on strengthening U.S. backing for Israel. Evangelical activists present themselves as born-again Christians who are assisting in the fulfillment of God's eternal plans, starting with the Rapture, which will ascend them into heaven, and ending with the Tribulation and Armageddon's battle, which will lead to disastrous effects on the world stage. Evangelical focus on rebuilding the Second Jewish Temple in Jerusalem is intended to facilitate the return of Jesus from heaven to earth to begin a thousand-year era of peace and harmony, which thus explains the evangelicals' enthusiastic support for Israel. Those who are affiliated with evangelical trends in my classes often point to links between their Christian theology and the course of history, which is expected, in accordance with their own interpretations of Christianity, to reach its end in ways that are referenced in sacred texts such as the books of Genesis, Daniel, and Revelations.[1]

Issues relating to the war on terror and democracy-promotion plans for the Arab region—which are common topics in courses relating to today's Middle East politics—are particularly popular among students who were, or remain, in the military. Students in those classes are urged to critically assess and evaluate the United States' inability and/or unwillingness to conclude a peace settlement between Israel and the Palestinians. This essay reflects on themes addressing my teaching experiences at several universities with the intent of featuring the benefits of cooperative and analytical learning, mainly when supported by case studies and simulations that highlights the value of human interactions among political opponents in the context of classroom settings.

As a student at Birzeit University in the West Bank in the early 1980s, I experienced firsthand exposure to Israel's military-occupation interventionist policies that, among other things, hindered Palestinians' educational institutions and undermined their academic endeavors.[2] Throughout my graduate studies in the United States, however, I became more exposed to an open and free academic life, which provided me with an opportunity to understand and value liberal education. This learning environment also prepared me to become a more independent and dynamic individual in my future career as a university professor. Although I have always had clear and often strong views on most controversial topics surrounding Middle East politics, I was taught that my personal beliefs and biases should not influence my students in classroom activities, especially on matters relating to Palestinian issues. I therefore assumed that my role as an educator should primarily be confined to facilitating a free learning atmosphere that enhances students' capacities for critical reflections, creative individuality, and the ability to communicate cooperatively with each other. In managing classroom activities, I have been, and remain, in favor of developing procedures underlining the student-centered approaches in the process of teaching and learning rather than settling for the more commonly used practice that emphasizes the central role of the faculty in classroom discussions. While it has always been my main duty to help students improve their academic standards, I have often felt a need to encourage them—without influencing their beliefs—to become active in ways that would benefit disadvantaged communities across societies.

The first time I taught a Middle East politics class in the late 1980s as a graduate teaching assistant, I realized how difficult it was to distance my personal beliefs from topics raised in the classroom. I recall having an Israeli student in that class who expressed views that are usually associated with right-wing Israeli policies. Initially, the student was not participating, and I was reluctant to pressure her to contribute to class discussions—perhaps because of my limited experience in teaching at the time. However, she soon became involved in class activities, especially during a discussion addressing Palestinian nationalism and the PLO versus political Zionism and Israel. The Israeli student obviously disagreed with views expressed in the reading materials and instead responded with Zionist propaganda that denies the existence of Palestinian nationalism.[3] As a Palestinian, I felt the need to counter her views by highlighting the Palestinian narrative, which is often downplayed by the U.S. media, society, and political establishment. Being the teacher in the classroom, however, it was difficult for me to present the Palestinian narrative without appearing biased and dismissive of the student's opinion. While keeping in mind that I should remain neutral, I stated to the class that the Israeli student's ideas are only reflective of one among many other views and arguments that are present across both the Israeli and Palestinian divide. The student may have felt satisfaction about being able to communicate the pro-Israeli narratives in a setting such as Cincinnati, Ohio, which is not typically evangelical but is more supportive of Israel than of Palestinians. I remember talking to her almost daily after class, where I felt a moderation in her approach to the Israeli-Palestinian conflict. For instance, while she continued to express frustration with the PLO, viewing it as a terrorist organization, the student was willing to understand how Palestinians feel about the Israeli soldiers, who were at the time crushing the First Intifada in the occupied Palestinian territories. At the personal level, we had a good degree of communication. The student lived less than an hour from where I was born and raised in the West Bank. Yet, despite decades of conflicts and years of fruitless negotiations, basic communications between individuals and communities along the Israeli and Palestinian divide were, and remain, almost nonexistent. The absence of social interactions at the individual and community levels has been a major obstacle in the pursuit of reconciliation between the two sides, where trust remains also nonexistent. Contacts between Israelis and Palestinians have been heavily reliant on already-established official security and diplomatic routes that are usually administered between Israeli military generals and politicians, on the one hand, and Palestinian elites, notably prominent former political activists and prisoners, on the other.[4]

My first full-time teaching experience lasted for four years (1995–99) at a university in Cyprus, which has been divided along the Greek and Turkish Cypriot ethnic and religious lines since the 1974 Turkish invasion of the country. Although the case of Cyprus may be different, it was useful to establish parallels between the two Cypriot communities, on the one hand, and Israelis and Palestinians, on the other. Both examples, along with the Irish conflict, were used as case studies in my international relations and diplomacy courses. Being on the Turkish Cypriot side of the island, other topics addressing Turkish and Middle Eastern politics were also explored. Although Turkey has been considered as one of the rising democracies in the region, many taboos still exist in Turkish politics, including topics critical of Atatürk's secular legacy, the Kurdish question and the PKK's activities, and controversies regarding the

Armenian genocide. Meanwhile, in Cyprus, unlike in the case of the Israeli-Palestinian conflict, the UN had implemented what was known at the time as confidence-building measures that aimed at bringing the Greek and Turkish Cypriot communities closer to each other as a step toward resolving the Cyprus conflict. On two occasions, I attended student-centered gatherings that were sponsored by the UN at the buffer zone in the divided city of Nicosia. While attending those sessions, I heard arguments and counterarguments raised by different students speaking on behalf of their own group and the larger communities. Their views were consistent with established narratives on the Cyprus question and thus reflective of examples of the pain and suffering inflicted on each side by the other. The two narratives were almost opposites of each other, not just in content but also in their use of different vocabularies, dates, maps, and dramatic stories. Given my background, I could not avoid making parallels with the Israeli-Palestinian narratives, in which each side also applies different interpretations of history, events, vocabularies, and stories. From the Greek Cypriot viewpoint, the Turkish invasion and occupation of the northern side of the island has been and remains the key obstacle preventing a resolution for the Cyprus conflict. However, for the Turkish Cypriots, events that preceded the Turkish intervention—namely, the Greek Cypriot coup attempt to unify the island with Greece—were far more critical and detrimental to the fate of the Turkish Cypriot community. With regard to the future of the island, the two sides clashed on unanswered questions surrounding the call for political equality between the two communities, the fate of Turkish settlers who came to the island after 1974, and the island's future relations with Greece and Turkey as the two guarantor powers. Because there were both Turkish and Greek Cypriot refugees on the island, claims and counterclaims assessing the personal losses and sufferings in relation to the refugees were the most painful part of the debates. As far as the stylistic nature of the discussions, the two groups have hardly listened to each other. Each individual participant was focused on addressing the grievances of his or her own community in a forceful way against the other. As time progressed, toward the end of the debate, the power of human interaction began to surface. Students from the divided island, who began to tell touching stories about their own sufferings at the individual and community levels, began now reacting positively to the stories of their opponents. A majority of the students agreed that regardless of which side they were affiliated with, the reality on the ground reveals that both communities have suffered a degree of victimization from the other side. After two hours of interactions, the two sides became more focused on the damaging effects of the conflict on their communities. As I watched the students—whether they were Turkish or Greek Cypriots—hugging and exchanging contact information with each other, I realized that human interactions should never be underestimated and must always remain part of the official diplomatic setting, which has generally downplayed the importance of confidence building between the two communities. When given a chance, those students from the two conflicting sides have managed to relate to each other positively and effectively, regardless of whether they agree with each other's politics. I also learned that if and when human beings bring that missing part of their humanity into the setting, they may have more hopeful views about resolving their conflicts.[5]

While teaching at Qatar University, which is quite traditional, it was important for me not to include in reading materials or classroom discussions topics that are considered offensive or unacceptable in relation to Arab and Muslim cultures. This was particularly relevant to issues surrounding gender equality, sexual orientations, a critical view of religious beliefs and conducts, and personal information relating to political elites in the country. The university campus had been divided into a male/female setting where gender interactions at the students' level were nonexistent. The presence of strict rules and procedures concerning gender relations on campus had not been controversial for most students. They were aware of the need for such restrictions to accommodate the conservative tribal and religious background of the country's inhabitants. At the same time, however, the students' daily exposure to Western social media that is unrestricted in the country and their extensive travel to the West may have contributed to their Westernization, without their having to necessarily feel pressured to abandon their traditional cultural upbringing. On the issue of religion, namely, the Sunni-Shi'a divide in the Muslim world, most students were surprisingly vocal in presenting their own ideological views, which were mostly critical of what they perceived as a Shi'a threat to their Sunni-oriented setting. Topics relating to gender and religious thought were also addressed by the students in class discussions only in ways that were in conformity with the dominant views in the country. As far as politics is concerned, although the Qatari political system is nondemocratic, almost all Qatari students whom I have seen over the years have been quite supportive of their own government. While being educated about the achievements of democratic institutions, rules, and procedures in different parts of the world, those students were also aware that an inclusive democratic system in Qatar may deprive them of many of their secured and unique privileges. They therefore were supportive of their government in part because it was able and willing to provide them with most of their needs and services at a symbolic cost. The wealth of the country and the small size of its population made it possible for them to experience one of the highest standards of living worldwide. Although the presence of constraints continued to influence my teaching responsibilities at the university, in reality most restrictions appear to be irrelevant or obsolete to those students participating in debates and discussions in the classrooms. Perhaps having experienced similar background to the other students at Qatar University may have enticed them to express their views openly and freely, without fear of being misjudged.

One incident at the university that was out of the norm, however, occurred while I was proctoring an exam for my students in a classroom where I found a customized textbook on the table. I began skimming through its collections of chapters and articles, which seemed unrelated to each other. I was particularly interested in one of its sections relating to the Israeli-Palestinian conflict. There, among other articles, I saw an essay titled "The Protocols of the Elders of Zion," which included the full text of that document.[6] I took the book home and then brought it back during the next class session to ask my students if they had ever taken this class or seen this textbook. A few of the students had indeed taken the class as part of their College of Arts and Sciences general requirements and were assigned that same textbook for the class. I asked them if they had known that the essay regarding the "Elders of Zion" was fabricated antisemitic propaganda that is false and should not be addressed as factual or legitimate reading in a classroom setting, unless the purpose is to critically explore its fallacies and reveal the historical reasons that created such materials. The students' reaction seemed indifferent about the issue. I continued my discussion with them about antisemitism, Nazism, and fascism in Europe and asked them questions concerning whether they believe that Arabs and Muslims would gain any benefits by defending European antisemitic and racist policies or by denying the Holocaust. Although they continued to express general indifference about the subject matter, their views changed when the discussion included reference to the Islamophobia that is spreading in the West. I felt it was my duty as an educator to direct the students to be more consistent in their approach to these topics and not to be selective in their humanity when it comes to examples of racism, whether it is antisemitism or Islamophobia. Eventually, they were convinced that both antisemitism and Islamophobia should be treated as deplorable. I also tried to inform my students that justifying acts of antisemitism by pointing to Israel's military occupation policies directed against Palestinians in the occupied territories—which may have been the argument underlined in the customized textbook—is not convincing. Antisemitism and the Holocaust were the result of deeply rooted ideologies and policies that were directed against Jews as religious and cultural communities across Europe. However, the issue of the Israeli-Palestinian conflict is mainly a product of a territorial conflict between two competing nationalist settings, where one side denies the claims of the other. Whether antisemitism and Islamophobia are the same or similar has in recent years became a subject of intense debates.[7]

My final example is based on a class that I taught for a nonprofit organization known as the Junior State of America (JSA), held at summer campus in various locations in the country. Although the class was more about international relations, I tried to focus it on U.S. foreign policy toward the Middle East. I introduced into the classroom debates a policy simulation case that relates to U.S. foreign policy with regard to the Israeli-Palestinian "peace process." The simulation assignment was to be carried out in the form of debates between three groups addressing the issue of whether the United States should change its policy toward Israel and the Palestinians. Each student in the class was assigned a specific role to play in relation to his or her own group. The discussion was intended to help students learn from one another how and why the resolution to the conflict between Israel and the Palestinians has been so elusive. I assumed that the simulation would fail to propose fundamental changes in the already-existent U.S. policy toward the peace process, given the presence of solid popular backing for Israel in the country. However, perhaps due to the fact that the students in this program were culturally and ethnically diverse, along with being more liberal and secular oriented compared to the students at my university in Oklahoma, the sympathy they expressed for the Palestinians was overwhelming. On the basis of my experience at other college settings in the country, I am typically more accustomed to seeing religiously oriented, parochial, and less diverse students who usually support Israel regardless of the effects of its policies on the Palestinians. Prior to the debate date, the students were given assigned reading materials that address arguments and counterarguments relating to the Israeli-Palestinian conflict in general and U.S. policy with regard to the peace process in particular.[8] The students were expected, on the day of the debate, to present ideas reflective of the views of three main political trends, including (1) a pro-Israeli perspective, (2) a pro-Palestinian perspective, and (3) those perspectives reflective of various views held by U.S. politicians, advisers, and the public at large.

The simulation was designed to reflect the level of an undergraduate classroom setting at a U.S. college campus. Although students were instructed to follow the procedures carefully, they were informed that they should be able to freely present their own views and arguments. They were also free to vote in ways that were reflective of their own beliefs. At the end of the debate, the students voted overwhelmingly to endorse the resolution to revise U.S. policy toward Israelis and Palestinians. In so doing, the students took fundamental risks with regard to revisiting and revising U.S. foreign policy in the region. This was unconventional and perhaps contrary to the established wisdom and frame of reference concerning the U.S.-Israel alliance.

During the debate, the students underlined points that were central to the failure of U.S. mediation efforts to resolve the Israeli-Palestinian conflict. It was obvious that the ongoing peace process between Israel and the Palestinians has problems relating to its procedures, contents, and participants. The debates were focused on the George W. Bush and Barack Obama administrations' policies regarding the peace process. Although other players such as the UN, Russia, and the EU may have been involved in procedures concerning the process, the United States has had by far the most prominent role in managing almost all bilateral negotiations between Israel and the Palestinians. The students assessed areas of consistencies and inconsistencies between the Bush and the Obama administrations' policies and concluded that the differences between the two administrations were marginal and procedural. Both presidents supported the two-state vision, to be reached through direct negotiations between the two sides. Both presidents also believed that they must only play the role of facilitator, not enforcer, for the peace process to continue and that it would be expected to lead to the creation of a peaceful, democratic, and demilitarized Palestinian state alongside Israel. However, given the inequality between the Israeli and Palestinian sides, the framework of negotiations, as endorsed by the United States, may have mainly helped Israel to maintain the status quo situation in the Palestinian territories.

Students who were supportive of the Palestinian side warned that the U.S. failure to become more active, and evenhanded, in resolving the conflict not only would unleash more violence in the Palestinian territories but might further discredit the Palestinian Authority (PA) while enhancing the popular appeal of Islamists among Palestinians. Other students, who were more affiliated with the Israeli side, also warned, for different reasons, that the U.S. failure to implement the two-state plan as a way to resolve the Israeli-Palestinian conflict may advance the one-state scenario as the only remaining option to address the changing realities of Israeli-Palestinian politics. In a one-state setting, the Palestinian population of the occupied territories will have to become citizens of Israel in a binational state. Those students argued that backing Palestinian statehood within the framework of the two-state idea may be the last resort to prevent the inclusion of Palestinians into Israeli society, which Israel considers to be a demographic and political threat to the Jewish identity of the country. They also argued that the U.S. support for a Palestinian state should be viewed by the supporters of Israel as being more motivated by a need to resolve Israel's security and demographic threats than to satisfy Palestinians' aspiration for statehood. Other pro-Israeli students rejected both scenarios—the one- and two-state ideas—in favor of the continuation of the status quo, which is most damaging for the Palestinians. Pro-Palestinian students argued forcefully against the permanence of the status quo situation. It was in that context that the students became more sympathetic with the Palestinians.

Students who expressed ideas reflective of U.S. policy makers and advisers focused on identifying the realist approach to international affairs that is mainly concerned with the pursuit of fundamental U.S. national interests in the region. At the domestic level, those students addressed interest-group activities such as those of the American-Israeli Public Affairs Committee (AIPAC) and Protestant evangelical groups that have historically influenced U.S. policy making to favor Israel rather than the Palestinians. They realized that most U.S. politicians, irrespective of their party affiliation, are oriented to back Israel unconditionally. The absence of major changes in President Obama's policy toward the Israeli-Palestinian conflict may have shown, in this context, that U.S. foreign policy making is not subject to contestations or divisions when handling Israel and the Palestinians. As far as U.S. policy in the larger Middle Eastern setting is concerned, the students outlined that the United States had historically focused its attention on preserving political stability across the region, accessing the region's oil resources, and containing external threats to U.S. dominance in the Middle East. While attempting to preserve U.S. interests in the Middle East as well as its credibility in world affairs, the students suggested that a successful and lasting peace between Israel and the Palestinians would be significantly helpful for the fulfillment of U.S. interests.

On the basis of students' own assessment of the contents and procedures of the peace process, most of them expressed opinions pointing to the Palestinians being the weak party in the context of negotiations. At the same time, those students also raised concerns and criticisms of the Palestinian side by pointing to the presence of a high degree of corruption in Palestinians' institutions. The continued geopolitical divisions among Palestinians living in the West Bank and those in Gaza also undermines Palestinians' claims vis-à-vis the United States and Israel. Students who expressed views that are affiliated with pro-Palestinian activists, such as the Justice for Palestine and Boycott, Divestment and Sanctions (BDS) groups, centered the blame primarily on the continuation of Israel's military occupation of the Palestinian territories for all of the challenges that Palestinians still face. They indicated that U.S. backing of Israel at all costs and irrespective of Palestinians' interests should raise alarming questions about U.S. credibility and honesty in mediating a just and lasting peace in the region. By the end of the debate, the students had educated each other through the use of this and other simulation techniques as to how to express their informed opinions critically and cooperatively. They were also able to develop, and express, their own understanding of, and appreciation for, the benefits of diversities of opinions, beliefs, ideas, and ideals in the framework of a vigorous classroom discussion.

This essay has tried to shed light on examples of classroom topics, debates, and views relating to different cultures, societies, and educational settings. Throughout the discussion, I have emphasized that—especially in the realm of politics—individuals and groups should not underestimate the power of human interactions in the process of managing conflict resolutions. Whether our nature as human beings is fundamentally good or bad has indeed puzzled the human race for centuries. The classroom experience does not answer issues concerning human nature, but it reveals that under the right circumstances, the value of individual and group interactions can be far more useful than official policies managed by political opponents who may often intimidate each other. Although it is always essential to allow students to think for themselves and learn from each other, an educator should in certain situations, such as the ones addressed in this essay, make sure that the topics are academically sound and accurate. Although subjects surrounding historical fabrications and unfounded conspiracies are often addressed in classroom settings, an educator must be able to critically identify and explain the issues and encourage the students to approach such information and analysis in critical and meaningful ways. I conclude that whatever educational system or approach emerges from the process of learning and teaching is bound to fail if educators are not able to communicate freely and cooperatively with each other and with their students, within the framework of their own institutional and, preferably, multicultural setting.

Notes

1. For more on evangelicals' popular appeal in the United States and their backing for Israel, see Jeremy D. Mayer, "Christian Fundamentalists and Public Opinion towards the Middle East: Israel's New Best Friends?," *Social Science Quarterly* 85, no. 3 (2004): 695–712; see also Husam Mohamad, "Protestant Evangelicals and U.S. Policy towards Israel," in *End of Days: Essays on the Apocalypse from Antiquity to Modernity*, ed. Karolyn Kinane and Michael A. Ryan (Jefferson, NC: McFarland, 2009), 199–220.
2. See more about the Israeli Military Order No. 854, cited in an article written by the acting president of Birzeit University at the time: Gabi Baramki, "Palestinian University Education under Occupation," *Palestine-Israel Journal* 3, no. 1 (1996): 37–43.
3. I recall using Fred J. Khouri's textbook *The Arab-Israeli Dilemma* (Syracuse, NY: Syracuse University Press, 1985).
4. For more on this issue, see Hussain Agha, Shai Feldman, Ahmad Khalidi, and Zeev Scheff, *Track-II Diplomacy: Lessons from the Middle East* (Cambridge, MA: MIT Press, 2003).
5. See a newly published edited book by James Ker-Lindsay, *Resolving Cyprus: New Approaches to Conflict Resolution* (London: I. B. Tauris, 2015), which highlights key issues and controversies raised by both sides of the divided island.
6. The *Protocols* were published in full in a customized textbook designed for college students. I do not recall the title of the textbook or the class that the book was assigned to.
7. For more on the comparison between the two, see Farid Hafez, "Comparing Anti-Semitism and Islamophobia: The State of the Field," *Islamophobia Studies Journal* 3, no. 2 (2016): 16–34.
8. For example, students looked at historical documents in Walter Laqueur and Barry Ruben, eds., *The Arab-Israeli Reader: A Documentary History* (New York: Penguin, 2008). They have also reviewed a number of journal and newspapers articles relating to the Israeli-Palestinian conflict. Those articles have included, among others, Ian Lustick, "Two-State Illusion," *New York Times*, September 14, 2013; Leila Farkash, "The One State Solution and the Israeli-Palestinian Conflict: Palestinian Challenges and Prospects," *Middle East Journal* 65, no. 1 (2011): 55–71; Douglas Little, "Pathways to Peace: America and the Arab-Israeli Conflict," *Middle East Journal* 67, no. 3 (2013):

476–78; Robert O. Freedman, "The Bush Administration and the Arab-Israeli Conflict: The Record of Its First Four Years," *Middle East Review of International Affairs* 9, no. 1 (2005); and George W. Bush, excerpts from an address to the members of the Knesset in Israel, May 15, 2008, *Journal of Palestine Studies* 37, no. 4 (2008): 186–88.

How Resources Shape Pedagogy
ISRAEL STUDIES AT CAIRO UNIVERSITY

MENNA ABUKHADRA

Cairo University began offering Hebrew classes in the 1920s with the opening of the university. At first, classes were limited to ancient Biblical Hebrew, as the main purpose of teaching Hebrew was to make comparative studies generally between Arabic and Hebrew and specifically between the Qur'an and the Bible. In the 1950s, after the evolution of political events and the establishment of Israel, Cairo University decided it was necessary to focus more on teaching Zionism and the establishment of Israel as a state in the region. During that period, the teaching of Modern Hebrew began in the Department of Oriental Languages as an independent specialty. Since then, teaching about Israel at Cairo University has made a lot of progress and has faced many problems and obstacles. Here I outline the beginning of Israel studies instruction at Cairo University, define the history of the development of various specialties and disciplines, and explore the various problems facing the pedagogy of Israel studies today in Egypt. At the heart of this essay is a discussion of available resources and the ways in which materials influence what is taught and the ways in which information is framed.

Cairo University was inaugurated as a civil university on December 21, 1908, in a ceremony held at Shura Council Chamber, which was attended by Khedive Abbas II and several statesmen. On the evening of the inauguration day, professors began giving lectures; some of the lectures were about the Hebrew language.

Due to World War I, the university's building moved to Saray Mohamed Sedki, El-Azhar Square, El-Falaki Street, to save expenses. But because there was no permanent headquarters allocated to lectures at the time, lectures were given in various halls that were advertised in daily newspapers, such as the hall of the Shura Council of the laws, high school club, and Dar-el-Garida until the university moved to El-Khawaja Nestor Ganaklis Sarai, which is the current site of the American University. Cairo University struggled to stand on its feet. As a result of this unstable situation, Hebrew-language instruction was very weak and undeveloped.

The 1920s—specifically 1925—marked a great development in the history of Cairo University, including the establishment of the basic buildings of the university in its new location (in Giza). Thus, Cairo University was declared a public university, and a decree was issued to establish Cairo University as the Egyptian University, which was composed of four faculties: Faculty of Arts, Faculty of Science, Faculty of Medicine, and Faculty of Law.

Teaching the Hebrew language started at the exact same year as the establishment of the Faculty of Arts, which was the first faculty situated at Cairo University in its new location. It started in the Department of Arabic and Oriental Languages, and its study was limited initially to Biblical Hebrew, as by that time the main purpose of Hebrew language instruction was to make comparative studies between Arabic and Hebrew, viewing them as two main Semitic languages with a common origin, sharing similarities in grammar and consonant sounds.

The first generation of professors teaching the Hebrew language at Cairo University appeared in 1925, and the first Hebrew educational textbook was titled *Hamatmon* (The treasure, 1926), by Mohammed Badr, who learned Hebrew, Aramaic, and Urdu at Edinburgh University and wrote this book after his return to Egypt. The book presents the basic grammar of the Hebrew language, focusing mainly on a comparison between the Arabic and Hebrew languages. But without Hebrew-language printing presses in Egypt, the book's publication encountered significant difficulties. The author confirmed in the introduction to his book that he was motivated to write it because of the absence of any educational book for teaching the Hebrew language to Arabs.

The second textbook teaching Hebrew in Cairo University was titled *Alasas* (The basis), which was released by a group of professors at Cairo University that included Mohammed Atia Alebrashy and Ali Anani. The book consists of two parts. The first part focuses on the strong correlation between Hebrew and Arabic and the statement of the similarities between both of them and other Semitic languages. The second part focuses on the general grammar of Hebrew, with a detailed study of some of the books of the Old Testament from a linguistic perspective.

The Development of the Discipline

The absence of Zionism from the map of Jewish studies in Egypt did not last long. In the 1950s, the evolution of political events and the establishment of Israel as an independent state marked a big change in the field in Egypt. It became necessary to keep up with events, to learn Modern Hebrew and focus more on teaching about Israel. By that time, the Department of Oriental Languages was separated from the Department of Arabic Language, and a new phase in Hebrew teaching began. But Egyptians were unfamiliar with the contemporary language in use, and the Department of Oriental Languages employed Saied Harb, a Palestinian who migrated to Egypt in the early 1950s and whose Hebrew had been learned while living among Israelis. Harb developed the curricula and used the same books being employed to teach Hebrew to Jews, such as *Ale Lisrael* (Migrate to Israel) and the international Linguaphone program. Among Harb's students were many of the future Egyptian professors of Modern Hebrew.

Professors Farouk Gody and Zakia Roshdy then expanded the curriculum from language instruction to a wider diversity of fields that included Modern Hebrew literature and Israeli political history. These developments in teaching Modern Hebrew language helped the professors in the department read Hebrew books in various disciplines. This became the foundation for Israel studies at Cairo University. Today, there is a significant number of academic staff and faculty running the Modern Hebrew language program and other courses in different fields of Israel studies, including the history of Zionism and Israeli politics, Israeli society, and other Jewish studies courses including medieval Hebrew literature, Judaism, Talmud, Mishna and Gmara, and Old Testament criticism.

This significant shift in Israel studies led to the emergence of a new generation of highly qualified graduates with an advanced level of education in Israel studies. As a result, the graduates of Cairo University were the prime candidates for any job requiring knowledge of Israeli society, Israeli policy, and Modern Hebrew language not only in Egypt but also in other parts of the Arab world, as programs expanded to Jordan, Bahrain, Saudi Arabia, and other Gulf states. Furthermore, many of those students enrolled in master's and PhD programs in different Israel studies' specialties then worked as academics in other Egyptian universities. Hence, teaching Israel studies subsequently expanded to include other universities throughout Egypt. Today there are thirteen Egyptian universities that teach Hebrew.

The Incentives behind Israel Studies in Egypt

The successive wars between Arabs and Israel significantly influenced the development of the teaching of Modern Hebrew language and the orientation of Israel studies at Cairo University. The 1948 Palestine War, the 1956 Suez War, the June 1967 Six-Day War, the 1969–70 War of Attrition, the October 1973 Yom Kippur War, the 1982 Lebanon War, and the 1991 Gulf War affected Israel studies in general and teaching Zionism in particular, making it a program for "studying the enemy." This idea not only influenced the teaching of Hebrew language but also extended to include other specialties in the department, including literature, religion, history, and society. For example, in teaching literature, professors focused on poems, stories, and novels dealing with the Israeli-Palestinian conflict, identifying the political position of authors and their support for Palestinians and criticism of their own government. In teaching religion, the focus was on the negative sides of Judaism, such as teaching laws that impose harsh restrictions on women and that can be contrasted with the more lenient laws of the Qur'an, such as in matters of divorce. Also in teaching history, the focus was on the complicated issues experienced by Jewish communities abroad and how they occupied the land of Palestine in the modern era.

Yet despite university students pursuing Israel studies with great interest, the faculty's knowledge was acquired at an extended remove, as there were no direct interactions between Egyptian and Israeli institutions, and what could be learned in Egypt came from reading Arabic books, Egyptian newspapers, and Egyptian media. As a result, scholars were heavily influenced by Israel's image in Arab culture in general and Egyptian culture in particular.

The Development of the Definitions of Zionism among Arab Scholars

The strained political relations between Arab countries and Israel affected the way Egyptian scholars defined Zionism in negative terms in their writings during the 1950s, 1960s, and 1970s, for example:

> Zionism is a racist ideology that allows Jews from anywhere in the world to go to Israel-Palestine to claim superior rights to the land and government there at the expense of the indigenous non-Jewish Palestinians.
> —Professor Mostafa Alsaadany, *A Spotlight on Zionism* (1957)

> Zionism is an expression of imperialism.
> —Professor Yehia Namy, *This Is Zionism* (1969)

Some Egyptian scholars used the United Nations General Assembly Resolution in 1975, defining Zionism as "a form of racism and racial discrimination" (Professor Mahmoud Semida, *The Strategy of the Zionist Literature to Terrorise Arabs* [1978]). But generally in the Department of Oriental Languages at the Faculty of Arts, Egyptian scholars did not focus on teaching Zionism by teaching politics or history; they actually focused on understanding it by analyzing Modern Hebrew literature. They chose poems, short stories, and novels as source materials for defining Zionism and Zionists, trying to understand the Israeli mentality. Yet this too led to negative framing of Israelis. For example, Egyptian professors used Hebrew poems to direct sharp criticism at traditional Jewish institutions, such as focusing on the explanation of Levirate marriage law in Judaism and discussing how this law represents an obvious disrespect of women.

However, in recent years, there has been a significant change in the attitude toward both Israel and Judaism. These have been primarily driven by the technological advances in communications in the modern era, which have represented a major milestone in the development of Israel studies at Cairo University. As it is no longer difficult to listen to the Hebrew language spoken by Israelis or to read Israeli newspapers online, it has become easy to see everything that goes on in Israeli society and to follow Israeli events moment by moment, and most importantly, it has become possible to watch Israeli television and to chat with Israelis.

In the past few years, when it has become easy to surf the internet and get all the information you seek in any field or specialty, the image of Israel as an enemy has changed. Academics in the Department of Oriental Languages began improving the curriculums, and the subject of the Israeli-Palestinian conflict is no longer the main issue of Israel studies at Cairo University. (I am not saying that it has disappeared completely; it is still there, but it is no longer the central focus of Israel studies.) Instead courses are more focused on Israel as a neighboring country regardless of its political status. For example, they examine Israel as an advanced state, consider its educational system, and analyze the personal nature of Israeli people, the most prominent Israeli writers, sports in Israel, and the customs and traditions of Israelis. The categorical rejection of Israel no longer exists, and while Egyptians continue to criticize Israel's policies toward Palestinians, they also support the two-state solution, which means that Egyptians accept Israel's existence.

After the revolution of January 25, 2011, Israel studies had a boom in Egypt. The reason for that was Arabs' desire in general and Egyptians' in particular to provide the world with information about events in Tahrir Square in Egypt. Many students at Cairo University were interested in showing their distinctiveness and good command of the Hebrew language and their ability to communicate with Israeli people. Heba Hamdy Abuseif, a Cairo University student, appeared on Israeli television—Channel Ten—as an on-camera journalist, reporting on the news of the Egyptian revolution moment by moment. Israeli newspapers commented on her excellent Hebrew, wondering how an Arabic Egyptian student in Cairo University had reached this level of Hebrew proficiency. What proved of particular note to Israeli audiences was that she was a Muslim woman, wearing hijab, indicating a relative détente between religious Egyptians and the Israeli state.

Moreover, Israel has been able to use social media successfully in order to improve its image in the eyes of Arabs. The Israeli Ministry of Foreign Affairs has created a

Facebook page named "Israel in Arabic," which provides information on the State of Israel in Arabic and provides updates on its activities to the general public. Other institutions have also established similar Facebook pages, such as that for Avichay Adraee, the spokesman for the Israel Defense Forces to the Arabic media. Private individuals have also created outreach efforts such as the page "Israel without Censorship," whose posts are directed at Arabs. These social media outreach efforts post articles focusing on the similarities between Arabs and Israelis in music, religion, customs and traditions, and so on. Moreover, on International Women's Day, some of the private pages celebrate and honor the achievements of women from Israel and the Arab world.

Oftentimes, these pages make an effort to focus more on introducing the real image of Israel that Arabs are not familiar with and to use the space for outreach and recruitment to events, such as a conference organized by the Israeli Ministry of Foreign Affairs, which invited Arab journalists and bloggers to participate in order for them to know more about Israel, Israeli society, Israeli nature, and Israeli culture. These pages also show respect for Arabs and Muslim culture and send blessings and greetings to Muslims on Friday (the Muslim holy day of the week), and along with posting the traditional greeting of "Gomaa Mobaraka," one of the pages shared a video of Israeli people greeting Muslims in the Arab world for a blessed Ramadan.

This technological revolution, especially in the past two decades, directly affects what Egyptian scholars teach about Israel. It affects their research and their curriculums, and it has totally changed the way Israel is studied in Egypt, paralleling other changes toward teaching Hebrew and about Israel in the Arab world. However, in spite of this remarkable development, there are still many obstacles that stand in the way of Israel studies at Cairo University. The majority of these are related to the problems of accessing resources, security issues, and psychological barriers.

The lack of direct communication with Israeli universities, as there is no cultural normalization with Israel, is among the most central problems. The students of Cairo University do not have any opportunity to travel to complete their studies in Israel or even to attend conferences or seminars at Israeli universities, which adversely affects Israel studies in Egypt. Moreover, the lack of scholarships awarded by global universities to the academic staff of the Department of Oriental Languages or even to the students has led to the slow progress of Israel studies at Cairo University.

One of the biggest problems faced by both students and professors is the difficulty of accessing Hebrew books from Israel. Most buy Hebrew books through the Israeli academic center in Cairo, but as the majority of the Egyptian public is skeptical about dealing with this institution, not to mention that not everyone is allowed to visit it, they try to find other ways to purchase Hebrew books from Israel. Some try communicating with the Egyptian embassy in Israel, asking officials to buy books for them, and wait for one of the embassy staff to travel, which is quite a lengthy process. Others ask Palestinian students learning in Egypt or Palestinian families living there to bring Hebrew books after their visit to the country. Recently, it became possible to buy Hebrew books online, although it takes a lot of money and a lot of time, and sometimes orders may never be delivered to the buyer; even this partial access, however, has addressed part of the problem.

The growing number of students choosing to learn Hebrew in Cairo University has also affected the needs of the program. In the 1960s, according to official statistics, the number of students in the Department of Oriental Languages was 24. In 2017, the number reached 1,676! This huge increase in the number of students far exceeds the available space and appropriate teaching aids.

Problems Facing Israel Studies at Cairo University (Based on Personal Experience)

As a student at Cairo University since 2004 and then as a lecturer starting from 2009, I have personally seen many of the problems that face Israel studies in Egypt. Moreover, I am following in the footsteps of my father, Zainelabideen Abukhadra, who was also a professor of Hebrew language and literature at Cairo University.

For my father, who belonged to the older generation that witnessed the series of Israeli-Arab wars and the landmark peace agreement between Israel and Egypt (1979), his original motive behind learning Hebrew was to know the language of "the enemy." He joined the university as a student in 1969, then started working as a lecturer in the Department of Oriental Languages and Literature in 1973. Resources and materials were scarce, and Israeli newspapers were treated as a valuable commodity. Learning the language was a struggle, but he persisted and taught his family the basics of Hebrew and practiced speaking in Hebrew in everyday life and over the phone with his colleagues. Above all, his desire for perfection led him to extend his studies to address other fields related to Israel. As a result, he was the first one to be awarded his PhD in Modern Hebrew literature in Cairo University, after years of research studies focusing only on religion and comparative studies between Arabic and Hebrew.

As a consequence of my family's domestic environment, I was attracted to the field, but for me the most interesting aspects were not in the political realm but in literature and culture. I see in my students and among the peers who studied with me a wide range of interests in pursuing Hebrew language and Israel studies. Tourism, particularly in Sharm El Sheikh, which is a popular destination for many Israeli tourists, has driven the need for Hebrew language skills. But even closer to home in Cairo, tourism at historic Jewish sites including synagogues and the old Jewish areas in Cairo and Alexandria brings Israeli tourists, who also then have needs for guides at other attractions and museums. Journalism is a major industry for Hebrew speakers, and some Egyptian e-journals and websites[1] are based mainly on translating Israeli newspaper articles (*Haaretz, Yedioth Ahronoth, Maariv, Israel Hayom*, etc.) into Arabic.

In 2001, a decision was made to launch an Egyptian television channel that broadcasts entirely in Hebrew, Nile TV. "Our aim is to reach Hebrew speakers who may only know about Arab problems with Israel from an Israeli point of view, and by broadcasting to this audience, we can clarify Egypt's position on the Middle East," said Hasan Aly, the head of Nile TV.[2] Moreover, some Egyptian talk shows are specifically dedicated to covering Israeli news, such as *Bel'ebri Alsarieh*[3] and *Bel'ebri* (both in Hebrew).[4]

In addition, many of the students also go on to work for military intelligence: there is an institute of the Egyptian army called *Ma'had Alqowat Almosallah* (the armed forces institute) that offers Hebrew classes to anyone in the Egyptian public who wants to study Modern Hebrew language, whether for military purposes or for any other reasons.

Despite this growing interest in the Hebrew language as one of the main requirements for a variety of jobs in Egypt, and the increasing opportunities available to find resources, there are still challenges for Israel studies at Egyptian universities due to limited exchange programs and the lack of opportunity for study in Israel.

Notes

1. Examples include websites based mainly on translating Israeli newspapers into Arabic, such as www.ehtelalnews.com. Also, other Egyptian websites devote a special section for translating Israeli newspapers, such as www.youm7.com and www.dotmsr.com.
2. Nicole Veash, "Egypt to Beam Hebrew TV Show into Israeli Homes," *Christian Science Monitor*, December 12, 2001, www.csmonitor.com/2001/1212/p7s1-wome.html.
3. This TV show is focused mainly on adding Arabic subtitles to Israeli documentary videos and movies, so that Arab audiences can understand. And it also provides readings and analysis of Israeli newspapers. For further information, see the official Facebook page for show: www.facebook.com/bel3abri/posts/495639260566828.
4. This TV show covers Israeli society news by reading and analyzing Israeli newspapers. For further information, see 'Amr Waly, "A New TV Show Called *Bel'ebri* on Alnahar TV," *dotmsr*, December 13, 2015, http://beta.dotmsr.com.

Where to Begin?

TEACHING THE CONFLICT AT SAN DIEGO STATE UNIVERSITY, JEWISH HISTORY, AND JOHN LE CARRÉ'S *THE LITTLE DRUMMER GIRL*[1]

PETER C. HERMAN

> "Begin at the beginning," the King said gravely, "and go on 'til you come to the end: then stop."

Where does one begin to teach a conflict that has, by one account, been going on since 1946 and, in another, since biblical times? Adding to the difficulties, while San Diego State University has a healthy number of student activists on either side (both Students for Justice in Palestine and Students Supporting Israel have thriving memberships at the university), the fact is, in my experience at least, most English majors have only the vaguest notion of the history and the players. They often have an indistinct impression that Israel does mean things to Arabs and that Arabs have done mean things to Jews but little notion of the conflict's extensive history. In short, how does one responsibly teach the Arab-Israeli conflict to students who know next to nothing about it? (And by "responsibly," I mean giving a more or less dispassionate, accurate version of events that takes into account the both sides' perspectives.) To that end, I have devised a section of my "Literature of Terrorism" class that is devoted to giving students a sense of the long and complicated history of the conflict and how that history makes its way into fiction, in particular, John le Carré's brilliant and underestimated 1983 novel *The Little Drummer Girl*.

But before we delve into fiction, I take a week (two seventy-five-minute classes) to give my students two PowerPoint lectures illustrating the background, thereby also giving students time to read le Carré's rather lengthy novel. I also assign a chapter, "Lydda, 1948," from Ari Shavit's *My Promised Land*.[1] My assumption is that unless you know something of the history, any fiction dealing with the Arab-Israeli conflict will not make a great deal of sense. My second assumption is that the conflict has very deep and complicated roots, with multiple avenues leading to the present situation.

The first lecture, "From Abraham to Auschwitz in 75 Minutes," gives a pocket history of the Jews from Genesis through to the creation of Israel in 1948. I start with Genesis and ancient Israel because contemporary Judaism for centuries regards Israel, and in particular Jerusalem, as its ancient homeland. To understand why so many Jews are invested in Israel, one has to begin with the country's cultural-religious significance. Genesis 12:1–2 gives the mythic origin of the Jewish people: YHWH says to Abraham, "Get thee out of thy country . . . unto a land that I will show thee; And I will make of thee a great nation," while Joshua, Judges, Samuel 1 and 2, and Kings 1 and 2 detail the history of ancient Israel (combining myth and fact). The point of what might seem like a Hebrew-school lesson of little consequence is not so much the success of Davidic or Solomonic Israel, let alone present-day Israel's supposedly historical right to Judaea and Samaria, but the subsequent conquest of ancient Palestine by the Babylonian, Greek, and Roman Empires and the exiles that followed, culminating in the diaspora after the failure of the Bar Kohkba revolt against Rome in AD 70. This event, I tell my class, had two essential consequences. First, the dispersal of the Jews over a very wide geographic area, including Europe, the Mediterranean, North Africa, and Babylonia; and second, the hope of eventually returning to Israel, as exemplified by the conclusion of the Passover service: "Next year in Jerusalem." I also illustrate the effect of the Roman suppression of the revolt by showing a few slides of the temple's ruins and what subsequently came to be known as the "Wailing Wall."

In addition to this primer of Jewish history, I include an element that is sure to disturb some members of the class, only a small proportion of whom are Jewish: the rise of Christianity and its concomitant internalization of antisemitism. At roughly the same time that the Jews dispersed, Christianity developed as a religion, and the Gospels included antisemitic elements. John, for example, writes of the Jews, "Ye are of your father the devil, and the lusts of your father ye will do. He was a murderer from the beginning, and abode not in the truth, because there is no truth in him. When he speaketh a lie, he speaketh of his own: for he is a liar, and the father of it" (8:43–44). What started as a rhetorical ploy to differentiate the new cult of Christianity from its parent religion, Judaism, soon became enshrined in Christian thinking from the Church Fathers through to Martin Luther and beyond. To demonstrate, I show a quotation from the Emperor Constantine, whose conversion to Christianity completed the religion's ascendance, expressing his distaste for the Jews:

> At this meeting the question concerning the most holy day of Easter was discussed, and it was resolved by the united judgment of all present, that this feast ought

to be kept by all and in every place on one and the same day. For what can be more becoming or honorable to us than that this feast from which we date our hopes of immortality, should be observed unfailingly by all alike, according to one ascertained order and arrangement? And first of all, it appeared an unworthy thing that in the celebration of this most holy feast we should follow the practice of the Jews, who have impiously defiled their hands with enormous sin, and are, therefore, deservedly afflicted with blindness of soul.[2]

Next, I present a few choice quotes from Martin Luther's *On the Jews and Their Lies* (1543), for example,

I had made up my mind to write no more either about the Jews or against them. But since I learned that these miserable and accursed people do not cease to lure to themselves even us, that is, the Christians, I have published this little book, so that I might be found among those who opposed such poisonous activities of the Jews who warned the Christians to be on their guard against them. I would not have believed that a Christian could be duped by the Jews into taking their exile and wretchedness upon himself. However, the devil is the god of the world, and wherever God's word is absent he has an easy task, not only with the weak but also with the strong. May God help us. Amen.[3]

Antisemitism also permeated European visual culture, as demonstrated by a series of slides illustrating the iconography of antisemitism from the Middle Ages through to a nineteenth-century American political cartoon showing a crucified Uncle Sam with a sign on top of him saying, "This is the U.S. in the hands of the Jews."[4] This lecture concludes with a quote from Adolf Hitler taken from *Mein Kampf*—"the personification of the devil as the symbol of all evil assumes the living shape of the Jew"[5]—a single slide on the Holocaust, and a newspaper declaring the birth of Israel in 1948. In sum, Hitler's antisemitism has its roots in Christian antisemitism.

I am very aware that this lecture largely reproduces the traditional Zionist narrative of the Jewish diaspora ending in catastrophe due to Europe's and Christianity's long-standing hatred of the Jew: the creation of Israel, a Jewish homeland, being the only answer to the Holocaust. The next class, however, significantly complicates this view by looking in more detail at the region's demographic history and subsequent political events.

Students are always surprised to learn that Palestine was ruled by the Ottoman Empire from the sixteenth century through to 1918. After establishing that fact, I go over three essential developments in the nineteenth and early twentieth centuries: the waves of government-sponsored, anti-Jewish riots in the Russian Empire and the concomitant rise of both nationalism and Zionism (if every other people has a nation, why not the Jews?); the carving up of the Middle East by the various colonial powers in 1918 (the Sykes-Picot Agreement), with Britain getting responsibility for Palestine; and the successive waves of immigration to Palestine caused by the pogroms in Russia and elsewhere. The last is especially important, and I use a graphic (taken, I admit, from Wikipedia) to illustrate how the increasing numbers of Jews changed the region's demography and why the Arabs determinedly resisted both the rising Jewish presence and the Balfour Declaration.

I point out that European Jews regarded immigration as moving to a haven safe from the depredations of antisemitism but that the Arabs regarded the same as an alien invasion, and they deeply resented the British government's decision to declare their sympathy for a Jewish homeland without taking into consideration the views of the region's inhabitants. As a 1918 Palestinian petition to the British government says, "We always sympathized profoundly with the persecuted Jews and their misfortunes in other countries, . . . but there is wide difference between such sympathy and the acceptance of such a nation . . . ruling over us and disposing of our affairs."[6] The next few slides bring the class up to 1948, Israel's creation by an act of the United Nations, and the subsequent attempt, first by the Palestinian Arabs in Israel and then, after that failed, by a joint invasion of Israel by Egypt, Jordan, Syria, Iraq, and Lebanon, to destroy the new state.[7]

And here, I stress, we find the origin of the opposing narratives: Zionists look at the repopulating of Palestine with Jews and the creation, in 1948, of the State of Israel as homecoming ("Next year in Jerusalem") and just recompense for the Holocaust. Palestinians look at the same events and see foreign powers imposing their will and their own displacement by an alien people. To give due credence to the Palestinian side, I ask students to read alongside this lecture Ari Shavit's chapter "Lydda, 1948," which describes the events at Lydda (the original Arabic name for what is now called Lod) as "our black box. In it lies the dark secret of Zionism," meaning that if the Arabs remained, Israel would not, could not exist: "If Zionism was to be, Lydda could not be. If Lydda was to be, Zionism could not be."[8] Therefore, the Arabs of this town were expelled just as the Jews were expelled many centuries earlier: "And as the military governor watches the faces of the people marching into exile, he wonders if there is a Jeremiah among them to lament their calamity and disgrace."[9]

I bring this lecture to a close by illustrating Israel's post-1948 history with a list of Israel's wars and a series of maps: the original, UN partition; the 1949 armistice (in which Israel gained about 50 percent more territory than originally given); Israel's borders before and after the 1967 war; Jerusalem pre- and post-1967; the 1973 Yom Kippur War cease-fire line; and the 1979 borders after Israel and Egypt signed a peace treaty.[10] The lecture concludes with slides illustrating statements from Iran

Overview of Palestine's Demographics from the First Century to the Mandate Era

Year	Jews	Christians	Muslims	Total
Early 1st c.	Majority	—	—	~ 2,500
Early 4th c.	Majority	Minority	—	> 1st c.
5th c.–11th c.	Minority	Majority	—	> 1st c.
End 12th c.	Minority	Minority	Majority	> 225
14th c.	Minority	Minority	Majority	150
1533–1539	5	6	145	157
1690–1691	2	11	219	232
1800	7	22	246	275
1890	431	57	432	532
1914	94	70	525	689
1922	84	71	589	752
1931	175	89	760	1,033
1947	630	143	1,181	1,970

NOTE: Estimates by Sergio Della Pergola, "Demography in Israel/Palestine: Trends, Prospects, Policy Implications," paper presented at the IUSSP XXIV General Population Conference, Salvador de Bahia, August 2001, drawing on the work of Roberto Bachi, *The Population of Israel*, World Population Year 1974 (Jerusalem: CICRED, 1975). Figures in thousands.

SOURCE: Wikipedia, "Demographic History of Palestine (Region)," https://en.wikipedia.org/wiki/Demographic_history_of_Palestine_(region).

and Hamas expressing their desire to wipe Israel off the map, for example, Mohammad Ali Jafari, the commander in chief of the Iranian Revolutionary Guard: "The Revolutionary Guards will fight to the end of the Zionist regime. . . . We will not rest easy until this epitome of vice [i.e., the State of Israel] is totally deleted from the region's geopolitics."[11]

With all this complicated backstory now under their belts, the students and I embark on analyzing le Carré's book. The novel concerns a group of Mossad agents who recruit an actress named Charlie (Charlene) to play the lover of a Palestinian terrorist, Michel, in order to find, and then kill, his brother, Khalil, the leader of a particularly effective cell of terrorists. Le Carré, however, carefully sets out the motivations of both Israelis and Palestinians.

At one end, we have the leader of the Mossad squad, variously known as "Schulmann," "Marty," and "Kurtz." He is, as his German counterpart, Alexis, realizes, "possessed by a deep and awesome hatred."[12] This hatred, however, far from irrational, results directly from recent Jewish history. Kurtz (as he is generally known) represents all the reasons why Israel exists and why the country feels so embattled. He chooses a particular safe house in Munich because "northward the windows gave a grimy view of the road to Dachau," and "nearer at hand, [the Mossad agents] could point out to Kurtz the very spot where, in more recent history, Palestinian commandos had burst into the living quarters of the Israeli athletes, killing some immediately, and taking the rest to the military airport, where they killed them too" (39–40). Looking at the stone tablet commemorating the eleven victims of an attack that "shocked the world," Kurtz "needlessly" orders the group, "So remember that" (41). Kurtz personally experienced what he tells his group to remember. Staring out of the window of a plane flying from Munich to Berlin, he recalls how he made this journey with his mother "and the hundred and eighteen other Jews who were crammed into their truck, ate the snow and froze, most of them to death" (46). Le Carré passes over Kurtz's experience in the camp, describing instead his life in general terms: "somewhere in the fields the Sudeten boy who was himself had [sic] starved and stolen and killed, waiting without illusion for another hostile world to find him" (46). He finds his way to Palestine, where "Kurtz's war [against those who destroy the Jews] had just begun" (46).

On the other side of the scale, le Carré gives us Khalil, the terrorist mastermind, the man Kurtz says is "the best operator they produced for years" (44). But le Carré departs from the usual depictions of terrorists by not depicting Khalil as a barbarian or a madman.[13] Instead, le Carré gives the reader an intelligent, "beautiful" man possessed of such charismatic presence that "he could not have walked into a restaurant without the talk dying round him" (493). He also has a sense of humor about himself: after finishing constructing the bomb, he lays it carefully inside the case: "'I need spectacles,' he explained with a smile, and shook his head like an old man. 'But where should I go for them—a man like me?'" (498). Everything about him, in other words, commands the reader's sympathy.

Which is not to say that le Carré romanticizes Khalil or downplays the horrific violence this man causes. Or the hypocrisy of it. As Khalil says, "our brother Arabs kill us, the Zionists kill us, the Falangists kill us" (497), but the Jews are the only objects of his murderous attention because they are "the real enemy" and not his "brother Arabs" (498). Le Carré, at the book's start, also graphically describes the death and maiming caused by one of Khalil's bombs. When Khalil quotes his friend Capt. Tayeh, saying, "But if we make a few bombs—kill a few people—make a slaughterhouse, just for two minutes of history" (498), we are meant to be properly horrified. But just as the first PowerPoint lecture gives students a better idea of Kurtz's motivations, the second, including the Shavit chapter, allows students to understand what would lead this handsome, intelligent, sensitive man to a life of utter destruction: the Palestinian dispossession following 1948. Khalil's great dream is not a massacre; it is repossession of the land the Palestinians lost, at the cost of Israel's existence: "We take ships to the borders. Planes. Millions of us. Like a great tide which nobody can turn back.... Then all together, we march into our homeland, we claim our houses and our farms and our villages, even if we have to knock down their towns and settlements and kibbutzim in order find them" (498).

Between Kurtz and Khalil, there is no middle ground, no compromise possible. Neither grants the other the slightest legitimacy. They may respect each other as adversaries, but each seeks to destroy the other and what the other represents.

Charlie's agent runner, Gadi Becker (she knows him as "Joseph"), however, occupies what Kurtz himself calls "the middle ground. . . . Because he has the reluctance that can make the bridge. Because he ponders" (48). Kurtz means that Becker can give Charlie the proper backstory, the proper narrative to fool the people she needs to fool to reach Khalil, because he can sympathize with both the Zionist and Palestinian narratives. In a remarkable act of ventriloquism, Becker takes on the role of Charlie's Palestinian lover, and he recites to her the Palestinian narrative of forced dispossession and Zionist atrocities, such as the events at Deir Yassin.[14] While the Israelis call the 1948 war the "War of Independence," the Palestinians name it something else altogether, a name that points to an entirely different narrative (the one covered in the second lecture): "I refer to the war of '48 as 'the Catastrophe.' Never the war—the Catastrophe" (225). Becker does not simply recite the narrative of his enemy; he seems to passionately believe every word of it, so much so that Charlie "could not tell whether Joseph or Michel was replying, and she knew he did not mean her to" (225). This is what Kurtz means when he says that Becker "ponders": he understands that there are two narratives underlying the conflict and sympathizes with both.

When I last taught this section, after we finished our discussion of *The Little Drummer Girl*, a student asked me just as the class was breaking up, "So who's right?" I said to myself, "My work here is done."

Notes

1. Ari Shavit, *My Promised Land: The Triumph and Tragedy of Israel* (New York: Random House, 2013), 99–132.
2. Eusebius of Caesarea, "The Life of the Blessed Emperor Constantine," Internet Medieval Source Book, https://sourcebooks.fordham.edu/basis/vita-constantine.asp.
3. Martin Luther, *The Jews and Their Lies*, Jewish Virtual Library, www.jewishvirtuallibrary.org/martin-luther-quot-the-jews-and-their-lies-quot.
4. The image can be found in the Wikipedia article "History of Anti-Semitism in the United States," https://en.wikipedia.org/wiki/History_of_antisemitism_in_the_United_States.
5. Adolf Hitler, *Mein Kampf* [*My Struggle*] (New York: Houghton Mifflin, 1969), 293.
6. Quoted in Robert O. Freedman, *Israel's First Fifty Years* (Gainesville: University Press of Florida, 2000), 96–97.
7. For a comprehensive and unsparing history, see Benny Morris, *1948: The First Arab-Israeli War* (New Haven, CT: Yale University Press, 2008).

8. Shavit, *My Promised Land*, 108.
9. Ibid., 123.
10. My original web source for these maps is no longer extant. However, each can be found using Google and Google Image.
11. Quoted in Jeffrey Goldberg, "The Iranian Regime on Israel's Right to Exist," *Atlantic Monthly*, March 9, 2015, www.theatlantic.com/international/archive/2015/03/Iranian-View-of-Israel/387085/.
12. John le Carré, *The Little Drummer Girl* (1983, repr., New York: Penguin, 2011), 30. All subsequent quotations from the novel refer to this edition and are cited parenthetically in the text.
13. See Robert Appelbaum and Alexis Paknadel, "Terrorism and the Novel, 1970–2001," *Poetics Today* 29, no. 3 (2008): 387–436.
14. Deir Yassin was a small village outside Jerusalem. On April 9, 1948, Jewish forces not only conquered the town but committed atrocities in the process. See Morris, *1948*, 225–28.

Jerusalem

HOLY CITY OF CONFLICT AND DESIRE

RACHEL FELDHAY BRENNER

I teach a course that studies the significance of Jerusalem in the Arab-Israeli conflict. The holiness that the three Abrahamic religions attribute to the city played a crucial role in shaping their foundational theological principles. The course proposes that close attention to these articles of faith and the ways in which they interrelate and inform history is essential to the understanding of the competitive desires for ownership of the city that underlie the intractable conflict over Jerusalem and the Holy Land.

I have taught the class a few times. The student composition varies: in the fall semester, I teach it to freshmen as part of the First-Year-Integration Program (FIG), and in the spring semester, I teach it to mixed classes of sophomores, juniors, and seniors. With regard to religious affiliation, the students have been mainly Christians of Catholic and Protestant denominations and non-Orthodox Jews. I have also had a small number of Muslim students. But age or religious affiliation notwithstanding, the students generally have very little, if any, knowledge of the political situation or even of the geography of the Middle East, and quite often they are ignorant about their own religious faiths, let alone the ways in which faith underlies the conflict.

Indeed, the students usually acknowledge their former lack of knowledge in the concluding assignment of the course, which consists of an oral presentation followed by a written final essay. The assignment requires an examination of the personal impact of the course. The students may focus on issues such as gaining knowledge; better understanding of the region and its religious complexities; evolution/change of personal ideological, political, religious views, and attitudes; increased level of interest in religion/politics; and possible future plans that relate to the course study. Very often, almost uniformly, the presentation begins with the student's admission that his or her enrollment in the course was motivated by the realization of having very little knowledge of the subject coupled with keen interest in this particular area of study, often triggered by personal or family experience. The students like this assignment and take it very seriously; as a rule, the presentations show good internalization of the material as well as interesting introspective appreciations of the emotionally and intellectually transformative impact of the study.

With regard to content and methodology, the class follows a two-pronged trajectory. Whereas the instruction of the core subject of the religious-historical roots of the conflict constitutes the major portion of the session, the class starts with each student's brief report of the news from the region. I start with the latter. The rationale for the requirement of news reports derives from my strong belief that the pedagogy of liberal education should raise the consciousness of and the interest in world events. Thus, the routine of reporting current events three times a week aims to instill a sense of curiosity about the world, which I hope will inculcate the habit of following the news. The requirement to state the provenance of the reported news item intends to draw attention to the issue of authenticity and reliability of the report. The recent debates over the phenomena of "fake news" and "alternative truth" have highlighted the importance of the source of information.

The events, reported consistently as they develop, illuminate the complexity of the Middle East at large and at the same time confirm the course's premise of the indelible role of religion in politics. For instance, the recurring news of the war in Syria relates to the war against ISIL and its religious radicalism. The idea of the caliphate as well as the enmity and warfare between the religious divisions of the Sunni and the Shiite denomination illuminates the importance of religion in local politics and international relations. It should be noted that the PowerPoint presentation of a Middle East map and of maps of the particular locations in the reported events, which I show as the reports are being presented (I usually anticipate the news items and have the maps ready), familiarize the students with the geographic location of the area under discussion.

In the midterm exam, I include a question, which was not discussed in the review for the exam, about the benefits of the news reports. That the response is overwhelmingly positive might be credited to the wish to "please the teacher"; however, the students' capacity to substantiate their positive answer with three news items that they remember and to explain their significance points to the effectiveness of this exercise. I have also noticed another unintended merit of the news presentation: over time, a number of the students have become quite eager to talk among themselves about the news before the class. Even though they might just try to avoid repetition of the same news item, I consider such exchanges a positive social interaction, as the conversations disrupt, even if for a short while, the constant (obsessive?) preoccupation with electronic devices.

Now I turn to the discussion of the core subject of the course: the religious roots of the Israeli-Arab conflict. The Socratic method of my instruction intends to stimulate critical thinking. The instruction is based on assigned readings for every class. I have found that shorter pieces are more effective, and so the syllabus specifies the texts or parts of texts to be read and summarized. These materials can be found online, but I also have a reader that students can purchase. Short, about ten sentences long, summaries of the assigned texts are due before class. I grade and return them the next session. I take this opportunity to make the students work on their writing. The summaries ensure that the students have some understanding of the materials, which enables the class's engagement in dialogic exchange and analytical examination of the concepts in the texts.

The first segment of the course focuses on the Jerusalem-related theological premises of each religion and the ways in which the contentious interrelation of these ideas contributed to a course of history that eventually produced the Israeli-Arab conflict.

We begin with a discussion of the relativity of a historical representation. On the one hand, as Martin Goodman's "Jews and Judaism in the Second Temple Period" points out, the predominantly Christian documentation of the period underscores the historians' intention to advance the perspective of the fulfillment of Jesus's prophesies about the destruction of Jerusalem;[1] on the other hand, the Jewish author Flavius Josephus admits in his preface to *The Wars of the Jews* the impact of his grief over the destruction of the Temple and Jerusalem on his documentation of the events. In both cases, faith in the holiness of the city and in the mythical signification of its destruction has affected the historical narrative. Not only does the juxtaposition of the Christian and Jewish perspectives of the holiness of the Temple and of Jerusalem elucidate the subjectivity of the historical representation of a factual event; our examination of the discrepancy between the perceptions of the event also leads to essential questions: How did the theological conceptualizations of the destruction shape each religion's specific attitude to Jerusalem and the Holy Land? How did the mythical attributes of Jerusalem in each religion set in motion a historical process that led to the emergence of the Israeli-Arab conflict?

We begin with the Jewish foundational myth of the covenant. The divine promise of the land to the Chosen People, which was conceived in the Babylonian exile, factored in the pattern of exile and return. Thus, the content of covenant between God and His People informed the mind-set of persistent longing and desire for the Promised Land, which centered on the repossessing of Jerusalem and rebuilding of the Temple. It was eventually the ages-long cultivation of the memory of the land, mainly through mandatory study of the Talmud and daily repeated liturgy, that produced the Zionist actualization of return.

We continue with the Christian foundational myth of Jesus, which, written up in the Gospels decades after his death, decreed the holiness of Jerusalem as the site of Passion, Crucifixion, and Resurrection. The destruction of the Jewish Temple proved the validity of the new covenant, which superseded the old covenant and made it possible to imprint Jerusalem with Jesus's story, authenticated by concrete loci, such as the Via Dolorosa and the Church of the Holy Sepulcher. Most significantly, the myth of the Second Coming, which would redeem Earthly Jerusalem into Heavenly Jerusalem, depended on the acceptance of the Savior by Jews, the witness-people. This article of faith constituted the theology of contempt, which produced a centuries-long history of Jewish persecutions aimed at the conversion of the Jews.

We conclude this segment of the course with an examination of the foundational myth of Muhammad's miraculous Night Journey from Mecca to Jerusalem and his Ascension to heavens from Haram al-Sharif (Temple Mount), a myth that instituted Jerusalem as the third holy city in Islam. The conquest of Jerusalem from Byzantium, which established centuries of almost-uninterrupted Muslim rule over the city, created a theologically adverse situation for both Christians and Jews, which bore historical consequences. For the Christians, the Muslim rule over the city of Christ precluded the advent of Heavenly Jerusalem, which resulted in a history of attempts to reconquest the city, most notably the Crusades. For the Jewish people, the Muslim takeover of the holiest site of the Jewish religion, as signified by the renaming of Temple Mount as Haram al-Sharif (The Noble Sanctuary), communicated the finality of the Temple destruction. The construction of the Dome of the Rock and the al-Aqsa Mosque on Haram al-Sharif eliminated irrevocably the Jewish hope to rebuild the Temple.

The study of the foundational myths of the three religions and the historical consequences of their Jerusalem-oriented theologies in antiquity and the Middle Ages is followed by the examination of Christian-Jewish relations in the European Diaspora. I ground this part of the course on the premise that Jewish history in Europe, which led to the emergence of modern Zionism, must be understood in the context of the religious and cultural transmutations of Europe in the aftermath of the medieval period.

The Spanish Reconquista provided Jews with the choice between expulsion and coerced conversion and represented an extreme implementation of the theology of contempt. The schism of the Reformation marked an extended era of intensified hatred and persecution of the Jews, whose refusal to convert thwarted Luther's hopes for the fulfillment of the prophecy of the Second Coming. Nonetheless, the Treaties of Westphalia, which initiated the concept of nation-state, weakened the hegemony of religion and led to the transformative historical and civilizational events of the Enlightenment, the French Revolution, and the Napoleonic wars. These dramatic developments in western Europe, which brought forth the ideas of humanism and scientific progress, eventually freed the Jews from their communal-religious segregation; the Emancipation, which abolished the ghettoes, made it possible for western European Jews to enter Christian society and consequently, as it seemed for a short while, to eliminate religion and its theological tenets as framers of Christian-Jewish history. Putting trust in the new era of religious and ethnic tolerance, Jews engaged in creating their own Enlightenment movement, the Haskalah. The recognition of the illusion of Jewish integration into Christian society persisted longer in western than in eastern Europe, where the failure of the Emancipation and the incessant persecutions proved the futility of Jewish hopes. The exacerbation of the antisemitic climate, fueled by the intensifying nationalistic movements and the racist ideas of social Darwinism, transformed the centuries-old theology of messianic longing for return to the land into the ideology of Jewish nationalism, which took the form of the Zionist movement.

Political Zionism, which actualized centuries-long Jewish yearnings for Jerusalem, consisted of *maskilim*, educated, secular Jews who had been yearning to enter the world of progress and modernity. And so, while the overarching idea of return referred to the ancient biblical covenantal promise, the conceptualization of the Zionist project drew on the ideas of enlightened Christian Europe that Zionists admired and wished to emulate. This paradoxical situation emerges in the profiles of the Zionist founding fathers. Grounding our discussion in primary sources, especially Arthur Herzberg's *The Zionist Idea: A Historical Analysis and Reader*, we trace the impact of the European thought on the Zionists' vision of the society they sought to establish in the land.[2]

In general, Zionists followed either of the modern systems of belief: the ideology of humanism, which promoted the inclusionary values of equality, empathy, and justice; and the ideology of nationalism, which promoted ethnic, religious, and cultural exclusion. On the one hand, we read thinkers such as Ahad Ha'Am, Yitzhak Epstein, and Martin Buber, who saw the return as an opportunity for Jewish social and spiritual revival in the creation of a new Jewish culture. The settlement in the land enabled the Jewish returnees to combine the biblical principles of social justice, as propagated by the prophets of Israel, with the present-day progressive humanistic ideals of solidarity and brotherhood/sisterhood of all human beings, which could include the Arab inhabitants of the land. On the other hand, Theodor Herzl, Max Nordau, Eliezer Ben Yehuda, and Ze'ev Jabotinsky subscribed to the idea of statehood modeled after western Europe. Their ideological orientation, which prevailed and which shaped the history that led to the conflict, combined the biblical myth of the powerful, militant Kingdom of David with the present-day idea of colonial nationalism. The returning Jews could bring Western civilization and prosperity to a declining Ottoman Empire. Their vision of a nation-state of Jewish majority, united by belief in Jewish sovereignty, self-defense, economic self-sufficiency, and cultural exclusivity, signaled an intentional exclusion of the Arab population.

The arrival of Zionism in Ottoman Palestine both as a representative of the superior Western civilization and as the rightful beneficiary of the covenantal promise of the land opens the final stage of our discussion. This concluding segment extends from the First and Second Aliyah to World War I and the collapse of the Ottoman

Empire, ending in the Balfour Declaration. We focus on the extent to which the clash of the emerging national identities of the arriving Jews and Palestinian Arab inhabitants reignited the theological disagreements of the three religions over Jerusalem and the Holy Land.

The ideological orientation of the Jewish immigrants, represented by the phrase "A Land without People to a People without Land," originally coined by Christian Zionists in the nineteenth century, emblematized the exclusionary perception of the newcomers with regard to the native inhabitants of the land. The fact that the Jews were purchasing the land—a phenomenon that caused increasing anxiety for the Arab-Ottoman intellectuals and politicians—not only exposed the incongruity of the slogan but also created a situation that presaged the conflict. However, the theological context of the phrase implies a religious aspect in the growing hostility between the two nations.

Since the "land without people" signifies the Holy Land, and the "people without land" are the Jews, the subtext of the phrase denotes the symbolical emptiness of the land, which, according to the stipulations of the covenant, has been waiting for its absent rightful owners. The Arab response to the Jewish covenantal claim to the land, as discussed in Jonathan Marc Gribetz's *Defining Neighbors: Religion, Race, and Early Zionist-Arab Encounter*, reinforces the religious aspect of the emerging conflict.[3] Gribetz's elaboration on the refutation of the Jewish covenantal claim to the land by Ruhi al-Khalidi and other Ottoman intellectuals is of particular significance, as it reconnects with the Christian world. Al-Khalidi's argument that the Jews forfeited their right to the land when they accepted Emancipation, which endowed them with new national identities, premises the national character of the covenant. Identification of the Jews as Western nationals annuls the covenant and thereby the Jewish claim to the land. At the same time, the centuries-long Muslim rule in Jerusalem, where Haram al-Sharif features al-Aqsa, the third holy mosque, affirms the Muslim ownership of the land.

The theologically historical argumentation over the Zionist repossession of the land did not remain strictly in the Muslim-Jewish sphere. The response of the Christian Church was divided. Catholics sided with the Palestinian rejection of the Jewish claim to the land. The Vatican preferred to have the holy places under Muslim rule. The possibility that the holy places and especially Jerusalem, the locus of Crucifixion and Resurrection, might be under the rule of the Jews, who persist in their disbelief and blindness to the true Messiah, was a theological anathema to the Catholic Church. However, British Protestants, and especially Christian Zionists, took a diametrically differing theological approach to the Jewish return to the land. They perceived Zionism as a harbinger of the Second Coming; it was a hopeful sign that the ingathering of the exiles may precipitate the conversion of the Jews, which would herald the advent of Heavenly Jerusalem. British Protestants followed their theological convictions with a political act the importance of which cannot be overestimated. While political factors in the British government's decision should not be ignored, Christian Zionism played an important role in the 1917 Balfour Declaration, which promised "a national home in Palestine to the Jewish people."

The Balfour Declaration represented a pivotal event that set in motion the modern national version of the hundreds-years-long interminable religious contention over Jerusalem and the Holy Land. The theological underpinnings of the inception of this crucial document remind us that the national conflict cannot be fully understood unless the theological differences of the three religious traditions over the holiness of Jerusalem are recognized and acknowledged.

To conclude, the foregoing narrative does not by any means cover the entire course; rather, it offers an outline for a study of the religious aspect of the conflict. In other words, it is intended as a template that might facilitate teaching the conflict from the theological perspective, which encompasses the three religions. I believe that the combination of the core course and the current events might prove quite a useful strategy to underline the relevance of the past to the understanding of the present. For instance, a discussion of today's unflinching support of Israel by the U.S. Right, which boasts a large Christian Zionist constituency, or conversely an examination of the exacerbating crisis concerning the right of Palestinian Muslims and Israeli Jews to worship on the Temple Mount–Haram al-Sharif may find the perspective offered in the preceding analysis helpful. As I am writing these words on May 9, 2017, the media reports that Recep Tayyip Erdoğan, the Turkish president, has just urged Muslims to make a pilgrimage to the al-Aqsa Mosque as an act of protest against the occupation. And so it goes . . .

Notes

1. Martin Goodman's "Jews and Judaism in the Second Temple Period," in *The Oxford Handbook of Jewish Studies*, ed. Martin Goodman (New York: Oxford University Press, 2002), 36–52.
2. Arthur Herzberg, ed., *The Zionist Idea: A Historical Analysis and Reader* (New York: Doubleday, 1959).
3. Jonathan Marc Gribetz, *Defining Neighbors: Religion, Race, and Early Zionist-Arab Encounter* (Princeton, NJ: Princeton University Press, 2014).

Teaching the Value of Conflict

INTELLECTUAL HOSPITALITY,
HUMANISTIC PEDAGOGY, AND
THE POETRY OF YEHUDA AMICHAI

HOLLI LEVITSKY

I teach at Loyola Marymount University, a small liberal arts college in the Jesuit tradition. My students are bright, global citizens, arriving at our picture-perfect Los Angeles campus from countries as distant—and different—as Uruguay, Malaysia, and Saudi Arabia. They come to study film or business or political science on a bluff overlooking the city lights on one side, the Pacific ocean on the other. Muslim, Jewish, and Christian students all make use of an interdenominational prayer center named for the Catholic Marymount tradition. While the outer view is singularly serene and commanding (the university is also called "University of Silicon Beach" for its location by the beach and inside a high-tech hub), students' internal lives are forged by a dynamic set of processes influenced by their experience with different or contrary religious traditions, political beliefs, and/or value systems. When students come to my classroom, they may or may not know much about Israel or Palestine or the history of the region, but they know about their own tensions and conflicts and, like college students everywhere, are concerned about the future. They can try to lead a safe life "on the bluff" and engage only with others like themselves. Or they can use the time to seek opportunities for personal growth as they further their education on specific topics. Enter the two-week summer immersion course in Israel, where the study of Israel *in* Israel becomes the embarkation for a deeper journey into their inner lives, shaking up their certainties, challenging their beliefs, and energizing their critical thinking skills, on the landscape of an ancient and holy land that is encumbered with aspirations and anxieties of its own.

Our students are dynamic beings, and our teaching should reflect that. This is not a new thesis; in 1993, Gerald Graff suggested in *Beyond the Culture Wars* that teaching the conflicts around academic issues prepares students to understand how knowledge becomes established and eventually accepted.[1] Conflict is the focus of much of our work in the university literature classroom. We tell students to identify the conflict in a literary work as a starting point to understanding its meaning; the key to the success of a literary work may well be how authentically the unfolding and resolution of the central conflict or problem is undertaken by the author. Conflicts are not always resolved—indeed, the lack of resolution may be what in fact makes a story great. But the idea of helping students "evolve" as critical thinkers through consideration of conflict and disagreement—that is, to understand how knowledge becomes established, eventually accepted, and then critiqued—is as old as teaching itself.

Even as we imagine engaging college students anew in the conflicts of the stories we teach, they are already participating—wittingly or not—in external and internal conflicts of one sort or another outside the classroom. They may face gender and other sexual-identity issues, financial and employment issues, family discord, or other age-related issues. On a daily basis, they are in contact with so many others, from different religions, countries, and political beliefs. Yet we rarely engage the dynamic process of identity formation that is the result of their quotidian conflicts.

Through study of a complex and dynamic topic, in a complex and dynamic country, my course "Literature and Faith in the Holy Land: Encountering the Other" addresses the complexity and dynamism of the individual college student. At its basic level, this upper-division course offers a means through which personal conflict comes into contact with literary conflict. Given Israel's history, its landscape offers an additional level of conflict that can become a powerful pedagogical tool.

The course was created specifically to satisfy a university-wide core requirement for an "Integrations" course, a category meant to serve as a culminating experience for junior and senior students as they develop a more mindful engagement with the world. These more advanced students "integrate the knowledge and skills gained in the [earlier Core] Foundations and Explorations courses and their major courses, and apply them to a range of questions of contemporary significance" (from the university's website). Study-abroad courses can fulfill this requirement in unique ways, bringing college students to sites of contest and conflict. Engaging with multiple historically weighted sites, students come to know a landscape from many angles. As they engage with the sites and learn about the associated issues, they move from "banking" knowledge to mindful and active engagement with the world.[2]

In the rest of the essay, I outline the scholarship that informed the course's development, provide the details of the course syllabus, examine one assignment more closely, and offer a universal lesson from the experience.

Theoretical Underpinnings

There are primarily two areas of inquiry that inform the pedagogy of this course. The first, from the philosophy of Paulo Freire, a Brazilian educator and philosopher and a leading advocate of critical pedagogy, addresses human growth through engagement with the world. Freire's work anchors the course objectives to my university's promise to "educate the whole person," which I take to mean that mind, body, and spirit are all present in a university education.[3] Applying Freire's concept of "praxis"—that action springs forth from reflection—extends our notion of engagement with the other from a static dimension to a dynamic and transformative encounter. Freire's pedagogical model of active reflecting helped me establish universal course objectives: that students should know what engagement is, be able to initiate such engagement with others, and value such engagement for personal growth. Freire says, "No one is born fully formed: it is through self-experience in the world that we become what we are."[4] The acquisition of an authentic and representational voice, developed through guided study in the literature classroom, gives college students the freedom to make alliances or seek allegiance. The next step toward self-identification, engagement with the world, is a necessary and powerful component for human learning and culture to evolve. For Freire, evolution involves struggle, and "without a sense of identity, there can be no real struggle."[5] Such site-specific encounters with a teacher and his or her students gives birth not just to new friendships and bonds but to a more vivid and engaged sense of self as well.

The second area of inquiry, from the discipline of hospitality studies, examines spaces of "intellectual hospitality" and grounds the course objectives in the university's mission to engage in ethical discourse and to embrace the search for values. The concept of hospitality is extended to include all encounters that may beckon/beg a conflict: self and self-image (values and beliefs); self and other (including teacher, classmates, tour guide, Israelis, and others with whom we engage in Israel); self and society (Israeli government and policies, culture, language, religion); self and nature (natural and constructed sites, ancient and modern); self and technology (access, virtual life, blogging, website creation, etc.); even self and the supernatural (mystical traditions). In applying the concept of "intellectual hospitality" to the course, we broaden conventional concepts of hospitality to include encounters between holders of different religious, political, and social views and holders of different national, professional, and other identities, whose exchange of their differing views is done with compassion, kindness, and curiosity—opening up a space of intellectual hospitality. While the course is deliberately crafted to be interfaith, interdisciplinary, and international in scope, the primary objective is to engage in encounters that interrogate students' own certainties through the eyes of the other, even as we are guided by the Judeo-Christian concept of hospitality—that is, the imperative to treat the stranger kindly, since we were all once "strangers in a strange land."

Course Objectives, Readings, and Other Assignments

Reading, writing, and oral assignments were designed to address these main course objectives (which can be easily adapted): (1) to understand hospitality as an encounter with another through compassion, kindness, and curiosity; (2) to be able to generate such hospitality with others, including classmates and strangers; (3) to value such hospitality as a means to intellectual, spiritual, and emotional growth; (4) to be able to reflect on, discuss, and analyze these encounters through literature and oral, written, individual, and group responses.

Reading assignments include the following essays and poetry, all bound in a course pack for easy carrying:

- David Patterson, "'Where Is Your Brother?': Jewish Teachings on the 'Stranger'" (in *Encountering the Stranger: A Jewish-Christian-Muslim Trialogue*, ed. Leonard Grob and John K. Roth [Seattle: University of Washington Press, 2012], 38–49)
- Henry F. Knight, "Canopies of Hospitality: Post-Shoah Christian Faith and Making Room for Others" (in Grob and Roth, *Encountering the Stranger*, 50–63)
- Mary C. Boys, "This I Believe" (in *Trialogue and Terror: Judaism, Christianity, and Islam after 9/11*, ed. Alan L. Berger [Eugene, OR: Cascade Books, 2012], 121–33)
- Selected poems from Yehuda Amichai, *The Selected Poetry of Yehuda Amichai* (ed. and trans. Chana Bloch and Stephen Mitchell [Berkeley: University of California, 1996])

The preceding essays ground the course in its "faith" component and primarily speak to the first and second objectives: to examine the questions at the heart of the Judeo-Christian concept of hospitality and to engage personally with those questions through encounters with various others. The poetry of Yehuda Amichai and the students' writing/oral assignments speak more to the third and fourth objectives: to evolve as a result of such engagements and to gain written and oral literacy, and a deepened understanding of the topic, through the course work.

In addition to the readings and several short essay assignments asking students to respond to the readings, the course requires a presentation based on a site visit and its connection to an assigned Amichai poem; an original poem written in the style of Amichai's "Autobiography, 1952"; and a concluding assignment that uses an Amichai poem and the essay by Mary Boys to assess whether the course objectives have been achieved.

The daily itinerary includes visits to significant, diverse religious sites; cultural sites that afford both historical context and an enriched understanding of the diversity of voices in Israel; civic and national sites that reveal the political and governmental structures of Israel; and locations across Israel that offer insights into the visible and invisible geographical boundaries operating in the Middle East. In addition, we arrange encounters with Israelis from different religious traditions, ethnicities, professions, and political points of view. The study trip includes a wide range of learning modes, including formal talks and lectures, discussions, site-specific poetry readings, guided visits to sites, student presentations, blogging, filmmaking, and journaling. Students are continually invited to think about and discuss connections between the experiences and their own values and traditions.

Concluding Assignment and Sample Student Responses

The final course assignment is to write a brief essay, within which students name a belief or conviction they held, a "place where they are right," to quote Amichai, and then discuss a moment or event that challenged that belief or conviction.[6] The challenge may or may not have come from the course experience. We discuss their responses in our class meeting on the final evening.

For our final in class session, which one year coincided with Lag B'Omer, we sit in a circle on the beach. That year, the sun was just beginning to set across the Kinneret from where we sat. We could smell the bonfires and could see the dotted flickering lights on the hills across the lake. A team of students had purchased firewood and threw logs on our own bonfire as it gathered force and pulled us together. My heart felt flooded with the holiday lights and the goodwill of the group. The combined intensity of the date, location, course content, and our gathering as a community was a unique and rare opportunity to act on shared and intentional intimacy. I thought of Leonard Cohen's tribute to the shared holiness of humanity, the song "Anthem," with the lines, "There's a crack in everything / that's how the light gets in"—his trenchant reframing of a well-known idea from a kabbalist text. Cohen is referring to the idea that "sparks of holiness" are to be found in everything existing. The light, or sparks, may be liberated by the intentional acts of conscious men and women. That our discussion of students' deeply held beliefs was correspondent with a national holiday of light, in which we too were participating, connected their—our—intellectual, spiritual, and emotional lives with the throbbing and dynamic life of an ancient people and a rich but anxious nation.

As I sought to capture each sensation (the sound and smell of the sea, the light and heat of the bonfire, the nervous rustling of students settling down for a class), I compared my own concern about whether my students were "seeing the light" with Amichai's feeling about the "place where we are right." His poems had been a roadmap for our journey through the Holy Land. The title of his poem "The Place Where We Are Right" rang in my ear as much as the lines of the poem. The course itinerary focuses on the act of encountering and the ethics of hospitality, but the course outcomes address the students' ability to reflect and analyze such encounters, from the place "where we are right."

Amichai writes,

> From the place where we are right
> flowers will never grow
> in the Spring.
> The place where we are right
> is hard and trampled
> like a yard.
> But doubts and loves
> dig up the world
> like a mole, a plough.
> And a whisper will be heard in the place
> where the ruined
> house once stood.[7]

When Amichai's poem was written, it offered a poignant but also helpful reminder to Israelis to avoid the hard and unyielding ground of self-righteousness in favor of the fertile growth that comes from listening to each other's "doubts and loves." Like many secular Israeli poets, Amichai struggled with religious faith. In the poetry that we had been reading all week, he references God and the religious experience. But the certainties of religious and national Zionism were, for him, abstracted by the challenges of his life as a soldier in three wars. War was the painful encounter that put Zionism—and righteousness—to the test.

One by one, students stood from their place within the circle and read their brief essays. They named the belief they held, told a story about how it was challenged, and sat down. Some students found their voice early; others waited anxiously for the right moment to stand among their peers and direct them to the place "where we are right." My task was not to silence the questions that would emerge from their encounters but to engage them, to listen carefully to them, and to help the students see what new possibilities might emerge from them.

Not all students drew on the trip for their story, though all stories were clearly informed by the trip. Students revealed central values they held, such as "encouraging love and positivity [to] rid our lives of the toxicity of judgment on one another" (Ellen); or "Respect is a gateway into encountering the 'other.' If we respect others that do not practice what we practice or look like us, or live like us, we create an inclusive environment" (Irene); or "I want children to know someone is truly on their side and will fight for them" (Dorothy). Samantha put it directly: "To love another human being, a stranger, is to recognize your shared humanity."

Every student narrated a particular moment in which they had to shift from a "place where we are right." But in light of the focus of this essay, one student in particular stands out for her expression in response to the heart of the assignment: that is, to listen to each other's doubts and loves and to evolve from that experience. The student was the child of Ethiopian parents in Los Angeles who were practicing Seventh-Day Adventists. Malía was a complacent churchgoer "who carried her doubts as firmly as her convictions." The Jesuit university, with its diverse student population, taught her how to "listen to the other." She explained what she realized through her new friendships: "I no longer saw my version of humanity as the belief or practice that was so dear to my heart that I couldn't understand how others could not also believe in it." On her trip abroad, she writes, "I had an inner dialogue, an encounter in the depth of my personal religiousness, and have met another religious experience on that intimate level. I learned that there is some degree of truth in all religions that promote the wellness of self and others in a practiced and sensible manner." This inner dialogue, in which she related intimately to a different religious practice, is most profound for its formation of a more realized and mature adult identity. She concludes her essay by sharing the ways in which the experience in Israel transformed her. She changed and has become an agent of change. She addresses her peers in the circle directly: "My daily activities are now shaped on exploring other religions, engaging in interfaith dialogue, with you all as my partners in interreligious conversation and developing more knowledge of myself as well as 'the other,' whatever the subject at hand."

As I listened to each student speak, I sought to find in their words a sense that they had all been transformed somehow by facing the other in an imperfect encounter. The heated religious and political landscape of Israel created the perfect opportunity for students to think about and to test their own values. The beach, bonfire, bonhomie, and Lag B'Omer holiday offered them a safe and inviting space to share their views and to open themselves up to doubt, uncertainty, and love. As women and men for others, they were sharing their gifts of knowledge, seeking to pursue justice, and showing concern for those who saw—or felt—things differently.

Conclusion

Amichai's point about avoiding self-righteousness reminds me of my goal to teach behaviors that reflect critical thought and responsible action on moral and ethical issues. Within a proper context, guided engaged discussion about conflict leads to deeper understanding of the historical and other significant but often overlooked details of the conflict and a greater willingness—indeed a readiness—to be open to positions outside one's own.

Notes

1. Gerald Graff, *Beyond the Culture Wars: How Teaching the Conflicts Can Revitalize American Education* (New York: Norton, 1993).
2. Paulo Freire, *Pedagogy of the Oppressed* (New York: Continuum, 2000).
3. Paulo Freire, *The Politics of Education: Culture, Power, and Liberation*, trans. Donald Macedo (Westport, CT: Bergin and Garvey, 1985).
4. Paulo Freire, *Paulo Freire at the Institute*, ed. Maria de Figueiredo-Cowan and Denise Gastaldo (London: University of London, Institute of Education, 1995).
5. Freire, *Politics of Education*, 186.
6. Yehuda Amichai, "The Place Where We Are Right," in *The Selected Poetry of Yehuda Amichai*, ed. and trans. Chana Bloch and Stephen Mitchell (Berkeley: University of California Press, 1996), 34.
7. Ibid.

Teaching Pluralism via the Arab-Israeli Conflict at a Catholic University

JEFFREY BLOODWORTH

Catholics should be good at globalization. Members of a "universal church" with an international reach and mission, Catholics were globalizers before globalization became chic. In the case of my Catholic university, we temporarily lost sight of this fact. Our "liberal core" was littered with parochial literature, theology, philosophy, and history courses. As for study abroad, we scarcely possessed a program.

Ten years ago, my university rediscovered its roots and made "globalization" a central tenet of its strategic plan. Lacking a large endowment, the university utilized its Catholic advantages. Indeed, Catholic universities have entrée to a global system of schools, priests, and church infrastructure. For me (and one would assume for most every professor at a Catholic college), that meant a link to a Catholic community in Jordan and free housing, service opportunities, and instant community connections.

For three consecutive summers, I led a study trip to Israel, Palestine, and Jordan. Every trip varied in its student composition and goals. Students exploring the Arab and Israeli communities they encountered and studying the Arab-Israeli conflict firsthand were the constants.

Students

My university is financially healthy because we emphasize engineering, health sciences, and a sundry of preprofessional programs. Though smart and intellectually curious, these students possess less knowledge about and inherent interest in the Middle East. Thus, attracting students to the trip is cumbersome. Affordability is a significant selling point. For $2,500, students get airfare and six weeks of room and board. Thus, staying in Jordan as opposed to Israel was premised on one factor: cost. Jordan is profoundly less expensive than Israel. Once parents are convinced that Jordan is not Afghanistan (geography is not a strong suit for many), I can generally recruit five to ten students.

During my first trip, I was able to tie the venture into a class. In that class, students learned the basic narrative of the Arab-Israeli conflict along with basic Hebrew and Arabic. The advantages of preparing students with historical content and language skills are obvious. Less noticeable in their value are the relationships, which are constructed over the course of a semester. Because preprofessional programs are so jam-packed with requirements, many students do not have room for electives. Thus, out of sheer necessity, I have also led trips not tied to a class. In all the ventures, I have discovered that the quality of the student, as opposed to enrollment in a course, is the independent variable. Good students ask questions, want to understand the context, and are observant.

Trip Goals

"Globalization" is an ambiguous term. At my university, "globalization" means advancing pluralism. As a Catholic university, we want students to engage with diverse viewpoints, to seek understanding across religious and ethnic divides, and to engage in dialogue with those who are different. Six weeks of service learning in Jordan and traveling to Israel and Palestine offer a perfect opportunity to engage with Arabs and Jews and study the Arab-Israeli conflict firsthand.

With regard to the latter, the Arab-Israeli conflict is an ideal setting to assess complicated narratives and appreciate the humanity of individuals across religious lines. Jordan offers students a chance to live among Arabs, Muslims, and Christians. Israel gives them an opportunity to meet Jewish and Arab Israelis and experience a complicated social and political situation.

To be sure, leading a trip that is tied to a class is ideal. Those students have invested sixteen weeks in learning the material and reading books about the region. In my experience, however, once students enter the region, they are thirsty for context. Informal explanations and discussions give them enough perspective to process their experience.

Madaba

For five weeks, we live in Madaba, Jordan. Forty minutes from Amman and twenty minutes from Mount Nebo, the city of one hundred thousand is big enough to offer variety but small enough to be cozy. The town is an ideal home base, and students very quickly take to it and learn the best hookah haunts and falafel joints.

Madaba is famous for its archaeological treasures and is home to a significant Arab Christian community and Catholic schools, in which my students volunteer. It is in the schools that students make connections with Muslim (and Christian) students that quickly translate into invitations for teas, dinners, and all sundry manner of social activities. In the evenings, we also volunteer at a community center, where students "teach" conversational English. Students are very busy performing their volunteer activities. As a result, I assess them by watching their "classes" and ensuring that they are prompt, friendly, and professional.

I cannot speak for all of Jordan. But in Madaba, nearly every young person can converse in English. Though English is taught intensively in both the public and private schools, Jordanians claim that they learn the language from movies and YouTube. Thus, my students who have studied Arabic get very little practice, because young Jordanians want to speak English.

As a result of our volunteer activities, students are constantly invited into homes for social occasions of all sorts. Meaningful in all manner of ways, the social interactions enable students to meet the trip's primary goal: engagement. My students have interacted with Jordanians from a variety of backgrounds and degrees of religious devotion. In their six weeks of living and working with Jordanians, they come to appreciate Arabs as individuals in all of their complexities. The significant time and amount of social interaction results in unexpected challenges.

Madaba is a majority-Muslim city with a noteworthy Christian past and population. We live in a Christian neighborhood and work in a Catholic school. Some, though not all, Christians harbor resentments toward their Muslim neighbors. During dinners and coffees, these select Jordanians (including an occasional priest) pepper their musings about the Middle East, politics, and the Arab-Israeli conflict with anti-Muslim diatribes. On top of this, Jordanians divide themselves into "Jordanian Jordanians" and "Palestinian Jordanians." With the former regularly impugning the behavior of the latter, students are privy to a regular diet of stereotypes and chauvinism.

Counteracting these asides calls for conversations and discussions. It is imperative that trip leaders hold constant debriefing sessions with students. This is the opportunity to teach about the region's history and offer context.

Madaba offers opportunities to engage with Arabs. However, my students come to Jordan with significant life experience with Muslims. My university is located in a small Rust Belt city. Once a bastion of the white working class, it is now home to a growing population of Muslims and Arabs. Thus, the city's younger generation has grown up in a mixed cultural atmosphere that has fostered friendships and dating across religious and ethnic lines.

As a refugee resettlement, my city is unique. But as a city with a growing Arab American and Muslim population, it is similar to many other locales. Added to this is my university's burgeoning international student population, of whom a large proportion are Arab. Prior to the trip, my students have many Muslim and Arab friends but possess almost no experience with Jews or Judaism. This reality inevitably influences their views on the Arab-Israeli conflict.

Arab-Israeli Conflict

The five weeks of service in Jordan is a life-altering experience for the sons and daughters of the Rust Belt and profoundly affects their impression of the region. Marinating in the attention and friendship of their newfound Jordanian friends, students encounter a variety of misinformation about Israel. Christian Arabs proffer a range of opinions but are generally predisposed to support the state's existence. Jordanians of non-Palestinian descent also run the gamut of views but increasingly favor peace and, by extension, Israel's existence. But most Jordanians of Palestinian ancestry are staunchly anti-Israel. This means that my students encounter lots of bias against Israel, and they enter Israel with some of these attitudes.

To counteract students' newfound yet substantial antipathies toward Israel, I assign Donna Rosenthal's *The Israelis: Ordinary People in an Extraordinary Land* (Simon and Schuster, 2008). This book offers the Israel that transcends the struggle and eradicates stereotypes. The work offers an overview of Israel's history, but it also features stand-alone chapters in which Rosenthal delineates the various peoples, Jewish and non-Jewish, who populate the nation and the issues that animate their lives (beyond the conflict). In this way, *The Israelis* humanizes an entire nation. My gentile students who once knew nothing of Judaism and Jewish history enter Israel with real knowledge.

After our service in Jordan, we conclude our study trip by traveling to Israel. Armed with an intellectual foundation about Israel's complexities, flaws, and admirable qualities and a recently acquired pro-Arab bias, students are unsettled. I have discovered that many students in this situation will opt to flee their cognitive dissonance by ignoring complexity in one of two ways. Some students prefer a Manichean world in which Israelis are the oppressors and Palestinians are the oppressed. Others will attempt to ignore the politics and treat Israel as an opportunity for air-conditioning and alcohol.

To counteract the tendencies of both groups, a varied and intentional itinerary is of upmost necessity. Dealing with the Manicheans comes first. Thus, I avoid the Allenby/King Hussein Bridge crossing, the busiest of all the border entries. There students would see the travails involved for Palestinians who cross from Jordan into the West Bank. Crowded, unruly, and tense, Allenby is a crummy introduction to Israel.

To avoid this experience, I opt for the Jordan River/Sheikh Hussein crossing. This entails a much-longer drive than would Allenby, but it is worth it for the stress avoided. Once we cross into Israel, this circuitous route introduces students to an unexpected Israel. As opposed to Allenby, where you drive through the West Bank and past the settlements into Jerusalem, Sheikh Hussein connects to the Galilee.

With the crossing complete, it is worth the money to secure a small bus and driver for a tour of the Galilee. In general, I disdain guided tours for students. For the Galilee, an afternoon driving tour not only melts away the stress but also is an ideal way to see the rolling countryside. We end the first day in Nazareth. The unofficial Arab capital of Israel is not only inexpensive but a good introduction to Arab-Israeli life.

In Israel, tour buses abound. Tours are fine venues for some student travel. But in Israel, it is important for students to travel like Israelis, to interact with people and see the world from their vantage point. In addition, public transport is plentiful and relatively inexpensive (for Israel). A public bus from Nazareth to Tel Aviv takes you to the heart of Tel Aviv in approximately two hours.

Avoiding the primary flashpoints of the conflict on your first day temporarily solves the Manichean issue. Tel Aviv introduces a conundrum of another sort: Spring Break. Miami in Hebrew, Tel Aviv offers beaches, bars, and a nightlife that can induce Spring Break behavior. Study trips need not be utterly sober (pun intended) experiences without fun. It is important that students socialize with Israelis and enjoy Tel Aviv's beaches, bars, and boulevards. At the same time, one needs an itinerary for Tel Aviv to remind students that they are just that, students, who are there primarily to learn.

Strolls to the Old City in Jaffa, people watching in the Carmel Market, and meetings with professors and journalists keep students engaged and (largely) out of trouble. Brandeis University's Schusterman Center for Israel Studies has been key in establishing a wealth of potential contacts. Thus, setup for these meetings consists of some emails and is utterly doable. In addition to these meetings, students walk the streets of Tel Aviv and experience the hubbub and the mundanity of normal Israeli life. It is vital that they understand that Israel, and life, is more than the conflict.

After two days in Tel Aviv, I take students to Bethlehem. Though I teach at a Catholic institution, we go to Bethlehem for nonreligious reasons. Catholic ties give us access to comfy, inexpensive accommodations. Moreover, we stay with and among Palestinians. We tour Bethlehem and see the town's historic sites, but we are there for the people. Catholic connections mean Catholic schools; for us, that entails invitations to dinners and parties in the homes of schoolteachers. These are multireligious affairs filled with music, hookah, and divine food. Nothing humanizes Palestinians more.

Bethlehem also offers an opportunity to experience the darker side of the occupation. Rather than hire a driver to bring us to Jerusalem, we travel to the Old City as Palestinians do. On my trip, I include a crossing by foot from Bethlehem into Jerusalem (the Bethlehem 300 checkpoint crossing). Through this, students experience the indignities and tight security experienced by Palestinians.

Using the Bethlehem 300 checkpoint crossing offers a depressing window into the world of the occupation. On certain days and at particular times, the crossing can take hours. I believe in experiential learning, but there are limits. Thus, I avoid Friday crossings and other high-traffic days and times. Trip leaders can always ask cab drivers, waiters, and pedestrians for advice. In a pinch, there are other checkpoint crossings with significantly shorter waiting periods.

Jerusalem might not be representative of Israel and Israeli life, but it is the apex of our study tour. As such, we spend several days touring the Old City and its immediate environs. For student accommodations, nothing beats the Seven Arches Hotel. Sitting high atop Mount Olive, Seven Arches offers a stunning view of the Old City. An Arab-owned entity, the once-posh establishment has grown a tad shabby. Clean with a courteous staff, the hotel offers very inexpensive rates with ready access to the Old City. A motley clientele of Muslim pilgrims and budget travelers (and an occasional company of IDF soldiers) makes Seven Arches even more appealing.

Of central importance has been checking calendars for significant dates. In the midst of making hotel reservations, booking drivers, and herding cats (the students), it is easy to overlook important dates. One student trip to Israel reminded me of this important fact. We arrived in Jerusalem and planned a day of touring the Old City. The problem was that it was June 5 (Naksa Day, or the Setback), the date Palestinians commemorate the 1967 war. In the Old City, Naksa features protests, a beefed-up IDF presence, and tension galore. During our tour, there was no violence, just mounds of anxiety. Visiting the Old City during a national holiday was extraordinarily educational, but it was not an experience one should repeat intentionally.

Tour guides abound in the Old City. There is much to recommend in the way of a good guide: they know the nooks and crannies of the Old City, can explain the significance of churches and ruins, and shoo away pesky vendors. Despite these advantages, I never use them. College students are generally uninterested in trivia and much prefer the opportunity to explore.

Outcomes

The six-week trip is emotionally exhausting. I assess students' engagement by monitoring their social calendar and volunteer activities in Jordan. If the students are not utterly wearied, then I know they have been halfhearted in their engagement. In fact, I have had only one student who did not fully commit to the experience. As a result of the trip's structure, student outcomes are difficult to assess. Five weeks in Jordan humanize the Arab "other." Ten days in Israel are scarcely equal time. However, the entire journey is designed to inculcate values of pluralism. After six weeks of witnessing Jordan's internal divisions and the Israeli-Palestinian conflict, students appreciate complexity and the necessity for eschewing simple answers in the quest for coexistence.

Teaching about the Establishment of Israel in Florida's Public Schools Using Primary Sources

TERRI SUSAN FINE

The establishment of the State of Israel in 1948 provides opportunities for students to learn about the contemporary experience of a nation establishing its independence. In this essay, I review Florida Department of Education (FDOE) requirements focusing on student learning about Israel and related subjects through the lens of middle school (grades 6–8) U.S. civics, high school (grades 9–12) world history, and high school U.S. history. Specific focus is given to teaching with primary sources for achieving curricular objectives.

This essay reviews required instructional benchmarks, literacy skills requirements, and educational mandates about Israel and related subjects in Florida. Using primary sources to teach required content is also discussed. Together, I outline requirements for Florida middle and high school student learning about Israel and related subjects in three disciplinary realms (U.S. civics and government, U.S. history, world history) across grades 6–12 using materials that fulfill state literacy skills requirements. These are among the skills that I use to train teachers in high school and middle school and that may be relevant for approaching the conflict in university education courses.

Teaching in Florida's K–12 Public Schools

The FDOE outlines its teaching requirements through standards and benchmarks in all subjects.[1] Academic standards identify the knowledge and skills in each content area that students are expected to learn once they fulfill the learning benchmarks included in that standard. A benchmark is a narrowly focused learning objective that generally combines a task (e.g., describe, identify, explain) with specific content.

Grade levels in Florida are provided for each middle school grade (6, 7, 8), while all high school subjects are presented as grades 9–12 and not specific to any grade. Benchmarks include the subject area, grade level, and standard, going from the broad subject area to the specific learning objective. For example, benchmark SS.912.W.8.6 would be read as "SS": social studies (subject); "912": grades 9–12; W: world history (social studies domain); and 8: "Recognize significant events and people from the post–World War II and Cold War eras" (standard). From there, the number 6 ending the benchmark identifies the specific learning objective. For example, SS.912.W.8.6 represents the benchmark "Explain the 20th century background for the establishment of the modern state of Israel in 1948 and the ongoing military and political conflicts between Israel and the Arab-Muslim world." "Explain" is the task, while the remainder of the statement is the content associated with that task. Teachers may encounter several content requirements within any benchmark, such as this example, in which students learn about the establishment of the State of Israel and the ongoing conflict in the Middle East.

High school U.S. history and middle school U.S. civics[2] are the two social studies subjects tested statewide in Florida. Students must take these courses and take the statewide exam administered every spring. Both subjects include content that relates to the establishment of modern Israel. The exams associated with each subject are written based on item (test question) specifications adopted by the FDOE. Each benchmark specification includes content associated with that benchmark for testing purposes. Item specifications include a "stimulus attribute," which lists the type of materials that may be included in any question. The stimulus attribute for each item specification in U.S. history and civics includes "historical and contemporary documents and other relevant stimuli (e.g., maps, timelines, charts, graphs, tables)."

Together, students in Florida's public schools learn content within set subjects, standards, and benchmarks. Subjects tested statewide allow items to be developed using one or more stimuli that may include historical or contemporary primary source documents.

Florida Teaching Requirements about Israel and Related Subjects

In this essay, I explore an approach to teaching about the establishment of modern Israel in 1948 using three primary source documents. The FDOE has determined that students will learn about the establishment of modern Israel in high school world history. The U.S. history course includes related topics supporting this world history content. Middle school civics also introduces students to topics that support their later high school learning about the establishment of Israel. The following is a description of Florida benchmarks focusing on Israel and related subjects and pertinent benchmark clarifications. Subjects tested statewide may include content-focus terms that further clarify expectations of student learning.

MIDDLE SCHOOL CIVICS

Benchmark: "SS.7.C.1.4: Analyze the ideas (natural rights, role of the government) and complaints set forth in the Declaration of Independence."

Standard: "Demonstrate an understanding of the origins and purposes of government, law, and the American political system."

Benchmark clarifications: "Explain the concept of natural rights as expressed in the Declaration of Independence"; "Identify the natural rights specifically expressed in the Declaration of Independence (life, liberty, and the pursuit of happiness)"; "Analyze the relationship between natural rights and the role of government."[3]

HIGH SCHOOL WORLD HISTORY

Benchmark: "SS.912.W.8.6: Explain the 20th century background for the establishment of the modern state of Israel in 1948 and the ongoing military and political conflicts between Israel and the Arab-Muslim world."

Standard: "Recognize significant events and people from the post World War II and Cold War eras."

Benchmark clarifications: "Identify the reasons why both Jews and Arab-Muslims claim the territory known as Palestine including the development of Zionism and the Balfour Declaration in 1917"; "Explore the rationale behind the United Nations' Partition Plan and how Jews and Arab-Muslims responded."[4]

HIGH SCHOOL U.S. HISTORY

Benchmark: "SS.912.A.6.1: Examine causes, course, and consequences of World War II on the United States and the world." "SS.912.A.6.3: Analyze the impact of the Holocaust during World War II on Jews as well as other groups."[5]

Standard: "Understand the causes and course of World War II, the character of the war at home and abroad, and its reshaping of the United States' role in the post-war world."

Benchmark clarifications: "Identify and/or evaluate the causes and consequences of World War II both domestically and internationally"; "Evaluate the long-term influences of the war on both domestic and international affairs."[6]

In addition to these standards and benchmarks, the Florida legislature enacted a Holocaust education mandate in 1994. The mandate includes a focus on the history of the Holocaust.[7] Unlike the standards and benchmarks described here, the educational mandate does not specify a subject or grade level in which the Holocaust must be taught.

In the next section, I show that the Israel declaration includes language establishing a connection between the establishment of the state and the targeting of Jews in the Holocaust. It is appropriate, then, that I include a discussion of the Florida Holocaust education mandate.

Teaching about the Establishment of Israel Using Historical and Contemporary Primary Source Documents

In this section, I explore three primary source documents to support teaching about the establishment of modern Israel: a presidential memo, the U.S. Declaration of Independence, and the Israeli Declaration of Establishment.

On May 14, 1948, President Harry Truman approved and signed the following statement: "This Government has been informed that a Jewish state has been proclaimed in Palestine, and recognition has been requested by the (provisional) government thereof. The United States recognizes the provisional government as the de facto authority of the new state of Israel."[8] This statement establishes the official U.S. position toward Israel. Deconstructing this contemporary primary source supports students' learning about Israel's independence while enhancing their information literacy and critical thinking skills.

Specifically, this statement outlines the relationship between Israel and the United States upon Israel's declaration. Article II, Section 3, of the U.S. Constitution states that the president "shall receive Ambassadors and other public Ministers." The U.S. Supreme Court has interpreted this provision to mean that the president (and not Congress) recognizes foreign nations. Recognition shapes foreign policy decisions.[9] Truman clarifies that a foreign nation requesting recognition does not ensure it; it is up to the president to confer that recognition as part of the president's Article II powers.

Truman's statement connects well to the preamble of the U.S. Declaration of Independence, which ends with, "To prove this, let Facts be submitted to a candid world." Florida middle school civics instruction includes the U.S. Declaration of Independence. Focusing on the reasons that the American colonists sought international recognition in their declaration of independence supports students' understanding as to why newly independent nations seek such recognition, including trade opportunities, diplomatic relations, and military protection.

The preamble of the U.S. Declaration of Independence also supports student learning about Israel's Declaration of Establishment through its emphasis on natural rights philosophy. The U.S. declaration identifies natural rights in the preamble (life, liberty, pursuit of happiness).[10] The Israel declaration also embraces a natural rights focus, including, "The State of Israel . . . will be based on freedom, justice and peace as envisaged by the prophets of Israel" and "This right is the natural right of the Jewish people to be masters of their own fate, like all other nations, in their own sovereign State."[11] Natural rights are guaranteed to individuals by virtue of their existence alone. Natural rights, because they are unalienable, may not be denied or taken away by government. Instruction about the principle of natural rights is enhanced when teaching with the U.S. and Israeli declarations.

To this point, I have described using two U.S.-based primary source documents (one historical, one contemporary) to teach about the Israel declaration. The third document to be examined is the Declaration of Establishment of the State of Israel in English translation. The Israel declaration provides both historical and contemporary reasons for statehood. The seven reasons outlined in the Israel declaration help students develop a better sense of ongoing issues shaping relations between Arabs and Israelis in Israel, U.S.-Israel foreign policy, and relations between Israel and the Arab-Muslim world, each of which supports and reinforces Florida educational benchmarks.[12]

Each reason is provided in the table on the following page, with a connection to Florida instructional benchmarks.[13] Each rationale provides insight as to why the framers of the Israeli declaration justified their independence. This diversity of rationales helps students understand why conflict continues over the legitimacy of Israel's statehood, why U.S. foreign policy toward Israel and the Middle East varies among U.S. presidents, and continued United Nations focus on the Arab-Israeli conflict. U.S. presidential elections also focus on one or more of these issues, such as the role of the U.S. supporting negotiations between Israel and the Palestinians and larger international security concerns.

The seven reasons also provide teachers the opportunity to bring an interactive learning activity about the establishment of the State of Israel to the classroom. Specifically, the seven reasons could be given to all students, and the class would be divided into seven groups. Each group would summarize one reason and identify two political strengths associated with that reason (e.g., justifying Israel's control of the West Bank, justifying opposition to proposals trading land for peace, justifying opposition to United Nations Security Council resolutions). This approach would help students shape arguments about Israel in U.S. politics and on the international stage. The "report-out," in which students share the outcomes of their small group discussions, helps students learn about all seven reasons.[14]

Rationale for independence in the Israel Declaration of Establishment	Connected benchmark clarification included in instructional benchmarks
"The Land of Israel was the birthplace of the Jewish people. Here their spiritual, religious and political identity was shaped. Here they first attained to statehood, created cultural values of national and universal significance and gave to the world the eternal Book of Books."	While not directly applicable, sixth-grade world history benchmarks include SS.6.W.2.9: "Identify key figures and basic beliefs of the Israelites and determine how these beliefs compared with those of others in the geographic area." This rationale supports instruction about the Israelites' beliefs.
"After being forcibly exiled from their land, the people kept faith with it throughout their Dispersion and never ceased to pray and hope for their return to it and for the restoration in it of their political freedom."	"Identify the reasons why both Jews and Arab-Muslims claim the territory known as Palestine including the development of Zionism and the Balfour Declaration in 1917." (Benchmark clarification from SS.912.W.8.6)
"Pioneers, defiant returnees, and defenders, they made deserts bloom, revived the Hebrew language, built villages and towns, and created a thriving community controlling its own economy and culture, loving peace but knowing how to defend itself, bringing the blessings of progress to all the country's inhabitants, and aspiring towards independent nationhood."	"Identify the reasons why both Jews and Arab-Muslims claim the territory known as Palestine including the development of Zionism and the Balfour Declaration in 1917." (Benchmark clarification from SS.912.W.8.6)
"In the year 5657 (1897), at the summons of the spiritual father of the Jewish State, Theodore Herzl, the First Zionist Congress convened and proclaimed the right of the Jewish people to national rebirth in its own country."	"Identify the reasons why both Jews and Arab-Muslims claim the territory known as Palestine including the development of Zionism and the Balfour Declaration in 1917." (Benchmark clarification from SS.912.W.8.6)
"This right was recognized in the Balfour Declaration of the 2nd November, 1917, and re-affirmed in the Mandate of the League of Nations which, in particular, gave international sanction to the historic connection between the Jewish people and Eretz-Israel* and to the right of the Jewish people to rebuild its National Home."	"Identify the reasons why both Jews and Arab-Muslims claim the territory known as Palestine including the development of Zionism and the Balfour Declaration in 1917." (Benchmark clarification from SS.912.W.8.6)
"The catastrophe which recently befell the Jewish people—the massacre of millions of Jews in Europe—was another clear demonstration of the urgency of solving the problem of its homelessness by re-establishing in Eretz-Israel the Jewish State, which would open the gates of the homeland wide to every Jew and confer upon the Jewish people the status of a fully privileged member of the community of nations.... Survivors of the Nazi holocaust in Europe, as well as Jews from other parts of the world, continued to migrate to Eretz-Israel, undaunted by difficulties, restrictions and dangers, and never ceased to assert their right to a life of dignity, freedom and honest toil in their national homeland."	"Identify and/or evaluate the causes and consequences of World War II both domestically and internationally." (Benchmark clarification from SS.912.A.6.3)
"On the 29th November, 1947, the United Nations General Assembly passed a resolution calling for the establishment of a Jewish State in Eretz-Israel; the General Assembly required the inhabitants of Eretz-Israel to take such steps as were necessary on their part for the implementation of that resolution. This recognition by the United Nations of the right of the Jewish people to establish their State is irrevocable."	"Explore the rationale behind the United Nations' Partition Plan and how Jews and Arab-Muslims responded." (Benchmark clarification from SS.912.W.8.6)

* Eretz is the Hebrew word for "land"; this phrase translates to "Land of Israel."

Instruction using one or more of these reasons may also be helpful for teaching course content while fulfilling stimulus attribute requirements. For example, a critical reading of the reason focusing on the Holocaust will help students learn about the causes and consequences of World War II while promoting critical thinking about the connection between the Holocaust and the establishment of Israel in the U.S. history course. Several reasons directly support high school world history instruction including the focus on Zionism, the Balfour Declaration, the United Nations partition plan, and Arab-Muslim claims. The focus in U.S. history on the Holocaust also provides teachers with an opportunity to fulfill Florida's Holocaust education mandate.

Conclusion

Challenges face instructors teaching about Israel. It is a complex subject affected by sensitivities and disagreements about the causes and consequences of issues facing the region. These concerns shape discussions about appropriate paths forward for Israel, the Palestinians, the Middle East peace process, U.S.-Israel relations, and the role of the United States in the United Nations.

Florida social studies instructional requirements include teaching about Israel and related subjects while middle school civics and high school U.S. history end-of-course statewide assessments include items requiring the interpretation of historical and contemporary primary source documents. Teaching about Israel using the primary sources presented here supports student learning in ways that promote critical thinking, fulfill content requirements, and enhance literacy skills.

Notes

1. Each state provides required standards and benchmarks, although these terms are not always used and, if used, are not necessarily used in the same context across states.
2. Referred to as "civics" from this point forward.
3. Florida Department of Education, *Civics End-of-Course Assessment Test Item Specifications* (2012), 24.
4. Florida Department of Education, *Florida Interim Assessment Item Bank and Test Platform, Item Specifications, Social Studies, World History, Grades 9–12* (2013), 70.
5. These benchmarks are presented together because the U.S. History End of Course Assessment is designed so that certain benchmarks are assessed together with other benchmarks.
6. Florida Department of Education, *U.S. History End-of-Course Assessment Test Item Specifications* (2010), 40–41.

7. The full text of the statute is available at www.flsenate.gov/laws/statutes/2011/1003.42, accessed May 28, 2017.
8. Harry S. Truman, "Statement by the President Announcing Recognition of the State of Israel," May 14, 1948, American Presidency Project, www.presidency.ucsb.edu/ws/index.php?pid=12896. A photograph of the artifact showing Truman's edits may be found at the Truman Presidential Library and Museum website: www.trumanlibrary.org/whistlestop/study_collections/israel/large/documents/index.php?documentdate=1948-05-14&documentid=48&pagenumber=1 (accessed May 28, 2017). Teachers may find that the authenticity of the artifact will foster students' interest.
9. See *Zivotofsky v. Kerry*, 576 U.S. ___ (2015).
10. Benchmark SS.7.C.1.4.
11. Provisional Government of Israel, Official Gazette: Number 1; Tel Aviv, 5 Iyar 5708, 14.5.1948 Page 1 (in English translation).
12. Middle and high school U.S. government benchmarks also include student learning about forms and systems of government. Instructors may opt to use Israel as a case study to fulfill these requirements, although a focus on Israel is not required to fulfill these instructional requirements.
13. The benchmarks associated with the benchmark clarifications provided here are presented in the "Florida Teaching Requirements about Israel and Related Subjects" section of this essay.
14. Bridget Arend, "Making the Most of 'Reporting Out' after Group Work," *Faculty Focus*, February 1, 2016, www.facultyfocus.com/articles/effective-teaching-strategies/making-the-most-of-reporting-out-after-group-work/.

The Personal and the Political

When the Outside World Intrudes on the Sacred Class Space

Feeding Minds

USING FOOD TO TEACH THE ARAB-ISRAELI CONFLICT

ARI ARIEL

Introduction

Food is among the best tools for unsettling static notions of identity and for humanizing others. Ironically, this is because we tend to think about food in fixed ethnic terms. The more we study foodways, however, the clearer it becomes that they are among the most hybrid of practices. This realization then helps us to question other ways we categorize foods and the peoples who eat them. For those of us interested in helping students disrupt the binaries that often plague discussion of the Arab-Israeli conflict, foodways can be invaluable.

In the classroom setting, before discussing a specific dish or culinary practice, it is important to emphasize the importance of foodways to political, social, and cultural studies, lest students fall into the trap of thinking that "it's just food." I usually start with a few historical examples to stress this point. I remind students that Christopher Columbus set out on his famous journey looking for spices and that sugar played a fundamental role in both the transatlantic slave trade and the development of an industrial economy in Great Britain.[1] I also ask students to consider Manning Nash's definition of ethnicity. For Nash, commensality is one of three fundamental ethnic boundary markers. He defines it as "the propriety of eating together indicating a kind of equality, peership, and the promise of further kinship links stemming from the intimate acts of dinning together, only one step removed from the intimacy of bedding together."[2] The role of food in identity formation is also highlighted in scholarship in the fields of Jewish studies and Middle Eastern studies.[3] Once students appreciate how important food and foodways are to understanding the world around us, we can talk about food in the context of Israel/Palestine. This essay uses one specific dish, hummus, to suggest several ways that food can be useful in teaching the conflict.

Hummus and the Arab-Israeli Conflict

Over the past decade or so, hummus has been an important part of narratives of the conflict. This has included an ongoing competition for the Guinness world record for the largest dish of hummus in the world, a Lebanese attempt to trademark the term *hummus* in the European Union (EU), and calls to boycott Sabra Dipping Company made by advocates of the Boycott, Divestment and Sanctions (BDS) movement. BDS is attracting an ever-increasing amount of attention in the U.S. media, and American celebrities have often been involved in public debate about Sabra. Stephen Colbert joked during his first episode as host of *The Late Show* that in order to get the show, he had to swear a blood oath on a demonic amulet and "make certain regrettable compromises." The amulet then appeared in a product placement for Sabra, one of the show's sponsors. Soon after, in February 2016, the Palestinian American hip hop artist DJ Khaled was criticized by BDS activists for performing at a Super Bowl event sponsored by Sabra. Hummus, it seems, is becoming more and more embedded in coverage of Israel/Palestine. To many students, however, food seems apolitical. It is, therefore, a perfect entryway into the topic.

Hummus and Nationalism

Both scholarly literature and journalistic work regularly portray the Arab-Israeli and/or Israel-Palestine conflict(s) as national. Likewise, college syllabi often frame courses on the topic in terms of two competing nationalist movements. However, for students (and for specialists too), nations and nationalisms are hard to understand. Food can help. We all, rather intuitively, categorize foods as ethnic or national: lasagna is Italian, mole is Mexican, sushi is Japanese, and so on. Of course, we sometimes debate the authenticity of a particular dish, but this matters little to the overall system, which requires that foods are linked with specific ethnic or national groups. In turn, these groups claim special rights of ownership over particular foods or dishes.

How, then, is hummus linked to group identity? Recently Lebanese chefs and businesspeople have claimed ownership of hummus in two ways: first, by making the largest dish of hummus in the world and, second, through an attempt by the Association of Lebanese Industrialists (ALI) to trademark the term *hummus* in the EU.[4] In order to receive the trademark, Lebanon first has to register hummus as Lebanese through one of three EU schemes designed to protect product names from misuse or imitation.[5] In so doing, Lebanon would be claiming that hummus is, by definition, Lebanese. On both fronts of the hummus wars, as this conflict has been called, the Lebanese claim is aimed primarily against Israel. The trademark attempt stems from the fact that large Israeli companies dominate the hummus market. According to ALI, Israeli companies have appropriated and are selling a Lebanese dish and are therefore stealing tens of millions of dollars annually from Lebanon. When the campaign began, Fadi Abboud, the head of ALI in 2008, was also involved in an effort to break the record for the largest dish of the chickpea dip. He noted, "I thought the best way to tell the world that the hummus is Lebanese is to break the *Guinness Book of Records*."[6]

This raises a host of questions that are productive in the classroom. Is hummus exclusively Lebanese? Might hummus also be Israeli? Why is it important for countries to claim a distinct national cuisine? Must each nation have a distinct national culture? Must this culture be recognizable to both insiders and outsiders? When is adopting a cultural practice from another group appropriation? What happens when national cultures overlap, for example, if a food is shared by several nations? And how does political conflict impact shared cultures?

While the Lebanese hummus claim is clearly part of a conflict between "Arabs" and "Jews," it also highlights the ambivalence of national cultures, both Arab and Israeli. To trademark hummus, Lebanon must assert that hummus is exclusively Lebanese. Facebook groups linked to, or supportive of, the campaign are titled "Fight to Keep Hummus and Tabouli LEBANESE No one else's"; "Hummus and Tabbouleh are 100% Lebanese"; "Hummus, Tabouli, Baba Ghanouj are LEBANESE NOT ISRAELI!!"; "Hummus is a LEBANESE invention (TM)"; and "Hummus is Lebanese." Each of these groups, in its description section, notes specifically that hummus is not Israeli. However, Abboud himself has noted that hummus, along with the other dishes under dispute, is not solely Lebanese, that it might be equally Palestinian or Syrian, for example: "Hummus might be debatable, in any case we will be happy if the Palestinians win."[7] Or speaking about falafel, Abboud said, "We have a dialogue as to the subject of falafel, whether it is Lebanese, Syrian, or Palestinian, but the dispute is not between us, it's clear that the dispute is not among the Arabs. I have no problem with falafel being Palestinian or Lebanese. I have a problem with it being Israeli."[8] The Lebanese national hummus claim is thus weakened by the unresolved tension between state nationalisms (Lebanese, Syrian, etc.) and a broader Arab nationalism. If Lebanon is a nation with a distinct culture, how are we to understand that this culture is shared by other Arab nations? Here Arab nationalism itself becomes an obstacle to the Lebanese trademark project.

At the same time, the Lebanese claim also makes a statement about Israeli identity—that Israel is European, despite the fact that Jews of European descent make up a minority of the population of the country. Even while noting that Arab Jews "eat the same food as other Arabs," including hummus, Abboud asserts, "with all due respect, I didn't know German Jews or Polish Jews knew anything about hummus."[9] Here Abboud is arguing that Israeli is defined by Ashkenazi/European culture, and since hummus is an Arab dish, it cannot be Israeli. But he too quickly writes off the question of Middle Eastern Jews. If Syrian Jews can become Israeli, why can hummus not become Israeli too? How does a dish move from one group or culture to another? Are pathways important? That is, does the question of hummus as Israeli depend on whether the dish entered Israeli-Jewish culinary culture with Middle Eastern Jews or was taken from Palestinian cuisine?

On the Israeli side, the hummus wars underscore a tension between Jewishness and Israeliness. The 2010 Israeli Guinness record (later bested by a Lebanese team) was set not by an Israeli Jew but by Palestinian Israeli chefs in the town of Abu Ghosh. Commenting on the record, the celebrity chef Haim Cohen noted, "It's funny because it's not the Israelis in Israel that are doing the hummus, it's the Arabs, the Israeli Arabs that are doing the hummus."[10] Again, this raises numerous questions that will provoke classroom discussion: How is Israeli identity linked to Jewishness? Can a non-Jew be Israeli? What is the distinction between citizenship and nationality? What is the relationship between Arab/Palestinian citizens of Israel to the state? To national ideology? If Arab citizens are Israeli, can hummus, an Arab dish, be Israeli?

Hummus and BDS

BDS stands for Boycott, Divestment and Sanctions, and its activists and supporters call for a boycott of Israel until the country complies "with international law and Palestinian rights." As part of this general call to boycott Israeli products, there has been a call to boycott Sabra hummus, primarily in food cooperatives and on college campuses. In food co-ops, the movement's success has been limited. In 2010, the Olympia Food Co-op in Washington State became the first to vote in favor of boycotting Israeli products. Soon after, several members of the co-op filed a lawsuit against it, claiming that board members enacted the boycott in violation of co-op policy. As of August 2016, the case is still making its way through the court system. In 2012, members of the Park Slope Food Coop in Brooklyn voted down a referendum to join the BDS movement and to stop selling Sabra products. In 2015, the board of directors of the GreenStar co-op in Ithaca, New York, rejected a similar referendum before it came to a vote because according to New York State human rights law, it is unlawful to "discriminate against, boycott or blacklist, or to refuse to buy from, sell to or trade with, any person, because of the race, creed, color, *national origin*, sexual orientation, military status or sex of such person."[11] Anti-BDS activists are now trying to block boycotts in the courts. In June 2015, when President Obama signed the Trade Promotion Authority legislation into law, it included a provision making it one of the "principal negotiating objectives of the United States" to "discourage politically motivated actions to boycott, divest from, or sanction Israel."[12]

On college campuses, the BDS movement has had more success, winning student divestment votes in several University of California schools, the University of New Mexico, and others. Boycotting Sabra has proved more difficult. At DePaul, Wesleyan, and UC Riverside, Sabra hummus was briefly removed from shelves but was then restocked along with an alternative brand so that consumers would have two choices. Vassar College Campus Dining decided to do the same.

In September 2015, I gave a talk at Boston University titled "Hummus Wars: Buying and Boycotting Middle Eastern Foods." About a month before the talk, in response to an advertisement listing that title and a brief description, I received an email from a member of the public, stating, "Before I commit [to attending] I need to ask a necessary question in todays [sic] antisemitic BDS environment. . . . The word 'boycott' appears in the text of the explanation. . . . Please tell me this is not a BDS talk in regards to Hummus. . . . I have had enough exposure to this antisemitic anti-Israel tactic as we have recently seen in Spain. If it is about Hummus and our similiar [sic] cultural beliefs that unite us then great." Neither the title not the description suggested that I was taking any position on the boycott.[13] The responder seems to suggest that mere mention of boycott, in even the most general terms, is tantamount to a declaration of antisemitism. In my opinion, declaring contentious topics off-limits is antithetical to the intellectual environment that we should create on college campuses and does a great disservice to our students.

Not only does the BDS movement's call to boycott Sabra raise interesting questions about dealing with contentious topics in the classroom; it also provides an opportunity to discuss political activism on college campuses and in U.S. society at large. Moreover, BDS is frequently in the media, and it is preposterous to ignore this topic in courses on Israel/Palestine. Hummus is a productive way to talk about boycott through a product that most students know.

Wherever one stands on the issue of BDS, the Sabra case raises important questions about political activism and the United States–Israel relationship. What kind of political action should be encouraged/discouraged on college campuses? Under what circumstances is boycott a legitimate political tool? Why have New York State and U.S. legislatures taken steps to make BDS illegal? Is this legislation, perhaps, unconstitutional? Does it matter where "Israeli" products are made? The GreenStar co-op referendum suggested a possible distinction between goods produced in Israel and those from the West Bank. How do we determine the national identity of a corporation? Sabra was founded in New York in 1986 and has always sold its products on the U.S. market. In 2005, the Israeli food manufacturer Strauss acquired 51 percent of the company. Then in 2007, Pepsico acquired 50 percent. It is now a joint venture between Pepsico and Strauss. The company is based in Queens, New York, and Virginia. So it might be fair to ask if Sabra is Israeli at all. BDS activists target Sabra because they say it supports the Israeli army, but Sabra itself does not appear to contribute anything to the Israel Defense Forces. On the other hand, Strauss does support soldiers in the IDF. According to the company's website, it provides funds "for welfare, cultural and educational activities, such as pocket money for underprivileged soldiers, sports and recreational equipment, care packages, and books and games for the soldiers' club."[14] If this support is primarily for soldiers' personal benefit, is that the same as support for Israeli military policies? Where should the line between the two be drawn?

Conclusion

Together, the hummus wars and the Sabra BDS campaign raise questions about nationalism and conflict, cultural appropriation, political activism on college campuses, freedom of speech, boycott and economic partnerships, and the U.S.-Israeli relationship, just to name a few. Certainly you could raise these issues in other ways. However, my goal in this essay was to demonstrate that a seemingly banal dish of pureed chickpeas can provide multiple entry points into the study of the Arab-Israeli conflict. Many other foods can be used to teach the conflict or Israeli history and society. Falafel has long been a contentious topic, as has anything labeled "Israeli." Is Israeli couscous really *maftul* or *moghrabieh*? Is Israeli salad Arab salad? Or why not use *amba* to teach Jewish history in Iraq or *shakshuka* to talk about North African Jews in Israel? Make food part of your students' "hunger" for knowledge!

Notes

1. Gary Paul Nabhan, *Cumin, Camels, and Caravans: A Spice Odyssey* (Berkeley: University of California Press, 2014); Sidney W. Mintz, *Sweetness and Power: The Place of Sugar in Modern History* (New York: Penguin Books, 1986).
2. Manning Nash, *The Cauldron of Ethnicity in the Modern World* (Chicago: University of Chicago Press, 1989), 11.
3. For two recent examples, see Nefissa Naguib, *Nurturing Masculinities: Men, Food, and Family in Contemporary Egypt* (Austin: University of Texas Press, 2015); and Yael Raviv, *Falafel Nation: Cuisine and the Making of National Identity in Israel* (Lincoln: University of Nebraska Press, 2015).
4. For a more detailed account of the hummus wars, see Ari Ariel, "The Hummus Wars," *Gastronomica: The Journal of Food and Culture* 12, no. 1 (2012): 34–42.

5. For more on the EU schemes, see European Commission, "EU Quality Logos," accessed August 17, 2018, http://ec.europa.eu/agriculture/quality/schemes/index_en.htm
6. "Give Chickpeas a Chance: Why Hummus Unites, and Divides, the Mideast," NPR, July 18, 2016, www.npr.org/sections/thesalt/2016/07/18/483715410/give-chickpeas-a-chance-why-hummus-unites-and-divides-the-mideast.
7. "Hummus War Looms between Lebanon, Israel," *USA Today*, October 7, 2008, http://usatoday30.usatoday.com/news/world/2008-10-07-lebanon-israel_N.htm.
8. "Israel and Lebanese Foods . . . Attack on Heritage" *Al Jazeera*, October 8, 2008.
9. Ibid.; Carolynne Wheeler, "Hummus Food Fight between Lebanon and Israel," *Telegraph*, October 11, 2008, www.telegraph.co.uk/news/worldnews/middleeast/3178040/Hummus-food-fight-between-Lebanon-and-Israel.html.
10. "Haim Cohen on the New Israeli Cuisine, Interview by Joan Nathan, March 24, 2010." This video was part of an online seminar given by the New York Times Knowledge Network and the Israeli Consulate in New York, titled *The New Israel Cuisine*.
11. New York State, "New York State Human Rights Law," accessed August 17, 2018, www.dhr.ny.gov/law; emphasis added.
12. S. 995, 114th Congress (2015–16), available at www.congress.gov/bill/114th-congress/senate-bill/995/text.
13. The advertisement described the talk as follows: "Focusing on the Guinness World Record for the largest serving of hummus, as well as attempts to trademark hummus and calls for its boycott, this talk will use food to highlight questions of ethnic and national identity, examining food as an arena of conflict and coexistence."
14. Ron Friedman, "Strauss Reposts IDF-Support Commitment on Website," *Jerusalem Post*, December 14, 2010, www.jpost.com/Defense/Strauss-reposts-IDF-support-commitment-on-website.

Letting Politics into the Israeli-Palestinian Relations Classroom

MIRA SUCHAROV

This is the story of one professor's personal, intellectual, and pedagogical evolution. The story is anchored in issues of pedagogy and raises questions about personal and professional identity, including where social capital is generated and how it can sustain and shape teaching practices. It is not necessarily a flattering story. But I hope that the telling of it will open new possibilities for how to address the politics of Israel/Palestine in the Israeli-Palestinian relations course classroom.

• • •

Anyone who has suffered from panic attacks quickly learns that trying to shove the panic away by sheer force of will is a recipe for disaster. The trick is to relax into the panic while quietly observing and acknowledging it until it gradually subsides. The alternative—pushing the sensation away in an inevitably panicky way—gives rise to a vicious cycle of intensifying panic.

It has taken me fifteen years of teaching Israel-Palestinian relations in the political science classroom to realize a great irony: I am a political scientist, but I have attempted to shut out politics from the classroom altogether. This binary approach—that what we do in the classroom is necessarily different from what students might choose to do in the student union building or what faculty might do in the faculty lounge or on social media or in the op-ed pages—is neither helpful nor accurate. It is not helpful in that it restricts the understanding of politics to the tasks of explanation and understanding—both relevant and important aims, to be sure, but certainly not the sum total of what the study of politics and Israeli-Palestinian relations actually is. And this approach is not an accurate accounting of what really goes on because it obscures the actual role of personal politics in our teaching. Even if our overall political subjectivity does not completely cloud how we interpret the evidence, it cannot but inform the courses we design and the questions we ask.

I have also come to realize that barricading the door against politics was actually intensifying the threat I felt—whether real or imagined—from the activist invasion. Like the panic attacks, it was a vicious cycle. I had attempted to set the boundaries of inquiry by fiat. We are not going to play the "blame game," I used to tell students on the first day of the course. We are not going to discuss, in the context of analyzing Israeli and Palestinian actions, who is "right" and who is "wrong."

Later in the term, if a student vocalized disdain over a certain moment in Israeli-Palestinian history—such as when one student expressed anger that the same Ariel Sharon we had learned about in the context of the Sabra and Shatila massacre was now (then) Israel's prime minister—I would feel my cheeks getting hot. In trying to promote a value-free classroom, I was on the defensive. I knew my private defensiveness was not a helpful pedagogical position, and yet I was having trouble shedding it. Later, I wrote and spoke to my peers about what I had learned about the value of "letting" students bring their emotions and politics into the classroom rather than implicitly seeking to ban these urges. But I also realized I was paying lip service to this aim, rather than doing much to actually facilitate it.

In a previous article on the role of subjectivity in teaching, I recounted a particularly challenging semester in which the ongoing conversation between my students and me erupted into a disjuncture of silence and misunderstanding during a tense encounter spurred by an unplanned conversation on the nature of Israeli democracy. One of the things I fear most when teaching the politics of Israel/Palestine is an assumption by students that I am shilling for one side or another. That fear came alive that day, and my teaching turned brittle.[1]

Part of what had been driving the tense buildup, I suspect, was a misguided attempt on my part to balance against what I sensed from class discussion early on in the term was a particular perspective toward the issue held by a majority of the students, or at least by a handful of vocal ones. Trying to even out the scales is ultimately a losing strategy. It can feel frantic and reactive as the sands shift. And it undermines an authentic teaching voice.

I finished that semester feeling raw and vulnerable, so much so that when I was invited by my university's educational development center to present a session to my peers on "teaching controversial topics," I declined. While I consider myself an extremely comfortable public speaker, I was quite certain I would not be able to get through a workshop on that topic without breaking down. (Indeed I had openly wept uncontrollably at a social gathering some weeks earlier when family friends, my parents' age, softly inquired—on the heels of seeing some discussion on my social media feed about my classroom challenges—how my semester had been.)

My approach has now evolved. Rather than demand that students check their activism at the door—and silently pray that they will not raise questions that make *me* feel unmoored—I have carefully and deliberately opened the door to politics. Rather than hope that students do not raise the "A" word (for "apartheid"), I now assign an academic article discussing the potential utility of the term in the Israel case, and I assign additional perspectives to ensure multidimensionality. Rather than keep my syllabus free of activist language, I have included contentious topics such as BDS (Boycott, Divestment and Sanctions). Next year I plan to add a section on intersectionality, pinkwashing (the accusation by human rights activists that Israel uses its relatively progressive record on LGBTQ rights to divert attention from its oppressive policies toward Palestinians), and more discussion on the distinction between justice and peace. This might also mean increasingly moving outside my discipline to generate course material, since political science and international relations research on Israel/Palestine tends to avoid some of these more politicized issues (again, the great irony I recounted earlier and about which I will have more to say shortly).

Rather than push students to consider activism as wholly distinct from the understanding-and-explanation approach I otherwise use in the classroom, this year I invited students to share their experiences with their peers of doing activism and to identify what they have learned from it. I am still careful, however, not to preach. I hope that my verbal disclaimers at various points in the class discussion—if I feel that drawing on personal examples might be misinterpreted as advocating a certain position—have the desired effect. However, I can never be sure.

A recent successful class session was one in which we carefully and deliberately analyzed the many dynamics of activism that we observe out there—on campus and social media and so on. Rather than gird myself for attacks, I took a more confident and relaxed position: I peppered the students with as many polarizing statements, labels, and clichés as I could think of, telling them that I was eager to get their reactions and response. I told them that I had been called a "JINO" (Jew in Name Only) on a Facebook thread not long ago. I asked them whether they think there is more pressure on individuals to conform to their own group's dominant opinion if that is the side that considers itself oppressed. I recounted a recent debate that ensued from one of my columns on the politics of Linda Sarsour, a Brooklyn-based Palestinian American activist in the Palestinian solidarity and women's movements. Referencing another recent op-ed I had written, I told them about my personal struggles with whether to identify with BDS—and the effect of Israel's new travel ban (barring anyone who has called for any kind of boycott—whether BDS or a boycott of settlement products only) on my personal political evolution. In rapid-fire motion, absorbed in the way that advocates of "flow" describe, where one is completely caught up in one's task, I guided the students through an analytical journey across the landscape that I comfortably inhabit out of the classroom and that I had been afraid would be imported into the classroom without my ability to write the script first.

This year, there were a few other changes I made that may have helped alleviate the building pressure in the classroom. During the semester prior, the one that was particularly tough, I had forgotten to do something I usually do: begin the course with an open and honest discussion of my background, positionality, and subjectivity. The following semester I introduced the course with an improvised monologue about the many complexities within my package of personal-political identity—my deep yet fraught attachment to Israel; my ambivalent connection to organized religion; my journey to find belonging in my own community while resisting pressure to conform. "Just because someone is Jewish (or Arab or Palestinian)," I said, "does not mean that you can predict their politics. It is complex, and we are going to explore these complexities—this semester—together."

On the syllabus this year, I included some disclaimers. In what now feels to me like a rear-guard action that I hope I might one day feel I can remove altogether, I wrote, "You may find that throughout class conversation, I might challenge you to see another 'angle' of the issue (whatever angle that might be at the time). But keep in mind that my attempt to enable you to consider another angle—whatever angle that might be in the context of the discussion—does not necessarily correspond to my personal opinions of the issue. And it certainly does not reflect any attempt on my part to 'defend' or 'promote' one side or another."

And I added something I had previously avoided in my earlier attempt to present the course as simply trying to "understand the actions of each side." Instead, this year I wrote the following: "Amidst all these important discussions, however, we will have to keep in mind the issue of power. While the course examines the contemporary relationship between Israel and the Palestinians in light of historical dynamics, we will keep in mind the fact that Israel is currently the occupying power."

When a course goes better than it did the previous year, one cannot ultimately discount minor changes and elements of chance. There were little things—largely out of my control—such as the new semester's classroom having windows. Daylight helped to lighten the mood, perhaps. And there was the fact that last semester my classroom had not come equipped with a chalkboard. Because of that, I did not have the chance to turn my back on the class for a moment to write down a concept, organize my thoughts, and regroup. And this semester there was less talking and whispering. Students spaced themselves out more across the rows. The dynamic just seemed lighter and less imposing.

Then there is the story of the shifting and fickle gods to which professors—at various points in their personal, political, and intellectual evolution—pray. When I first started out in this profession, it seemed there was no higher calling than asking explanatory questions. "Why did Israel pursue the Oslo agreement?" "Why did Arafat adopt a two-state solution orientation when he did?" Perhaps owing to my particular graduate training at a Washington, DC-based university, I had internalized the fact/value distinction to a fault. It followed that if you wanted to make prescriptive arguments—what should Israel (or the United States or Canada or the Palestinian Authority) do in a given case—you could do so, as long as those arguments flowed from a record of evidence and as long as it was called "policy." This means that if you were going to argue that the United States should push for negotiations or sanctions or war in any given case, you needed to know under what conditions any of these forms of statecraft work—reasonable enough, except that it effectively excludes certain kinds of more ethically based questions from being asked in the first place.

In turn, disciplinary norms dictated that one could advocate for a certain set of policies as long as it was to serve the "national interest" (usually of the United States). This strict separation between fact and value—with policy advocacy being relegated to the national interest of the United States (though as a Canadian scholar now living and working in Canada, I suppose I could extend that ethos to Canadian foreign policy)—made North American scholars who desperately wanted to see justice, dignity, and equality in Israel/Palestine particularly vulnerable to charges of inappropriately politicizing one's scholarship. The result, in my own teaching, was fifteen years of teaching a strictly explanatory approach to Israeli-Palestinian relations and desperately hoping that students did not try to smuggle politics in.

It took several years of active op-ed writing (in *Haaretz*, the *Forward*, the *Globe and Mail*, and elsewhere) for me to ease into a new scholarly and professional identity—one that put prescriptive arguments front and center. It has been a gradual transition to helping my students develop their own prescriptive voice. I now typically assign op-ed writing assignments to my students. I also ask them to create a Facebook page (with their own name hidden behind the page title) to assess a particular analytical issue, providing analysis and commentary. There too they have the opportunity of making strong, normative arguments—as long as they connect those claims to a research question and as long as they ground their analysis in evidence and logical reasoning. And while in my own op-ed writing I too need to adhere to the demands of evidence and logic, I can also introduce ethical concerns as I see them. The op-ed form lends itself to a broader array of values to be served when posing questions and constructing arguments.

Finally, there is the issue of social capital. It is possible that as I have developed new communities of professional friends and acquaintances, I have developed a more rights-forward voice in both my writing and my teaching, a voice that embraces discourses of human rights and justice. I have begun to mine these dynamics in another reflexive piece and am still trying to understand how my own personal and professional identities affect my pedagogical commitments—and vice versa. I suspect it will be an ongoing process.[2]

Perhaps calling rights-forward discourse a "blame game" was misguided from the start. Perhaps it revealed a lack of confidence in my own ability to guide students through these charged debates. Retreating to explanatory questions felt safer. And now, I realize, it is time to step outside that safety zone and expand the kinds of questions I am willing to ask, together with my students. Sometimes I wonder why this lesson took so long for me to learn. Perhaps it is age and maturity. Perhaps it was the results of one particularly challenging semester that forced me to ask myself some tough questions. Whatever it is, I realize that refining our pedagogy is a lifelong approach, after all.

Notes

1. Stacy Douglas, Betina Kuzmarov, Karen Schwartz, Mira Sucharov, and Sarah L. Todd, "Teaching Subjectively: Interdisciplinary Insights," *Canadian Journal for the Scholarship of Teaching and Learning* 7, no. 2 (2016): article 4.
2. Mira Sucharov, "Feeling My Way along the Seam Line of Jerusalem," *Journal of Narrative Politics* 3, no. 2 (2017): 120–30.

Seeing the Israeli

TEACHING PALESTINIAN STUDENTS

MYA GUARNIERI JARADAT

The student lingered after class, straightening her hijab, taking her time to pack her satchel, waiting for the others to leave. When the room was empty, she approached me: "You're Jewish, right?"

I did not respond. I taught freshman English composition in an American program at a Palestinian university in the West Bank. The campus was in a village just outside the Israeli-built separation barrier. Some of our students were refugees who longed to see the villages and homes that their grandparents fled in 1948, when the Jewish state was established. Most braved checkpoints on their way to campus every day; clashes with Israeli soldiers occurred by our gates on a regular basis; sometimes the army made incursions onto campus, firing tear gas. Students had friends and family who had been held under administrative detention without charge or trial in Israeli prisons; some had, themselves, seen the occupiers' jails. They had lost land to settlements and loved ones to political violence. A handful bore scars from incidents they would rather forget.

And there I was: a reminder.

"You're Jewish, right?" I had been warned by administrators not to address such questions head-on, not to be too open about the fact that, yes, I am a Jew who holds an Israeli ID. One administrator told me that I ought to tell students that it was none of their business, a response that seemed, to me, rude and dishonest. It also struck me as patronizing, the assumption behind such an answer being that students were not sophisticated enough to understand that one could be at once a Jew and an Israeli and believe in universal human rights. Further, it seemed to clash with the type of work that was asked of students in first-year comp. We had an integrated curriculum with the first-year seminar (FYSEM); their comp assignments often led them to draw out the larger implications and themes of their personal experiences by using the literary texts they read in FYSEM. We held that writing leads to thinking, not the other way around; our process-oriented approach to writing meant that students wrote multiple drafts of each essay, workshopping them together in class and with me as they progressed. Sharing and trust were integral to the classroom environment. How could my students feel comfortable sharing intimate details about their lives if I refused to answer even the most basic questions about my own, particularly when they were questions that, thanks to Google and my work as a journalist and writer, most of them already knew the answers to?

"You're brave to be here," the girl continued, not waiting for my response. "Anyone could bring a gun to campus and shoot you."

Was that a compliment? Or a threat? I was not sure. I laughed and headed toward the hallway. She walked with me. I kept my eyes on the ground, watching the tips of her black Converse sneakers dart out from her floor-length *jelbab*, then retreat again to their hiding place under the fabric. I had spent the better part of two years doing the same—keeping my identity under wraps, only to have it surface again and again.

•••

FYSEM set the bulk of the reading assignments; the English comp instructors determined some short, supplementary texts. While some of our students were native English speakers—either because they had spent a significant amount of time in the United States or because they had an American parent—most were not. Accordingly, we tried to limit their number of readings; we also preferred our students to engage deeply with a smaller number of texts rather than superficially with many. In the fall semester in FYSEM, students read Gilgamesh, Genesis, and the Gospel of Luke, among other texts; spring found the students immersed in Plato's *Republic*, Hayy ibn Yaqzan, and *Hamlet*. In comp, students read everything from Anne Lamott's "Shitty First Drafts" and Alain de Botton's "On Travel" to "Thirst" by Nawal El Saadawi and Mahmoud Darwish's poem "Write down, I am an Arab." All of these readings were approved beforehand by an American administrator who represented the American college and its interests in the "cooperative program" with the Palestinian university.

In English composition, every class meeting began with a short, low-stakes writing task; for the most part, these were relatively open-ended. Upon completion, students were encouraged to share—mindful of their participation grade, many did. Just as politics permeated their lives, it often seeped into their low-stakes writing: a student who had been stopped by Israeli soldiers at a flying checkpoint on her way to campus, for example, wrote about her experience and shared it with the class. Another who had been arrested at a protest against Israel's use of administrative detention did the same. There was the girl who, years before, found herself trapped in Gaza when she and her parents went to visit family there, and the Israelis refused to issue them the necessary permits to return to the West Bank. It was endless.

An integrated curriculum meant that larger paper assignments—the guidelines of which we referred to as "prompts"—were developed with FYSEM faculty as well as the aforementioned administrator. In other words, there was a lot of oversight. And though a stated goal of the program was to enhance "the prospect for peace and cooperation," our prompts were sometimes overtly political:

> Recall a moment from your life when you experienced justice or injustice. Begin your paper by rendering the experience as vividly as possible so the reader has a strong sense of what you went through; then interpret the experience through the lens of one of the definitions of justice offered in *The Republic*.

> The Gospel of Luke is full of instructions on how to live one's life. Pick two instructions or parables that interest you. Argue whether or not these teachings or parables are applicable to contemporary society. Can Jesus's advice and teachings be followed in the particular place and moment you live in? Why or why not? Use examples from your life as well as from the broader political context to make your argument.

In other cases, it was not hard for students to take things in a political direction if they so desired. Take, for example, the following excerpt from the prompt for their spring-semester research paper about Muslim Spain: "Thinking about the sources we have looked at in class—as well as any preliminary research about Muslim Spain you might do on your own—what grabbed your interest? For example, you might consider . . . Christian-Muslim conflict; coexistence between Jews, Muslims, and Christians; cultural exchange between the three groups."

Of course, we were not looking for students to simply swallow and regurgitate information. They had done that the previous year for their high school matriculation exam, known as *tawjihi*. The Palestinian educational system relies on rote; we were trying to cultivate critical thinkers. The skills that students learned in FYSEM and first-year comp were crucial to reaching this goal; the aims of the spring-semester research paper dovetailed with those of the program itself: "After you have picked an area you'd like to learn more about, try to develop an open-ended, probative question to guide your research. It should be a question that cannot be answered with a simple 'yes' or 'no.' It should be something that makes you dig deeper, it should force you to develop an argument. Your question might not have an answer or it might have more than one, conflicting answer. The idea is for you to wrestle with the topic, using outside sources, and to offer an argument, counterargument, and supporting evidence."

But in the black-and-white world of the Israeli-Palestinian conflict, advocating such nuanced thinking was nothing short of radical. This did not always go over well in the conservative West Bank, particularly when one's instructor was a Jew holding an Israeli ID.

⋯

Through the analysis and discussion of published texts and students' own writing, they became skilled at identifying strong theses, argument, counterargument, supporting details and evidence, and the correct usage of appropriate, reliable sources; they could also recognize the lack thereof. While most of the published texts we read were not inherently political, students' writing often was. Accordingly, conversations sometimes veered in that direction, even though I tried to keep the class focused on the tools of argumentative writing. In those cases, I attempted to use peer learning to avoid talking politics myself, throwing questions out to the class in hopes that they would guide each other to the answer. ("If the student is arguing that Jesus's teachings can't be followed in the context of the occupation of Palestine, what would the counterargument be?") But as most of my students were less than a year out from an educational system based on rote learning, things such as counterargument did not always come easy. Sometimes I had to spell the counterargument out; I also had to explain that claims such as "dozens of Palestinians die because of the occupation every day" need to be fact-checked and backed up with numbers and reliable sources. And because gross generalizations and inaccuracies open one's argument to attack, if they could not produce a reliable source to prove such a claim, they needed to reconsider their language.

With first-year students, it was a bit like Russian dolls: opening one topic meant explaining another. What was a reliable source anyway? We had to talk about that, too. Was the Hamas website, for example, a reliable source? Probably not. Did B'Tselem keep up-to-date and accurate statistics about the human toll of the occupation? It certainly did.

"What is B'Tselem?" a student asked.

I explained that it is an Israeli NGO that, among other things, documents human rights abuses in the occupied territories. That such an organization exists was shocking to some of my students, particularly those who conflated Judaism with Zionism and who had a narrow view of both; it confused those who believed that all Jews and all Israelis support the occupation and other right-wing policies. I saw a window of opportunity to complicate their ideas. Naively, perhaps, I believed the hype about the program I was teaching in. I believed that, as a Palestinian administrator put it, "it is precisely through the kind of education which can make us better human beings that we can achieve a state of mutual respect, concern for each other, and a just peace." I believed in the U.S. college's slogan, that its institution is "a place to think."

I rattled off the names of a few more Israeli NGOs, suggesting that my students look them up online. On another occasion, I presented students with an image of Shimon Yehoshua, a *mizrahi* (Jew from Arab or Muslim land) who was shot to death by Israeli police in 1982 as the state attempted to evict him and his family from public housing in south Tel Aviv. Their home was slated for demolition, and the land would be used for a more profitable venture—a process known in Hebrew as *pinui-binui*. Without the explanation, my students thought the man was a Palestinian, fighting the army during the First Intifada. I told them the short version of Yehoshua's story and encouraged them to learn more about the *mizrahim* and about their conflicted identity and place in this conflicted land. In the words of one of the administration-approved prompts, I wanted them to "develop . . . open-ended, probative" questions, questions "that cannot be answered with a simple 'yes' or 'no.'" Their questions should, I believed, "have more than one, conflicting answer." I wanted them to "wrestle with" every "topic." This is how one becomes a writer. This is how one becomes a thinker.

And if I am to be honest with myself, I have to say that I also offered them up these nuances and complexities because I was tired of hearing about *al yahud*, the monolithic Jews. At some point, right or wrong, it became personal.

I had a number of bright students who got me and got what I was doing. They understood that addressing the Zionist or right-wing Israeli claims was essential to closing the holes in their own argument. They also got that hyperbolic statements exaggerating the death toll attributable to the occupation just opened up their writing to attack.

But some did not understand. Some thought that simply giving airtime to the Israeli narrative meant advocating it. As an instructor, it was a lose-lose situation: if I did not teach students how to address holes in their argument by using counter-argument, I would be remiss in my duties. But as a Jew who holds an Israeli ID, my attempts to present the "Israeli side of things" were sometimes misunderstood.

If, say, a Palestinian instructor was nudging them in this direction, it might have been fine. But because of the skin that I am in, it was not. After I had resigned to follow my soon-to-be-husband to Florida, an American administrator chided me for my classroom discussions about B'Tselem and *mizrahim*. "Mya, you're Israeli," she said. "You can't say things like that to Palestinian students."

We were at a café in Jewish West Jerusalem, near her apartment. "Ah, ken?" (Oh, yeah?), I asked her. "So how was I supposed to teach them counterargument?"

And never mind that I had advocated publicly for both BDS and a one-state solution, a democratic polity that would stretch from river to sea, a place where Jews and Arabs would be equal citizens. Never mind that I had moved to Bethlehem, an area of the West Bank governed by the Palestinian Authority, that I took the same minivans to school as my students, passing through the same checkpoints; never mind that I would eventually marry a Palestinian, whose surname I now bear. At the end of the day, to some of my students, I was nothing but a Jew and an Israeli. A suspect.

• • •

But I did not realize this—or maybe I refused to—until the 2014 war with Gaza, when the same student who had warned me that "anyone could bring a gun to campus" began to send "anonymous" emails to the student body and faculty about my "aggressive and unprofessional" actions. I had already resigned my post for fall, but I was set to teach a course at the end of summer. The administration wrung its "cooperative program" hands: my evaluations had always been strong; my students had showed great progress in their writing; had I stayed, an American administrator had promised to make me director of first-year writing. And now, as Gaza bled and the West Bank boiled, there were emails claiming that I was a Zionist and that I had lived in a settlement, that, in asking students to differentiate between Jews and Israelis and Zionists, by teaching them how to acknowledge and address the Israeli counterarguments, I had been attempting to brainwash them. These same letters included vague threats, saying that I had been spotted in Beit Sahour and Jerusalem and that I had better apologize to my Palestinian students if I planned on setting a foot on campus again. So on and so forth.

A number of students emailed me to offer their support—including one who had never taken a class with me but had heard about me and who hoped "one day . . . to have the honor of meeting and learning from" me. I was touched. I continue still today to be heartened by the former students who keep in touch with me: all young women, all brilliant, critical thinkers whose inner and outer lives are colored with complexity. More than a few of these former students have become fine writers. One has begun working as a journalist already. Another, whose wedding I attended in Ramallah, has written a novel. I would like to think that to these students, I was much more than "a Jew" and "an Israeli." I have to believe I was their teacher.

• • •

Just before the summer course began, I received a one-line email from the administration asking me not to teach the class. A Jewish Israeli colleague who had been an instructor in the program for three years and who was already listed on the fall schedule received a nearly identical email minutes after mine—a writer and well-connected member of the media with prestigious publications under his belt, he was bullied into signing a nondisclosure form.

I left the West Bank two weeks after that one-line email, to join my then-fiancé, now-husband in Florida. I was sad to go. But I was also relieved. My experiences made me understand that I had been working and living in an impossible situation. I no longer believe in a one-state solution. Nor do I believe in two states either. There will be no peace between the river and the sea.

Teaching the Palestinian-Israeli Conflict in the Community College Classroom

SUSAN JACOBOWITZ

Queensborough Community College, where I am an associate professor in the English department, is a public, open-admission two-year college in the borough of Queens, located in the most diverse county in the United States.[1] The students come from all over the world. Many are immigrants or the children of immigrants and are the first in their families to go to college. The college comprises nearly equal populations of African Americans, Caucasians, and Latinos, representing 139 nations of birth and eighty-seven languages. Queensborough is one of the twenty-four campuses of the City University of New York, the largest urban public university in the United States.

My scholarship focuses on creative work by sons and daughters of survivors and issues of trauma and its inheritance across the generations. Much of my identity has been shaped around being the daughter of a Holocaust survivor. When I teach introduction to literature courses, I usually include a small unit on Holocaust literature and share with my students a little bit about my own background and work.

I realized that there was a tremendous interest in Jews, the Holocaust, and the historical background and context I would introduce and that there were experiences in the pasts of my own students that made them connect very strongly and engage with the course material: grandparents who had survived Japanese occupation, parents who had fled revolutions in Latin America, family or personal histories shaped by refugee experiences, war and displacement, or direct experiences of prejudice, discrimination, and persecution. I often had classrooms where there were no Jewish students but where there was an intense interest in and curiosity about Jews and the Jewish experience.

Because our students come from all over the world and have experienced so much, I thought they would also be very interested in the foundation of Israel and the history of the Palestinian-Israeli conflict, which we could explore through literature.

There was a natural connection to Israel that had developed for me through doing Holocaust-related work. I often had students who were Muslim, some of whom were connected to the Middle East. I felt less confident about my ability to teach the Palestinian perspective and Palestinian history and literature. But a unique opportunity presented itself through the Brandeis Summer Institute for Israel Studies (SIIS), which was intended to help faculty develop courses that involved Israel. I applied to be part of the summer 2006 cohort, with the aim of creating a special topics course: "The Literature of the Palestinian-Israeli Conflict." The fellowship involved two weeks of intensive study with scholars and experts at Brandeis University in Boston and then a week of travel and study in Israel, where we met with representatives of the Israeli government, visited a settlement in the West Bank, and toured the security wall. We also had the opportunity to travel with Elie Rekhess, a scholar of the political history of Arabs in Israel, to the Triangle Area—a predominantly Arab region of Israel—where we visited a mosque and were introduced to Arab civic, religious, and community leaders in Umm al-Fahm, a city located twenty kilometers northwest of Jenin in the Haifa District.

Course Goals and Description

My goal was to offer a course that would provide insight into the Palestinian-Israeli conflict through a study of texts and materials incorporating multiple disciplines and genres and representing as wide an array of voices, experiences, and perspectives as I could construct. I was very focused on providing background and context. I chose two texts, *The Arab-Israeli Conflict* by Kirsten E. Schulze (Routledge, 2013) and *The Yellow Wind* by David Grossman (Random House, 2016), partially because they were comprehensive, compact, and inexpensive. Because textbooks are difficult for our students to afford and because I wanted to provide access to a wide array of materials, I also assembled a reader.

I organized the special topics course along chronological lines, so that we would conclude with what was most current. I began with historical Jewish and Muslim connections to the Land of Israel.[2] Next, students studied the history of pogroms and Jewish persecution in Europe and the development of Zionism.[3] They studied immigration and learned about life in the Yishuv, reviewing excerpts from *The Plough Woman: Records of the Pioneer Women of Palestine*, edited by Mark A. Raider and Miriam B. Raider-Roth (Brandeis University Press, 2002); poetry by Rachel; and the Balfour Declaration. For the class on the war in 1948, students supplemented the readings in Schulze with the Declaration of Israel's Independence, David Ben-Gurion's diary page describing events as they unfolded, and S. Yizhar's short story "The Prisoner" (in

The Oxford Book of Hebrew Short Stories, ed. Glenda Abramson [Oxford University Press, 1996]).

I also utilized several films. *Four Friends* (2000), directed by Esther Dar, tells the story of four women—Selma Dejani, daughter of an Old Palestinian Muslim family; Wadad Shihade, a Palestinian Christian, originally from Jaffa; Olga Belkind, daughter of a prominent Zionist family; and Sharona Aharon, from the heart of cosmopolitan Tel Aviv—who were roommates at an Anglican boarding school in Jerusalem in 1939. Fifty years after they had left, they met for a reunion. For Olga and Sharona, the establishment of the State of Israel in 1948 was the fulfillment of a dream, but for Selma and Wadad, it spelled the beginning of a lifelong tragedy.

Students also watched the documentary *The Forgotten Refugees* (2005, directed by Michael Grynszpan), which recounts the history of Jewish communities of the Middle East and North Africa and their demise in the face of persecution following the creation of the modern State of Israel in 1948. In an attempt to give voice to Palestinian experience and show some of the realities of life on the West Bank for those who are living under occupation, I also used *Rana's Wedding* (2002) and *Paradise Now* (2005), two films directed by Hany Abu-Assad. *Rana's Wedding* depicts the challenges of a young Palestinian woman as she attempts to reach her boyfriend and marry to avoid having to emigrate to Egypt with her father. *Paradise Now* tells the story of two Palestinian friends recruited by a terrorist group to become suicide bombers in Tel Aviv.

Hany Abu-Assad's films highlight the day-to-day indignities and frustrations for Arabs living in the West Bank, showing life under occupation involving restricted movement and constant logistical challenges, economic struggle, and circumscribed possibilities, particularly for young people. *Paradise Now* attempts to show the kind of hopelessness and despair that leads young men to volunteer to be suicide bombers; it also shows the leaders within the movement that recruited them to be indifferent to their plight. I wanted the students to be able to distinguish between the different realities and challenges for the two Arab populations, depending on whether they lived within Israel and were citizens or were living in the West Bank under occupation. Gaza was changing hands as I was teaching the course, with the Israeli withdrawal in 2005, but I tried to give the students a sense of what the challenges were for young people growing up in Gaza as well. It is one of the most densely occupied patches of land on the planet, and the residents of Gaza do not hold passports since they are not citizens of any state. Students read excerpts from Amira Hass's *Drinking the Sea at Gaza: Days and Nights in a Land under Siege* (Holt, 2000), written by an Israeli journalist who went to Gaza in 1993 to cover a story, and ended up staying.

At this point, students were also reading "Memory of Place: Re-Creating the Pre-1948 Palestinian Village," from Susan Slyomivoc's *The Object of Memory: Arab and Jew Narrate the Palestinian Village* (University of Pennsylvania Press, 1998), to understand the trauma of Palestinian expulsion; A. B. Yehoshua's "Facing the Forests"; and selected Palestinian poetry. They continued to explore the meaning of exile as they read "Shadow Cities" by André Aciman, "The New Nomads" by Eva Hoffman, and "No Reconciliation Allowed" by Edward W. Said, all from *Letters of Transit: Reflections on Exile, Identity, Language, and Loss*, edited by André Aciman (New Press, 1999).

I incorporated a focus on the Arab national minority through readings from *The Other Side of Israel: My Journey across the Jewish-Arab Divide*, by Susan Nathan (Knopf Doubleday, 2007), an exploration of the legal status of the Arab-Palestinian community in Israel, and eight policy guidelines regarding the Arab population in Israel. In the Schulze text, students read about the 1967 war, the 1973 war, the Lebanon War, the intifada, and the Middle East peace process and reviewed the Palestinian National Charter: Resolutions of the Palestine National Council, July 1–17, 1968. I tried to incorporate women's experience as well, including the readings "Growing Up Female and Palestinian in Israel," by Manar Hassan, translated by Sharon Ne'eman; and "Homefront and Battlefront: The Status of Jewish and Palestinian Women in Israel," in *Israeli Women's Studies: A Reader*, edited by Esther Fuchs (Rutgers University Press, 2005). It seemed important to incorporate gender as a focus and look at the ways in which women's lives are affected when a society is either intensely patriarchal or highly militarized or both.

To come into the present, students read an interview with Ami Ayalon, from *The Other Israel: Voices of Refusal and Dissent* (ed. Tom Segev, Roane Carey, and Jonathan Shainin [New Press, 2004]); Amos Oz, "Good Guys and Bad Guys" (*Forward*, June 2, 2006, 13); Mahmoud Darwish, "The Palestinian People's Appeal on the 50th Anniversary of the Nakba" (June 14, 1998, http://rula1234.tripod.com); excerpts from Hamas's "The Covenant of the Islamic Resistance Movement" (August 18, 1988, The Avalon Project: Documents in Law, History and Diplomacy, http://avalon.law.yale.edu); George Soros, "Blinded by a Concept" (*Boston Globe*, August 31, 2006); David Grossman's address on the anniversary of the assassination of Yitzhak Rabin (November 6, 2006, http://IMEMC.org); and Lisa Beyer, "The Big Lie about the Middle East" (*Time*, December 18, 2006).

Reflection

While I was an SIIS fellow and preparing to teach this course, I was cautioned that I might encounter a lot of resistance in the form of support for Palestinians and anti-Jewish or anti-Israel backlash, which was presented along with the argument that being anti-Israel or anti-Zionist should be viewed as a/the new form of antisemitism. Faculty at other campuses had encountered these kinds of problems, and some of them felt quite embattled. Working in a diverse environment—knowing that I would have Muslim and Arab students from different countries and perhaps only a smattering of Jewish students—I wondered what the atmosphere in the class would be like and what kind of reaction the course would provoke on campus.

As I planned my course, one goal included ensuring that Palestinian history and perspectives would have equal time on the syllabus and in class discussion/assignments in order to facilitate a more complex understanding of the conflict. My own introduction to the subject had been the novel *Exodus* by Leon Uris in high school. From a Jewish or a Holocaust perspective, it is impossible not to understand the creation of Israel as a tremendous opportunity for the Jewish people to realize a dream of statehood and achieve a more normalized existence. I wanted to be sure that my own connection to Israel through family and religion did not compromise my ability to be objective or compassionate. And while I anticipated confrontation in class, I was shocked to discover that the students generally reacted with apathy toward the situation of Palestinians. Few expressed either sympathy or concern. When I asked students to explain their reactions, some told me that they just did not have any associations with Palestinians or the conflict; some Muslim students told me that they had not been raised to feel sympathy for Palestinians.

As I came to understand more about the realities of the conflict, the biggest challenge was personal. The more scholarly material I read, the more I became conscious of the many ways in which Palestinians had been discriminated against by the Israeli state through institutional measures such as urban planning, infrastructure, the control of water resources, and the development of "facts on the ground."[4]

The intersection of my personal history with the course became surprising for me. I identified with the Palestinian experience of suffering and discrimination. As the daughter of a Holocaust survivor who was given opportunities in the United States, I understood that I was the beneficiary of a system in which my father had been allowed to flourish. In contrast, I saw that the Palestinians within Israel have limited opportunities for advancement. Being told that Arabs have it better in Israel even with second-class status than they do in many other Middle Eastern countries did not really seem like the point to me. It seemed similar to arguments about *dhimmitude*, the status of minorities under Islam during the Ottoman period, in which Jews were a protected minority yet one that was discriminated against. While I understand that some kind of protective status is better than none, this seems like an inadequate compromise. Clearly the ideal should be equality.

I was also disturbed by the rhetoric around population transfer that I was exposed to through the lectures and published material of Sergio Della Pergola, a professor of demography who has written extensively on Palestinian and Jewish/Israeli population shifts. His concern with the lower birth rate of Israeli Jews and higher birth rate among Israeli Arabs and Palestinians in the West Bank led him to advocate an idea known as "population transfer." It proposed that borders could change overnight if Israel swapped out the Triangle Area, where there is a large number of Palestinian settlements, in exchange for some of the larger Jewish settlements—cities, really—in the West Bank. Israeli Arabs would go to bed as Israeli citizens one night and wake up the next morning stripped of their Israeli citizenship, now being Palestinian citizens.[5] The focus was on maintaining a Jewish majority in Israel so that Israel would remain a Jewish state and on trying to create a foundation for a two-state solution. The idea of depriving people of their citizenship—particularly without their consent—is a very difficult one for me. I do not believe that any objection to any Israeli policy is just a new form of antisemitism, but it is difficult and increasingly uncomfortable to criticize Israeli governmental policies within the U.S. Jewish community. I am concerned about the rights of Palestinians and what a never-ending conflict means for Jews and the State of Israel. I am also concerned about Israel's security and survival.

I taught the course, which I developed several times, as a special topics upper-division elective. The students were bright, committed, and mature. But I came to feel overwhelmed by the complexity and intensity of what I was teaching, and I felt that the preparation and study that I had embarked on in order to prepare to teach the class left me far from being an expert. Literature does not exist in isolation. It is connected to a time, to a place, to people, to moments—to individual stories. I always find myself teaching a lot of history: I have graduate degrees in both history and literature. I find it impossible to think of either discipline without feeling that they are entwined. With regard to the Middle East, the challenge is almost overwhelming. It is a part of the world we as Americans know very little about. In addition to history, it is important to understand something of the religions and cultures that are involved; it involves political science and sociology as well. I wanted the class to be interdisciplinary. But such hopes meant that students were being asked to absorb a tremendous amount of history, context, and background very quickly, in order to be able to evaluate a wide range of materials: primary source documents, films, memoirs, diaries, short stories, poetry. The level of complexity made me wonder if the class would not be more appropriate as a graduate seminar—this was a course for second-year community college students. While the student evaluations for the course were positive, it was difficult to feel certain about what students were getting from the experience.

Since I stopped teaching the course, things have only become more complicated. Israel faces very real challenges and existential threats. The occupation continues. While I do not support the BDS movement and have argued against it, I am discouraged by the bleak human rights situation. I am very concerned when people say that Israel can remain either a democratic state or a Jewish state but not both. It is a haunting dilemma, and there seems to be no immediate resolution.

I was walking through the main parking lot on campus recently when I was hailed with the familiar "Hey, professor!" I turned around and recognized a young man who had taken "The Literature of the Palestinian-Israeli Conflict." "Do you still teach that class?" he asked me. "It was one of the best classes I ever took." I felt very emotional, thinking of all of the time, effort, and anxiety that had gone into the class. I was grateful to receive the feedback. It made me realize that, however daunting and complex the subject matter, students are up to the challenges. They will be the agents of change in the world, and they should know as much as they can about the history of the region and the origins of its conflicts, in order to more productively focus on resolution, peace, and hope.

Notes

1. According to the Endangered Language Alliance (ELA), there are as many as eight hundred languages spoken in New York City, and nowhere in the world has more than Queens, "the capital of language diversity."
2. To explore historical Jewish connections to the Land of Israel, students reviewed Psalm 137; the Gemara excerpt "Kethuboth"; "A Longing to Return to the Land of Israel," by Yehudah ha-Levi; Mishna, tractate Pe'ah chapter 1 (Soncino edition); and Yiddish Letters in the Cairo Geniza (circa 1560–70). Students were introduced to pre-Islamic Arabia and Islam, reading "Muhammad the Prophet," an excerpt from *Islam: Beliefs and Observances*, by Caesar E. Farah (New York: Barron's, 2000); "A New Power in an Old World," from *A History of the Arab Peoples*, by Albert Hourani (Cambridge, MA: Harvard University Press, 2002); and "The Shape of the Holy—Jerusalem under Three Religions," by Nimrod Luz, *Journal of the American Oriental Society* 120, no. 1 (2000): 108.
3. They read excerpts from Arthur Hertzberg's *The Zionist Idea: A Historical Analysis and Reader* as well as Max Nordau's "Jewry of Muscle," Chaim Nahman Bialik's "The City of Slaughter," and Andrei Shapiro's "The Kishinev Pogrom." As the students progressed through the Schulze text, beginning with "The Origins of the Arab-Israeli Conflict," they also read from the reader: "The Economic Basis for Arab/Jewish Accommodation," by S. Ilan Troen, from *Imagining Zion: Dreams, Designs, and Realities in a Century of Jewish Settlement* (New Haven, CT: Yale University Press, 2003).
4. Troen, *Imagining Zion*.
5. I also felt a lot of concern about the idea of casting out citizens because of the fear that the expanding numbers were threatening and that there would be a large cost involved in providing health care and education to "undesirable" communities. Because the Arab birth rate was higher, there was the cost of sending children to school, etc.

Grappling with the Arab-Israeli Conflict at a Historically Black College and University

REFLECTIONS ON AN ACCIDENTAL JOURNEY

ROLIN MAINUDDIN

Located in Durham, North Carolina, North Carolina Central University (NCCU) is a historically black college and university (HBCU). Even though research is enthusiastically promoted on campus and is now a requirement for tenure and promotion, NCCU is still primarily a teaching institution. According to campus website information, with a small minority of Asians and Hispanics and 11 percent of European descent, 75 percent of the students are African Americans.

Parallels have been drawn within social justice movements between African Americans and Palestinians as victims of oppression. Given the campus population's deep awareness of the legacy of slavery and the experience of subjugation and racial injustice in the United States, there is a sense of solidarity among students with the Palestinian people. For most students, this attitude stems from social identification rather than knowledge of the Middle East. However, knowledge production can become a competitive game over contested issues by the parties involved. Thus, it is imperative to impress on students the importance of critically examining the assumptions and arguments for different theoretical perspectives and metanarratives. My challenge in teaching is making students aware of cognitive dissonance and having them engage in critical thinking.

Given my cross-cultural living experience (I was raised in South Asia and went to high school in the Bahamas) and background in political science, my own journey to understand religious conflicts helps inform my approach to teaching. In South Asia, I became aware of Hindu-Muslim riots with loss of lives. Growing up in

Muslim-majority Bangladesh, where Zionism is viewed as an enigma, if not anathema, I had to overcome the views I was raised with and to regard the practical implications of Zionism for both its supporters and its opponents.

Most of the students who gravitate toward my "Middle Eastern Politics" course are political science majors. Some have taken the required survey course in comparative politics or international politics or both. In addition to essays in midterm and final examinations, I require a ten- to twelve-page paper for my upper-level elective course. In subscribing to an interactive mode of teaching, I have the goal of moving students beyond the descriptive (What? When? Where? Who?) to the analytical level (How? Why?). In stressing attention to relevant concepts, I urge students to organize their thoughts within a conceptual framework.

"Where is the Middle East?" I generally begin with that question as I project an online map of the region. In particular, students are asked to think about the "Middle" of the "Middle East." Puzzling looks lead me to rephrase by asking, from whose perspective? Then I clarify: from which part of the world is the region to the east of? The class responds "Europe," and occasionally one student may narrow the answer to "Britain." That takes me to introduce the concept of "Eurocentrism," with passing reference to European colonization, in addressing the "Middle East" name of the region.

I note that scholars with an "Afrocentric" perspective have challenged the inclusion of North Africa, located on the continent of Africa, as part of the Middle East. I continue to inform the class that scholars now refer to West Asia as the Middle East and North Africa (MENA). Yet, in the United States, the premier scholarly organization for that region is the "Middle East Studies Association" (MESA), and a prominent think tank is the "Near East Institute" (NEI). Both are Eurocentric names, I add. In giving a hint about politics pertaining to that region, I point out that MESA has a pro-Palestinian leaning and NEI is pro-Israel.

"Does the United States have any interest in the Middle East?" Students quickly respond "oil," and occasionally someone adds "Israel." I follow up with the question, "Given that Arab countries are important members of the Organization of the Oil Exporting Countries (OPEC), what explains U.S. interest in Israel?" If there is a silence, I inject, "democracy," to which someone may add, "Israel lobby," after a pause.

Having distinguished different types of democracy in my lower-level "Comparative Politics" course, I review with the class the concept of "pluralist democracy" in reiterating that lobbying by interest groups is legal in the United States. I mention as examples not only the American Israel Public Affairs Committee (AIPAC) but also the National Association for the Advancement of Colored People (NAACP) and other interest groups.

Looking inward, I ask the class to tell me in one word what is considered the most divisive issue in the United States. Upon clarifying that I mean historically the most socially divisive issue, after some pause, one or two students will respond, "race." Nodding in agreement, I broaden their horizon by noting that social tension revolve around other issues in non-Western parts of the world. I continue on that in the Middle East, religion has been a bone of contention.

In introducing students to the concept of "monotheism," I note the contribution of the Middle East with three monotheistic religions, each of which can be traced back to the Prophet Abraham (Ibrahim in Arabic): Judaism, Christianity, and Islam. I add that most of the Arabs practice Islam (though a minority are Christians); the majority people in Israel are of Jewish faith.

In view of the "Wahhabism" misnomer, I list the different theological schools in Islam: Ja'fari, Hanafi, Maliki, Shafi'i, and Hanbali. Thereafter, I observe that it is more appropriate to identify Muhammad ibn Abd al-Wahhab with the conservative Hanbali school in Saudi Arabia. Sometimes I follow up with debunking "fundamentalism," another misnomer that is in circulation.

A few students may express interest in the Shi'a-Sunni divide in Islam. I clarify that the Shi'a-Sunni division is over leadership succession after the death of Prophet Muhammad. With Iran being in the news in recent years, students know that it is a Shi'a-majority country. I inform them that Bahrain also has a Shi'a majority and that Lebanon has a significant Shi'a population. In response to my question about three major ethnic groups in the Middle East, after a while the class identifies Arab, Persian, and Turkish people. In responding to the question of which is the only Jewish country in the world, generally at least one person in the class knows that it is Israel.

This is the general introduction to MENA when I teach the "Middle Eastern Politics" course. Although I have been teaching an undergraduate course in the Middle East for over twenty years, my training was not in area studies. I got into this by accident.

Accidental Journey

If I have to teach a course in the Middle East, I thought to myself, I had better prepare myself for the task. With that in mind, I pursued a threefold strategy: a teaching philosophy that incorporates self-learning, lifetime membership in MESA, and book reviews to increase my knowledge about the region. Thus, my journey has been a continuous extended education. In the process, I benefited from attending guest lectures, workshops, and seminars. The imperative of Arabic language became clear to me for both learning about the Arab Middle East and understanding Islam. Being born into a Muslim family did not make me knowledgeable in Islam. Thus, in the early 2000s, I enrolled in Arabic-language courses at the University of North Carolina at Chapel

Hill. However, with a teaching load of four courses, it was difficult to continue for more than three semesters. Nevertheless, the experience made me aware of the importance of alphabetical roots for word derivation in the Arabic language.

During a brief discussion of current affairs at the beginning of my "Middle Eastern" Politics class one semester, a Muslim student remarked that "Islam is a religion of peace"—a counterargument developed against Islamophobia. This is where a rudimentary knowledge of Arabic vocabulary comes in handy in correcting the misconception. Emphasizing that *Islam* means "submission," I pointed out that the Arabic words for "war" and "peace" are *harb* and *salaam*, respectively. I added that both the greetings *salaam* (Arabic) and *shalom* (Hebrew) mean "peace." Yet Muslim Arabs and Jewish Israelis have been in conflict for over half a century. Then I asked the class to think whether the Arab-Israeli conflict is over religion or land.

The 2005 Islam Workshop at the Dar al-Islam Teachers Institute in Abiquiu, New Mexico, was a great learning experience about Muslim history, including in Africa, and Islamic theology. Later, in 2014, participation in the Summer Research Laboratory on Middle East and Islamic Studies at the University of Illinois, Urbana-Champaign, introduced me to Ibadi Islam, prevalent in Oman. Also, a 2006 NCCU faculty travel grant to Sana'a provided useful insights into Yemen. From there, a personal side trip to Makkah (Mecca) for *umrah* (truncated *hajj*, pilgrimage) gave me a glimpse of Saudi Arabia. These experiences enlightened me about the region. However, it was the two trips to Israel and the Palestinian Territories that exposed me to the complexity of the Israeli-Palestinian conflict.

Multilayered Complexity

An invaluable experience was the 2001 seminars abroad program in Israel and Jordan with a Fulbright-Hays fellowship funded by the United States Department of Education. The visit to the Old City of Jerusalem gave a firsthand look at the Western Wall and the Haram al-Sharif (Noble Sanctuary) or Har ha-Bayit (Temple Mount). The overhead-projector slides that I developed as part of my project for the field trip helped me to explain to students the danger of adjacent locations of the religious sites in an atmosphere of distrust and contention.

I add another reality check in remarking that the Israeli enthusiasm for archeological excavation underneath the Noble Sanctuary (Temple Mount) is resented by the Palestinians. I explain that the Israeli position, based on a new notion of horizontal sovereignty, is adamantly rejected by the Palestinians, who adhere to the traditional view of vertical sovereignty. The compact environment of the Old City, proximity of the holy sites, and antagonistic views help students to get a peek into the tense relationship between the Israelis and the Palestinians. Slowly, the complexity of the situation on the ground starts to sink in for my students.

Attending the 2015 Brandeis Summer Institute for Israel Studies (SIIS) gave me another opportunity to visit Israel and the Palestinian Territories. I took advantage of the SIIS seminars to learn about the broad philosophical perspectives within Zionism.

The Palestinian issue has been simmering for generations. Why? I answer that question in the class with attention to three concentric circles. First, the Palestinians are Arab, and the coethnic Arabs are numerically the largest group in the Middle East. Second, the future of Jerusalem is a sentimental issue for Muslims around the globe. Finally, the Israeli occupation is resented by people in the wider developing world. This three-tier support for the Palestinians needs to be juxtaposed with the Jewish people in Israel, many of whom (or their families) have made aliyah (immigrated) to that country, as well as the Jewish diaspora's historical insecurity due to violence that Jews have experienced in Europe, the Middle East, and around the world.

In 2002, a colleague asked me to give a talk, "The Arab-Israeli Conflict," in his class at Elon University. After the Q&A session following my presentation, a student who identified herself as Jewish came forward and thanked me for my "balanced views." I characterized the Arab-Israeli peace process as an "S-curve" phenomenon: the initial phase is slow, followed by a rapid acceleration, thereafter leveling off at a plateau. The antagonistic relationship that resulted in three Arab-Israeli wars (1948, 1956, and 1973) was only cracked in 1979 with the Egyptian-Israeli peace treaty. Many years passed before the 1993 Oslo Accords between Israel and the Palestine Liberation Organization, which were quickly followed by the 1994 Israeli-Jordanian peace treaty. An Israeli-Syrian peace treaty has not yet materialized, and Palestinian statehood remains uncertain. My students have found the aforementioned framework helpful in making some sense of the slow pace of the peace process.

Engaging students in the classroom has its own challenges. However, developing a new course could mean walking through a minefield for faculty. Given the strong emotions on both sides of the aisle regarding the Palestinian issue, it has been my steadfast policy not to teach a course in the Arab-Israeli conflict. As part of my commitment for the SIIS fellowship, I incorporated a section on Israel (and added two readings) in my "Comparative Politics" survey course and developed the syllabus for a new "Israeli Politics" course. In the process of getting the syllabus approved through the department curriculum committee, I was asked to include the "Palestinian perspective." Designed to be an upper-level sequel to the "Comparative Politics" survey course, I explained that a section on the Israeli-Palestinian peace process would not fit the domestic focus of the proposed "Israeli Politics" course. There were other episodes. Whereas one colleague urged me to incorporate a book by Benjamin Netanyahu, another colleague was emphatic about delegitimizing Israel. Let me add that these colleagues were neither Arab nor Muslim but from different sides of the conservative-liberal ideological spectrum.

Being identifiably Muslim (my last name is a giveaway) apparently warrants caution in speaking engagements. While giving a public talk, "Islamic Communities around the World," at the invitation of the North Carolina Department of Public Instruction (Raleigh, North Carolina) in 2003, it appeared that two people in the audience came to monitor me. Their Jewish and Muslim identities were given away by *kippah* and hijab, respectively. Thus, I also live at the intersection between identity politics and scholarship.

Having appreciated my earlier talk, "Reform in the MENA Region," in 2011, the Emerald Pond Retirement Center (Durham, North Carolina) invited me back for another topic later that year, "Israel and Palestine." However, the second time was an unpleasant experience for me with a few (not all) Jewish members of the audience. On another occasion, I had to cancel the idea of a class discussion with my students by a professor from the Hebrew University of Jerusalem when an African American Muslim student was adamant about publicly accusing the guest speaker of racism on account of Israeli government policy toward Africa.

There is no escape from the Arab-Israeli conflict. In recent years, I have been focusing on the Gulf Cooperation Council (GCC) countries in my "Middle Eastern Politics" course. When a Muslim Arab student unexpectedly asked me to talk about the Palestinian issue in class, despite the topic clearly not being related to GCC domestic politics, I took half an hour to address the matter in order to avoid any future interruption.

Course Development

Even though I have stayed away from teaching a full course on the topic, I did incorporate the Arab-Israeli conflict on two occasions. The essence of the protracted conflict was captured for my class by pointing to the title of a textbook by Deborah Gerner, *One Land, Two Peoples: The Conflict over Palestine* (Westview, 1991). In addition to using the S-curve phenomenon as the framework for the peace process, I asked the class to think about the concept of "cognitive dissonance," the psychological process of ignoring information that contradicts an individual's own perspective.

The Israeli and Palestinian psyches were juxtaposed for students in discussing two chapters from Tamara Wittes's edited volume *How Israelis and Palestinians Negotiate: A Cross-Cultural Analysis of the Oslo Peace Process* (United States Institute of Peace

Press, 2005): "Surviving Opportunities: Palestinian Negotiating Patterns in Peace Talks with Israel," by Omar Dajani; and "Israeli Negotiating Culture," by Aharon Klieman. It was gratifying to find scholarly contributions by both an Israeli and a Palestinian. Borrowing from Dajani, who previously served as a legal adviser to the Palestinian negotiating team, the class discussed implications of the Palestinian distinction between a transitional framework with expectations of the Israeli government fulfilling its obligations and a subsequent comprehensive settlement with a Palestinian state in tackling all outstanding issues. In the tension between diplomatic and security subcultures, I informed students in citing Klieman that the security subculture strongly influences Israeli negotiating positions. Seeing gloomy faces, I tried to cheer up the class by pointing to normalization of diplomatic relations between the United States and Vietnam after a devastating war and the emergence of a "security community" in Europe, whereby European countries no longer fear invasion from one another.

For my "Middle Eastern Politics" course (during the 2006–7 academic year), one of the two required readings was Shlomo Ben-Ami, *Scars of War, Wounds of Peace: The Israeli-Arab Tragedy* (Oxford University Press, 2006). The textbook covers the phased land strategy of Zionism, the military ethos in Jewish history, the misreading of fleeting opportunities, the encapsulation of a cold peace, the grinding peace process, and the challenges of an endgame. It was noteworthy that the strategy of marginalizing or jettisoning the Palestinian issue by embedding it within a neighboring Arab country turned out to be futile. The book is written by a former Israeli foreign minister, and its insight into negotiations and the "capsule theory" provided a good foundation for a lively class discussion.

In spring 2017, I taught my "American Foreign Policy" course with a Middle East focus. The textbook by Richard Mansbach and Kirsten Taylor, *Challenges for America in the Middle East* (CQ, 2017), has three chapters devoted to the Israeli-Palestinian conflict. They address the evolution of the relationship, the failure of the peace process, and challenges for a viable peace. Interestingly, the textbook focuses narrowly on the Palestinians rather than Arabs at large. The one-state versus two-state solution, settlement expansion, and refugee return issues generated a good debate.

In Lieu of a Conclusion

If I were to develop an undergraduate academic course on the Arab-Israeli conflict in the future, the goal would be to ascertain both continuity and change regarding the peace process. The objective would be to have the course conceptually grounded, to juxtapose opposing views, and to address selective issues with attention to how and why. A lucidly written suitable textbook is Abdel Monem Said Aly, Shai Feldman, and Khalil Shikaki, *Arabs and Israelis: Conflict and Peacemaking in the Middle East* (Palgrave Macmillan, 2013). The course would include two types of activities for students for a deeper understanding of the challenges: simulation to explore peace negotiation dynamics, and team debate for robust articulation of different perspectives.

Thinking Differently and Creating New Paradigms

Teaching Israel/Palestine without Repeating History

Teaching Israel/Palestine Studies

LIORA R. HALPERIN

The university promises to be a space where all students, from whatever standpoint, revisit comfortable or axiomatic assumptions. When we teach history, we are asking students to probe assumptions about the past, to understand the evolution of a present situation from multiple perspectives, and to gain the tools to understand (and participate in, if they wish) a conversation about the appropriate future directions for Israel and Palestine. How can we create an institutional foundation for this kind of thinking, this kind of conversation, this kind of learning?

I would suggest that the way we frame this project is important—indeed, thinking critically about why and how we use the terms we do is part of the conversation itself, part of recognizing and owning the fact that we are charting a course between multiple, often competing visions. Therefore, though multiple framings may be appropriate even within a single class, I want to use this essay to argue for the importance of framing what I am teaching as the history of "Israel/Palestine," not the history of Israel alone, Israel and the Arab world, or Israel and the Middle East.

For me, the study of Israel/Palestine is not about establishing two entities and presenting a history that is parallel. I want to emphasize that these histories are not parallel, whether in the features of their stories or in the power relations between them at different phases and their relations with other global actors. For me it is important not to suggest that students must understand them as equal and to encourage everyone to get beyond the "both sides" framing. What they are—and this is the inarguable—is interwoven, historically, symbolically, and logistically.

With the theme of interwovenness in mind, I want to argue that Israel/Palestine framing (Palestine/Israel would be equally fitting) is appropriate for five main reasons and to direct these remarks in particular to the Israel studies field, where courses are often offered with a primary or sole focus on Israel.

1. *History.* The study of the State of Israel, like the study of the Middle East as a whole, requires the study of pre-1948 Ottoman and Mandatory Palestine. I would

argue that calling this "pre-State Israel" is highly anachronistic. Palestine before 1948 has its own history and politics that needs to be studied in its own right, without projecting later events back onto the past. Moreover, during the period before 1948, both Jews and Arabs (and everyone else) referred to this land as Palestine. Israel is wrapped up with its own Palestinian past, the geographic, legal, and political conditions that preceded the state of Israel. Decisions, infrastructure, and laws from before 1948 still have meaningful presence and effects today.

2. *Overlapping symbolism.* The bit of land that most Israelis consider Israel from a national/cultural (if not political) standpoint and most Palestinians consider Palestine is the same piece of land, mostly defined according to the British Mandatory borders.[1] These imaginings are common even among those who accept limits on sovereignty in the present or the conceivable future or who would agree that, at present, "Israel" or "Palestine" does not constitute the whole land for political purposes. For all attempts to divide the land and despite the pre-1967 borders, few people have taken on the Green Line or the divisions between areas A, B, and C as part of collective memory. While on more official maps, actual political lines are often (though not always) visible, more symbolic maps, intended to play on emotions, almost never show lines. Such maps are politically misleading, but they point honestly to the fact that political realities do not reflect collective, emotive imaginings.

3. *Interconnection.* Some people contrast Israel "inside the Green Line" with Palestine (the West Bank and Gaza or, more accurately, the areas under partial Palestinian control in areas A and B). Sometimes these entities are depicted as clearly delineated and nonoverlapping. These delineated zones, based on the 1949 cease-fire lines (or pre-1967 borders), were the basis for Palestinian self-determination in the 1993 Oslo Accords. When Mahmoud Abbas has gone to the UN in recent years to receive forms of recognition for a Palestinian state, he is imagining that this state is the West Bank and Gaza. Many of those who are committed to an eventual two-state solution understand that the land will be formally divided, with an international border between the two.

However, in the current reality, neither the West Bank nor Gaza is a freestanding entity. This means that to move between parts of Palestine (in this sense), one needs to move through Israel, with the attendant Israeli military presence, and to move people or goods into or out of Gaza, one in most cases needs to interact with Israelis. These territories are also linked to Israel by a shared currency, shared water resources, and other infrastructure linkages. Tel Aviv beaches get polluted when Gaza's sewage-treatment plans are damaged and not fixed. This means that for the purposes of studying "Palestine," one necessarily has to study how it has been shaped and limited and constrained by Israel; it also means that for the purposes of studying "Israel," one has to be aware of the ways that Israel is intertwined with Palestine. Even were Palestine to become a separate state, Israel and Palestine will nonetheless always be linked.

4. *Shared global context.* Israeli and Palestinian histories have been historically subject to larger regional and global pressures. The breakup of empires, the evolution of nationalism, the shifting balance of powers in the region and globally, changes to world commodity markets, the emergence of new technologies of communication, transportation, and warfare: all have affected both Israelis and Palestinians, though they have had differential effects. The tiny territory of Israel/Palestine has never existed as an isolated unit; indeed, it has been buffeted and meaningfully shaped by patterns and trends much larger than itself, global trends with local implications. When we study the differential effects of such trends, we understand the separate paths of Israeli and Palestinian development, but we also can speak relationally, understanding how peoples and territories are linked for reasons that transcend local politics, policies, ideologies, and desires.

5. *Connection of Israel and Palestine for scholars and for researchers.* Though one may make pretensions to study Israel without Palestine or Palestine without Israel, on the basis of one's topic of interest, the practice of scholarship requires facing both Israel and Palestine. Scholars of Palestine often must make their way through contemporary Israel, its politics and bureaucratic structures, in order to access archival records. Scholars often must know both Arabic and Hebrew. A scholar of Israelis will confront the population of Palestinians in Israel, the legacies from the Ottomans and British, or the reshaping of the geography of the state that was enabled by and occurred in the wake of Israel's destruction of Palestinian villages in 1948. Scholars face the fact that Israeli politics have long been shaped by Palestinian politics. All scholars of this land are necessarily wrapped up in the politics and pressures that derive from the occupation, whatever their take on its future. Though the range of questions, the historical comparisons, and sources in question will be different, these fields are necessarily part of the same broader conversation. Israel studies cannot ignore Palestine studies, and Palestine studies cannot ignore Israel studies—indeed, such scholars are part of some of the same larger conversations and often benefit from creating partnerships and acknowledging their interlinking research agendas.

Bringing Israel/Palestine Studies to the Classroom

How can these principles be put into practice in the classroom? How do we encompass these various pieces of history without speaking about a simple binary of "the Israeli narrative" and "the Palestinian narrative"?

I bring three larger principles with me into my teaching in a large U.S. public university setting, mainly in classes of twenty to forty students who are taking my courses either to fulfill distribution requirements or as part of history, international studies,

Jewish studies, or other humanities or social sciences major. In some cases, the students have some Jewish studies or Middle Eastern studies background, but in many cases, they are encountering the study of Israel/Palestine for the first time in my courses.

1. There are not two sides: each of the normally recognized sides has numerous internal divisions and splits, along class or religious lines, as well as with regard to the ideological understanding of the national project, its purpose and its importance. When we encompass both Palestinian and Israeli perspectives, understanding the multiplicity of sides (or sides within sides) is key.
2. Positions need to be taken on their own terms, ideally through reading primary sources and trying to understand the motivations of the writers. It does not matter whether we personally agree with what we are reading—we need to read what we read in context, in light of questions about contingency, causality, influence, and change over time.
3. It is important that students feel that they can form their own conclusions and pursue whatever politics they want to pursue outside of class but that everyone from any position benefits from returning to the history and reading sources, understanding that no position comes out of nowhere.

Let me give the example of two assignments that I have done that aim to move in the direction of these goals. The first is an exercise that asks students to reconstruct a scholarly debate between contemporary academics, and the second involves the creation of a time line that reflects the historical consciousness of historical actors in the past. These assignments ask students to understand the multiple perspectives that have shaped both the history of the region and its modern interpretations; to explore the historical places, moments, and events that appear, with key variations, across narrative divides; and to understand Israel/Palestine through several different analytical frameworks, frameworks that often lead to highly divergent conclusions.

Debate Assignment

The essence of moving between discussions of "Israel" and "Palestine" is by cutting between views that suggest that only one of these categories is primary and the other is secondary. One could attempt to simply present a "balanced" perspective, which lays out two stories side by side, but such approaches imply a level of parallelism and equality that does not reflect reality.

In the past, I have chosen to work with three survey histories. The first is by a writer who focuses on Israel, situating it within the history of Zionism and broader

Jewish history, and follows primarily the Jewish story through its history. The second is by a writer who focuses on Palestine, situating this land and its population primarily within a history of trends and developments in the Middle East. The third is a globally focused history that places developments in Israel/Palestine within broader geopolitical processes. The specific titles can change as new books become available.

At the beginning of the semester, we consider the starting premises of each book: Where does each book begin geographically? When does it begin? Who are the most important actors? Is it a history that focuses on ideas? On economic conditions? On global politics? Already we see that answers to these questions determine what material is considered at length and what is relegated to the sidelines. As the semester goes on, we read about major historical moments, for example, early Zionist settlement, World War I, and the Balfour Declaration; the Arab Revolt of 1936–39; and the United Nations partition plan from each textbook. What is different? Where do the authors agree on facts but present them differently? Where do they use different words to describe the same thing? Are they disagreeing about what happened? About how to describe what happened? Or about what is most important? Students find that for the most part, these three internationally regarded scholars agree on the facts, but their choice of emphasis or their choice of descriptions give very different ideas of what happened and why and what conclusions we are asked to draw.

For one of the central assignments of the semester, students have to imagine that the three scholars have been invited to campus for a panel discussion about what is the right way to teach the history of Palestine/Israel: the students are asked to write the transcript of the conversation that they believe would ensue at this event. Students need to correctly capture the respective positions of the three scholars, root their statements in historical specifics (because of course the scholars themselves would do so), and make clear their differences from one another. They can stage arguments that they think would occur and have scholars make the most compelling argument they can. They are to serve as the moderator of this discussion, which means they get to pose tough questions of individuals, direct the conversation, and challenge those whose answers they think are insufficient. Students are incredibly creative with this assignment.

Time Line Assignment

If the dialogue assignment is about understanding scholars' approaches and understanding that differences in scholarly opinion are about differences in emphasis as well as differences in interpretation, the time line assignment helps students get into the mind-set of historical actors themselves. By the end of the semester, students should be aware that many events happened, many things occurred, but should also be aware that different people historically would have placed emphasis on different events or would have incorporated the same events in different ways into their telling of the past.

In this assignment, students have to choose a perspective, describe that perspective, and then make a time line of the most important events in history for that person's narrative of the past. A written assignment asks students to defend their choices of what they included and also to consider what events they left off the time line and why. This assignment helps students move beyond the more simplistic idea of an "Israeli perspective" or a "Palestinian perspective" and consider how events have different meanings or are more or less important for people depending on their different backgrounds, location, education, class level, or type and degree of political affiliation.

These two assignments share a focus on perspective. In a land where different perspectives seem to yield realities that have nothing to do with one another, in which individuals and groups seem to be living in alternate realities, these assignments take seriously some of these perspectives and help us discusses what approach to the past they yield. They also have the effect of helping students realize that actors, however much they may disagree or hate one another, are not living in separate realities: they are living in joint realities with shared events that, however, had and have very different meanings for different populations.

Conclusion

"Israel/Palestine studies" is an inherently unstable term. It has a slash in the middle, which can mean "and," "or," "in relationship with," or "in conflict with." It is all these things at the same time. The very instability of the framing, the fact that it sounds odd and makes us ask, "What's Israel/Palestine?" opens a series of conversations. These conversations are not prologue; they constitute the essence of seriously considering our object of study. What is the relationship between past realities and present ones? How do perception, symbolism, narrative, and dreams about a place intersect with (or contradict) political realities? How do groups that are deeply separate, in some cases deeply unequal, interact, share resources, or move within space? How does the process of answering these questions force us, as students and teachers, to cross boundaries ourselves, contend with boundaries that cannot be crossed, and gain the resources to make conclusions? How do we set up exercises that let us understand competing perspectives even if we hate and disagree with those perspectives? How do we recognize that while there are things that are simply untrue, there are many more things that are true for some people but not others, that are true if one makes certain starting assumptions or that fit within one analytical perspective and not another.

We live in an environment in which the stakes are not theoretical or academic; they are real, they affect real people. Some of our students are making choices daily about which group of people most needs their sympathy, money, or energies and making decisions about who should be condemned, pressured, criticized, and how. As students navigate their own approach to these questions, they benefit from their professors acknowledging the intersecting nature of these stories. The more our universities can be places in which we ask about these intersections, the more informed we can be as viewers of news, intelligent commentators, and people making change on the ground.

Notes

1. Israelis normally include the Golan Heights in their mental map of Israel, while Palestinians, using the British Mandate borders that did not include the Golan Heights, do not.

Teaching Israel/Palestine

A CONTRAPUNTAL READING OF SAVYON LIEBRECHT'S "A ROOM ON THE ROOF" AND GHAREEB ASQALANI'S "HUNGER"

PHILIP METRES

This essay comes out of my experience teaching Israeli and Palestinian literatures in counterpoint at John Carroll University since 2006. John Carroll University is a small Jesuit Catholic liberal arts university that draws most of its students from the Midwest, particularly in Northeast Ohio. Interestingly, the university is situated in University Heights, right between an entirely Jewish Orthodox community and a robustly Catholic community. Over the ten years of the course's existence, "Israeli and Palestinian Literatures" has fulfilled a variety of liberal arts / humanities core requirements, which has contributed to its robust enrollment. Despite the tiny population of Middle Eastern and Jewish students at John Carroll, the course has become a place where these students—and others interested in issues of justice seeking and peace making—can meet to learn more about this divided land and the people's narratives that coclaim it.

•••

> There were no guns at the PLO Research Center, no ammunition, and no fighters. But there was evidently something more dangerous—books about Palestine, old records and land deeds belonging to Palestinian families, photographs about Arab life in Palestine, historical archives about the Arab community in Palestine, and, most important, maps—maps of pre-1948 Palestine with every Arab village on it before the state of Israel came into being and erased many of them. . . . You could read it in the graffiti the Israelis boys left behind on the Research Center Walls: *Palestinian? What's that?* And *Palestinians, fuck you*, and *Arafat, I will hump your mother*.[1]

This essay, reprinted by permission of the copyright owner, the Modern Language Association of America, originally appeared in "Teaching (beyond) the Conflict: A Contrapuntal Reading," *Teaching Modern Arabic Literature in Translation*, 62–78.

At the heart of Palestinian narratives, to echo Edward Said, is the question of the "permission to narrate" itself.[2] In other words, in light of the power of the Zionist narrative of Israel—articulated so effectively (and resembling the American settler-colonial story) and backed so fiercely by U.S. imperial interests and institutions—Palestinian stories seem to disappear. This erasure was made literal again in 2014, when Diane Sawyer reported that Israelis had been attacked by Palestinian bombs, while showing footage of Palestinians in Gaza being bombed by Israel.[3] Yet even Thomas Friedman, long considered an imperial cheerleader by the political Left, notes that the very fact of Palestinian history presented such a threat to Israel's narrative that the first place the Israel Defense Forces headed, on invading Beirut in 1982, was to the PLO Research Center, in order to abscond with its archive.

This perverse situation animates my ongoing critical thinking and rethinking of how I teach Palestinian literature—and how this literature comes to be produced, circulated, and received. Since 2006, I have been teaching it in a contrapuntal fashion with Israeli literature, mostly in a course called "Israeli and Palestinian Literatures" but also in more recent courses: "Peacebuilding and Literature," "Studies in Postcolonial Literature." These experiences, and my reflection on the continued dispossession of Palestinians in Israel/Palestine, have led to my critical negotiation between the frames and aims of postcolonial theory, on the one hand, and peace-building theory, on the other. Although I began teaching "Israeli and Palestinian Literatures" with the purpose of highlighting the moral imagination evident in both literatures, I became increasingly uneasy that I was leaving students with the false impression that the conflict was as symmetrical as the authors' exercise in moral imagination. I found that I needed to foreground the tension between exploring the moral imagination and accounting for the vast asymmetry of power between Israel and the Palestinians. Not surprisingly, because of a keener attention to the asymmetry in sectors of the wider public, larger numbers of students are entering the class with knowledge of the Palestinian story.

This essay explores, first, the rationale for teaching Palestinian literature using a contrapuntal method and makes a case for a peace-building pedagogy that still accounts for the fact that Israel maintains almost complete hegemony over Palestinian life in Israel and the occupied territories. Second, I demonstrate the possibilities of contrapuntal analysis of Savyon Liebrecht's story "A Room on the Roof," told from the point of view of an Israeli woman who hires three Palestinians to build a room for her, alongside Ghareeb Asqalani's story "Hunger," which tells the story of Sa'id, a Palestinian worker, from his point of view.[4] Finally, I render explicit the promise and perils of teaching Palestinian literature in this way, highlighting the complication of "teaching while Arab" in the United States, which has itself changed since I began teaching (I began after 9/11). Through a critical reflection on my experience teaching this class and on the ways in which I have been situating myself in relation to the material, I hope to provide a resource to others who would like to teach Palestinian or Israeli literature from a framework that looks for and anticipates a transformation of the conflict and the establishment of a just peace.

Why Teach Palestinian and Israeli Literatures Contrapuntally?

Because I focus on Palestinian and Israeli literatures together in my class, I actively court cognitive dissonance—my own and the students'—enacting what Said, in *Culture and Imperialism*, calls "contrapuntal reading."[5] Contrapuntal reading requires a shift from the harmonizing ethos of the comparative literature model toward a cacophonous framing of literatures alongside each other—not necessarily in dialogue but in the context of both. In Said's words, "this global, contrapuntal analysis should be modeled not (as earlier notions of comparative literature were) on a symphony but rather on an atonal ensemble" (318), one that "emphasize[s] and highlight[s] the disjunctions, not to overlook and play them down" (146).

Said's contrapuntal reading represents a third way of reading postcolonial literature and the literature of empire, the first two being the politics of blame and the politics of colonial triumphalism. Said articulates a path that will enable us, reading the story of Palestine through Palestinian and Israeli literature, to see how "intertwined and overlapping histories" (19) already exist and to offer ways to begin imagining a just peace.

Said's contrapuntal reading rhymes well with John Paul Lederach's *The Moral Imagination*, whose subtitle is "The Art and Soul of Building Peace."[6] Lederach enumerates the moral imagination's four disciplines as "the capacity to imagine ourselves in a web of relationships that includes our enemies; the ability to sustain a paradoxical curiosity that embraces complexity without reliance on dualistic polarity; the fundamental belief in and pursuit of the creative act; and the acceptance of the inherent risk of stepping into the mystery of the unknown that lies beyond the far too familiar landscape of violence" (5).

Lederach's emphasis on the need for cultivating empathy, curiosity, creativity, and courage might appear to be ineffectual liberalism, given the obstacles that Palestinians face. But his work reminds us that peace requires as much preparation as war. In fact, peace building is probably more difficult, given the human propensity for exacting revenge and acting out of fear. Said's contrapuntal reading and Lederach's theory of the moral imagination meet at the intersection where we "imagine ourselves in a web of relationships that includes our enemies." Including one's enemies, of course, does not require one to accept their conditions. In contrast to the mainstream liberal discourse of peace making, Lederach argues that we should resist the assumption that peace-building is merely a balancing of perspectives, that there can be no normalization or reconciliation without justice: "We must understand and feel the landscape of protracted violence and why it poses such deep-rooted challenges to constructive change. In other words we must set our feet deeply into the geographies and realities of what destructive relationships produce, what legacies they leave, and what breaking their violent patterns will require, . . . [and] we must explore the creative process itself, not as a tangential inquiry, but as the wellspring that feeds the building of peace" (5).

If we do not analyze fully and remorselessly the nature of destructive relationships, if we do not understand and address what has fueled the conflict and oppression, we risk moving too quickly to a false or unjust peace. To read contrapuntally is to hear with both ears, to see with both eyes, outside the frames offered by mainstream media or ideological propaganda. It does not mean, in the case of Israel/Palestine, to seek balance or coexistence at all costs; on the contrary, as Marcy Knopf-Newman has explored in *The Politics of Teaching Palestine to Americans*, coexistence projects have tended to obfuscate the causes of Palestinian resistance, to undermine historical analysis, and to normalize oppression.[7] Peace-building must define peace through prisms of both justice and security. Situating itself critically and empathically at the point of intersection of national frames, it must resist the binarism that wars and sectarianism require.

Background Research

"Israeli and Palestinian Literatures," an introductory-level course, emerged from my study and teaching of war literature, postcolonial theory, and peace studies. Through a contrapuntal reading of literary and historical narratives of Israel/Palestine, with a special emphasis on works that activate or embody the moral imagination, I try to model for students how literature might contribute to a real peace process, one that addresses the crucial final-status issues, especially the plight of Palestinian refugees. I want to show that understanding the politics of representation can provide a way to see that conflicts are not eternal and inevitable but historically specific and therefore resolvable.

In my initial research, I was stunned by the cultural intervention of both Palestinian and Israeli literatures. Considered together, they offer critical insights into how the relationship between the Israeli state and the Palestinians has affected and is affecting both sides. Because my focus in this essay is on Palestinian literature, it is important for me to point to Israeli writers who have undergone unsparing self-criticism, bearing witness to the pain of Palestinian dispossession (beginning with the 1948 Nakba (catastrophe) and through the continuing occupation, particularly after the 1967 Naksa (setback), becoming voices of conscience that hark back to the Hebrew prophetic tradition. S. Yizhar (the pen name of Yizhar Smilansky) in particular merits attention for his *Khirbet Khizeh*, an unvarnished portrayal of the destruction of a Palestinian village by Israeli forces in 1948.[8] Other writers, such as Amos Oz and David Grossman, have explored the moral damage of the military occupation of the West Bank and Gaza Strip. At their best, they not only have represented the contradictions of Israeli society and the moral ugliness of occupation and dispossession but also, at moments, have challenged their own liberal Zionist (yet often Orientalist) frames of reference.

I disagree with Elias Khoury's incisive but too quickly dismissive reading of Israeli literature's representations of Palestinians: "How is the Palestinian represented? Either he doesn't speak because he is deaf and dumb and exists only in Hannah's dreams in [Amos Oz's] 'My Michael'; or the Palestinians are part of the geography, as in Yizhar, or even for Oz in his short story 'Nomad and Viper.' In Yehoshua, the Palestinian is mute or a child, like Na'im in 'The Lover.' Even with David Grossman—the most open of the writers—in, say, 'The Smile of the Lamb,' the Palestinian is an insane character."[9] Khoury is largely correct but collapses the question of engaging otherness with the question of representing the other. Both "The Prisoner," by Yizhar, and "Nomad and Viper," by Oz, can be read easily as deconstructions of Israeli Orientalist attitudes toward Palestinians. Khoury's reading of Khilmi in *The Smile of the Lamb* is reductionist; Khilmi may be half mad, but he is also a wise and loving proponent of nonviolent resistance (cf. "Vexing Resistance"). Khoury also misses key authors who have engaged Palestinian reality in ways that are far more nuanced, and show far more solidarity, than Grossman's portrayal, such as Savyon Liebrecht (in "The Road to Cedar City") and Aharon Shabtai (in *J'Accuse*). A contrapuntal reading of such works can be mobilized as part of an effort that goes beyond representing what has been called the beautiful soul of Zionism to explore the damage done by the racist othering of Palestinians.

Palestinian literature has struggled in its diverse locations against the dispossession, Israeli occupation, and the cultural, economic, and military siege that people have lived through since 1948. Palestinian writers such as Ghassan Kanafani, Emile Habibi, Mahmoud Darwish, Taha Muhammad Ali, and Sahar Khalifeh, when read alongside Israeli writers challenging the official Zionist myth-narrative of Israeli history, illuminate the human cost of the conflict to Palestinians (and the moral cost to Israelis) despite the ongoing erasure of Palestinian history. These writers help us see the predicaments of Palestinian lives that are increasingly hemmed in by what Jeff Halper has called the "matrix of control"—his term for the legal, economic, and military frameworks that suffocate Palestinian existence in Israel, the West Bank, and Gaza.[10]

Palestinian writers dramatize how radicalism emerges from conditions of extreme privation and psychological humiliation. Kanafani's *Men in the Sun* and Khalifeh's *Wild Thorns*, for example, confront how Palestinians' politics has contributed to and complicated their suffering, how the struggle to satisfy personal desires or family needs can be in conflict with national aspirations.[11] Finally, throughout the corpus of Palestinian writing—as Khoury has noted—we are witness to moments of the moral imagination in which the humanity of Palestinians and Israelis alike is represented.

Contrapuntalism in Practice

In the course, we alternate between Israeli and Palestinian texts and perspectives in specific periods: from the beginnings to 1948, 1948–67, 1967–93, 1993–2000, 2000 to the present. For the first period, we establish the complexity of the origins of the Israel-Palestine conflict, the problem of navigating radically different framings of that history. The first week, students read four brief accounts of Israeli history—a BBC article, an orthodox Zionist take, and that of Ilan Pappé, an anti-Zionist Israeli historian. They then read early Israeli patriotic war poems and Yizhar's story "The Soldier" and consider the debates in Israel regarding the narrative about what happened in 1948 and how Yizhar describes the Israeli soldier's treatment of Arabs. The following week, they read four Palestinian historical accounts of 1948, including the website complement to Walid Khalidi's *All That Remains*, a documentary history of the 1948 Nakba and the hundreds of destroyed villages of Palestine. This exploration, laying bare the contestedness of history itself, is followed by poems and a story, such as Kanafani's *Men in the Sun* or *Returning to Haifa*, which show how 1948 affected the lives of Palestinians.

Students often try to guess my political point of view and are surprised when they fail to figure me out: there is no easy way for them to find definitive answers (e.g., about who is right and who is wrong) or to predict what will happen next in a story. Reading contrapuntally and cultivating the moral imagination involve an ethos of openness and a willingness to refuse the fatalism of received narratives. Though the course admittedly employs an aspirational frame—the final unit is called "Prospects for Peace"—it suggests that history is fundamentally contingent, always in the making; further, it proposes that our positionality is never neutral and that our empowerment involves the loss of the invisibility of U.S. privilege.

The contrapuntal strategy is valuable because students learn more when they are challenged with contrary viewpoints. They are given greater agency to explore the complex longings and sufferings of Palestinians and Israelis as fellow human beings. Contrapuntal reading also provides inoculation against the virus of racism (whether it be anti-Arab or anti-Jewish), not only because literature activates the moral imagination but also because, at its best, it creates characters irreducible to ideology and stereotype. At the end of my course, students will know the hunger and desperation of Sa'id, from "Hunger," and the ethical uncertainty of the unnamed Israeli female narrator of "A Room on the Roof," who must confront her fantasies and fears about the Palestinian laborers whom she has hired. Students will know these characters better than they may ever know an actual Palestinian or Israeli.

A Case Study: The Post-1967 Occupation in "A Room on the Roof" and "Hunger"

In an article in the *New York Times* written nearly fifty years after the 1967 Arab-Israeli War, Jodi Rudoren explores the "double-edged sword" of Israeli jobs for Palestinian workers. If Palestinian laborers once helped build the State of Israel, now their labor supports the illegal settlement of the West Bank. Hassan Jalaita, a mechanic, repairs jeeps for the Israeli army in the Mishor Adinim Industrial Zone inside the West Bank. According to Jalaita, "I feel like I'm not a human being—we are serving the occupation."[12] This dilemma—between earning a living to support one's family and refusing to help an occupying power—has been an ongoing vexation for Palestinian workers. During the 1970s and 1980s, after the 1967 war and before the First Intifada, according to Philippa Strum, who uses 1989 figures, about "120,000 laborers were bussed daily to work in Israel, 55% of whom work in construction, the rest in agriculture and industry. Unskilled day labor from the West Bank and Gaza represents 6.5% of the total Israeli work force."[13]

Given the asymmetrical power relationship in which Israelis and Palestinians find themselves, it is not surprising that encounters between them tend to confirm stereotypes and biases about the superiority of one's own culture and the inferiority of the other. Liebrecht's "A Room on the Roof" and Asqalani's "Hunger" both undermine these stereotypes and biases, staging two different encounters, intensely subjective and politically inflected, between Palestinian construction workers and Israeli overseers, in ways that explore how people are challenged by the complex humanity of the other. In both stories, there are crucial moments in which the moral imagination burgeons, but no false reconciliations take place and no panaceas are offered.

In "A Room on the Roof," set in Israel after 1967 during the period of a housing boom, an Israeli woman hires Palestinian workers to build a room on her roof while her husband, Yoel, is away. The central drama of the story, told from her point of view, concerns her struggle to maintain her authority over the workers, whom she feels she cannot trust, and her desire at the same time to be generous to them. Her sudden interest in one of the Palestinians, Hassan, teeters on the verge of (and nearly falls into) romantic love.

"A Room on the Roof" clearly alludes to Virginia Woolf's *A Room of One's Own*, and the story revolves around othernesses—the otherness of female subjectivity in a patriarchal society, the otherness of working-class Palestinians in bourgeois Israeli society. It is almost too easy to read the main character as an allegory for the Israeli state. After all, her independence requires the constant assertion of authority, yet she is an insecure, vulnerable person who has difficulty showing kindness and generosity. She swings between wanting to offer the workers coffee and the use of her kitchen or bathroom and refusing them the money they need to complete the job.

At one point, she has let them use the bathroom but begins to fear that they are readying a terrorist operation, because the knapsack is "the kind that Yoel used to extricate from the storeroom when his unit was called up for maneuvers" (52). It turns out that they are going to a wedding in nearby Tulkarem. For most American students, the narrator becomes a kind of medium by which they measure their own fear of and fascination with the other. They see, in Liebrecht's selectively omniscient exploration of the Israeli woman's thoughts, their own socially constructed thoughts about Palestinians.

The woman slowly shifts from seeing the three Palestinians as "a single person" (44) to being stunned by Hassan's gentleness with her baby son, Udi:

> She heard Hassan talking softly to the baby in Arabic, like a man who loves to talk to his child, in a caressing voice, the words running together in a pleasant flow, containing a high beauty, like the words of a poem in an ancient language which you don't understand, but which well up inside you. Udi, lying tranquilly on his chest, reached out toward Hassan's dark face, and Hassan put his head down toward the little fingers and kissed them. She, stunned by the sight, stood where she was and looked at them, as the tremor inspired by fear gradually died down, and another, new kind of trembling, arose within her, seeing something that, even as it happens, you already yearn for from a distance, knowing that when it passes nothing like it will happen again. And, as though dividing themselves, her thoughts turned to Yoel, whose eyes examined his son with a certain remoteness. Since the baby's birth he had never clasped him to his body and was careful not to wet his clothes or have them smell of wet diapers. (53–54)

The woman, utterly taken aback by Hassan's interaction with her baby, sees how the baby does not care about his background, just his gentleness. Then she is surprised to learn that Hassan can speak English better than she can, that he studied it at the American University of Beirut, and that because of difficulties in life, he had to discontinue his studies (54–55). The "new kind of trembling" she feels is akin to the vulnerability of attraction. We sense that real change is possible in her, yet we are also aware of the distance that divides Hassan and her. Liebrecht, echoing the moral imagination of each of these characters, encourages the circle of humanity to widen, initiating possibilities of reconciliation.

Yet things go wrong. The Palestinian workers do violate some of the woman's boundaries, and we never quite know if they have done it purposefully or, acting on their cultural codes, unconsciously. Are they cheating her, for example, or do they simply fail to understand her directions? Or do they feel that she does not understand what the room addition requires? As she grows afraid of her own vulnerability and lack of authority, her distrust and hostility reemerge. Hassan, insulted by her treatment of him, leaves and does not return, and the story ends, with the work finally done and the husband back but with her transformation incomplete. When Yoel comes home, she lies about having a "Jewish foreman" and hides the complexity of her feelings. She tells her husband about Hassan but does not name the man who "spoke to [Udi] softly and kissed his fingers" (63).

Her feelings shock her: "Suddenly she noticed the softness flowing into her voice, *betraying herself to herself*, and she added loudly, more stridently than she intended, 'But once they made some trouble about the money and tried to trick me by putting iron rods that were too thin. Arabs, you know'" (63; my emphasis). Although she knows better, she reverts to the stereotypes about Arabs prevalent in her culture, to reestablish solidarity with her husband and hide her emotional self-betrayal. This poignant ending shows the subtle ways in which people betray themselves and one another when they perpetuate the ethnocentric mechanisms of othering, the machinery of colonial oppression. But such introspection should not be fetishized: it can be merely a typical operation of the colonial imaginary and a demonstration of the colonizer's inherent moral and intellectual superiority to the colonized. For that reason, it is necessary to read Liebrecht's story alongside a Palestinian story that deals with the same scenario. A contrapuntal reading allows us to dilate that moment of epistemological opening.

Whereas "A Room on the Roof" depicts the complex ambivalence of an Israeli woman's relationship with Palestinians, Asqalani's "Hunger" dramatizes the complexity of the experience of workers who struggle with their complicity in a state-building project that ensures the erasure of their people. By seeing the inner and outer lives of Sa'id, a desperately hungry Gazan construction worker who labors in Israel, we understand better the behavior of the workers in Liebrecht's story. We learn about their physical exhaustion and angry helplessness—their struggle just to get to work every day. Most of all, we become aware of the social and spiritual shame felt by Palestinians who must work in Israel to feed their families. We see in a new light the hidden lives of Hassan, Salah, and Ahmad, who remain ciphers untranslatable to the Israeli woman.

"Hunger" capitalizes on fiction's ability to explore a character's inner thoughts, which the translation emphasizes by italicizing Sa'id's italicized inner monologue; it reveals that Sa'id has been in prison and has a revolutionary past but feels he must prostitute his revolutionary values in order to feed his children. The italicized monologue dramatizes the gap between the stoic exterior of its main character and the pain that seethes within him. Palestinians in Gaza, the story tells us, are imprisoned, behind bars, not only physically but psychically as well.

In contrast to the Israeli woman's slow recognition of a diversity of character among Palestinians in Liebrecht's story, Asqalani thrusts us into the conflicts in Palestinian society—for example, between those who suffer hunger, like Sa'id, and those with jobs or power in Gaza who ask "with distaste and condescension, 'Why don't you work in *Israel*?'" (381). Asqalani introduces us to complexity in Israeli society also: Sa'id is hired by an Israeli foreman and contractor named Shlomo, an Ashkenazi Jew, and later works with Azra, a Yemeni Jew who "speaks Arabic better than [he]" (385). The cross-national identification between Sa'id and Azra suggests how Israeli society has suppressed its Arab roots both in the Palestinian community and in the Mizrahi communities, which emigrated from the Arab world after the founding of Israel and often were treated as second-class citizens. Sa'id sees himself in Azra, whose pitiable, skeletal form feels like his own fate.

The skeleton motif, which weaves through the story, signifies both bodies and buildings, individuals and states. For Sa'id, avoiding the starvation of his children comes at an enormous cost: the building up of the State of Israel. When he recognizes Abu Mahmoud, a Palestinian foreman for whom he once worked, he feels the gulf between his ideals as a revolutionary and his reality as a father:

> *Abu Mahmoud, am I going to be sharing with you in the dressing up of this skeleton?* He remembered vividly the look of terror in the man's eyes the day he had torn up his work permit and thoughtlessly thrown it in his face. He had never attempted, that day, to hear his own stuttering, frightened words, nor had he sympathized with the terror he felt in his own heart. He had never realized, on that day, that the pain in children's eyes was stronger than a work permit and a measuring tape—stronger even than cement columns. (384; emphasis in the translation)

Sa'id understands that in order not to have a skeletal body and family, he must put flesh on the skeletons of buildings, on the bigger skeleton of Israel. These Palestinian construction workers are making houses on their former homeland, houses that they will never own and that will lessen the possibility of their return. He makes and is unmade by his labor; in his making, "he himself [will] become a skeleton withered by the wind" (383).

Interestingly, it is Azra who is the first to collapse from the work. Sa'id sees him as "this human skeleton" (385) who labors as the building rises, in stark contrast to the "fields of Majdal spread out like a green carpet that is forbidden to [the laborers]" (385). At the climax of the story, when the Yemeni Jew collapses, his body is "slumped over the cement mix, face downward" (387). It is as if the building itself came to drown him. Sa'id reflects later that between him and Azra, "there's no difference, no difference at all" (387). In this epiphanic moment, what binds the two men is not their language but their sharing in tormenting, oppressive labor, in which the workers literally are consumed in the process of building.

The story ends with Shlomo's firing of everyone—after his derisive comments about the crew and Sa'id's attempt to attack Shlomo physically in response to the insults. Yet, as in "A Room on the Roof," there is a glimmer of the moral imagination, and the possibility of a cross-national movement against economic and political oppression remains in the mind. Despite the smoke and dust that cover the workers from Shlomo's departing car—images of our greater human transience—Asqalani lays bare the pain of Palestinians living in statelessness, not without their humanity but with a keen despair.

Reading these two stories in a contrapuntal fashion compels students to engage critically with and feel empathy for the predicament of Palestinians and Israelis, through the irreducibly particular portraits of Asqalani's Sa'id and Liebrecht's unnamed narrator. It also reveals how the United States and Israel are connected by privilege (and by blind spots). My predominantly white students often identify with the Israeli woman's fascination with and fear of her Palestinian workers. Encountering an analogous story from the Palestinian point of view makes them question the epistemological limits that inhere in political privilege.

The Perils of Teaching Palestine as an Arab American

At the Radius of Arab American Writers conference in 2010, Michael Malek Najjar articulated the parallelism between the outing of queers and the outing of Arab Americans after the terrorist attacks of 9/11.[14] Despite my own visible invisibility as a person who identifies as Arab but often is not recognized as such, I too felt exposed and vulnerable in those days in 2001. At the same time, 9/11 provoked me into action, into coming out publicly not just as a progressive but also as an Arab American who stands in solidarity with Arabs at a time when we have been the objects of suspicion and even hatred. My coming out was an experience both terrifying and empowering.

The level of fear that accompanied my entering the public sphere in the 1990s to protest the brutal economic sanctions against Iraq and to decry house demolitions and land confiscations in Palestine was considerable. I received a string of anonymous hate mail after being quoted in the local newspaper. Because of my personality, I dread the moment when an argument goes from a simmer to a boil or when a friend's face twists when I say something that disturbs his or her picture of the world or vision of me. I am well aware of the deep division between my Jewish and Palestinian friends and of how the victims of history often do not feel saintly toward one another or toward themselves.

I bring together my personal, political, and pedagogical responsibilities through this course. I developed it despite my desire to run away and be invisible in my privilege of distance and unrecognizability—partly because, as Miguel de Unamuno once wrote, "sometimes, to remain silent is to lie."[15] I bring out this example of myself both because it may help others in an analogous position and because the challenges we face when writing about erased histories in the academy are shared beyond our specific positions.

A peace-building pedagogy fosters future peace builders and encourages academic honesty and openness. In developing my approach, I have benefited from the work of other scholar-teachers who work in this field, Marcy Jane Knopf-Newman in particular. Knopf-Newman's strategies, articulated in *The Politics of Teaching Palestine to Americans*, differ from mine but have helped me sharpen my analyses. Her chapter "Separate and Unequal: On Coexistence" offers a valuable deconstruction of coexistence narratives that efface the radical asymmetries of power at the heart of the problem (65–102).

In 2007, I was emailed by a member of the local Jewish community to ask about my course, which was new then. This community is robust and diverse; Judith Butler, now a major Jewish voice for the Boycott, Divestment and Sanctions Movement (against Israel), grew up and studied in it. The "concerned citizen" who contacted me must have accessed my online archive of resources and student projects. She wanted further information about the course but questioned its study of both Israeli and Palestinian literatures. She then rejected my invitation to visit my class, arguing that there was no such thing as Palestinian literature or, for that matter, a Palestinian people. She sent a letter of complaint to my department chair and administrators at my university, accusing me of preaching antisemitism, teaching propaganda, and brainwashing my students. She demanded that the course be canceled.

I was heartened that the chair of my department immediately supported my course and me. After a careful vetting of the course and the correspondence, my dean did as well. Colleagues who teach similar courses have not always been so fortunate. Steven Salaita lost his tenured position at the University of Illinois in 2014, allegedly because of the "lack of civility" in his tweets during Israel's 2014 attack on Gaza.[16] His case was settled at the end of 2015 for almost $1 million, but he was not reinstated in the position he was scheduled to take up at that university.[17] The concerned citizen was wrong about the heart of the matter: my course offers students an opportunity to confront racism in themselves and their society, inviting them into imaginative empathy with the people on both sides of the wall, people who struggle under the burdens of fear and despair, terror and oppression. Though students of course always want answers, my course offers more questions than answers, but it provides them with resources to begin working out their own responses.

The concerned citizen caused a dark night of the soul for me, in which I questioned all the choices of my course as well as my ability to deal with such flammable material. I was painfully aware that although I know quite a bit about the Palestinian-Israeli conflict and the peoples in it, I will always be learning, not only about the subject of its literature but also about how ideology and trauma affect people. My introspection led me to consider from a new angle how the course, however subtly, invariably reflects my own perspectives on and framing of the conflict, on how the course concentrates on certain questions and not others—for example, the funding of terrorist groups by regional players or Hamas's failure to disavow the antisemitism of its founding charter.

I continue to revise the course to reflect my evolving understanding of the conflict. I believe that a historical wrong was perpetrated against Palestinians and continues in the form of occupation and dispossession. I also believe that Israelis have an important story to tell and that anyone interested in Palestinian rights must also be interested in the human rights of Israelis and fight anti-Jewish and anti-Arab hatred wherever it is found. I believe that a just peace is possible.

The personal and professional risks of teaching courses in North American university classrooms dealing with the Palestinian experience are worth taking. As teachers, we must plant the seeds for critically engaged and empathetic global citizens who are not afraid to ask difficult questions about the future of Israel/Palestine and the U.S. relation to the conflict between Palestinians and Israelis. Simply reading the literary and historical narratives of Palestine and Israel and discussing them in class will not solve the conflict, but it will offer students an intimate window onto the geographies of violence and, more important, into the moral imagination. May fugitive moments of that imagination slip through the crevices of the walls promoted by ideologues and fundamentalists—all those who benefit from perpetuating this untenable yet seemingly intractable war.

Notes

The author would like to thank Adam Rovner for providing me with the original Hebrew quotations. Rovner also offered an additional interpretation of the translation of the Hebrew that is of interest here. The verb *masgir* is translated by Green as "betraying," which is accurate but carries different connotations in English. The verb in Hebrew indicates "handing someone over" but typically to a legal authority; the same verb is used for an extradition. It can also mean to "give oneself away" in the sense of

exposing inner thoughts or feelings: this meaning is perhaps better than "betray" in the passage here.
1. Thomas L. Freidman, *From Beirut to Jerusalem* (New York: Macmillan, 1995), 159.
2. Edward Said, "Permission to Narrate," *Journal of Palestine Studies* 13, no. 3 (1984): 27–48.
3. "Outrage Turns to Satire after ABC News Misidentifies Palestinian Victims," *Al Jazeera*, 10 July 2014, http://stream.aljazeera.com/story/201407101217-0023919; Rania Khalek, "ABC News Tells Viewers That Scenes of Destruction in Gaza Are in Israel," *Electronic Intifada*, 9 July 1014, http://electronicintifada.net/blogs/rania-khalek/abc-news-tells-viewers-scenes-destruction-gaza-are-israel.
4. Ghareeb Asqalani, "Hunger," in *Anthology of Modern Palestinian Literature*, ed. Salma Khadra Jayyusi (New York: Columbia University Press, 1992), 380–88; Savyon Liebrecht, "A Room on the Roof," in *Apples from the Desert: Selected Stories*, trans. Marganit Weinberger-Rotman et al. (New York: Feminist Press at CUNY, 1998), 39–64. Subsequent quotations from these sources are cited parenthetically in the text.
5. Edward Said, *Culture and Imperialism* (New York: Vintage Books, 1993), 66. Subsequent quotations from this source are cited parenthetically in the text.
6. John Paul Lederach, *The Moral Imagination: The Art and Soul of Building Peace* (New York: Oxford University Press, 2005). Subsequent quotations from this source are cited parenthetically in the text.
7. Marcy Jane Knopf-Newman, *The Politics of Teaching Palestine to Americans* (New York: Palgrave Macmillan, 2011), 66. Subsequent quotations from this source are cited parenthetically in the text.
8. S. Yizhar, *Khirbet Khizeh*, trans. Nicholas de Lange and Yaacob Dweck (New York: Farrar, Straus and Giroux, 2015).
9. Elias Khoury, "A Boycott on Institutions Is a Good Thing for Israelis," interview by Maya Sela, *Haaretz*, 5 June 2014, www.haaretz.com/jewish/books/.premium-1.597182.
10. Jeff Halper, *An Israeli in Palestine: Resisting Dispossession, Redeeming Israel* (London: Pluto, 2010), chap. 6.
11. Philip Metres, "Vexing Resistance, Complicating Occupation: A Contrapuntal Reading of Sahar Khalifeh's *Wild Thorns* and David Grossman's *The Smile of the Lamb*," *College Literature* 37, no. 1 (2010): 81–109.
12. Jodi Rudoren, "In West Bank Settlements, Israeli Jobs Are Double-Edged Sword," *New York Times*, 10 February 2014, www.nytimes.com/2014/02/11/world/middleeast/palestinians-work-in-west-bank-for-israeli-industry-they-oppose.html?_r=0.
13. Philippa Strum, "West Bank Women and the Intifada: Revolution within the Revolution," in *Palestinian Women of Gaza and the West Bank*, ed. Suha Sabbagh (Bloomington: Indiana University Press, 1998), 71.
14. Michael Malek Najjar, "Going It Alone: Arab American Drama and the Politics of Solo Performance," paper presented at the Radius of Arab American Writers Conference, Ann Arbor, MI, June 4, 2010.

15. Quoted in "Miguel de Unamuno," Wikipedia, accessed 11 May 2016, http://en.wikipedia.org/wiki/Miguel_de_Unamuno.
16. David Moshman and Frank Edler, "Civility and Academic Freedom after Salaita," *JAF: AAUP Journal of Academic Freedom* 6 (2015), www.aaup.org/sites/default/files/MoshmanEdler.pdf.
17. Jodi Cohen, "University of Illinois OKs $875,000 Settlement to End Steven Salaita Dispute," *Chicago Tribune*, 12 November 2015, www.chicagotribune.com/news/local/breaking/ct-steven-salaita-settlement-met-20151112-story.html.

Israeli Narratives
CHARTING NEW TERRITORIES

SHIRI GOREN

I always bring maps to the first session of my "Israeli Narrative" seminar. Although there are plenty of digital maps available online, I prefer physical, paper ones—four or five of them, all contemporary. Maps are useful, first of all, because even in my Ivy League institution, it does not hurt to remind students of the exact location of the Middle East and which countries and territories are part of it. At a time when an American president announces, shortly after arriving in Israel from Saudi Arabia, that he "just got back from the Middle East," basic geography seems an issue worth stressing.[1] Second, even beyond contemporary geopolitics, maps give me a productive starting point for the seminar.

The map I find most useful was distributed several years ago by the Consulate General of Israel in New York. Israel is marked in yellow; the West Bank and Gaza are also captured in yellow, a shade lighter yellow. Technically, the map is accurate, but it does not take a cartographer to see the problem. Although I am often tempted to hold the map up in the air and ask, "What's wrong with this picture?" my aim is to model not only critical thinking but also tolerance. Thus, I simply ask students to look carefully at all the maps and try to identify any unique features or elements that seem interesting to them. Students take their time. While there is often one first-year and a couple of seniors, the majority of the group usually consists of sophomores and juniors. One thing their experience at Yale has taught them is that no matter how casually a question is worded, just like Chekov's gun, a map in the first class must "fire" in the final paper. They usually have no idea how accurate their instincts are.

The yellow-territory map—a tangible evidence for a misleading authority—illustrates what the seminar is all about. This classroom activity of comparing different maps exemplifies how one or few details can lead to a creation of multiple, often highly competing interpretations. This activity becomes a point of departure for thinking about the potential relativity of truth—a complex issue to come to terms with for an adolescent, however bright. This is the exact moment when we begin to talk about narratives and stories, those of the past and those of the present, and how they often compete to shape the future.

Pedagogical Approaches and Goals

"Israeli Narratives" is a course that aims to help students become more fluent in conversing about Israel (and Palestine) and developing a critical framework for their own thinking about the region. With regard to methodology, the seminar uses literary and other cultural texts as a lens through which to examine what we later term "the Israeli condition." This term encompasses the Hebrew word *Hamatzav* and what scholars sometimes label "The Israeli State of Emergency," but it also relates to other themes that the political crisis often overshadows, especially when viewed from the outside.

The readings and films focus on contemporary representations of social and domestic Israeli space, in an attempt to construct an informed perspective. The discussion includes topics and theories of personal and collective identity formation, war and peace, ethnicity and race, migration, nationalism, and gender and queer culture.

Another goal I set for the seminar is for students to learn how to approach and how to think about literary and visual materials and to equip them with tools to conduct such a textual and visual analysis. Throughout the semester, students are introduced to critical concepts in literary, culture, and visual theory. Subsequently, the class discussion—which I will say more about soon—models the type of textual examination and close reading that students will then be expected to demonstrate in their independent work.

The emphasis on fictional texts derives from my own training as a literary and cultural scholar but also from the sense that when it comes to contested topics such as Israel, and particularly the Israeli-Palestinian conflict, fictional narratives seem to pose less of a "threat" to students. While personal politics, preconceptions, and religious beliefs tend to stand in the way of critically examining, say, an op-ed or even an academic article, fiction does not carry similar baggage. The very idea that a creative text is fictional—regardless of the authenticity of the reality it presumably represents—helps students to connect with it, both intellectually and emotionally. Similarly, visual narratives—short and full feature films, as well as selected episodes of television series—provide a clear path into a foreign culture by introducing a human condition that is often not too difficult to empathize with. Many students, as we know all too well, react extremely positively to visual stimulations, and the course syllabus is constructed with this notion in mind.

Another element that helps bridge political and conceptual gaps is humor. Throughout the semester, I encourage students to share with me and with their peers humorous clips about Israel and how its leaders' actions are perceived through American eyes. I have my own clip from *The Daily Show*, which I usually screen during the first or second sessions. This piece was broadcast in 2007 and featured John Oliver, then a correspondent on the show. Titled "Oliver's Travels: Israel," the segment lists many of the stereotypes and assumptions that Americans make about Israelis. The content is still so relevant that the main method through which students become aware of the decade that has passed since the production of the clip is through the receding hairlines of John Oliver and Jon Stewart. (Sacha Baron Cohen recent controversial character of retired Israeli Colonel Erran Morad, from the Showtime series "Who is America" will likely serve a similar purpose in the coming semester).

Course Activities and Assignments

Beyond the comic meditation on the news, students take turns in preparing brief weekly news reports that one student shares in the beginning of each class. The assignment calls for finding information on one or two hard news items that occurred during that week, as well as one interesting or "light" news item. The presentation is intended to be short—three to four minutes—but requires careful thinking and preparation. Students share their reports using information gleaned from at least three different news websites. They then comment on the differences in the coverage of each event. Such differences could be vast or minor: tone of reporting, headlines, length, selection of visuals, and language used to describe the people related to the news event ("terrorists," "prisoners," or "political detainees"; "victims," "citizens," or "settlers"; "West Bank" or "Occupied Territories"; etc.). By comparing stories created by various news sites and paying attention to details and nuances of language, students refine their interpretative skills and advance their ability for textual close reading. This assignment also trains them to be critical media consumers, regardless of the issues at stake. I introduced this activity long before "fake news" had become a critical media issue with far-reaching implications for U.S. domestic and international politics. Still, the pedagogical motivations for adding this graded task as a regular component in the course align well with contemporary concerns. This assignment also provides a useful way for the articulation of our own professional ethics as educators. News reports keep the class members informed about political developments in Israel and the region. They allow students to add a personal touch when they pick a lighter news item (from technological innovation to interesting surveys, beauty pageants, and the Eurovision song competition), again providing them with paths into a foreign culture. Above all, the news reports assist students in finding their own ways and independence in framing, and reframing, their thinking about the subject.

Another way through which to expand students' exposure to the different narratives that continue to fuel the Israeli-Palestinian conflict emerges from activities and events outside the classroom. As many other universities, Yale is a hub of cultural, social, and political activity, local, domestic, and international. There are always more lectures, performances, discussion groups, concerts, roundtables, art exhibits, literary readings, and film screenings than one could possibly attend. This dynamic intellectual atmosphere is a major draw for students and faculty alike. In my teaching, I constantly search for creative ways to incorporate aspects of this richness into the curriculum. Throughout the semester, students in "Israeli Narratives" are required to attend two campus events—any events—that relate to Israel/Palestine or the Middle East. Students report back both verbally in class and in writing. They create an "event report" by answering a set of guided questions leading them to contextualize the events and then reflect on them. Even before approaching the content, students need to provide information about the speaker/artist/author/performer, the organizer (a department or program? student organization? library? museum?), and the targeted audience (students? faculty? community members?). In addition to a brief summary of the content and general observations, other prompts such as "questions that remain unanswered" encourage reflective thinking. The questions that students need to address before sharing their observations with the class provide scaffolding for critical reflection on the event. For the course instructor, the format of this assignment has two added benefits. First, she is able to better protect her time by not having to attend all the relevant events by herself. Second, she does not have to judge the academic merit of each and every gathering organized by a student advocacy group, since the students themselves assume that agency now. In order to accommodate different types of learners and personalities, students can choose not to speak about the event in front of their peers and instead provide their analysis only in writing. Still, in my experience, almost all students choose to speak in front of the class and take great ownership in their newfound cultural analysis skills. This activity has proven so productive that in recent years we have instituted it in all of our Hebrew Program classes.

Backward Mapping and Design

More typical assignments of reading and viewing materials in preparation for class discussion and writing academic papers form the lion's share of the course work. I take a few minutes, usually at the beginning of each class, when students are particularly alert, to talk about the reading for the following week. Students get one or two questions or themes to think about while reading. This helps focus the reading and better prepare them for the discussion. Students also need to write one response paragraph in relation to these questions. They post their responses on the discussion board of the course's online learning platform that we use. Writing the short paragraphs and making them available for peers to read has become a successful mechanism: it ensures reading the materials in a way that does not make students feel like they do "busy work"; it forces students to consider the texts in a participatory manner as they read and respond to peers' observations; and finally, it enables the class discussion to begin at a more advanced point. In other word, the brief written engagement with the readings before class allows me to be more efficient with "warm-up" questions and quickly get into the more profound and critical ones.

The expectations from written assignments also progress gradually. Students need to apply the detailed feedback they receive on the short paper task in writing their midterm papers. Likewise, the different stages of the final paper require them to use the analytical tools and practices that they have acquired throughout the term and sharpened in the early writing assignments. In addition, for every high-stakes paper (i.e., midterm and final), students have the option of submitting drafts and getting comments prior to the final submission. This practice emphasizes that writing is a process. It encourages students to avoid conceiving and writing their papers in "one sitting" and teaches them how to incorporate academic feedback in their work.

...

I purposely do not include here specific information on the actual texts and scholarly articles that appear on the syllabus. It is not because they are not important or less relevant. On the contrary, they are the most meaningful components of the seminar, and my syllabus is available online for anyone to look at. My aim, rather, is to think through the pedagogical method of backward mapping and design.[2] To that end, I was trying to model here, on a small scale, what the mechanics of using backward design would look like in a course such as "Israeli Narratives." This goal derives directly from the overall mission of this volume, as I understand it: creating a metanarrative that enhances our thinking and expands the conversation on how we teach the Israeli-Palestinian conflict in U.S. universities today. This complex topic presents academic professors with the opportunity to be thoughtful and intentional about the objectives of their courses. The practice of goal setting must be followed by a close examination of the design of the class, the nuts and bolts of each assignment, before delving into the content. This stage tends to be somewhat counterintuitive, in particular for us, faculty in the humanities, but it is worth spending time thinking about our course building blocks before beginning a conversation about particular texts.

Going back to the maps from the first class, part of understanding the premise of the Israeli-Palestinian conflict requires an acknowledgment of the narrative division that exists in both historical and popular imagination. The history of the Jewish war of independence and the history of the Nakba, the Palestinian disaster, were created—and to this day exist—separately, as if they do not depict the same events. This understanding accounts, for example, for the apparent gap in both Israeli and Palestinian schoolbooks, which often completely ignore the history of the other side. A material understanding of the epistemological aspects of the conflict, such as those that emerge, for example, from working with maps, leads to the type of intercultural competency that our students strive for and are capable of achieving. "Fiction is not life," I keep reminding my students, and while there is certainly a need to reintroduce the gap between fiction and reality, a narratological understanding of the complexities of the conflict can go a long way.

Notes

1. "The Secretary of State has done an incredible job. We just got back from the Middle East. We just got back from Saudi Arabia." Donald Trump in a meeting in Jerusalem with Israeli president Reuven Rivlin, May 22, 2017. See a recording of the quote on YouTube: www.youtube.com/watch?v=UaS633dA6Kc&feature=youtu.be.
2. For information and examples on backward design, see Grant Wiggins and Jay McTighe, *Understanding by Design* (Alexandria, VA: Association for Supervision and Curriculum Development, 2005).

Women On-Screen

TEACHING GENDER BUT NOT HISTORY

RACHEL S. HARRIS

In spring 2017, I taught a new class on women and cinema. It was a response to several professional frustrations about the way in which I was teaching the Arab-Israeli conflict. I wanted to move away from a fetishization of the conflict as an unusual and unique situation that had little overlap with other regions or situations. I was tired of treating culture as the poor sibling of political science and history—whose fields I was raiding for resources to historicize and contextualize readings of film and literature. And most of all, I was exasperated by the sidelining of women's experience, and domestic and social issues, from the central conversations about the conflict. While Israel studies as a discipline has a rich and growing resource bank in women's studies and gender studies, I had not been using these in my teaching, even though I had been using them in my research.

It was precisely this conversation about women, and women's filmmaking in particular, that transcended national boundaries. It not only offered parallels between Muslim, Christian, Jewish, and Druze women but also extended into other conversations happening within the Middle East about women, tradition, religion, and filmmaking—and into global conversations about violence, women's role in the public space, human trafficking, foreign workers, child care, pay equity, institutionalized discrimination, women's education, women's health care and control over their own bodies, and the ongoing hegemony of patriarchy. And these were all subjects that were also part of an international conversation about women making films that represent women's experience.

More than anything, I was tired of devoting huge chunks of class time to describing history, time I robbed from sharing texts and analyzing them with the students. I wanted this class to provide a new model for myself. Building on my own recent research on women in Israeli cinema and the book that I had recently completed, I decided that I would teach the class as a film course about feminist filmmaking by Israelis and Palestinians by focusing on the language of the medium. Using *Israeli Women's Studies: A Reader*, edited by Esther Fuchs (Rutgers University Press, 2005), as the only secondary text, students were assigned weekly readings. This provided students with the background, which included some social history but generally focused on women's experiences—the texts, like everything else for this course, were not concerned with the facts of history but the ways in which the consequences of history played out.

Each class I gave a lecture with clips from films that had in some ways engaged with the weekly topic, and we discussed not the historical and social reality but the representation of this reality on-screen. I then showed a film in class that complemented the discussion, and the students were assigned an additional film for viewing at home. These were films that either were available at the library on DVD or were streamed through it or could be found on YouTube, Netflix, Amazon streaming, the Israel Film Center (www.israelfilmcenter.org), or the production company Go2Films (www.go2films.com).

This model meant that rather than spending the majority of the class discussion on the historical and social context, we focused on the cinematic context. We analyzed the shots, what was on the screen and what was left out, the mise-en-scène, the costumes, the soundtracks, the plots, and the characters. We talked about the groupings of characters and power structures. We talked about access in interviews and documentary films. We discussed bias and perspective. We talked about the films' agendas and their presumed audience. We did everything except talk about history, and as a result, we talked about art.

That is, we discussed feminist filmmaking.

To help students access this visual language and train them in the medium rather than the content, I spent the first class talking through a PowerPoint presentation of stills. The screen grabs came from films that we would view over the course of the semester or were related to our future topics. I broke down each image slowly, asking where the camera was, who was looking, and who was being looked at. We discussed women's status given their level of dress, or undress, their positioning in the room, and the kind of room in which they were positioned. We discussed class, race, and ethnicity. Without moving characters, dialogue, or music to distract them, the students were forced to focus on film as a visual medium—not just an alternative way to communicate fact or plot—and it developed their critical thinking skills, rapidly changing their perspective on the movies.

Since I particularly wanted to focus on feminist filmmaking and its development since the mid-1990s, at the start of the second class, I screened the short video "The Bechdel Test for Women in Movies" (www.youtube.com/watch?v=bLF6sAAMb4s), a production by Feminist Frequency, in which Anita Sarkeesian explains the underlying principles. The Bechdel test, which has become shorthand for referring to whether a film is women friendly, has three criteria: (1) Are there two or more women in the film? (2) Do they have names? (3) Do they talk to each other about something other than a man? The short video highlights the huge number of Hollywood films that do not meet this basic test. (There is also a Hebrew remake of this video that focuses on Israeli films.) This video gave the students touchstones to look out for that, on the one hand, considered women's presence on-screen while, on the other, highlighted the problems of such a test, as it provided no evaluative analysis that judged whether those films portrayed women in a positive or empowering way.

Now armed with a toolbox of new skills, the students were ready to encounter one of the course's primary goals: to explore the diverse experiences of women within Israeli and Palestinian societies. Each class, following the film screening, students would practice their skills, reading what they had just watched in critical ways that focused on the text's visual (and aural) examination of the topic—paying careful attention to the handling of gender.

The topics we covered included many that I have taught in other contexts, usually starting with an outline of the historical experience, before introducing texts that engaged with it. But in this case, determined not to repeat this conventional engagement with text by teaching it through a historical context, I dived right in! Over the course of the semester, we covered the kibbutz, Zionist pioneering, militarism, religion, ethnic diversity, and the conflict over the land. But reading these from a feminist perspective changed how we engaged with these topics.

I started with the kibbutz and the propaganda films made for the Jewish National Fund and the Jewish Agency. I showed women's marginalization on the screen even as the films celebrated gender equality. Using Michal Aviad's documentary *The Women Pioneers* (2014) and Hadar Freidlich's *The Beautiful Valley* (2011), we considered women's experiences of these foundational Zionist experiments. These films challenged the ideology of the kibbutz's important place in Israeli society by pointing to women's exclusion and alienation, their relegation to conventional domestic roles, and the isolation that they experienced.

This gendering of the Arab-Israeli conflict meant that we continually looked to the impact of facts on the ground rather than the political maneuverings that created them. Thus, putting *Lemon Tree* (2008), *Free Zone* (2005), and *Syrian Bride* (2004) in conversation focused on films that depict Palestinian, Druze, and Jewish women's shared experiences of the conflict. These films address borders, fences, and separation; they focus on women's alienation from their own children due to the physical and emotional barriers that the conflict causes. But they also address the women's marginalization within their own communities by a controlling patriarchal establishment and their isolation from one another because of the national divisions caused by the conflict. Such a conversation changes the focus from why the conflict is occurring to what its impacts are, particularly for women.

The week we studied the army, we looked at films that depict women within the military, contrasting the image of the pretty CHEN (Women's Corps) soldier with later films such as *Room 514* (2012) and *Zero Motivation* (2014), in which women are rough, tough, and aggressive. The accompanying chapters in the reader addressed gendered violence and the connection between that and the militarism within Israeli society. Many of the films that depict women within the army have rape scenes, and we considered the role of such scenes, the ways in which they serve to situate women within a society that sees men as women's protectors. The following week, I followed with a class on women's activism, considering feminist responses to sexual violence and rape, particularly the ways in which women make films differently than men, using the documentary *Brave Miss World* (2013) and the feature film *Invisible* (2011).

When discussing women and religion, I screened several films in which women depict religion from within the community both positively, as with *Fill the Void* (2012), and critically, as with *3 Times Divorced* (2007) and *Gett: The Trial of Viviane Amsalem* (2014). This parallel between the ultra-Orthodox community and Islamic religious authorities highlights the systemic control of domestic issues by men and shows the shared experiences of women that transcend religious divisions between Jews and Muslims. Thus the course also offers a way to focus on areas of overlap in religious women's feminism and the shared female experience for both secular and religious women within the region. By bringing *Lady Kul El Arab* (2008), a film about a Druze woman participating in both Arab and Israeli beauty contests, I was able to expand our conversation to include other groups within Israel contesting traditional patriarchal systems and striving for female independence.

Though there have been several female Palestinian documentary filmmakers since the early 2000s, the first feature film was made by Annemarie Jacir in 2007. Like female Mizrahi filmmakers and female filmmakers within Israel more generally, the need to represent female experience in all its diversity has grown dramatically in the past decade. I chose several films such as *Or: My Treasure* (2004) and *Sandstorm* (2016) that showed women's communities of suffering. I imagine that with the growth of women's filmmaking, there will be new films and more works to consider, leading to regular updates to my syllabus each time I offer this course. Toward the end of the semester, we directly focused on the ways women's activism is now using cinema as a mode of protest, not only against the occupation and the conflict but also on other issues such as foreign workers (*Noodle* [2007] and *Jellyfish* [2007]), human trafficking, prostitution, and the expression of women's independence and sexuality.

For me, the course was an experiment. Could I bring my research into the classroom? Could my own activist work, which has been focused on empowering women and highlighting gender discrimination, find a space in my teaching? Could I develop students' critical thinking skills, add complexity to a reading of the Arab-Israeli conflict, and also develop their knowledge of a discipline providing them with skills and language? The reality was that by taking a different approach, I was able to combine these goals. The students loved the course and begged for it to be offered again. They all reflected on the change to their viewing patterns outside the work we had been doing within the classroom, but they also reflected on their change in attitude toward women's experience, discrimination, and challenges. They came to view the conversation around foreign workers and accusations of rape differently, topics that were current in the news in the wake of the most recent U.S. presidential elections. As we discussed sexual harassment and discrimination through Israeli cinematic representations, two public scandals were being covered in the press, the first involving the rape of a student by a football player who had been protected by his university, the second involving cover-ups of sexual harassment at Fox News. These later became the first public inklings of the #MeToo movement that followed. The students felt comfortable raising these topical issues during our meetings, drawing direct parallels between what they were learning and what was taking place outside the classroom. Thus, the course succeeded in bringing together global topics of interest with local issues that were of direct relevance to the students, using the Arab-Israeli conflict and filmmaking about it as a case study, rather than siloing it as a unique and remote example. Yet the representation of diversity and the discussions of complexity relating to "the situation" in Israel/Palestine also provoked the students' interest in gaining a deeper understanding of the Middle East, with many students commenting that they hoped to take another course about the region in the future.

As someone who has always taught culture within a social and historical context, it has been rewarding to see that I can do so while also helping students develop a love for my field. I no longer have to choose between content and methodology. I hope that the students I had this year will be a little different in the world as a result of this course, that they will look a little closer at the screen and think a little harder about the ways in which information is presented to them. And I really hope that I teach the course again.

Conclusion

How What We Teach Changes (and Changes Us)

Teaching beyond the Conflict

JOEL S. MIGDAL

I have taught courses on Israel and Israelis. And I have offered ones on Palestine and Palestinians. But I have never actually given a course on the Arab-Israeli, or Israeli-Palestinian, *conflict*. As I sat down to write this essay, I began to ponder why I have so studiously avoided a class with that title or even steered clear of making *The Conflict* a central part of other courses. After all, in my teaching on Israel, Palestinians play a significant role, and the same is true for Israelis, Jews, and Zionism in my classes on Palestinians. And courses on the conflict are big draws in many universities across the country. Why not simply teach the Arab-Israeli conflict? The answer to that question is embedded in my understanding of the dynamics of Arab-Jewish engagement. How I came to approach these dynamics with students began, I think, with the very origins of the field of Israel studies, in the Hebrew University of Jerusalem's Department of Sociology.

The towering figure of that department for decades was S. N. Eisenstadt, one of the world's most prominent sociologists of the twentieth century. I first encountered Shmuel (as all who knew him called him) in a graduate seminar at Harvard University when he was a visiting professor in the Social Relations Department there and I was a second-year graduate student in government. His class was far and away the best and most memorable seminar I ever took. Eisenstadt was mesmerizing—brilliant, encyclopedic in his knowledge, and big, big, big in his ideas. He seemed to swallow articles in one gulp, rather than read them, but somehow still remembered every detail. The sheer audacity of his theories took my breath away.

In an odd way, the class also gave me a chance to discover my own voice. As dazzled as I was by Eisenstadt, the man and the teacher, I found his theoretical perspective on social change unsatisfying. The theories were grand, to be sure, but they seemed to overreach, collapsing disparate phenomena into huge, abstract sociological categories and homogenizing them in ways that made me cringe. In that respect, Eisenstadt fell very much into the camp of the leading sociologist of the middle decades of the twentieth century, Talcott Parsons. Like Parsons, Eisenstadt seemed to take the politics out of politics, emphasizing broad consensus around values and societal equilibrium, rather than the squabbling among social groups and the instability that seemed so prominent to me at the height of the Vietnam War and riots in U.S. cities in the tumultuous 1960s. He focused on the values of national leaders, rather than the people in the streets.

Eisenstadt avoided the friction and the frazzle, and I saw little but strife around me in the United States at the tail end of the 1960s. The class, to my delight, gave me the opportunity to begin to articulate how I saw the world—words such as *struggle*, *conflict*, *discord*, *hostility*, and *domination* were at the forefront of my thinking. Around me, I saw not consensus or equilibrium—so prominent in the thinking of Eisenstadt and the social sciences generally at the time—but intense tugs-of-war over daily practices and fundamental values. I saw not elites whose values purportedly molded society but ordinary people putting their own stamp on social life. I began to figure out what it was that I had found so jarring in Eisenstadt's approach. For all this, I was eternally grateful to Shmuel, and we became lifelong friends.

Back in Eisenstadt's hometown of Jerusalem, he was a larger-than-life scholar, hovering over his own department and the other social science faculties at the Hebrew University, indeed over all the social sciences in Israel. Not only did he write general treatises on social theory, modernization, and world civilizations among other grand topics, but he also was one of a handful of social scientists who pioneered the field of Israel studies. Two of his early works paved the road for the new field: a book he published in the early 1950s titled *The Absorption of Immigrants: A Comparative Study Based on the Jewish Community in Palestine and the State of Israel*[1] and a huge tome a decade or so later called simply *Israeli Society*.[2] He also wrote numerous other books and multiple articles on Israel over the years.

As in Eisenstadt's general social theories, value sharing, stability, and institution building triumphed over clashing interests, irreconcilable differences, and conflict. He focused on the center, rather than the periphery. Eisenstadt's approach to studying Israel permeated the curriculum of social science courses in Israeli universities. Perhaps too simplistically, I would characterize that thinking as "Jews picking themselves up by the bootstraps to build a new national state." In the spirit of much of the social science writing at the time in comparative sociology and comparative politics, Eisenstadt's account fed off and fed into the nationalist stories and myths that leaders and followers alike reveled in.

Nationalists' accounts tend to ignore or downplay international and regional factors affecting their societies: "We have written our own story." That word "we" is itself problematic: it tends to exclude contending accounts, and it is prone to write minorities and marginal groups out of the story entirely. In this sort of social science, Arabs in Palestine and Arab countries were by no means negligible to the Israeli experience. But they were what social scientists would label as exogenous variables, meaning that they were outside factors, demanding Israel's attention but by no means shaping the core of what Israeli society was becoming.

Another founder of Israeli sociology, Yonathan Shapiro, began chipping away at Eisenstadt's approach in a book that caused an intellectual storm in Israel, *The Formative Years of the Israel Labor Party*.[3] Like Eisenstadt, Shapiro emphasized the role of central institutions and leaders in shaping Israel. But Shapiro also saw the deep impact on the dominant Israel Labor Party of Russian political culture and particularly the different types of participation by early Zionist leaders in Palestine in the failed Russian Revolution of 1905 and the successful Bolshevik Revolution in 1917. He did not gloss over internal conflicts, although it was still an account about the national elite.

One of the first people to challenge Eisenstadt's approach directly was a student of his and later collaborator of mine, Baruch Kimmerling. Kimmerling came to the infant state of Israel as a child and was part of the generation that grew up in the midst of multiple wars and attacks and, then as a young adult, experienced daily the corrosive effects on Israeli society and politics of the occupation of the territories conquered in the June 1967 war. He was baffled by the Eisenstadt-inspired curriculum in the Hebrew University Sociology Department. How could it include so little on the conflict, he asked, and how could it pay such meager attention to Arabs in Israeli society? How could Eisenstadt's seemingly seminal work, *Israeli Society*, barely contain any references to Israel's Arab population?

Kimmerling's critique was not simply that Arab citizens constituted a growing and significant share of the Israeli population, reaching one in five Israelis, although that alone would have been a telling indictment of the existing approach to studying Israeli society. Nor was it that one cannot ignore an occupation that stretches on without end in sight, although that too would undercut much of the social science of the time. Rather, Kimmerling stressed that it is impossible to understand Israel, and particularly the Jewish population of Israel, without taking into account the profound effect Arabs have had on Jewish culture and society (and Jews on Arab society).[4]

Israel's institutions, practices, and beliefs, Kimmerling argued, are more than the product of innovative Zionist leaders having a common vision and meeting the challenges they faced with ingenuity and verve. No, Israel's politics, society, and culture are in good measure the outcome of the engagement of two distinct, but deeply intertwined, groups, Jews and Arabs. Kimmerling was in his own work less interested in the violent conflict between Jews and Arabs in Palestine and Israel than in the ongoing direct and indirect encounters between the two and how such engagement shaped and reshaped each group. He saw Jewish and Palestinian societies as mutually constitutive. He also felt that the ongoing wars and threats were carving out an outsized role for the Israeli military in society and politics.[5] This violence also created areas of uncertainty, what Kimmerling called a frontier, where the creation of stable institutions was stymied.[6] In short, the everyday engagement of Palestinian Arabs and Jews and the ongoing belligerent relations with Israel's neighbors were being internalized in Israel, shaping and transforming society, politics, and culture.

I began my own research and teaching on Palestinians and Israelis at Tel Aviv University in the early 1970s. It was a time when my discipline, political science, was paying increasing attention to how states could be understood as autonomous actors, forcing their will on pliant societies. If one wanted to understand social change, the place to start was with the state's laws, rules, and use of violence.

But when I started researching in the West Bank in the early years of the occupation, I found something quite different. The vaunted Israeli state, coming off its extraordinary victory in the 1967 war, was not having an easy time dictating policy in West Bank villages. It certainly was changing everyday life in these villages in dramatic fashion, but often in ways that its policy makers did not at all anticipate. To my eyes, the military administration was sputtering and halting, full of false starts and, at best, only partially successful policies. Lower-level officers had to work with village leaders to get anything done, and even then there was no guarantee that outcomes would at all reflect what policy makers had created on the drawing board. In fact, it seemed to me that Palestinian village society was shaping the military administration as much as the military was shaping Palestinian society.

As I taught courses related to my research and as I spoke to soldiers in the wake of the 1973 war, I began to question old theories and to think about how states and the societies that they purportedly govern may be intertwined in unexpected ways. What went on in poor villages could affect the state and its operations deeply, even as the state wittingly and unwittingly transformed life in the villages.

I started discovering historians and social scientists writing on Arabs and Jews who sidestepped the conflict—at least the wars and battles—in favor of other forms of Arab-Jewish engagement. Many of these studies shared my own skepticism with the tendency in political science and other disciplines to valorize the modern state and portray society as pliant. The works I admired began to move from a predominant focus on elites, centers, and national politics to social history, ordinary citizens, and peripheries. Zachary Lockman, for example, focused on laborers, writing an important book on the failed attempts to forge an alliance of Jewish and Arab workers at the end of the Ottoman period and in the British Mandate in Palestine.[7]

In a seminal work, Deborah Bernstein distanced herself from writers, such as Anita Shapira, the grande dame among Israeli historians, who portrayed Jewish society in the Mandate period as self-formed and standing alone, and even from Lockman, whom she saw as overemphasizing Jewish-Arab cooperation among workers. Writing on labor in Palestine, Bernstein demonstrated how a split labor market led to far more conflict than cooperation between Jewish and Arab workers.[8]

A more recent example of studying early Jewish-Arab engagement at the grassroots level and beyond the purview of the violent conflict is Menachem Klein's important book *Lives in Common: Arabs and Jews in Jerusalem, Jaffa, and Hebron*.[9] Authors such as Lockman and Klein tended to put a bit too much weight on the level of Jewish-Arab cooperation, bordering at times on nostalgia for a small slice of the past. But they did succeed in documenting engagement that went well beyond shooting at, or dominating, one another.

These studies—and others, such as Gershon Shafir's influential book *Land, Labor and the Origins of the Israeli-Palestinian Conflict, 1882–1914*—bore in on the prestate era.[10] A number of these works attempted to demonstrate a lost moment in Arab-Jewish encounters—a fork in the road where, for a variety of reasons, Arab-Jewish cooperation was the path *not* taken. Such writing frequently presumes a mythical "critical juncture," a magical moment in which history could have ended up entirely differently. A future of great promise was somehow lost forever. I am skeptical of these sorts of premises; I suspect that they may wistfully whitewash intercommunal relations that were complex mixtures of true friendships and positive collaboration, concurrent with smoldering hostility, limited association, and ongoing dissension. My own doubts aside, though, these works pioneered in opening the door to regarding Arab-Jewish engagement as existing on a canvas that is much larger than simple out-and-out conflict.

In recent years, other scholars have extended research on Arab-Jewish interaction into the post-1948 period in new and exciting ways. To take one excellent example, Moriel Ram and Meirav Aharon-Gutman wrote a piece based on ethnographic research in a synagogue in the heart of the ethnonationally mixed city of Acre.[11] Demographic shifts have left the remaining, mostly Mizrahi Jews in the center of the Old City increasingly surrounded by fellow citizens who are Palestinian Arabs. These Jews expressed their discomfort with the growing dominance of their Arab neighbors as well as frustration over their inability to generate a minyan (quorum of ten men) on most weekday mornings.

In this context, Jewish religion itself changed. The synagogue became more than a place of worship; it symbolized a final (and failing) stronghold of the effort of Jews to dominate urban space in the center of Acre. In the words of one member, "If we're not here, Hamas will be."[12] Beyond the synagogue's meaning in the context of tense

Arab-Jewish relations in the city, its character changed in another way, as well. Like many synagogues in Israel, the one in Acre represented a particular immigrant community, Tunisian Jews. But with the changing demographics, the synagogue was forced to corral Jews from other communities in order to make a minyan, thereby changing the very makeup and character of the *tsibur*, the synagogue community.

The article also points to how Palestinian-Jewish and Arab-Israeli relations have inexorably interacted with intracommunal relations among Jews. As Aharon-Gutman pointed out to me in a personal communication, the relations between Ashkenazi and Mizrahi Jews have been key to understanding Jewish-Palestinian relations and conflict, as well as the Arab-Israeli conflict. "After all," she noted, "the Jews who were settled in abandoned Arab homes were Mizrahi Jews. The people who were settled along the borders in large numbers were Mizrahi Jews. The young men and women of the Border Police and the new (and interesting) Kfir Brigade who are in the first line of fire are Mizrahi Jews. And the list continues."

In Israel itself in recent years, Jewish-Arab engagement has been Janus-like. Since the beginning of the Al-Aqsa Intifada in 2000, day-to-day interactions have been fraught with tension and, frequently, outright hostility. Acre's tense relations are not an exception. Many Palestinians citizens have distanced themselves from ordinary interactions with Jews, as an unwritten rule against "normalization" has gained momentum. Many Jews have shunned and excluded Arabs in multiple settings. A competition for the national domination of space has been ongoing.

At the same time, Palestinians and Jews have increasingly shared public and commercial space. The two groups have coexisted, if not always happily, in supermarkets, parks, beaches, promenades, city streets, and more. Jews could not help but interact with Palestinian pharmacists in the ubiquitous Super-Pharms and Arab doctors in nearly every hospital. Academics and businesspeople from the two groups have collaborated on a daily basis.

All these interactions have had a drip, drip, drip effect on institutions, slowly transforming the groups themselves and general Israeli institutions. The signs of such mutual transformation are ubiquitous. Zionist political parties have become more nationalistic in a backlash against the more obvious presence of Palestinians in day-to-day life. Soccer matches have become hotbeds of deafening hatred.

At the same time, a host of new social enterprises and nonprofits have championed coexistence. A network of six schools in Israel called Hand in Hand have taught Arab and Jewish students together in bilingual settings. Other Arab and Jewish schools have built cooperative or joint programs. Universities have developed special programs to advance entering Arab students' Hebrew to an academic level. Jews and Palestinians sit side by side in universities throughout the country. Several Palestinian authors have written their novels and essays in Hebrew, while a handful of Jewish writers have chosen to write in Arabic. A number of Mizrahi Jews have adopted the hyphenated identity of Arab-Jew.

Some of these phenomena remain marginal and may prove to be ephemeral. Others may have cutting-edge power. What they reflect in total is the inability of either group to maintain insularity; Palestinians and Jews have been shaped, in some important measure, by the actions—even the mere presence—of the other.

On the broader canvas of the Middle East, relations between Israel and neighboring Arab countries have had similarly contradictory and complex effects. Of course, teaching the Arab-Israeli conflict demands a different set of readings and approach from teaching Palestinian-Jewish relations in Israel. Still, many issues on how to think about engagement beyond bombs and bullets are similar. In the broader Middle East, joint production zones, shared intelligence, increased trade, and shared security concerns have demanded attitudinal and institutional changes on both sides of the divide. Not coincidentally, social protests broke out in Israel just as the Arab Spring reached its peak. Israel studies, including the teaching of Hebrew, has gained a foothold at a number of Arab universities, and Arab studies has continued to be a central component of Israeli universities' humanities and social science curricula.

At the same time, academics have had little contact across boundaries (meeting in third-party sites might be a partial exception). Cross-border tourism has remained pitifully low. School curricula and mass media have denigrated the other side. But even these negative and non-interactions have had their own impact on fundamental norms and key institutions on the two sides.

Palestinians and Jews in Israel and Arabs and Israelis in the wider Middle East have had deep and lasting effects on one another. The changes in each have gone beyond the parameters of the violent conflict, per se. Aside from studying the all-too-frequent wars, the invidious terrorism, and state countermeasures, room exists for university courses that capture the complex ways that the two sides have transformed each other. My own avoidance of a course called the "Arab-Israeli Conflict" rests on confidence that the conflict can be contextualized in a broader setting of critical interactions.

The literature on Arab-Jewish engagement that could be assigned in classes examining this broader canvas is growing. It is rich enough to offer students a broad palette of research, case studies, and more general works. To be sure, this literature is still limited. It remains difficult to assess how—and how much—Arab-Jewish interactions have shaped the politics, culture, and institutions of Palestine and Israel and of other countries in the Middle East. But it seems to me that confronting those lacunae in class will only enrich students' understanding of, and curiosity about, this intractable conflict and the complex engagement of Jews and Arabs that it has spawned.

Notes

1. S. N. Eisenstadt, *The Absorption of Immigrants: A Comparative Study Based Mainly on the Jewish Community in Palestine and the State of Israel* (1954; repr., Westport, CT: Greenwood, 1975).
2. S. N. Eisenstadt, *Israeli Society* (New York: Basic Books, 1967).
3. Yonathan Shapiro, *The Formative Years of the Israeli Labor Party: The Organisation of Power, 1919–30* (Beverly Hills, CA: Sage, 1976).
4. Baruch Kimmerling, *The Interrupted System: Israeli Civilians in War and Routine Times* (New Brunswick, NJ: Transaction Books, 1985); Kimmerling, *Social Interruption and Besieged Societies: The Case of Israel* (Amherst, NY: Council on International Studies, State University of New York at Buffalo, 1979).
5. Baruch Kimmerling, "Patterns of Militarism in Israel," *European Journal of Sociology* 34, no. 2 (1993): 196–223.
6. Baruch Kimmerling, *The Israeli State and Society: Boundaries and Frontiers* (Albany: State University of New York Press, 1989).
7. Zachary Lockman, *Comrades and Enemies: Arab and Jewish Workers in Palestine, 1906–1948* (Berkeley: University of California Press, 1996).
8. Deborah S. Bernstein, *Constructing Boundaries: Jewish and Arab Workers in Mandatory Palestine* (Albany: State University of New York Press, 2000).
9. Menachem Klein, *Lives in Common: Arabs and Jews in Jerusalem, Jaffa, and Hebron* (New York: Oxford University Press, 2014).
10. Gershon Shafir, *Land, Labor and the Origins of the Israeli-Palestinian Conflict, 1882–1914* (New York: Cambridge University Press, 1989).
11. Moriel Ram and Meirav Aharon-Gutman, "Strongholding the Synagogue to Stronghold the City: Urban-Religious Configurations in an Israeli Mixed-City," *Tijdschrift voor Economische en Sociale Geografie* 108, no. 5 (2017): 641–55.
12. Ibid., 651

Time Line

THE ARAB-ISRAELI CONFLICT IN HISTORICAL CONTEXT

The following time line of the Arab-Israeli conflict offers a two-hundred-year history of events in the region. It is not meant to be a comprehensive account of every event but rather to provide a general overview that helps contextualize the conflict not only in relation to Jewish, Israeli, and Palestinian history but also in light of the rise of national movements, the collapse of empire, and the developments of the modern age.

References to world events are provided as a reminder that the Arab-Israeli conflict has often served as a stage on which global politics are played out. At times, they are also provided to help situate this particular conflict on a time line of world history with which students may have more familiarity.

In the layout of the time line, each page represents a decade divided into years, running from left to right. Events are separated into geographic areas (World, United States, Middle East, Ottoman Empire, Israel/Palestine, Eastern Europe/Russia, Western Europe). In addition, there are rows marked "Jews" and "Palestinians," though the latter row only appears after the fall of the Ottoman Empire in 1922.

Jewish historical events globally are included as a way to explain periods of immigration to Palestine and later Israel, information that appears in the row "Aliyah." The time line also provides a counterpoint of Jewish experiences, developments, and encounters with antisemitism that may be relevant in understanding Jewish diasporic attitudes toward Israel.

The land of Israel/Palestine is at the center of the chart in a gray row. Where Palestinian history or Jewish history overlaps with the history of the land, the gray row often extends up or down to accommodate these entries.

Spelling, particularly of places, uses the current "official" translated names as they are found on English-language maps or in general usage. As a result, there is no consistency of transliteration. Names of significant individuals who have impacted Zionism, Jewish history, Palestinian nationalism, and the history of the Middle East are marked in bold and are in light-gray boxes. These can be found throughout the time line, though the dating of their location is very approximate.

I hope you may find this time line useful for both situating the conflict in historical context and providing resources for student learning.

	1820	1821	1822	1823	1824	1825	1826	1827	1828	1829
World		Wallachian Uprising		Austria, Russia, and Prussia authorize French troops to enter Spain to destroy the liberal revolution there and reestablish the rule of Spanish King Ferdinand VII (1823)		Panic of 1825; stock market crashes by 80 percent		In London, Parliament extends tolerance, passing the Catholic Emancipation Bill, making it possible for Catholics to hold public office. Jews still cannot hold office, as oath requires swearing "upon the true faith of a Christian" (1829)		
United States	United States now world's largest cotton producer					Erie Canal is completed	Construction of Baltimore-Ohio railroad, first in United States	New York passes law emancipating slaves		
Middle East			Egyptian conquest of Sudan (1821–24)						First official newspaper published in Egypt: *al-Waqā'i'al-Masriya* (1828)	
Ottoman Empire	Following Wahabi War (1811–18), Ottomans now in control of Arabian Peninsula	Greek War of Independence against Ottoman rule (1821–29); Greeks massacre Jews					Ottoman Janissaries stage uprising; sultan disbands the elite guard	Ottoman naval defeat at Navarino	Turban banned and fez introduced	
Israel/Palestine			Nineteenth-century Orientalist art movement includes Palestine on tourist route; numerous artists from Europe and the United States travel and re-create exoticism and biblical scenes					Moses Montefiore makes first of many visits to Palestine		
Jews	German Jews begin to immigrate to United States in significant numbers		First Jewish periodical published in the United States: *The Jew*			Under Tsar Nicholas 1, Jews are oppressed (1825–55); Mordecai Manuel Noah founds Ararat, a Jewish city of refuge on Grand Island in the Niagara River near Buffalo, New York	Last auto-da-fé of Spanish inquisition; Maryland Assembly passes the "Jew Bill", removing restrictions that prevented Jews from holding public office	Cantonist Decrees enforce conscription of Jewish boys as young as 12 for at least 25 years		
Eastern Europe / Russia	Vilna Gaon followers move in large numbers to Palestine (beginning in 1808); later joined by Jewish immigrants from Arab world, anticipating 1840, 5600 in the Jewish calendar, when they believe the Messiah will arrive						Russo-Persian War; Persia cedes Armenia to Russia			
Western Europe		Napoleon dies		Steam-powered shipping begins				Beethoven dies		Oxford University wins first Boat Club interuniversity boat race.

	1830	1831	1832	1833	1834	1835	1836	1837	1838	1839
World										Lord Shaftesbury takes out advertisement in the *Times* suggesting return of Jews to Palestine and introduces the phrase "a land without people for a people without land" British take Aden (1839)
United States	Andrew Jackson signs Indian Removal Act	Trail of Tears (1831–50) Nat Turner rebellion					Texas declares independence from Mexico			
Middle East	Baghdad is devastated by plague and floods; Mamluk rule ends, and Ottomans reign					***Sultan Mahmud II, "The Reformer" (1808–1839): disbands Janissaries***				Sultan Abdulmejid comes to power and will spend the next three decades fighting the rise of nationalist movements spreading from Europe, hoping that reforms can impact change instead (1839)
Ottoman Empire	France invades Algeria, takes from Ottoman Empire	*Moniteur Ottoman*, first official newspaper of the empire, published in Istanbul in French		Egypt declares independence from Ottoman rule; Muhammad Ali Pasha of Egypt occupies Palestine; Ottomans reassert control (1832–40)						First reforms (*tanzimat*) giving equal rights to all groups in the Ottoman Empire, but new groups seek independence, including Tunisia, Romania, and Bulgaria
Israel/Palestine			Hebrew printing revived in Safed		Arab revolt "Peasants Revolt" in Palestine against Egyptian taxation and erosion of millet system privileges (1834)			Earthquake in Galilee area kills thousands in Safed and Tiberias		First consulate (British) opens in Jerusalem
Jews	Jews emancipated in Belgium and Greece		Jews emancipated in Canada		Jews emancipated in Netherlands			Moses Montefiore elected sheriff of London	Rebecca Gratz establishes the first Hebrew Sunday school in Philadelphia	Jews emancipated in Ottoman Empire
Eastern Europe / Russia		Cholera in Europe kills 900,000					Jewish printing censored			
Western Europe	July Revolution in France			Spanish Inquisition abolished		Communist league formed in Paris			***Samson Raphael Hirsch (1808–1888): writes Nineteen Letters on Judaism, advocating knowledge of secular culture***	

	1840	1841	1842	1843	1844	1845	1846	1847	1848	1849
World	First postage stamp	Treaty of London: halts Russian advancement into Ottoman territory						Greenwich Mean Time adopted by the railway in Britain but does not become official until 1880		California Gold Rush
United States		*Sir Moses Montefiore (1784–1885)*		First major wagon train on the Oregon Trail brings 1,000 westward		US President James Polk invokes the concept of Manifest Destiny, announcing to Congress that the Monroe Doctrine should be strictly enforced and western settlement pursued (1845)	US-Mexican War			
Middle East		Muhammad Ali rises to power in Egypt, eventually advancing to Syria, but Europe sides with Ottomans and pushes him back to Egypt, where he remains under Ottoman control					Israel Joseph Benjamin (1818–1864) travels through Africa and the Middle East in search of the ten lost tribes of Israel (1846–55), writes *Eight Years in Africa and Asia*			
					Abdul Hamid I (1839–1861): launches the Tanzimat period of Ottoman reforms					
						Baron Lionel Rothschild (1808–1879)				
Ottoman Empire						Ottoman currency reform on European model				
	Educational reforms, including compulsory primary school; new academies pose threat to Ulama (religious authorities)									
Israel/Palestine		Nineteenth-century fascination with the Holy Land leads European and American travelers to visit; more than 500 travelogues are written								Christ Church established in Jerusalem, first Protestant church in Near East
Jews	Damascus blood libel		Israel Salanter (1810–83) develops the Musar Movement in Vilna	12 men in New York set up B'nai B'rith	Dissolution of Kahal (Executive Board of Kehilla, Jewish Community)	The Reform Society founded in Berlin	English Jew elected to Parliament, unable to serve due to oath restriction		Wave of revolutions begin in Europe; Jews support efforts hoping for legal emancipation Friedrich Engels and Karl Marx write *The Communist Manifesto*	First High Holiday services held in San Francisco
Eastern Europe / Russia	Government schools set up for Jews in Russia as an attempt to control Jewish beliefs					*Judah Alkalai (1798–1878): Orthodox rabbi begins campaigning in Europe for a mass return to the Holy Land*				Wissotzky tea factory founded in Moscow; by early 20th century is largest tea manufacturer in the world
Western Europe		*The Jewish Chronicle*, oldest Jewish newspaper, is established in London				Great Famine in Ireland				

	1850	1851	1852	1853	1854	1855	1856	1857	1858	1859
World			Floods in China kill 50 million (1851–66)			Introduction of telegraph; Panama railway crosses from Atlantic to Pacific	Treaty of Paris; Moldavia and Bessarabia taken from Russians and made autonomous	Indian mutiny against British rule		Darwin's *Origin of Species*
United States	California becomes 31st state	*New York Times* founded				Singer sewing machine patented		*Dred Scott* case		First productive oil well drilled in Titusville, PA
Middle East				Britain and the Arab sheikhdoms of the Persian Gulf sign the Perpetual Maritime Truce, becoming Trucial States, recognizing British power in the Gulf, while Britain leaves them to autonomous rule (1853); they will join together later, in 1971, and become UAE						
Ottoman Empire					Russians invade Ottoman Empire; Crimean War (1853–56)		Tanzimat reforms include building roads and canals		Ottoman land code leads to systematic reforms including in Palestine; owners must now register land plots; unfarmed land can be returned to state; land can be dedicated "religious"; land registration remains legally binding in Israel today	
Israel/Palestine	James Finn and his wife found the British Society for the Promotion of Jewish Agricultural Labour in the Holy Land			George Gawler founds "Association for promoting Jewish Settlement in Palestine"		Using funds by Judah Touro, Moses Montefiore buys an orchard on the edge of Jaffa to train Jewish agriculturalists				
Jews		Washington Hebrew Congregation is established, the first synagogue in the District of Columbia	Mount Sinai, first Jewish hospital in United States, founded	Abraham Mapu publishes *Ahavat Zion*	*Haskalah (Jewish Enlightenment; 17th–19th centuries across Europe)*		Russia stops conscripting Jewish children		The Mortara Affair; Eduardo Mortara is kidnapped	
Eastern Europe / Russia					Russia's Nicholas I in conflict with France's Napoleon III over rights to the holy sites in Jerusalem	Alexander II becomes Russian tsar; less oppressive regime means Jewish elite increasingly participate in intellectual, cultural, and economic life (1855)			*Heinrich Graetz (1817–1891): writes History of the Jews, portraying Jews as a nation*	More Jews are given rights outside the Pale of Settlement
Western Europe	Emperor Franz Joseph I brings in new tolerant regime in Austro-Hungarian Empire that invites religious freedoms and leads to growth of Jewish community					Sir David Salomons becomes the first Jewish Lord Mayor of London (1855)			Full emancipation of the Jews in Britain; Lionel Rothschild can finally take seat as first Jewish MP (1858)	

	1860	1861	1862	1863	1864	1865	1866	1867	1868	1869
World						Celluloid invented	Alfred Nobel invents dynamite; Banking crisis in London	Canada founded		Suez Canal opens
United States	Abraham Lincoln elected president	US Civil War (1861–65) General Ulysses S. Grant bars Jewish traders from doing business with his army; Lincoln later revokes the ban	*Judah P. Benjamin (1811–1884): First Jew to be elected to the U.S. Senate (Louisiana) and first to hold a Cabinet position (for the Confederacy)*	Gettysburg Address		Abraham Lincoln assassinated	Ku Klux Klan is formed in Tennessee to maintain white supremacy			One of the first acts of the women's suffrage movement, a Women's Suffrage Law passes in the territory of Wyoming (1869)
Middle East	Mount Lebanon civil war in Syria; 20,000 Christians killed by Druze, villages and churches destroyed (1860)		Creation of autonomous Lebanon	Egyptian cotton becomes valuable commodity, leading to veiled protectorate by Britain.						
Ottoman Empire	Large migration of Middle East Christians to United States begins (1860–1920)			Foundation of the Ottoman bank		Young Ottomans: Secret society aiming for revolution		France, Britain, and Austria intervene in Ottoman reforms	*Sultan Abdul Aziz I (r. 1861–76): deposed and found dead*	
Israel/Palestine	*Mishkenot She'ananim, first Jewish settlement outside Jerusalem, built by Moses Montefiore (1860)*				Beginning of wave of US Protestant pilgrimage to Holy Land (1865–1941)	Beginning of the British Palestine Exploration Fund and the German *Der Deutsche Verein zur Erforschung Palästinas* for the scientific study of the region		Mark Twain visits Palestine; in 1869, publishes *Innocents Abroad*, concluding area is uninhabited desert		Mahane Israel built outside Jerusalem walls for and by Maghrebi Jews
Jews	Israelite Universelle founded in France to defend Jewish rights all over the world and to provide vocational training throughout North Africa and the Ottoman Empire (1860)		Moses Hess writes *Rome and Jerusalem: The Last National Question*	General Ulysses S. Grant issues General Order No. 11 expelling Jewish civilians from Kentucky, Tennessee, and Mississippi				Full emancipation for Jews in Austro-Hungarian Empire (1867); First rabbinical college established in United States: Maimonides College in Philadelphia (1867); Contact between Western and Ethiopian Jews is renewed (1867)		
Eastern Europe / Russia				Polish uprising suppressed by Russia, which becomes more suspicious of minorities and nationalist efforts (1863)						
Western Europe			First German workers' party founded by Jewish intellectual Ferdinand Lassalle (1863)		*Mendele Mokher Sforim (Sholem Abramovitz; 1836–1917): first Yiddish writer; first story 1864*			Benjamin Disraeli (1804–1881) becomes Britain's first "Jewish" prime minister, though baptized as a Christian		

	1870	1871	1872	1873	1874	1875	1876	1877	1878	1879
World				Japanese mission to Europe; opens up kingdom		South Africa becomes largest diamond producer	Bell invents telephone	Queen Victoria becomes Empress of India; now has greatest number of Muslims under her control in the world (1877)		
United States	Blacks given the right to vote; first African American sworn into office (1870)									
	Jim Crow laws brought into effect throughout the South (1870s–1880s), creating segregation between blacks and whites; upheld in 1896 by the US Supreme Court (1870)									
		Great Fire of Chicago (1871)								
	Susan B. Anthony, women's suffragette, illegally casts a ballot at Rochester, New York, in the presidential election to publicize the cause of a woman's right to vote (1872)									
Middle East	Crémieux Decree grants Jews in Algeria French citizenship (not extended to Muslims) (1870)									
				Persian Shah meets Crémieux and promises to improve Jewish conditions and support education, but antisemitic attacks continue (1873)						
Ottoman Empire	**Sultan Murad V (r. 1876): rules for three months; deposed by ministers; dies 1904**		The Sanjak of Jerusalem (Mustariffe of Jerusalem) is established as administrative district	Periods of drought and famine in Anatolia, harsh winter, lead to major financial collapse		Insurrections in Herzegovina spreads to Bosnia; Ottoman Empire gives full equal rights to Jews	Armed revolt in Bulgaria triggers Balkan revolutionary movement (1876); Ottoman sultan deposed (1876); Palestinian representatives from Jerusalem attend the first Ottoman parliament in Istanbul (1876); Ottoman constitution proclaimed (1876)	Ottoman war with Serbia and then Russia	Treaty of San Stefano; Parliament suspended and Tanzimat is over	
Israel/Palestine	Mikveh Israel Agricultural school established by Charles Netter				Meah She'arim established outside Jerusalem city walls (1874)				Founding of Petach Tikvah, the first agricultural colony (moshava) in Palestine	
Jews	Earliest "Zionist" groups first appear in Europe, often called "Lovers of Zion" ("Zionism" coined only in 1890s)	Anglo-Jewish Association created		American Reform synagogues organize as movement (1873–75)	Emancipation in Switzerland means *Jews are now emancipated in all of western and central Europe*				**Sultan Abdul Hamid II (r. 1876–1909): pressured to institute a constitutional era; deposed in 1909, and dies 1918**	The term "antisemitism" is coined by Wilhelm Marr, a German political agitator
			Ahad Ha'am (1856–1927): Hebrew essayist, advocate for cultural Zionism				**Theodor Herzl (1860–1904): journalist who organized and oversaw the development of political Zionism and the creation of the World Zionist Organization**			
Eastern Europe / Russia	Abolition of the ghettos in the unification of Italy brings emancipation for Jews (1870)				Military exemption for study leads many Jews to enter state learning institutions (1874)		The Russians conquer Uzbekistan and occupy the northern part of Kyrgyzstan (1876)			
							George Eliot publishes *Daniel Deronda*			
Western Europe	Franco-Prussian War (1870–71)					The Gilded Age has major economic growth in northern and western United States; high wages lead to massive migration from economically depressed Europe (1874–96)			Congress of Berlin; Alliance Israelite Universelle represents all Jews; Serbia, Romania, Bulgaria become independent, with Jewish emancipation; Bosnia and Herzegovina occupied by Austria-Hungary; eastern provinces occupied by Russia (1878)	
	Germany unified and emancipates Jews (1871)									

	1880	1881	1882	1883	1884	1885	1886	1887	1888	1889
World		Construction of the Panama Canal begins			France annexes Vietnam	Mid-1880s: Western powers engage in land grab in Africa			Brazil overthrows its monarchy and becomes a republic	
United States		Clara Barton named president of the American Red Cross		Emma Lazarus (1849–1887) writes *The New Colossus*			Statue of Liberty built (1886); Haymarket riot and bombing in Chicago, IL, over general strike pushing for eight-hour work day (1886)			First issue of the *Wall Street Journal* published
Middle East	Ahmed Arabi leads nationalist coup d'etat, leading to Egyptian Arab Nationalism	French occupy Tunisia	British occupy Egypt; 50 Europeans massacred at Alexandria		British and Egyptians fight Sudanese in Mahdist War (1881–99)					
Ottoman Empire		After borrowing funds from Europe, sultan fails to pay back debt; Europe claims access to natural resources		Ottoman railway expansion connects empire to western Europe, eventually becoming Orient Express from Vienna to Istanbul and Baghdad				Palestine divided by Ottomans into the districts (*sanjaks*) of Jerusalem, Nablus, and Acre; the first was attached directly to Istanbul, the others to the *wilayet* of Beirut (1887)		Ahmed Riza organizes students: "Young Turks"
Israel/Palestine		Jews migrate to Palestine from Yemen (1881–82) Eliezer Ben-Yehuda arrives in Palestine	Rishon LeZion, Rosh Pina, and Zikhron Ya'akov are founded First BILU settlers arrive		Hartuv: Land bought by Lord Aberdeen for Russian Jewish refugees near Beit Shemesh is supposed to lead to their conversion to Christianity; 12 years later, the land is bought and settled by Jews from Bulgaria (1884)					
Jews		*Eliezer Ben Yehuda (1858–1922): revitalizes and modernizes the Hebrew language; writes first modern dictionary*	Baron Edmond de Rothschild begins financially backing Jewish settlement in Palestine Leon Pinsker publishes *Autoemancipation*	Jews in Vienna constitute 10 percent of the total population and 12 percent by 1890	Hovevei Zion conference in Kattowice	Sir Nathaniel Meyer Rothschild becomes first Jewish member of the House of Lords in the British Parliament	Split in Reform Movement with "historical positivism" Judaism, which eventually becomes Conservative Movement	The Jewish Theological Seminary established in New York for "enlightened Orthodoxy" (eventually, the Conservative Movement)		
Eastern Europe / Russia	Russian Tsar Alexander II assassinated (1881) **Waves of pogroms** in Russia (1881–82): triggers mass emigration to Europe, South Africa, South America, and especially North America; Zionist activities increase, and small numbers of pioneers move to Palestine (1881)		May Laws restrict Jewish settlement	**Blood libel in Tiza Eslar (Hungary)**	Anti-Jewish riots in Bulgaria		*Ha-Yom* first Hebrew daily newspaper published in St. Petersburg	New restrictions on Jews including quotas for education		Jews officially allowed to live in Finland; previously had restricted residency that required three-month checks and could only deal in secondhand clothes
Western Europe				Period of significant industrialization across Europe, encouraged by international trade and resources from newly acquired territories						Eiffel Tower built
Aliyah				First Aliyah begins: 1882–84, comprising Romanian and Russian Jews						

	1890	1891	1892	1893	1894	1895	1896	1897	1898	1899
World							Klondike gold rush		First airship	Boer War (1899–1902)
United States			New York Stock Exchange panic triggers a recession			Lumière brothers launch cinematograph			Spanish-American War (1898)	
Middle East			First Arabic-language newspaper, *Kawkab Amrika* (Star of America), published in United States (1892)					The Cairo Genizah is opened to European scholar-explorers	The Egyptian book *The Liberation of Women* stimulates public debate on the need to emancipate women in Egypt (1899)	
Ottoman Empire					Armenian revolts, suppressed by Ottomans (1894–96)		Abortive coup d'etat; conspirators exiled, including Freemasons, Jews, and Dönmeh	Ottoman-Greek War (1897)		
Israel/Palestine	Rehovot established Mishmar Hayarden established	Jaffa railway station is first train terminus in the Middle East; line ran to Jerusalem; closed in 1948 Ahad Ha'am visits Palestine		Bukharians arrive in Palestine and establish own community after "May Laws" instituted in Bukhara, Russia			Metula established	Lumière brothers film Palestine	First Hebrew-speaking kindergarten opens in Rishon LeZion Mahanayim (1898–1912)	
Jews		**Corfu blood libel (1891)** Baron De Hirsch (1831–1896) sets up the Jewish Colonization Association (JCA) to resettle European Jews in Argentina and the United States; large-scale Russian Jewish emigration takes off (1891) Russian government approves creation of the Society for the Support of Jewish Farmers and Artisans in Syria and Palestine, known as the Odessa Committee (1891)		Nathan Birnbaum coins term "Zionism"	Jewish workers organize Jewish socialist groups throughout Poland, including Warsaw and Vilna (1894–96); they begin to publish the first Yiddish circular on May Day 1895; but from 1895, they being to clash with Russian Jewish worker groups (1894)		Theodor Herzl calls for modern political Zionism in *The Jewish State*	Forerunner to Yeshiva University established in New York for America's Orthodox movement (1897) The Bund, first Jewish socialist party, established in eastern Europe (1897) First Zionist Congress held in Basel, Switzerland: Members agree, "Zionism aspires to establish a homeland for the Jewish people" (1897) Census of Poland has Jews at 1.32 million, 14 percent of total Polish citizenry (1897)		The *Jewish Daily Forward* newspaper is established in New York
Eastern Europe / Russia		Jews expelled from Moscow								
Western Europe				Antisemitic parties win 16 seats in German national elections	The Dreyfus Affair (1894–1906): A Jewish captain in the French army is framed for treason; in 1898, Émile Zola publishes letter *J'accuse* defending Dreyfus, leading to new trial and pardon			Anti-Jewish riots in Prague		**Hilsner Affair blood libel, Bohemia**
Aliyah					First Aliyah continues: 1890–91, from Russia;					

	1900	1901	1902	1903	1904	1905	1906	1907	1908	1909
World	Boxer Rebellion in China against Western imperialism			Wright brothers' first powered flight	Russo-Japanese War (1904–5)			Bubonic plague in India kills 1.3 million		First flight across the Channel
United States	*Solomon Schechter (1847–1915): architect of American Conservative Judaism; head JTS*						San Francisco earthquake kills 1,000 / Peak of Jewish immigration to the United States (1906–7)		Model T Ford rolls off production line	
Middle East			Wahhabi leader Abd al-Aziz ibn Saud recaptures a major city in Saudi Arabia, beginning a 30-year campaign to unify the Arabian Peninsula (1902)			Ottoman-controlled Northern Yemen and British-controlled Southern Yemen officially divided (1905) / Naguib Azoury publishes *The Awakening of the Arab Nation* (1905)	Persian constitutional revolution		Oil discovered in Persia (Iran) / Hijaz railway opens / Young Turk revolution	First recorded use of the term "Palestinian" for Arabs in Palestine as distinct group appears in Farid Georges book *Palestine, Hellenism, and Clericalism*
Ottoman Empire		Theodor Herzl asks to meet with Sultan Abdul Hamid II and offers to buy an interest in Jewish colonization of Palestine but is rebuffed (1901)							*Al Karmil*, Arabic-language anti-Zionist newspaper, founded in Palestine; lasts until 1948; under Sadij Nassar	
Israel/Palestine		JNF established at Fifth Zionist Congress for the acquisition of land for Jewish settlement in Palestine		*Yitzhak Shami (1888–1949): Palestinian-Jewish author; wrote in Hebrew and Arabic*		First Hebrew high school, the Herzliya Gymnasium, in Jaffa	Bezalel art school founded in Jerusalem by Boris Schatz			Founding of al-Muntada al-Adabia, the Arab literary club that becomes incubator for Arab national movement; dominated by Nashashibi family / Founding of Tel Aviv, previously Ahuzat Bayit
Jews	Blood libel in Konitz	Hebrew Immigrant Aid Society established (1902)	"Uganda controversy" at Sixth Zionist Congress / Kishniev Pogrom: 49 Jews killed, 92 severely wounded		Russian tsarist secret police behind the antisemitic *Protocols of the Learned Elders of Zion*, fiction that "shows" global Jewish conspiracy, a key myth of antisemitism; later spreads (1904)				*Yehuda Burla (1886–1969): Israeli author, Ottoman Jew; head of the Arab Department of the Histadrut*	
Eastern Europe / Russia			Lenin becomes leader of the Bolsheviks	State-sanctioned pogroms in Russia by "Black Hundreds" kill thousands, a huge escalation (1905–7)	Russian Revolution (1905)		Millions starve in Russian famine	*Chaim Nahman Bialik (1873–1934): Hebrew national poet; chronicles Kishniev pogrom in poem*		
Western Europe	Sigmund Freud publishes *The Interpretation of Dreams*	French separation of church and state	Queen Victoria dies	500,000 Jews leave Russia (1903–7); 90 percent go to United States	Construction of Panama Canal begins (ends 1914)			*A. D. Gordon (1856–1922): Founded Hapoel Hatzair; followed a non-Marxist Socialist-Zionist agenda; believed in redeeming the land through agriculture of Eretz Ysrael*		
Aliyah	First Aliyah continues: 1900–1903, from Russia and eastern Europe; totaling 40,000 Jews			The Second Aliyah (1903–14): Immigration by mostly Socialist Zionists from eastern Europe; they begin the labor and kibbutz movements, adopt Modern Hebrew as their language						

	1910	1911	1912	1913	1914	1915	1916	1917	1918	1919
World		Chinese Republic proclaimed	*Titanic* sinks, killing 1,513		World War I (1914–18); Panama Canal opens		***Henrietta Szold (1860–1943): sets up Hadassah, the Women's Zionist Organization of America; in 1933, sets up Youth Aliyah to bring German children to Palestine***		Spanish flu kills 20 million worldwide	Woodrow Wilson 14-point peace plan
United States		146 women die in the Shirtwaist Factory fire in New York		Anti-Defamation League founded		Leo Frank lynched				
Middle East		Italians conquer Tripoli		***Hussein bin Ali, Sharif of Mecca (1853/4–1931): proclaims Arab Revolt***	Britain enters Iraq and occupies Baghdad in 1917	McMahon-Hussein correspondence (1915–16); Turks commit genocide of Armenians (1915–17)	Arab revolt in Hijaz begins against Ottoman Empire (1916–24)		End of Ottoman rule in Arab lands	Egyptian Revolution
Ottoman Empire	***Sultan Mehmed V (r. 1909–18)***		First Balkan War; Emergence of pan-Turkism	Second Balkan War	Ottoman alliance with Germany				***Sultan Mehmed VI (r. 1918–22): last sultan of the Ottoman Empire; dies in exile in Sanremo, Italy, 1926***	
Israel/Palestine	Degania, first kibbutz set up in Galilee (1909–10)	*Filastin* daily newspaper founded in Jaffa; First Jewish hospital opens in Haifa			Arthur Ruppin buys land on Mount Scopus to create the Hebrew University	The Zion Mule corps become auxiliary Jewish forces in British army, organized by Jabotinsky and Trumpeldor (1915); forced to withdraw from Gallipoli in disastrous campaign; become foundation for Jewish Legion (1917–21)		Britain's General Allenby conquers Palestine, ending 400 years of Ottoman rule	Palestinian delegates meet in Syria at the Al-Nadi Al-Arabi club in Damascus to affirm commitment to Greater Syria with Palestine as southern province	King-Crane Commission
Jews		Beilis blood libel in Kiev (1911–13)	Agudat Israel Orthodox anti-Zionist movement is founded; in 1948, becomes a political party in the State of Israel; Fez riots: local soldiers attack Jewish quarter in Morocco, and Jews take refuge in sultan's gardens		The American Jewish Joint Distribution Committee (the Joint) is established to aid European Jews			Balfour Declaration: British Foreign Minister formally pledges support for the establishment of a Jewish home in Palestine	Jewish Legion (1917–21)	By the end of the Ottoman Empire, there were estimated to be 56,000–82,000 Jews in Palestine, out of a total population of approximately 600,000
Eastern Europe / Russia							Britain and France secretly sign the Sykes-Picot Agreement with Russian collusion, dividing the Ottoman Empire into spheres of their own influence (1916)		Russian Revolution leads to civil war (1918–21); widespread pogroms against Jews	
Western Europe		***Sarah Schenirer (1883–1935): pioneers education for Orthodox girls***								Weimar Republic founded in Germany
Aliyah		Second Aliyah continues (1903–14)								Third Aliyah (1919–23)

	1920	1921	1922	1923	1924	1925	1926	1927	1928	1929
World	Prohibition begins; Women get the vote	First helicopter	Gandhi's noncooperation policy in India (1922); BBC launched (1922)			Three million die in Chinese famine		*The Jazz Singer*, first "talkie"		*Louis Brandeis (1856-1941): becomes first Jewish Supreme Court Justice in 1865*; Stock market crashes on Wall Street, beginning the Great Depression (1929-39)
United States		United States dramatically cuts immigration	Quotas limiting Jews at US universities							
Middle East	Turkish War of Independence; When Faisel I fails to secure greater Syria, at San Remo peace conference, Palestinian delegate recognizes need to change plans and reject identification as southern Syrian province (1920); Third Arab Congress meets in Haifa; calls for Palestinian self-determination; founds Palestinian Arab Executive (1920); General Union of Palestinian Students (GUPS) established (early 1920s); officially launched in Cairo in 1959; one of the first Palestinian institutions (1921); Transjordan set up on three-quarters of Britain's Palestine Mandate (1922)					Accession of Reza Shah, first ruler of Pahlavi dynasty	*Yaacov Ben-Dov (1882-1968): a pioneer of cinematography in Palestine*; Ibn Saud adopts title of king and, in 1932, proclaims Saudi Arabian kingdom; Lebanon, a French mandate, becomes a semiautonomous state	Treaty of Jeddah between Britain and Ibn Saud recognizes independence over the kingdom of Hejaz and Nejd	The Muslim brotherhood is founded in Egypt	
Ottoman Empire		Turkey established, thereby ending Ottoman Empire (1922)								
Palestinians	Fifth Palestinian National Congress, meeting in Nablus, agrees to economic boycott of Zionists (1922); Creation of the Supreme Muslim Council, advisory board in charge of Muslim religious affairs in Mandate Palestine; dissolved in 1951 by Jordanians (1922)					*Haj Amin al-Husseini (1897-1974): Palestinian nationalist and mandatory leader in Palestine; Mufti of Jerusalem, 1921-48*				*Abd al-Qadir al-Husayni (1907-1948): leader of the Army of the Holy War 1948*
Israel/Palestine	Jews and Arabs given right to run own internal affairs by British (1920); Jews establish Histadrut and Haganah, network of schools, health care, synagogues, and social services (1921)		League of Nations formally confirms Britain's Mandate for Palestine (1922); British propose draft constitution, conditional on Arab legislative counsel accepting principles of Balfour Declaration (1922); Bnei Akiva youth movement established (1922)		Technion, first institute of technology in Palestine, opens in Haifa	Hebrew University of Jerusalem opens (1926)	Britain imposes immigration quotas on Jews to Palestine (1926)	Jericho earthquake 287 estimated to have been killed	Arab riots in Palestine; attacks in Jerusalem, Jaffa, Tiberias and Safed; massacre in Hebron (1929); Work begins on port in Haifa (1929)	
Jews	Battle of Tel Hai; Joseph Trumpeldor killed (1920); Riots in Palestine (1920-21)		First exhibition of Eretz Yisrael art organized by new generation, including Nahum Gutman, Reuven Rubin, and Pinhas Litvinovsky (1922)		Baruch Agadati choreographs "Hora"			*Mordechai Kaplan (1881-1983): founds Reconstructionist Judaism*; Austria denies Jews a place in higher education, but Hungary commits to doing away with antisemitism	Massena blood libel (upstate New York)	Jewish Agency created at Sixteenth Zionist Congress
Eastern Europe / Russia			Russia renamed USSR				Stalin takes power in USSR	Trotsky expelled from USSR		Birobidzhan, an autonomous Jewish area of eastern Siberia, is set up (1928)
Western Europe		Munich Putsch	Mussolini's fascists take power in Italy; Michael Collins assassinated in Ireland	Irish Civil War (1922-23); First Nuremberg rally by Nazis						
Aliyah	Third Aliyah continues: about 35,000 mainly from Russia and Hungary arrive in Palestine; expand agricultural settlements and develop urban centers					*Manya Shochat (1881-1961): mother of the collective settlement movement; forerunner of kibbutz movement*; Fourth Aliyah: 82,000 mostly Polish Jews, of whom 23,000 leave (1924-28)				
Eastern Europe / Russia (writers)	*Dvora Baron (1884-1956): Pioneering Jewish writer, noted for use of Modern Hebrew*									

	1930	1931	1932	1933	1934	1935	1936	1937	1938	1939
World				Dachau concentration camp built		Italy invades Ethiopia	Edward VIII abdicates British throne to marry divorcée Wallis Simpson		Japan withdraws from the League of Nations	World War II (1939–45)
United States			Franklin D. Roosevelt elected president	Albert Einstein leaves Germany for United States	The Mother Mosque, first mosque built in United States in Cedar Rapids, Iowa (1934)					
Middle East	Oil exploration develops in the Gulf and what later becomes UAE (1930s–1950s)		Iraq becomes independent		Women in Turkey earn full voting rights		Anglo-Egyptian treaty, recognizing independence of Egypt (1936); Reza Shah (Iran) bans the veil and insists on Western dress (1936)		Oil discovered in Saudi Arabia	
Palestinians	Arab Executive leads demonstration in Haifa, but leader Musa Kazim al-Husayni is beaten by police (1933); British Shaw Palestinian Commission of Inquiry finds 1929 riots result of Arab fears of Jewish immigration (1930); Hope-Simpson report finds insufficient land for agriculture for increased Jewish migration (1930)	Passfield white paper limits Jewish immigration and insists on recognition of Palestinian rights; but in 1931, Ramsey MacDonald in letter to Chaim Weizmann retracts white paper (1930)			***Sheikh Izz ad-din al Qassam (1881–1935): Syrian Muslim preacher and militant opponent of Zionism; guerrilla who attacks British and Jewish targets***		Arab National Congress at Bludan, Syria, attended by 450 delegates from Arab countries, rejects partition proposal and demands end to Mandate, a stop to Zionist immigration, and a prohibition of transfer of Palestinian lands to Zionist ownership (1936)			
Israel/Palestine		Pinchas Rutenberg sets up hydroelectric plant at Nahariyim on Jordan River (1930); Irgun Tzva Leumi (Etzel) set up (1931)	Influx of European artists leads to two new movements, French impressionism and postimpressionism, based in Tel Aviv, and German avant-garde expressionism, based mainly in Jerusalem (1933); Impact of Bauhaus artists begins to be felt (1933)			British kill Sheikh Izz ad-Din al-Qassam, and followers initiate general strike that becomes violence the following year	Peasants Revolt (1936–39): 5,000 killed and 15,000 wounded by British; Arab Higher Committee established by Haj Amin; outlawed in 1937	British Peel Commission recommends partition of Palestine (1936); British dissolve Arab Higher Committee and all Palestinian political organizations; five Palestinian leaders deported; Haj Amin al-Husseini escapes to Lebanon (1936); Irgun bomb Arab targets throughout Palestine (1937–39)		MacDonald white paper, restricting Jewish immigration to Palestine; Irgun bombs kill 38 Arab Palestinians and wound 44 in Haifa and Jerusalem
Jews	***Ze'ev Jabotinsky (1880–1940): founder of Revisionist Zionism***	Betar, the revisionist youth movement, establishes a naval school in Riga	First Maccabiah Games held in Israel	First Hebrew feature film, *Oded Hanoded*; **The Holocaust (1933–45)**	2,000 Jews expelled from Afghanistan and forced to live in the wilderness	Nuremburg Laws deprive Jews of civil rights			19 Jews killed in Tiberias Pogrom	
Eastern Europe / Russia	Habimah Theatre moves from Russia to Israel supported by Margot Klausner, who will later create first Israeli film studio at Herzliya (1931)			Britain admits 75,000 Jews (1933–39)			Stalin begins to execute Jewish intellectuals	Kristallnacht: Jewish property destroyed in Germany (1937); Kindertransport rescue operation brings thousands of Jewish children to Britain from Germany (1938–40)		
Western Europe			General strike in France against rise of fascism	Weimar Republic falls; Adolf Hitler becomes German chancellor		Hitler begins to expand his dictatorial powers upon the death of Hindenburg	Leon Blum is elected the first Jewish prime minister of France (1936); Spanish Civil War (1936–39)		Germany annexes Austria	Italy invades Albania
Aliyah	Fifth Aliyah (1929–39): Mostly German refugees, including many educated professionals and intellectuals; unaccompanied children arrive in Youth Aliyah, 250,000 in total									

	1940	1941	1942	1943	1944	1945	1946	1947	1948	1949
World			World War II continues (1939–45)			Atomic bombs dropped on Hiroshima and Nagasaki, ending war in Asia (1945); Nuremburg Trials of Nazi war criminals (1945–46)		India and Pakistan become independent (of British Empire)	UN adopts Universal Declaration of Human Rights; Mahatma Gandhi assassinated	NATO founded; People's Republic of China established
United States		In December, Japan bombs Pearl Harbor; United States enters World War II (1941)			Franklin D. Roosevelt dies in office; Harry Truman becomes president (1944); Bess Myerson becomes the first Jewish woman to win the Miss America Pageant (1945)				United States recognizes Israel	
Middle East		Allied powers invade Iran and force Reza Shah into exile	Britain forces Egypt's King Faruq to appoint a pro-British prime minister		France grants Lebanon full independence; Stern Gang murders Lord Moyne, British resident minister of state, in Cairo (1944)	League of Arab States formed (1945); Jordan becomes independent (1945)			Arab-Israeli War (1948–49) (Israeli War of Independence); Lehi and Etzel massacre 120 Arabs in Deir Yassin; four days later, Arabs respond by massacring 77 Jews in medical convoy	
Palestinians	*Raghib al-Nashashibi (1881–1951): wealthy landowner and public figure; mayor of Jerusalem, 1920–34*	Haj Amin al-Husseini collaborates with fascist Italy and Nazi Germany; makes radio broadcasts encouraging Muslim support of Nazis				Ernest Bevin issues white paper announcing continued Jewish immigration into Palestine after exhaustion of 1939 white paper quota (1945); Anglo-American Committee report declares "private armies" illegal, recommends admission of 100,000 Jews into Palestine and abolition of Land Transfers Regulations; Palestinians strike in protest (1946); Anglo-American Conference in London produces Morrison-Grady Plan proposing federal scheme to solve Palestine problem; Zionist and Palestinian leaders reject the plan (1946)		Bevin refers Palestine problem to UN, which recommends partition; Jewish Agency accepts, but Arab Higher Committee rejects plan; Palestinian exodus during war becomes known as "Al Nakba" (the catastrophe; 1947–49)		
Israel/Palestine	Stern Gang breaks away from Etzel and forms Lehi (1940); "Canaanites," new art movement, impacts literature, visual and plastic arts; led by Yonatan Ratosh, Amos Kenan, Aharon Amir, and Benjamin Tammuz (1940s); Italy bombs Mandate Palestine, particularly port cities and refineries; 137 killed in bombing of Tel Aviv (1940–41)					King David Hotel, British headquarters, bombed by Irgun, killing 91 and injuring 46 (1945); UN General Assembly partition of Palestine leads to heightened civil conflict in Palestine (1946); First caves with Dead Sea Scrolls discovered (1946)		4,515 refugees on ship *Exodus* refused entry to Palestine	STATE OF ISRAEL DECLARED	Armistice ending the war signed at Rhodes; Israel joins UN as 59th member
Jews		Auschwitz Concentration Camp: gassing experiments on humans begin	Warsaw Ghetto Uprising		Allies liberate concentration camps (1944–45): Majdanek liberated by Soviets on July 23, 1944; Auschwitz, January 27, 1945; Buchenwald by Americans on April 11; Bergen-Belsen by British on April 15; Dachau by Americans and Ravensbrück by the Soviets on April 29; Mauthausen by Americans on May 5; and Theresienstadt by Soviets on May 8			Post-Holocaust mass migration of Jewish displaced persons; those immigrating illegally to Palestine who are caught are imprisoned by British; Sarah Levi Tannai (1910–2005), who had migrated to Israel from Yemen, forms Inbal dance troupe (1949)		
	The Holocaust continues (1933–45)			*Abraham Joshua Heschel (1907–72): leading Jewish theologian and philosopher*						
Eastern Europe / Russia					Postwar new communist regimes repress Jewish culture (1946)	Kielce Pogrom triggered by blood libel in Poland (1946)		Cold War (1947–91)		"Black Years" in Russia as Stalin wipes out Jewish culture and murders Jewish leaders and intellectuals (1948–53)
Western Europe	*Baruch Agadati (1895–1976): dancer, painter, choreographer, producer, and film director*			Mussolini arrested; Italy surrenders to allies (1943)						
Aliyah					Massive immigration to Israel from Arab countries and European refugees doubles Jewish population of the State of Israel (1.3 million; 1948–52)		8,000 illegal Jewish immigrants enter Palestine, known as Aliyah Bet (1944–47)			

	1950	1951	1952	1953	1954	1955	1956	1957	1958	1959
World		Color television introduced								Fidel Castro takes power in Cuba
United States	Korean War (1950–53)		Dwight Eisenhower elected president	Joseph Stalin dies; Khrushchev becomes first secretary and denounces Stalin's purges	Army-McCarthy hearings: series of congressional hearings on communism		Dwight Eisenhower reelected president			
Middle East	Jordan annexes West Bank following war; Palestinians double Jordan's population and are given full citizenship and parliamentary seats	Libya becomes independent Egypt occupies Gaza; Syria occupies Golan Heights	Military coup in Egypt; King Faruq abdicates Turkey joins NATO	Egypt becomes a republic Lebanese women gain the right to vote	Algerian War (1954–62) Britain agrees to leave Suez and end occupation of Egypt	***Gamal Abdel Nasser (1918–1970): president of Egypt; nationalized Suez Canal and called for pan-Arab unity***	Sudan, Tunisia, and Morocco become independent World Bank and United States turn down funding Aswan Dam; Nasser nationalizes the Suez Canal	Tunisia becomes a republic	United Arab Republic (UAR) (1958–61): Union between Syria and Egypt Civil war in Lebanon Revolution in Iraq, which becomes a republic	Yasser Arafat founds Fatah, a terrorist organization
Palestinians					"The Lost Years" (1948–67): Fracturing and dispersal of Palestinian population leads to lack of leadership Some clandestine activity and organization, but groups appear in spotlight in 1960s		Kafr Qassim massacre by Magav Israel border police; 48 Palestinians killed	Traditional Palestinian elite that had dominated political activism and negotiations with British and Arab countries replaced with new generation of university graduates		
Israel/Palestine	Israel passes the Law of Return Proclaims Jerusalem capital	Beginning of Israel's reprisal raids to stymie Palestinian infiltrations and attacks, continues to 1956		Yad Vashem established (1953) Israel signs reparation agreement with Germany, leading to influx of foreign currency and economic stability (1953)			Suez Crisis and Suez Campaign Jews expelled from Egypt by government decree; 25,000 leave (1956)		Construction begins of Israeli nuclear reactor with French help	
Jews	***Gurit Kadman (1897–1987): pioneer of Israeli folk dancing; organizes first dance pageant at Kibbutz Dalia (1944), becomes regular event***				***Benjamin Tammuz (1919–1989): Israeli writer and artist***	***Shmuel Yosef (S. Y.) Agnon (1888–1970): Nobel laureate (1964), Hebrew novelist***		***S. Yizhar (Yizhar Smilansky) (1916–2006): Israeli writer and politician***	***Leah Goldberg (1911–1970): Hebrew poet, translator, scholar, and educator***	
Eastern Europe / Russia	***Natan Alterman (1910–1970): poet, playwright, journalist, and translator; highly influential in Zionist politics***						USSR invades Hungary			Khrushchev visits the United States, the first such visit by a Soviet leader
Western Europe					West Germany joins NATO			European Common Market, a precursor of the European Union, established		
Aliyah	Operation Ezra and Nehemiah brings almost all Iraqi Jews: 120,000 (1950–51)			Jewish immigration to Israel continues steadily until 1960; approximately 900,000 Jews arrive from Arab countries 1948–70; 50,000 Jews arrive from Poland 1954–60, when they are granted permission to leave; the large numbers cause the creation of *maabarot*, settlement camps						

	1960	1961	1962	1963	1964	1965	1966	1967	1968	1969
World	Mossad tracks down and captures former Nazi Adolf Eichmann	Eichmann is put on trial in Israel while world watches	Cuban Missile Crisis		**Golda Meir (1898–1978): teacher, politician, and Israel's fourth prime minister; Israel's only female prime minister**		Beginning of Cultural Revolution in China (1966–76)	UN peace resolution 242: "Land for Peace"	Tet Offensive begins in Vietnam, marking a turning point in the war	US astronauts land on Moon
United States	John F. Kennedy elected president; Paul Newman stars in Exodus			John F. Kennedy assassinated	Lyndon Johnson signs the Civil Rights Act	First US offensive in Vietnam		Martin Luther King and Robert Kennedy assassinated; Lyndon Johnson declines to run for president (1968)		Richard Nixon becomes president; Vietnam antiwar protests
Middle East	OPEC founded in Baghdad; Iranian shah recognizes Israel; Egypt and Iran break ties	Kuwait becomes independent	Yemen Civil War (1962–70); Egypt and Saudi Arabia intervene					Nasser closes Straits of Tiran to Israeli shipping (1967); Khartoum Resolution offering no recognition of Israel (1967); Yemen becomes independent (1967)		Libya becomes a republic
Palestinians	Jordan opposes Arab League's creation of a Palestinian national entity	*Mahmoud Darwish (1941–2008): Palestinian author and poet regarded as national poet*			League of Arab States Summit in Cairo; Palestinian Liberation Organization (PLO) founded	Popular Front for the Liberation of Palestine (PFLP) founded by George Habash; also creates armed wing, Abu Ali Mustapha Brigades (1967)		PNC Fedayeen take over PLO	Democratic Front for the Liberation of Palestine (DFLP) founded by Nayef Hawatmah	Yasser Arafat becomes chairman of the PLO, until his death in 2004
Israel/Palestine	International success of Hollywood film *Exodus* leads to official support by Israeli government of Israeli film industry		Excavations begin at Masada		Israel wins the Asia Soccer Cup, beating South Korea 2–1 in the final; Competition over fresh water from Jordan River exacerbates regional tensions	Israel Museum founded in Jerusalem; Teddy Kollek elected mayor of Jerusalem and serves 28 years	Water conflicts with Syria; S. Y. Agnon shares Nobel Prize for Literature with Jewish poet Nelly Sachs	Six-Day War (June 5–10); Second Palestinian exodus (Naksa), mostly from West Bank to Jordan	Israel's first television station is launched; War of Attrition with Egypt (1968–70); Battle of Karameh: Israel battles PLO forces in Jordan	Golda Meir becomes first woman prime minister in Israel
Jews	Jews active in US civil rights movement; more than half of all white freedom fighters are Jewish, and two-thirds of white volunteers in Freedom Summer are Jewish; Andrew Goodman and Michael Schwerner are murdered				Israel recognizes the Bnai Israel Jews of India as Jewish	R. Abraham Joshua Heschel marches in Selma with Martin Luther King Jr.		Jews applying to leave USSR for Israel but denied exit known as "refusnik" (singular); leads to international movement to advocate for Jewish emigration (1967–71)		AJS founded
Eastern Europe / Russia		Berlin Wall built between eastern and western Europe			Nikita Khrushchev removed from office, replaced by Leonid Brezhnev				Polish government outlaws Jewish language and institutions; USSR invades Czechoslovakia	Beginning of detente between USSR and the West
Western Europe										
Aliyah	Operation Yachin brings 120,000 Moroccan Jews to Israel as Morocco opens doors after restrictions imposed in 1956 had limited emigration							Small emigration from USSR limited by refusal to grant exit visas (1967–71)		

	1970	1971	1972	1973	1974	1975	1976	1977	1978	1979
World		India-Pakistan war (1971): leads to creation of Bangladesh	Massacre of 11 Israeli athletes at Munich Olympic Games by Black September	UN Peace Resolution 338 (1973); ceasefire overseen by Russia and US Arab oil embargo	Henry Kissinger manages Israeli, Egyptian, Syrian disengagement; excludes PLO	UN passes Resolution 3789 equating Zionism with racism	German revolutionaries and Palestinian terrorists hijack plane; German commandos storm hijacked plane in Mogadishu (1977)		Boat people arrive in Hong Kong from Vietnam	Margaret Thatcher becomes first female British prime minister
United States		*Edward Said (1935–2003): literature professor, public intellectual, and founder of postcolonial studies*	Richard Nixon wins reelection Watergate	Vietnam cease-fire; US troops leave Vietnam	Richard Nixon resigns over Watergate		Jimmy Carter becomes president		Edward Said publishes *Orientalism*	
Middle East	Nasser dies; Anwar Sadat becomes president of Egypt	Gulf states become independent Formation of Union of Arab Emirates	*Tawfiq Ziad (1929–1994): Palestinian poet and politician*		Turkey invades Cyprus; occupies northern part of island (1974)	Arab League Summit in Rabat: PLO recognized as the only representative of the Palestinians (1974) Saudi King Faisal assassinated (1975) Beginning of Lebanese civil war (1975–77); finally ends in 1990		Anwar Sadat becomes first Arab leader to visit Israel	Operation Litani: Israel incursion into Lebanon after Coastal Road Massacre; objective to push PLO beyond artillery range of the Galilee	Iranian Revolution; beginning of American hostage crisis Egypt and Israel make peace
Palestinians	PLO, led by Arafat, clashes with Jordanian authorities, expelled; "Black September"; Forced relocation to Lebanon PLO participates in Lebanese civil war			*Taha Muhammad Ali (1931–2011): Palestinian poet and short-story writer*		The United Nations establishes the Committee on the Exercise of the Inalienable Rights of the Palestinian People		UN creates annual International Day of Solidarity with the Palestinian People		Palestinian El-Funoun Dance Company established
Israel/Palestine	Hebrew art movement moves away from abstraction and begins to "Americanize" under "group of ten"	Terrorist attack on Lod airport by Japanese Red Army recruited by PFLP kills 26 and injures 80 (1972) West Bank Jewish settlement population reaches 10,600		Yom Kippur / October War (1973)	Golda Meir resigns Gush Emunim (right-wing Orthodox Jewish settler movement) established		Terrorists hijack Air France plane on route to Israel, forcing it down in Entebbe, Uganda; Israeli commandos rescue hostages	Anwar Sadat visits Jerusalem Menachem Begin elected prime minister from Likud	Begin offers Vietnamese boat people asylum in Israel (1978) Camp David Accords, encouraged by Jimmy Carter, between Israel and Egypt as background to peace; include Palestinian self-determination in Egypt (1978) Israel-Egypt Peace Treaty (1979)	
Jews				First Jewish national women's conference held in New York; 400 attend	*Simon Wiesenthal (1908–2005): Holocaust survivor, Nazi hunter, and author*		*Lilith*, Jewish feminist publication, begins		American neo-Nazi party marches in Skokie, Illinois	
Eastern Europe / Russia	Soviet Jews attempt to hijack a plane to Sweden; they are caught and sent to long prison terms (1970)		SALT I treaty, freezing the number of ballistic missile launchers held by the superpowers (1972)				*Yasser Arafat (1929–2004): chairman of the PLO, 1969–2004, president of Palestinian National Authority (1994–2004)*			
Western Europe									Israel wins Eurovision song contest with "A-ba-ni-bi"	Israel wins Eurovision song contest again with "Hallelujah"
Aliyah	First Russian Aliyah from Soviet Union brings tens of thousands per year, reaching peak in 1978–79, when 76,000 exit visas to Israel are granted in just two years									

	1980	1981	1982	1983	1984	1985	1986	1987	1988	1989
World			Falklands War between Britain and Argentina (1982)		Famine in Ethiopia (1983–85)	Achille Lauro hijacking; TWA hijacking			Libya blows up Pan Am flight over Lockerbie, killing hundreds	Tiananmen Square massacre
United States	Ronald Reagan elected president	Iranian hostage crisis ends			Ronald Reagan reelected president			Jonathan Pollard convicted of spying for Israel		
Middle East	Iran-Iraq War (1980–88)	Egyptian president Anwar Sadat assassinated	First Lebanon War against the PLO and Syria begins (1982); Israel is blamed for allowing Maronite Phalanges to massacre Palestinians in the Sabra and Shatila refugee camps (1982)						Al-Qaeda established by Osama bin Laden, who rules until assassination in 2011	
Palestinians	Palestinian Islamic Jihad (PIJ) established with aim of creating Islamic State; also creates military wing, al-Quds Brigade (1981); active in Gaza and West Bank, particularly active in Jenin and Hebron		PLO expelled from Beirut; Kahan Commission to investigate Sabra and Shatila massacre	PLO headquartered in Tunisia (1983–93); Arafat shifts approach from conflict to negotiation		*Emile Habibi (1922–1996): Israeli-Arab writer and politician who served in Knesset; believed in coexistence*	*Ghassan Kanafani (1936–1972): Palestinian author and leader of PFLP; assassinated by Mossad as a response to Lod airport massacre*	Hamas, a Palestinian Sunni Islamist organization, is founded; has a social service wing, Dawah, and a military wing, the Izz ad-Din al-Qassam Brigades (1987); it has been the de facto governing authority of the Gaza Strip since 2007	PNC in Algiers declares creation of a Palestinian State. Infers willingness to recognize Israel and renounce terrorism (1988); First Intifada (1987–91)	
Israel/Palestine	Israel annexes East Jerusalem (1980)	Israel bombs Iraqi nuclear reactor; United States sanctions Israel (1981); Makhteret (Jewish Underground; 1979–84): extremist right-wing Jewish group engages in attacks against Palestinians, including plot to blow up the Dome of the Rock	Israeli ambassador to UK attacked; Israel's withdrawal from Sinai complete and area returned to Egypt	Israel signs free trade agreement with United States; Kol Demama, disabled dance company, is formed	Creation of Shas political party under Sephardic R. Ovadiah Yosef	Israelis attack PLO in Tunis		*Yehuda Amichai: major Israeli poet and among the first to use colloquial Hebrew*		
Jews						Women rabbis are ordained by the Conservative Movement				
Eastern Europe / Russia		*Haim Gouri (1923–2018): Israeli poet, novelist, journalist, and documentary filmmaker*				Mikhail Gorbachev becomes Soviet president and introduces reforms that allow Jewish religion and culture (1985)			Perestroika and Glasnost	Communism falls in much of eastern Europe; Berlin Wall falls
Western Europe										
Aliyah		2,500 Ethiopian Jews resettled in Israel		"Operation Moses": In a secret mass airlift, 8,000 Ethiopian Jews brought to Israel from refugee camps in the Sudan (1984)		"Operation Joshua" brings 800 more Ethiopian refugees (1985)				Russian Aliyah: Approximately one million Jews migrate to Israel from former USSR and eastern Europe

	1990	1991	1992	1993	1994	1995	1996	1997	1998	1999
World	Nelson Mandela freed in South Africa after 27 years	UN resolution 4684 revokes the "Zionism is racism" resolution; Yugoslavian civil war		World Wide Web is made free and becomes popular due to usable graphic browser				Taliban takes control in Afghanistan (1997–98); Beginning of dot-com bubble, which ends in financial crash in 2000; Google founded (1998)		War in Kosovo
United States		Bill Clinton elected president (1992)	The first Jewish women senators, Dianne Feinstein and Barbara Boxer, are elected to the US Senate, representing California (1992)	US Holocaust Museum opens in Washington, DC (1993); Ruth Bader Ginsburg becomes first Jewish woman Supreme Court justice (1993)		Oklahoma bombing of US federal building	Bill Clinton reelected	Netflix launches with DVD subscription service		
Middle East		Iraq invades Kuwait, First Persian Gulf War			Israel-Jordan peace treaty; Palestinian Authority created	United States imposes oil sanctions against Iran	First Palestinian general elections; Arafat voted to head Palestinian national council	Global terror attacks dramatically increase		Islamic State of Iraq and the Levant (known as ISIS or ISIL) founded
Palestinians		Kuwaiti authorities pressure 200,000 Palestinians to leave Kuwait, partly a response to PLO alignment with Saddam Hussein	***Na'im Araidi (1950–2015): Druze academic and poet; wrote in both Hebrew and Arabic***	***Mahmoud Abbas (b. 1935): president of the Palestinian Authority***		***Sahar Khalifah (b. 1941): Palestinian novelist; founder of the Women's Affairs Center***	Palestinians first represented at Summer Olympics		***Hanan Ashrawi (b. 1946): Palestinian legislator, activist, and scholar; first woman on Palestinian National Council***	
Israel/Palestine		Madrid Peace Conference sponsored by United States and USSR	Yitzhak Rabin becomes Israeli prime minister	Oslo Accords signed between Yitzhak Rabin and Yasser Arafat; mutual letters of recognition exchanged	Yitzhak Rabin, Shimon Peres, and Yasser Arafat receive Nobel Peace Prize (1994); Baruch Goldstein massacres 29 and wounds 125 Muslims at prayer in the Cave of the Patriarchs (1994); Prime Minister Yitzhak Rabin assassinated at peace rally (1995)	Oslo II (Taba Agreement); creation of West Bank areas A, B, C and Palestinian Authority given limited control of A and B	Benjamin Netanyahu becomes Israeli prime minister	Hamas bombings in public places kill and maim hundreds in Tel Aviv and Jerusalem; PA works with Israelis to reduce threats of attack; Israeli air force helicopter crash kills 73	Israel-PLO Wye River Accord, enabling greater cooperation; Miss Israel Linor Abargil wins Miss World	Ehud Barak becomes Israeli prime minister; By end of decade, approximately 400,000 foreign workers in Israel; Shas win 17 seats
Jews	War in Bosnia leads to emigration of Jews to the West and to Israel; many children airlifted without families (1990)		Suicide bomb at Israeli embassy in Buenos Aires; 29 killed and 242 injured (1990)	Foreign Workers' Program (FWP) visas for industry and agriculture later expanded to include health-care services	Bombing of Argentine Israelite Mutual Association (Jewish community center) kills 85, injures hundreds; largest ever attack in Argentina (1994)			Creation of "Open Orthodox" movement by R. Avi Weiss (1997)		Creation of new Yeshiva Chovevei Torah
Eastern Europe / Russia		START I, limiting nuclear weapons, signed between superpowers (1991); Soviet Union dissolved (1991)								
Western Europe									Dana International wins Eurovision song contest with "Diva" (1998)	
Aliyah	Jewish Aliyah from Albania (1990); Ethiopian Aliyah: Operation Solomon brings 14,325 Jews in airlift over 36 hours (1990)						26,000 Moldovan Jews flee to Israel due to violence (1999–2002); Argentinian Aliyah (1999–2002): following political discord, approximately 10,000 arrive, though many more come to Israel without making Aliyah	***Sami Michael (b. 1926): Israeli novelist and journalist on boards of Arab communist newspapers in Haifa***	***Amos Gitai (b. 1950): major Israeli filmmaker***	

	2000	2001	2002	2003	2004	2005	2006	2007	2008	2009
World			Euro becomes legal tender in Europe	Skype launched	Facebook launched		Twitter launched	Netflix begins streaming		
United States	George W. Bush elected president	9/11: World Trade Center and Pentagon attacked; 2,996 killed	United States invades Afghanistan; George W. Bush supports creation of a Palestinian State	United States invades Iraq and topples Saddam Hussein	George W. Bush reelected president				Barack Obama elected president	
Middle East	Israel unilaterally ends occupation of southern Lebanon by withdrawing all forces; Camp David II peace talks end without resolution		Arab League Summit in Beirut; calls for full normalization with Israel if it withdraws to 1967 borders	Second Gulf War (Iraq War; 2003–11); United States issues "Road Map to Peace"; Looting of the Iraq museum			Lebanon War between Israel and Hezbollah	Deadliest year for US troops in Iraq		Obama gives speech in Cairo to restart US-Arab relations, souring relations with Israel
Palestinians		Al-Aqsa Intifada begins (2000–2005); The al-Aqsa Martyrs Brigades military wing of Fatah begins operating; responsible for numerous suicide-bomb attacks			Hamas leader Ahmed Yassin assassinated by Israelis	Mahmoud Abbas becomes president of the Palestinian National Authority	Second Palestinian legislative elections; Hamas wins	Palestinian civil war in Gaza between Hamas and Fatah; Hamas takes control		
					Hiam Abbas (b. 1960): Palestinian actor and director					
									Elia Suleiman (b. 1960): Palestinian-Christian filmmaker	
Israel/Palestine	Riots break out in October; Or Commission investigates Arab sector, concludes inequality and discrimination			Israel begins building barrier around West Bank known as "separation wall" or "security barrier" to reduce terrorist attacks; majority completed by 2006; Palestinians angered at annexing of additional Palestinian land by barrier as it is built; Israel's Supreme Court orders sections moved		Disengagement plan: Israel evacuates all settlers from Gaza; Beta Dance Troupe formed	Prime Minister Ariel Sharon goes into coma in office and never awakens		Operation Cast Lead: an extended conflict between Israel and Hamas to end rocket fire into Israel from Gaza	
			David Grossman (b. 1954): Israeli journalist and novelist		*Eran Riklis (b. 1954): major Israeli filmmaker*					
Jews									Yeshivat Maharat created for the ordination of Orthodox women; Sara Hurwitz first woman ordained by R. Avi Weiss, now dean of the yeshiva	
	Michal Aviad (b. 1955): feminist professor and filmmaker					*Sami Shalom Chetrit (b. 1960): Moroccan Hebrew poet, scholar, and peace activist*		*Ronit Elkabetz (1964–2016): Israeli writer, actress, and filmmaker; active as a Mizrahi feminist, president of Achoti, and Forum for Israeli Women Filmmakers and Television Artists*		
Eastern Europe / Russia										
Western Europe										
Aliyah		Argentinian Aliyah continues (1999–2002)								

	2010	2011	2012	2013	2014	2015	2016	2017	2018	2019
		Anne Marie Jacir (b. 1974): Palestinian filmmaker and poet		*Samir El-youssef (b. 1965): Palestinian-British novelist and critic*	*Ibtisam Ma'arana Menuhin (b. 1975): Israeli-Palestinian feminist documentary filmmaker*					*Sayed Kashua (b. 1975): Palestinian-Israeli author, journalist, and screenwriter; created Avoda Aravit TV series*
World						The Vatican recognizes the state of Palestine (2015)				
						ISIL terrorist attacks continue to threaten both East and West				
United States			Barack Obama reelected president				Hillary Clinton first woman to run for president of United States for a major party; Donald Trump elected president	White nationalists march at Charlottesville chanting Nazi slogans and waving swastikas	Donald Trump reaffirms recognition of Jerusalem as Israel's capital and moves US embassy; several smaller countries follow suit	
									U.S. stops funding UNRWA	
Middle East	Series of protests and demonstrations become known as the "Arab Spring"	Muammar Gaddafi, deposed leader of Libya, killed (2011)			ISIL drives Iraqi government forces out of western Iraq		Syrian refugee crisis reaches new highs; millions displaced	ISIL driven from Mosul, largest held city, by Iraqi forces		
		Egyptian Revolution (2011)								
		Beginning of Syrian Civil War, killing half a million Syrians (2011)								
		Iraq War ends (2011)								
Palestinians	Construction begins on Rawabi, the first planned Palestinian city	Palestinians hand over Gilad Shalit, an Israeli soldier, in exchange for 477 Palestinian prisoners in first phase of swap	UN upgrades Palestinians to "nonmember" observer state	*Suha Arraf (b. 1969): Palestinian screenwriter, producer, and director*		Unity government between Hamas and Fatah (2014–16)	Opening of the Palestinian Museum at Birzeit University, West Bank		Gaza border protests	
Israel/Palestine			Wave of African refugees arrives through Israel's border with Egypt coming from civil war in Sudan and Eritrea		Gaza War (Operation Protective Edge) (2014)		Escalation of violence in territories, fear of new intifada		Nationality Law passed; protests throughout country, including by Druze	
					Growth in the Israeli film industry culminates with 1.6 million ticket sales in Israel (2014)				David Grossman wins British Man Booker Prize for literature	
Jews	Rise in antisemitic attacks in Malmo, Sweden, include burning of synagogue; Jews begin to leave city	*Etgar Keret (b. 1967): Israeli writer known for short stories and graphic novels*		Sarcelles riots (France): Jewish businesses attacked with clubs and metal bars; Jewish Defense League forms line around synagogue to protect it (2014)			Increasing questions about antisemitism in the British Labour Party lead to Chakrabarti inquiry in 2016; findings rejected by British Jewish community due to unwillingness to accept evidence submissions; concerns that leader Jeremy Corbyn is unwilling to confront issue leads to the three Jewish newspapers publishing same editorial in unprecedented act (2006)		
				Hostages taken at the Porte de Vincennes siege of a kosher supermarket in France, part of a string of antisemitic attacks (2015)				United States excludes Jews in official statement on Holocaust Memorial Day, causing outrage (2017)		
				Jihadist kills guard outside main synagogue in Copenhagen during services (2015)						
Eastern Europe / Russia	New START signed between Russia and United States, reducing nuclear stockpiles (2010)									
Western Europe		*Hamy Abu Assad (b. 1961): Dutch-Palestinian film director*		200,000 French citizens live in Israel; the rise of antisemitism in France triggers wave of French Aliyah	10,000 Jews migrate to Israel from western Europe, largest number since 1948 (2015)				Netta wins Eurovision song contest with "Toy" (2018)	
Aliyah						Significant rise in Aliyah rates from 2014 onward				

Selected Bibliography

This selected bibliography offers suggestions for both primary and secondary texts, building on those suggested in the essays. This selection is useful both for student reading assignments and faculty preparing courses. All texts are in English or English translation (or for films, with English subtitles). Given that Israeli songs rarely come with subtitles, none are listed in the primary materials. However, the secondary sources on Israeli music list a number of artists whose music can be found online, on YouTube or through iTunes. Amy Horowitz's book *Mediterranean Israeli Music and the Politics of the Aesthetic* (Detroit: Wayne State University Press, 2010) comes with a CD that is a valuable resource for class use.

Primary Sources

HISTORICAL DOCUMENTS

Dowty, Alan, ed. *The Israel-Palestine Reader*. Cambridge, UK: Polity Press, 2019.
Hertzberg, Arthur, ed. *The Zionist Idea: A Historical Analysis and Reader*. Garden City, NY: Doubleday, 1959.
Kaplan, Eran, and Derek J. Penslar, eds. *The Origins of Israel, 1882–1948: A Documentary History*. Madison: University of Wisconsin Press, 2011.
Laqueur, Walter, ed. *The Israel-Arab Reader: A Documentary History of the Middle East Conflict*. 8th ed. New York: Penguin Books, 2016.
Rabinovich, Itamar, and Jehuda Reinharz, eds. *Israel in the Middle East: Documents and Readings on Society, Politics, and Foreign Relations, Pre-1948 to the Present*. 2nd ed. Waltham, MA: Brandeis University Press, 2008.
Smith, Charles, ed. *Palestine and the Arab-Israeli Conflict: A History with Documents*. 8th ed. Basingstoke, UK: Palgrave Macmillan, 2010.

LITERATURE

Multiauthor Edited Anthologies

Abu Saif, Atef, ed. *The Book of Gaza: A City in Short Fiction*. Manchester, UK: Comma, 2014.

Alareer, Refaat, ed. *Gaza Writes Back: Short Stories from Young Writers in Gaza, Palestine.* Charlottesville, VA: Just World Books, 2014.

Alcalay, Ammiel, ed. *Keys to the Garden: New Israeli Writing.* San Francisco: City Lights Books, 1996.

Alter, Robert, ed. *Modern Hebrew Literature.* West Orange, NJ: Behrman House, 1975.

al-Udhari, Abdullah, ed. *Modern Poetry of the Arab World.* Middlesex, UK: Penguin, 1986.

———, trans. *Victims of a Map: A Bilingual Anthology of Arabic Poetry.* London: Saqi Books, 1984.

Aruri, Naseer, and Edmund Ghareeb, eds. *Enemy of the Sun: Poetry of Palestinian Resistance.* Washington, DC: Drum and Spear, 1970.

Assadi, Jamal, ed. *The Story of a People: An Anthology of Palestinian Poets within the Green-Lines.* New York: Peter Lang, 2012.

Back, Rachel Tzvia, ed. *With an Iron Pen: Hebrew Protest Poetry 1984–2004.* Albany, NY: Excelsior Editions, 2009.

Bargad, Warren, and Stanley F. Chyet, eds. and trans. *Israeli Poetry: A Contemporary Anthology.* Bloomington: Indiana University Press 1986.

———, eds. *No Sign of Ceasefire: An Anthology of Contemporary Israeli Poetry.* Los Angeles: Skirball Cultural Centre, 2002.

Bell, Henry, and Sarah Irving, eds. *A Bird Is Not a Stone: An Anthology of Contemporary Palestinian Poetry.* Glasgow, UK: Freight Books, 2014.

Ben-Ezer, Ehud, ed. *Sleep Walkers and Other Stories: The Arab in Hebrew Fiction.* Boulder, CO: Lynne Rienner, 1999.

Burnshaw, Stanley, T. Carmi, Susan Glassman, Ariel Hirschfeld, and Ezra Spicehandler, eds. *The Modern Hebrew Poem Itself: A New and Updated Edition.* Detroit: Wayne State University Press, 2003.

Diament, Carol, and Lily Rattok, eds. *Ribcage: Israeli Women's Fiction.* New York: Hadassah, 1994.

Domb, Risa, ed. *New Women's Writing from Israel.* London: Vallentine Mitchell, 1996.

Dor, Moshe, and Barbara Goldberg, eds. *After the First Rain: Israeli Poems on War and Peace.* Syracuse, NY: Syracuse University Press, in association with Dryad, 1998.

Elmessiri, Abdelwahab M., ed. and trans. *The Palestinian Wedding: A Bilingual Anthology of Contemporary Palestinian Resistance Poetry.* Washington, DC: Three Continents, 1982.

Elmessiri, Nur, and Abdelwahab M. Elmessiri, eds. *A Land of Stone and Thyme: An Anthology of Palestinian Short Stories.* London: Quartet Books, 1996.

Glazer, Miriyam, ed. *Dreaming the Actual: Contemporary Fiction and Poetry by Israeli Women Writers.* Albany: SUNY Press, 2000.

Jayyusi, Salma Khadra, ed. *Anthology of Modern Palestinian Literature.* New York: Columbia University Press, 1992.

Keller, Tsipi, ed. and trans. *Poets on the Edge: An Anthology of Contemporary Hebrew Poetry.* Albany: State University of New York Press, 2008.

Nitzan, Tal, and Rachel Tzvia Back, eds. *With an Iron Pen: Twenty Years of Hebrew Protest Poetry.* Albany: State University of New York Press, 2009.

Raizen, Esther, ed. *No Rattling of Sabers: An Anthology of Israeli War Poetry.* Bilingual ed. Austin: Center for Middle Eastern Studies, University of Texas at Austin, 1995.

Ravikovitch, Dalia, ed. *The New Israeli Writers: Short Stories of the First Generation.* New York: Funk and Wagnalls, 1969.

Wallace, Naomi, and Ismail Khalidi, eds. *Inside/Outside: Six Plays from Palestine and the Diaspora.* New York: Theatre Communications Group, 2015.

Watts, Irene N., ed. *A Terrible Truth: Anthology of Holocaust Drama.* Vol. 1. Toronto: Playwrights Canada, 2004.

Single-Author Fiction, Poetry, Drama, and Memoir

Abdelrazaq, Leila. *Baddawi.* Charlottesville, VA: Just World Books, 2015.

Alcalay, Ammiel., eds. *Keys to the Garden: New Israeli Writing.* San Francisco: City Lights Books, 1996.

al-Qasim, Samih. *All Faces but Mine: The Poetry of Samih al-Qasim.* Translated by Abdulwahid Lu'lu'a. Syracuse: Syracuse University Press, 2015.

———. *Sadder than Water: New and Selected Poems.* Translated by Nazih Kassis. Jerusalem: Ibis, 2006.

Amichai, Yehuda. *Not of This Time, Not of This Place.* New York: Harper and Row, 1968.

———. *Poems of Jerusalem.* New York: Schocken, 1987.

———. *The Selected Poetry of Yehuda Amichai.* Berkeley: University of California Press, 2013.

Amichai, Yehuda, and Benjamin Harshav. *Yehuda Amichai: A Life of Poetry, 1948–1994.* New York: HarperCollins, 1995.

Ashery, Oreet, and Larissa Sansoor. *The Novel of Nonel and Vovel.* New York: Charta, 2009.

Behar, Almog. "Ana Min Al Yahoud—I'm One of the Jews." *Ha'aretz Magazine* 29 (2005): 24–26.

Castel-Bloom, Orly, and Dalya Bilu. *Dolly City.* Champaign, IL: Dalkey Archive, 2010.

Darwish, Mahmoud. "Edward Said: A Contrapuntal Reading: Translated by Mona Anis." *Cultural Critique*, no. 67 (2007): 175–82.

———. *If I Were Another: Poems.* New York: Macmillan, 2009.

———. *In the Presence of Absence.* Brooklyn, NY: Archipelago, 2012.

———. *Memory for Forgetfulness: August, Beirut, 1982.* Berkeley: University of California Press, 2013.

———. *Unfortunately, It Was Paradise: Selected Poems.* Berkeley: University of California Press, 2013.

Delisle, Guy. *Jerusalem: Chronicles from the Holy City.* New York: Farrar, Straus and Giroux, 2012.

El-youssef, Samir. *The Illusion of Return.* Brooklyn, NY: Melville House, 2008.

———. "The Levant: Zone of Culture or Conflict?" *Levantine Review* 1, no. 2 (2012): 200–204.

———. *A Treaty of Love: A Novel.* London: Halban, 2008.

Gilad, Seliktar. *Farm 54.* Wisbech, UK: Fanfare, 2011.

Glidden, Sarah. *How to Understand Israel in 60 Days or Less*. Montreal: Drawn and Quarterly, 2016.
Gouri, Haim, and Stanley F. Chyet. *Words in My Lovesick Blood = Milim Be-Dami Ha-Holeh Ahavah*. Detroit: Wayne State University Press, 1996.
Grossman, David. *Sleeping on a Wire: Conversations with Palestinians in Israel*. New York: Farrar, Straus and Giroux, 2003.
———. *The Smile of the Lamb*. New York: Macmillan, 1990.
———. *The Yellow Wind*. New York: Random House, 2016.
Halkin, Hillel. *A Strange Death*. New York: Toby, 2010.
Jayyusi, Salma Khadra, and Trevor Le Gassick. *The Secret Life of Saeed: The Pessoptimist*. Northampton, MA: Interlink Books, 2002.
Kanafani, Ghassan. *Men in the Sun: And Other Palestinian Stories*. Washington, DC: Three Continents, 1995.
———. *Palestine's Children: Returning to Haifa and Other Stories*. Boulder, CO: Lynne Rienner, 2000.
Kashua, Sayed. *Dancing Arabs*. New York: Grove, 2004.
———. *Let It Be Morning*. New York: Black Cat, 2006.
———. *Second Person Singular*. New York: Grove, 2012.
Keret, Etgar. *Kneller's Happy Campers*. New York: Random House, 2009.
———. "Pastrami." *New Yorker*, November 20, 2012.
Keret, Etgar, and Samir El-youssef. *Gaza Blues: Different Stories*. Sydney: Picador Australia, 2006.
Keret, Etgar, and Assaf Hanuka. *Pizzeria Kamikaze*. Gainesville, FL: Alternative Comics, 2006.
Keret, Etgar, and Miriam Shlesinger. *Suddenly, a Knock on the Door*. New York: Farrar, Straus and Giroux, 2012.
Keret, Etgar, Miriam Shlesinger, and Sondra Silverston. *The Nimrod Flipout*. New York: Farrar, Straus and Giroux, 2006.
Khadra, Yasmina. *The Attack*. New York: Nan A. Talese / Doubleday, 2005.
Khalifeh, Sahar. *The Inheritance*. Oxford: Oxford University Press, 2005.
———. *Wild Thorns*. London: Al Saqi, 1985.
Koestler, Arthur. *Thieves in the Night: Chronicle of an Experiment*. New York: Macmillan, 1967.
Kurzweil, Amy. *Flying Couch: A Graphic Memoir*. New York: Carapault / Black Balloon, 2016.
Le Carré, John. *The Little Drummer Girl*. London: Hodder and Stoughton, 1983.
Lerner, Michael. *Best Contemporary Jewish Writing*. San Francisco: Jossey-Bass, 2001.
Libicki, Miriam. *Jobnik! An American Girl's Adventures in the Israeli Army*. Coquitlam, BC: Real Gone Girls Studios, 2008.
———. *Toward a Hot Jew*. Seattle: Fantagraphics Books, 2016.
Liebrecht, Savyon. *Apples from the Desert: Selected Stories*. New York: Feminist Press at CUNY, 2000.

Michael, Sami. *A Trumpet in the Wadi*. New York: Simon and Schuster, 2003.

Michael, Sami, and Imre Goldstein. "On Being an Iraqi-Jewish Writer in Israel." *Prooftexts* 4 (1984): 23-33.

Modan, Rutu. *Exit Wounds*. Montreal: Drawn and Quarterly, 2007.

Muhammad Ali, Taha. *Never Mind: Twenty Poems and a Story*. Jerusalem: Ibis Editions, 2000.

———. *So What: New and Selected Poems (with a Story), 1971–2005*. Translated by Peter Cole, Yahya Hijazi, and Gabriel Levin. Port Townsend, WA: Cooper Canyon, 2006.

Naji, Ali, and Joe Sacco. *A Child in Palestine: The Cartoons of Naji Al-Naji*. New York: Verso, 2009.

Nevo, Eshkol. *Homesick: A Novel*. Champaign, IL: Dalkey Archive, 2010.

Nusseibeh, Sari. *Once upon a Country: A Palestinian Life*. New York: Farrar, Straus and Giroux, 2007.

Oz, Amos. *How to Cure a Fanatic*. Princeton, NJ: Princeton University Press, 2010.

———. *In the Land of Israel: Essays*. Boston: Houghton Mifflin Harcourt, 1993.

———. *Israel, Palestine and Peace: Essays*. Boston: Houghton Mifflin Harcourt, 1995.

———. *Where the Jackals Howl and Other Stories*. New York: Random House, 1992.

Oz, Amos, and Nicholas Robert Michael De Lange. *My Michael*. Boston: Houghton Mifflin Harcourt, 2005.

Pascal, Julia. "Crossing Jerusalem." *Crossing Jerusalem and Other Plays*. London: Oberon, 2003.

Pekar, Harvey Waldman J. T. *Not the Israel My Parents Promised Me*. New York: Hill and Wang, 2012.

Ravikovitch, Dalia, and Chana Bloch. *A Dress of Fire*. London: Menard, 1976.

Ravikovitch, Dalia, Chana Bloch, and Chana Kronfeld. *Hovering at a Low Altitude: The Collected Poetry of Dahlia Ravikovitch*. New York: Norton, 2009.

Sacco, Joe. *Footnotes in Gaza*. New York: Metropolitan Books, 2009.

———. *Palestine*. Seattle, WA: Fantagraphics Books, 2001.

Shabtai, Aharon. *J'Accuse*. New York: New Directions, 2003.

Shamieh, Betty. "The Black Eyed." *The Black Eyed & Architecture*. New York: Broadway Play Publishing, 2009.

Shammas, Anton. *Arabesques*. New York: Harper and Row, 1988

Sobol, Joshua. *Ghetto*. Translated by David Lan. London: Hern, 1989.

———. "Shooting Magda (The Palestinian Girl)." In *Modern Jewish Plays*, edited by Jason Sherman. Toronto: Playwrights Canada, 2006.

Somekh, Sasson. *Baghdad, Yesterday: The Making of an Arab Jew*. Ibis Edition, 2007.

Spiegelman, Art. *Maus: A Survivor's Tale*. New York: Pantheon Books, 1986.

———. *Maus II: A Survivor's Tale: And Here My Troubles Began*. New York: Pantheon Books, 1991.

Tolan, Sandy. *The Lemon Tree, an Arab, a Jew, and the Heart of the Middle East*. New York: Bloomsbury, 2006.

Urian, Dan. *The Arab in Israeli Drama and Theatre.* Translated by Naomi Paz. Amsterdam: Harwood, 1997.

Watts, Irene N. *A Terrible Truth: Anthology of Holocaust Drama.* Vol. 1. Toronto: Playwrights Canada, 2004.

Yakin, Boaz, and Nick Bartozzi. *Jerusalem: A Family Portrait.* New York: First Second, 2013.

Yehoshua, Abraham B. *Facing the Forests.* Tel Aviv: Institute for the Translation of Hebrew Literature, 1968.

———. *The Lover.* London: Halban, 2012.

———. *Mr. Mani.* Boston: Houghton Mifflin Harcourt, 1993.

Yizhar, S. *Midnight Convoy and Other Stories.* Tel Aviv: Institute for the Translation of Hebrew Literature, 1969.

———. "The Prisoner." In *Modern Hebrew Literature*, edited by Robert Alter, 294–310. West Orange, NJ: Behrman House, 1975.

Zach, Natan. *The Static Element: Selected Poems of Natan Zach.* Translated by Peter Everine and Shulamit Yasny-Starkman. New York: Atheneum, 1982.

Zuabi, Amir Nizar. *I Am Yusuf and This Is My Brother.* London: Bloomsbury, 2010.

Secondary Sources

Abdel-Malek, Kamal. *The Rhetoric of Violence: Arab-Jewish Encounters in Contemporary Palestinian Literature and Film.* New York: Palgrave Macmillan, 2005.

Abdel-Malek, Kamal, and David C. Jacobson, eds. *Israeli and Palestinian Identities in History and Literature.* New York: St. Martin's, 1999.

Adoni, Hanna., Dan Caspi, and Akiba A. Cohen. *Media, Minorities, and Hybrid Identities: The Arab and Russian Communities in Israel.* Cresskill, NJ: Hampton, 2006.

Akash, Munir. *Mahmoud Darwish: The Adam of Two Edens.* Syracuse, NY: Syracuse University Press, 2000.

Alcalay, Ammiel. *After Jews and Arabs: Remaking Levantine Culture.* Minneapolis: University of Minnesota Press, 1993.

Almog, Oz. "From 'Blorit' to Ponytail: Israeli Culture Reflected in Popular Hairstyles." *Israel Studies* 8, no. 2 (2003): 82–117.

———. *The Sabra: The Creation of the New Jew.* Berkeley: University of California Press, 2000.

Alpher Yossi, *Periphery: Israel's Search for Middle East Allies.* Lanham, MD: Rowman and Littlefield, 2015.

Aly, Abdel Monem Said, Shai Feldman, and Khalil Shikaki, eds. *Arabs and Israelis: Conflict and Peacemaking in the Middle East.* New York: Macmillan, 2013.

Ankori, Gannit. *Palestinian Art.* London: Reaktion Books, 2013.

Ariel, Ari. "The Hummus Wars." *Gastronomica: The Journal of Food and Culture* 12, no. 1 (2012): 34–42.

———. *Jewish-Muslim Relations and Migration from Yemen to Palestine in the Late Nineteenth and Twentieth Centuries.* Boston: Brill, 2014.

———. "Mosaic or Melting Pot: The Transformation of Middle Eastern Jewish Foodways in Israel." In *The Global History of Jewish Foodways: A History*, edited by Hasia Diner and Simone Cinotto, 91–114. Lincoln: University of Nebraska Press, 2018.

Armbrust, Walter. *Mass Mediations New Approaches to Popular Culture in the Middle East and Beyond.* Berkeley: University of California Press, 2000.

Armstrong, Karen. *Jerusalem: One City, Three Faiths.* New York: Knopf, 1996.

Ashplant, T. G, Graham Dawson, and Michael Roper, eds. *The Politics of War Memory and Commemoration.* London; New York: Routledge, 2000.

Ashuri, Tamar. *The Arab-Israeli Conflict in the Media: Producing Shared Memory and National Identity in the Global Television Era.* New York: Palgrave Macmillan, 2010.

Avruch, Kevin, and Walter P. Zenner, eds. *Critical Essays on Israeli Society, Religion, and Government.* Albany: SUNY Press, 1997.

Azaryahu, Maoz, and Ilan Troen, eds. *Tel-Aviv, the First Century: Visions, Designs, Actualities.* Bloomington: Indiana University Press, 2011.

Ball, Anna. *Palestinian Literature and Film in Postcolonial Feminist Perspective.* New York and Abingdon: Routledge, 2012.

Barak-Erez, Daphne. *Outlawed Pigs: Law, Religion, and Culture in Israel.* Madison: University of Wisconsin Press, 2007.

Ben-Ami, Shlomo. *Scars of War, Wounds of Peace: The Israeli Arab Tragedy.* Oxford: Oxford University Press, 2007.

Ben-Ari, Eyal, and Yoram Bilu, eds. *Grasping Land: Space and Place in Contemporary Israeli Discourse and Experience.* Albany: SUNY Press, 1997.

Ben-Ari, Eyal, Zeev Lerer, Uzi Ben-Shalom, and Ariel Vainer. *Rethinking Contemporary Warfare: A Sociological View of the Al-Aqsa Intifada.* Albany: SUNY Press, 2010.

Ben-Shaul, Nitzan S. *A Violent World: TV News Images of Middle Eastern Terror and War.* Lanham, MD: Rowman and Littlefield, 2006.

Ben-Yehuda, Nachman. *The Masada Myth Collective Memory and Mythmaking in Israel.* Madison: University of Wisconsin Press, 1995.

Berg, Nancy E. *Exile from Exile: Israeli Writers from Iraq.* Albany: SUNY Press, 2012.

———. *More and More Equal: The Literary Works of Sami Michael.* Lanham, MD: Lexington Books, 2005.

Berger, Alan L. *Trialogue and Terror: Judaism, Christianity, and Islam after 9/11.* Eugene, OR: Wipf and Stock, 2012.

Berman, Russell A. "Beyond Engaged Literature: Samir El-youssef's the Illusion of Return." *Telos* 2017, no. 181 (2017): 198–203.

Bernard-Donals, Michael, and Janice W. Fernheimer, eds. *Jewish Rhetorics: History, Theory, Practice.* Waltham, MA: Brandeis University Press, 2014.

Bernstein, Deborah S. *Constructing Boundaries: Jewish and Arab Workers in Mandatory Palestine.* Albany: SUNY Press, 2000.

Bernstein, Deborah S. *Pioneers and Homemakers: Jewish Women in Pre-State Israel.* Albany: SUNY Press, 2012.

Bilu, Yoram, and Eliezer Witztum, 2000. "War-Related Loss and Suffering in Israeli Society: An Historical Perspective." *Israel Studies* 5, no. 2 (2000): 1-32.

Boullata, Kamal, and Mirène Ghossein. *The World of Rashid Hussein, a Palestinian Poet in Exile.* Detroit: Association of Arab-American University Graduates, 1979.

Brenner, Michael. *Zionism: A Brief History.* Princeton, NJ: M. Wiener, 2003.

Brenner, Rachel Feldhay. *Inextricably Bonded: Israeli Arab and Jewish Writers Re-visioning Culture.* Madison: Wisconsin University Press, 2003.

Caplan, Neil. *The Israel Palestine Conflict: Contested Histories.* Chichester, UK: Wiley-Blackwell, 2009.

Cleveland, William L. *A History of the Modern Middle East.* 4th ed. Boulder, CO: Westview, 2009.

Cohen, Hillel, and Haim Watzman. *Year Zero of the Arab-Israeli Conflict 1929.* Waltham, MA: Brandeis University Press, 2015.

Cohen, Jessica, Adriana X. Jacobs, and Adam Rovner. "Prose, Poetry, and the Heresy of Normalcy: New Voices in Contemporary Hebrew Literature." *World Literature Today* 89, nos. 3–4 (2015): 60–63.

Cohen, Nir. *Soldiers, Rebels, and Drifters: Gay Representation in Israeli Cinema.* Detroit: Wayne State University Press, 2012.

David, Joseph E., ed. *The State of Israel: Between Judaism and Democracy: A Compendium of Interviews and Articles.* Jerusalem: Israel Democracy Institute, 2003.

Dekel, Tal. "From First-Wave to Third-Wave Feminist Art in Israel: A Quantum Leap." *Israel Studies* 16, no. 1 (2011): 149–78.

———. *Transnational Identities: Women, Art and Migration in Contemporary Israel.* Detroit: Wayne State University Press, 2016.

Divine, Donna Robinson. *Exiled in the Homeland: Zionism and the Return to Mandate Palestine.* Austin: University of Texas Press, 2009.

Downey, Anthony. *Dissonant Archives: Contemporary Visual Culture and Competing Narratives in the Middle East.* London: I. B. Tauris, 2015.

Dowty, Alan. "Is Israel Democratic? Substance and Semantics in the Ethnic Democracy Debate." *Israel Studies* 4 (1999): 1–15.

———. *Israel/Palestine.* 4th ed. Cambridge, UK: Polity, 2017.

———. *The Jewish State: A Century Later; Updated with a New Preface.* Berkeley: University of California Press, 1998.

Eid, Muna Abu. *Mahmoud Darwish: Literature and the Politics of Palestinian Identity.* London: I. B. Tauris, 2016.

Eisenstadt, S. N. *The Absorption of Immigrants: A Comparative Study Based Mainly on the Jewish Community in Palestine and the State of Israel.* Glencoe, IL: Free Press, 1955.

———. *Israeli Society.* London: Weidenfeld and Nicolson, 1967.

Elad-Bouskila, Ami. *Modern Palestinian Literature and Culture*. New York: Routledge, 2014.

Elizur, Yuval, and Lawrence Malkin. *The War Within: Israel's Ultra-Orthodox Threat to Democracy and the Nation*. New York: Overlook, 2013.

Eshel, Ruth. "A Creative Process in Ethiopian-Israeli Dance: Eskesta Dance Theater and Beta Dance Troupe." *Dance Chronicle* 34, no. 3 (2011): 352–87.

Farsakh, Leila. "The One-State Solution and the Israeli-Palestinian Conflict: Palestinian Challenges and Prospects." *Middle East Journal* 65, no. 1 (2011): 55–71.

Feige, Michael. "Introduction: Rethinking Israeli Memory and Identity." *Israel Studies* 7, no. 2 (2002): v–xiv.

———. *One Space, Two Places: Gush Emunim, Peace Now and the Construction of Israeli Space*. Jerusalem: Magnes, 2002. In Hebrew.

———. "Peace Now and the Legitimation Crisis of 'Civil Militarism.'" *Israel Studies* 3, no. 1 (1998): 85–111.

———. *Settling in the Hearts: Jewish Fundamentalism in the Occupied Territories*. Detroit: Wayne State University Press, 2009.

Feige, Michael, and Eyal Ben-Ari. "Card Games and an Israeli Army Unit: An Interpretive Case Study." *Armed Forces & Society* 17, no. 3 (1991): 429–48.

Feldman, Keith P. *A Shadow over Palestine: The Imperial Life of Race in America*. Minneapolis: University of Minnesota Press, 2015.

Fernheimer, Janice W. *Stepping into Zion: Hatzaad Harishon, Black Jews, and the Remaking of Jewish Identity*. Tuscaloosa: University of Alabama Press. 2014.

Fibich, Felix, and Sara Levi-Tanai, eds. *Seeing Israeli and Jewish Dance*. Detroit: Wayne State University Press, 2011.

Fischbach, Michael R. *The Middle East in Crisis*. New York: Foreign Affairs, 2002.

———. *The Peace Process and Palestinian Refugee Claims: Addressing Claims for Property Compensation and Restitution*. Washington, DC: United States Institute of Peace Press, 2006.

Freedman, Robert O. "The Bush Administration and the Arab-Israeli Conflict: The Record of Its First Four Years." *Middle East Review of International Affairs* 9, no. 1 (2005). www.rubincenter.org/meria/2005/03/freedman.pdf

———. "George W. Bush, Barack Obama and the Arab-Israeli Conflict from 2001 to 2011." In *Israel and the United States*, 36–78. New York: Routledge, 2018.

———. *Israel's First Fifty Years*. Gainesville: University Press of Florida, 2000.

Freire, Paulo. *Pedagogy of the Oppressed*. New York: Bloomsbury, 2018.

Friedman, Thomas L. *From Beirut to Jerusalem*. New York: Macmillan, 1995.

Fuchs, Esther, ed. *Israeli Feminist Scholarship: Gender, Zionism, and Difference*. Austin: University of Texas Press, 2014.

———, ed. *Israeli Women's Studies: A Reader*. New Brunswick, NJ: Rutgers University Press, 2005.

Fuhrer, Ronald. *Israeli Painting: From Post-Impressionism to Post-Zionism*. New York: Overlook, 1998.

Furani, Khaled. *Silencing the Sea: Secular Rhythms in Palestinian Poetry.* Stanford, CA: Stanford University Press, 2012.

Gavison, Ruth. *Conditions for the Prosperity of the State of Israel: "Where there is no vision, the people cast off restraint"—A Meta-Purpose for Israel and its Implications.* Haifa: Metzilah and the Samuel Neamam Institute, The Technion, 2007.

———. "'Jewish and Democratic'? A Rejoinder to the Ethnic Democracy Debate." *Israel Studies* 4 (1999): 44-72.

Gelvin, James L. *The Israel-Palestine Conflict: One Hundred Years of War.* Cambridge: Cambridge University Press, 2005.

Gerner, Deborah J. *One Land, Two Peoples: The Conflict over Palestine.* New York: Routledge, 2018.

Gertz, Nurith. *Myths in Israeli Culture: Captives of a Dream.* London: Vallentine Mitchell, 2000.

Gluzman, Michael. *The Politics of Canonicity: Lines of Resistance in Modernist Hebrew Poetry.* Stanford, CA: Stanford University Press, 2002.

Golan, Galia. *Israel and Palestine: Peace Plans and Proposals from Oslo to Disengagement.* Princeton, NJ: Markus Wiener, 2008.

Graff, Gerald. *Beyond the Culture Wars: How Teaching the Conflicts Can Revitalize American Education.* New York: Norton, 1993.

Gribetz, Jonathan Marc. *Defining Neighbors: Religion, Race, and the Early Zionist-Arab Encounter.* Princeton, NJ: Princeton University Press, 2014.

Grob, Leonard, and John K. Roth. *Encountering the Stranger: A Jewish-Christian-Muslim Trialogue.* Seattle: University of Washington Press, 2013.

Hahn Tapper, Aaron J., and Oren Kroll-Zeldin. "Paulo Freire and the Israeli-Palestinian Conflict: The Pedagogy of a Social Justice and Experiential Educational Program in Israel and Palestine." *Revista Internacional de Educación para la Justicia Social* 4, no. 1 (2015): 71–88.

Halper, Jeff. *An Israeli in Palestine: Resisting Dispossession, Redeeming Israel.* London: Pluto, 2010.

Harris, Rachel S. "Between the Backpack and the Tent: Home, Zionism, and a New Generation in Eshkol Nevo's Novels *Homesick* and *Neuland*." *Shofar* 33, no. 4 (2015): 36–59.

———. "Forgetting *The Forgotten Ones*: The Case of Haim Gouri's 'Hanishkahim.'" *Journal of Modern Jewish Studies* 8, no. 2 (2009): 199–214.

———. *An Ideological Death: Suicide in Israeli Literature.* Evanston: Northwestern University Press, 2014.

———. "Israeli Literature in the 21st Century: The Transcultural Generation: An Introduction." *Shofar* 33, no. 4 (2015): 1–14.

———. "Palestinian Counter-Hero: Samir El-youssef's Anglo-Palestinian Fiction." *Telos* 2017, no. 181 (2017): 176–97.

———. *Warriors, Witches, Whores: Women in Israeli Cinema.* Detroit: Wayne State University Press, 2017.

Harris, Rachel S., and Ranen Omer-Sherman, eds. *Narratives of Dissent: War in Contemporary Israeli Arts and Culture*. Detroit: Wayne State University Press, 2013.

Hatuka, Tali. *Violent Acts and Urban Space in Contemporary Tel Aviv: Revisioning Moments*. Austin: University of Texas Press, 2010.

Helman, Anat. *Becoming Israeli: National Ideals and Everyday Life in the 1950s*. Waltham, MA: Brandeis University Press, 2014.

———, ed. *Jews and Their Foodways*. New York: Oxford University Press, 2015.

———. *Young Tel Aviv: A Tale of Two Cities*. Waltham, MA: Brandeis University Press, 2012.

Herman, Peter C., ed. *Literature and Terrorism*. Cambridge: Cambridge University Press, 2018

Hertzog, Esther, Orit Abuhav, Harvey E. Goldberg, and Emanuel Marx. *Perspectives on Israeli Anthropology*. Detroit: Wayne State University Press, 2009.

Horowitz, Amy. *Mediterranean Israeli Music and the Politics of the Aesthetic*. Detroit: Wayne State University Press, 2010.

Ibish, Hussein. "Why Israel Simultaneously Both Is and Is Not a 'Jewish State.'" Miftah.org, March 20, 2010. www.miftah.org/Display.cfm?DocId=21890&CategoryId=5.

Israëlian, Viktor Levonovich. *Inside the Kremlin during the Yom Kippur War*. University Park: Penn State University Press, 1995

Izraeli, Dafna N. "The Zionist Women's Movement in Palestine, 1911–1927: A Sociological Analysis." *Signs: Journal of Women in Culture and Society* 7, no. 1 (1981): 87–114.

Jamal, Amal. *The Arab Public Sphere in Israel: Media Space and Cultural Resistance*. Bloomington: Indiana University Press, 2009.

Kaplan, Eran. *Beyond Zionism*. Albany: SUNY Press, 2017.

Kaschl, Elke. *Dance and Authenticity in Israel and Palestine: Performing the Nation*. Boston: Brill, 2003.

Keren, Zvi. *Contemporary Israeli Music*. Tel Aviv: Bar Ilan University Press, 1980.

Khalidi, Rashid. *Palestinian Identity: The Construction of Modern National Consciousness*. New York: Columbia University Press, 2010.

Khalidi, Walid, and Sharif S. Elmusa. *All That Remains: The Palestinian Villages Occupied and Depopulated by Israel in 1948*. Washington, DC: Institute for Palestine Studies, 1992.

Kimmerling, Baruch. *Clash of Identities: Explorations in Israeli and Palestinian Societies*. New York: Columbia University Press, 2008.

———. *The Interrupted System: Israeli Civilians in War and Routine Times*. New Brunswick, NJ: Transaction Books, . 1985.

———. *The Israeli State and Society: Boundaries and Frontiers*. Albany: SUNY Press, 1989.

———. *Social Interruption and Besieged Societies: The Case of Israel*. Amherst, NY: Council on International Studies, SUNY at Buffalo, 1979.

Kimmerling, Baruch, and Joel S. Migdal. *The Palestinian People: A History*. Cambridge, MA: Harvard University Press, 2003.

Klein, Menachem. *Lives in Common: Arabs and Jews in Jerusalem, Jaffa and Hebron.* London: Hurst, 2014.

Knopf-Newman, Marcy Jane. *The Politics of Teaching Palestine to Americans: Addressing Pedagogical Strategies.* New York: Springer, 2011.

Kronfeld, Chana. *The Full Severity of Compassion: The Poetry of Yehuda Amichai.* Stanford, CA: Stanford University Press, 2015.

Kronish, Amy. *Israeli Film: A Reference Guide.* Westport, CT: Praeger, 2003.

Kurtzer, Daniel C. *Pathways to Peace: America and the Arab-Israeli Conflict.* New York: Palgrave Macmillan, 2012.

Lassner, Jacob, and S. Ilan Troen. *Jews and Muslims in the Arab World: Haunted by Pasts Real and Imagined.* Lanham, MD: Rowman and Littlefield, 2007.

Lebow, Alissa. *The Cinema of Me: The Self and Subjectivity in First Person Documentary.* London: Wallflower, 2012.

Lederach, John Paul. *The Moral Imagination: The Art and Soul of Building Peace.* Oxford: Oxford University Press, 2005.

Lesch, David W. *The Arab-Israeli Conflict: A History.* New York: Oxford University Press, 2008.

Levy, Lital. *Poetic Trespass: Writing between Hebrew and Arabic in Israel/Palestine.* Princeton, NJ: Princeton University Press, 2014.

Lockard, Joe. "Somewhere between Arab and Jew: Ethnic Re-Identification in Modern Hebrew Literature." *Middle Eastern Literatures* 5, no. 1 (2002): 49–62.

Lockman, Zachary. *Comrades and Enemies: Arab and Jewish Workers in Palestine, 1906–1948.* Berkeley: University of California Press, 1996.

Lomsky-Feder, Edna, and Eyal Ben-Ari. *The Military and Militarism in Israeli Society.* Albany: SUNY Press, 1999.

Loshitzky, Yosefa. *Identity Politics on the Israeli Screen.* Austin: University of Texas Press, 2001.

Lustick, Ian. "Two-State Illusion." *New York Times*, September 14, 2013.

Lynch, Paul, Jennie Germann Molz, Alison McIntosh, Peter Lugosi, and Conrad Lashley. "Theorizing Hospitality." *Hospitality & Society* 1, no. 1 (2011): 3–24.

Mann, Barbara E. *A Place in History. Modernism, Tel Aviv, and the Creation of Jewish Urban Space.* Stanford, CA: Stanford University Press, 2006.

Mansbach, Richard W., and Kirsten L. Taylor. *Challenges for America in the Middle East.* Thousand Oaks, CA: CQ, 2016.

Marcus, Alan S., Scott Alan Metzger, Richard J. Paxton, and Jeremy D. Stoddard. *Teaching History with Film: Strategies for Secondary Social Studies.* New York: Routledge, 2018.

Martegani, Fiammetta. *The Israeli Defence Forces' Representation in Israeli Cinema: Did David Betray His Soldiers?* Newcastle upon Tyne, UK: Cambridge Scholars, 2017.

Matar, H. "The Curse of Topicality: Samir El-youssef, *In the Country of Men*." *New Statesman* 135, no. 4803 (2006): 58.

Mattawa, Khaled. *Mahmoud Darwish: The Poet's Art and His Nation.* Syracuse, NY: Syracuse University Press, 2014.

Mazie, Steven V. *Israel's Higher Law: Religion and Liberal Democracy in the Jewish State*. Lanham, MD: Lexington Books, 2006.

McCloud, Scott. *Understanding Comics: The Invisible Art*. Northampton, MA: Kitchen Sink, 1993.

Migdal, Joel S. *Shifting Sands: The United States in the Middle East*. New York: Columbia University Press, 2014.

———. *Through the Lens of Israel: Explorations in State and Society*. Albany: SUNY Press, 2001.

Mizrachi, Beverly. *Paths to Middle-Class Mobility among Second-Generation Moroccan Immigrant Women in Israel*. Detroit: Wayne State University Press, 2013.

Morag, Raya. *Waltzing with Bashir: Perpetrator Trauma and Cinema*. London: I. B. Tauris, 2013.

Morris, Benny. *The Birth of the Palestinian Refugee Problem Revisited*. 2nd ed. Cambridge: Cambridge University Press, 2004.

———. *1948: A History of the First Arab-Israeli War*. New Haven, CT: Yale University Press, 2008.

Nassar, Hala Khamis, and Najat Rahman, eds. *Mahmoud Darwish: Exile's Poet*. Northampton, MA: Olive Branch, 2008.

Nelson, Cary. *Dreams Deferred: A Concise Guide to the Israeli-Palestinian Boycott and the Movement to Boycott Israel*. Bloomington: Indiana University Press / MLA Members for Scholars' Rights, 2016.

Nelson, Cary, and Gabriel Noah Brahm, eds. *The Case against Academic Boycotts of Israel*. Detroit: Wayne State University Press, 2014.

Neumann, Boaz. *Land and Desire in Early Zionism*. Waltham, MA: Brandeis University Press, 2011

O'Brien, Conor Cruise. *The Siege: The Saga of Israel and Zionism*. London: Weidenfeld and Nicolson, 1986.

Ofrat, Gideon. *One Hundred Years of Art in Israel*. New York: Basic Books, 1998.

Omer-Sherman, Ranen. *Imagining the Kibbutz: Visions of Utopia in Literature and Film*. University Park: Penn State University Press, 2016.

———. *Israel in Exile: Jewish Writing and the Desert*. Urbana: University of Illinois Press, 2006.

———. "Paradoxes of Jewish and Muslim Identities in Israeli Short Stories." *Peace Review* 22, no. 4 (2010): 440–52.

Oren, Michael B. *Six Days of War: June 1967 and the Making of the Modern Middle East*. New York: Ballantine Books, 2003.

Oren, Tasha G. *Demon in the Box: Jews, Arabs, Politics, and Culture in the Making of Israeli Television*. New Brunswick, NJ: Rutgers University Press, 2004.

Pappe, Ilan. *A History of Modern Palestine: One Land, Two Peoples*. Cambridge: Cambridge University Press, 2004.

Parfitt, Tudor, and Yulia Egorova, eds. *Jews, Muslims, and Mass Media: Mediating the "Other."* London: Routledge Curzon, 2004.

Patel, Eboo. *Interfaith Leadership: A Primer*. Boston: Beacon, 2016.
Peleg, Yaron. *Israeli Culture between the Two Intifadas a Brief Romance*. Austin: University of Texas Press, 2008.
Penslar, Derek J., and Anita Shapira. *Israeli Historical Revisionism: From Left to Right*. New York: Routledge, 2013.
Peri, Yoram. *Telepopulism: Media and Politics in Israel*. Stanford, CA: Stanford University Press, 2004.
Peteet, Julie. "Male Gender and Rituals of Resistance in the Palestinian Intifada: A Cultural Politics of Violence." *American Ethnologist* 21, no. 1 (1994): 31–49.
Rabinovich, Itamar. *The Lingering Conflict: Israel, the Arabs, and the Middle East, 1948–2011*. Washington, DC: Brookings Institution Press, 2011.
Ram, Moriel, and Meirav Aharon Gutman. "Strongholding the Synagogue to Stronghold the City: Urban-Religious Configurations in an Israeli Mixed-City." *Tijdschrift voor Economische en Sociale Geografie* 108, no. 5 (2017): 641–55.
Ram, Uri. *The Globalization of Israel: McWorld in Tel Aviv, Jihad in Jerusalem*. New York: Routledge, 2013.
Ramraz-Ra'ukh, Gilah. *The Arab in Israeli Literature*. London: I. B. Tauris, 1989.
Raviv, Yael. *Falafel Nation: Cuisine and the Making of National Identity in Israel*. Lincoln: University of Nebraska Press, 2015.
Regev, Motti, and Edwin Seroussi. *Popular Music and National Culture in Israel*. Berkeley: University of California Press, 2004.
Reisz, Matthew. "Samir El-youssef: At Home with the Heretic." *Independent*, January 19, 2007.
Roniger, Luis, and Michael Feige. "From Pioneer to Freire: The Changing Models of Generalized Exchange in Israel." *European Journal of Sociology/Archives Européennes de Sociologie* 33, no. 2 (1992): 280–307.
Rosenberg-Friedman, Lilach. *Birthrate Politics in Zion: Judaism, Nationalism, and Modernity under the British Mandate*. Bloomington: Indiana University Press, 2017.
Rosenthal, Donna. *The Israelis: Ordinary People in an Extraordinary Land*. New York: Simon and Schuster, 2003.
Rotberg, Robert I., ed. *Israeli and Palestinian Narratives of Conflict: History's Double Helix*. Bloomington: Indiana University Press, 2006.
Rowland, Robert C. *Shared Land/Conflicting Identity: Trajectories of Israeli and Palestinian Symbol Use*. East Lansing: Michigan State University Press, 2003.
Rowland, Robert C., and David A. Frank. "Mythic Rhetoric and Rectification in the Israeli-Palestinian Conflict." *Communication Studies* 62, no. 1 (2011): 41–57.
Rozin, Orit. *A Home for All Jews: Citizenship, Rights, and National Identity in the New Israeli State*. Waltham, MA: Brandeis University Press, 2016.
———. *The Rise of the Individual in 1950s Israel: A Challenge to Collectivism*. Waltham, MA: Brandeis University Press, 2011.
Rubin, Avshalom. *The Limits of the Land: How the Struggle for the West Bank Shaped the Arab Israeli Conflict*. Bloomington: Indiana University Press, 2017.

Sabbagh, Suha. *Palestinian Women of Gaza and the West Bank*. Bloomington: Indiana University Press, 1998.

Sa'di, Ahmad H., and Lila Abu-Lughod. *Nakba: Palestine, 1948, and the Claims of Memory*. New York: Columbia University Press, 2007.

Said, Edward W. *Culture and Imperialism*. New York: Vintage, 2012.

———. "Permission to Narrate." *Journal of Palestine Studies* 13, no. 3 (1984): 27–48.

———. *The Question of Palestine*. London: Routledge and Kegan Paul, 1980.

Sayigh, Yezid. "Arafat and the Anatomy of a Revolt." *Survival* 43, no. 3 (2001): 47–60.

Schulman, Sarah. *Israel/Palestine and the Queer International*. Durham, NC: Duke University Press, 2012.

Schulze, Kirsten E. *The Arab-Israeli Conflict*. New York: Routledge, 2013.

Segev, Tom. *The Seventh Million: The Israelis and the Holocaust*. New York: Hill and Wang, 1993.

Segev, Tom, and Arlen Neal Weinstein. *1949: The First Israelis*. New York: Free Press, 1986.

Sela, Avraham. "Civil Society, the Military, and National Security: The Case of Israel's Security Zone in South Lebanon." *Israel Studies* 12, no. 1 (2007): 53–78.

Sela, Avraham, and Alon Kadish, eds. *The War of 1948: Representations of Israeli and Palestinian Memories and Narratives*. Bloomington: Indiana University Press, 2016.

Sered, Susan. *What Makes Women Sick? Maternity Modesty, and Militarism in Israeli Society*. Waltham, MA: Brandeis University Press, 2000.

Shafir, Gershon. *A Half Century of Occupation: Israel, Palestine, and the World's Most Intractable Conflict*. Berkeley: University of California Press, 2017.

———. *Land, Labor, and the Origins of the Israeli-Palestinian Conflict, 1882–1914*. Cambridge: Cambridge University Press, 1989.

Shamir, Ronen. *The Colonies of Law: Colonialism, Zionism and Law in Early Mandate Palestine*. Cambridge: Cambridge University Press, 2000.

Shapira, Anita. *Israel: A History*. Hanover, NH: University Press of New England, 2012.

———. *Land and Power*. Oxford: Oxford University Press, 1992.

Shapira, Anita, and Ora Wiskind-Elper. "Politics and Collective Memory: The Debate over the 'New Historians' in Israel." *History and Memory* 7, no. 1 (1995): 9–40.

Shapiro, Yonathan. *The Formative Years of the Israeli Labor Party: The Organisation of Power, 1919–1930*. Beverly Hills, CA: Sage, 1976.

Shavit, Ari. *My Promised Land: The Triumph and Tragedy of Israel*. New York: Spiegel and Grau, 2013.

Shaw, Tony. *Cinematic Terror: A Global History of Terrorism On Film*. London: Bloomsbury, 2015.

Sheffer, Gabriel, and Oren Barak. *Israel's Security Networks: A Theoretical and Comparative Perspective*. Cambridge: Cambridge University Press, 2013.

———, eds. *Militarism and Israeli Society*. Bloomington: Indiana University Press, 2010.

Shemer, Yaron. *Identity, Place, and Subversion in Contemporary Mizrahi Cinema in Israel*. Ann Arbor: University of Michigan Press, 2013.

Shlaim, Avi. *Israel and Palestine: Reappraisals, Revisions, Refutations*. London: Verso, 2009.

Shohat, Ella. *Israeli Cinema: East/West and the Politics of Representation*. 2nd ed. London: I. B. Tauris, 2010.

Shoshan, Malkit. *Atlas of the Conflict: Israel-Palestine*. Rotterdam: Uitgeverij 010, 2010.

Smooha, Sammy. "Is Israel Western?" In *Comparing Modernities: Pluralism versus Homogeneity: Essays in Homage to Shmuel N. Eisenstadt*, edited by Eliezer Ben-Rafael and Yitzhak Sternberg, 413–42. Boston: Brill, 2005.

———. "The Model of Ethnic Democracy: Israel as a Jewish and Democratic State." *Nations and Nationalism* 8 (2002): 475–503.

Soloveichik, Aaron. "The State of Israel: A Torah Perspective." *Tradition: A Journal of Orthodox Jewish Thought* 25, no. 2 (1990–90): 1–11.

Spiegel, Nina S. *Embodying Hebrew Culture: Aesthetics, Athletics, and Dance in the Jewish Community of Mandate Palestine*. Detroit Wayne State University Press, 2013.

———. "New Israeli Rituals: Inventing a Folk Dance Tradition." In *Revisioning Ritual: Jewish Traditions in Transition*, edited by Simon J. Bronner, 392–418. Portland, OR: Littman Library of Jewish Civilization, 2011.

Spiro, Melford E. *Gender and Culture: Kibbutz Women Revisited*. New York: Routledge, 2017.

Stein, Rebecca L., and Ted Swedenburg, eds. *Palestine, Israel, and the Politics of Popular Culture*. Durham, NC: Duke University Press, 2005.

Strum, Philippa. "Women and the Politics of Religion in Israel." *Human Rights Quarterly* 11 (1989): 483–503.

Sucharov, Mira. *The International Self: Psychoanalysis and the Search for Israeli-Palestinian Peace*. Albany: SUNY Press, 2005.

Susser, Asher. *Israel, Jordan and Palestine: The Two-State Imperative*. Waltham, MA: Brandeis University Press, 2012.

———. *The Rise of Hamas in Palestine and the Crisis of Secularism in the Arab World* Waltham, MA: Brandeis University Press, 2010.

Szobel, Ilana. *A Poetics of Trauma: The Work of Dahlia Ravikovitch*. Waltham, MA: Brandeis University Press, 2013.

Talmon, Miri, and Yaron Peleg, eds. *Israeli Cinema: Identities in Motion*. Austin: University of Texas Press, 2011.

Taub, Michael. "The Challenge to Popular Myth and Conventions in Recent Israeli Drama." *Modern Judaism* 17, no. 2 (1997): 133–62.

Tayler, Marilyn R. "The Transformation from Multidisciplinarity to Interdisciplinarity: A Case Study of a Course Involving the Status of Arab Citizens of Israel." *Issues in Interdisciplinary Studies*, no. 32 (2014): 28–52.

Tessler, Mark A. *A History of the Israeli-Palestinian Conflict*. 2nd ed. Bloomington: Indiana University Press, 2009.

Troen, S. Ilan. "De-Judaizing the Homeland: Academic Politics in Rewriting the History of Palestine." *Israel Affairs* 13, no. 4 (2007): 872–84.

———. *Imagining Zion: Dreams, Designs, and Realities in a Century of Jewish Settlement*. New Haven, CT: Yale University Press, 2003.

Troen, S. Ilan, and Rachel Fish, eds. *Essential Israel: Essays for the 21st Century*. Bloomington: Indiana University Press, 2017.

Trottier, Julie. "Water and the Challenge of Palestinian Institution Building." *Journal of Palestine Studies* 29, no. 2 (2000): 35–50.

Turki, Fawaz. "The Future of a Past: Fragments from the Palestinian Dream." *Journal of Palestine Studies* 6, no. 3 (1977): 66–76.

Uzer, Umut. "Turkish-Israeli Relations: Their Rise and Fall." *Middle East Policy* 20, no. 1 (2013): 97–110.

Weiss, Susan M., and Netty C. Gross-Horowitz. *Marriage and Divorce in the Jewish State* Waltham, MA: Brandeis University Press, 2013.

Wittes, Tamara Cofman. *How Israelis and Palestinians Negotiate: A Cross-Cultural Analysis of the Oslo Peace Process*. Washington, DC: United States Institute of Peace Press, 2005.

Yosef, Raz. *Beyond Flesh: Queer Masculinities and Nationalism in Israeli Cinema*. New Brunswick, NJ: Rutgers University Press, 2004.

———, eds. *Deeper than Oblivion: Trauma and Memory in Israeli Cinema*. New York: Bloomsbury, 2013.

———. *The Politics of Loss and Trauma in Contemporary Israeli Cinema*. New York: Routledge, 2011.

Yudkin, Leon I. *Escape into Siege: A Survey of Israeli Literature Today*. Vol. 1. London: Routledge and Kegan Paul, 1974.

Zalmona, Yigal. *A Century of Israeli Art*. Aldershot, UK: Lund Humphries, 2013.

Zanger, Anat. *Place, Memory and Myth in Contemporary Israeli Cinema*. London:: Vallentine Mitchell, 2012.

Zerubavel, Yael. "The Forest as a National Icon: Literature, Politics, and the Archaeology of Memory." *Israel Studies* 1, no. 1 (1996): 60–99.

———. "The 'Mythological Sabra' and Jewish Past: Trauma, Memory, and Contested Identities." *Israel Studies* 7, no. 2 (2002): 115–44.

———. "The Politics of Interpretation: Tel Hai in Israel's Collective Memory." *AJS Review* 16, nos. 1–2 (1991): 133–60.

———. *Recovered Roots: Collective Memory and the Making of Israeli National Tradition*. Chicago: University of Chicago Press, 1995.

Annotated Filmography

Finding videos on demand (VOD), also known as streaming, is often the easiest way to access films. Many come with subtitles in a variety of languages including French, Russia, Spanish, and Turkish. Netflix has also recently added a service that "dubs" many of these films when using the site. Buying DVDs through Amazon or other international services offers repeat access and is often a more reliable and less expensive long-term solution if you plan to use the films repeatedly. But be aware that when buying DVDs in Israel or at Ben Gurion Airport, films may not have English subtitles. They are usually marked on the box cover, and so it is worth checking if you plan to screen the films to students who do not have the requisite languages to follow without subtitles. The streaming options are country specific, with the widest selection available in the United States.

Websites

Amazon, www.amazon.com: Amazon has films available for purchase as DVDs. Amazon Prime also has streaming.

Fandor, www.fandor.com: Has a small selection of films available for streaming.

Go2films, www.go2films.com: Offers films through both streaming and DVD purchase.

Israel Film Center Stream, www.israelfilmcenterstream.org: A streaming service for purchasing individual films.

iTunes, www.apple.com: Offers a selection of streaming films for rental or purchase. Currently the search function dos not filter by country, and it is easiest to search by film title.

Kanopy: A streaming service for public libraries and educational institutions that has a large selection of films including a significant number of Israeli and Palestinian documentaries and films about the conflict. These can usually be accessed through your university library and streamed remotely.

Ma'aleh film school, www.maale.co.il: Offers films by the school's students in DVD and VOD; an excellent source for short films.

Netflix, www.netflix.com: Has a changing selection of approximately twenty to twenty-five Israeli/Palestinian films. These can be filtered through the search function as "Israeli" and "Palestinian."

Palestine Campaign, www.palestinecampaign.org/films/films-about-palestine/: Offers links to Palestinian-made films or films about the conflict.

Ruth Films, www.ruthfilms.com: Offers films for purchase and streaming.

Steven Spielberg Jewish Film Archive, https://en.jfa.huji.ac.il: Has a vast collection of historical documentary films that can be accessed through its online portal, which links to a YouTube channel.

The Toronto Jewish Film Foundation, ww.j-flix.com: Has a library of Toronto Jewish Film Festival (TJFF) films for streaming (only availabe in Canada); access is currently free.

Vimeo, https://vimeo.com: Filmmakers often upload their works here, though many are password protected.

YouTube, www.youtube.com: Many Israeli and Palestinian films can be found free on YouTube, particularly older documentaries and shorts, but they do not always have subtitles. There is also the option to pay for some films, and these generally do have subtitles.

Selected Films

Ajami. 2009. Directed by Scandar Copti and Yaron Shani, 124 minutes: Five overlapping story lines in the impoverished Arab-Christian and Arab-Muslim neighborhood of Ajami in Jaffa.

AKA Nadia. 2015. Directed by Tova Ascher, 115 minutes: A Palestinian Israeli woman living under a false identity as a Jewish Israeli is forced to confront her past.

Atalia. 1984. Directed by Akiva Tevet, 90 minutes: A war widow living outside social mores on the kibbutz must choose between her daughter and her lover.

Attack, The. 2012. Directed by Ziad Doueri, 102 minutes: A Palestinian Israeli emergency room doctor must confront the fallout from a suicide bomb.

Avenge but One of My Two Eyes. 2005. Directed by Avi Mograbi, 100 minutes: Documentary about the treatment of Palestinians by the Israeli army.

Beaufort. 2007. Directed by Joseph Cedar, 131 minutes: A group of Israeli soldiers stationed at a historic Lebanese outpost wait tensely for their withdrawal.

Berlin/Jerusalem. 1989. Directed by Gitai, 99 minutes: Two interconnected stories of women in the 1930s, one set in Berlin, the other in Palestine, both observing the violence in the societies around them.

Bethlehem. 2013. Directed by Yuval Adler, 109 minutes: Drama following the complex relationship between an Israeli Secret Service officer and his teenage Palestinian informant.

Beyond the Walls. 1984. Directed by Uri Barbash, 103 minutes: Palestinian and Jew must ally in the Central Prison to confront the corrupt governor and his regime of terror.

Born in Deir Yassin. 2017. Directed by Neta Shoshani, 63 minutes: The evolution of the village of Deir Yassin, which was conquered in a highly controversial and pivotal battle in 1948 and then turned into the government-owned psychiatric hospital in 1951.

Brave Miss World. 2013. Directed by Cecilia Peck, 98 minutes: Documentary following Linor Abargil's road from Miss World to international rape-prevention activist.

Bubble, The. 2006. Directed by Eytan Fox, 117 minutes: Drama following the diversity and youth culture of Tel Aviv. As gay and straight, Arab and Jew meet and revel in the hedonistic city, the Second Intifada looms in the background.

Budrus. 2011. Directed by Julia Bacha, 70 minutes: Follows a Palestinian leader who unites Fatah, Hamas, and Israelis in an unarmed movement to save his village from destruction. Success eludes them until his fifteen-year-old daughter jumps into the fray.

Censored Voices. 2015. Directed by Mor Loushy, 84 minutes: Documentary tracing the reactions of soldiers to the 1967 Six-Day War, recorded a week after the battles, with follow-up interviews fifty years later as the tapes are rediscovered.

Checkpoint. 2003. Directed by Yoav Shamir, 80 minutes: Documentary following soldiers at the checkpoints to the West Bank during the Second Intifada.

Children of the Sun. 2007. Directed by Ron Tal, 70 minutes: Documentary following the generation raised in the children's houses in the kibbutz and imagined to be the ideal Hebrew youth.

Cup Final. 1991. Directed by Eran Riklis, 105 minutes: Drama about an Israeli soldier kidnapped by a small PLO unit in Southern Lebanon. Despite political differences, the men share an interest in soccer and the World Cup.

Dancing in Jaffa. Directed by Hila Medallia, 100 minutes: Documentary following the renowned ballroom dancer Pierre Dulane's visit to his hometown and his efforts to teach Jewish and Arab children to dance together.

Diameter of the Bomb. 2007. Directed by Andrew Quigley and Steven Silver, 96 minutes: Documentary about a group of disparate people in Israel and the occupied territories, all connected by a single catastrophic suicide bomb.

Dimona Twist. 2015. Directed by Michal Aviad, 71 minutes: Documentary tracing the experiences of women who arrived in Israel in the 1950s and 1960s and were sent to Dimona, a new settlement in the desert.

Discordia. 2004. Directed by Ben Addelman and Samir Mallal, 68 minutes: When Benjamin Netanyahu is scheduled to give a speech at Concordia University in Montreal, the reaction from the student body is swift and sudden.

Divine Intervention: A Chronicle of Love and Pain. 2005. Directed by Elia Suleiman, 92 minutes: Surreal drama about Palestinian lovers from Jerusalem and Ramallah, who are separated by a checkpoint and arrange clandestine meetings.

Every Bastard a King. 1968. Directed by Uri Zohar, 100 minutes: An American reporter and his girlfriend are trying to get to know the real Israel by meeting locals when war breaks out and their driver (Yehoram Gaon) receives his call-up notice. The film's long battle sequence in the desert used military equipment and troops from the Six-Day War.

Exodus. 1960. Directed by Otto Preminger, 208 minutes: Hollywood epic tracing the creation of the State of Israel in 1948 and the immigration of Jewish refugees from Europe.

Fictitious Marriage, A. 1988. Directed by Haim Buzaglo, 90 minutes: Drama about an Israeli who is mistaken as a Palestinian laborer and passes as a mute until he has to make a decision about whether to trust his new friends.

Five Broken Cameras. 2013. Directed by Emad Burnat and Guy Davidi, 94 minutes: Documentary about a Palestinian farmer's chronicle of his nonviolent resistance to the actions of the Israeli army.

500 Dunams on the Moon. 2002. Directed by Rachel Leah Jones, 48 minutes: Documentary about Ein Hod, a Palestinian village whose villagers were expelled when Israelis captured it in 1948.

Forgotten Refugees, The. 2005. Directed by Michael Grynszpan, 49 minutes: Documentary that recounts the history of Jewish communities of the Middle East and North Africa and their demise in the face of persecution following the creation of the modern State of Israel in 1948.

For My Father. 2008. Directed by Dror Zahavi, 101 minutes: A suicide bomber becomes dependent on the kindness of strangers when his explosives will not detonate, giving him time to meet some of the people he is targeting.

Four Friends. 1999. Directed by Esther Dar, 61 minutes: Four women who went to an Anglican boarding school in Mandate Palestine meet fifty years later.

Gatekeepers. 2012. Directed by Dror Moreh, 101 minutes: Interviews with all the surviving heads of the Shin Beit (Israel's internal security service).

Gett: The Trial of Viviane Amsalem. 2015. Directed by Ronit Elkabetz, 115 minutes: The third film in the Viviane Amsalem trilogy. Elkabetz offers a powerful performance of a woman seeking a divorce from the Beit Din (Jewish religious law courts) in this courtroom drama.

Green Fields. 1989. Directed by Isaac Zepel Yeshurun, 92 minutes: A family of expats must examine the gap between their imagination and the reality when they drive through the West Bank to attend a young man's graduation from army training.

Green Prince, The. 2014. Directed by Nadav Schirman, 101 minutes: The son of a Hamas leader spies for Israel. This documentary is built around interviews with Mosab Hassan Yousef, on whose book the film is based, and Gonen Ben Yitzhak, his Israeli intelligence handler.

Halfon Hill Doesn't Answer. 1976. Directed by Assi Dayan, 92 minutes: HaGashash HaHiver, a famous Israeli comedy trio, satirize the Israel Defense Forces in this cult classic.

Hamsin (Eastern Wind). 1982. Directed by Daniel Wachsmann, 88 minutes: Contested land ownership in a farming village between Jewish landholders and their Palestinian neighbors plays out in the relationship between the Jewish daughter and her brother's Arab friend, ending in tragedy.

He Walked in the Fields. 1967. Directed by Yosef Millo, 90 minutes: Based on a novel (and a play) by Moshe Shamir about the 1948 war, Uri (Assi Dayan) must choose between his family on the kibbutz and the Palmach.

Hide and Seek. 1980. Directed by Dan Wolman, 90 minutes: In 1946, twelve-year-old Uri reports his teacher Balaban as a suspected spy when he observes him meeting with a young Arab man. Only later does he discover that Balaban's interest in the young Arab is romantic rather than political.

Hill 24 Doesn't Answer. 1955. Directed by Thorold Dickinson, 101 minutes: Through a series of flashbacks, we learn how four soldiers came to defend a hill against Arab forces in a battle during the 1948 war. This mostly English-language production was the first full-length Israeli feature film.

Human Resources Manager. 2010. Directed by Eran Riklis, 103 minutes: When a woman remains in the city morgue as the unclaimed victim of a suicide bomb, her previous employer must journey to her family home to return her body.

In Between. 2016. Directed by Maysaloun Hamoud, 103 minutes: Three Palestinian women living together in Tel Aviv must find the balance between tradition and modernity.

Inch'Allah. 2012. Directed by Anaïs Barbeau-Lavalette, 102 minutes: A Canadian doctor finds her sympathies sorely tested while working in the conflict-ravaged Palestinian territories.

Invisible. 2011. Directed by Michal Aviad, 90 minutes: Two women raped by the same man meet thirty years later. This personal violence is framed around the violence and militarism of men in Israeli society and the rape of Palestinian lands.

Jaffa. 2009. Directed by Keren Yedaya, 106 minutes: In the heart of Jaffa, star-crossed lovers struggle to be together.

Jenin, Jenin. 2003. Directed by Mohammed Bakri, 54 minutes: Documentary about the massacre in Jenin and the local inhabitants' vision of what happened.

Junction 48. 2016. Directed by Udi Aloni, 95 minutes: A Palestinian hip-hop musician and his girlfriend make music against the miserable backdrop of their slum and the patriarchal values of Palestinian society.

Kaddish for a Friend. 2010. Directed by Leo Khasin, 93 minutes: An unlikely friendship develops in Berlin between an eighty-four-year-old Jewish war veteran and a Palestinian boy from Lebanon.

Lady Kul el Arab. 2008. Directed by Ibtisam Mara'ana, 56 minutes: Duah Fares is the first Druze woman to participate in the Miss Israel competition. But what sets out as a documentary about a beauty pageant becomes a study in the conflict for a woman who has to choose between international success and her family's culture.

Land without Borders. 2007. Directed by Michael Alalu, 62 minutes: On a quest to find faith in the possibility of a two-state solution, Baram travels around the West Bank speaking with the Palestinians and Jewish settlers living there.

Late Summer Blues. 1987. Directed by Renen Schorr, 101 minutes: High school students on the eve of conscription consider the cost of the War of Attrition.

Law in These Parts, The. 2011. Directed by Ra'anan Alexandrowicz, 101 minutes: Through interviews with local and Supreme Court judges, this documentary explores the history of Israel's military legal system in the occupied Palestinian territories of the West Bank and Gaza Strip.

Lemon Tree. 2009. Directed by Eran Riklis., 106 minutes: Drama about Salma (Hiam Abbas), who loses access to her family lemon grove when the ministry of security moves nearby. It is a tense drama about security needs and human costs.

Life According to Agfa. 1992. Directed by Assi Dayan, 100 minutes: One night in a small Tel Aviv pub serves as a microcosm for Israeli society and the all-encompassing dominance of the country's militarism.

Maytal. 1996. Directed by Yael Kipper Zaretsky, 51 minutes: Maytal is severely wounded and her brother killed in a terrorist attack. The documentary follows six months of her rehabilitation.

Mirror Image. 2013. Directed by Danielle Schwartz, 11 minutes: Short film wrestling with Jewish complicity in the Nakba. Jewish grandparents are forced to tell the story of their crystal mirror, originally stolen from a Palestinian village in 1948.

Munich. 2005. Directed by Steven Spielberg, 164 minutes: Historical drama following the Israeli agents tracking down the men who perpetrated the terrorist attack against Israeli athletes at the 1972 Munich Olympic Games.

My Michael. 1975. Directed by Dan Wolman, 95 minutes: Based on a novel by Amos Oz, the film follows the relationship of a couple whose psychology reflects the state of siege in the city of Jerusalem leading up to the Six-Day War (1967).

1913: Seeds of Conflict. 2015. Directed by Ben Loeterman, 60 minutes: Documentary tracing the breakdown of the Ottoman Palestinian identity of Jews and Arabs and the rise of nationalism and the conflict. In English and available on YouTube.

Noodle. 2007. Directed by Ayelet Menahemi, 90 minutes: An air stewardess (Mili Avital) twice widowed by Israel's wars must help the Chinese boy in her custody reunite with his mother.

No. 17. 2003. Directed by David Ofek, 76 minutes: The search for the unidentified seventeenth victim of a bus bomb becomes a journey through the humanity of the Arab-Israeli conflict.

Omar. 2013. Directed by Hany Abu-Assad, 96 minutes: A young Palestinian agrees to work as an informant after he is tricked into an admission of guilt in the wake of an Israeli soldier's killing.

One of Us. 1989. Directed by Uri Barbash, 110 minutes: Drama about a Palestinian guerrilla who is taken into custody after killing several Israeli soldiers at an army outpost. But his death in captivity is treated as a murder investigation, and a military official must find out the truth.

Out in the Dark. 2012. Directed by Michael Mayer, 96 minutes: Romantic thriller about the relationship between a Palestinian and an Israeli man who have to defy their societies to be together.

Paradise Now. 2005. Directed by Hany Abu-Assad, 90 minutes: Following two suicide bombers on their last day before the attack, this drama presents the multiple perspectives on terror attacks among Palestinians.

Rabin, the Last Day. 2015. Directed by Amos Gitai, 153 minutes: Following the last days of President Yitzhak Rabin in office and the politics that led to his assassination in 1995.

Rana's Wedding. 2002. Directed by Hany Abu-Assad, 90 minutes: Seventeen-year-old Rana has one day to choose a husband from a preselected list approved by her father or leave with him for Egypt. Can she find her forbidden love, Khalil, in time?

Road to Jenin, The. 2005. Directed by Pierre Rehov, 53 minutes: This documentary was made as a counternarrative to *Jenin, Jenin*, presenting an alternative view of the battle as a conflict against militants rather than a massacre of innocents.

Rock the Casbah. 2012. Directed by Yariv Horowitz, 94 minutes: A group of young Israeli soldiers are stationed in the West Bank at the start of the Second Intifada. Each side is watching the other in fear and wondering if they can make a human connection.

Room 514. 2012. Directed by Sharon Bar-Ziv, 91 minutes: A female investigator, against the advice of her male superiors, investigates whether a male officer abused his power in the West Bank and beat an Arab family. This tense thriller offers a brutal look at the military's culture of masculinity and silence.

Sandstorm. 2017. Directed by Elite Zexer, 87 minutes: Two Bedouin women must confront their fate and face the patriarchal forces around them.

Settlers, The. 2016. Directed by Shimon Dotan, 107 minutes: This documentary explores the lives of settlers in the West Bank.

Seven Minutes in Heaven. 2011. Directed by Omri Givon, 94 minutes: Drama about a woman (Reymonde Amsallem) struggling with PTSD after she survives a suicide bomb on a bus.

Shining Stars. 2008. Directed by Yael Kipper Zaretsky, 61 minutes: Twelve years after filming *Maytal*, Zaretzky follows Maytal again as she embarks on fertility treatment, but the medicalization process reawakens her posttrauma from the terrorist attack in 1996.

Siege. 1969. Directed by Gilberto Tofano, 100 minutes: A young war widow (Gila Almagor) raises her son in the shadow of her husband's death while trying to build a new life and defy social expectations for her public role as a living memorial to her dead husband.

Song of the Siren. 1994. Directed by Eytan Fox, 90 minutes: Based on a best-selling feminist novel by Irit Linur, this romantic comedy about yuppie advertising executives in Tel Aviv is set against the background of the Gulf War.

Strangers. 2007. Directed by Guy Nattiv and Erez Tadmor, 85 minutes: A Palestinian and an Israeli meet on a train and watch the World Cup (2006) together in Paris, but their romance is disrupted by the Lebanon War.

Syrian Bride. 2004. Directed by Eran Riklis, 97 minutes: A Druze bride must cross the border to Syria to meet her husband on her wedding day, never to return. As her family says good-bye, old conflicts must be faced.

Take 3. 2016. Directed by Ayelet Bechar, 15 minutes: After a Palestinian man is forced from his home during the 1948 war, he returns to see it again and visit his father's grave.

Tale of Love and Darkness, A. 2015. Directed by Natalie Portman, 95 minutes: Adapted from the autobiographical novel by Amos Oz, this film is set against the backdrop of the British Mandate and the early years of the State of Israel.

They Were Ten. 1961. Directed by Baruch Dienar, 105 minutes: A band of pioneers sets out to start a settlement in the late nineteenth century but must face Ottoman bureaucracy, a hostile landscape, and an unwelcoming Arab village.

3 Times Divorced. 2007. Directed by Ibtisam Mara'ana, 74 minutes: Documentary following a Palestinian woman's battles with Shariah law inside Israel and her precarious status as a noncitizen experiencing domestic abuse.

Time of Favor. 2002. Directed by Joseph Cedar, 102 minutes: Thriller exploring the tense relationship between religious nationalists and the military, loosely based on a real-life plot by religious extremists in the *makhteret* (underground).

Time That Remains, The. 2009. Directed by Elia Suleiman, 109 minutes: An examination of the creation of the State of Israel and its present situation from a Palestinian perspective.

Troupe, The. 1978. Directed by Avi Nesher, 112 minutes: Musicians in a military troupe contend with bombing and the influences of American antiwar music while entertaining the troops.

Unsettling. 2018. Directed by Iris Zakai, 70 minutes: A pop-up film studio becomes a social laboratory for encounters with camera-shy (but not conflict-averse) Israeli settlers on the West Bank.

Villa Touma. 2014. Directed by Suha Arraf, 85 minutes: In the family villa in Ramallah, three unmarried Christian sisters have hidden away, ignoring the changing times, until their niece Badia arrives.

Walk on Water. 2004. Directed by Eytan Fox, 103 minutes: Eyal, a Mossad agent, is sent to hunt an aging Nazi but is forced to confront his fears and prejudices along the way.

Waltz with Bashir. 2008. Directed by Ari Folman, 90 minutes: In graphic form, this film is a study in trauma and memory. An Israeli film director interviews fellow veterans of the 1982 invasion of Lebanon and the massacre at the Sabra and Shatila refugee camps. Unable to remember, he uses their narratives to reconstruct his own memories of the conflict.

Wedding in Galilee. 1987. Directed by Michel Khleifi, 113 minutes: In exchange for granting a Palestinian family a pass from the curfew so that they can celebrate a wedding in style, the local Israeli military authorities insist on attending. But not everyone agrees that the father should have asked or that the soldiers should attend. In the heat and revelries, tempers flare.

West Bank Story. 2005. Directed by Ari Sandel, 21 minutes: Musical short that presents the Arab-Israeli conflict through the metaphor of dueling falafel stands. It won Best Short Film at the Academy Awards. In English and available on YouTube.

West of the Jordan River. 2018. Directed by Amos Gitai, 84 minutes: Interspersing footage from interviews with Yitzhak Rabin and contemporary settlers in the West Bank, Gitai explores the nature of the fifty-year-old occupation.

Wild West Hebron. 2013. Directed by Nissim Mossek, 96 minutes: In a violent corner of the West Bank, Palestinians, Israeli settlers, and antioccupation activists clash. At the center is Yohanan Sharet, a man who has attacked Palestinians and activists but is now facing his settler neighbors, who want to drive him off the land.

Woman Pioneers, The. 2012. Directed by Michal Aviad, 52 minutes: Diaries and letters of women from the Second Aliyah shine a light on Zionist-socialist ideology and its feminist failings.

Wooden Gun. 1979. Directed by Ilan Moshenson, 95 minutes: In 1950s Israel, a children's game turns vicious when one child wants to defend a Holocaust survivor. This study in nationalism and militarism highlights tensions in the early state.

Write Down, I Am an Arab. 2014. Directed by Ibtisam Mara'ana, 73 minutes: This documentary offers a study of the poet Mahmoud Darwish.

Yana's Friends. 1999. Directed by Arik Kaplun, 90 minutes: A Russian woman arrives in Israel just as the Gulf War begins. Sheltered by her neighbors, she begins a romance while learning about the wars that came before.

Yellow Asphalt. 2001. Directed by Dan Verete, 97 minutes: Three intersecting episodes that chronicle the daily encounters of Israelis and Bedouins living and working near one another. The film particularly focuses on women's situation within patriarchal power structures.

Zero Motivation. 2014. Directed by Talya Lavie, 101 minutes: In this black comedy about a group of female IDF soldiers, we see women in the human resources office on a remote and desolate military base hate each other, the army, their commanding officer, and the mundane tasks they are assigned.

Contributors

RACHEL S. HARRIS is Associate Professor of Israeli Literature and Culture at the University of Illinois Urbana-Champaign in the Program in Comparative and World Literature and the Program in Jewish Culture and Society. Her books include *An Ideological Death: Suicide in Israeli Literature* (2014) and *Warriors, Witches, Whores: Women in Israeli Cinema* (Wayne State University Press, 2017). She is coeditor of *Narratives of Dissent: War in Contemporary Israeli Arts and Culture* (Wayne State University Press, 2011) and *Casting a Giant Shadow: The Transnational Shaping of Israeli Cinema* (forthcoming). She is the series editor for the Dalkey Archive Press Hebrew Literature Series. Harris has edited journal special issues on contemporary Israeli literature, Jewish women's bodies, religious Jewish women's feminism and art, and Russian Jews since 1970. She serves on the board of the Association of Israel Studies and is cochair of the Women's Caucus of the AJS.

•••

MENNA ABUKHADRA is an Israel Institute postdoctoral fellow at the University of Cambridge and a lecturer of Hebrew language and literature at Cairo University. She was awarded her BA in Oriental languages and literature and MA and PhD in Modern Hebrew language and literature from the Department of Oriental Languages, Cairo University. Her primary research interests include studying the relation between Modern Hebrew literature and Jewish heritage.

ARI ARIEL is a historian of the modern Middle East at the University of Iowa, with a particular focus on Jewish communities in the Arab world and Mizrahi communities in Israel. His interests include ethnic, national, and religious identities, migration, and foodways. He is the author of *Jewish-Muslim Relations and Migration from Yemen to Palestine in the Late Nineteenth and Twentieth Centuries* (2014), which analyzes the impact of local, regional, and international events on ethnic relations in Yemen and on Yemeni migration patterns. He has also published on the "hummus wars" and on Middle Eastern Jewish culinary history.

BEVERLY BAILIS is a visiting scholar at Brooklyn College, where she teaches courses in Hebrew language and literature. She specializes in Modern Hebrew, Jewish literature, and gender studies. She has taught at the Jewish Theological Seminary, the Women's League for Conservative Judaism, the JCC in Manhattan, and other adult education programs in New York City. Her articles appear in journals such as *Prooftexts*, the *Forward*, and *Prospect: A Journal of Art and Writing in Landscape Studies*. She is preparing her dissertation, *Fantasies of Modernity: Representations of the Jewish Female Body in Hebrew Literature*, as a book manuscript.

RUSSELL A. BERMAN is the Walter A. Haas Professor in the Humanities at Stanford. His books include *The Rise of the Modern German Novel: Crisis and Charisma* (1988) and *Enlightenment or Empire: Colonial Discourse in German Culture* (1998), both of which won the Outstanding Book Award of the German Studies Association. Some of his other books include *Anti-Americanism in Europe: A Cultural Problem* (2004), *Fiction Sets You Free: Literature, Liberty, and Western Culture* (2007), and *Freedom or Terror: Europe Faces Jihad* (2010). He has also edited translations including Ernst Jünger's novel *Eumeswil* and Carl Schmitt's *Land and Sea*. In his books and many articles, Berman has written widely on German literary and cultural history of the nineteenth and twentieth centuries, critical theory, and cultural dimensions of transatlantic relations, as well as on topics between Europe and the Middle East. A senior fellow at the Hoover Institution and at the Freeman Spogli Institute for International Studies, he is also the editor of *Telos, a Journal of Critical Theory*, and he served as the 2011 president of the Modern Language Association.

JEFFREY BLOODWORTH is Professor of History and a codirector of the School of Public Service & Global Affairs at Gannon University (Erie, PA). He specializes in twentieth-century political history. His book *Losing the Center: The Decline of American Liberalism 1968–1992* (2013) was nominated for the Ellis W. Hawley and Frederick Jackson Turner Awards. In addition, he has published articles and op-eds in *Political Science & Politics*, *Wisconsin Magazine of History*, the *Historian*, the *Pacific Northwest Quarterly*, *Just Security*, the *St. Louis Post-Dispatch*, the *Wichita Eagle*, and additional journals and newspapers. Bloodworth has received grants and fellowships from presidential libraries, research repositories, and educational institutes throughout the United States as well as Germany, Israel, Poland, and the Ukraine. The recipient of the 2016–2017 Excellence in Teaching Award from the Gannon University Student Government Association, he has led travel trips to Haiti, Poland, Israel, Jordan, Egypt, Great Britain, Germany, and Denmark.

RACHEL FELDHAY BRENNER is the Max and Frieda Weinstein-Bascom Professor of Jewish Studies and Professor of Modern Hebrew Literature at the Center for Jewish Studies at the University of Wisconsin–Madison. She has published widely on responses to the Holocaust in Jewish Diaspora literature, Israeli literature, and Polish literature and has held fellowships at the Hebrew University, the Oxford Center for Hebrew and Jewish Studies, the United States Holocaust Memorial Museum, and the Institute for Research in Humanities in the University of Wisconsin–Madison). Her books include *Writing as Resistance: Four Women Confronting the Holocaust: Edith Stein, Simone Weil, Anne Frank, and Etty Hillesum*; *Inextricably Bonded: Israeli Jewish and Arab Writers Re-Visioning Culture*; and *The Freedom to Write: The Woman-Artist and the World in Ruth Almog's Fiction* (in Hebrew). Her latest book, *The Ethics of Witnessing: The Holocaust in Polish Writers' Diaries from Warsaw, 1939–1945*, was published in 2014. It received the University of Southern California Book Prize in Literary and Cultural Studies. She is a past president of the Association of Israel Studies.

CAITLIN CARENEN is Professor of History at Eastern Connecticut State University. Her first book, *The Fervent Embrace: Liberal Protestants, Evangelicals, and Israel* (2012), examined the role of religion in the formation of the U.S.-Israeli alliance. Her current book project examines U.S. popular and policy responses to international terrorism in the 1970s and 1980s. In addition to teaching the Arab-Israeli conflict, she teaches courses on foreign policy, religion, and terrorism.

DONNA ROBINSON DIVINE is the Morningstar Family Professor of Jewish Studies and Professor of Government Emerita at Smith College, where she taught a variety of courses on Middle East politics. Her books include *Women Living Change: Cross-Cultural Perspectives; Essays from the Smith College Research Project on Women and Social Change*, *Politics and Society in Ottoman Palestine: The Arab Struggle for Survival and Power*, *Postcolonial Theory and the Arab-Israeli Conflict*, and *Exiled in the Homeland: Zionism and the Return to Mandate Palestine*. Named the Katharine Asher Engel lecturer at Smith College for the 2012–13 academic year in recognition of her scholarly achievements, she was also designated as Smith's Honored Professor for the excellence of her teaching. She is currently serving as President of the Association for Israel Studies and as an Affiliate Professor at Israel's University of Haifa.

ALAN DOWTY is Emeritus Professor of Political Science, University of Notre Dame. He was formerly Kahanoff Chair Professor of Israel Studies at the University of Calgary, 2003–6 and president of the Association for Israel Studies, 2005–7. His books include *The Limits of American Isolation* (1971), *Middle East Crisis: U.S. Decision Making in 1958, 1970, and 1973* (1984), *Closed Borders: The Contemporary Assault on Freedom of Movement* (1987), *The Jewish State: A Century Later* (1998; 2nd ed., 2001), and *Israel/Palestine* (2005; 4th ed., 2017)

JANICE W. FERNHEIMER is Associate Professor of Writing, Rhetoric, and Digital Studies as well as the Zantker Charitable Foundation Professor and director of Jewish Studies at the University of Kentucky. She is the author of *Stepping into Zion: Hatzaad Harishon, Black Jews, and the Remaking of Jewish Identity* (2014) and coeditor, with Michael Bernard-Donals, of *Jewish Rhetorics: History, Theory, Practice* (2014). She has published widely in peer-reviewed journals including *Rhetoric Society Quarterly, College English, Journal of Communication and Religion, Computers and Composition Online, Argumentation and Advocacy, Journal of Business and Technical Communication, Technical Communication*, and *Oral History Review*. In collaboration with the author/illustrator J. T. Waldman, she is currently researching and writing a historical-fiction graphic novel, *America's Chosen Spirit*, based on oral histories that detail Jewish influences on the Kentucky bourbon industry. Along with her research collaborator, Beth L. Goldstein, she is collecting oral histories for the Jewish Heritage Fund for Excellence (JHFE) Jewish Kentucky Oral History Project, a repository of oral histories for Jewish Kentuckians.

TERRI SUSAN FINE is Professor of Political Science at the University of Central Florida, where she also serves as associate director of the Lou Frey Institute and content specialist for the Florida Joint Center for Citizenship. At the Florida Joint Center for Citizenship, she is responsible for training teachers to advance content literacy, infusing content into civics teaching and ensuring its accuracy, developing sample assessment items for teacher and student use, and overseeing the content development of a student review website for the high-stakes statewide civics exam required of all public middle school students in Florida. She is a Brandeis University Schusterman Center fellow and an affiliated faculty member at the University of Haifa. Her primary research and teaching interests focus on American political participation and political communication including public opinion, voting and elections, voting rights, and voting systems. Her publications have appeared in several academic journals and as chapters in books.

OLGA GERSHENSON is Professor of Judaic and Near Eastern studies at the University of Massachusetts Amherst, where she is also on the Film Studies faculty. She is a multidisciplinary scholar with interests at the intersection of culture, history, and film. She is the author of *Gesher: Russian Theater in Israel; A Study of Cultural Colonization* (2005) and *The Phantom Holocaust: Soviet Cinema and Jewish Catastrophe* (2013). She edited a collection, *Ladies and Gents: Public Toilets and Gender* (2009), and a special issue of *East European Jewish Affairs* about new Jewish museums in postcommunist Europe. Her current research deals with emerging genres in Israeli cinema. Along with her academic work, she curates film series, consults for festivals, and has a lively lecture schedule at universities, conferences, and museums around the world.

SHIRI GOREN is the director of the Modern Hebrew Program at Yale University. Her teaching and research areas include Hebrew and Israeli literature and culture, film and media theory, Yiddish literature, and gender studies. She is also active in the field of second-language acquisition, working on projects related to community-based teaching, as well as the intersection of language and foreign-culture pedagogy and digital humanities. Goren is the coeditor of the volume *Choosing Yiddish: New Frontiers of Language and Culture* (Wayne State University Press, 2013). She is currently working on the manuscript "Creative Resistance: Literary Interventions in the Israeli-Palestinian Conflict," which explores how violence affects real and imagined spaces in Israel of recent years. The book focuses on novels by the authors Orly Castel-Bloom, Gabriella Avigur-Rotem, Ronit Matalon, and Sayed Kashua, as well as films, documentaries, and TV series. Goren has also recently published on the issue of assessment in Hebrew-language acquisition. She is a member of the Executive Steering Committee of the National Association of Professors of Hebrew (NAPH). She is a twice-elected senator of the inaugural Faculty of Arts and Sciences Senate at Yale (2015–20) and is an elected member of the senate executive council (2017–19).

LIORA R. HALPERIN is Associate Professor of International Studies, History, and Jewish Studies and the Jack and Rebecca Benaroya Endowed Chair in Israel Studies at the University of Washington in Seattle. Her first book, *Babel in Zion: Jews, Nationalism, and Language Diversity in Palestine, 1920–1948*, was the 2015 winner of the Shapiro Prize for Best Book in Israel Studies.

PETER C. HERMAN is Professor of English Literature at San Diego State University. He has edited *Critical Contexts: Terrorism and Literature* (2018), and his book *Literature and Terrorism from the Gunpowder Plot to 9/11: Representing the Unspeakable* is forthcoming. Other publications include a contextual edition of Thomas Deloney's 1596 proto-novel, *Jack of Newbury* (2015); *The New Milton Criticism* (2012), coedited with Elizabeth Sauer; *Destabilizing Milton: "Paradise Lost" and the Poetics of Incertitude* (2005); and *"Royal Poetrie": Monarchic Verse and the Political Imaginary of Early Modern England* (2010; *Choice* Outstanding Academic Title).

SUSAN JACOBOWITZ is Associate Professor of English at Queensborough Community College, part of the City University of New York. Her research areas include second-generation literature and performance art, Australian Jewish and immigrant writing, conflicts and challenges of Jewish identity, and graphic texts. She has participated as a scholar in workshops and seminars at Yad Vashem in Jerusalem and at the United States Holocaust Memorial Museum in Washington, DC. Her scholarship has been published in Australia, the United States, Germany, Brazil, Israel, and India, with articles and reviews appearing in *Shofar: An Interdisciplinary Journal of Jewish Studies, Studies in American Jewish Literature, Ilha Do Desterro: A Journal of English Language, Literature in English and Cultural Studies, Australian Journal of Jewish Studies, East European Jewish Affairs, Post Script: Essays in Film and Humanities, Journal of American Ethnic History, Clio: A Journal of Literature, History, and the Philosophy of History*, and *Philip Roth Studies*.

MYA GUARNIERI JARADAT is an American-Israeli journalist and writer. The author of *The Unchosen: The Lives of Israel's New Others* (2017), her reportage, commentary, essays, and fiction have appeared in numerous media outlets and literary journals.

ELLEN W. KAPLAN is Professor of Acting and Directing at Smith, a Fulbright scholar, and an actress, director, and playwright. She has directed and performed in China, Israel, and Costa Rica and was a guest professor at Tel Aviv University and the University of Theatre and Film in Bucharest, Romania, and was Distinguished Artist/Scholar at Hong Kong University, where her play *Livy in the Garden* was performed at the Robert Black Theatre in 2016. Ellen's other plays include several on Jewish themes, including *Cast No Shadow*, about the legacies of the Holocaust, which premiered at the Jewish State Theater of Bucharest, and *Pulling Apart*, about the Second Intifada, which won a Moss Hart Award, as well as plays about Justine Wise Polier, Charlotte Salomon, and Anzia Yezierska. Her most recent play is *Someone Is Sure to Come*, which combines voices from men and women on death row and was presented in New York City in 2016. Her book chapter on creativity and trauma will be published in *Performing Psychologies*.

OREN KROLL-ZELDIN is the assistant director of the Swig Program in Jewish Studies and Social Justice and Term Assistant Professor in the Department of Theology and Religious Studies at the University of San Francisco. He is also the director of Beyond Bridges: Israel-Palestine with the Center for Global Education at USF and the Center for Transformative Education.

P. R. KUMARASWAMY teaches Israeli politics at the School of International Studies, Jawaharlal Nehru University, New Delhi, India, and is the author of *India's Israel Policy* (2010), *Historical Dictionary of the Arab-Israeli Conflict* (2015), and *Squaring the Circle: Mahatma Gandhi and the Jewish National Home* (2018). In 2009, he established the Middle East Institute, New Delhi, and serves as its honorary director (www.mei.org.in), and in 2018, he has taken over as the managing editor of *Indo-Judaic Studies*.

JACOB LASSNER, former director of Jewish Studies at Northwestern University, is the Phillip M. and Ethel Klutznick Professor Emeritus of Jewish Civilization in the Departments of History and Religion. He has been a member of the Institute of Advanced Study (Princeton), a fellow of the Hebrew Union College Biblical and Archeological School (Jerusalem), and a member of the Rockefeller Institute in Bellagio, Italy; the Harvard centers of Jewish and Middle East studies; and the Oxford Center for Hebrew and Jewish Studies, where he was Skirball fellow for Jewish-Muslim relations. He was also a longtime research affiliate of the Moshe Dayan Centre at Tel Aviv University. Lassner is a recipient of awards from the Guggenheim Foundation, the National Endowment for the Humanities, and the Social Science Research Council. He has authored and/or coauthored eleven books and recently completed a twelfth. In addition, he was curator of a prize-winning museum exhibition on the Cairo Geniza, an extraordinary cache of documents revealing the life of Jews in the lands of Islam. His written articles and refereed presentations on Near Eastern history and Jewish-Muslim relations number more than 150. In recognition of his scholarship, he was awarded the honorary degree Doctor of Humane Letters (Honoris Causa) by the Hebrew Union College–Jewish Institute of Religion and elected president of the American Oriental Society, America's oldest scholarly society devoted to a specific discipline. In 2013, he became the second recipient of the prestigious Franz Rosenthal Prize for a lifetime of distinguished contributions to Semitic and Islamic studies.

HOLLI LEVITSKY is founder and director of the Jewish Studies Program and Professor of English at Loyola Marymount University in Los Angeles. She has been a fellow at the Center for Advanced Holocaust Studies at the United State Holocaust Memorial Museum, a Fulbright Distinguished Chair in American literature in Poland, a fellow at the Brandeis Summer Institute for Israel Studies, and the Florida International University Exile Studies Writer in Residence. She is an affiliated professor of the University of Haifa. She works primarily in the areas of Jewish American literature, Holocaust studies, and exile studies and has published dozens of articles, book chapters, and essays in these areas. Most recently, she is the coeditor of two volumes, *The Literature of Exile and Displacement: American Identity in a Time of Crisis* (2016) and *Summer Haven: The Catskills, the Holocaust, and the Literary Imagination* (2015).

ROLIN MAINUDDIN is Associate Professor of Political Science at North Carolina Central University. He received his PhD in political science from the University of Kansas. Before earning two master's degrees in political science and administrative studies from Ohio University, he completed graduate and undergraduate education in international relations from the University of Dhaka (Bangladesh). His research interest is in international security and religious violence. A former president of the North Carolina Political Science Association, he served as associate editor (Middle East) of the *Journal of Third World Studies* (renamed *Journal of Global South Studies*). Mainuddin serves on the editorial board of the *International Journal of South Asian Studies* (India) and the *Journal of Global South Studies*. Also, he is on the Executive Board of the Triangle Institute for Security Studies in North Carolina. In addition to editing a book, *Religion and Politics in the Developing World: Explosive Interactions* (2002), his articles have appeared in the *Asian Journal of Peacebuilding*, the *Indian Journal of Asian Affairs*, the *Journal of Political Science, Government and Politics* (online), the *Journal of Third World Studies*, the *Mid-American Journal of Politics*, *Middle East Policy*, and *Military Review*.

ADIA MENDELSON-MAOZ is Associate Professor of Israeli Literature and Culture and the chair of the Department of Literature, Language and Arts at the Open University of Israel. She investigates the multifaceted relationships among literature, ethics, politics, and culture, mainly in the context of Hebrew literature and Israeli culture. Mendelson-Maoz is the author of numerous articles in books and journals, including *Social Jewish Studies*, *PHILOSOPHIA*, *Shofar*, *Social Identities*, *JLT: Journal of Literary Theory*, *Israel Studies Review*, and *Women Studies*. She has published three books, *Literature as Moral Laboratory* (2009, in Hebrew), *Multiculturalism in Israel—Literary Perspectives* (2014), and her latest book, *Borders, Territories, and Ethics: Hebrew Literature in the Shadow of the Intifada* (2018).

PHILIP METRES is the author of ten books, including *Shrapnel Maps* (forthcoming 2020), *The Sound of Listening* (essays, 2018), *Pictures at an Exhibition* (poems, 2016), *Sand Opera* (poems, 2015), *I Burned at the Feast: Selected Poems of Arseny Tarkovsky* (translations, 2015), *A Concordance of Leaves* (2013), and *To See the Earth* (2008). A recipient of the Lannan Literary Award, two NEA Awards, two Arab American Book Awards, the Watson Fellowship, the Creative Workforce Fellowship, and the Cleveland Arts Prize, he is Professor of English and director of the Peace, Justice, and Human Rights program at John Carroll University.

JOEL S. MIGDAL is the Robert F. Philip Professor of International Studies in the Jackson School of International Studies at the University of Washington. He was the founding chair of the school's International Studies Program. He was formerly an associate professor of government at Harvard University and a senior lecturer at Tel Aviv University. His books include *Peasants, Politics, and Revolution*; *Palestinian Society and Politics*; *Strong Societies and Weak States*; *State in Society*; *Through the Lens of Israel*; *The Palestinian People: A History* (with Baruch Kimmerling); and, most recently, *Shifting Sands: The United States in the Middle East*. He received the University of Washington's Distinguished Teaching Award and Graduate Mentor Award, as well as the Governor's Writers Award.

HUSAM MOHAMAD is Professor of Political Science at the University of Central Oklahoma. He previously taught at Zayed University in the UAE, Qatar University, the Eastern Mediterranean University in Cyprus, and the Junior State of America foundation. Husam was the recipient of the Fulbright Scholar Award in 2008. His teaching interests focus on comparative politics, political theory, and international relations. He has published several journal articles, book chapters, reviews, and short communications addressing Israeli-Palestinian relations, U.S. policy toward the Arab and Muslim world, democratization in Arab politics, and Islamist movements across the Arab region.

CARY NELSON is Jubilee Professor of Liberal Arts & Sciences at the University of Illinois at Urbana-Champaign and an affiliated professor at the University of Haifa. His more than thirty authored or edited books include many on modern poetry. His most recent book is *Dreams Deferred: A Concise Guide to the Israeli-Palestinian Conflict and the Movement to Boycott Israel*.

RANEN OMER-SHERMAN is the Jewish Heritage Fund for Excellence Endowed Chair in Judaic Studies at the University of Louisville. He is the coeditor of the journal *Shofar* and the author or editor of five books including *Diaspora and Zionism in Jewish American Literature* (2002), *Israel in Exile: Jewish Writing and the Desert* (2006), *The Jewish Graphic Novel: Critical Approaches* (2008), *Narratives of Dissent: War in Contemporary Israeli Arts and Culture* (2013), and most recently *Imagining Kibbutz: Visions of Utopia in Literature and Film* (2015), as well as numerous essays on Jewish writers from Israel and North America. He was a founder of a desert kibbutz, served as a combat soldier in the IDF, and worked for many years as a desert guide in Sinai and Israel.

ASHLEY PASSMORE is Assistant Professor of German and International Studies at Texas A&M University. Her recent articles include "The Artful Dodge: The Appearance of the Schnorrer in German Literature" (*Journal of Austrian Studies*) and "Their Feet Will Become Fins Again: Theodor Herzl's View of Darwinian Transformation" (*Israel Studies*). She is currently working on a monograph called "Common Ground" about the reevaluation of the idea of "Diaspora" for third-generation Israelis and German Jews. In 2014, she was awarded a fellowship by the Schusterman Center for Israel Studies at Brandeis University.

RANDALL G. ROGAN is Professor of Communication at Wake Forest University. Rogan's research program is forensic discourse analysis of crisis negotiations and author identification. He is recognized as an international expert and researcher in crisis negotiation. Of particular noteworthiness, his analysis of written documents was central in the investigation and arrest of the Unabomber. Further, his research focuses on the communication-based analysis of terrorist narrative and recruitment strategies, along with particular attention to the discourse of jihadism, its foundational jurisprudence, and the ideology for jihad against democracy.

MARTIN B. SHICHTMAN is the director of Jewish Studies and Professor of English Language and Literature at Eastern Michigan University. He has been a fellow at the United States Holocaust Memorial Museum and at Brandeis University's Schusterman Center for Israel Studies. He received of a Mellon Partnership grant with Smith College for Jewish Studies programming and has directed several National Endowment for the Humanities Summer Seminars for School Teachers and an NEH focus grant teaming faculty from EMU with teachers from Detroit's Mumford High School. Shichtman has been the recipient of grants from the Covenant Foundation, the Academic Engagement Network, and the Jewish Federation of Greater Ann Arbor. He has directed five summer seminars for schoolteachers at the Holocaust Memorial Center Zekelman Family Campus in Farmington Hills. He is coauthor (with Laurie A. Finke) of *Cinematic Illuminations: The Middle Ages on Film* (2009) and *King Arthur and the Myth of History* (2004). He coedited *Culture and the King: The Social Implications of the Arthurian Legend* (1994) and *Medieval Texts and Contemporary Readers* (1987). He has published thirty-five scholarly articles and has presented more than one hundred papers at international, national, and regional conferences.

MIRA SUCHAROV is Associate Professor of Political Science at Carleton University, where she is also a provost teaching fellow. She is the author of *The International Self: Psychoanalysis and the Search for Israeli-Palestinian Peace* (2005) and *Public Influence: A Guide to Op-Ed Writing and Social Media Engagement* (2019). She publishes on pedagogy, Jewish identity, and Israel-Palestine, and her op-eds have appeared in *Haaretz*, the *Forward*, the *Globe and Mail*, the *Daily Beast*, and the *Toronto Star*. She is currently coeditor (with Chaya Halberstam) of *AJS Perspectives*.

MARCELA SULAK is Associate Professor of English Literature and Linguistics at Bar-Ilan University, where she teaches American literature, creative writing, and literary translation. Her poetry collections include *Immigrant* (2010), *Decency* (2015), *Mouth Full of Seeds* (2019), and *City of Skypapers* (2020). She has coedited *Family Resemblance: An Anthology and Exploration of 8 Hybrid Literary Genres*. Her fourth book-length poetry translation, *Twenty Girls to Envy Me: The Selected Poems of Orit Gidali* (2016), was long-listed for the 2017 PEN Award for Poetry in Translation.

MARILYN R. TAYLER is Professor Emerita in the Department of Political Science and Law at Montclair State University in New Jersey. She holds a JD from Seton Hall University and a PhD in Latin American literature from Rutgers University. Her current scholarship is focused on interdisciplinary studies and Israel studies. She has most recently written for the journals *Issues in Interdisciplinary Studies* and *Law, Culture and the Humanities* and the book *Case Studies in Interdisciplinary Research*. She is the author or editor of more than forty-five articles, books, and other writings.

UMUT UZER is an associate professor in the Department of Humanities and Social Sciences at Istanbul Technical University. He has published on Turkish foreign policy, Turkish nationalism, Israeli-Turkish relations, and Arab perceptions of the Cold War in *Middle East Policy*, *Israel Affairs*, *Turkish Studies*, the *Journal of Muslim Minority Affairs*, and the *Journal of South Asian and Middle Eastern Studies*. He is the author of two books: *An Intellectual History of Turkish Nationalism: Between Turkish Ethnicity and Islamic Identity* (2016) and *Identity and Turkish Foreign Policy: The Kemalist Influence in Cyprus and the Caucasus* (2011). From 2007 to 2010, he was a postdoctoral fellow at Harvard's Center for Middle Eastern Studies. Uzer has taught at Smith College, the University of Maryland University College, the Fashion Institute of Technology (SUNY), the University of Utah, Boğaziçi University, and Eastern Mediterranean University. He was affiliated with the Centre for European Policy Studies (CEPS), a think tank in Brussels, and was a visiting professor at the University of Antwerp. Earlier, he was a research assistant at the Foreign Policy Institute, Ankara, researching the Middle East peace process and the Arab-Israeli conflict.

AMY WEISS is the director of the Center for Holocaust and Genocide Education at the College of Saint Elizabeth. She also teaches American history and the Arab-Israeli conflict at City College, part of the City University of New York (CUNY). Her research and publications focus on the intersections of American Jewish history, Israel studies, and Jewish-Christian relations, including her current book manuscript on Jewish-Protestant interfaith alliances and the Arab-Israeli conflict.

SHAYNA WEISS is the associate director of the Schusterman Center for Israel Studies at Brandeis University. Previously she served as the Distinguished Visiting Scholar in Israel Studies at the United States Naval Academy. Her research interests include religion and the Israeli public sphere as well as the politics of Israeli popular culture. Weiss has published in the *Journal of Israeli History* and the *Journal of Jewish Film & New Media*. She is currently working on a book manuscript about gender segregation in the Israeli public sphere.

Index

Page numbers in *italics* indicate maps or tables. Titles of specific works will be found under the author's name. Surnames beginning with *Al-* or *El-* are alphabetized under *A* or *E*, but terms beginning with *al-* or *el-* are alphabetized under the main portion of the word (al-Qaeda, for instance, is under *Q*).

1948 War (War of Independence), xv, 8; Cairo University, influencing Israel studies at, 229; comparative literature, teaching empathy through, 101; competing narratives of, 142; in contrapuntal teaching of Israeli and Palestinian literatures, 323; dramatic Palestinian and Israeli presentations of, 82–83; fictional literature in interdisciplinary studies, using, 110–11; map of Israel/Palestine, *xxx*; terminology for, 32, 109, 241; U.S. Naval Academy, teaching narratives of war at, 128–32. *See also* Nakba

1956–57 (Sinai Campaign / Suez War), 8, 9, 229

1967 War (Six-Day War; June War; Naksa), 9–10; Arab conclusions drawn from, 9–10, 13; Cairo University, influencing Israel studies at, 229; competing narratives of, 142; contrapuntal reading on, 324–28; India and, 212; Israeli and Palestinian poetry on, 157–58, 168; Kanafani's "Returning to Haifa" and, 102; map of Israel/Palestine, *xxx*; West Bank, interaction of Israeli state with, 350

1969–70 War of Attrition, 229

1973 War (Yom Kippur War; October War), 11, 212, 229

1982 War (Lebanon War), 129, 136–37, 158, 159–60, 194, 229, 319

1991 Gulf War (first), 229

2014 Israel-Gaza conflict (*Miv'tzah Tzuk Eitan* or Operation Protective Edge; Gaza War), 39, 57n2, 77–78, 293

Abbas, Hiam, xiii
Abbas, Mahmoud, 312
Abbas II (Khedive), 227
Abboud, Fadi, 277
Abdelrazaq, Leila, *Baddawi* (2015), 30, 31, 34
Abdul Hamid II (Sultan), 208
Abramson, Glenda: *The Oxford Book of Hebrew Short Stories* (1996), 296; *The Writing of Yehuda Amichai* (1989), 159
absolutes and "sides," student need for, 22–23, 24, 53, 100, 261, 283
Abu-Assad, Hany, xiii, 143, 296
Abu Eid, Muna, 170
Abu Hanna, Hanna, "The Desire's Squint," 170
Abukhadra, Menna, xxii, 227, 233, 405
Abukhadra, Zainelabideen, 233
Abulhawa, Susan, 70
Abu Saif, Atef, ed., *The Book of Gaza* (2014), 39
Abuseif, Heba Hamdy, 231
academic freedom, 197, 198, 199–200n9
Aciman, André, 297
Acre, ethnographic study of city center synagogue in, 351–52
activism and scholarship, 187, 197–99, 217, 282–87
Adler, Yuri, 143
administrative/faculty issues: Arab American teaching Palestine, perils of, 329–30; course design and, 305–6; Jewish instructor working with Palestinian students, 288–93. *See also* continuing education for instructors; personal history
Adorno, Theodor, 191
Adraee, Avichay, 232
African American experience of racism, 95, 96, 98n12, 131, 301–8
Agnon, S. Y., 67, 68
Aharon-Gutman, Meirav, 351–52
AIPAC (American-Israel Public Affairs Committee), 223, 302
Ajami (film; 2009), 54, 396
AKA Nadia (film; 2015), 396
Akash, Munir, 158, 174n9
Aladdin Project, 209
al-Aqsa Brigades, 61

417

Al Aqsa (Second) Intifada (2000–2005), xvi, 28, 87
Alareer, Refaat, ed., *Gaza Writes Back* (2014), 39
Alebrashy, Mohammed Atia, 228
ALI (Association of Lebanese Industrialists), 276–77
Ali, Taha Muhammad, 69, 161–63, 177n29, 322; "Empty Words," 162–63; "Fooling the Killers," 161–62; "Sabha's Rope," 161; *So What: New and Selected Poems, 1971–2005*, 161
al-Khalidi, Ruhi, 248
al-Naji, Naji, *A Child in Palestine* (2009), 31
al-Qasim, Sami, 165–66, 168–69; *All Faces but Mine* (2015), 168; "Buchenwald," 165–66; *Sadder than Water* (2006), 168
Alsaadany, Mostafa, *A Spotlight on Zionism* (1957), 230
Al-Sab'awi, 'Abd-Al-Karim, "Three Poems to Palestine," 167
Alter, Robert, ed.: *Modern Hebrew Literature* (1975), 43; *The Poetry of Yehuda Amichai* (2015), 159
Alterman, Natan, 69
Aly, Abdel Monem Said, Shai Feldman, and Khalil Shikaki, *Arabs and Israelis* (2013), 117, 308
Aly, Hasan, 234
ambiguous/complex subject matter. *See* complex/ambiguous subject matter, teaching
American-Israel Public Affairs Committee (AIPAC), 223, 302
American University, Cairo, 227
Amichai, Yehuda, 151–59, 161, 169, 174n9, 253–55, 257; "I Guard the Children," 158; "Jerusalem, 1967," 157–58, 159; "The Place Where We Are Right," 255; "Songs of Zion the Beautiful," 159; "The U.N. Headquarters in the High Commissioner's House in Jerusalem," 155–57
Amir, Dvora, "Woodcut of a Landscape," 165
Amiry, Suad, 70
Anani, Ali, 228
Anne Frank House, 209
antisemitism: anti-Zionism as, 196; BDS associated with, 279; Christian/European, 236–37, 246–47; conspiracy theories about Israel and Jews, 206–8, 221, 224–25; Darwish's "Identity Card" read as, 95–96; in India, 212; "The Protocols of the Elders of Zion," 221, 225n6; Russian, 237–38; in social media, 208
Anusrour, Abdelfattah, *Handala* (2011), 85, 86
Arab American teaching Palestine, perils of, 319, 328–30
Arabic. *See* language issues and abilities; literature (as discipline); writing and rhetoric (as discipline)
Arab-Israeli conflict, teaching. *See* teaching the Arab-Israeli conflict
Arab Jews, Mizrahi identification as, 99, 105, 353

Arab Labor (television show), 54
Arab League, 129
Arab Legion, 8, 10
Arab nationalism, 4, 5–7, 10, 277
Arab Revolt (Peasant's Revolt; 1936–39), xv, 315
Arab Revolt of Sharif Hussein (1916), 206
Arabs: Ashkenazi/European culture, association of State of Israel with, 277–78; Christian Arabs, 6, 38, 260, 261; pan-Arabism, 10; Turkey and, 203–4, 206
Arab Spring, 216, 231, 353
Arafat, Yasser, 183, 286, 318
Araidi, Naim, 151
Ariel, Ari, xxii, 275, 405
Armstrong, Karen, *Jerusalem* (1996), 43, 49
Arraf, Suha, xiii
Ashery, Oreet, and Larissa Sansoor, *The Novel of Nonel and Vovel* (2009), 31
Ashkenazi, 38, 46, 277–78, 327, 352
Ashur, Dorit, 68–69
Asqalani, Ghareeb, "Hunger," 319, 323–28
Association of Lebanese Industrialists (ALI), 276–77
Atalia (film; 1984), 396
Atatürk, Mustafa Kemal, 203
Attack, The (film; 2012), 54, 396
Attrition, War of (1969–70), 229
Avenge but One of My Two Eyes (film; 2005), 396
Aviad, Michal, 341
Avidan, David, 69
Ayalon, Ami, 297

Back, Rachel Tzvia, ed., *With an Iron Pen* (2009), 165, 172
backward mapping and design, 337–38
Badr, Mohammed, *Hamatmon* (The treasure, 1926), 228
Baghdad Pact (1958), 203
Baha'i, xx, 213
Bailis, Beverly, xx, xxi, 90, 405
Baldwin, James, *Notes of a Native Son* (1955), 195
Balfour Declaration (1917), xii, 7, 205, 212, 214, 248, 249, 267, 295, 315
Bangladesh, 302
Barghouti, Mourid, "The Balcony," 167
Barghouti, Omar, 197, 199–200n9
Bar-Ilan University, Israel, 72–80
Baron Cohen, Sacha, 335
Barriers (film; 2010), 54, 118
Bartley, Aryn, 45
BBIP (Beyond Bridges: Israel-Palestine), 180–85
BDS movement. *See* Boycott, Divestment, and Sanctions (BDS) movement
Beaufort (film; 2007), 396

Beautiful Valley, The (film; 2011), 341
Bechdel Test for Women in Movies, 340–41
Bedouin, xvii, xxi, 5, 38, 66, 67, 183
Begin, Menachem, 135
Behar, Almog, 97
Ben-Ami, Shlomo, *Scars of War, Wounds of Peace* (2007), 24, 307
Ben 'Ami (Berkman), Tamar, 152
Ben-Gurion, David, 295
Ben Gurion University, 66
Ben Yehuda, Netiva, 70
Berdichevsky, Micha Josef, 67
Berkman (Ben 'Ami), Tamar, 152
Berlin/Jerusalem (film; 1989), 396
Berman, Russell A., xx, xxi, xxii, xxiii, 187, 197, 405–6
Bernstein, Deborah, 351
Bertozzi, Nick, and Boaz Yakin, *Jerusalem* (2013), 30
Bethlehem (film; 2013), 143, 396
Beyond Bridges: Israel-Palestine (BBIP), 180–85
Beyond the Walls (film; 1984), 396
Bialik, Chaim Nahman, 67, 151, 171, 300n3
bias and bias perception, 24, 43–45, 48–49, 107
Bilkent University, Turkey, 207
BirZeit University, West Bank, 217
Black Lives Matter, 98n12
Bloch, Chana, 155, 175n17
Bloodworth, Jeffrey, xxii, xxiv, 258, 406
Bluwstein, Ra'hel (Ra'hel), 171, 295
Boğaziçi University, Turkey, 205, 207
Boianjiu, Shani, 70
Bonaparte, Napoleon, xv, 246
borders, boundaries, and barriers: creative writing graduate courses, Bar-Ilan University, 72–80; film, depictions of land/territory in Israel/Palestine through, 133–39; wall between West Bank and Israel, 134, 137–38
Born in Deir Yassin (film; 2017), 396
Borrowed Identity, A (film; 2014), 65
Boston University, 279
Botton, Alain de, 289
Boycott, Divestment, and Sanctions (BDS) movement, xxii, 115, 196–97, 199–200n9, 224, 276, 278–80, 284, 292, 299, 329
Boys, Mary C., 253
Brandeis University, xiii, 118, 262, 295, 305
Brave Miss World (film; 2013), 342, 396
breakout groups. *See* discussion groups/small groups/breakout groups
Brenner, Rachel Feldhay, xx, 243, 406
British (Palestine) Mandate, xi–xii, xxiv, 6–8, 205, 238, 312, 315, 350
Brown, George Francis Graham, xi

B'Tselem, 291, 292
Bubble, The (film; 2006), 54, 396
Budrus (film; 2011), 134, 137–38, 397
Bush, George W., 222, 223
Butler, Judith, 329

Cairo University, Egypt, 227–34
CAMERA (Committee for Accuracy in Middle East Reporting in America), 117
Carenen, Caitlin, xix, xxiii, 21, 407
Castel-Bloom, Orly, 70
Catholic universities, teaching pluralism at, 258–64
Censored Voices (film; 2015), 397
Center for Global Education, University of San Francisco, 182
Chancellor, Sir John, xi
Checkpoint (film; 2003), 397
CHEN (Women's Corps) soldiers, 342
Chetrit, Sami Shalom, xiii, 97
Children of the Sun (film; 2007), 397
Christian Arabs, 6, 38, 260, 261
Christianity: antisemitism and, 236–37, 246–47; evangelical, xxii, 21, 29, 52–53, 216–17, 218, 223, 248–49; in India, 211; Jerusalem and foundational myth of, 245–46, 248–49; Palestinian poetry invoking, 165–66, 167; Second Coming, 246, 248; Zionism, Christian, 196, 248–49
Chute, Hillary, 41–42n35
cinema. *See* film
City College (CUNY), 133
classroom skills, xviii, xxiii. *See also* bias and bias perception; complex/ambiguous subject matter, teaching; critical thinking
Cleveland, William, *A History of the Modern Middle East* (2009), 204
Clurman, Harold, 82
cognitive dissonance, 261, 301, 306, 320
Cohen, Leonard, "Anthem" (song), 254
Colbert, Stephen, 276
Cold War, xv, 213, 266
Collins, Martha, *White Papers* (2012), 74, 75
Columbus, Christopher, 275
Columbus Day controversy, 131
comics. *See* graphic narratives/comics
Committee for Accuracy in Middle East Reporting in America (CAMERA), 117
communications (as discipline), using Arab-Israeli conflict to teach, 114–20
community college students, developing course for, 294–300
comparative conflict analysis, 182
comparative literature, teaching empathy through, 99–107

comparative teaching of Jewish-Israeli, Arab-Israeli, and Palestinian poetry, 147–72; aesthetic standards and, 149–50, 173n5; Darwish and Amichai, 151–59, 161, 174n9; dating of poetry, 176–77n25, 177n29; defining, 148; goals and principles, 147–51; historical application of implied parallelism, problems associated with, 170; Holocaust in, 148, 165–66; language and translations, 150, 151, 155, 156, 158–59, 168–69, 173n7, 174n9; occupation of West Bank and Gaza Strip, poems addressing, 159–68; as political poetry, 150, 169, 178–79n54; versus teaching them separately, 148, 149, 173n7; terminology and classification of poets, 170–71, 172–73n1

competing narratives, xii, xviii; community college students, developing course for, 295–97; defining, 142; empathy through comparative literature, teaching, 99–107; experiential learning and, 180–85; extremists in, 125; film as means of teaching, 141–45; framing Israel/Palestine, 311–17; graphic narratives/comics, using strategic juxtaposition in, 31–34, 39; interwovenness of Israel/Palestine, 311–14; land/territory in Israel/Palestine, film depictions of, 133–39; political science course, focus on competing narratives in, 123–26; U.S. Naval Academy, teaching 1948 War at, 128–32; of Zionism, 238. *See also* comparative teaching of Jewish-Israeli, Arab-Israeli, and Palestinian poetry; contrapuntal teaching of Israeli and Palestinian literatures; Zionism and the novel

complex/ambiguous subject matter, teaching: absolutes and "sides," student need for, 22–23, 24, 53, 100, 261, 283; BBIP (Beyond Bridges: Israel-Palestine) syllabus and, 183; comparative literature, teaching empathy through, 99–107; comparative teaching of poetry and, 149; critical analysis, overriding emotional convictions with, 22–23; in feminist filmmaking course, 342; parallelism of Israel/Palestine narratives, implied, 170, 311; personal political history and, 285, 291–93; in upper-division history/honors colloquium course, 21–27; using graphic narratives/comics, 28, 37–40; using Sacco's *Palestine*, 49–50

composition. *See* language issues and abilities; literature (as discipline); writing and rhetoric (as discipline)

conflict: comparative conflict analysis, 182; learning from, 251, 257, 320–21, 347–53; looking beyond, 347–53; teaching conflict interaction/negotiation, 114–20

conspiracy theories about Israel and Jews, 206–8, 221, 224–25

Constantine (Roman emperor), 236–37

contextualization, xviii, xxi–xxii, 257. *See also specific academic institutions and locales*

continuing education for instructors: Arabic, learning, 303–4; contrapuntal teaching of Israeli and Palestinian literatures, background research for, 321–22; Dar al-Islam Teachers Institute, Abiquiu, New Mexico, 304; faculty travel grants, 304–5; SIIS (Summer Institute for Israel Studies), Brandeis University, xiii, 118, 262, 295, 305; Summer Research Laboratory on Middle East and Islamic Studies, University of Illinois, Urbana-Champaign, 304

contrapuntal teaching of Israeli and Palestinian literatures, 318–30; Arab American teaching Palestine, perils of, 319, 328–30; background research for, 321–22; Liebrecht's "A Room on the Roof" and Asqalani's "Hunger," 319, 323–28; rationale for, 319, 320–21; syllabus and reading assignments, 323–24

counterargument, teaching, 290–93

covenant, Jerusalem and foundational myths of, 245–46, 248

creative writing: Open University of Israel literature course, 70; Shaindy-Rudoff Graduate Program, Bar-Ilan University, 72–80

crisis and hostage negotiation, 115–16

critical thinking: assessing, 53; composition/writing taught as means to, 288–93; conflict, learning from, 257; emotional convictions, overriding, 22–23; in feminist filmmaking course, 343; film used to teach, 51–56; homeland, studying Israeli and Palestinian stage representations of, 88; "how" of conflict versus "why," focus on, 58–62; in "Israeli Narratives" course, 334; political advocacy in the classroom and, 197–99; primary sources, focusing on, 129; Socratic method and, 244–45; targeted skills, 55–56; Texas A&M, Critical Thinking Seminars at, 52. *See also* complex/ambiguous subject matter, teaching

Crumb, R., 45

Crusades, 16, 86, 159

CUNY (City University of New York), 133, 294

Cup Final (film; 1991), 397

Cyprus: India and, 213; teaching Arab-Israeli conflict in, xxii, 218–20; Turkey and, 203, 213, 218–19

Dahbour, Ahmed, 171
Dajani, Omar, 307
Dancing in Jaffa (film; 2013), 54, 397
Dar, Esther, 296
Dar al-Islam Teachers Institute, Abiquiu, New Mexico, 304

Darwish, Mahmoud, xx, 67, 69, 90–97, 151–59, 161, 164, 165, 169, 171, 174–75n12, 174n9, 297, 322; "A Beautiful Woman from Sodom," 152; *Birds without Wings* (1960), 177n25; "A Caller of the Dove," 174n9; "The girl / The scream," 154–55, 157; "Identity Card" ("Write It Down, I Am an Arab"), 91, 94–97, 153, 175n14, 289; "In Praise of the High Shadow," 158; *Leaves of the Olive Tree* (1964), 153, 177n25; *Lesser Roses* (1986), 158–59; *Mural* (2000), 174n9; "Oh Father, I Am Joseph," 159; "Passport," 91–94; "Rita and the Rifle," 152; "Rita's Winter," 152–53; *The River Dies of Thirst* (2008), 154; "A Soldier Dreams of White Tulips," 152; "A State of Siege," 174n9; "Those Who Pass between Fleeting Words," 151–52; *Unfortunately, It Was Paradise* (2013), 158, 159, 174n9; *Why Did You Leave the Horse Alone* (1995), 174n9

Davis, Jordan, 174n9

debates: frameworks used by different scholars, comparing, 314–15; on two-state solution, 23, 25–26; on U.S. policy toward Israel and Palestinians, 221–24

Declarations of Independence: Israel Declaration of Establishment, 268–69, 270, 295; Palestinian, 97n2; U.S., 267–69

Deir Yassin, 241, 242n14

Delisle, Guy, *Jerusalem* (2012), 30, 31, 33

Della Pergola, Sergio, 298–99

demographics: India, religious demographics of, 210–11, 213; Israel/Palestine, population distribution in, *xxxi*; Palestinian demographics, first century to Mandate era, *239*; population transfer, 298–99, 300n5

DePaul University, 279

Der Stürmer, 45–46

Diameter of the Bomb (film; 2007), 397

diaspora, Jewish, 81

Dickinson, Thorold, 143

Dimona Twist (film; 2015), 397

discussion groups / small groups / breakout groups: drama, teaching Arab-Israeli conflict through, 83; for film as means of teaching competing narratives, 144–45; group-process sessions in BBIP (Beyond Bridges: Israel-Palestine) syllabus, 183; immersive study-abroad program, 254–56; U.S. Naval Academy, teaching 1948 War at, 130; for Zionism and the novel, 188

discussion questions: for film as means of teaching competing narratives, 144, 146n3; student framing of, 24–25

diversity, xx–xxi; contextualizing presentations by students addressing, 38–39. *See also* other, the, and otherness

Divine, Donna Robinson, xix, xxii–xxiii, 58, 407

Divine Intervention (film; 2005), 397

DJ Khaled, 276

"documentary poetics" workshop, Bar-Ilan University, 74–76

Donohoe, William A., Randall G. Rogan, and Sandra Kaufmann, eds., *Framing Matters* (2011), 116–17

Dotan, Shimon, 134, 135

Dowty, Alan, xx, 123, 407; *Israel/Palestine* (2017), 34, 126; *The Israel/Palestine Reader* (2019), 126

drama (as discipline): homeland, Israeli and Palestinian stage representations of, 81–88; literature for Arab and Jewish students in Israel and, 68–69

Druze, xx, xxi, 38, 79, 151, 339, 341, 342

dual narrative learning. *See* competing narratives

Eastern Michigan University (EMU), 43, 47–48

Egypt: in 1973 War, 11; Gaza strip, occupation of, after 1948 War, 8; Israel studies at Cairo University, 227–34; Nile TV (Hebrew channel), 234; peace treaty of 1978 with Israel, 5, 11, 13; revolution of 2011 in, 231; in Sinai campaign (1956–57), 8, 9

Eisenstadt, S. N., 347–49; *The Absorption of Immigrants* (1955), 348; *Israeli Society* (1967), 348, 349

ELA (Endangered Language Alliance), 300n1

El-Asmar, Fouzi, "The Wandering Reed," 166

Eliot, George, *Daniel Deronda* (1876), 188

Elmusa, Sharif S., and Walid Khalidi, *All That Remains* (2008), 323

Elon University, North Carolina, 305

El Saadawi, Nawal, 289

El-youssef, Samir, *Illusion of Return* (2008), xiii, 194–95, 197

emotion: critical analysis, overriding emotional convictions with, 22–23; depressing nature of studying Arab-Israeli conflict, 26; homeland, Israeli and Palestinian stage representations of, 84; in multidisciplinary course focused on critical thinking, 61–62. *See also* personal history

empathy through comparative literature, teaching, 99–107

EMU (Eastern Michigan University), 43, 47–48

Endangered Language Alliance (ELA), 300n1

English. *See* language issues and abilities; literature (as discipline); writing and rhetoric (as discipline)

Enlightenment, 246–47

Erciyes University, Kayseri, Turkey, 207

Erdoğan, Recep Tayyip, 204, 249

essays. *See* writing/research assignments

ethnographic study of city center synagogue in Acre, 351–52

Eurocentrism, 302
Europe: antisemitism, Christian/European, 236–37, 246–47; Ashkenazi/European culture, Arab association of State of Israel with, 277–78; Jews, political emancipation of, xv, 246–47
evangelical Christianity, xxii, 21, 29, 52–53, 216–17, 218, 223, 248–49
event reports, 336
Every Bastard a King (film; 1968), 143, 146n3
existential problem, Arab-Israeli conflict viewed as, 3–4, 15–17
Exodus (film; 1960), 143, 146n3, 397
experiential learning, xxii–xxiii, 180–85. *See also* travel/study-abroad programs
extremists, in competing narratives, 125
Eytan, Eytan, "The Rain Is Ready to Fall," 165

Facebook, xiii, 22, 27, 48, 72, 232, 234n3, 277, 284, 286
fact/value distinction, 286
faculty. *See* administrative/faculty issues; continuing education for instructors
falafel, 32, 259, 277, 280
Falah, Dahlia, "Thursday at Angel's Bakery," 165
Fatah, 138
FDOE (Florida Department of Education), 265–71
Federal Bureau of Investigation (FBI), Crisis Hostage Negotiation Unit and Behavioral Sciences Unit, 115
Feige, Michael, 139n3
Feldman, Keith P., 96
Feldman, Shai, Abdel Monem Said Aly, and Khalil Shikaki, *Arabs and Israelis* (2013), 117, 308
feminist filmmaking course, 339–43
Feminist Frequency, 340
Fernheimer, Janice W., xix, xxi, 28, 407–8
fiction. *See* literature (as discipline); *specific authors*
Fictitious Marriage, A (film; 1988), 397
Fill the Void (film; 2012), 342
film: annotated filmography, 395–403; Bechdel Test for Women in Movies, 340–41; community college students, developing course for, 296; competing narratives, as means of teaching, 141–45; conflict interaction, using Arab-Israeli conflict to teach, 118; critical thinking, used to teach, 51–56; feminist filmmaking course, 339–43; graphic narratives/comics and, 32, 137; land/territory in Israel/Palestine depicted through, 133–39; Open University of Israel, Palestinian cinema course, 68. *See also specific films by title*
Fine, Terri Susan, xxiii, 265, 408
First Gulf War (1991), 229
First Intifada (1987), xvi, 151, 218, 324

First World War, xv, 9, 173n5, 203, 206, 227, 247, 315
First Zionist Congress, Basel, 208
Fisher, Roger, 117
Five Broken Cameras (film; 2013), 54, 397
500 Dunams on the Moon (film; 2002), 398
Flavius Josephus, *The Wars of the Jews*, 245
Florida Department of Education (FDOE), 265–71
Folger, Joseph P., Scott Poole, and Randall K. Stutman, *Working through Conflict* (2013), 116
Folman, Ari, 134, 136; *Waltz with Bashir: A Lebanon War Story* (with David Polonsky; 2009), 137
food and foodways, 32, 79, 275–80
Forché, Carolyn, 158
Forgotten Refugees, The (film; 2005), 296, 398
For My Children (film; 2009), 54
For My Father (film; 2008), 398
foundational myths of Abrahamic religions, 245–46, 248–49
Four Friends (film; 1999), 296, 398
framing Israel/Palestine, 311–17
Frank, Anne, 36, 209
Frank, David. *See* Rowland, John, and David Frank
Free Zone (film; 2005), 341
Freire, Paulo, 252
French Revolution, xv, 246
Friedlich, Hadar, 341
Friedman, Thomas, 319
Fuchs, Esther, ed., *Israeli Women's Studies: A Reader* (2005), 297, 339
Fulbright-Hays fellowship, 304

Gandhi, Mahatma, 117, 211
Gaon, Boaz, 104
Gatekeepers (film; 2012), 398
Gaza Strip: after 1948 War, 8; comparative study of poetry addressing occupation of, 159–68; defined, xxvn8; interwovenness of Israel/Palestine and, 312; in Sinai campaign, 8, 9; two-state solution, difficulties faced by, 14; West Bank Palestinians compared, 296
Gaza War (Israel-Gaza conflict / *Miv'tzah Tzuk Eitan* or Operation Protective Edge; 2014), 39, 57n2, 77–78, 293
GCC (Gulf Cooperation Council) countries, 306
Geertz, Clifford, 129
Gemayel, Bashir, 136
gender. *See* women
general education requirements, xxxiii, 43, 141–42
general familiarity versus in-depth knowledge of students, 22, 23, 29, 52–53, 115, 206, 235, 243–44
Gerner, Deborah, *One Land, Two Peoples* (1991), 306
Gershenson, Olga, xx, 141, 408

Gett: The Trial of Viviane Amsalem (film; 2015), 342, 398
Ghareeb, Edmund, and Aruri Naseer, eds., *Enemy of the Sun* (1970), 168, 172, 176n25
Gitai, Amos, 143
Glidden, Sarah, *How to Understand Israel in 60 Days or Less* (2010), 25, 30–31, 34, 35–37, 39, 41n25
global context, Israel/Palestine sharing, 313
globalization, 258, 259
Gluzman, Michael, 149
Gody, Farouk, 229
Golan Heights, 9, 11, 13, 317n1
Goldstein, Baruch, 125
Goodman, Martin, 245
Goren, Shiri, xx, xxi, xxiii, 332, 408–9
Gottesman, Shoshana, 106–7
Gouri, Haim, 69
Govrin, Michal, 70
Graff, Gerald, *Beyond the Culture Wars* (1993), 251
graphic narratives/comics, 28–40; about complex/ambiguous subject matter, 28, 37–40; comics vocabulary, teaching, 33, 34, 41–42n35; course overview, 31–37; film and, 32, 137; narrative and interpretation, using strategic juxtaposition of, 31–34, 39; reading assignments, 25, 30–31, 32–34, 39; reasons for using, 30; students, curricula, and disciplines, 29–30; writing assignments, 34–35; in "Zionism and the Novel" course, 189. *See also specific texts by author*
Greek Wars of Independence (1821–27), xiv
Green, Katie, 118
Green Fields (film; 1989), 398
Green Line, 10, 76, 138, 169, 185, 312
Gregory, Alex, 100, 101
Gribetz, Jonathan Marc, *Defining Neighbors* (2014), 248
Grossman, David, 84, 297, 322; *The Smile of the Lamb* (1990), 322; *The Yellow Wind* (2016), 295
group-process sessions in BBIP (Beyond Bridges: Israel-Palestine) syllabus, 183
Grynszpan, Michael, 296
Gulf Cooperation Council (GCC) countries, 306
Gulf War (first; 1991), 229
Gutmann, Assia, 155

Habibi, Emile, xiii, 78, 322
Haganah, 129
Hahn, Kimiko, *Toxic Flora* (2010), 74
Haifa University, 66, 67
Halfon Hill Doesn't Answer (film; 1976), 398
Halkin, Hillel, 59, 60
Halper, Jeff, 322
Halperin, Liora R., xii–xiii, xx, 311, 409

Hamas, 10, 15–16, 61, 117, 138, 204, 239, 291, 297, 351
Hamatzav, 334
Hamsin (film; 1982), 143, 398
Handal, Nathalie, 67
Hand in Hand (school network), 352
Haram al-Sharif / Temple Mount, Jerusalem, 246, 249, 304
Harb, Said, 229
Harris, Rachel S., xx, 339, 409
Harshav, Benjamin and Barbara, 156, 175n17; *Yehuda Amichai: A Life of Poetry, 1948–1994*, 159
Harvard University, 347
Haskalah, 247
Hass, Amira, *Drinking the Sea at Gaza* (2000), 296
"Hatikvah" (Israeli national anthem), 4, 180–81
Havy ibn Yaqzan, 289
HBCUs (historically black colleges and universities), 301–8
Hebrew. *See* language issues and abilities; literature (as discipline); writing and rhetoric (as discipline)
Hebrew University of Jerusalem, 347, 349
Hebron: Goldstein massacre of Muslims in, 126; Jewish presence in, after 1967 War, 10
Herman, Peter C., xx, 235, 409
Hermoni, Matan, 70
Herzberg, Arthur, ed., *The Zionist Idea* (1959), 25, 247
Herzl, Theodor, 208; *Old New Land* (1902), 189
He Walked the Fields (film; 1967), 398
Hezbollah, 16
Hide and Seek (film; 1980), 398
hijab and veiling, 47–48, 231
Hill 24 Doesn't Answer (film; 1955), 143, 398
Hinduism, 210, 213
historically black colleges and universities (HBCUs), 301–8
historical perspectives on Arab-Israeli conflict, xiv–xvii, xix, 3–18; development of Israeli-Palestinian problem, 7–8; as existential conflict, 3–4, 15–17; political and military developments after 1948, 9–12; as political dispute, 3, 13–14; rise of Zionism and Arab nationalism, xv, 4–7; roots of, 4–7; time line, 356–75. *See also specific wars and events*
history (as discipline), xix–xx; of complex/ambiguous subject matter, 21–27; considering actions and motivations in historical context, 22–23; feminist filmmaking course not focusing on history, 339–43; framing Israel/Palestine in, 311–17; introductory surveys and general introductions in nonhistory classes, 23–24, 34, 109, 188, 235–39, 295–96, 323; land/territory in Israel/Palestine, film depictions of, 133–39; literature intertwined with, 299; social studies requirements of FDOE

history (as discipline) (*continued*)
(Florida Department of Education), 265–71; Turkey, teaching Middle Eastern politics in, 203–9; upper-division history course / honors colloquium course, 21–27; U.S. Naval Academy, teaching 1948 War at, 128–32
Hitchens, Christopher, 48
Hitler, Adolf, *Mein Kampf* (1925), 237
Hoffman, Eva, 297
Holocaust, xxiii; in BBIP (Beyond Bridges: Israel-Palestine) program, 184; Christian/European antisemitism and, 237, 238; community college students, developing course for, 294–95, 298; in comparative teaching of poetry, 148, 165–66; FDOE (Florida Department of Education) on, 267, 268; graphic narratives / comics used to teach, 32, 33, 34, 39; India and, 211, 212; International Holocaust Remembrance Day, 208; Israel, teaching literature to Arab and Jewish students in, 71; Kanafani's "Returning to Haifa" and, 102, 103; Qatar University, teaching Arab-Israeli conflict at, 216, 220–21; survival and personal history, 294, 298; Turkey, teaching Middle Eastern politics in, 206, 208–9; in "Zionism and the Novel" course, 190, 191
honor killing, 48
Horkheimer, Max, 191
hostage and crisis negotiation, 115–16
Human Resources Manager (film; 2010), 399
hummus, 32, 275–80
Hussein, Rashid, 151, 166–68, 171, 172; "At Zero Hour," 166–67; "Jerusalem . . . And the Hour," 168; "Tent #50 (Song of a Refugee)," 166, 167
Husseini, Shajid, 70
hybrid writing, 78–79

Ibadi Islam, 304
Ibsen, Henrik: *A Doll's House* (1879), 69; on Jewish statelessness, 81
IDF (Israeli Defense Forces), 9, 31, 32, 39, 46, 102, 107, 118, 129, 136, 232, 263, 280, 319, 403
In Between (film; 2016), 399
Inch'Allah (film; 2012), 399
Independence, War of. *See* 1948 War (War of Independence); Nakba
Independence Day (in State of Israel), 109, 180–81
India: in East-West ideological debates, 212–13; religious demographics of, 210–11, 213; teaching Arab-Israeli conflict in, 210–15
integrated curriculum, 288–90
integrational coursework, 251
intellectual hospitality, concept of, 252–53, 256
interdisciplinary studies, xix–xx; fictional literature in, 108–12; honors colloquium course, 21–27; immersive study-abroad program, 250–57; Repko's interdisciplinary research process, 108
interest groups and lobbying, 4, 223, 302
International Holocaust Remembrance Day, 208
International Women's Day, 232
interpretation. *See* competing narratives
intersectionality, 284
interwovenness of Israel/Palestine, 311–14, 347–53
introductory courses: graphic narratives / comics, use of, 29–30; historical introductory surveys and general introductions in nonhistory classes, 23–24, 34, 109, 188, 235–39, 295–96, 323; upper-division history course / honors colloquium course, 21–27
Invisible (film; 2011), 342, 399
Iranian antipathy toward Israel, 238–39
ISIL (Islamic State of the Levant), 10, 16, 244
Islam: 1967 War and resurgence of, 10; basic theology instruction in Judaism and Islam, providing, 23; existential problem, Arab-Israeli conflict viewed as, 3–4, 15–17; in HBCU (historically black college and university) courses, 303; Ibadi Islam, 304; in India, 211, 213; Jerusalem and foundational myth of, 246, 249; Jews and Judaism as viewed by, 14; peace, viewed as religion of, 304; Spanish Reconquista, 246; Sunni-Shi'a divide, 216, 220, 244, 303; Turkey, teaching Middle Eastern politics in, 203–9; Ummah, concept of, 6, 10, 15–16; Wahhabism, 303
Islamic Jihad, 10, 16
Islamic State of the Levant (ISIL), 10, 16, 244
Islamophobia, 221, 304
Israel. *See* State of Israel
Israel-Gaza conflict (*Miv'tzah Tzuk Eitan* or Operation Protective Edge / Gaza War; 2014), 39, 57n2, 77–78, 293
Israeli-Arab conflict, teaching. *See* teaching the Arab-Israeli conflict
Israeli Defense Forces (IDF), 9, 31, 32, 39, 46, 102, 107, 118, 129, 136, 232, 263, 280, 319, 403
Israel studies: at Cairo University, 227–34; fictional literature in, 108–12; graphic narratives / comics, use of, 29–30; origins of discipline, 347. *See also* Jewish studies
Istanbul Technical University, 204

Jabotinsky, Vladimir, *The Five* (1935), 189
Jacir, AnneMarie, 342
Jacobowitz, Susan, xxiii, 294, 409–10
Jacobson, Howard, *The Finkler Question* (2010), 195–96, 197
Jafari, Mohammad Ali, 239

Jaffa (film; 2009), 143, 399
Jalaita, Hassan, 324
Japanese Red Army (JRA), 103–4
Jaradat, Mya Guarnieri, xxii, xxiii, 288, 410
Jayyusi, Salma Khadra: *The Anthology of Modern Palestinian Literature* (ed.; 1992), 43; "Dearest Love II," 168
Jellyfish (film; 2007), 342
Jenin, Jenin (film; 2003), 399, 400
Jerusalem: after 1967 War, 9–10; division after 1948 War, 8; foundational myths of Abrahamic religions and, 245–46, 248–49; map, *xxxiii*; in peace negotiations, 12; poetry about, 173; religious significance, course on, 243–49; Temple Mount / Haram al-Sharif, 246, 249, 304; two-state solution, difficulties faced by, 14
Jewish studies, 29–30, 73, 141–45, 228–29, 275, 314. See also Israel studies
Jews: Acre, ethnographic study of synagogue in city center of, 351–52; Arab association of State of Israel with Ashkenazi/European culture, 277–78; Ashkenazi, 38, 46, 277–78, 327, 352; Cairo University, Israel studies at, 230, 231; covenant, Jerusalem and foundational myth of, 245–46, 248; Haskalah, 247; homeland, Israeli and Palestinian stage representations of, 81–88; in India, 210–11; Islamic views of, 15; in Open University of Israel literature course, 65–71; Palestinian students, Jewish instructor working with, 288–93; political emancipation in Europe, xv, 246–47; Sacco's *Palestine*, stereotypes in, 45–46; Turkey, knowledge of/ relationship with Jews and Israel in, 204, 206–9; in Turkey, 208–9. See also antisemitism; Mizrahi
JINO (Jew in Name Only), 284
John Carroll University, 318
Johnson, Willa, 98n13
Jordan: Arab Legion, 8, 10; Catholic travel/study-abroad program based in, 258–61; occupation of Palestine after 1948 War, 8; peace treaty of 1994 with Israel, 5, 11, 13, 305
Josephus, *The Wars of the Jews*, 245
JRA (Japanese Red Army), 103–4
JSA (Junior State of America), 221–24
Jubran, Salim, "A Refugee," 167
Judaism: basic theology instruction in Judaism and Islam, providing, 23; Cairo University, Israel studies at, 230, 231; covenant, Jerusalem and foundational myth of, 245–46, 248. See also antisemitism
Junction 48 (film; 2016), 399
June War. See 1967 War
Junior State of America (JSA), 221–24
Justice for Palestine, 224
Just Vision, 138

Kaddish for a Friend (film; 2010), 399
Kanafani, Ghassan, 67, 103–4, 322; *Men in the Sun* (1995), 322–23; *Palestine's Children* (2005), 102; *Returning to Haifa* (1969), 102–4, 323
Kaplan, Ellen W., xxii, 81, 410; *Pulling Apart* (2004), 87
Kashua, Sayed, xiii, 65, 67, 70, 197; *Dancing Arabs* (2002), 65; *Second Person Singular* (2010), 65, 192–94, 195
Kaufmann, Sandra, William A. Donohoe, and Randall G. Rogan, eds., *Framing Matters* (2011), 116–17
Kedma (film; 2002), 143, 146n3
Keret, Etgar, "Pastrami," 39
Khalidi, Ismael, *Tennis in Nablus* (2010), 86
Khalidi, Walid, and Sharif S. Elmusa, *All That Remains* (2008), 323
Khalifeh, Sahar, 70, 322; *Wild Thorns* (1985), 322–23
Khalil, Hannan, *Plan D* (2010), 83
Khoury, Elias, 322, 323
Khoury, Nidaa, 169
Khulud, Khamis, *Haifa Fragments* (2015), 106
Kimmerling, Baruch, 349–50
Kirsch, Adam, 159
Klein, A. M., *The Second Scroll* (1951), 189–92
Klein, Menachem, *Lives in Common* (2014), 351
Klieman, Aharon, 307
Knight, Henry F., 253
Knopf-Newman, Marcy, *The Politics of Teaching Palestine to Americans* (2011), 321, 329
Koestler, Arthur, *Thieves in the Night* (1967), 102–3
Kolosov, Jacqueline, 78
Kroll-Zeldin, Oren, xxi, xxii, xxiv, 180, 410
Kronfeld, Chana, 158
Kumaraswamy, P. R., xxi, 210, 410–11
Kurds, 213
Kurzweil, Amy, *Flying Couch* (2016), 30, 31
Kuwait, Iraqi invasion of (1991), 11

Lady Kul el Arab (film; 2008), 342, 399
Lamott, Anne, 289
land/territory in Israel/Palestine: film depictions of, 133–39; overlapping symbolism and physical interconnection of, 312. See also *specific locations*
Land without Borders (film; 2007), 399
language issues and abilities: Cairo University, Hebrew-language instruction at, 227–29; in comparative teaching of poetry, 150, 151, 155, 156, 158–59, 168–69, 173n7, 174n9; ELA (Endangered Language Alliance), 300n1; film subtitles and, 137; hybridity, expressing, 79; instructor's knowledge of Arabic, 303–4; of literature students at Open

language issues and abilities (*continued*)
University of Israel, 67, 69, 70, 71; *Ma'had Alqowat Almosallah* (the armed forces institute, Egypt), Hebrew instruction at, 234; New York City, language diversity in, 300n1; Palestinian/Israeli relations and, 353; poetry in translation, 95–97, 150, 151, 155, 156, 158–59, 168–69, 173n7, 174n9; Shaindy-Rudoff Graduate Program, Bar-Ilan University, 73; U.S. Naval Academy, students studying Arabic at, 127–28; in "Zionism and the Novel" course, 188

Laor, Yitzhak, "Memory of Three Dead," 165

Laqueur, Walter, *The Israel-Arab Reader* (1969), xiii

Lassner, Jacob, xix, 3, 411

Late Summer Blues (film; 1987), 399

Latowicki, Tali, 165

Law in These Parts, The (film; 2011), 399

Lawrence, T. E., *Seven Pillars of Wisdom* (1926), 206

Lebanese hummus, 276–77

Lebanon War (1982), 129, 136–37, 158, 159–60, 194, 229, 319

le Carré, John, *The Little Drummer Girl*, xx, 235, 239–41

Lederach, John Paul, *The Moral Imagination* (2005), 320–21

Lemon Tree (film; 2009), 54, 341, 399

Lerner, Motti, *At Night's End* (2011), 86

Levi, Tikva, xiii

Levin, Hanoch: *Murder* (1997), 87; *The Patriot* (1982), 84; *Queen of the Bathtub* (1970), 84; *You and Me and the Next War* (1968), 84

Levinas, Emmanuel, 170

Levitsky, Holli, xxiv, 250, 411

Libicki, Miriam: *jobnik!* (2008), 31; *Toward a Hot Jew* (ed.; 2016), 30, 34

Liebrecht, Savyon, 70; "The Road to Cedar City," 322; "A Room on the Roof," 319, 324–28

Life According to Agfa (film; 1992), 400

literature (as discipline), xx–xxi; community college students, developing course for, 294–300; comparative literature, teaching empathy through, 99–107; drama courses as means of communicating, 68–69; fictional literature in interdisciplinary studies, 108–12; history intertwined with, 299; immersive study-abroad program, 250–57; Israel, teaching literature to Arab and Jewish students in, 65–71; "Israeli Narratives" course, 333–38; poetry of Palmach and State generations in Israel, 69–70; San Diego State University, le Carré's *Little Drummer Girl* at, 235–41. *See also* comparative teaching of Jewish-Israeli, Arab-Israeli, and Palestinian poetry; contrapuntal teaching of Israeli and Palestinian literatures; creative writing; Zionism and the novel; *specific authors*

lobbying and interest groups, 4, 223, 302

Lockman, Zachary, 351

Loshitzky, Yosefa, 143

Lotan, Gilad, 53

Loyola Marymount University, 250

Lukács, Georg, 188–89

Luke, Sir Harry Charles, xi, xxivn2

Luther, Martin, 236, 246; *On the Jews and Their Lies* (1543), 237

Lydda, 238

Machsom Watch, 118

Madrid conference (1988), 12

Ma'had Alqowat Almosallah (the armed forces institute, Egypt), Hebrew instruction at, 234

Mainuddin, Rolin, xx, xxiii, 301, 411–12

Makhuli, Salim, 167

Mandate Palestine, xi–xii, xxiv, 6–8, 205, 238, 312, 315, 350

Mansback, Richard W., and Kirsten L. Taylor, *Challenges for America in the Middle East* (2017), 307

Mansour, Reda, 151

maps, as pedagogical tools, 23, 25, 133, 238–39, 244, 266, 302, 333–34, 338

Mara'ana, Ibtisam, xiii

Marx, Karl, *Theses on Feuerbach* (1888), 198

Marxism, 175n14, 191, 194

Masalba, Nur, 130

Masalha, Salman, 151

Matalon, Ronit, 70

Mattawa, Khaled, 174–75n12

Mavi Marmara incident (Gaza flotilla, 2010), 204

Maytal (film; 1996), 399, 401

McCloud, Scott, *Understanding Comics* (1993), 30, 33, 34

Meital, Oreet Meital, "October 2000," 165

MEMRI (Middle East Media Research Institute), 117

MENA (Middle East and North Africa), 302, 303

Mendelson-Maoz, Adia, xxii, 65, 412

MESA (Middle East Studies Association), 302, 303

#MeToo movement, 343

Metres, Philip, xx, 317, 412

Michael, Sami, 105; *Doves in Trafalgar* (2005), 104

Middle East, defining, 302

Middle East and North Africa (MENA), 302, 303

Middle East Media Research Institute (MEMRI), 117

Middle East Studies Association (MESA), 302, 303

Middle East Technical University, Turkey, 207

Migdal, Joel S., xx, 347, 412–13

military: IDF (Israeli Defense Forces), 9, 31, 32, 39, 46, 102, 107, 118, 129, 136, 232, 263, 280, 319, 403; students in military studying Arab-Israeli conflict, 128–32, 217, 234; women in, 342
Mirror Image (film; 2013), 400
Mitchell, Stephen, 155, 175n17
Miv'tzah Tzuk Eitan or Operation Protective Edge (Israel-Gaza conflict / Gaza War; 2014), 39, 57n2, 77–78, 293
Mizrahi: Arab Jews, identification as, 99, 105, 353; Darwish, reading Mizrahi writers with, 97; *The Forgotten Refugees* (film; 2005), 296, 398; nationalist associations of hummus and, 278; Palestinian-Jewish relations and, 351–52; teaching Palestinian students about, 291–92
mock debates. *See* debates
Modan, Rutu, 197; *Exit Wounds* (2008), 31, 38, 189
Mohamad, Husam, xxi–xxii, 216, 413
Mongols, 16
Montclair State University, 108
Moodle, 144
Morrar, Ayed, 138
Morris, Benny, *Righteous Victims* (1999), 109–12, 124, 130
movies. *See* film
multiple narratives. *See* competing narratives
Munich (film; 2005), 400
Muslim Brotherhood, 16, 204
My Michael (film; 1974), 143, 400

NAACP (National Association for the Advancement of Colored People), 302
Nadler, Mei-Tal, 69–70
Najjar, Michael Malek, 328
Nakba: competing narratives of, 142; in Darwish's poetry, 92; defined, 9; dramatic presentations of, 82–83; graphic narratives / comics used to teach, 32, 33, 34, 39; Israeli recognition of, 321; teaching literature to Arab and Jewish students in Israel and, 71; as terminological issue, 109, 241; U.S. Naval Academy, teaching 1948 War at, 128–32. *See also* 1948 War (War of Independence)
Nakba law, 131
Naksa. *See* 1967 War (Six-Day War; June War; Naksa)
Namy, Yehia, *This Is Zionism* (1969), 230
Napoleon Bonaparte, xv, 246
Naqqash, Samir, 105
narrative and interpretation. *See* competing narratives
Naseer, Aruri, and Edmund Ghareeb, eds., *Enemy of the Sun* (1970), 168, 172, 176n25
Nash, Manning, 275

Nathan, Susan, *The Other Side of Israel* (2007), 297
National Association for the Advancement of Colored People (NAACP), 302
nationalism: Arab, 4, 5–7, 10, 277; hummus and group identity, 276–78; in India, 212; international and regional factors, tendency to downplay, 348–49; in multidisciplinary course focused on critical thinking, 59, 60, 62n3. *See also* Palestinian Arabs and Palestinian national consciousness; Zionism
National Outlook Movement, 208
natural rights philosophy, 269
Naval Academy, United States, 128–32
Nazis, 36, 46, 82, 103, 173n5, 190, 210, 212, 221
NCCU (North Carolina Central University), 301–8
Near East Institute (NEI), 302
Ne'eman, Sharon, 297
NEI (Near East Institute), 302
Nelson, Cary, xx, 147, 413
Netanyahu, Benjamin, 135, 204, 305
Neve Shalom / School for Peace, 87
New Historians / new Israeli historiography, 130–31
news reports, 244, 335–36
9/11 attacks, 28, 319, 328
1913: Seeds of Conflict (film; 2015), 400
Nitzan, Tal, 165
Noodle (film; 2007), 342, 400
Nordau, Max, 300n3
normalization, 11, 13, 197, 232, 298, 307, 321, 352
North Carolina Central University (NCCU), 301–8
No. 17 (film; 2003), 38, 400
novels. *See* literature (as discipline); Zionism and the novel; *specific authors*
Nusseibeh, Sari, *Once upon a Country* (2007), 24, 25, 27

Obama, Barack, 222, 223–24, 278
occupied territories, xvi, xxvn8, 10. *See also* Gaza Strip; West Bank
October War (1973 War; Yom Kippur War), 11, 212, 229
oil in Middle East, xv, 212, 302
Oliver, John, 335
Omar (film; 2013), 143, 400
Omer-Sherman, Ranen, xx, xxiii, 99, 413
One of Us (film; 1989), 400
one-state solutions, 223, 292, 293, 307
online course materials, 117–18, 144, 245, 340
On the Frontline (film; 2002), 54
Open University of Israel, 65–71
Operation Protective Edge or *Miv'tzah Tzuk Eitan* (Israel-Gaza conflict / Gaza War; 2014), 39, 57n2, 77–78, 293

Orientalism, 45, 204, 205, 322
Or: My Treasure (film; 2004), 342
ORSAM (Center for Middle Eastern Strategic Studies), Ankara, 207
Oslo Accords (1993), 11–12, 13, 61, 129, 131, 286, 305
Osman, Jena, *The Network* (2010), 74
other, the, and otherness, xviii; Catholic universities, teaching pluralism at, 258–64; communication and conflict interaction, using Arab-Israeli conflict to teach, 114–20; community college, developing course for diverse environment of, 294–95, 297–98; creative writing graduate courses, Bar-Ilan University, 72–80; Darwish's poetry, taught in transnational academic environment, 90–97; engaging with versus representing the other, 322; homeland, Israeli and Palestinian stage representations of, 81–88; intellectual hospitality, concept of, 252–53, 256; Jewish instructor working with Palestinian students, 288–93; in Liebrecht's "A Room on the Roof," 324–25; literature course for Arab and Jewish students in Israel, 65–71; in multidisciplinary course focused on critical thinking, 62n3; Palestinian-authored texts, using, 31
Ottoman Empire, xiv–xv, 5–6, 59, 203, 205, 206, 208, 237, 247
Out in the Dark (film; 2012), 54, 400
Oz, Amos, 59, 82, 86, 297, 322; *How to Cure a Fanatic* (2010), 82; *My Michael* (2005), 65, 322; "Nomad and Viper," 322
Özal, Turgut, 203

PA (Palestinian Authority), 12, 223
Pakistan, 211
Palestine (British) Mandate, xi–xii, xxiv, 6–8, 205, 238, 312, 315, 350
Palestine Liberation Organization (PLO), xv, xvi, 10–12, 97n2, 136, 204, 217, 305
Palestinian Arabs and Palestinian national consciousness: African American experience of racism and, 95, 96, 131, 301–8; after 1948 War, 8; historical development of, xv, 7–8, 248; homeland, Israeli and Palestinian stage representations of, 81–88; India and, 212; Israeli jobs for Palestinian workers, 324–28; Jewish instructors working with Palestinian students, 288–93; in multidisciplinary course focused on critical thinking, 60; in Open University of Israel literature course, 65–71; Oslo Accords and, 11–12; Turkey and, 204, 205, 208; Zionism and, 218
Palestinian Authority (PA), 12, 223
Palestinian demographics, first century to Mandate era, *239*
Palestinian-Israeli conflict, teaching. *See* teaching the Arab-Israeli conflict
"Palestinian Jordanians," 260
Palestinian Media Watch (PMW), 117
Palestinian refugees, xxvn7, 12, 14, 85, 109–12, 126, 131, 136, 167, 181, 183, 184, 194–95, 260
Palestinian Wedding, The (1982), 169
pan-Arabism, 10
papers. *See* writing/research assignments
Pappé, Ilan, 323
Paradise Now (film, 2005), 38, 296, 400
parallelism of Israel/Palestine narratives, implied, 170, 311
Parsons, Talcott, 348
partition plan, UN (1947), 7–8, 124, 205, 212, 267
Pascal, Julia, *Crossing Jerusalem* (2002), 88
Passmore, Ashley, xxi, xxii, xxiii, 51, 413
Patterson, David, 253
peace, Islam viewed as religion of, 304
peace process, xvi, 12, 205, 221–24, 271, 297, 305–7, 321
Peasant's Revolt (Arab Revolt; 1936–39), xv
Pekar, Harvey, and J. T. Waldman, *Not the Israel My Parents Promised Me* (2012), 30
PEP (progressive except on Palestine) position, 145
Pepsico, 279–80
personal history, xviii, xxii, xxiii; academic instruction and personal views, separating, 187, 197–99, 217–18; Arab American teaching Palestine, perils of, 319, 328–30; Cairo University, Israel studies at, 233–34; changing perspectives of instructor and, 288–93, 297–300; classroom use of, 107, 282–87; community college students, developing course for, 294–95, 297–300; complex/ambiguous subject matter, teaching, 285, 291–93; cross-cultural living experience and, 301–2; Cyprus, effects of Greek/Turkish divide in, 218–30; Holocaust survival and, 294, 298; of Jewish instructor working with Palestinian students, 288–93; in multidisciplinary course focused on critical thinking, 61–62; overriding emotional convictions with critical analysis, 22–23
Peter, Sinai, 104
PFLP (Popular Front for the Liberation of Palestine), 103–4
Phalangists, 135
pinkwashing, 284
pinui-binui, 292
Plan C, 129, 132n2
Plan D (*Tochnit Dalet*), 129–32, 132n2
PLO (Palestine Liberation Organization), xv, xvi, 10–12, 97n2, 136, 204, 217, 305
PLO Research Center, Beirut, 318, 319

pluralism. *See* other, the, and otherness
PMW (Palestinian Media Watch), 117
"poetic prosody, genre, and form" workshop, Bar-Ilan University, 76–78
poetry. *See* literature (as discipline)
political science (as discipline): activism and, 282–87; competing narratives, focus on, 123–26; HBCU (historically black college and university) courses, 301–9; states as autonomous actors and, 350; Turkey, teaching Middle Eastern politics in, 203–9; U.S. Naval Academy, teaching 1948 War at, 128–32
political Zionism, 4–5, 189, 218, 247
politics, xviii, xxii, xxiii; Arab American teaching Palestine, perils of, 319, 328–30; BDS movement, xxii, 115, 196–97, 199–200n9, 224, 276, 278–80, 284, 292, 299, 329; foodways and, 275–80; homeland, Israeli and Palestinian stage representations of, 86–87; Jewish instructor working with Palestinian students, 288–93; modern political dispute, view of Arab-Israeli conflict as, 3, 13–14; political poetry, comparative teaching of, 150, 169, 178–79n54; power and power analysis, 285, 319, 324; scholarship and activism, 187, 197–99, 217, 282–87; shifts in political empathy over time, 60; Zionism and the novel, teaching, 187, 196–99
Polonsky, David, and Ari Folman, *Waltz with Bashir: A Lebanon War Story* (2009), 137
Poole, Scott, Joseph P. Folger, and Randall K. Stutman, *Working through Conflict* (2013), 116
Popular Front for the Liberation of Palestine (PFLP), 103–4
population. *See* demographics
post-Zionist perspective, 142–43
power and power analysis, 285, 319, 324
PowerPoint, 235, 240, 244, 340
praxis, Freire's concept of, 252
Preminger, Otto, 143
presentations: conflict interaction, using Arab-Israeli conflict to teach, 117; event reports, 336; for film as means of teaching competing narratives, 145; on films used to teach critical thinking, 51, 54–55; graphic narratives / comics, contextualizing presentations by students using, 38–39; immersive study-abroad program, 253–56; Jerusalem, course on religious significance of, 243–44; news reports, 244, 335–36; for Zionism and the novel, 187–88
primary sources, 128–29, 138, 247, 265–71
principled negotiation, 117
progressive except on Palestine (PEP) position, 145
"Protocols of the Elders of Zion, The," 221, 225n6
proximal knowledge, 98n13

Qabbani, Nizar, 173n7
al-Qaeda, 10, 16
Qatar University, 216, 220–21
Queensborough Community College (CUNY), 294

Rabin, Yitzhak, 87, 297
Rabinovich, Itamar, and Jehuda Reinharz, eds., *Israel in the Middle East* (2008), 25
Rabin, the Last Day (film; 2015), 400
Rabinyan, Dorit, 70
Rachamim, Yechezkel, xiii
Rachel, tomb of, 10
racism: African American experience of, 95, 96, 98n12, 131, 301–8; contrapuntal reading as inoculation against, 323; Qatar University, teaching Arab-Israeli conflict at, 221; Zionism equated with, 213–14, 230
Ra'hel (Ra'hel Bluwstein), 171, 295
Rahman, Najat, 98n8
Raider, Mark A., and Miriam B. Raider-Roth, eds., *The Plough Woman* (2002), 295
Ram, Moriel, 351
Rana's Wedding (film; 2002), 296, 400
Rasheed, Harun Hashim, "We Will Return One Day," 167
Ravikovitch, Dahlia, 69, 159–63, 168, 177n28; "The Horns of Hittin," 159–60; "The Story of the Arab Who Died in the Fire," 160–61; *The Third Book* (1969), 159
reading assignments: Catholic travel/study-abroad program, teaching pluralism through, 261; community college students, developing course for, 295–97; comparative literature, teaching empathy through, 101–6; for comparative teaching of poetry, 148–49; conflict interaction, using Arab-Israeli conflict to teach, 116–17; contrapuntal teaching of Israeli and Palestinian literatures, 323–24; for debate on U.S. policy toward Israel and Palestinians, 222; "documentary poetics" workshop, Bar-Ilan University, 74, 75; for fictional literature in interdisciplinary studies, 110–11; for film as means of teaching competing narratives, 143, 144; film used to teach critical thinking, 54; graphic narratives / comics, 25, 30–31, 32–34, 39; for HBCU (historically black college and university) courses, 307–8; homeland, Israeli and Palestinian stage representations of, 82–83; immersive study-abroad program, 253–54; "Israeli Narratives" course, 336–37; Jerusalem, course on religious significance of, 245, 247; literature students at Open University of Israel, 68; multi-disciplinary course focused on critical thinking, 59; "poetic prosody, genre, and form" workshop,

reading assignments (*continued*)
  Bar-Ilan University, 77; for political science course focused on competing narratives, 123–25; primary sources, 128–29, 138, 247, 265–71; Turkey, teaching Middle Eastern politics in, 204; for upper-division history course/honors colloquium course, 23–25, 26; U.S. Naval Academy, teaching 1948 War at, 128–29, 130–31; Zionism and the novel, 189–96. *See also specific texts, by author's name*
refugees, Palestinian, xxvn7, 12, 14, 85, 109–12, 126, 131, 136, 167, 181, 183, 184, 194–95, 260
Reinharz, Jehuda, and Itamar Rabinovich, eds., *Israel in the Middle East* (2008), 25
Rekhess, Elie, 295
reliable source, defining, 291
religion: basic theology instruction in Judaism and Islam, providing, 23; in feminist filmmaking course, 342; in HBCU (historically black college and university) courses, 303; immersive study-abroad program, 250–57; India, religious demographics of, 210–11, 213; Jerusalem, course on religious significance of, 243–49; student tendency to read Arab-Israeli conflict as religious war, 21. *See also specific faiths*
Rensselaer Polytechnic Institute, 29
Repko, Allen, *Introduction to Interdisciplinary Studies* (2014), 108
research assignments. *See* writing/research assignments
resources and pedagogy, relationship between, 227, 232–33
rhetoric. *See* writing and rhetoric (as discipline)
right of return, xxvn7, 12, 14
Riley, Karen, 102
Road to Jenin, The (film; 2005), 400
Rock the Casbah (film; 2012), 400
Rogan, Randall G., xxii–xxiii, 114, 414; *Framing Matters* (ed., with William A. Donohoe and Sandra Kaufmann; 2011), 116–17
Room 514 (film; 2012), 342, 401
Rose Metal Press, 78
Rosenthal, Donna, *The Israelis* (2008), 261
Roshdy, Zakia, 229
Rowland, John, and David Frank: "Mythic Rhetoric" (2002), 32–33; *Shared Land/Conflicting Territory* (2002), 32, 34
Rudoren, John, 324
Rukeyser, Muriel, *Book of the Dead* (1938), 74
Russia: antisemitism in, 237–38; UN partition plan and Soviet Union, 212
Russian (Bolshevik) Revolution (1917), xv, 349
Russian Revolution (1905), 349
Russo-Turkish Wars, xiv

Sabra and Shatila massacre (1982), 96, 136, 137, 283
Sabra Dipping Company, 276, 279–80
Sacco, Joe: *Footnotes in Gaza* (2009), 31, 44; *Palestine* (2001), xx, 30, 43–50
Sadabad Pact (1937), 203
Said, Edward W., 59–60, 297, 319; *Culture and Imperialism* (2012), 320; *Orientalism* (1978), 45
Salaita, Steven, 329
Samuel, Maurice, xi
Sandel, Ari, 32
San Diego State University, 235–41
Sandstorm (film; 2017), 342, 401
Sansoor, Larissa, and Oreet Ashery, *The Novel of Nonel and Vovel* (2009), 31
Santos Perez, Craig, *From Unincorporated Territory* (2008), 74
Sarkeesian, Anita, 340–41
Saunders, Alan, xi
Sawyer, Diane, 319
Sayigh, Mai, 169
Scarry, Elaine, 82
School for Peace/Neve Shalom, 87
Schueftan, Dan, xiii
Schulze, Kirsten E., *The Arab-Israeli Conflict* (2013), 295, 297
Schusterman Center for Israel Studies and Summer Institute, Brandeis University, xiii, 118, 262, 295, 305
Second (Al Aqsa) Intifada (2000–2005), xvi, 28, 87
Second Coming, 246, 248
Second World War, xv, 7, 131, 173n5, 184, 189, 211, 266, 267, 271
Seliktar, Galit and Gilad, *Farm 54* (2011), 30
Semida, Mahmoud, 230
Settlers, The (film; 2016), 134–35, 401
Seven Minutes in Heaven (film; 2011), 401
Sfar, Johann, 99, 100
Shabtai, Aharon, 163–64, 168; *J'Accuse* (2003), 163, 322; "J'Accuse," 163; "Lotem Abdel Shafi," 164; "The Moral, It Seems, Doesn't Come with a Smile," 164; "The Reason to Live Here," 163; "Summer 1997," 163; "To Dr. Majed Nassar," 164; "To My Friend," 164; "Toy Soldiers," 163–64; "2006," 163; *War & Love/Love & War* (2010), 163
Shadmi, Koren, "Snapshots from Israel," 39
Shafir, Gershon, *Land, Labor and the Origins of the Israeli-Palestinian Conflict, 1882–1914* (1989), 351
Shaheen, Mohammed, 174n9
Shaindy-Rudoff Graduate Program, Bar-Ilan University, 72–80
Shamieh, *The Black Eyed* (2007), 85–86
Shammas, Anton, 67, 151; "Prisoner of Sleeping and Waking," 166

Shapira, Anita, 351
Shapiro, Andrei, 300n3
Shapiro, Yonathan, *The Formative Years of the Israel Labor Party* (1976), 349
Sharif Hussein, Arab Revolt of (1916), 206
Sharon, Ariel, 135, 282
Shavit, Ari, *My Promised Land* (2013), 235–36, 238
Shichtman, Martin B., xx, 43, 414
Shikaki, Khalil, Abdel Monem Said Aly, and Shai Feldman, *Arabs and Israelis* (2013), 117, 308
Shining Stars (film; 2008), 401
Shoah. *See* Holocaust
Shofman, Gershon, 67
Shomali, Amer, 31
Shulman, David, 101–2
"sides" and absolutes, student need for, 22–23, 24, 53, 100, 261, 283
Siege (film; 1969), 401
SIIS (Summer Institute for Israel Studies), Brandeis University, xiii, 118, 262, 295, 305
simulation assignments. *See* debates
Sinai campaign (1956–57), 8, 9, 229
Sinai Peninsula, 9, 11, 13
Six-Day War. *See* 1967 War (Six-Day War; June War; Naksa)
Slyomivoc, Susan, *The Object of Memory* (1998), 296–97
small groups. *See* discussion groups / small groups / breakout groups
Smilansky, Yizhar. *See* Yizhar, S. (Yizhar Smilansky)
Smith, Charles D., *Palestine and the Arab-Israeli Conflict* (2013), 23–24, 205
Smith College, 59, 62n1, 81, 206
Snir, Reuven, 159
Sobol, Jonathan: *Ghetto* (1989), 82; *Shooting Magda (The Palestinian Girl)* (1985), 84–85
social capital, 282, 286–87
social identity theory, 182–83
social interactions between conflicting parties, encouraging, 218, 219–20, 232, 260
social media: antisemitism in, 208; classroom use of, 39, 59, 286; Facebook, xiii, 22, 27, 48, 72, 232, 234n3, 277, 284, 286; influence of, 57n2, 206; Israeli use of, 231–32; Qatar University students and, 220; Twitter, 39, 53, 329
social studies requirements of Florida Department of Education (FDOE), 265–71
sociology (as discipline), 347–50
Socratic method, 23, 244–45
Soloveichik, Aaron, 59
Song of the Siren (film; 1994), 401
Soviet Union. *See* Russia
Spanish Reconquista and expulsion of Jews, 246

Spiegelman, Art, *Maus* (1986), 33–34, 39, 44
State of Israel: Arab states, evolving relationship with, 5, 11–12; Ashkenazi/European culture, Arab association with, 277–78; Catholic travel/study-abroad program moving from Jordan to, 261–63; conspiracy theories about Israel and Jews, 206–8, 221, 224–25; creation of, xvi, 5, 8; creative writing courses in, 70, 72–80; Declaration of Establishment, 268–69, 270, 295; FDOE (Florida Department of Education) requirements for learning about, 265–71; "Hatikvah" (national anthem), 4, 180–81; homeland, Israeli and Palestinian stage representations of, 81–88; Independence Day in, 109, 180–81; India, teaching Arab-Israeli conflict in, 211–15; literature for Arab and Jewish students in, 65–71; Military Order No. 854, 225n2; Palestinian workers, Israeli jobs for, 324–28; social media, use of, 231–32; threat of Palestinian narrative to, 318–19; Turkey and, 204, 206–9; United States and, 268, 278–79, 302, 319; wall between West Bank and, 134, 137–38
State University of New York (SUNY) Albany, xiii
Steinberg, Jacob, 67
Stewart, Jon, 335
Strauss (food manufacturer), 279–80
Strum, Philippa, 324
student debates. *See* debates
student presentations. *See* presentations
Students for Justice in Palestine, 235
students' general familiarity versus in-depth knowledge, 22, 23, 29, 52–53, 115, 206, 235, 243–44
Students Supporting Israel, 235
study abroad. *See* travel/study-abroad programs
Stutman, Randall K., Joseph P. Folger, and Scott Poole, *Working through Conflict* (2013), 116
Sucharov, Mira, xx, xxii, xxiii, 282, 414
Suez Canal (1869), xiv–xv, 9
Suez War / Sinai campaign (1956–57), 8, 9, 229
suicide bombings, xii, xvi, 32, 38, 85–86, 125, 296
Sulaiman, Khalid A., *Palestine and Modern Arab Poetry* (1984), 179n5
Sulak, Marcela, xix, 72, 414–15; *Family Resemblance* (ed., with Jacqueline A. Kolosov; 2015), 78
Suleiman, Elia, xiii, 143
Summer Institute for Israel Studies (SIIS), Brandeis University, xiii, 118, 262, 295, 305
Summer Research Laboratory on Middle East and Islamic Studies, University of Illinois, Urbana-Champaign, 304
Sunni-Shi'a divide, 216, 220, 244, 303
SUNY (State University of New York) Albany, xiii
Sykes-Picot Agreement (1918), 238

syllabus: adjustment for current events, 39; BBIP (Beyond Bridges: Israel-Palestine), 182–85; community college students, developing course for, 295–97; for comparative teaching of poetry, 150; contrapuntal teaching of Israeli and Palestinian literatures, 323–24; creation of courses, xii–xiv, xviii–xix, xx; feminist filmmaking course, 339–40; for film as means of teaching competing narratives, 142–44; film used to teach critical thinking, 53–54; for graphic narratives / comics, 31–37; HBCU (historically black college and university) courses, 302–8; immersive study-abroad program, 253–54; "Israeli Narratives" course, 334–37; Jerusalem, course on religious significance of, 244–49; le Carré's *Little Drummer Girl*, teaching, 235–41; multidisciplinary course focused on critical thinking, 59; for political science course focused on competing narratives, 123–26; for upper-division history course / honors colloquium course, 23–26; U.S. Naval Academy, teaching 1948 War at, 129–31; for Zionism and the novel, 187–89

Syrian Bride (film; 2004), 341, 401
Syrian refugee crisis, 216

Take 3 (film; 2016), 401
Tale of Love and Darkness, A (film; 2015), 401
Tammuz, Benjamin, "The Swimming Race" (1951), 105
Tan'ee, Shlomo, "Rains," 165
Tatour, Dareen, "Resist my people, resist them," 72–73, 80
tawjihi, 290
Tayler, Marilyn R., xix–xx, 415
Taylor, Kirsten L., and Richard W. Mansback, *Challenges for America in the Middle East* (2017), 307
teaching the Arab-Israeli conflict, xi–xxiv; conflict, learning from, 251, 257, 320–21; conflict, looking beyond, 347–53; creation of courses for, xii–xiv, xviii–xix, xx; different historical, ideological, and disciplinary perspectives on, xvii–xviii, xix–xx (*see also specific disciplines*); diversity issues and, xx–xxi; general familiarity versus in-depth knowledge of students, 22, 23, 29, 52–53, 115, 206, 235, 243–44; history and significance of conflict, xiv–xvii, xix (*see also* historical perspectives on Arab-Israeli conflict); maps, *xxix–xxxiv*; pedagogical framework, xviii–xxiv; resources and pedagogy, relationship between, 227, 232–33; social justice issues and, xxi; terminological issues in, xxi (*see also* terminology); time line, 356–75
Tel Aviv University, 67

Temple Mount / Haram al-Sharif, Jerusalem, 246, 249, 304
terminology: for 1948 War, 32, 109; "Israeli Narratives" course examining, 335; poets, classification of / terminology for, 170–71, 172–73n1; in teaching the Arab-Israeli conflict, xxi; for wall between West Bank and Israel, 138
term papers. *See* writing/research assignments
territory/land in Israel/Palestine: film depictions of, 133–39; overlapping symbolism and physical interconnection of, 312. *See also specific locations*
Tessler, Mark, *A History of the Israeli-Palestinian Conflict* (2009), 124
Texas A&M University, 51, 52–53
They Were Ten (film; 1961), 401
3 Times Divorced (film; 2007), 342, 401
time line, 356–75
time line assignment, 315–16
Time of Favor (film; 2002), 401
Time That Remains, The (film; 2009), 143, 401
Tochnit Dalet (Plan D), 129–32, 132n2
Tolan, Sandy, *The Lemon Tree* (2006), 25
Touma, Khalil, 169
translations. *See* language issues and abilities
travel/study-abroad programs, xxiv, 232; BBIP (Beyond Bridges: Israel-Palestine), 180–85; Catholic universities, teaching pluralism at, 258–64; checkpoint crossings and itineraries, 180–82, 185, 261–63; faculty travel grants, 304–5; Loyola Marymount immersive study program, 250–57; SIIS fellowships for instructors, xii, 118, 262, 295, 305
Troupe, The (film; 1978), 402
Truman, Harry, 268
Trump, Donald, 333, 338n1
Trumpet in the Wadi (film; 2001), 143
Tuqan, Fadwa, 70, 169
Tuqan, Ibrahim, 171
Turkey: Arabs, relationship with / knowledge of, 203–4, 206; Cyprus and, 203, 213, 218–19; Erdoğan urging Muslim pilgrimages to Jerusalem to protest occupation, 249; Israel and Jews, relationship with / knowledge of, 204, 206–9; Jews in, 208–9; not considered as part of Middle East, by Turkish people, 205, 207; Ottoman Empire and, xiv–xv, 5–6, 59, 203, 205, 206, 208, 237, 247; Palestinian Arabs, sympathy for, 204, 205, 208; Russo-Turkish Wars, xiv; teaching Middle Eastern politics in, 203–9
Turki, Fawaz, 59
Twitter, 39, 53, 329
two-state solutions, 13–14, 23, 25–26, 293, 299, 307

Ummah, 6, 10, 15–16
UN. *See* United Nations (UN)
Unabomber, 115
Unamuno, Miguel de, 329
United Nations (UN): General Assembly Resolution defining Zionism as racism, 230; partition plan (1947), 7–8, 124, 205, 212, 267
United States Holocaust Memorial Museum, 209
United States Naval Academy, 128–32
University of Ankara, 207
University of California at Riverside, 279
University of Firat, Turkey, 207
University of Illinois at Urbana-Champaign, xiii, 304
University of Iowa, 52
University of Kentucky, 29, 30
University of Marmara, Turkey, 207
University of Maryland University College, 206
University of Massachusetts, 141
University of Michigan, 43
University of New Mexico, 279
University of Notre Dame, 123
University of Sakarya, 207
University of San Francisco, 182
University of Texas at Austin, 28, 29
Unsettling (film; 2018), 402
UN Watch, 117
Urian, Dan, 84
Uris, Leon, *Exodus* (1958), 107, 298
Ury, William, 117
Uzer, Umut, xxi, 203, 415

VALUE (Valid Assessment of Learning in Undergraduate Education) rubric, 53
Vassar College, 279
Victims of a Map (1984), 158, 168
Vietnam War, 148, 307, 348
Villa Touma (film; 2014), 402
violence: comparative teaching of poetry and, 148; conflict interaction, using Arab-Israeli conflict to teach, 114–20; gender-based, 75–76; graphic narratives/comics used to discuss, 28, 46; homeland, Israeli and Palestinian stage representations of, 85–86; Kimmerling on, 349–50; in multidisciplinary course focused on critical thinking, 60–61; poetry, (mis)reading, 72–73

Wahhabism, 303
Waldman, J. T., and Harvey Pekar, *Not the Israel My Parents Promised Me* (2012), 30
Walk on Water (film; 2004), 402
wall between Israel and West Bank, 134, 137–38
Waltz with Bashir (film; 2008), 54, 134, 136–37, 402

War of Attrition (1969–70), 229
War of Independence. *See* 1948 War (War of Independence); Nakba
Wedding in Galilee (film; 1987), 402
Weiss, Amy, xix, xx, 133, 415
Weiss, Shayna, xxiii, 127, 415
Weissbort, Daniel, 173n2
Wesleyan University, 279
West Bank: in 1967 War, 9; administrative divisions, xxxii; after 1948 War, 8; comparative study of poetry addressing occupation of, 159–68; defined, xxvn8; Gaza Palestinians compared, 296; interaction of Israeli state with, 350; interwovenness of Israel/Palestine and, 312; as Israeli bargaining chip, 13; Jewish instructor working with Palestinian students in, 288–93; Jewish settlements in, 10, 18n2, 61, 125, 134–35; in Oslo Accords, 12; two-state solution, difficulties faced by, 13–14, 293; wall between Israel and, 134, 137–38
West Bank Story (film; 2005), 32, 402
Wild West Hebron (film; 2013), 402
Williams, William Carlos, 154; "Asphodel, That Greeny Flower," 74
Wittes, Tamara, ed., *How Israelis and Palestinians Negotiate* (2005), 306–7
Wolkin, David, 35, 36
Woman Pioneers, The (film; 2012), 341, 402
women: Bechdel Test for Women in Movies, 340–41; in *Budrus* (film; 2009), 138; community college students, developing course for, 297; in creative writing workshops at Bar-Ilan University, 72, 75–76, 79, 80; feminist filmmaking course, 339–43; hijab and veiling, 47–48, 231; homeland, Israeli and Palestinian stage representations of, 85–86; International Women's Day, 232; in Liebrecht's "A Room on the Roof," 324–25; literature students at Open University of Israel and, 66, 69, 70; #MeToo movement, 343; Qatar University, gender division at, 220; in Sacco's *Palestine*, 46–48
Wooden Gun (film; 1979), 402
Woolf, Virginia, *A Room of One's Own* (1929), 324
workshops: in BBIP (Beyond Bridges: Israel-Palestine) syllabus, 183; crisis and hostage negotiation exercise, 115–16; "documentary poetics" workshop, Bar-Ilan University, 74–76; homeland, Israeli and Palestinian stage representations of, 83; "poetic prosody, genre, and form" workshop, Bar-Ilan University, 76–78
World Summit on Counter-Terrorism, 115
World War I, xi
World War II, xv, 7, 131, 173n5, 184, 189, 211, 266, 267, 271

Wright, C. D.: *One with Others* (2010), 74; *One Big Self* (2007), 74
Write Down, I Am an Arab (film; 2014), 402
writing and rhetoric (as discipline): graphic narratives/comics, use of, 29–30, 32–33; Jewish instructor working with Palestinian students, 288–93; "Zionism and the Novel" course designed to apply to, 187
writing/research assignments: conflict interaction, using Arab-Israeli conflict to teach, 118–19; Darwish, teaching poetry of, 97; discussion questions, student framing of, 24–25; "documentary poetics" workshop, Bar-Ilan University, 74, 75; for film as means of teaching competing narratives, 144, 145; on films used to teach critical thinking, 51; film used to teach critical thinking, 53–54, 56; graphic narratives/comics, 34–35; HBCU (historically black college and university) courses, 302; immersive study-abroad program, 253–54; "Israeli Narratives" course, 337; Jerusalem, course on religious significance of, 243; Jewish instructor working with Palestinian students, 289; multidisciplinary course focused on critical thinking, 59; on wall between West Bank and Israel, 138; for Zionism and the novel, 187
Wycliffe Hall (University of Oxford) students, and Arab rioting in Mandate Palestine (1929), xi–xii, xxiv

Yad Vashem, 183, 184, 209
Yakhlif, Yahya, *A Lake beyond the Wind* (1998), 104–5
Yakin, Boaz, and Nick Bertozzi, *Jerusalem* (2013), 30
Yale University, 333, 336
Yana's Friends (film; 1999), 402
Yehoshua, A. B., 197; *Facing the Forests* (1968), 297; *Mr. Mani* (1993), 189
Yehoshua, Shimon, 291–92
Yellow Asphalt (film; 2001), 403
Yeshurun, Avot, "Passover on Caves," 170

Yishuv, 129, 130, 171, 295
Yizhar, S. (Yizhar Smilansky), 322; *Khirbet Khizeh* (1949), 101–2, 110–12, 321–22; "The Prisoner" (1949), 105, 295–96, 322; "The Soldier," 323
Yom Kippur War (1973 War; October War), 11, 212, 229
Young, James E., 141

Zach, Natan, 69
Zayyad, Tawfiq, 67; "Cuba," 166; "On the Trunk of an Olive Tree," 167; "The Skull Harvest," 168; "Taxation," 168
Zero Motivation (film; 2014), 342, 403
Ziad, Tawfiq, 169
Zionism: Amichai's "The Place Where We Are Right" and, 255; Balfour Declaration as legal foundation for, 7; Cairo University, Israel studies at, 227, 228, 230–33; Christian/European antisemitism and, 236–37, 246–47; Christian Zionism, 196, 248–49; competing narratives of, 238; FDOE (Florida Department of Education) on, 267; First Zionist Congress, Basel, 208; historical development of, xv, 4–5; Indian and Bangladeshi views of, 213–14, 302; Jerusalem, course on religious significance of, 246–48; Kanafani's "Returning to Haifa" and, 102–3; in multidisciplinary course focused on critical thinking, 59, 60; Palestinian national consciousness and, 218; political Zionism, 4–5, 189, 218, 247; post-Zionist perspective versus, 142–43; racism, equated with, 213–14, 230; Russian antisemitism and, 237–38; Turkey, teaching Middle Eastern politics in, 205, 207, 208
Zionism and the novel, 187–99; current events and political activism, 187, 196–99; genre, addressing novel as, 188–89; reading assignments, 189–96; syllabus, requirements, goals, and principles, 187–89
Zuabi, Amir Nuar, *I Am Yusuf and This Is My Brother* (2009), 82–83